RUSSIAN CONSTRUCTIVISM

CHRISTINA LODDER

# RUSSIAN
CONSTRUCTIVISM

YALE UNIVERSITY PRESS · NEW HAVEN AND LONDON · 1983

In memory of my father, Reginald James Lodder

Designed by Faith Brabenec Hart
Filmset in Monophoto Times Roman and printed in Great Britain by
Butler & Tanner Ltd, Frome, Somerset

Library of Congress Cataloging in Publication Data

Lodder, Christina, 1948–
  Russian constructivism.

  Bibliography: p.
  Includes index.
  1. Constructivism (Art)—Soviet Union. 2. Art,
  Russian. 3. Art, Modern—20th century—Soviet Union.
I. Title.
N6988.5.C64L63 1983   709′.47   83–40002
ISBN 0-300-02727-3

PREFACE

My desire to learn more about Russian Constructivism was prompted by seeing Tatlin's flying apparatus, the *Letatlin*, being reconstructed by Martin Chalk in Newcastle in 1968; it has been sustained in the years since I began this work by the help, advice and encouragement I have received from various individuals and institutions.

My research in the Soviet Union was made possible by a British Council Exchange Scholarship to the art history department of the University of Moscow. I should like to express my gratitude to the head of that department, Professor Dmitrii Vladimirovich Sarab'yanov, and to my Soviet supervisor, Rafael' Samuilovich Kaufman. I am most grateful to the Soviet Ministry of Higher Education for permission to work in Soviet archives and to the staff of those archives, in particular the Central State Archives of Literature and Art in Moscow, the Manuscript Department of the Russian Museum in Leningrad and the Manuscript Department of the Lenin Library in Moscow. The library staffs of the Lenin Library, the Tret'yakov Gallery and the Russian Museum in Leningrad were most helpful and I owe a great deal to their help and diligence in tracking down rare publications. I also owe much to the staffs of the British Library, the library of the Victoria and Albert Museum and the New York Public Library.

In addition I am exceedingly grateful to the many Soviet scholars and specialists in this field who have advised, taught and helped me, in particular, Alina Vasil'evna Abramova, who has been exceedingly generous in imparting much of her knowledge and material, as well as much of her time in discussing the problems of Russian Constructivism with me. Evgenii Fedorovich Kovtun and Alina Vasil'evna Povelikhina in Leningrad gave me much invaluable advice on the period as a whole and I am also very indebted to the tremendous help I received from Elena Zhukova, Boris Mikhailov and Vasilii Rakitin. The artist, Vladimir Avgustovich Stenberg, one of the few Constructivists who was still alive, gave me fascinating first-hand accounts of his involvement with INKhUK, OBMOKhU and the VKhUTEMAS. The families and friends of other Russian artists have been particularly helpful, and I should like to acknowledge my great debt to Mrs Miriam Gabo, Mai Petrovich Miturich, Nina Konstantinovna Bruni, Varvara Aleksandrovna Rodchenko, Elena Borisovna Murina, Evgenii Borisovich Pasternak, Andrei Ivanovich Leonidov, Anna Aleksandrovna Leporskaya, Viktor Borisovich Shklovskii, Aleksandr Lavrent'ev, Ekaterina Drevin, and Tat'yana and Dmitrii Borisov. Several private galleries and collectors in the West have been very helpful in giving me access to works and reproductions. In particular I should like to thank Mr George Costakis, Mrs Annely Juda, Frau Antonina Gmurzynska, Monsieur Jean Chauvelin, Mrs Rosa Esman and Mr and Mrs Leonard Hutton. Public galleries and museums have also been most generous, especially Yale University Art Gallery, New Haven, the

Solomon R. Guggenheim Museum, New York, the Museum of Modern Art, New York, the Tate Gallery, London, the Stedelijk Museum, Amsterdam, and the Moderna Museet, Stockholm. In addition I am grateful to Andrei B. Nakov, Herman Berninger, David Elliot, Oleg Prokofiev, Troels Andersen, Szymon Bojko, the Arts Council of Great Britain and the Society for Cultural Relations with the USSR, London. Finally, I should like to thank my supervisor at the University of Sussex, Miss Beryl Williams, who encouraged my research, and I should like to say a particular thank you to Dr Catherine Cooke of Cambridge University without whose friendship and help the thesis which forms the main substance of this volume would never have been written.

In preparing this volume for publication I am grateful for the comments and discussion provided by my colleagues at St Andrews Robin Spencer, Roger Keys and Paul Crowther, and by Richard Davies, Julian Graffy, Angelica Rudenstine, John Milner and Briony Fer. For their kindness and patience in wrestling with the illegibilities of my writing and the difficulties of the Russian language I should like to thank Jennifer Sturtridge who typed the original manuscript and Joyce Quinn and Dawn Waddell who coped with the revisions to the original text. The Inter-Library Loan Staff of the University of St Andrews have enabled me to pursue obscure lines of enquiry and I am most grateful to them for their apparently limitless patience and perseverance. My gratitude is also due to the British Academy which in financing a study trip to the United States in the summer of 1982 to commence a new area of research enabled me also to settle some outstanding queries and gain new insights which have enriched this volume.

I should like to thank Faith Hart and John Nicoll for all their help in making the publication of this work a reality; and finally all my family and friends who have maintained my momentum when the logistics of this work seemed overwhelming.

Specific photographic credits include: Herman Berninger, *Oeuvre catalog. Jean Pougny (Iwan Puni)*, Tübingen (Verlag Wasmuth), 1962 (plates 1.14, 1.17); L. Zhadova, *V. E. Tatlin*, Moscow (Sovetskii khudozhnik), 1977 (plate 1.2); S. Khan-Magomedov, 'U istokov sovetskogo dizaina', *Technicheskaya estetika*, No. 2, 1980 (plates 4.10–15, 4.16–18); S. Khan-Magomedov, *Pionere der sowjetischen Architektur*, Dresden (V.E.B. Verlag), 1983 (plate 2.20); S. Lissitzky-Kuppers, *El Lissitzky*, Dresden, 1967 (plates 5.13–14, 5.16); and L. Zhadova, 'Tatlin', in *Sovetskoe dekorativnoe iskusstvo 77/78*, Moscow, 1980 (plate 7.10). I am also grateful to A.D.A.G.P. for permission to reproduce the works of Ivan Puni (plates 1.14–15: © A.D.A.G.P., Paris).

CONTENTS

INTRODUCTION

RUSSIAN CONSTRUCTIVISM posited an entirely new relationship between the artist, his work and society. This radical reassessment of artistic activity was a direct response to the experience of the Russian Revolution of 1917 and of the ensuing Civil War. The far-reaching and utopian aspirations which inspired those artists who adhered to Constructivism were embodied in works like Tatlin's Monument to the Third International, but despite the great interest and enthusiasm generated at different times for such works and ideas in the West, precise knowledge of these has remained elusive. In Western literature Constructivism has been portrayed as a movement primarily concerned with aesthetics. Ever since the West first became aware of the artistic developments of post-revolutionary Russia in 1922, at the Erste Russische Kunstausstellung in Berlin, it has viewed Russian Constructivism pre-eminently as an art movement. In reality it was something much wider: an approach to working with materials, within a certain conception of their potential as active participants in the process of social and political transformation.

The first step towards a coherent Western account of the early modernist movement in Russia was provided by Camilla Gray in her book of 1962, *The Great Experiment: Russian Art, 1863–1922*. In opening up a new area of research it was perhaps inevitable that there would be inaccuracies and confusions here, but some of them did touch upon central issues. This was especially evident in her account of Constructivism, where Gabo and Pevsner who never embraced a utilitarian aesthetic were grouped with Tatlin, Rodchenko, Stepanova and Popova, and the differences between what were designated the various 'versions' of Constructivism were not elucidated.

This confusion and the tendency to interpret Constructivism as a purely 'artistic' phenomenon was continued in the work of George Rickey, whose *Constructivism: Origins and Evolution* appeared in New York in 1967. Rickey defined 'Constructivist' as a term referring to

> the work of a group of Russians between 1913 and 1922, which include Tatlin, Malevich, Rodchenko, El Lissitzky, Naum Gabo, Antoine Pevsner, and briefly, Wassily Kandinsky. Their work is, in general, geometrical and non-mimetic. It refers also to the Dutch art which resembled that of the Russians but did not derive from it, to the ensuing painting and sculpture in Europe and America which emanated from the two groups, including 'Concrete Art' and 'Kalte Kunst', and to much of the work done in such groups as 'Cercle et Carré', 'Réalités Nouvelles' and 'American Abstract Artists'. The term will also encompass more recent work characterised by such neologisms as 'hard-edge', 'post-painterly abstraction' and 'primary structures', as well as the most all-embracing European term, 'new tendency', which was a cry of mutual recognition rather than a definition of style.[1]

The confusion of this catholicity was clarified in Stephen Bann's compilation *The Tradition of Constructivism*, published simultaneously on both sides of the Atlantic in 1974. Bann acknowledged that 'in Russia the development of Constructivism led very swiftly beyond the traditional genres of the plastic arts into the wider fields of planning and design for a revolutionary society',[2] but his further discussion was then conducted primarily in conventional Western art-historical terms. The result of stressing those dimensions which did have a Western parallel was a conception that left little place for the factor of 'social construction' which was the essential element distinguishing Soviet Constructivism's move into these wider fields.

Although no satisfactory overall account of Constructivism has appeared in the West, or in Soviet Russia, Soviet scholars have produced a valuable series of articles as a result of detailed archive investigations, which have gone a long way to help clarify certain points in the development of the Constructivist movement. The initial task of opening up the field was performed during the early 1960s by Alina Vasil'evna Abramova, who presented the first detailed and coherent accounts of the careers of Tatlin, Rodchenko and the Stenberg brothers and of various areas of work in the Higher Artistic and Technical Workshops. As a pupil of I. Matsa, a Hungarian who went to live in Russia in the 1920s and who in 1933 compiled the first and still crucially valuable collection of documents from the artistic activity of this period,[3] Abramova represents a link directly back to the people and the reality of this period. Subsequent research by such scholars as L. Marts, N. Adaskina, L. Zhadova, A. Lavrent'ev, E. Murina and A. Strigalev have moved investigations further in specific areas. This step towards a more thorough understanding of Constructivist work took place against a background of investigations into the wider artistic heritage of the Russian avant-garde over the same period. Especially important here has been the work of S. O. Khan-Magomedov, E. Kovtun, A. Povelikhina and V. Rakitin. This work by Soviet scholars has prepared the way for a detailed reworking and synthesising of whole movements, such as I have attempted here for Constructivism.

*   *   *

Constructivism first emerged both as an artistic practice and as a term for this practice in the Russian artistic world at the beginning of the 1920s. The term seems to have appeared in print for the very first time in the catalogue for the exhibition entitled *The Constructivists: K. K. Medunetskii, V. A. Stenberg, G. A. Stenberg*, held at the Poets' Café (Kafe Poetov), Moscow, in January 1922.[4] The exhibits comprised spatial structures made from real materials with a very strong industrial emphasis. The nature of these constructions was explained in the declaration of the three artists printed in the catalogue. This stated unequivocally that all artists should now 'go into the factory, where the real body of life is made', and asserted that 'this route is called Constructivism'. The artists wrote of Constructivism as 'the highest springboard for the leap into universal human culture' and juxtaposed it to art and aestheticism which they considered corrupting: 'The Constructivists declare art and its priests to be outlaws.' In a rather vague form this declaration gave expression to most of the basic principles that were developed by Constructivism: the call for the artist to go into the factory; the recognition that the factory is the real creative force in the world; the impediment that conventional concepts of art and practising artists represent to such a link between art and life, and therefore the call for their banishment; and the identification with a new political and social order. The artists' declaration that 'Constructivism will lead humanity to master a maximum of cultural values with the minimum expenditure of energy' shows that Constructivism was seen to represent the culture of the future, although it is not specifically linked in this statement with communist ideology.

As the accompanying declaration makes clear, this first use of the term 'Constructivism' links it to the concept of the merging of art and life through mass production and industry. Constructivist activity is equally clearly being juxtaposed to the concept of creating a 'work of art' with the result that the validity of such purely artistic activity is strongly denied. Since Constructivism's first appearance in print related it to a functional aesthetic it is to be presumed that this is an accurate rendition of the meaning of the term as understood at its inception.

Such an interpretation is confirmed by the way the First Working Group of Constructivists, officially set up in March 1921, used the term. This group consisted of Aleksei Gan, Aleksandr Rodchenko, Varvara Stepanova, Karl Ioganson and the Constructivists who wrote the declaration of January 1922, Vladimir Stenberg, Georgii Stenberg and Konstantin Medunetskii. As the group made clear in its programme, it set out to 'involve its members in the revolutionary inventive work of the Constructivists, who . . . have decided to realise the communist expression of material structures'.[5] This aim involved a complete rejection of the art work as a product of the old order and hence irredeemably individualistic and bourgeois.

> Art in the past stood in the place of religion.
> It arose from the main spring of individualism.[6]

Therefore art as such had no place in the new society. In its stead 'intellectual production' would serve the new communist collective by fusing the formal experience gained from making abstract constructions in three dimensions with the ideology of Marxism and the constraints of industrial production. The programme stated explicitly that Constructivists should enter the factories armed with an approach based on communism.

From this it may be concluded that the term 'Constructivism' arose in Russia during the winter of 1920–1 as a term specifically formulated to meet the needs of these new attitudes towards the culture of the future classless society. Strictly speaking, the term should not be used with reference to those works of art which were made prior to the Revolution, completely free of any utilitarian content or social commitment on the part of the artists who produced them. On the other hand the three-dimensional works of the pre-revolutionary period did provide the formal language of the movement and applying the word 'construction' to them recognises such a relationship.

To solve the problem of a term which will emphasise the relationship between the two periods and yet still express the differences between them, I have adopted the term 'non-utilitarian constructions' to describe those works conceived without the implicitly ideological, industrial and social commitment of the Constructivists. Nakov used the term 'laboratory period',[7] presumably because the term 'laboratory work' was used by the Constructivists to denote those formal abstract researches which were undertaken with an ultimately utilitarian aim in mind.[8] However, this term is too closely linked with a specific historical period and particular type of work to be used properly with reference to the abstract three-dimensional works of the pre-revolutionary period and to those of a purely aesthetic nature created after the Revolution. The term 'non-utilitarian construction' is therefore used to describe such works throughout this study.

Another set of terminological confusions has bedevilled the existing literature on Constructivism. In retrospect it is easy to interpret the aims of the Constructivists as those of artists wanting to become 'designers'. Belonging to a period before the modern concept of design had fully emerged, the Constructivists used a multiplicity of terms to describe the precise nature of the activity they envisaged, and the nature of the design task. The theoretical statements and debates of the period are therefore exceedingly confusing.

One of the most common terms encountered and one that is particularly difficult is '*proizvodstvennoe iskusstvo*' or 'production art'. As I shall point out in Chapter Three it was used in a variety of ways. In essence it denoted an artistic involvement with the mass-produced industrial object. This involvement, however, could be of many different kinds. On the one hand it embraced the artist who merely applied a superficial decoration to an already manufactured object; on the other it included the Constructivist approach which envisaged an artist equipped with the necessary technical knowledge to enable him to produce an object the form of which was perfectly suited to its function and to the mechanical process by which it was produced. Because the term 'design' had not emerged, the design process the Constructivists envisaged was often referred to as *khudozhestvennoe konstruirovanie*. This term can be literally translated as 'artistic construction', but it differs from the English expression in that it denotes the process of assembling the artistic elements of the object. *Khudozhestvennaya promyshlennost'* literally means 'artistic production'. Normally in Russian this denotes the general participation of art as *proizvodstvennoe iskusstvo* in industry – and like that term is not identified with any particular approach to this participation. However, it is generally used to describe applied art which consists of an artistic decoration applied to an already completed object entailing changes in the form of the decorated object only with consideration for its decorative potential – such as is consistent with a craft approach, although it can also be used to describe all the in-between ranges culminating in the complete fusion of the production and artistic process. Where possible I shall indicate precise meanings in a given context, or indicate the difficulties of interpretation involved.

I have used the system of transliteration employed by the *Oxford Slavonic Papers* with the alteration that both a soft sign and a hard sign are represented by a single diacritical mark. Russian surnames have generally been rendered according to this system. Hence, Kandinsky becomes Kandinskii. However, where other forms have become well established as in Lissitzky or Chagall and this system would render them unrecognisable it has not been adopted. There are exceptions such as Ivan Puni, where I have chosen to retain the strict transliteration of the original Russian instead of the later Jean Pougny. In the case of artists like Klutsis who were non-Russian yet who spent the largest part of their active lives in Russia I have used the Russian transliteration rather than the native form of the name, which in this case would be Klucis.

*   *   *

This study of Russian Constructivism does not pretend to be an exhaustive account of the Constructivist movement in Russia. It is merely an attempt to identify and delineate the principal themes of the movement and its main stages of development. Naturally, a lot more research needs to be done among the rich sources of Soviet archives, and I hope that this study will be followed by more detailed investigations. My intention has been merely to establish a factual framework within which these can legitimately take place. There are naturally portions of the story where the primary source material with which I have worked corroborates rather than refutes accounts hitherto assembled. But even these can now be traced back to their original documentation. In other areas, the documentation has produced an entirely different interpretation.

I will not summarise the detailed argument of each chapter. In its briefest form the story line is a simple one. The 'non-utilitarian' constructions of the pre-revolutionary period provided the formal vocabulary for Constructivism. The identification of the formal language and work in materials with the revolutionary tasks of propaganda, agitation and later with creating the new communist environment and harnessing it to the power of industry occurred during the few years immediately following the October Revolution of 1917. It led to the theoretical debates conducted within the INKhUK (Institut khudozhestvennoi kul'tury – Institute of Artistic Culture) and formulations of a new concept of the role of art and of the artist. The ideal of the 'artist-constructor' and the 'artist-engineer' emerged.

The realisation of this ideal was entrusted to the VKhUTEMAS (Vysshie gosudar-stvennye khudozhestvennye i tekhnicheskie masterskie – Higher State Artistic and Technical Workshops) where the formal, ideological and technical elements of the Constructivist approach were taught. In addition Constructivist artists attempted to design everyday objects for mass production. These will be examined together with the results of the Constructivists' sorties into theatrical design and graphic design.

It has always been assumed that Constructivism consisted entirely of those works inspired by the forms of contemporary machine technology which have usually been associated with the term. In this study I will put forward the hypothesis that in addition to this mechanical dimension there is a phenomenon that I have chosen to call Organic Constructivism. Rooted in the work of the pioneering figure Vlad-imir Tatlin, it derived its inspiration from the organic forms found in natural phenomena.

The traditional interpretation of the decline of Russian avant-garde activity in general and of Constructivism in particular has always been that of a vital artistic activity cut off in its prime by a repressive and reactionary regime. The final chapters of this study therefore centre upon the question of the nature of this decline, and posit a different interpretation of Constructivism's demise. I argue that the re-emergence of that very Realism which has traditionally been juxtaposed to Constructivism struck a chord which was already potentially resonant in Construc-tivism's own development, and which logically emerged from the new technological aesthetic that it espoused. One of the most prominent manifestations of this was the use of photomontage. Constructivism's adaptability and this continuity are emphasised by summarising the subsequent, albeit obscure, careers of Constructiv-ism's erstwhile leading members, after modernism as a whole fell into disfavour in the Soviet Union, in the early 1930s. This study ends with Constructivism's recep-tion in the West and the way in which the Russian movement's social, political and industrial imperatives became subsumed within the aesthetic dimension of the Western movement.

1 NON-UTILITARIAN CONSTRUCTIONS: THE EVOLUTION OF A FORMAL LANGUAGE

THE FIRST non-utilitarian constructions in Russia were made by the artist Vladimir Evgrafovich Tatlin in 1913, when he stopped creating two-dimensional compositions of painterly elements on the plane of the canvas and began experimenting with the construction of small three-dimensional objects made from materials such as metal, wood and glass. Tatlin, who is credited with being 'the founder of Constructivism', has a dual claim to this title.[1] Not only did he play a decisive role in the development of Constructivism proper after the Revolution of 1917 with his Monument to the Third International, of 1920, but he also undoubtedly initiated the work on non-utilitarian constructions which preceded it.

This initial phase of making small-scale abstract art works from combinations of materials in three dimensions generally came to an end between 1920 and 1921 when a strong utilitarian dimension started to emerge in the work of Tatlin and other Constructivist artists. This general trend is subject to certain qualifications. Not all artists who had been engaged on the creation of non-utilitarian constructions adopted the utilitarian imperative. For those who did, the total abandonment of making abstract art works for the exclusive production of more utilitarian structures proceeded at different rates. Some artists who eventually became Constructivists only began to create abstract three-dimensional works after 1920–1. Other future Constructivists continued such formal experimentation after this date. However, this second period is broadly distinguishable as that in which this type of abstract activity tended to take the form of 'laboratory work'.

The Constructivists used the term 'laboratory work' to describe formal investigation – usually in three dimensions but sometimes in two – which was undertaken not as an end in itself, nor for any immediately utilitarian purpose, but with the idea that such experimentation would eventually contribute to the solution of some utilitarian task. Theoretically, therefore, 'laboratory work' consisted of artistic explorations into the component elements of form, material, colour, space and construction, which were initiated not for their own sake, but with the longer-term purpose of establishing the objective bases of artistic criteria, and general laws of their interrelationships, so that these could be exploited later in the design process.

Although laboratory work was not necessarily harnessed directly to design work, or to the solution of a specific design task, it did provide the artistic bases for such work, and often suggested completely new approaches to it. At the same time the investigations which comprised laboratory work were direct continuations of these artists' previous work in the area of non-utilitarian constructions. It is these continuities which are of particular relevance for understanding Constructivism, and therefore it is apposite to commence this study not with a theoretical exposition of the non-utilitarian constructions themselves but with an examination of their development from the point of view of the formal language which they ultimately provided for the movement into utilitarian tasks.

1.1. V. Tatlin, *The Bottle: A Painterly Relief* (*Butylka. Zhivopisnyi rel'ef*), 1913, wallpaper, wood, metal, glass. Whereabouts unknown. [First reproduced in Gray, *Great Experiment*, 1962.]

VLADIMIR TATLIN

Although Tatlin occupies a central position for the development of Constructivism, any attempt to establish the precise details of his life and artistic development immediately encounters difficulties. These uncertainties relating to factual information would be fewer had not a large quantity of Tatlin's private papers been lost soon after his death in 1953. According to Abramova, the concierge, who was impatient to clear his room, threw many important items on the rubbish heap.[2] Some of his paintings and papers and one wing of the *Letatlin*, his flying machine, were rescued by Tatlin's friend Sara Lebedeva, the sculptress, but much was lost. This accidental loss compounded previous losses caused by the dislocation and disruptions of the 1930s and the Second World War. However, a great deal of the scarcity of surviving works, not only by Tatlin but by other Constructivists too, can be attributed to the Constructivists themselves. Their attitude of disclaiming the importance of the artist's creative individuality made them more than usually careless of their own creations.

Nevertheless certain facts do emerge with some clarity. We know for instance that Tatlin was born in Moscow in 1885 and grew up in the Ukraine. His father was an engineer and his mother a poetess who died when he was two years old. Tatlin seems to have had a very unhappy childhood and ran away to sea at a fairly young age. It is significant that his initial artistic training commenced in 1902 when he started painting icons under the direction of Levenets and Kharchenko.[4] That same year Tatlin entered the more academically orientated Moscow School of Painting, Sculpture and Architecture (Moskovskoe uchilishche zhivopisi, vayaniya i zodchestva) where he studied until 1904.[5] This period of study seems to have been interrupted by more adventures as a sailor.

Between 1904 and 1909 Tatlin studied at the Penza Art School under the artist Afanas'ev, who was a member of the Society of Travelling Art Exhibitions (Tovarishchestvo peredvizhnykh khudozhestvennykh vystavok, active 1870–1923). Known as Itinerants or Wanderers (Peredvizhniki), these artists were committed to creating an art relevant to Russian reality which would describe contemporary conditions and social problems. Although stylistically embedded in Realism, the national, social and political commitment of these artists may have had an impact on Tatlin. Later Tatlin described Afanas'ev as one of the three artists who had influenced him most. He named the other two as Pablo Picasso and Mikhail Larionov.[6] After graduating from Penza, Tatlin spent a year, 1909–10, at the Moscow School of Painting, Sculpture and Architecture, but he does not seem to have completed the course. About this date he began to be closely associated with the then leaders of the Russian avant-garde, Mikhail Larionov and Natalia Goncharova. Through them he became acquainted with the latest developments amongst Western and native progressive artists. Subsequently he exhibited works with the Russian avant-garde at the Donkey's Tail exhibition (Oslinyi khvost) of 1912, and at the Knave of Diamonds (Bubnovyi valet) and the Union of Youth (Soyuz molodezhi) in 1913–14.[7]

As far as can be ascertained, the first relief or in Tatlin's terms 'painterly relief' (*zhivopisnyi rel'ef*), was *The Bottle* of *c.* 1913 (plate 1.1).[8] The artistic impulse for the reliefs has usually been attributed to the visual stimulation provided by Picasso's reliefs which Tatlin saw when he visited the latter's studio in Paris in 1913–14.[9] This is an attractive explanation, since it provides a satisfactory link between two apparently different phases of Tatlin's artistic activity. Moreover, Tatlin himself later stressed that Picasso was one of the three painters who had influenced him most, and in 1919 Tatlin underlined the importance of his Parisian visit when he wrote, 'I have studied in France'.[10] This emphasis suggests that the Parisian experience was a formative one for Tatlin so that some of the ideas to which it exposed him need to be summarised.

Tatlin would already have been acquainted with Cubism before his visit to Paris, through the Shchukin Collection in Moscow and through Cubist contributions to Russian exhibitions. Le Fauconnier had exhibited with the Knave of Diamonds in 1910-11 and Picasso had himself shown Cubist works at that group's exhibitions of 1912, 1913 and 1914 held in Moscow.[11] But in Paris Tatlin was able to see Picasso's collages and the more extended reliefs which Picasso had developed from his experiments with collage of the previous year, when he and Braque had begun to utilise various scraps of paper and other materials in their otherwise painted compositions. The first collage was Picasso's *Still Life with Chair-Caning* (1912) into which he had incorporated a piece of oilcloth, overprinted to imitate chair-caning.[12] From this he had gone on to frame the painting with a piece of rope, and by early 1913 he was working with bits of paper, cloth, zinc and tinfoil. In 1912 Braque also produced the first *papier collé* in a drawing entitled *Compotier et verre* to which he affixed three pieces of wallpaper imitating wood panelling.[13]

The invention of collage revolutionised the concept of what constituted a work of art, proving that 'this monster beauty is not eternal' and extending the range of accepted materials from which a work of art could be made.[14] 'One can paint with whatever one likes, with pipes, postage stamps, postcards or playing cards, candle sticks, pieces of oilcloth, detachable collars, painted paper, newspapers.'[15] Material which until then had been considered of little or no value was utilised in the creation of art. The very uselessness and refuse quality of this material seemed to have been suitable to the Cubists' purpose: 'We sought to express reality with materials we did not know how to handle, and which we prized precisely because we knew their help was not indispensable to us, that they were neither the best nor the most adequate.'[16]

However, collage should not be regarded as an entirely accidental development from Cubism. It was inherent in the Cubists' conception of their works as self-contained constructed objects:[17] 'The Cubist *collages* and *papiers collés* are in a sense exactly that – objects built up of various substances and materials, a protest against the conventional oil painting ... the strips of paper, fragments of canvas and other materials that the painters applied to their pictures emphasised in a very concrete way their weight and solidity as material objects.'[18] Picasso went on from his explorations of the possibilities of collage to make totally three-dimensional constructions from paper and cardboard, some of which incorporate or represent musical instruments.[19] These belong to the period 1912-13 and therefore Tatlin may have seen them when he visited Picasso.

The collage technique had its own history in Russian art independent of Tatlin. It was also adopted by the Russian Cubist movement. Malevich had incorporated various collage elements into his pre-Suprematist paintings such as *Woman at a Poster Column* (1914).[20] In 1916 Rozanova composed and Kruchenykh entitled a series of completely abstract illustrations consisting almost entirely of cut-out pieces of coloured tissue paper arranged on sugar paper for the album *The Universal War*.[21] Stepanova followed this in 1919 with her hand-made book *Gaust Chaba* which consisted of collages and poems, stuck and written onto newspaper and published in a limited edition of fifty copies.[22]

These experiments postdate Tatlin's work but remain firmly within the concept of collage as inaugurated by the *papiers collés* of Braque and the collage works of Picasso, and they seemed to have derived from Russian experiments with Cubism rather than from the impact of Tatlin's work with its overwhelming stress on the three-dimensional presence of the material.

There is evidence to suggest that Tatlin may have been experimenting with a Cubist analysis of form, at least in his drawings, prior to his departure from Russia in 1913. Two sketchbooks preserved at the Central State Archives of Literature and Art (TsGALI) in Moscow contain the draft of a letter concerning Tatlin's proposed trip to Berlin and Paris together with some Cubist-inspired figure draw-

1.2. (facing page left) V. Tatlin, *A Cubist Drawing*, *c*. 1913, pencil on paper, 43 × 26 cm. Leaf 79 from an album of Tatlin drawings in the Central State Archive of Literature and Art, Moscow.

1.3. (facing page right) V. Tatlin, *The Nude* (*Naturshchitsa*), 1913, oil on canvas, 143 × 108 cm. Tret'yakov Gallery, Moscow.

1.6. Peasant woodcut (*lubok*) of the 18th century.

1.7. *Icon of the Virgin of Vladimir*, 12th century. Tret'yakov Gallery, Moscow.

1.4. (facing page left) V. Tatlin, *Panel No. 1* (*Doska No. 1*), 1917, tempera and gilt on board, 105 × 57 cm. Tret'yakov Gallery, Moscow.

1.5. (facing page right) V. Tatlin, *The Sailor: A Self-Portrait* (*Moryak. Avtoportret*), 1911–12, oil on canvas, 71·5 × 71·5 cm. Russian Museum, Leningrad.

ings.[23] These sketches which consist of sitting or standing figures are schematic in their cubic structure (plate 1.2). In some, Tatlin's approach can be compared to that of Hermetic Cubism in the manner in which he has reinterpreted the original structure. Presuming that the date of the draft letter contained in this sketchbook approximates to the date of the sketches, then these Cubist works could be attributed to the period just before, or just after, his trip to Germany and France.

In the light of this, the painterly reliefs, which exploit and extend the principle of collage as developed by Cubism, could be seen to be a logical continuation of these Cubist interests. Without this artistic interest in Cubism, Tatlin's 'painterly reliefs' remain an apparently inexplicable change of direction, seemingly lacking any solid artistic basis in his previous work. However, the sketches cannot be accurately dated since it is known that Tatlin preserved drawings and papers haphazardly, and in his concern to compile an archive economically often made copies of later letters on earlier drawings and vice versa.[24] This suggests that it would be difficult to draw any firm conclusions from the juxtaposition of a Cubist drawing and the text of a letter of 1913. The problems could be clarified by the presence of a Cubist painting in Tatlin's oeuvre. However, the earliest paintings that correspond most closely to a Cubist definition are his panel paintings such as *Panel No. 1* (plate 1.4), which is a work of 1917.[25] Since this postdates, rather than predates, Tatlin's work on the reliefs, *Panel No. 1* cannot serve as evidence that Tatlin was working in any type of Cubist medium prior to the trip to Paris. What the existence of the Cubist sketches establishes beyond doubt is that Tatlin was experimenting with Cubist analysis at some time just before, just after or at the same time as he began working on the reliefs.[26]

Among the paintings that immediately preceded the 'painterly reliefs' were *The Nude* of 1913 (plate 1.3) and *The Sailor: A Self-Portrait* of 1911–12 (plate 1.5).[27] Neither of these is a Cubist work. Despite the use of perspectival distortions and a tendency towards the analysis of form into facets and planes, these are curvilinear, as is the treatment of mass. These qualities, together with the powerful monumentality of these paintings, point to native sources of inspiration such as the traditional popular art of the Russian woodcut (plate 1.6), the *lubok* (*lubochnaya kartina*), and the icon with its spiritual images. The influence of the latter is especially evident in *The Nude*, where the image is analysed in curved planes and is pressed close to the picture plane in a way that is characteristic of these devotional objects (plate 1.7). Moreover, the painting technique that Tatlin employed in this work is strongly reminiscent of icon painting. Composed of three colours, ochre, red and cobalt blue (subtle variations of the three primaries), applied flatly to the canvas in the manner of icons, the image has been given substance by the addition of white highlighting and black shading applied schematically to the base colour. Such similarities of approach to the modelling of form and handling of space prompted Tatlin's colleague the art critic Nikolai Punin to assert that 'the influence of the Russian icon on Tatlin is undoubtedly greater than the influence upon him of Cézanne or Picasso'.[28]

That Tatlin should have been influenced by icons is not surprising. As a young man his initial training in art had been with icons, he had worked in icon studios both in Moscow and in Yaroslavl', and therefore he had a first-hand knowledge of icon painting techniques.[29] Tatlin's interest in icons would undoubtedly have been further stimulated by the exhibition of icons held in Moscow in 1913 to celebrate the three hundred years of Romanov rule in Russia. Although the exhibition included manuscript illumination, embroidery and metalwork, it was the icons that won the interest and enthusiasm of the reviewers in the contemporary art journal *Apollon*.[30] In addition, the Russian Futurist movement to which Tatlin belonged had become very interested in native Russian artistic traditions and Primitivism as manifest in peasant and children's art, employing icons, *lubki* and children's drawings directly as sources of inspiration for their artistic activity.[31]

11

The impact of this traditional Russian material that was receiving attention in Moscow during the 1910s was almost certainly one of the factors leading to the genesis of the painterly reliefs. According to the evidence of Berthold Lubetkin, Tatlin had told him several times 'how inspired by the icons he started to drill his boards, mounting on them rings, screws, bells, marking and screwing the background, gluing abacus beads, mirrors, tinsels, and arriving at a shimmering dangling and sonorous composition', and that the specific source of this stimulus was the major exhibition of icons held in Moscow in 1913. ' "If it wasn't for the icons", he used to tell me, "I should have remained preoccupied with water-drips, sponges, rags and aquarelles." '[32]

One aspect of the icon that may have stimulated Tatlin in his move towards creating three-dimensional constructions through the combinations of various materials, was the elaborately worked ceremonial frame, usually made from valuable metals and encrusted with precious stones, which enclosed the image. The

1.8. V. Tatlin, *Selection of Materials: Counter-Relief (Material'nyi podbor. Kontr-rel'ef)*, 1916, galvanised iron on wood, 100 × 64 × 24 cm. Tret'yakov Gallery, Moscow.

sculptor and critic Waldemars Matveys (who wrote under the pseudonym Vladimir Markov) stressed this aspect of the icon as an important precedent for the new sculpture.

Let us remember the icons; they are embellished with metal halos, metal casings on the shoulders, fringes and incrustations; the painting itself is decorated with precious stones and metals, etc. All of this destroys our contemporary conception of painting ... Through the resonance of the colours, the sound of the materials, the assemblage of textures [*faktura*], we call the people to beauty, to religion, to God ... The real world is introduced into [the icon's] creation only through the assemblage and incrustation of real, tangible objects. And this seems to produce a combat between two worlds, the inner ... and outer.[33]

The expressive qualities of the materials of the icons may have produced a very similar effect on Tatlin. Certainly Tatlin's interests in the resonance of materials

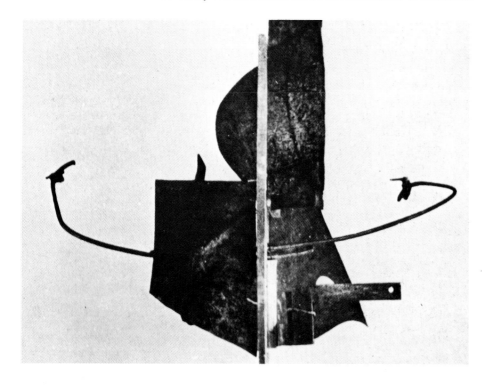

1.9. *Central Relief, c.* 1914–15. Whereabouts unknown. [First reproduced in Gray, *'Great Experiment*, 1962.]

and the materiality of the object were constant factors in his work, and on the basis of this Punin argued that there was no sharp break in Tatlin's work between the paintings and the reliefs. Punin had stressed Tatlin's constant interest in colour as material and in pigment as a structural element, demonstrated initially in his approach to the surface textures (*faktura*) of the painting and his varied manipulation of the pigments.[34] In paintings like *The Sailor: A Self-Portrait*, Tatlin mixed different media and combined accidental effects of liquid colour with thickly impastoed oil paint.

Tatlin's reliefs similarly exploited the inherent properties of the materials used, their interrelationships, and the qualities of their surface textures, which seem to have been as central a concern as the reliefs' spatial dimension. Materials were either used in states which almost approximated to that of being found (apparently only marginally altered for the composition) or else worked in a manner consistent with their natural state and requiring only the minimal intervention by the artist, hence the metal conical shape in *Selection of Materials: Counter-Relief* of 1917 (plate 1.8), and the bending and hammering of the metal in *Central Relief* of 1914–15 (plate 1.9).

Tatlin does not seem to have used techniques such as casting, and in this context it is interesting to read Valentina Khodasevich's account of Tatlin producing some reliefs for the Tramway V exhibition in 1915. Initially Tatlin wanted to use the rear leg of a piano, although finally he used refuse items collected from the cellar: 'I should like to take things you no longer need – glass, wood, bark, pieces of metal and copper would be good, and anything else which might catch my fancy.'[35] Khodasevich describes Tatlin working with this material:

He used a saw, an axe, a chisel, wire, nails, canvas stretched over sub-frames, coloured paper, paints, brushes, a spray, a kerosene lamp to blacken different surfaces for shadow … He chopped, planed, cut, broke off pieces of glass, diluted size, and for a long time feasted his eyes on a scrap of sheet metal and it was generally clear that he was fired with inspiration. He drilled holes into primed canvases which I had prepared for portraits and pushed in some wire with which he fixed chocks, wood, and crushed paper, repeating 'Marvellous. Beautiful. We will colour some bits and darken others with smoke.'[36]

The earliest of all Tatlin's known reliefs, *The Bottle* (plate 1.1), also had the simplest structure. Although the work is believed no longer to exist, it is evident from the single extant photograph that it was primarily painterly in character. Tatlin's concern had been to analyse the material, i.e. the glass and the shape of the bottle, in a three-dimensional way. The neck of the bottle silhouette is placed against a circular shape which seems to represent the internal shape of the bottle as viewed from above. According to Camilla Gray the material covered by the wire filigree was a piece of 'curved polished metal'; however, Ivan Puni, who would have had the opportunity presumably to study the work at first hand, identified this element as a piece of glass.[37] As glass, combined with the metal netting, this component of the relief presents a clear investigation of the ambiguity of the glazed volume of the bottle and of its almost transparent structure. The curve of the outline form of the bottle is repeated in the sweeping curve of the metal section below it. To the right of that is what appears to be a section of wallpaper.[38] Its rectangular pattern may be no more than a general indication of the everyday environment in which drinking occurs, but it relates the bottle to the real world very directly and emphasises the narrative and representational character of the work as a whole. This was not an abstract relief. Although the bottle is fragmented to reveal its external and internal structure in accordance with the general principles of Cubist analysis and three-dimensional collage, it is still identifiable. The relief, concerned to analyse the shape and the materials of a real object, has not developed into a completely abstract analysis of form and material. The photograph suggests that the whole composition is held within the rectangular picture frame and that it has been built outwards from this two-dimensional plane. The work's relationship with the surrounding spatial environment develops only to a limited extent in the curvilinear surface of the metal which juts forward from the picture plane. As such this work represents only a tentative experiment towards a bolder relationship with space.

In the next series of reliefs about which we have documentary evidence, the properties and interrelationships of the materials replace the narrative content. Whereas the first relief, *The Bottle*, was primarily concerned with investigating the qualities of the still life of the bottle, its form and material, the later reliefs were more concerned with the interrelationships and properties of the materials themselves. *Painterly Relief belonging to I. A. Puni* (plate 1.10) and *Painterly Relief, the property of A. A. Ekster* (plate 1.11), both of 1913–14, are very similar to each other.[39] Although they are completely abstract they only establish a very limited relationship with the surrounding space. They both remain firmly within the format of the picture frame, but in plate 1.10 it is clear that the diagonally placed strip of wood breaks the line of the rectangular foundation board from which it appears to

1.10 V. Tatlin, *Painterly Relief belonging to I.A. Puni* (*Zhivoposnyi rel'ef priobreten I. A. Puni*), 1913–14. Whereabouts unknown. [Reproduced in *Vladimir Evgrafovich Tatlin*, 1915.]

1.11. V. Tatlin, *Painterly Relief, the Property of A. A. Ekster* (*Zhiboposnyi rel'ef sobstv. A. A. Ekster*), 1913–14. Whereabouts unknown. [Reproduced in *Vladimir Evgrafovich Tatlin*, 1915.]

1.12. V. Tatlin, *Selection of Materials: Iron, Stucco, Glass, Asphalt* (*Material'nyi podbor. Zhelezo, shtukatura, steklo, gudron*), 1914. Whereabouts unknown. [Reproduced in Punin, *Tatlin* (*Protiv kubizma*), 1921.]

have been built. Later Tatlin completely discarded the rectangular frame and abandoned entirely the practice of using a flat foundation surface that limited him to a basically one-directional involvement with space.

This movement into three dimensions beyond both picture plane and picture frame is more strongly evident in *Selection of Materials: Iron, Stucco, Glass, Asphalt* of 1914 (plate 1.12).[40] Although the square frame is still present, the elements project further beyond it than in any of the previous reliefs. The dramatic forward jutting of the triangle begins to produce a far more active relationship with the

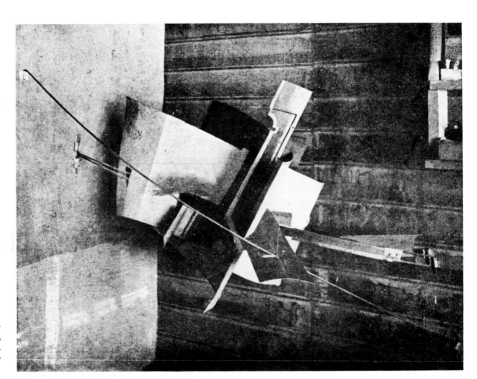

1.13. V. Tatlin, *Corner Counter-Relief* (*Uglovoi kontr-rel'ef*), 1914–15. Whereabouts unknown. [Reproduced in *Vladimir Evgra-fovich Tatlin*, 1915.]

surrounding space. The triangle straddles a square-sectioned wooden rod which is itself set into the plaster surface at an angle producing a counteracting movement to that of the triangle. Below and above the latter is a contrasting curve of metal enclosing and continued in a curved sheet of glass. The glass is narrower at the bottom than at the top, resembling a truncated cone. Tatlin also used this form reversed, in the later *Selection of Materials: Counter-Relief* (plate 1.8).[41]

Tatlin had initially used the terms 'painterly relief' (*zhivopisnyi rel'ef*) or 'selection of materials (*material'nyi podbor*) to describe these works. He adopted the term 'counter-relief' (*kontr-rel'ef*) only after the exhibition of his works in 1914.[42] The new term did not denote an intensification of the relief qualities of these works or any plastic deepening, but referred to the more intense relationship they formed with the surrounding spatial environment, in other words, their outward expansion into space and their movement towards encapsulating the real spatial environment. It seems that Tatlin considered that the prefix '*kontr*-' suggested this increased tension and energy in the same way that the impact of a 'counter' attack was more forceful than an attack.[43] This terminology was obviously heavily dependent upon the martial atmosphere of the First World War and the consequent popularity of military terms in civilian life.

Tatlin's next works developed outwards into space, resulting in the complete liberation of the work from the wall and its almost completely free suspension in space. The first corner counter-relief (*uglovoi kontr-rel'ef*) seems to have been made in 1914–15.[44] As far as can be judged from photographs, the corner or central relief in plate 1.9 creates a less complex relationship with space than the corner counter-relief of plate 1.13.[45] In the latter the whole construction is strung along an axial wire. The two curving sheets of metal form two diagonally intersecting planes, one of which is again intercut at right angles to the side. The other elements embellish this basic structure. Two elegantly curving supports, one of which is of thick metal with an arrowhead type of decoration, the other wire, form elegantly intersecting lines as they suspend the construction between the two walls of the corner.

The whole construction appears to obey the injunctions of Boccioni's *Technical Manifesto of Futurist Sculpture* (1912):

16

We must take the object which we wish to create and begin with its central core. In this way we shall uncover new laws and new forms which link it invisibly but mathematically to an EXTERNAL PLASTIC INFINITY. This new plastic art will then be a translation, in plaster, bronze, glass, wood or any other material, of those atmospheric planes which bind and intersect things ...

Sculpture must, therefore, make objects live by showing their extensions in space as sensitive, systematic and plastic; no one still believes that an object finishes off where another begins or that there is anything around us - a bottle, a car, a house, a hotel, a street - which cannot be cut up and sectionalised by an arabesque of straight curves.[46]

Moreover the counter-relief fuses with its environment in exactly the same way: 'LET'S SPLIT OPEN OUR FIGURES AND PLACE THE ENVIRONMENT INSIDE THEM.'[47] The fixing of the supports performs both a utilitarian and an artistic function integrating the wall into the sculpture. The walls perform the role of additional planes. Boccioni had stressed that various types of material could be utilised to indicate planes: 'transparent planes, glass, strips of metal sheeting, wire, street-lamps or house-lights may all indicate planes'.[48] Tatlin had utilised these types of materials, but divorced them from any associative function. He had analysed 'the manifestations of material as such and its consequences - movement, tension and their interrelationship'.[49] Here in Tatlin's use of contemporary materials and in his exploration of materials in their spatial environment there is a new emphasis which is not present in the words of the Futurist manifestos. It is difficult to assess the influence of Futurism but it is possible that prior to making the corner counter-reliefs Tatlin may have read the *Technical Manifesto of Futurist Sculpture* or heard it discussed in Russian artistic circles.[50] Certainly Futurist ideas were current in Russia. It is also possible that, while in Paris, Tatlin may have seen the exhibition of Boccioni's work on display from 20 June until 16 July 1913 at the Galerie La Boétie, which included *The Development of a Bottle in Space* and *Unique Forms of Continuity in Space*. Furthermore, the exhibition was reviewed and Boccioni's ideas explained in the September edition of the art journal *Apollon*.[51]

Whatever the extent of Tatlin's knowledge of Boccioni and his manifesto, the influence of the Italian's ideas was probably stronger than his visual example. Although Punin insisted that Italian Futurism had 'practically no relevance to Tatlin',[52] the coincidence of Boccioni's ideas expressed in the *Technical Manifesto of Futurist Sculpture* and the actual construction of the reliefs seems unlikely to have been totally fortuitous. Moreover, in a peculiarly Russian movement developed from Futurism by Mikhail Larionov in 1913 and called Rayism (*luchizm*) there was a concept of the fragmentation of the object and its relationship to its spatial environment which may have been more influential in Tatlin's immediate cultural context than the rather remote examples of the Italians.[53] Propounded by Larionov in 1913, Rayism represented for its author a synthesis of Cubism, Futurism and Orphism. In 'Rayists and Futurists: A Manifesto' of 1913 the Rayist approach was described in the following terms: 'Rayist painting has in view spatial forms, arising from the intersection of reflected rays from different objects.'[54] Its concentration not upon the object itself but upon the lines in space between the objects and the spatial extension of the object had an obvious corollary in the spatially active material elements of the corner counter-reliefs.

However, although Tatlin at one time had been a close colleague of Larionov and had done illustrations for Futurist publications,[55] the booklet he distributed at the 0.10 exhibition in Petrograd in 1915, and which therefore can be assumed to have had his approval, stressed his present artistic independence and complete non-alignment: 'He does not belong to Tatlinism, nor to Rayism, nor to Futurism, nor to the Wanderers, nor to any other similar group.'[56] The very fact that 'Tatlinism' could already be spoken of in this way was clear recognition that Tatlin already had some cult following of his own from which he wanted to dissociate himself, and that he was already recognised among the highly innovative Russian avant-garde as a man of identifiably new ideas.

In the works leading up to and including *Corner Counter-Relief* (plate 1.13) Tatlin had explored the formal elements which were to become dominant in further experiments in non-utilitarian construction and later in Constructivism proper. The counter-reliefs which he exhibited in Petrograd at 0.10 The Last Futurist Exhibition of Paintings in 1916, had an immediate impact on the frenetic activity of his fellow artists.[57]

> Tatlin's reliefs became known in Petrograd this autumn; the naive inventor opened the doors of his painting and relief workshop to let the public see the latest new thing. Larionov - the most enterprising of the scandal-makers - quickly took Tatlin's caprice and gave birth to 'plastic rayonism' [Rayism] for the exhibition, tacking together a composition of pieces of wood, planks, rope, coloured paper, bits of cloth, bottles, etc. ... each tries to put his work on exhibition last to prevent competitors from borrowing his caprices ... They nail together absolutely anything: soiled gloves, a bit of cheap top hat - and call it 'self-portrait of Mayakovskii' or similar ...
>
> On the wall assigned to Larionov, there happened to be a fan. Someone started it up. Larionov was called to admire the new effect given to his construction. He approved hugely and set some strings and nails on the fan.[58]

Such frolics had more in common with the alogical use of chance factors characteristic of Cubist collage and its successors such as Dada montages, than with Tatlin's logical progression forward in his study of materials, their interrelationships and internal tensions and of 'volumes in their real spatial relationships'.[59]

PARALLEL EXPERIMENTS

While Larionov's work was a mere playing with Tatlin's new ideas, there were other artists who explored them more seriously, though in several very different directions. Of those who later became Constructivists, by far the most important was Aleksandr Rodchenko. Other artists, notably Ivan Puni, Ivan Klyun and Lev Bruni, contributed to the enlargement of the new formal vocabulary at this stage. Petr Miturich followed a more personal path, as did the brothers Naum Gabo and Antoine Pevsner, whose conception of the nature and role of 'the art object' led them into emigration at the moment when the Constructivist movement emerged with a utilitarian content.

Among those artists working in three dimensions, Puni and Klyun were conducting experiments parallel to Tatlin but derived directly from their investigations with Cubism rather than from Tatlin's example. As far as can be gauged these experiments were of a limited three-dimensionality and in approach remained essentially painterly. Puni, working from an interest in Synthetic Cubism and Cubist collage, produced a more three-dimensional work in his compilation of materials *The Card Players* (wood, tin, wallpaper, other materials - plate 1.14) which he exhibited at the Tramway V exhibition in Petrograd in 1915.[60] At the same exhibition Puni showed a work that consisted solely of a plane of canvas to which a hammer was attached. The clarity of this construction presenting the *objet trouvé* intact seems directly related to the more Suprematist-inspired constructions, such as *Painterly Sculpture* (plate 1.15), like those that Puni exhibited at the 0.10 exhibition in Petrograd in December 1915 (Nos. 98, 120).[61] These derived their formal inspiration from Malevich's Suprematist works, which had been shown publicly for the first time at this exhibition. Puni's interest in these was clearly concentrated upon the painterly form depicted three-dimensionally, and on the

1.14. I. Puni, *The Card Players* (*Igroki v karty*), 1913-14, wood, wallpaper, tin and other materials, Whereabouts unknown. [Reproduced in review of Tramway V exhibition.]

1.15. I. Puni, *Painterly Sculpture* (*Zhivoposnaya skul'ptura*), 1915, montage of various materials, 36 × 24 cm. Private collection.

1.16. I. Klyun, *A Cubist at her Toilet* (*Kubistka za tualetom*), 1915, collage of iron, wood, *objets trouvés*. Whereabouts unknown. [Reproduced in *Ogonek*, 16 January 1915.]

1.17. I. Klyun, *Rapidly Passing Landscape* (*Probegayushchii peizazh'*), c. 1914–15, painted wood, wire, porcelain. Tret'yakov Gallery, Moscow. [Reproduced in a review of March 1915.]

1.18. I. Klyun, *Construction*, c. 1916. Whereabouts unknown. [Photograph: © George Costakis 1981.]

formal content of the compositions, rather than on the materials from which they were constructed.

Puni asserted in the declaration he issued at this exhibiton, that 'a painting is a new conception of abstracted real elements devoid of meaning.'[62] In accordance with this maxim Puni used three-dimensional form to emphasise the separateness of the component pictorial elements and to explore their formal relationships without reference to their textural or spatial potential.

Klyun's approach to the three-dimensional was very similar to that of Puni. Klyun also became a Suprematist, publishing in company with Malevich a Suprematist declaration at the 0.10 exhibition and making constructions inspired by the pure unbroken geometric forms of Suprematism. In his statement of 1915 he announced that 'our sculpture is pure art . . . it has no content, there is only form'.[63] However, prior to this, Klyun had experimented with both Cubism and Futurism. *A Cubist at her Toilet* (plate 1.16) retained a very close relationship to the anecdotal quality of the representational object (using the *objet trouvé* to emphasise this), and adhered to the essentially static quality of Cubist analysis.[64] The dynamism of Futurism, however, entered into Klyun's work in reliefs such as the *Rapidly Passing Landscape* of 1914–15 (wood, wire, porcelain - plate 1.17),[65] which was constructed on the principle of a strong cutting diagonal intersecting the vertical. This dislocation emphasised through the use of vibrant colours displaced the echoing forms to suggest movement. Both of these works extend the formal vocabulary of two dimensions into three but do not create any new aesthetic vocabulary from this transposition. This observation also holds true for the Suprematist reliefs which Klyun constructed. The manner in which Klyun's later three-dimensional work utilised Suprematist forms is very evident from plate 1.18. The composition is painterly and the use of a limited three-dimensionality adds a spatial quality to the work and creates a composition in space without opening up the interior of form to any dynamic interaction with the surrounding space. This is equally true of those compositions, projected but apparently not built, where the Suprematist forms are intended to be completely liberated from the picture plane and exist completely independently in space, as in the designs Klyun executed for a monument to the artist Ol'ga Rozanova who died in 1918.[66] These designs seem to have been conceived as Suprematist compositions but in three dimensions rather than two. The geometric forms of Suprematism extend into space without space being incorporated into and transforming the nature of those formal elements, and without their material nature being any more than a means towards their three-dimensional realisation. In the same way the process of constructing the object does not find any expression in the completed work. The absence of these material and structural interests and potential areas of development in using Suprematist forms three-dimensionally underlies the difficulties of using this vocabulary of coherent form and colour established in painting for work with materials in three dimensions. Despite these limitations in creating Suprematist constructions there was tremendous potential in constructively exploring the structure of Euclidean geometric forms in space. This is displayed in the intensity and rigour of later investigations by artists like Rodchenko in constructions such as the ellipse (plate 1.32), discussed below, where the internal structure of that form is analysed and developed in space. The greater implications of this work only highlight the comparatively rigid parameters set by the application of the ideal forms of Suprematism to three dimensions in the works described above. Those parameters were perhaps inherent in the Suprematist conception of the painting as pure emotion and pure form.

At the same time a brief flirtation with Cubist collage, and with extended collage in the form of constructions of limited three-dimensionality, was a fairly common feature of the wide range of artistic experiment of this period in Russia. It embraced artists who later remained firmly within a figurative and painterly tradition, such as Lev Aleksandrovich Bruni.

According to Rodchenko's recollections of Tatlin's The Store exhibition in Moscow in 1916, Bruni showed a broken up barrel of cement and a pane of glass that had been pierced by a bullet.[67] Such sensationalist exploitation of the chance and contrived *objet trouvé* to arouse public indignation had little in common with Tatlin's serious investigations. Yet Bruni was undoubtedly influenced by Tatlin, whom he had known well since 1915, and he did pursue more serious explorations of materials and their spatial interrelationships. At present only two examples of such works are known, through photographs. The earlier experiment is *Painterly Work with Materials* of 1916 (plate 1.19), apparently made from wood and metal, as well as other materials.[68] This has none of the narrative content of a Cubist construction, yet it has a very definite painterly quality. It is of only limited three-dimensionality and it is held tight within its rectangular picture frame. The later work is *Construction* of 1917 (plate 1.20), made of celluloid, aluminium, iron, glass and cloth (?).[69] Although it was an open structure which stood freely in space and incorporated space fully within itself, this construction did not establish a dynamic relationship with that spatial environment. Apparently constructed on a triangular base, the perspex, glass, cloth and metal all form planes; and it is this investigation of planes and transparency that provides the dominant focus of the work. It has not been possible to establish whether these two works represent Bruni's total output of non-utilitarian constructions. However, what can be established is that Bruni at no point devoted his energies exclusively to such tasks. Concurrent with his abstract work in three dimensions he was producing figurative canvases, and ultimately in the 1920s he devoted himself entirely to such creations.[70]

1.19. L. Bruni, *Painterly Work with Materials* (*Zhivopisnaya rabota materialov*), 1916. Whereabouts unknown. [Reproduced in *Izobrazitel'noe iskusstvo*, No. 1, 1919.]

1.20. L. Bruni, *Construction*, 1917, celluloid, aluminium, iron, glass, etc. Whereabouts unknown. [First reproduced in Gray, *Great Experiment*, 1962.]

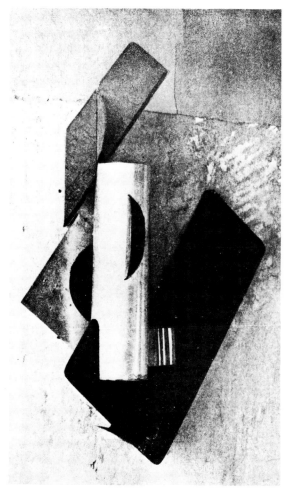

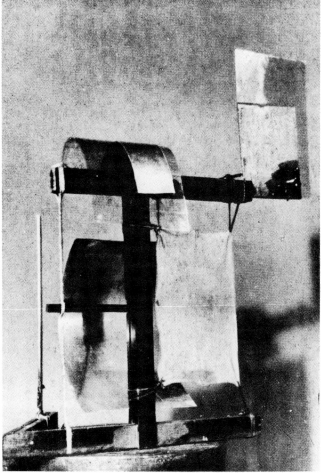

Bruni's experiments were closely echoed by those of Shapiro. The only surviving photograph of Shapiro's work is of *Selection of Materials: Glass, Iron, Wood* of 1921 (plate 1.21). Although spatially more ambitious than Bruni's construction, it displays a basic similarity of approach.[71] Both of these artists clearly based their work on Tatlin's ideas and contributed to the enlargement of the new formal vocabulary. It is therefore appropriate that they were both to assist him with the Monument to the Third International. The Brunis, who lived next door to Tatlin at the former Academy of Art in Petrograd while he was constructing the model for the monument, helped him paint it silver ready for exhibition for November 1920.[72] Shapiro was one of Tatlin's assistants in constructing the model, and he also signed the declaration that accompanied its exhibition in Moscow in 1920.[73]

ALEKSANDR RODCHENKO

Tatlin's most immediate follower was Aleksandr Rodchenko.[74] Son of a theatrical stageworker, Rodchenko had encountered Futurism during his art school career in Kazan', and entered the Moscow avant-garde circles in 1915–16. As far as can be determined, Rodchenko began working on combinations of material elements in three dimensions in 1918. In that year he wrote a short note stating that 'constructive and spatial composition in "real" space becomes completely detached from the flat plane'.[75] Rodchenko is presumably referring to his own work, since Tatlin had already achieved this three years before, in 1915, with the corner counter-reliefs. However, Rodchenko did add a new dimension to the concept of the counter-relief by making constructions which would 'fold and unfold'.[76] It is difficult to establish precisely which works he was describing in this note. However, at the Tenth State Exhibition of 1919 Rodchenko exhibited some works entitled *White Non-Objective Sculpture*.[77] It is possible that this title refers to the untitled work illustrated originally in *Kino-Fot* where it is dated 1918, and here reproduced in plate 1.22.

These 'sculptures' seem to have been rather complicated combinations of regular and irregular rectilinear geometrical elements. Plate 1.23 shows clearly how the interest was focused not so much upon the structural qualities of the materials as on the expressive quality of the component geometrical elements. Tracing his own development in 1921, in his manuscript 'The Line',[78] Rodchenko related these works to his purely painterly investigations of line and colour. He argued that when painting became non-objective it concentrated on studying its own essence and therefore rejected traditional painterly techniques. From this arose on the one hand Rodchenko's works with rule and compasses leading to his linear studies and line constructions on canvas (plate 1.24), and on the other, his monochromatic canvases such as *Black on Black* (plate 1.25).[79] Whereas the *Black on Black* represented a *tabula rasa*, Rodchenko's work with the line led directly to the three-dimensional constructions. Concerning the works he produced in 1917–18 he wrote: 'Lately I have been working exclusively on the construction of forms and the systems of their construction, and I have started to introduce LINE into plane as a new element of construction.'[80]

Subsequently in 1919 and 1920 Rodchenko executed a series of works using pieces of wood of equal length. Using these standard elements he produced a series of standing constructions entitled *Spatial Object* one of which was reproduced in *Kino-Fot* with the dating 1919 (plate 1.26). Here the modular nature of the component elements led to a great simplification of the structure. More complicated investigations were represented by the dense constructions using rectangular wooden sections resembling wooden bricks, such as those illustrated in plates 1.27 and 1.28. Here the emphasis was not upon the delineation of space, but on the definition of mass through complex combinations of standard units.

1.21. T. Shapiro, *Selection of Materials: Glass, Iron, Wood*, 1921, glass, iron, wood. Destroyed. Photographed in Tatlin's studio, Leningrad. [Photograph: A. B. Nakov.]

1.22. A. Rodchenko, *White Non-Objective Sculpture* (*Belaya bespredmetnaya skul'ptura*), 1918. Whereabouts unknown. [Reproduced in *Kino-Fot*, No. 5, 1922.]

1.23. A. Rodchenko, *White Non-Objective Sculpture* (*Belaya bespredmetnaya skul'ptura*), 1918. Whereabouts unknown.

1.25. (facing page top left) A. Rodchenko, *Black on Black* (*Chernoe na chernom*), 1918, 81·9 × 79·4 cm. Collection, The Museum of Modern Art, New York. Gift of the artist, through Jay Leyda.

1.26. (facing page middle left) A. Rodchenko, *Spatial Object* (*Prostranstvennaya veshch'*), 1919. Whereabouts unknown. [Reproduced in *Kino-Fot*, No. 2, 1922.]

1.27. (facing page right) A. Rodchenko, *Spatial Construction* (*Prostranstvennaya konstruktsiya*), 1920, standardised units of wood. Whereabouts unknown.

1.24. A. Rodchenko, *Line Construction*, 1918 oil on board, 47 × 36·2 cm. Private collection, Switzerland. [Photograph: Courtesy Annely Juda Fine Art, London.]

1.28. (facing page) A. Rodchenko, *Spatial Constructions* (*Prostranstvennye konstruktsii*), 1920–1, standardised units of wood. Whereabouts unknown.

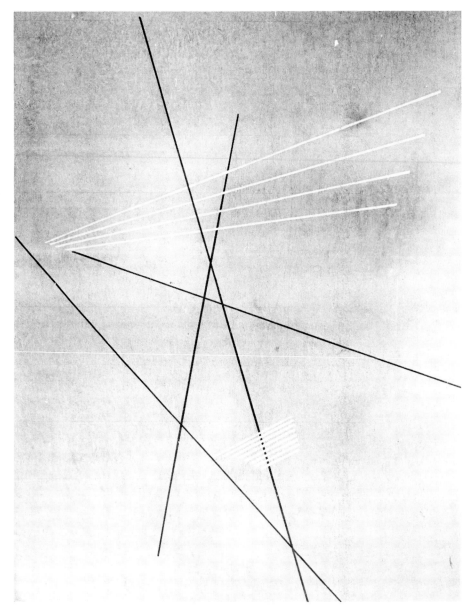

A continuation of the experiments represented by plate 1.26 is found in the series of spatial constructions Rodchenko exhibited for the first time at the third exhibition of the Society of Young Artists (OBMOKhU) which opened in Moscow on 22 May 1921.[81] These works, entitled variously *Spatial Construction* (plate 1.29)[82] and *Spatial Object* (plate 1.30),[83] seem to have been made in the second half of 1920 or early 1921 although not exhibited until May 1921. At the exhibition these three-dimensional structures were suspended from a central wire, as can be seen in plate 2.16, where the hexagon, ellipse, triangle and portion of the circle are visible. In all there seem to have been five constructions: a triangle, a hexagon (plate 1.29), a square (plate 1.30), a circle (plate 1.31) and an ellipse (plate 1.32).[84] They were all made of plywood, and painted silver, presumably to imitate metal.[85] They all shared a common method of construction. Concentric geometrical shapes were cut from one single flat piece of plywood. These concentric elements were then arranged within each other and rotated from a two-dimensional plane into a three-dimensional space to form a spatial composition held in position by the use of wire. After exhibition, the wires could be removed and the construction collapsed back into a flat plane for storage. This can be seen in plate 1.33, where Rodchenko, in his

РОДЧЕНКО. 1921 г.
Пространственная конструкция.

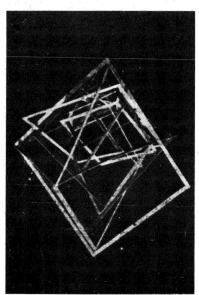

specially designed work-suit, is seen against a background of these stored constructions. The exploration in this way of the growth potential of a single geometric
form in space possessed an inherent dynamism which was increased by the free
movement of the construction on the wire from which it hung. Moreover, in these
explorations of combinations of similar geometric forms there is for the first time
a clear example of how the mode of production and the principle of economy of
material, which later became central tenets of the Constructructivist doctrine, were
being treated as significant constraints upon the creation of the art object. According to the reminiscences of Vladimir Stenberg, Rodchenko played lights onto the
constructions at the third OBMOKhU exhibition to intensify the spatial effects produced and to enhance the reflective qualities of the silver painted surfaces and the
potential movement of the construction on its single suspending wire.[86]

These constructions, experimenting with Euclidean geometry, and particularly
with the spatial potential of line, although following a line of development initiated
in 1919 before the concept of 'laboratory work' had been formulated, represent a
transition towards the practical definition of such work. In the month prior to the
third OBMOKhU exhibition, Rodchenko had been instrumental in organising the

First Working Group of Constructivists, which had enshrined the idea that 'construction is the system by which an object is realised from the utilisation of material together with a predetermined purpose'.[87] Rodchenko's hanging constructions seem to represent a significant point of transition towards such a stance, dealing as they do with the type of structural problems which became pre-occupations of 'laboratory work'. However, when they were made they were not necessarily conceived as 'laboratory work' by Rodchenko, in strict accordance with the Constructivists' later definition. Although their creation undoubtedly aided the development of Rodchenko's utilitarian conception of construction in the spring of 1921, they do not seem to represent any immediate culmination of Rodchenko's evolution towards a utilitarian stance in terms of practical activity. In September 1921, for example, at the $5 \times 5 = 25$ exhibition where the five artists, Aleksandra Ekster, Lyubov' Popova, Varvara Stepanova, Aleksandr Vesnin and Aleksandr Rodchenko, each exhibited five works, Rodchenko's exhibits included three canvases that apparently bore no relation whatever to the position formulated in March, but continued his purely painterly investigations of colour, consisting as they did of monochromatic canvases each in one primary colour.[88] This sustained

experimentation within delimited areas, but on several fronts simultaneously, is characteristic of the work of this period. Rodchenko is an extreme example, but the attempt to establish a precise chronology from fragmentary documentation is continually hampered by this parallelism.

1.33. A. Rodchenko dressed in his *prozodezhda* standing before his collapsed spatial constructions, *c.* 1924. [Photograph: Courtesy Galerie Gmurzynska, Cologne.]

PETR MITURICH

Whereas Rodchenko later became recognised and explicitly aligned as a Constructivist, the name of Petr Miturich has not traditionally been associated with Constructivism at all. Indeed, there is no documentary evidence to suggest that he ever used this term to describe his own work, or his approach. However, the first and only issue of the journal *Fine Art* (*Izobrazitel'noe iskusstvo*), which appeared in 1919, illustrated two works by Miturich that share some of the characteristics typical of three-dimensional art works belonging to the phase of non-utilitarian constructions (plates 1.34–5). These indicate a *de facto*, if temporary, affiliation to the movement, and a strong interest in the three-dimensional exploration of artistic elements. That interest does not seem to have been an exclusive one. Even during 1918–22 when Miturich was developing this interest in three-dimensional structures, he was also producing realistic works, such as the 1922 series of drawings of the village of Santalovo and of the dying Khlebnikov.[89] Nevertheless Miturich's three-dimensional experiments are worthy of note, because they do embody certain features that became prominent in his later design work.

Even those early non-utilitarian constructions were not mere imitations of Tatlin's work, but represented an independent approach to the three-dimensionality of the art object, arrived at through Miturich's own investigations of the ideas in Cubism and Futurism. His work prior to 1918 was characterised by a strong interest in the qualities of line, to the point where this feature is dominant even in his oils, such as his 1915 *Portrait of the Composer A. S. Lur'e* (plate 1.36).[90] The outlines of the figure and the chair in which he is sitting bear only a general

1.34. P. Miturich, *Spatial Painting No. 12* (*Prostranstvennaya zhivopis' No. 12*), 1918. Destroyed. [Reproduced in *Izobrazitel'noe iskusstvo*, No. 1, 1919.]

1.35. P. Miturich, *Spatial Painting No. 14* (*Prostranstvennaya zhivopis' No. 14*), 1918. Destroyed. [Reproduced in *Izobrazitel'noe iskusstvo*, No. 1, 1919.]

relationship to the forms produced by the areas of colour. In this painting line and colour are being emphatically treated as separate pictorial elements.

The art critic Nikolai Punin later detected in this portrait Miturich's break with Impressionism and his first experiments with dynamism.[91] This development of dynamism in Miturich's work may have had some connection with the hazardous methods of producing the folk woodcuts with which the Futurists experimented. Following the traditional process, the outline was printed from the cut block and was then coloured by hand in such a manner that sometimes the broad areas of colour bore little relationship to the black-printed outlines.

It may not be inaccurate to assume that it was this interest in the investigation of pictorial elements and their interaction which led to Miturich's experiment in 1916 with collage in *The Child* (plate 1.37).[92] Constructed from canvas on cardboard, the collage elements were derived from pieces of wood, coloured paper, staples and pieces of birch bark. Devoid of Cubist formal analysis and lacking the rich ambiguities of Cubist collage, the collage elements in this work all relate directly to the representational depiction of physical forms, and are merely used to replace more traditional media of depiction: the round piece of paper denoting the child's head is a central example. Miturich stressed the pictorial nature and function of these elements rather than their intrinsic material qualities and internal tensions. There seems therefore to be only a very remote relationship between this work and the first of Miturich's three-dimensional works, which appeared in 1918.

These compositions which Miturich called spatial graphics (*prostranstvennye grafiki*) were in effect his first constructions and he worked on them between 1918 and 1922.[93] They were produced at the same time as he was experimenting with Cubo-Futurism in his two-dimensional works. For instance, in the geometrically structured *Our March* (plate 1.38) Miturich exploited the intersecting planes and volumes and the geometrically diminishing lettering to intensify the dynamism of the composition.[94] These interests were echoed in two three-dimensional works of 1918, *Spatial Painting No. 12* (Plate 1.34) and *Spatial Painting No. 14* (plate 1.35).[95] Neither of these is shown in the photograph of Miturich's Moscow studio taken in 1920 (plate 1.39). This shows three large constructions which seem to have been labelled 18, 19 and 20 by Miturich himself to correspond to the numbering system he employed to catalogue his oeuvre.[96] This is the only photograph of *Spatial Painting No. 19*, whereas there is an additional photograph of *No. 18*. *No. 20* is the most well documented of all: there are two photographs, including plate 1.40, that show the work from different angles, as well as the view in the photograph of Miturich's studio. These three views provide the most complete impression of the plastic presence of these three-dimensional works.[97] Miturich's spatial paintings employ most directly the visual language of Cubism and Futurism and are his most explicitly geometrical three-dimensional works. They are primarily rectilinear and angular although also employing curvatures. *No. 18* (see plate 1.39), composed of two intersecting curves (a problem that had been a dominant interest in Tatlin's corner counter-reliefs, e.g. plate 1.13), is more opened out than *No. 19* and *No. 20* (plates 1.39–40), the prevailing interest being the external intersection of the volumes and the relationship which these in turn set up with the spatial environment. On the other hand most of the spatial paintings tended to preserve rather more enclosed interiors, locked within their own definitions of volumes.

An additional visual complexity was provided by the fact that the surfaces of the component geometrical elements were painted with hatching strokes which, as far as can be discerned from the photographs, delineated areas of light and shade on the component elements. This introduced an additional ambiguity because this painted shading contradicted the shadows thrown by the material presence of the shapes themselves. This hatching therefore imposed a formal organisation on the constructions which was additional to that provided by the three-dimensional forms themselves. As in *Portrait of the Composer A. S. Lur'e* (plate 1.36), where the

1.36. P. Miturich, *The Composer A. S. Lur'e* (*Kompozitor A. S. Lur'e*), 1915, oil on canvas, 1020 × 1015 cm. Russian Museum, Leningrad.

1.37. P. Miturich, *The Child* (*Rebenok*), a portrait of the artist's son Vasi, 1916, collage and oil on canvas, 385 × 300 cm. Russian Museum, Leningrad.

1.39. (right) View of Miturich's studio c. 1921.

30

graphic element was divorced from the colour, in these spatial paintings the dynamic element was provided by the discrepancy between the graphic element (the hatching) and the material element (the construction).

This type of hatching was directly related to that employed in *Our March* (plate 1.38) and in the spatial paintings of 1918 such as *No. 12* and *No. 14* (plates 1.34–5). However, in this connection it is perhaps also relevant that Miturich served in a military camouflage department during 1920 in Moscow.[98]

Much less angular in their basic conception were the second type of constructions which also date from the same period and which seem to have been produced simultaneously with the spatial paintings. The works of this second category were called spatial graphics (*prostranstvennaya grafika*) or spatial posters (*prostranstvennyi plakat*). These were explicitly inspired by the striving to find a visual equivalent for the Futurist transrational poetry of Velimir Khlebnikov.[99] Miturich had first met Khlebnikov in Petrograd in 1916, but had read his poetry prior to this.[100] Their acquaintance was renewed in Moscow in 1921 when Miturich returned from the front.[101] The friendship was crucial to Miturich, and the ideas and poetry of Khlebnikov inspired much of his later artistic work. More specifically they provided the direct content of the spatial posters. Referring to them later Miturich stated: 'The spatial compositions which I devised in large quantities were my main occupation. This work developed from my acquaintance with the work of Velimir Khlebnikov. I accompanied my compositions with drawings of Velimir's poems, striving to serve him with all means available.'[102] These spatial compositions were made of paper and cardboard and were destroyed by Miturich before he and Khlebnikov left to visit Miturich's wife in the village of Santalovo in the Novgorod district.

1.38. P. Miturich, *Our March* (*Nash Marsh*), cover for music, 1918, watercolour and gouache on paper, 360 × 340 cm. Literary Museum, Moscow.

'Not long before we left I destroyed all my spatial constructions. Made of paper and cardboard, they were not long-lasting; they would have rapidly become discoloured with smoke and lost their shape. I did not want them to continue their existence like that whomever they had belonged to.'[103] Apparently Khlebnikov was displeased at the destruction of these works, but prior to taking this step Miturich did have the foresight to photograph them.[104]

The three-dimensionality of these works was considerably less than that of the previous spatial paintings. For example, *Spatial Poster No. 29* (plate 1.41), dated 1921, in contrast to the previous work, is built out from a flat plane. The paper seems to have been merely folded and moulded into the required shapes based on interacting diagonals forming cone shapes. The poem and the graphic elements merely intensify the effects of the highlights and shadows created by the folds.

In *Spatial Poster No. 37* of 1921 (plate 1.42), using Khlebnikov's poem 'Bobeobi', Miturich experimented with the use of extraneous elements to the folded flat sheet. The ridges and segments of the angular surfaces produced were altered by the application of irregular rectangular elements painted black. *Spatial Graphics No. 46* (plate 1.43) was an imposition of basically curvilinear forms onto a rectangular construction. Here the spatial structure set up by the three intersecting wooden

1.40. P. Miturich, *Spatial Painting No. 20* (*Prostranstvennaya zhivopis' No. 20*), 1918, destroyed.

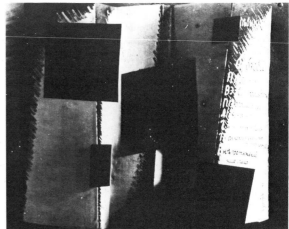

1.41–2. P. Miturich, *Spatial Posters No. 29 and No. 37* (*Prostranstvennye plakaty No. 29 i No. 37*), 1921, destroyed.

1.43. P. Miturich, *Spatial Graphics No. 46* (*Prostranstvennaya grafika No. 46*), 1921, wood and wire, c. 98 × 99 cm. Private collection, Moscow.

planes is almost submerged behind the near-vegetable quality of the graphic forms that are superimposed upon them, and by the Emmenthal-like holes bored into the wood itself.[105] This destruction of the geometrical character of the construction was carried much further in *Spatial Graphics No. 48* (plate 1.44). The form was folded and glued into a completely organic shape, painted with curvilinear lines and pierced by holes cut in the paper. (This construction could be viewed either way up, as Miturich signified by signing it at both top and bottom.)

These formal researches display a strong interest in the organic quality of form, despite the obvious geometricity of some of the constructions. Miturich was not interested in the materials themselves, except as a graphic means, and he certainly was not interested in the sort of ideological function that materials play in Cubist collage. The material is used merely to achieve the extension of the graphic elements into space: the point extended into the line, and the line in turn defining the plane. Miturich was interested in how these graphically derived elements interact spatially with defined forms, and the dominant formal language which seems to emerge in his work towards the later constructions, of 1921, is curvilinear. A more light-hearted exploration of the spatial potential of line is seen in the series of cubes that Miturich created (plate 1.45). These interests received a greater development in his subsequent design work, discussed in Chapter Seven, to which I have given the term 'Organic Constructivism'.

1.44. P. Miturich, *Spatial Graphics No. 48* (*Prostranstvennaya grafika No. 48*), 1921, destroyed.

NAUM GABO AND ANTOINE PEVSNER

At this point it is necessary to consider the work of the brothers Naum Gabo and Antoine Pevsner whose names in the West are synonymous with Constructivism. In view of the confusion which has prevailed over their role in Russian Constructivism it is necessary to follow through in outline the whole period of their work that is relevant to Russian developments.

Both had received a substantial part of their higher education in Western Europe. Pevsner had studied art in Paris intermittently from 1911, where he had experimented with Cubism. Gabo on the other hand had received a predominantly scientific education in Munich, where he had attended courses in medicine and the natural sciences as well as engineering. This scientific diet had been supplemented by attending Wölfflin's art history lectures. It was at Wölfflin's instigation that Gabo visited Italy in 1913 to study the classics.[106] He also visited Paris where he became acquainted with the ideas and visual achievements of Cubism. On the outbreak of war Gabo went to Scandinavia whence he returned to Russia after the February Revolution of 1917. In the following year Pevsner became a professor at the reorganised Moscow State Free Art Studios where Gabo (who did not have an official teaching position) shared his studio and seems to have held seminars. Gabo left Moscow for Berlin in 1922 and helped organise the three rooms of abstract art at the First Russian Art Exhibition (Erste Russische Kunstausstellung) which opened in Berlin in October of that year.[107] Pevsner followed his brother abroad in 1923. Neither of them returned to Russia.

During the brothers' stay in Russia, Pevsner's artistic explorations were limited to the two-dimensional plane of the canvas. Although he called these paintings 'constructions', it was only after having left Russia, and then under the guidance and with the encouragement of Gabo, that Pevsner began to extend his experiments to work in three dimensions with real materials.[108] Gabo, on the other hand, had produced his first three-dimensional constructions during the First World War while he was in Scandinavia. The first of these was his *Constructed Head No. 1* of 1915 (plate 1.46). Employing wood and his 'stereometric method', Gabo sought to present space as 'an absolute sculptural element' so that the 'space in which mass exists was made visible'.[109] Subsequent works, such as his *Constructed Head No. 2* of 1916 (plate 1.47) made from galvanised iron painted with yellow enamel, and the *Torso* of 1917 (plate 1.48) made from sheet iron treated with sand, all retained a relatively close relationship with the object depicted, and yet, while remaining figurative, they continued to explore the object in terms of the incorporation of space and to extend the process of building up spatial parameters. The influence of Gabo's experimentation based on the figure is still discernible in one of his first

1.46. N. Gabo, *Constructed Head No. 1*, 1915, plywood, *c.* 54 × 32 × 31 cm. Collection Miriam Gabo, London.

1.45. (left) P. Miturich, *Cubes (Kubiki)*, *c.* 1920–1, ink and gouache on paper and cardboard, *c.* 5 × 5 × 5 cm. Private collection, Moscow.

1.48. N. Gabo, *Torso*, 1917, height *c*. 137 cm, exhibited in Berlin, 1922, as *Constructive Torso*. Whereabouts unknown.

non-figurative constructions of 1919. Made from printed cardboard, *Construction en creux* (plate 1.49), now lost, is known only through a reproduction which appeared in the Hungarian journal *Egység* in 1922.[110] It was reconstructed with a clearer geometry in 1921 using wood and plastic (plate 1.50). However, the earlier, more tentatively abstract version clearly seems to have been distilled from the experience with the heads and in particular *Head of a Woman* of 1916–17 (plate 1.51) which is now in the Museum of Modern Art, New York. *Construction en creux* thus provides a link between the earlier studies based on the human figure and the later, abstract explorations of form which embraced space more dynami-

1.47. (facing page) N. Gabo, *Constructed Head No. 2*, 1916, galvanised iron, originally painted with yellow ochre, 45 × 40·5 × 40·5 cm. Collection Miriam Gabo, London.

cally. Its transitional character is emphasised by the obvious use of colour and hatching to create ambiguities in the plays of forms giving the work a painterly character which underlined the Cubist lineage. Gabo first used transparent celluloid in his *Construction in Relief* of 1920 (plate 1.52) which also seems to have been among the first three-dimensional works in which Gabo explored a Euclidean geometric form.[111] By 1920 Gabo had thus clarified his formal vocabulary and found the transparent material which minimised the texturally associative and material interests of his constructions and permitted a purer concentration on the form in space.

It is clear that Gabo's works of this period in Russia, 1917–22, fall broadly within the category of non-utilitarian constructions. However, even at this stage, there were important differences between Gabo's constructions with their rather mathematical approach to form and the more emphatically textural, abstract work of Tatlin. Whereas Tatlin's starting point was an interest in the qualities of the materials and their juxtaposition and interaction in space, Gabo's was a precise analysis of the structure of form and its internal spatial implications. He began with the idea or image which he then executed in a suitable material. There was no exploitation of the *objet trouvé* or any chance combinations of materials. In Gabo's view, Tatlin's reliefs retained too many of the 'chaotic' characteristics of Cubism. He said later: 'Constructivism rejects both Cubism and Futurism. In that respect, I had quarrels even with Tatlin's group. The analytical character of Cubism and its chaotic compositions was not the thing which could satisfy us.'[112] The divergencies of approach which were apparent at this stage were later exacerbated, and it is clear from their own avowal that neither Gabo nor Pevsner embraced the nihilistic attitude towards art which accompanied the utilitarian and social dimension of Constructivism when it emerged as a movement in Russia in 1920–1. They made their disagreement quite explicit in their *Realistic Manifesto* of 1920.[113] It therefore would have been most unlikely for Gabo and Pevsner to have used the term 'Constructivist' (with all its ideological overtones) to describe their approach at this

1.49. N. Gabo, *Construction en creux*, 1919. Whereabouts unknown. [First reproduced in *Egység*, No. 2, 1922, p. 8, under title *Realist Composition (Realista kompozicio)*, dated 1919.]

1.50. N. Gabo, *Construction en creux*, 1921, plastic and wood, exhibited in Berlin, 1922, as *Relief encreux*. Whereabouts unknown, formerly Collection Comte de Noailles.

38

time. In fact, although the label 'Constructivist' was later applied to their work and Gabo and Pevsner both called themselves 'Constructivists', Gabo always stressed that the term had been first used to describe a utilitarian approach and that therefore it was not strictly applicable to either his work or himself. In 1948 he stated:

> My art is commonly known as the art of Constructivism. Actually the word Constructivism is a misnomer. The word Constructivism has been appropriated by one group of constructivist artists in the 1920s who demanded that art should liquidate itself. They denied any value to easel painting, to sculpture, in fine, to any work of art in which the artist's purpose was to convey ideas or emotions for their own sake. They demanded from the artist, and particularly from those who were commonly called constructivists that they should use their talents for construction of material values, namely in building useful objects, houses, chairs, tables, stoves, etc., being materialistic in their philosophy and Marxist in their politics, they could not see in a work of art anything else but a pleasurable occupation cherished in a decadent capitalistic society and totally useless, even harmful in the new society of communism.[114]

The evidence of Gabo's brother Aleksei Pevsner confirms this. He wrote that 'in Moscow ... at that time neither Antoine nor Gabo called themselves Constructivists. I know that Gabo protested strongly against any "isms" and that Antoine agreed with him. Gabo called the ideas he was standing for in art "constructive ideas" or "ideas of spatial construction".'[115] Gabo himself has intimated that instead of the term 'Constructivist' to describe his three-dimensional works in Russia, he used the word '*postroenie*' – a term denoting a structure that is 'built up' (as opposed to being carved out or moulded) and based on the Russian root '*stroit*'', to build, rather than '*konstruktsiya*' with its foreign root, 'to construct'. Western confusion was perhaps inevitable here, because the distinction was difficult to maintain in translation; both terms could easily be rendered in European languages by 'construction'. Later, when talking of his own work and that of his brother, Gabo emphasised that

1.51. N. Gabo, *Head of a Woman*, c. 1917–20, after a work of 1916, celluloid and metal on wood, 62·2 × 48·9 cm. Collection, The Museum of Modern Art, New York.

1.52. N. Gabo, *Construction in Relief*, 1920. Whereabouts unknown. [Reproduced in the catalogue of the Erste Russische Kunstausstellung, Berlin, 1922, under title *Model for a Spatial Construction C* (*Model for a Plastic Glass*).]

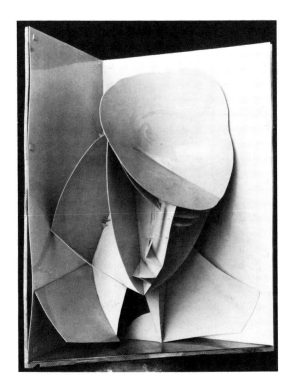

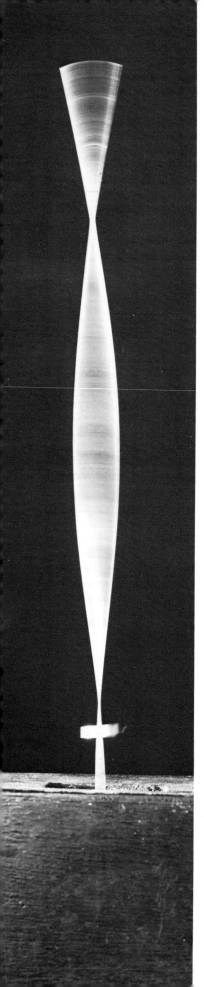

the word constructivism was not invented by us; it was given to us by critics and writers. There were no Constructivists until 1920. We all called ourselves constructors from the Russian word *postroyenia* [*sic*] meaning construction. Instead of carving or moulding a sculpture of one piece we built it up into space out of our imagination in the same way as an engineer does when he builds a construction.[116]

Gabo maintained the distinction by calling his art 'constructive' as opposed to 'constructivist'.[117] However, removed from the specific context of post-revolutionary Russia, it was a distinction which lost a lot of its *raison d'être*, especially as the creative impetus of Russian Constructivism declined towards the end of the 1920s and early 1930s and ceased to present an active alternative to the Western phenomenon.

The principles for Gabo's 'constructive technique'[118] and their theoretical bases were outlined most clearly in *The Realistic Manifesto* of 5 August 1920, written by Gabo but signed also by Pevsner. In Gabo's words, the *Realistic Manifesto*, so named because 'we were convinced that what we were doing represented a new reality', had for its most important ideas 'the assertion that art has its absolute, independent value ... as one of the indispensable expressions of human experience and as an important means of communication', and that 'space and time constitute the backbone of the constructive art'.[119]

The manifesto cited five 'renunciations and affirmations' which were to guide the creation of such an art so that 'the reality of the constant rhythm of the forces' in life and its objects was preserved. They were as follows:

1.   ... *in painting we renounce colour as a pictorial element ... it has nothing in common with the innermost essence of a thing.*
We affirm *that the tone of a substance,* i.e. *its light-absorbing material body, is the only pictorial reality.*
2. We renounce *in a line its descriptive value ...*
We affirm *the line only as a direction of the static forces and their rhythm in objects.*
3. We renounce *volume as a pictorial and plastic form of space ...*
We affirm *depth as the only pictorial and plastic form of space.*
4. We renounce ... *the mass as a sculptural element ... we take four planes and we construct with them the same volume as four tons of mass.*
Thus we bring back to sculpture the line as a direction and in it we affirm depth as the one form of space.
5. We renounce ... *static rhythms as the only elements of the plastic and pictorial arts.*
We affirm *in these arts a new element the kinetic rhythms as the basic forms of our perception of real time.*

These principles summarise the purely artistic implications of those three-dimensional works which Gabo produced in Russia and to a large extent of the phase of non-utilitarian constructions generally. In 1920 Gabo had extended the practical application of these principles in his work by making *Kinetic Construction* (plate 1.53), which consisted of a metal rod vibrating by means of a motor.[120] Gabo's interest in movement derived from his concern to make his three-dimensional work four-dimensional by incorporating the element of time into its construction. 'By time I mean movement, rhythm: the actual one as well as the illusory one.'[121]

The ideas expressed in the *Realistic Manifesto* also underlie some of the other projects with which Gabo experimented during the period of his stay in Russia. Most of these designs, like his *Project for a Radio Station* of 1919–20 (plate 1.54), did not get beyond the drawing stage. This design, in particular, remains a sketchy, spatially inarticulate and rather eclectic structure, growing from a base inspired by the Eiffel Tower, which Gabo would undoubtedly have seen on his visit to Paris in 1913. The project, which Gabo was to denounce in 1920 together with Tatlin's

Monument to the Third International as 'useless romanticism',[122] shows Gabo extending his artistic principles and methods to a wider arena. It indicates that he was not immune to those wider objectives which art acquired through its move out onto the streets during the revolutionary festivals. It is known that Gabo was involved in urban decorations for such events,[123] and projects such as the radio station suggest that he too was affected by the current concern with concepts of artistic synthesis and of art fusing with life. Gabo's *Project for a Radio Station* in this respect should be compared to the early kiosk projects of Rodchenko which, inspired by ideas of artistic synthesis, concentrated on the expressive qualities of form (plate 2.8). There is a marked similarity of approach between Rodchenko and Gabo here, both being concerned with expressive form rather than with the purely functional reorganisation of architectural spaces and entities. The *Project for a Radio Station* by Gabo can therefore be seen to correspond to that experimental stage which preceded the emergence of the First Working Group of Constructivists in March 1921. However, Gabo's project does not represent his willingness to espouse or espousal of the Constructivists' strictly utilitarian and anti-art position.

Gabo executed other projects which explored the similarities between constructive sculpture and architecture and he also worked on specifically architectural designs. His design for *Column*, conceived in Russia in 1920–1 but constructed in the West in 1923 (plate 1.55), was an immediate result of such investigations. Although its function was not specified, it was far more structurally articulate than the *Project for a Radio Station*. This could be attributed to the fact that as a project it had advanced beyond the sketch to the model stage. On the other hand, the *Column*'s relationship to technology was also more clearly expressed in the exploitation of new, transparent materials and a clear Euclidean geometry, which implies that Gabo's ideas in this area had matured considerably. Yet, Gabo's approach to this potentially utilitarian or social structure was primarily artistic, and *Column* is,

1.53. (facing page) N. Gabo, *Kinetic Construction* (*Standing Wave*) 1920, metal rod and electric motor, 61·5 × 24·1 × 19 cm. Tate Gallery, London.

1.54. N. Gabo, *Project for a Radio Station*, 1919–20, ink on paper. Whereabouts unknown. [Photograph: Miriam Gabo.]

1.55. N. Gabo, *Column*, 1923, glass, metal, wood (later perspex replaced the glass), 105·3 × 73·6 × 73·6 cm. Solomon R. Guggenheim Museum, New York.

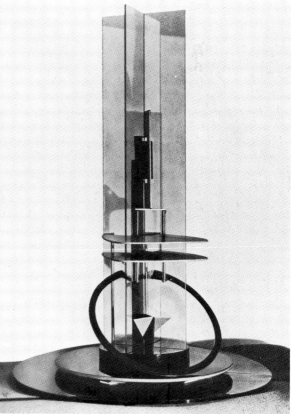

above all, an aesthetic object. Gabo did later participate in the solution of more utilitarian design tasks, even submitting a design for the Palace of Soviets competition in 1932, where he developed a very advanced structural engineering solution for the winged roof. However, his main concern was always the artistic. Gabo's projects were inspired by his expressed desire that 'art should attend us everywhere that life flows and acts'.[124] It was precisely art which remained for Gabo the supreme value. Although he was to embrace a wider context for his art, he never rejected artistic activity to devote himself solely to the utilitarian. For Gabo, art could spiritually and materially influence the environment, but it was not to be subsumed in the utilitarian. Gabo's ultimate aim was always spiritually didactic. He wrote: 'The aim of our time consists in creating a harmonious human being, and we strive in our works to educate the spirit in this direction.'[125] Gabo's constant dedication to the creation of art was the fundamental and irreconcilable difference between Gabo and the Russian Constructivists.

GUSTAV KLUTSIS

One of the students who exhibited with Gabo on Tverskoi Boulevard in August 1920 was Gustav Klutsis, who was then studying with Antoine Pevsner at the State Free Art Studios. Prior to this Klutsis had been working with Malevich and exhibited with the latter's UNOVIS group (Affirmers of the New Art – Utverditeli novogo iskusstva).[126] Klutsis' canvases from this period, such as *The Dynamic City* of 1919 (colour plate XIV), display a close affinity with the geometry of Suprematism and perhaps more especially with the architectural and three-dimensional emphasis of Malevich's architectural models and Lissitzky's compositions after 1919, with their three-dimensional geometric bodies floating in the absolute space of the Suprematist picture plane.

As an ardent member of the Bolshevik party and a fearless soldier in the Latvian Rifles Regiment, Klutsis enthusiastically embraced the new artistic tasks facing the consolidation of the Revolution in Russia. Later he wrote: 'After my abstract period, which ended in 1920-1, the line of my further development is the line of the development of agitational and mass art, which was then still called production art.'[127] Although he was not, as far as can be ascertained, ever a member of the First Working Group of Constructivists, Klutsis did call himself a Constructivist and was engaged on design work, beginning with his agitational stands for the Congress of the Third International in 1922.

Prior to commencing such practical work, Klutsis spent some time investigating the structure of geometric form in space through a series of drawings and small three-dimensional structures. *Spatial Construction* of 1920-1 (plate 1.56), consisting of skeletal rectangles telescoped inside each other, clearly continues the geometric interests of *Dynamic City*, while at the same time announcing the new concern with the internal structure of that geometry. The incorporation of different scales recalls Rodchenko's work, as does the suspension from a central wire. The slanting angle, reminiscent of *Dynamic City*, emphasises the dynamism which is concretely present here in the motion inherent in the construction. Made from wood, the nature of the material used is not exploited in this work. Although it is difficult to judge from the few photographs which survive of Klutsis' three-dimensional constructions, it seems that material considerations played no major role in the definition of these works. Klutsis' approach to form and material is reminiscent of Gabo's. On the other hand the minimal, skeletal type of construction Klutsis used does also suggest the influence of existing engineering structures. This technological bias is less evident in *Spatial Construction* of 1920-1 (plate 1.57), which is simpler in structure, indicating perhaps that it may have been made earlier than plate 1.56. There is no explicit utilitarian content in these works. Their motivation seems to have been

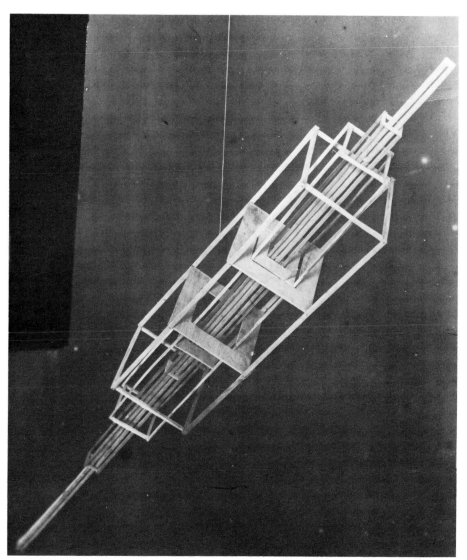

1.56. G. Klutsis, *Three-dimensional Construction, c.* 1920. Whereabouts unknown. [Photograph: © George Costakis 1981.]

1.57. G. Klutsis, *Three-dimensional Construction, c.* 1920. Whereabouts unknown. [Photograph: A. B. Nakov.]

purely artistic, as Klutsis explained: 'I worked exclusively with the aim of seeking new art forms and methods. *Faktura*, construction, colour experiments, all kinds of structures, fantastic constructions, fantastic cities.'[128] Therefore although Klutsis' constructions provided a basis for his later work in designing agitational tribunes they cannot be considered as 'laboratory work' for they were undertaken with no ultimately utilitarian aim in mind. The technological inspiration and yet purely formal nature of these researches is very apparent in the drawings. Whereas the constructions through being assembled in space from real materials inevitably possessed a structural coherence, the drawings, as for example plate 1.58, are often spatially ambiguous and structurally incoherent. Yet these works represent a very important aspect of Klutsis' investigations of spatial constructions and were probably more numerous than his actual three-dimensional constructions of which only a few are known through photographs.

For Klutsis, therefore, the two-dimensional format of the drawing was an important medium for investigating construction. Pevsner also produced works which he called 'constructions', although they were two-dimensional and entirely painterly in their execution. In Gabo's and Pevsner's circle, these were accepted as explorations of the principles of structure or *postroenie*. There was no doubt that spatial relationships could be explored and discussed in two-dimensional, tradi-

tional media, in particular through harnessing what *The Realistic Manifesto* called 'the tone or light-absorbing' quality of a substance. At the same time there were some artists who became Constructivists whose contribution was also made – both at this early stage and later – through essentially two-dimensional media.

LYUBOV' POPOVA AND VARVARA STEPANOVA

The most important of these artists who worked principally in two dimensions was Lyubov' Popova. Her starting points were Cubism, followed by Futurism.[129] These she interpreted as 'the problems of form' and 'the problem of the movement of colour'.[130] Her most extended three-dimensional work was *Jug on a Table* (*Plastic Painting*), *Relief* of 1915 (plate 1.59).[131] Made from oil paint and cardboard mounted on wood, this work also incorporates the lettering '2 LIR' and the *objet trouvé* element of a small wooden knob in the bottom left-hand corner.

Writing of this type of work in 1920–1 in connection with her work at the Museum of Artistic Culture (Muzei khudozhestvennoi kul'tury), Popova described it as a laboratory experiment concerned with solving the problem of painterly and volumetric space, the unity of which was produced by the real sculptural volumes and modulations of colour as a painterly surface.[132] Despite the emphatically painterly character of the work, it does possess certain affinities with Tatlin's early reliefs, especially *The Bottle*. Tatlin's influence is strikingly present in the structural conception and in the natural qualities of the component elements. The subdued Cubist palette Popova used focussed attention on the volumetric problems with which she was dealing. However, the main direction of Popova's work in its post-Cubist phase was a concern not with volume but with the plane, producing works such as *Painterly Architectonics* of 1919 (colour plate I).[133] In her own words, this work 'consists of three constructions: the colour, the volumetric and the linear. The volumetric is built from the intersection of the planes and their representation [*izobrazhenie*] in space. The space is not perspectival, therefore the colour construction and its gradations do not necessarily coincide'.[134] The dissonance created between the different planes of colour on the plane of the canvas produces tension and dynamism. The geometricity of the planes and the vibrant nature of the colour indicate the influence of Suprematism and the ideas of Malevich with whom she was associated in 1916 over the publication of the Suprematist journal *Supremus*.

However, Popova's work of 1920–1 moved away from Malevich's ideas and was characterised by more stridently structural interests. Such concerns were epitomised by the small woodcut she included in the exhibition catalogue *5 × 5 = 25* of 1921 (plate 1.60).[135] The full-scale works of this type were given the name spatial force construction (*prostranstvenno-silovoe postroenie*).[136] These investigations indicated, as Popova herself pointed out, that she had moved away 'from the analysis of the volume and space of objects (Cubism) towards the *organisation of these elements*, not as the means of representation, but as integral constructions (either colour-planar, volumetric-spatial or other material constructions)'.[137] She stressed that henceforth in her work 'the significance of each element (line, plane, volume, colour, material) of the representational vocabulary [*izobrazitel'noe sredstvo*] is formed by that concrete working of a given material'.[138] This last phrase stressed her approach to painting as a work concerned with the material organisation of the painterly elements, completely freed from any extraneous emotional or metaphysical content.

In 1921 Popova embraced the utilitarian position of Constructivism together with her colleagues Aleksandr Rodchenko and Varvara Stepanova. Later to collaborate with Popova on the design of textiles, Stepanova had followed a similar though far less intense artistic development. She pursued her structural concerns through analysing the movements of the human figure. Although her paintings

1.59. L. Popova, *Jug on a Table* (*Plastic Painting*), *Relief* (*Kuvshin na stole (plasticheskaya zhivopis')*. *Rel'ef*), 1915, oil on wood and cardboard, *objet trouvé*, 58·5 × 47 × 17 cm. Tret'yakov Gallery, Moscow.

1.60. L. Popova, *Print*, from *5 × 5 = 25. Katalog vystavki*, 1921. [Photograph: Courtesy Galerie Jean Chauvelin, Paris.]

remained primarily representational,[139] she had explored the potential of abstract collage in her *zaum'* book *Gaust Chaba*, already mentioned. It is indicative of her artistic interests that Stepanova's contribution to the exhibition catalogue *5 × 5 = 25* comprised a linocut of a jumping figure (plate 1.61).

Neither Popova nor Stepanova went beyond these two-dimensional media to full three-dimensional constructions. Later in their laboratory work all Constructivists worked in two-dimensional media as a basis for solutions to three-dimensional problems. Although it can be argued that the main bulk of the formal vocabulary was provided by real work in real materials, the two-dimensional treatments of space and form were clearly recognised to have a role in preliminary investigations.

*   *   *

This chapter has been concerned to chronicle certain developments in formal language; from these investigations into the combinations of materials in three-dimensional ways there are two major formal trends that emerge. First there is the trend epitomised by the works of Tatlin and Miturich. These were essentially non-schematic structures built up from real materials and, in Miturich's case, from graphic elements, which for him were the apparent starting point of the exploration of the more 'organic' geometry that is a central characteristic of their work. Tatlin's work was more concerned with the textural possibilities of materials themselves and their interrelationships. Both these bodies of work differ strongly in their formal conception from the more Euclidean rectilinear geometry which characterised the second formal trend, whose leading exponent was Rodchenko. The formal language of non-utilitarian constructions thus from the first embraced both Euclidean and 'organic' geometries.

Lying behind and sometimes cutting across this distinction was another – between different approaches to the actual process of conception and execution of the 'constructed' work. One approach was essentially that of 'discovery', in which the artists (the paramount example being Tatlin) allowed the material itself to play an important part in determining the form. The other approach, particularly present in the work of Rodchenko, possessed a 'pre-planned' element already allying it with the production process and logically facilitating the later move into design.

It should also be stressed that artists who experimented with three-dimensional non-utilitarian constructions did not always go on to become Constructivists, as for example Bruni, Puni and Klyun. It was, however, the corpus of work that has briefly been surveyed in this chapter that provided the visual language for Constructivism. These experiments were of great variety, but none as yet contained the idea of a practical purpose, far less, of a social one. The motivation for harnessing these non-utilitarian experiments to such ends came through the Revolution of 1917, and the way in which this new amalgam emerged is the subject of the next two chapters.

1.61. V. Stepanova, *Print*, from *5 × 5 = 25. Katalog vystavki*, 1921. [Photograph: Courtesy Galerie Jean Chauvelin, Paris.]

2 THE REVOLUTIONARY EXPERIENCE: FROM THE STUDIO INTO THE STREET

ON 7 NOVEMBER 1917 the Bolshevik Party took power in Russia and proclaimed the establishment of a socialist State. This Revolution occurred in a context of complete political and economic disruption, following the military disasters of the First World War. The February Revolution of 1917, which had removed the Tsar and created a democracy, had failed to deal effectively with the people's demands for Peace, Bread and Land. The establishment of Soviet power was rapidly followed by the inauguration of a whole new set of administrative institutions appropriate to the new State. Included amongst these was the People's Commissariat of Enlightenment (Narodnyi komissariat prosveshcheniya - usually known by its abbreviation Narkompros) under the direction of Anatolii Lunacharskii, responsible for the administration of education and the arts. The People's Commissariats as a whole were dedicated to building an entirely new economic, political, social and cultural structure in Russia. The performance of this task was hampered by the outbreak of the Civil War, which lasted intermittently from early 1918 until 1921, when the Red power of the Communist Party was reasonably secure against the forces of intervention and White aggression.[1]

The diverse experiences of this Revolution and the ensuing Civil War provided three essential ingredients for the development of Constructivism. It gave artists experience in agitation, it gave them practical experience in the running of artistic affairs, and finally it provided a revolutionary ideology: Marxist materialism. This chapter will primarily examine the agitational experience of the artists and their practical involvement in the formulation and administration of a new socialist culture. It will be argued that this practical experience provided the basis for the idea of the artist as agitator, the artist as transmitter of the socialist idea, and that this in turn led to the idea of the artist as creator of the new socialist reality. This identification of art and ideology could be seen to have its roots in the original welcoming of the Revolution by the artists. It was also generated and fostered by the way in which their co-operation was pragmatically welcomed by the Bolsheviks, and the way they were initially given a relatively free reign in the setting up and running of official cultural bodies concerned among other things with the formulation of new cultural values for the new society.

It was an exciting and exhilarating period. Despite the hardships, the food and fuel shortages, artists managed to express some of this excitement in the revolutionary festivals, decorating the streets and participating in the resultant synthesis of painting, sculpture, music and theatre that led to the idea of a new synthetic art which would not be divorced from life but fused with it. It is not surprising that in recalling this youthful time in their memoirs, members of the avant-garde stressed their acceptance of the Revolution and their immediate identification with it. Tatlin later wrote: 'To Accept or not accept the October Revolution. There was no such question for me. I organically merged into active creative, social and pedagogical life.'[2] Rodchenko likewise looked back from the early 1920s to his welcoming of the Revolution, stating, 'I became utterly engrossed in it with all my will.'[3] The composer Artur Lur'e described the effect it had not only on himself but on the whole artistic avant-garde around him.

> Like my friends – young avant-garde artists and poets – I believed in the October Revolution and immediately sided with it. Thanks to the support shown to us by the October Revolution, all of us, young artists – innovators and experimentalists – were taken seriously. At first boyish visionaries talked about being able to realise their dreams ... but in general neither politics nor power really intruded into pure art. We were given complete freedom in our field to do everything we wanted; it was the first time in history that there had been such an opportunity.[4]

These artists called themselves and were called 'Futurists'. This should not, especially in its post-October phase, be confused with the Italian movement. Futurism was a term used very loosely in Russia in the immediate post-revolutionary years to denote all avant-garde artists and poets. The artist Ivan Puni considered that it was closely related to the lines of Mayakovskii which appeared in the first number of *Art of the Commune*: 'The streets are our brushes, the squares our palettes.'[5] Puni argued that these lines inherently regarded art as the creation of life and he therefore defined Futurism as a 'clearly and definitely expressed tendency to go beyond the limits of the work of art enclosed within itself, i.e. the trend towards the liquidation of art as a separate discipline'.[6] Hence 'Futurism' was used almost synonymously with the term 'left art' (*levoe iskusstvo*), which, as Nikolai Punin pointed out in 1923, was an equally vague phrase, which did not denote any explicit commitment to a specific political position. He stated, ' "left art" where left is interpreted as a general commitment to revolutionary materialism is also a myth'.[7] This terminological confusion was preserved in the first commentaries on the period, produced in the late 1920s. Tugendkhol'd, for example, in his book *The Art of the October Epoch* of 1928, used the terms 'Futurist' and 'left artist' interchangeably.[8]

ARTISTS IN ADMINISTRATION

After the February Revolution, which was primarily liberal and democratic, Russian artists of all persuasions from the World of Art (Mir iskusstva) to the avant-garde took advantage of the new freedom to organise a Union of Art Workers (Soyuz deyatelei iskusstv) in Petrograd.[9] This artistically diverse body concentrated its attention primarily on the question of the Academy of Arts, and directed its energies towards destroying the hegemony that this body had previously exercised in the artistic and cultural life of Russia. After the second, October, Revolution, the less progressive elements which formed the majority in the Union of Art Workers refused to co-operate with Lunacharskii unless he guaranteed them complete independence from the Soviet of Worker, Peasant and Soldier Deputies,[10] which was the chief administrative organ of the State at this point. However, many of those artists, who for political reasons continued to refuse to work in the organisation of the artistic life of the new State, did agree to work in the Department of Museums and Conservation of Antiquities (Otdel muzeev i okhrany stariny), which subsequently became a stronghold of the less artistically progressive elements among the artists.[11] It was decided to keep this area separate from that of contemporary artistic affairs, which came under the control of the Fine Art Department (Otdel izobrazitel'nykh iskusstv – known by its abbreviation of IZO) set up at the beginning of 1918.[12] However, it should be noted that the mere fact of a government body designed to control artistic affairs meant a complete break with the liberal conception enunciated by the Union of Art Workers after February, and with the rather anarchic situation that had existed between the two Revolutions of 1917.

IZO was run by an Arts Board (Khudozhestvennaya kollegiya) which consisted of Shterenberg (president), Al'tman, Vaulin, Karev, Matveev, Punin, Chekhonin and Yatmanov.[13] It was an artistically eclectic and rather moderate body. Al'tman was a 'Futurist' and Punin was an apologist for the Futurists, but Chekhonin was a member of the World of Art group who later became famous for his translation of revolutionary symbols into the rather decorative language of that school. The Arts Board was later joined by Baranov-Rossine, Shkol'nik, Mayakovskii, Brik and five architects,[14] Mayakovskii becoming a member of IZO only in August-September 1918.[15]

A department of IZO was also set up in Moscow and was distinguished from that in Petrograd by its inclusion of a greater proportion of members from the more extreme sections of the avant-garde. There is not complete agreement over the membership of this Moscow Kollegiya of IZO. According to one source, it comprised Kuznetsov, Mashkov, Morgunov, Malevich, Zholtovskii, Dymshits-Tolstaya, Udal'tsova, Noakovskii, Fal'k, Rozanova, Shevchenko, Korolev, Konenkov and Kandinskii, under its president and the deputy head of IZO, Tatlin.[16] According to another, its members were Kuznetsov, Mashkov, Morgunov, Tatlin, Malevich, Zholtovskii, Dymshits-Tolstaya, Rozanova, Shevchenko, Ivanov, Korolev, Konenkov and Kandinskii. Co-opted members were Franketti, Fidler and Rodchenko.[17] In their report these artists described themselves as 'left' and 'centre', directly employing political terminology to describe their artistic affiliations. 'According to artistic trends, the members of the board belong to the artists of the left and centre (as the youngest, most productive and vital strength of the country).'[18] The Kollegiya was divided into two sections, one deliberative and one executive. Subsections dealt with schools, literature, art and production (*khudozhestvennaya promyshlennost'*), theatre, cinema, artistic construction (*konstruirovanie*) and architecture.[19]

The concrete work of IZO undertaken in the immediate post-revolutionary period from 1918 to 1920 included the organisation of twenty-eight exhibitions.[20] The main principle governing their organisation was the fact that they were held without any selection board restricting entry. This was reflected in their title: The State Free Exhibition (Svobodnaya gosudarstvennaya vystavka). The first of these was the First Exhibition of Petrograd Artists of All Trends (Pervaya vystavka vsekh napravlenii petrogradskykh khudozhnikov) which opened in the Winter Palace on 13 April 1919 and comprised 299 artists exhibiting a total of 1,826 works.[21] During the same period the Museums Office (Muzeinoe byuro) under the direction of Rodchenko (aided by Stepanova) acquired a total of 1,926 works by 415 artists. It also organised thirty museums in various Russian provincial towns to which it distributed a total of 1,211 works.[22] The Subsection of Artistic Work (Podotdel khudozhestvennogo truda), organised in May 1919, registered artistic organisations that would undertake Government commissions. By May 1920 it had eleven collectives on its books including Agit-poster (Agitplakat – Agitational poster), the Society of Young Artists (Obshchestvo molodykh khudozhnikov – OBMOKhU), and the Painting, Sculpture and Architecture Collective (Zhivskul'ptarkh). Over this period the Subsection commissioned 1,250 stencil posters for the anniversary of the Revolution; almost 2,000 for the Abolition of Illiteracy Campaign and 280 posters for various economic organisations. It also organised competitions for various projects, including a monument to Karl Marx and a more prosaically useful kiosk for selling books and journals.[23] IZO also contained an Art and Production Subsection (Khudozhestvenno-promyshlennyi podotdel). The programme for this department was devised by Ol'ga Rozanova who together with Rodchenko (her assistant for a time) visited studios, raised money and basically reactivated in Moscow, Petrograd and immediate provincial areas the craft workshops that had fallen into disuse over the war period.[24] One result of this craft-orientated activity was the First All Russian Exhibition of Art and Production

(Pervaya vserossiiskaya khudozhestvenno-promyshlennaya vystavka) of 1923. Although generally popular, this show was condemned by Tarabukin for being totally concerned with crafts and applied arts and therefore in his terms not answering the demands of a technological socialist society.[25]

As well as these more practical tasks performed by IZO, Narkompros was also confronted with the task of formulating the theoretical basis of a cultural policy for Socialist Russia. In 1919 IZO issued a general statement of its aesthetic position and discussed the nature and types of artistic forums which should be created.[26] Amongst those bodies intended for such a purpose was the Scientific and Theoretical Department of the Central Section of AKIZO (Akademiya izobrazitel'nykh iskusstv – Academy of Fine Arts). Its aims were widely defined as 'the organisation of the artistic life of the country from the point of view of the ideological, theoretical, practical, scientific and productive aspects'.[27] Conceived as an 'ideological centre', committed to the 'historical law of the closest dependence of art on the social and political condition of society', it asserted that 'intellectual production ... is a reflection of the ideology of the social and political moment, therefore the ideological programme ... is spontaneously linked with the present change in social and political conditions of life'.[28] The theoretical part of the programme was intended to establish and maintain contact with all new technological and scientific ideas, while 'questions relating to the science of art'[29] were to be dealt with by the Institute of Artistic Culture (Institut khudozhestvennoi kul'tury). The ideas which resulted from the debates conducted at INKhUK form the basis of Chapter Three.

Although the more progressive artists, the so-called Futurists, ran IZO this did not mean that their art was accepted as the official aesthetic or that their artistic policy was favoured by the Party. Derogatory assertions that IZO was 'Futurist' occurred as early as 24 November 1918. On that day a statement appeared in *Pravda* accusing the Department of misusing its two million roubles purchasing fund, because instead of buying respectable works of art by Benois or Golovin, it had bought works by 'the Futurists, that painterly movement the future of which is still an unsettled question'.[30] In his reply to this accusation Lunacharskii stressed that IZO was not guilty of favouritism or partiality and that its policy was to purchase works from all artists, irrespective of trend. However, he did explain that IZO was initially concentrating on acquiring works by those younger and officially less favoured artists who were now living in extreme poverty and whose works, although important and deserving of patronage, had been ignored during the rule of bourgeois taste, and were not as yet represented in museums. Lunacharskii concluded by asserting IZO's primacy in all affairs concerning art.[31] It is evident from these two articles that official party favour from the beginning inclined away from the avant-garde. This is confirmed by Lenin's angry response to the publication of Mayakovskii's poem *150,000,000* in an edition of 5,000: 'We need no more than 1500 copies for libraries and eccentrics.'[32] Evidently Lenin himself did not equate revolutionary fervour with Futurism. When he visited the VKhUTEMAS in 1921 he expressed surprise on learning that these ardent students described themselves as being simultaneously 'Futurists' *and* 'Communists'.[33]

AGITATION

In addition to their purely administrative work, the avant-garde artists of IZO were also responsible for carrying out the more practical tasks connected with political agitation. This included the work of decorating the city streets to celebrate the new revolutionary festivals, such as May Day and the anniversary of the October Revolution. Many of the artists who later became leading Constructivists are known to have been engaged on such activity. Popova contributed to the decorations of the building of the Moscow Soviet for May Day 1917, and although there

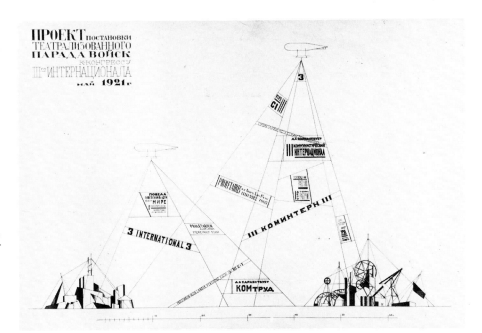

2.1. L. Popova, A. Vesnin, *Project for a theatricised military parade for the Congress of the Third International, entitled 'The End of Capital'* (*Proekt postanovki teatralizovannogo parada voisk k kongressu IIIgo Internatsionala*), May 1921, pen and ink on paper, 46 × 62 cm. Tret'yakov Gallery, Moscow. [Photograph: Courtesy the Arts Council of Great Britain.]

is no evidence that she was directly involved in any other decorations for the revolutionary festivals, she did collaborate with Aleksandr Vesnin in 1921 on a design for a mass festival.[34] This 'theatricalised military parade', planned for May 1921, was to take place on Khodyn' Field, Moscow, in honour of the Third International (Comintern) which met for its third congress in Moscow during the summer of 1921 (plate 2.1).[35] Ultimately the project was abandoned: 'Owing to the difficult economic situation of the country' the funds to finance the project were withdrawn.[36] So the cast of thousands, soldiers, planes, trains, tanks, gymnasts and military bands, never assembled to move from the enclosed and forbidding 'Fortress of Capitalism' on the left of the square to the open, skeletal structure of the 'City of the Future' on the right. However, as part of a more modest and less dramatic entertainment Popova co-operated with Aleksandr Vesnin on the decorations for Red Square to greet the delegates who attended the Third Congress of the Comintern.[37]

Another future Constructivist, Rodchenko, was elected (with Viktor Vesnin and E. Korotkov) to the committee commissioned to design the decorations for Red Square and the tomb of the fallen revolutionaries for May Day 1918.[38] Although there is no evidence to suggest that Rodchenko continued such design work, it is known that he was involved in the preparations for the second anniversary of the Revolution in 1919.[39] Tatlin, however, seems to have been only slightly concerned with such activity. The only known example of his participation in decoration work for the revolutionary festivals was his work with Dymshits-Tolstaya, Kuznetsov and Shaposhnikov designing a firework display for the centre of Moscow to mark the first anniversary of the Revolution.[40] While still serving in the army Miturich was also involved in decorating the Narkompros building and the entrance to the Winter Palace in Petrograd to mark the first anniversary of the Revolution.[41]

With the exception of Vesnin's and Popova's models for the 'End of Capital', I have been unable to trace any visual examples of the type of three-dimensional works which the future Constructivists created for the revolutionary festivals. A contemporary commentary suggests that these decorations were not successful: 'Those very counter-reliefs and constructed combinations of planes and materials which seem so acutely revolutionary at exhibitions, appear inadequate, too individual and even painterly when they are taken out onto the streets and squares. They seem like paintings hung out of doors.'[42] The failure of these constructed ensembles to be effective as revolutionary decorations may have been a contributory factor in the revolutionary experience of these artists which prompted a reassessment of the validity of such objects within the context of the new revolutionary way of life, leading ultimately to the rejection of art as such. At the same time the participation in such activities certainly reinforced the avant-garde's practical identification with the Revolution and its tasks, both immediate and long-term.

The Agitational Propaganda (Agitprop) Section of the Central Committee of the Communist Party directed the work of 453 institutions engaged on poster production. These included all the commissariats, various military organisations, various districts, cities and towns. Until April 1920, when the State Publishing House (Gosudarstvennoe izdatel'stvo) was set up, all posters were distributed by the Central Printing Office (Tsentropechat'). These posters ranged from being purely concerned with gaining immediate support for the Bolshevik cause to being part of the long-term educative task of conveying basic information to the Soviet masses.

In response to a request from the Red Army for artists to design posters, covers and brochures, the Moscow office of IZO resolved on 11 November 1918 to send Smirnov, Malevich, Rodchenko and Osmerkin from the 'left' and three artists from the 'right'.[43] Whether this resolution was implemented practically is difficult to establish. It is possible that Rodchenko was actually sent and did do design work for the Red Army, although there is no surviving evidence of the products of such activity. Undoubtedly Rodchenko as a member of the Moscow IZO was willing to do such work.[44]

Artists also executed propaganda and design tasks for other organisations such as the Trade Unions and the Chief Committee for Political Education under Narkompros (Glavnyi politiko-prosvetitel'nyi komitet Narkomprosa – Glavpolitprosvet). There are examples of poster designs by Popova from 1921 concerning the fight with illiteracy (plate 2.2). However, it has proved impossible to establish whether these were isolated products or merely one example of an intensive participation at this time in poster production.[45] Miturich was apparently also engaged to an indefinable extent on the production of posters, and he also designed the new emblem and money for the Soviet government.[46] Little is known about Stepanova's activities, but in 1919 she painted some slogans with stirring messages:

2.2. L. Popova, *Design for a poster 'Literacy is Light – Illiteracy is Darkness' (Eskiz plakata 'Uchen'e svet – neuchen'e t'ma')*, 1921.

> The Proletariat is the Creator of the Future
> Comrades, Take up your Hammers
> Build the Avant-Garde of Revolutionary Proletarian Art[47]

Posters for the Russian Telegraphic Agency, ROSTA, on which Mayakovskii and Lebedev worked also engaged the energies of Lavinskii for a while.[48]

As an extension of the agitational work in posters the idea was conceived of the agit-train (*agitpoezd* – agitational train) and the agit-ship (*agitparokhod* – agitational steamer), which would travel to areas near the front line during the Civil War as mobile agitational centres dispensing Bolshevik propaganda. As far as can be determined no Constructivist artists were specifically engaged upon painting the outside surfaces of such trains. (The walls of the train's carriages were painted so that while moving the train would resemble a moving poster.) The records of the Department of Agit-ships and -trains under the All Russian Central Executive Committee (Otdel agitpar-poezdov VTsIK), which began in 1920, named thirty artists who participated in this work, none of whom was a prominent member of the avant-garde.[49] However, it does appear that one agit-ship was decorated by a group of young artists working in Aleksandra Ekster's studio in Kiev.[50]

Frequently artists who had left the capital for the provinces were engaged in propaganda and agitational work. Lavinskii for instance was working in this area in Saratov some time between 1918 and 1920.[51] These random recorded examples of agitational work done by future Constructivists indicate that they were engaged in tasks of this political nature from the very beginning, while the new regime was still trying to overcome the capitalist threat during the Civil War and the period of foreign intervention. Agitation, however, was merely directed towards evoking an immediate response to a given situation. Propaganda was conceived as a far more permanent and educative process which should be integrally related to the construction of a new communist society in post-revolutionary Russia. The Plan for Monumental Propaganda launched in 1918 was therefore part of a whole vision and process aimed at creating a new communist Russia.

THE PLAN FOR MONUMENTAL PROPAGANDA

The Plan for Monumental Propaganda was inaugurated by Lenin.[52] It was Lenin's authorship which Lunacharskii stressed when he later presented the plan to the Moscow IZO and he explained that it proposed 'to set up monuments to outstanding persons in the field of revolutionary and social activity, philosophy, literature, science and art'.[53] The decree embodying this policy was signed by Lenin on 13 April 1918, and was published in *Izvestiya* and *Pravda* on the following day under the title 'The Removal of Monuments erected in Honour of the Tsars and their Servants, and the Production of Projects for Monuments to the Russian Socialist Revolution'.[54] A list of sixty-six distinguished figures worthy of such attention included Russian and foreign revolutionaries such as Marx, Engels, Spartacus, Danton, Robespierre, Bakunin and Robert Owen as well as Russian cultural figures such as Uspenskii, Dostoevskii, Rublev, Vrubel' and Skryabin.[55] The monuments, to be set up 'in suitable corners of the capital', were to 'serve the aim of extensive propaganda, rather than the aim of immortalisation'.[56] They were to be made of cheap temporary materials such as plaster and terracotta, although later it was hoped to replace them in more permanent materials. Primary consideration was to be given to 'the quantity and expressive qualities of these monuments'.[57] In addition it was planned to have ceremonial unveilings of the monuments which would be accompanied by speeches and music to make them into 'an act of propaganda and a small festival'. The educational nature of the monuments was reinforced by the provision of short biographies on the pedestals.[58]

This was Lenin's view of how art could most directly serve the masses and the new social order, and of how artists' creations could be most directly linked with the spirit of the future.[59] This conception undoubtedly reflected a utopian element which is confirmed by the evidence of Lunacharskii, who recorded that Lenin in his paper on art in the socialist city cited Campanella and his work *The City of the Sun*.[60] From Lunacharskii's account it seems that the Italian utopian thinker's ideas may have provided the direct inspiration for Lenin's Plan for Monumental Propaganda:

> Campanella in his 'City of the Sun' says that the walls of his fantastic socialist city are covered with frescoes which, serving the youth as a graphic lesson in natural science and history, arouse civil feelings and, in a word, participate in the business of raising and educating the new generation. It seems to me that this is far from being naive and with certain changes could be adopted by us and put into operation now ... I have called what I am thinking of monumental propaganda.[61]

Not only is a direct relationship made explicit in the above statement, but the fact that the erection of statues was to be accompanied by information of an educative character and that plaques containing slogans and citations were also to be distributed on the walls of the city[62] confirms the similarity of the ideas.

Lenin did, however, recognise that the plan would have to be adapted to Russian climatic conditions. 'Our climate hardly allows for the frescoes of which Campanella dreamed,' he wrote.[63] This did not necessarily entail a rejection of monumental painting. This medium was used primarily in the panels to decorate the cities for the great revolutionary festivals, the anniversary of the Revolution and May Day.[64] It was also used in the decoration of the agit-trains and agit-ships. The greatest possibilities in Russia, however, were seen to be in the erection of statues of famous men. These statues combined with plaques affixed to buildings, the ceremonial unveilings and festive musical accompaniments give the impression that the Plan for Monumental Propaganda advocated and embodied an idea of a synthesis of the arts, of painting, architecture, sculpture and music, on the streets of the city.[65] This concept of artistic synthesis and of taking art out into the streets had already been present in the decorations and activities of the revolutionary festivals. The Plan for Monumental Propaganda gave it a more permanent character.

Certainly the Plan for Monumental Propaganda was initially more productive in its negative aspect, the removal of Tsarist monuments, than in the erection of new ones. In Moscow on the eve of May Day 1918 the statue of General Skobolev was removed under the supervision of the sculptors Babichev and Korolev and on May Day itself the statue of Prince S. A. Romanov in the Kremlin was demolished.

Demolition went quickly, but construction was a relatively slow process. There were competitions for a monument to the fighter heroes who died during the German attack on Pskov, for a monument to Karl Liebknecht and Rosa Luxemburg and to Sverdlov.[66] From printed sources which unfortunately are not comprehensive the first statue, a monument to Radishchev, was erected in Petrograd on 22 September 1918. This was followed by one to Lassalle (7 October), Dobrolyubov (27 October), Marx (7 November), Chernyshevskii and Heine (17 November) and Shevchenko (29 November).[67] On 9 March 1919 a monument to Garibaldi was unveiled (plate 2.4).[68] In Moscow thirteen monuments were erected during 1918.[69] This is far from being an exhaustive list, and there were further monuments to Marx, Herzen, Chernyshevskii and many others erected in the larger major cities.[70]

2.3. V. Sinaiskii, Monument to Lasalle, Petrograd, 1918. [Reproduced in *Iskusstvo*, No. 3, 1933.]

2.4. The festive unveiling of K. Zalit's Monument to Garibaldi, in the presence of Lunacharskii, Petrograd, 1918. [Reproduced in *Iskusstvo*, No. 3, 1933, p. 166.]

Relatively few of the monuments are well documented but a comparatively large number are illustrated and they seem primarily to have followed the traditional pattern of monumental figurative portraiture. Such, for instance, is the bust by Sinaiskii of Lassalle erected on Nevskii Prospekt (plate 2.3). The philosopher's features are generalised and idealised. Matveev's bust of Karl Marx, erected in front of the Smol'ny Institute in 1918, was less academic and indulged a penchant for Cubist forms within a figurative format. However, neither of these was sufficiently innovative to refute the conclusion that the monuments had a revolutionary content without a particularly revolutionary artistic form, that apart from a restrained modernism the sculptural language they utilised could have been used for Tsarist monuments.

Tatlin's project of a monument later known as the Monument to the Third International was inspired by the desire to remedy such a situation, and to create a genuinely revolutionary monument for the new revolutionary society.

TATLIN'S MONUMENT TO THE THIRD INTERNATIONAL

As head of the Moscow IZO, Tatlin prepared and sent a report to the Council of People's Commissars, Sovnarkom, in June 1918 concerning the organisation and execution of the Plan for Monumental Propaganda in Moscow.[72] In this report, affirmed by Sovnarkom in July, Tatlin stressed the difficulty of speedily executing the project without endangering the artistic quality of the monuments produced, because he stressed 'the State, as it is now, cannot and must not be the initiator of bad taste'. His solution was to attract 'fresh and youthful artistic talents', supply them with all the materials they would need, abolish the old jury and introduce an 'international review' which would decide which projects should be executed in permanent materials.[73] In a letter, written probably towards the end of August 1918, Tatlin again stressed in relation to the monuments that they should be 'free creations in a socialist state'.[74] In this letter Tatlin referred to work 'not only on monuments to prominent figures but also on monuments to the Russian Revolution, monuments to a relationship between the State and art which has not existed until now'.[75] It is possible that he had already conceived the idea for his own monument although he became a participating artist only at the beginning of 1919.[76]

Tatlin was commissioned by the Moscow IZO early in 1919 to execute a project for a monument to the Revolution. However, he moved to Petrograd in the middle of 1919 to take charge of the Studio of Volume, Material and Construction at the Free Studios and he continued his work on it there.[77] The first information concerning Tatlin's ideas for the monument was presented in an article by Punin, 'About Monuments', in *Art of the Commune* on 9 March 1919.[78] Punin's statement, evidently directly based on conversations and correspondence with Tatlin, stressed Tatlin's rejection of the traditional figurative monument which could not change the face of the city in any fundamental way. The essence of Tatlin's conception put forward as an antithesis was that 'contemporary monuments above all must answer that general striving for synthesis of different types of art, such as we are observing at the moment'. Rejecting the idea that synthesis consisted in the architect building the structure, the painter painting it, and the sculptor decorating it, Tatlin nevertheless suggested that they should all three be engaged upon the design of monuments and that the end product should please all three.

In this article Punin also put forward Tatlin's basic outline concerning the form and the structure of the monument: 'The form of the monument will correspond to all invented artistic forms at the present time. In the present position of art these forms will obviously be cubes, cylinders, spheres, cones, segments, spherical surfaces, pieces of these, etc.' It seems at this point that Tatlin had not made any final decision concerning the basic overall shape of the monument because the description referred to a wing of the building being a ramp for motor cyclists. However, it is clear that he envisaged different geometrically shaped structures, allotted to specific functions, which whilst existing as separate entities would be interconnected by means of lifts. This implied a vertical separation in addition to a possible horizontal separation into different wings.

However, the article did not stress the plastic forms of the monument but the functional programme with which Tatlin had endowed it. This emphasis supports the idea that Tatlin's initial impulse was derived from the urge to create a truly revolutionary monument, responding to and expressing the dynamism of a socialist and revolutionary society. In this connection it should be noted that it was much later, probably not until mid-1920, that Tatlin conceived the idea of dedicating his monument not to the Russian Revolution but to the new Third International set up in 1919.[79]

It is evident from Punin's article that Tatlin had already decided prior to this that the monument should express dynamism, be dynamic and perform a dynamic function as an agitational and propaganda centre:

> As a principle it is necessary to stress that first all the elements of the monument should be modern technical apparatuses promoting agitation and propaganda, and secondly that the monument should be a place of the most intense movement; least of all should one stand still or sit down in it, you must be mechanically taken up, down, carried away against your will, in front of you must flash the powerful laconic phrase of the orator-agitator, and further on the latest news, decrees, decisions, the latest inventions, an explosion of simple and clear thoughts, creativity, only creativity.[80]

The element of dynamism was to pervade both the entire structure – the function, and the working of the monument, the apparatuses therein contained – and those working there. Nothing that hindered this celebration of dynamism could be permitted. 'Part of the simple forms (the cubes) must house lecture halls, gymnasiums, agitational rooms and other similar establishments . . . but these must not be museums, libraries, etc., because it is desirable to preserve the constant movement of these rooms.'[81]

Among other features specifically mentioned was a garage housing special motorcycles and cars to move and distribute agitational apparatus, a gigantic screen to show 'the latest news in the cultural and political life of the whole world', a radio station capable of transmitting world wide, a telegraphic and telephone exchange, a projector for throwing messages onto the clouds, art workshops and a printing shop.[82] This stress on the 'modern technical apparatus' and the dynamic qualities of technology amounted to what could be called a romanticisation of technology. Describing this approach, Tatlin asserted (via Punin) that 'the project . . . based on a synthesis of the technical achievements of our time, presents the opportunity of richly applying the new artistic forms to technology. The radio, screen and aerial, being elements of the monument, can also be the elements of the form.'[83] Given the emphasis on technological dynamism that has been described and this approach, it is not surprising that the forms eventually chosen for the supporting structure were a spiral and a dynamic diagonal and that the internal glass structures rotated on their axes.

Tatlin's project, as outlined by Punin, posited a dynamic alternative to the traditional monument. Tatlin's monument, wedded firmly to the dynamics of modern technology, was to perform a positive role in the process of change then going on in Russia. It was conceived as a revolutionary monument, performing a revolutionary function in a revolutionary situation. As such, it represented a reaction against the current practice of the Plan for Monumental Propaganda, although responding very positively to the utopian element in the idea of propa-

I. L. Popova, *Painterly Architectonics* (*Zhivopiskaya arkhitektonika*), 1918, 29·3 × 23·5 cm. Yale University Art Gallery, New Haven, Gift from estate of Katherine S. Dreier.

К. МЕДУНЕЦКИ

2.5. V. Tatlin, Tsarevich plate, painted by Chekhonin to Tatlin's design, 1922. [Reproduced in Matsa, *Sovetskoe iskusstvo*, 1933.]

2.6. V. Tatlin, G. Yakulov, et al., Detail of the Kafe Pittoresk, Moscow, 1917. [Reproduced in Salmon, *L'Art russe moderne*, 1928.]

II. K. Medunetskii, *Spatial Construction*, 1920, tin, brass, iron, aluminium, height 45 cm. Yale University Art Gallery, New Haven. Gift of Collection Société Anonyme.

ganda embodied in Lenin's plan. However, Tatlin's project could also be interpreted as a reassertion of Russian traditions.[84] Tatlin's paintings had been strongly influenced by old Russian icon and fresco painting, and the fact that this influence was still a potent force is evinced by the Tsarevich plate (plate 2.5), of 1919.[85] Russian history contained several examples of buildings being erected to commemorate specific events. The Cathedral of St Basil or of the Intercession of the Virgin was built (1554–60) by Ivan the Terrible to commemorate the conquest of Kazan'. Later, in St Petersburg, the Church of the Resurrection or of the Saviour of the Spilled Blood (1883–1907) was built to mark the spot where Tsar Aleksandr II was assassinated on 13 March 1881.

Tatlin had defined his task as that not only of synthesising the various branches of art but also of synthesising them with technology. 'The task .... is to find a single form, simultaneously architectonic, plastic, and painterly, which would have the possibility of synthesising the separate forms of these or other technical apparatuses.'[86] Before looking in detail at Tatlin's final version of his Tower, it is important to mention some of the artistic experiments that constitute its context.

Tatlin himself had already participated in one project which represented a first step beyond the totally non-functional constructions examined in Chapter One. He had worked with the artists Yakulov, Bruni and others on decorating Filippov's Kafe Pittoresk in Moscow in 1917 (plate 2.6).[87] This new café interior had been designed to manifest the elements of contemporary city life, to be 'a type of fair or street festival' and to provide a basis for a new style in all branches of art.[88] However, judging from the photographs, the finished product, visually exciting as it may have been, merely confirmed the eclectic nature of the artistic personalities involved and of the decorations produced. It had hardly achieved Filippov's aim to bring together 'the modern decorative ... scenic and musical arts' to create 'a beautiful tribune for the new aesthetic achievements in all fields of the arts and the propaganda of these among the masses'.[89] It was the first instance when the methods of working in three dimensions evolved in the non-utilitarian constructions were applied to a practical situation to create a total environment. The decorations were built onto the existing four walls and this naturally limited the scope for the variety of spatial relationships that could be created. This search for a new aesthetic had been related to technology and urbanism. However, during the Civil War period the idea of the synthetic work of art had been further fostered by the practical activity of the revolutionary festivals committed to a revolutionary content. The practice of painting panels to transform pre-revolutionary facades into revolutionary buildings for the festivals encouraged the idea of the artist producing a new, totally artistic environment. This new ideological element and the 'merging of life and art' made the experiment of the Kafe Pittoresk seem like 'a beautiful toy in the hands of grown-up people'.[90]

This utopianism infected such a stalwart of traditional culture as Lunacharskii. At the opening of the State Free Art Studios in October 1918 he expressed the dreams that inspired artists of the time: 'A brotherhood of artists and architects will be born and will create not only temples and monuments to human ideals but also complete artistic towns. To link art with life – this is the task of the new art.'[91] In the context of such enthusiasm everything seemed possible.[92] Immediate prototypes for such ideas were to be found in literature, such as Khlebnikov's poem 'The City of the Future' and Bogdanov's utopian novel *The Red Star*, which described the perfect socialist society and environment on a distant planet.[93] Lavinskii's plans for a projected City of the Future (*Gorod budushchego*, plate 2.7) were inspired by just such utopian concepts. He envisaged a town of glass and asbestos, built on springs in the sky.[94] The plan was ultra-rational, based on a circular grid system (addresses would be purely numerical) in conformity with principles he had distilled from engineering,[95] and in conformity also with his conception of his role not as 'a creator priest but a master executing a social brief'.[96]

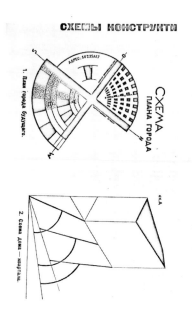

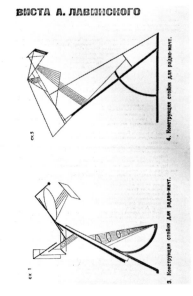

2.7. A. Lavinskii, *City of the Future: Plans* (*Gorod budush-chego. Skhemy*), 1922. [Reproduced in *LEF*, No. 1, 1923.]

2.8. A. Rodchenko, Design for a kiosk, 1922. [Photograph: Society for Cultural Relations with the USSR, London.]

The trend toward artistic synthesis found a more solidly practical manifestation in the organisation in May 1919 of a collective to deal with questions of synthesis between sculpture and architecture called Sinskul'ptarkh (Sintez skul'pturno-arkhitekturnyi – Sculptural and Architectural Synthesis) within the sculpture section of the Subsection of Artistic Work of IZO.[97] The aim was to create a synthesis of the spatial arts, and one of the first projects was a Temple to Intercourse between Nations (*Khram obshcheniya narodov*) intended for mass festivals. Towards the end of 1919 the painters Rodchenko and Shevchenko joined, and the committee was renamed Zhivskul'ptarkh (Zhivopisno-skul'pturno-arkhitekturnyi sintez – Painterly, Sculptural and Architectural Synthesis).[98] The group concentrated their attention on projects for buildings embodying the new social functions such as communal housing. In the various drawings for projects there was a very strong reliance on the formal language of avant-garde painting (plate 2.8), and structural coherence and viability were sacrificed to the expressive qualities of form.

It is within this artistic and ideological context that Tatlin's final version of his Tower should be viewed. By December 1919 the project seems to have been fully worked out, but there is no explicit indication that it was as yet dedicated to the Third International. This final design projected a structure 'built according to completely new architectural principles, from completely new architectural forms'.[99] It would stand four hundred metres high and straddle the broad river Neva in the centre of Petrograd. Tatlin was confident that 'modern technology fully allows for the possibility of constructing such a building'.[100]

This version of the Tower is known from the two facades reproduced in Punin's pamphlet of 1920-1, *The Monument to the Third International* (plates 2.9-10), from photographs of the model taken at the exhibition in Moscow (plates 2.11, 13), and from the description of the monument which Punin published in his pamphlet.[101]

Work on building the model began not earlier than March 1920, and it was completed before the third anniversary of the October Revolution.[102] Appropriately the model was exhibited from 8 November to 1 December 1920 in the hall of the studio in which it had been built.[103] It was apparently this model that was transported to Moscow towards the end of December and re-erected in the Hall of the Eighth Congress of the Soviets, which was discussing Lenin's Plan for the Electrification of Russia.[104] Before exhibiting the monument in Moscow Tatlin delivered a lecture with photographs to a meeting of the VKhUTEMAS students in their Paul Cézanne Club. According to Khardzhiev, this meeting took place between 16 and 18 December 1920. Gabo and Lissitzky were critical of the monument but

60

Mayakovskii defended it as a piece of engineering art and greeted it as 'the first monument without a beard' and 'the first object of October'.[105]

From the photographs the model appears to have been between 6 and 7 metres high.[106] The supporting external structure to be made of iron (but wood in the model) consisted of two separate spirals moving in the same direction around a strong diagonal axis. Within this structure four glass-skinned volumes were to be suspended. According to Punin's description,

> The monument consists of three great rooms of glass, erected with the help of a complicated system of vertical pillars and spirals. These rooms are placed on top of each other and have different, harmonically corresponding forms. They are to be able to move at different speeds by means of a special mechanism. The lower storey, which is in the form of a cube, rotates on its axis at the speed of one revolution per year. This is intended for legislative assemblies. The next storey, which is in the form of a pyramid, rotates on its axis at the rate of one revolution per month. Here the executive bodies are to meet (the International Executive Committee, the Secretariat and other executive administrative bodies). Finally, the uppermost cylinder, which rotates at the speed of one revolution per day, is reserved for information services: an information office, a newspaper, the issuing of proclamations, pamphlets and manifestos – in short all the means for inform-ing the international proletariat; it will also have a telegraphic office and an apparatus that can project slogans onto a large screen. These can be fitted around the axis of the hemisphere. Radio masts will rise up over the monument. It should be emphasised that Tatlin's proposal provides for walls with a vacuum (thermos) which will help to keep the temperature in the various rooms constant.[107]

Despite Tatlin's optimism at the project's technical viability, there is no indication from the drawings that exist as to how he conceived of the complex gearing system which these rotating structures would have required, linked together as they were within the open supportive framework by lifts.

2.9. V. Tatlin, *Drawing of the Monument to the Third International*, 1920. [Reproduced in Punin, *Pamyat' III Internatsion-ala*, 1920.]

2.10. V. Tatlin, *Drawing of the Monument to the Third International*, 1920. [Reproduced in Punin, *Pamyat' III Internatsion-ala*, 1920.]

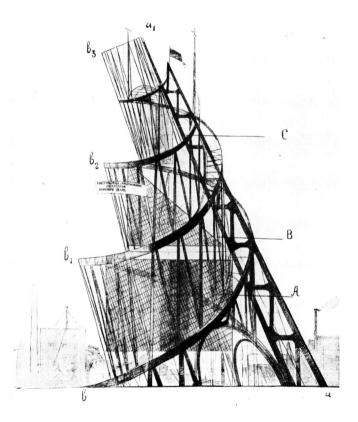

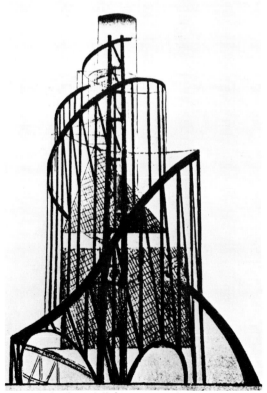

Confronted with this rather grandiose structure, Western commentators have sought an explanation in established artistic parallels. Obvious comparison has been made between the girder construction of the Eiffel Tower and that of Tatlin's monument.[108] Tatlin had visited Paris in 1913 and would almost certainly have seen Eiffel's structure. As Troels Andersen has pointed out, Eiffel and Tatlin were dealing with similar technological possibilities which made Eiffel's edifice an obvious starting point for Tatlin despite the differences in motivation (after all Eiffel built to demonstrate a method of construction, and Tatlin to illustrate the more abstract concept of communist revolution). Although Andersen questioned the validity of investigating the iconography of the Tower, he drew a contemporary parallel with Boccioni's *Development of a Bottle in Space* of 1912 (plate 2.12).[109] Elderfield, however, has traced the iconography of the spiral in the Tower from Bruegel's *Tower of Babel* to Rodin's *Tower of Labour*.[110] Arguing for a more contemporary and more technological source of inspiration, Kestutis Paul Zygas has suggested that the structures of the Baku oil derricks and the skeleton masts of ships may have influenced Tatlin.[111] Certainly, as a sailor himself, Tatlin may have been familiar with the type of marine craft Zygas describes. He would also have travelled extensively and may have visited Baku and seen the oil derricks. A first-hand experience of such structures would probably have been more influential than any knowledge gleaned as a child from his engineer father whom he disliked. Margit Rowell further suggests that functionally and visually the skeleton masts which were used on battleships prior to 1914, when Tatlin was frequently at sea, were a credible point of departure for the structure of Tatlin's monument. The armature of such masts had the form of a latticework cone constructed on the principle of the 'rotational hyperboloid', with the interior rigged for the raising or lowering of equipment and signal lights and radio transmitters fixed to the top. Tatlin may have been influenced by his nautical experience in this way. He had already worked on designs for Wagner's opera *The Flying Dutchman*, and in 1916 he suggested that Meierkhol'd use a 'great ship's mast with all the proper naval attributes – the rigging and observation turrets' – instead of a mystical tree in the film *Spirit Magic* (*Nav'i chary*).[112]

However, Tatlin himself, in his declaration accompanying the exhibition of the model of the monument in Moscow, specifically related the aesthetic principles of his Tower to his pre-revolutionary work in non-utilitarian constructions.

2.11. V. Tatlin, Model of the Monument to the Third International on exhibition in Moscow, 1920. [Reproduced in Punin, *Tatlin* (*Protiv kubizma*), 1921.]

2.12. U. Boccioni, *Development of a Bottle in Space*, 1912, silvered bronze, 38·1 × 19·9 × 59·4 cm. Collection, The Museum of Modern Art, New York, Aristide Maillol Fund.

2.13. V. Tatlin, Model of the Monument to the Third International on exhibition in Moscow, 1920, with Tatlin in foreground holding pipe. [Reproduced in Punin, *Tatlin* (*Protiv kubizma*), 1921.]

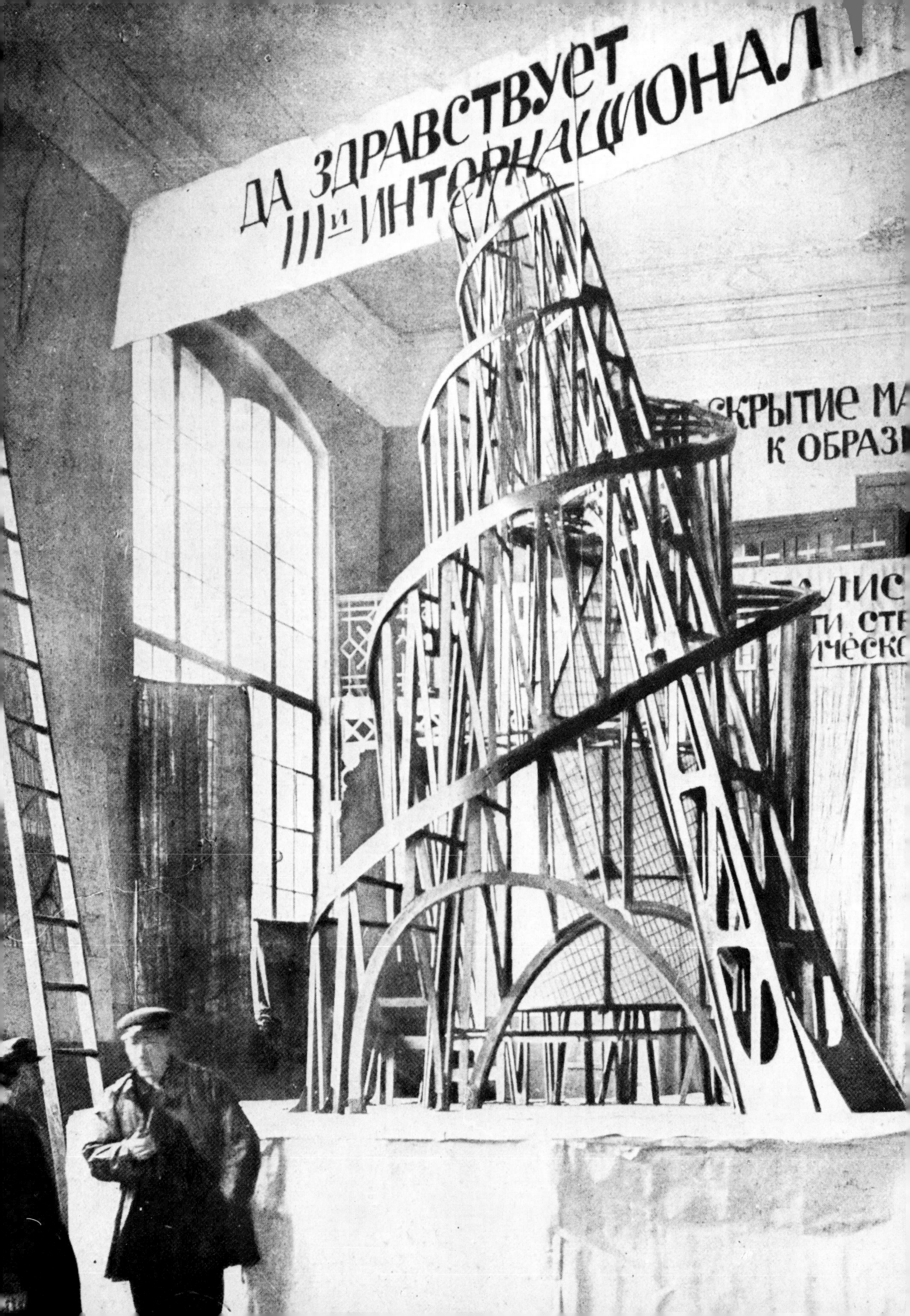
ДА ЗДРАВСТВУЕТ
III-и ИНТЕРНАЦИОНАЛ

In 1915, in Moscow, there was an exhibition of material and laboratory models (an exhibition of reliefs and counter-reliefs).

The exhibition of 1917 gave a series of examples of selections of materials, of more complicated investigations and demonstrations of material as such, and its consequences – movement, tension and their interrelationship.

This investigation of material, volume and construction made it possible for us, in 1918, to move towards creating an artistic form of a selection of the materials iron and glass as the materials of modern classicism, equivalent in their severity to marble in the past.

In this way there emerges the possibility of uniting purely artistic forms with utilitarian aims. An example: the Monument to the Third Communist International.[113]

In tracing the development of Constructivism, it is this continuity of formal inspiration in the work of Tatlin himself that is important. When a model of the monument was reconstructed for the exhibition of Tatlin's work at the Moderna Museet in Stockholm in 1968, it was revealed that the whole structure was built upon an inclined truncated cone, technically known as a frustum.[114] This was a recurrent form in Tatlin's early constructions, to be seen clearly in *Selection of Materials* of 1917 (plate 1.8) and less prominently in the glass shape of the earlier *Selection of Materials* of 1914 (plate 1.12). Tatlin's interest in curved planes is evinced from his earliest work, such as *The Nude* of 1913 (plate 1.3), and it is encountered in the very first reliefs such as *The Bottle* of the same year (plate 1.1). It continued to be a prominent feature of the corner counter-reliefs with which he moved out into three-dimensional space (plates 1.9 and 1.13). In 1932 he made his

2.14. Simplified model of Tatlin's Monument to the Third International in a street demonstration, *c.* 1927. [Reproduced in Gushchin, *Izo iskusstvo v massovykh proadnestvakh i deomonstratsiyakh*, 1930.]

interest in curvatures as a basis for architectural construction more explicit in his declaration 'Art into Technology'.

> There is normally a tension between simple rectilinear forms and forms determined by the simplest curves. In architecture the use of curves and forms determined by complicated curvatures created by a complicated movement, a straight line or a curve is still of a fairly primitive character; the whole thing is limited to a common section of the simplest forms...
>
> The artist shall in his work, as a counterpart to technology, present a succession of new relationships between the forms of the material. A series of forms determined by complicated curvatures will demand other plastic, material and constructive relationships – the artist can and must master these elements.[115]

The form of the monument could be seen at least partially as a result of Tatlin's work with the materials from which he constructed the model (i.e. wooden laths). With its curvilinear volumes and its juxtaposition of curved planes, and with the tensile curves of the supporting spirals, recalling strongly the elegantly curving wires supporting the hanging reliefs, the interaction of internal and external volumes which these define, and the very principle of the open structure embracing forms, fusing with the environment, the Tower resembles in its conception nothing so much as a gigantic counter-relief.

Despite Tatlin's stress on the utilitarian nature of his monument, he, as well as his contemporaries, recognised the symbolic nature of the Tower. Lissitzky wrote of it as a new revolutionary symbol – 'Here an ancient concept of form, as represented for example by the Sargon pyramid, was actually created in a new material for a new content' – and he imbued the materials themselves with symbolic qualities. He wrote, 'Iron is strong like the will of the proletariat. Glass is clear like its conscience.'[116] Trotskii upbraided Tatlin for his impracticality, his revolutionary romanticism and symbolism.[117] In the same way the architectural critic Khiger placed the Tower firmly within the context of that romanticism and symbolism which had dominated architectural thought between 1920 and 1922.[118] The architect Konstantin Mel'nikov is reported to have said, 'Our age is dynamic. Tatlin is making the spiral a modern symbol.'[119] This seems to have been one of Tatlin's conscious aims. According to the memoirs of A. A. Begicheva, Tatlin regarded the Tower as a symbolic structure. Talking to her during the period of his teaching in Kiev in the mid-1920s, he explained: 'My monument is a symbol of the epoch. Unifying in it artistic and utilitarian forms, I created a kind of synthesis of art with life.'[120] Moreover, from her memoirs it appears that the spiral was specifically chosen as a symbol of time and energy. She reports Tatlin as saying:

> I placed at its basis the screw, as the most dynamic form – a symbol of time: energy, lucidity, striving. The transparent construction from metallic forms has the form of a spiral – inclined at the angle of the earth. The inclined forms to the angle of the earth are the most stable, soft forms.[121]

As a symbol of the new century, it was natural that the different velocities of the internal volumes should be suggestive of a cosmic symbolism: the earth moving around the sun (a year), the moon orbiting the earth (a month) and the earth rotating on its own axis (a day).[122]

In his declaration Tatlin had stated that the results of 'uniting purely artistic forms with purely utilitarian aims' were 'models which stimulate inventions in the business of creating a new world and summon producers to take control over the forms of the new everyday life'. The role of the Tower was to be exactly this: a model which stimulated inventions. Against the background of emerging theoretical discussion, it acted as a practical crystallisation, helping to focus both the pre-revolutionary and post-revolutionary artistic experiences around utilitarian objectives.

In order to achieve this unity of the artistic and utilitarian, Tatlin wanted to continue to apply the methods of working with materials which he had developed in his counter-reliefs. For Tatlin this process had been intuitive rather than scientific or mechanical. As he stated in 'The Work Ahead of Us', and made even more explicit in 1932, he rejected the mechanical application of technique to art and stressed the organic relationship between material and its tensile capacity. He stressed that 'only as an outcome of the dynamic force resulting from these mutual relations is a vitally inevitable form born'.[123] In this conception of the intuitive understanding possessed by the artist, there is present an almost mystical element, which is related to the messianic conception of the artist's role, as creator and interpreter of the environment.

However, over the monument Tatlin had displayed a banner proclaiming a stirring message linking engineering creativity with art. Conventional wisdom has it that this banner read 'Engineers Create New Forms'.[124] All that is legible of the three line slogan in the extant photograph (plate 2.11) is:

Inzhenery mo[stov] ...	Engineers [of bridges?] ...
Delaite ...	Make ...
Izobretennoi ...	Invented ...

Many artists interpreted this statement, and Tatlin's position *vis-à-vis* the utilitarian task in 'The Work Ahead of Us', to represent a celebration of the machine and technology. Whereas Tatlin in his further work retained the intuitive approach to materials themselves and the forms they produced, these other artists took their starting point from the technological rhetoric and content of the monument, and moved on to seek their central disciplines from these sources. This approach and

2.15. View of the third OBMO-KhU exhibition, Moscow, May 1921. [Reproduced in Matsa, *Sovetskoe iskusstvo*, 1933, where it is erroneously dated 1920.]

a   b   c   d   e

path of development is typified by the work of certain future Constructivist members of the OBMOKhU group, which can be examined as a case study of the development outlined in this chapter from agitational tasks through to laboratory work for real constructions with a utilitarian aim.

OBMOKhU: THE SOCIETY OF YOUNG ARTISTS

The Society of Young Artists (Obshchestvo molodykh khudozhnikov– known by the abbreviated form of its name OBMOKhU) was set up in 1919.[125] Its founding members were N. Denisovskii, V. Komardenkov, S. Kostin, M. Eremichev, A. Zamoshkin, K. Medunetskii, A. Naumov, A. Perekatov, N. Prusakov, S. Svetlov and the Stenberg brothers Georgii and Vladimir, all of whom were students from the State Free Art Studios.[126] The aim of the group was initially agitational. They were not interested in creating easel paintings but in the execution 'of production tasks from the point of view of the new consumer in art'.[127] Initially they seem to have come together through their agitational work decorating the streets of Moscow for the revolutionary festivals. Medunetskii and the Stenberg brothers had decorated the Post Office on the Myasnitskaya for May Day 1918,[128] and they had all been involved in the decorations of the Rogozhsko-Simonovskii district of Moscow for the first anniversary of October, together with one student who remained outside the later group, Echeistov.[129] To facilitate their work they were given a metal workshop, where they prepared stencils for posters commissioned by the Committee for the Abolition of Illiteracy. Apart from their extensive work with agitational posters they also decorated the streets and station of Voronezh with

2.16. View of the third OBMO-KhU exhibition, Moscow, May 1921. [Reproduced in *Veshch'*, No. 1/2, 1922.]

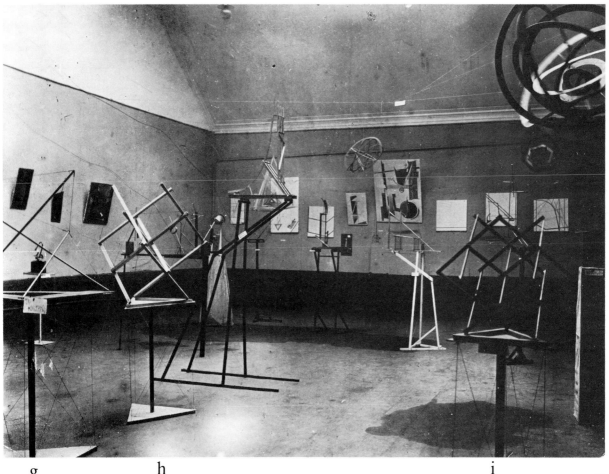

f

g   h   i

posters, and executed set designs for various theatrical productions in Moscow and in the provinces.[130] This is confirmed by Denisovskii's own description of their activity:

> We did posters for the All Russian Special Committee for the Abolition of Illiteracy, we executed the tasks of N. K. Krupskaya for Glavpolitprosvet, we did decorations for the travelling rural theatre, directed by Z. Raikh. We also produced seals, including a 'hammer and sickle', in a specially organised workshop. But primarily we turned out agitational posters.[131]

At their first exhibition in spring 1919 the exhibits consisted entirely of examples of their agitational work, and no figurative or abstract work relating to any formal investigations was displayed. Furthermore, to emphasise the collective nature of their creativity and organisation and to stress their rejection of individualism all the works exhibited were anonymous. In 1920 at the second exhibition the items exhibited were again preponderantly posters but some colour constructions (*tsvetokonstruktsii*) were included.[132]. The third exhbition of the OBMOKhU, which opened on 22 May 1921, was the famous exhibition which included work by Rodchenko and Ioganson, who were not among the original members of the group.[133] Fortunately it is documented with two photographs (plates 2.15-16) which provide two views of the exhibition. In these Rodchenko's constructions, described above, including a circle, an oval, a triangle and a hexagon, are all visible.[134]

The three-dimensional works by Medunetskii can be seen in plates 2.15-16 where their position is denoted by the letters *a* through *i* printed below or to the side. They can just be discerned in the photographs and they are the only works by Medunetskii known at present. In January 1922 he and the two Stenberg brothers exhibited their works at the exhibition of work of the Constructivists at the Kafe Poetov in Moscow. At the same time, in their declaration printed in the catalogue to that exhibition, they clearly announced their adoption of utilitarian objectives and their rejection of purely artistic activity. They had presented their constructions as 'laboratory work'. Medunetskii's exhibits at the third OBMOKhU exhibition consisted of interlocking metal shapes of a very precise geometrical nature. In his *Spatial Construction* of 1920-1 (colour plate II; *f* in plate 2.16), usually erroneously entitled *Construction No. 557* because of a mistaken report of its catalogue number at the 1922 Erste Russische Kunstausstellung in Berlin, these shapes thread through each other with a minimum of contact and their lines define the spatial parameters of the enclosed volumes.[135] Medunetskii used different metals in this work but chose not to exploit the textural possibilities of these materials but rather their colour values. The red rod juxtaposed with the yellow sheen of the brass triangle and the black base of the composition increased the weightlessness and dynamism of the whole. It is difficult to discern any immediately utilitarian content in this particular construction and this work in three dimensions inevitably belongs to the more theoretical and abstract aspects of laboratory work.

Construction *a*[136] (plate 2.15), in which slim metallic curved and straight bars delineated the spatial environment, represented an identical linear approach to the problem of spatial construction. Constructions *b*, *c* and *d* indicate that this was a common feature of all the works exhibited. Variations were produced by different thicknesses of bar and strip and by different geometrical shapes. The material varieties and qualities of Tatlin's reliefs were completely absent. Medunetskii's constructions seem not to have been built up in this sense but minimally joined together, characterising the clarity and precision of technological form.

This feature of Medunetskii's laboratory work was also very apparent in some of the Stenberg constructions, e.g. Cat. Nos. 11 and 6 (plates 2.17-18) also exhibited at the OBMOKhU.[137] Formally Medunetskii's constructions bear a closer relationship to some works by the Stenberg brothers (plate 2.20).[138] These are essentially linear

2.17. G. Stenberg, *Construction for a Spatial Structure No. 11* (*Konstruktsiya prostranstvennogo sooruzheniya No. 11*), 1920, iron, glass, wood. Whereabouts unknown.

2.18. V. Stenberg, *Construction for a Spatial Structure No. 6 (Konstruktsiya prostranstvennogo sooruzheniya No. 6)*, reconstruction of object of 1920. [Photograph: Courtesy Galerie Gmurzynska, Cologne.]

works which explore the development of line in three dimensions. Other works by Georgii and Vladimir Stenberg contain strong references to the materials, forms and articulations of existing technological structures such as bridges. Frequently using metal and incorporating glass, these works appear as completely abstract investigations of the potential of such structures in artistic terms. However, Vladimir Stenberg had stressed that these constructions were conceived as explorations towards the realisation of actual buildings. Such a consideration may underlie the fact that the stands were designed as integral parts of the constructions, continuing the interests of the work right through to the base and emphasising the radical potential of the new forms. This is particularly evident in plate 2.18.

As far as can be ascertained from the photographs of the exhibition, and the evidence of Vladimir Stenberg based on these, the constructions labelled *g*, *h* and *i* in plate 2.16 are works by Ioganson.[139] These suggest that Ioganson also was working with basically linear constructions, defining spatial parameters, rather than with massing material components. Fortunately, Moholy-Nagy illustrated one of Ioganson's works, as figure 93, in his treatise *The New Vision: From Material to Architecture*, originally published in Munich in 1929 and later in New York in

2.19. G. Stenberg, *Construction No. 2* (*Konstruksiya No. 2*), 1920, ink and gouache on paper. Russian Museum, Leningrad.

an English translation. This work by Ioganson (plate 2.21), whom Moholy-Nagy rather understandably calls Johansen, is dated 1921 and entitled *A Study in Balance*.[140] According to Moholy-Nagy, if the string was pulled the composition would change to another position while maintaining its equilibrium. This suggests that Ioganson was exploring the movement of geometrical skeletal structures in a rather more calculated and technical manner than Rodchenko was doing in his

2.20. V. Stenberg, *Construction*, 1920. [First reproduced in *Pionere der sowjetischen Architektur*, 1983.]

2.21. K. Ioganson, *Study in Balance*, c. 1920. [Reproduced in Moholy-Nagy, *New Vision*, 1930.]

hanging constructions. Ioganson's *Study in Balance* was exhibited at the third OBMOKhU exhibition and can be identified as construction g in plate 2.16. The jointing in other constructions exhibited by Ioganson at this exhibition implies that they too were able to be adjusted to other positions and that they were possibly collapsible. This suggests that the direct reference to existing engineering structures which is particularly strong in the work of the Stenberg brothers, is, in these works by Ioganson, focussed on a detailed study of the dynamic potential of the constructive interrelationships of the component elements of such engineering structures.

These types of structural interests which seem to have been the underlying concerns of Ioganson's work at this juncture also found expression in his theoretical statements delivered to the Institute of Artistic Culture (INKhUK) later in March 1922, in which he attacked the textural and accidental qualities of Tatlin's work and emphasised that laboratory work should be dealing with constructional problems of direct relevance to utilitarian tasks.[141]

Ioganson, Rodchenko, Medunetskii and Vladimir and Georgii Stenberg had all become members of the First Working Group of Constructivists set up on 18 March 1921.[142] In their works exhibited at the third OBMOKhU exhibition, which are among some of the first examples of 'laboratory work', there is a pronounced emphasis on the precision, clarity and economy of the geometric form. The relationship to technology is emphasised by these qualities. Although Tatlin's Tower pointed the way towards a new synthesis between the arts, and between art and technology, his method of working was based on the textural possibilities of materials as well as their formal presence. The ideas which he expressed in his Monument to the Third International have been interpreted by the OBMOKhU as a 'celebration of the machine' and in this dimension only. To them the organic form and texture of material has become less important and the stress on material, as worked and processed by machine technology, has become greater. The two trends which were evident in the non-utilitarian constructions have become distilled into one dominant trend – that of the geometric form in technologically processed material highly influenced by mechanical forms. The story of Constructivism from this point onwards is pre-eminently involved with technology and is concerned with what could be described as technological or mechanical form. The next phase of Constructivism's development was characterised by the attempt to build a theoretical basis for the harnessing of these technologically inspired formal explorations to the revolutionary tasks of creating a socialist environment.

3 TOWARDS A THEORETICAL BASIS: FUSING THE FORMAL AND UTILITARIAN

CHAPTER ONE traced how artists trained in conventional artistic media moved, on the basis of their experimentation with Cubist and Futurist ideas, towards a new category of art objects: the three-dimensional construction. Made from contemporary materials, these incorporated real space within themselves, fusing with their environment and expressing the spatial and dynamic aspects of twentieth-century urbanism and technology as perceived by the artists. These formal investigations added impetus to that trend in Russian art towards objectively defining the artistic component elements of the work of art which had received its initial impulse from the Union of Youth group (Soyuz molodezhi), whose pictorial experiments and theoretical examinations of Cubism and Futurism were well publicised by its journal of the same name and by its exhibitions, the first of which was held in St Petersburg in the spring of 1910. The formal basis of non-functional constructions developed by Tatlin and his followers fused with the revolutionary experiences of the artists (outlined in Chapter Two) to produce the beginnings of the theoretical principles which would eventually become Constructivism. This chapter now attempts to trace and document the evolution of Constructivism as a theory of design, placing it within the context of the general idea of production art which also emerged at this period.

Before moving on to examine in detail the literary and oral debates through which the theoretical ideas of the Constructivists evolved, it is appropriate to outline certain strands of the artistic context out of which these debates arose. The most important dimensions of this context to highlight here are the new attitude towards the relationship between art and the production process, and the roots of its connection with generally socialist attitudes.

In this period the critical move towards the formulation of a new design process was marked by the emergence of a new attitude towards the art object. This new attitude permeated all avant-garde activity of the pre-revolutionary period. It was a view which saw the work of art not as an entity primarily composed of inspirational, philosophical or emotional elements, but as an object composed of various material and artistic elements, organised by the artist according to specific laws and techniques.[1] In other words when the subject matter of the relief no longer referred however indirectly to an external object (i.e. ceased to be representational or to contain representational elements), the subject matter or content of the relief became the materials from which it was made, their interrelationships and their interaction with their immediate spatial environment. In this way the relief became an object in its own right, conditioned by various artistic laws, a product of these laws and of the activity of the artist. The creative process became directed towards the production of a 'real object . . . autonomous in its form and content'.[2]

In 1923 Arvatov described this new relationship between the artist and his work as being similar to that existing between a craftsman and the product of his labour:

The artist began to relate to the picture, not as a field for the illusionistic depiction of objects, but as a real object. He began to work on the picture as a worker in wood works on a piece of wood ... He became in his own way a specialist and the only difference was that for him the construction was an aim in itself.[3]

The objectivisation of the artistic process which Arvatov compared here to the craft production process, with these connotations carried by the words 'worker' and 'specialist', was the same idea that was also being connected up with the yet more impersonal and objective industrial production process. In the material conditions of Russia in the 1920s, with the poorly equipped workshops these people had at their disposal, this ambiguity between 'craft' and 'industrial' processes was always present.

At the same time as this *rapprochement* was taking place between the 'cultures' of art and industry, the newly emerging industrial technology was providing a concrete source of inspiration for art itself. Technology was not merely an implicit parallel, it also provided the thematics of Futurist paintings with their celebration of the dynamism of the modern city and the potential of modern machinery. Machines, speed and movement became the subject matter of art. At the same time, its products became used in the Cubist collage and the non-utilitarian constructions of Tatlin: here were real materials from the world of modern technology. The culmination of this cult of the machine was ultimately expressed in a theory which posited a very different attitude towards it. This attitude was embodied in the concept of 'production art' and the Constructivist approach to it, which are examined in this chapter.

Modernism in Russia, as in Europe, had its indigenous, but far more nationalistic, precursors in a renaissance of aesthetic interest in craft production. The main centres of this Russian Arts and Crafts movement were the country estates of Princess Tenisheva at Talashkino near Smolensk and of the industrialist Savva Mamontov at Abramtsevo, near Moscow.[4] Whilst deriving their basic impulse from the ideas of William Morris, they relied heavily for their artistic sources of inspiration on the artefacts of native Russian folk art, the motifs of which they combined with the stylistic devices of Art Nouveau.

In 1905 this developing Russian discussion of the relationship between art and industry gained further momentum from the ideas of P. S. Strakhov, when he delivered a lecture in St Petersburg entitled 'Technology and the Beauty of Life' ('Tekhnika i krasota zhizni'). This lecture was subsequently expanded into the book *The Aesthetic Tasks of Technology*. Presenting his argument in the form of a dialogue between Socrates and a pupil, Strakhov discussed the relationship between the aesthetic needs of the everyday environment and the expanding potential of mass production. He concluded that artists should receive a technical training, and engineers, an aesthetic one.[5] In this way the utopian conception of Morris was translated in Russia into industrial terms.

The socialistic political dimension of this whole movement was, of course, enormously complex in Russia as it was in the West. With the Bolshevik Revolution of 1917, however, this 'socialism' ceased to be a minority utopian aspiration and became the everyday social and theoretical reality. Marx and Engels had not formulated a coherent and systematic theory of socialist aesthetics and this vacuum permitted many differing and contradictory theories to be constructed upon the basis of their rather fragmentary remarks and writings.

After the Revolution, cultural and artistic theorists had to rely on their knowledge of the fundamental principles of dialectical materialism to solve questions relating to literature and art. These, as part of the ideological superstructure, were held to be determined by the economic and social substructure, i.e. by the relations of production. The ruling ideas in a given society were held to be the ideas of that ruling class.[6] Since art is unequivocally socially conditioned, and history is seen in terms of the struggle between social classes, art could be regarded as a weapon to be used in the struggle for the building of socialism. This idea was based on the general principles of Marxism, but ignored the fact that Marx and Engels had regarded art as being subject to its own laws as well as being socially conditioned. The main group that supported and developed this idea was the Proletarian Culture Movement known as Proletkul't (from Proletarskaya kul'tura), founded soon after October to put into practice ideas formulated prior to the Revolution by Bogdanov, Lunacharskii and Gor'kii, who had together founded the Workers' School at Capri. The Petrograd Proletkul't was set up 16–19 October 1917 and the Moscow Proletkul't in February 1918, both as independent mass working-class organisations with full autonomy in the cultural sphere.[7] Although the Proletkul't did not expound one consistent theory (there were differences over specific questions such as the cultural heritage and co-operation with bourgeois specialists),[8] the chief idea of Bogdanov was that the working class should advance toward socialism along three different and autonomous paths: the political, the economic and the cultural. Bogdanov maintained that although the proletariat had made progress in the realm of politics and economics it had not advanced at all in the field of culture. He did not differentiate between socialist culture and proletarian culture, the former being regarded as merely an extension of the latter. The creation of this culture should not be entrusted to the government,[9] which contained ideologically alien elements, but should be undertaken only by those who belonged to the ideologically immaculate elite of the working class, the membership of which was determined not by class origins but by political outlook. To Bogdanov, creative art was merely another form of labour and as such should use everyday, theoretical and practical techniques. Although he considered the role of art to be the organisation of social experience, in cognition as well as emotions and aspirations, he perceived the essential unity of the cognitive and aesthetic functions of art and advocated the critical study and assimilation of past culture. Some extremists within Proletkul't such as Gastev rejected the past completely and wanted to see the psychology and the art of the proletariat technicised.[10] This equation between technology and communist ideology was a dominant feature of one section of Proletkul't, and it may have influenced the Constructivists. Certainly it provided an ideological framework, which, as part of the whole debate on the nature of proletarian art, was part of the common currency of the immediate post-revolutionary intellectual climate. Moreover, the very question of production art was part of this wider debate: 'At the present time the question of the connection between art and industry has become an extensively discussed subject, as one of the fundamental questions of proletarian culture.'[11]

Before finally moving on into the Constructivist circles of this debate, it is necessary to recapitulate on some of the basic terminology in which the debate was conducted. The main terms which were being used to describe the design process were 'khudozhestvennoe konstruirovanie' (artistic construction), 'oformlenie' and 'formoobrazovanie' (both approximating to form-making), elucidated in the Introduction. As the experience of IZO, recounted in Chapter Two, indicated, the term 'khudozhestvennaya promyshlennost'' (artistic production) meant, in practical terms, applied art of a craft nature. Among the multiplicity of terms used to describe the envisaged involvement of art in industrial production, the most general was 'proizvodstvennoe iskusstvo' (production art). In its most precise usage, this denoted the complete fusion of the artistic and technological aspects of the productive process. This fusion was to be personified in an 'artist-constructor' who would possess both the artistic and the technical skills required to produce an object completely adapted to its total function. The chief difficulty of elucidation centres around the distinction between the approaches of the Constructivist (konstruktivist) and the Productivist (proizvodstvennik). Sometimes these labels are used as if they were completely interchangeable. When strictly defined, however, Constructivist seems to denote the artist who is trying to approach this fusion practically, by himself grappling with real form-making amongst materials, while the Productivist approached the problem of fusion from the standpoint of industry. He might be a theoretician, or he might be an artist who was seeking to achieve this unity by working in the factory on the production of real mass-industrial objects. The Productivist and the Constructivist were distinguished primarily by the difference in their relative commitments to the two halves of the art–industrial polarity. The inevitable result of this difference in their approaches to their common ideal of a 'production art' was a difference in their conception of the ideal itself. Both were in danger of retreating to relatively traditional positions. Constructivism was warned at the time to 'Beware of becoming a conventional artistic school' and the Productivist in the factory to 'Beware of becoming an applied artist-craftsman'.[12]

ART OF THE COMMUNE: THE FIRST STEPS

The first steps towards the development of these theories of a 'production art' were taken in the journal *Art of the Commune* published in Petrograd from December 1918 to April 1919.[13] As the official journal of IZO it expounded a whole range of ideas being raised among avant-garde artists who belonged to IZO. The journal was eclectic and not characterised by one set of aesthetic ideas:

> This was the time of storms and the onslaught of the working class, a time of happy attacks on the most inviolable 'cultural values', such as 'the Constituent Assembly', 'democracy', 'classless science and art' ... and it is understandable why, inspired with such atheistic enthusiasm, the then most conspicuous writings of the ringleaders of *Art of the Commune* were inspired with such atheistic fervour, from the poetic 'Orders to the Army of Art' by Mayakovskii, to the theoretical scrimmages of Brik, the Komfut romanticism of Kushner and even the relatively calm special articles of Punin, the heavy artillery of the paper.[14]

Mayakovskii's first 'Order to the Army of Art' printed on the first page of the first issue of the paper, exhorting artists to go out onto the streets because 'the streets are our brushes, the squares our palettes',[15] represented the minimum programme of the paper. Although *Art of the Commune* never formulated a coherent programme which could be called Constructivist, many of the concepts and terms which became crucial to the development of Constructivism were first summarily issued in the paper. As Chuzhak pointed out with hindsight in 1923:

> by instinct and in disunity, in a fantastically eclectic milieu ... all the most important words, used later, were employed in *Art of the Commune* ... but half were issued by accident ... Not only the practice of the paper, but also the whole practice of Futurism at this time, was almost entirely based on the 'agitational poster'.[16]

The chief exponents of the new ideas were Osip Brik, Boris Kushner and Nikolai Punin, and through their articles it is possible to trace the genesis of ideas that in their later ramification became Constructivism, production art and Productivism.

Brik's article 'A Drain for Art', which appeared in the very first issue of 1918, exhorted artists to abandon the misty ideas and the quagmire of bourgeois art and devote themselves instead to the creation of material objects. This he asserted was the essence of proletarian art: 'Do not distort, but create. Not idealistic vapours but matèrial objects ... we do not need your ideas ... art is like any other means of production.'[17] Brik like Kushner denied that art was related to spiritual values and asserted that it was like any other form of work: 'Art – this is simply work: knowledge, craft, skill.'[18] If art therefore was mere work with no higher spiritual attributes, the artist was stripped of his metaphysical garb too and revealed as 'now only a constructor and technician, only a supervisor and a foreman'.[19] This is almost certainly the first use of the word 'constructor' in print in connection with art. Its use was probably purely accidental and based on the use of the term in the building industry, juxtaposing the traditional concept of the artist to that of the constructor, the man who actually built objects.

An editorial extended this identification of art with work in the following terms: 'Art strives towards conscious creation; production towards the mechanical ... Production and art merge into one whole; creation and work – towards conscious work.'[20] These passages indicate a step forward to a different concept of art, towards the idea that art should not be concerned with the realm of philosophical or metaphysical ideas, but with action: 'Not ideas but a real object is the aim of all true creativity.'[21] The idea that art should be concerned with the material creation of objects was, as Chuzhak pointed out, 'the first stone of the maximum programme'.[22]

According to Chuzhak the next step was taken when Brik definitely placed art in the category of work, or more specifically in the category of industrial work, by referring to 'art as all production'.[23] 'The divided existence of art and production is not an established law. We see in this division a survival of bourgeois structures.'[24] This opened the way for the proposed fusion of art and production, the problem of art and production and the role it would assume. Punin made an attempt to distinguish between the old concept of applied art and the new concept of production art: 'It is not a matter of decoration, but of the creation of new artistic objects. Art for the proletariat is not a sacred temple for lazy contemplation but work, a factory, producing completely artistic objects.'[25] Punin did not offer a precise definition of 'the completely artistic object', or of the process that would contribute to its formation. However, he did reject the idea of art as passive contemplation, and suggested a positive activity to replace it. This positive alternative was expressed in the concept of the artistic object as the result of art's active participation in production.

These ideas did not win immediate acceptance, and the ensuing discussion which appeared in the paper indicates the extent to which the theories put forward by Punin, Brik and Kushner were still incomplete and defective. The crucial problem of how exactly art was to become part of industry had not been treated in any depth by these exhortatory articles in *Art of the Commune*. Therefore when criticising the concept of production art as it had so far evolved, Puni, Dmitriev and Baulin did not encounter much difficulty in demolishing the rather simplistic statements of Brik et al. The discussion was really opened by the artist Ivan Puni in an article, 'The Creation of Life', in the fifth issue of *Art of the Commune*, in which he expressed doubts as to the usefulness of the role that art could play in the productive process. He maintained that because of the fundamentally different natures of art and industrial production, the artist's attempts to co-operate with the machine would inevitably produce a merely 'applied art'. It would lead to a situation in which artists would apply decoration or decorative elements to an object, the form of which was totally determined by the function the object was to perform:

> art cannot be useful because this ultimately contradicts the undoubted general principle of 'utility' in contemporary industry ... because aesthetics do not govern life, but follow in the wake of it ... The construction of an object is completely dependent on its purpose, the artist may add only superfluous elements to this ... Here we don't need artists, but very good technicians and mathematicians ... all contemporary objects are beautiful and good, because the connection of their parts, the necessity of each part is dictated only by their usefulness, and the more purely this principle is carried out, the better the object is.[26]

Puni's argument that the artist was unnecessary to industry became a major weapon in the armoury of the anti-Productivists.[27]

The other major characteristic of the Productivist programme in its earliest development was the stress that was placed on the sociological, and the attempt to place the theory on a very strong sociological basis, by presenting it as 'proletarian'. Brik asserted that the working class, 'as the creative class, cannot sink into contemplation, cannot abandon itself to aesthetic experiences from a contemplation of the old. The study of artistic monuments must not turn into passive enjoyment, it must not leave the limits of scientific research.'[28]

Strangely, these ideas expressed in *Art of the Commune* received very little development in the journal *Fine Art*, the one and only issue of which was also published in 1919 by the Petrograd IZO. The absence of these ideas was so remarkable that Chuzhak called the journal 'a step backwards'.[29] However, the fact that Punin's article 'The Proletariat and Art' was signed and dated April 1918, and that the editorial was dated May 1918, suggests that in its conception and ideas *Fine Art* predated *Art of the Commune* even though it was published afterwards.[30] 'It contains no whiff of "production" and even an elementary idea of the object is missing.'[31]

The eclectic character of the journal is very indicative of the date of its conception in early 1918 and therefore provides an important insight into the early stage of the debate. Punin, for instance, in his article, stood very firmly by the idea of art as a method of cognition: 'Art is a weapon by the help of which humanity expands its vision, its experience, and in this way, its culture.'[32] This statement is in harmony with the tone of the editorial which also upheld a conception of art as the 'spiritual cognitive activity of humanity'.[33] After *Art of the Commune*, *Fine Art* and the various journals with the title *Art* had all ceased publication in 1919 there was a reduction in the number of artistic journals being published – the Proletkul't journal *Furnace* and the IZO journal *Artistic Life* do not significantly alter this situation – until 1923.[34] With the publication of *LEF* (*Journal of the Left Front of the Arts*) and *Russian Art* in 1923,[35] the artistic debate was recommenced in print, but until then the main centres for debate were the various artistic organisations such as IZO, the State Free Art Studios, and more especially the Institute of Artistic Culture set up in 1920.

INKhUK: THE INSTITUTE OF ARTISTIC CULTURE

The Institute of Artistic Culture (Institut khudozhestvennoi kul'tury – INKhUK) is of great importance, not simply because it was an arena for artistic debate, but also because as a direct result of these debates and theoretical developments the First Working Group of Constructivists (Pervaya rabochaya gruppa konstruktivistov) was set up within the Institute in March 1921. An examination of the history of INKhUK reveals the way in which the Constructivist aesthetic emerged, the role which the Institute played in this development and how this Institute, not specially set up as a Constructivist body, was gradually transformed into a centre of Constructivist theorising. It is therefore vital to examine the contribution that INKhUK made to the development of the design movement in Russia.

Unfortunately, an outline history of the Institute is all that can be attempted until the archive is made fully available. The early history of INKhUK given in the following pages has been pieced together from various published sources (the Institute's programme published in Moscow in 1920 and reports of its activities which appeared in the journals *Russian Art*, *LEF* and *Furnace*) and from certain scattered archive material which I have been able to see. Unfortunately the haphazard quality of the material has produced several important gaps in this history, but within these limitations the following account has been made as complete as possible.

Under the aegis of IZO Narkompros, INKhUK was established in March 1920, apparently on the initiative of and according to the programme and statutes worked out by Kandinskii.[36] The concept of 'artistic culture' had already been outlined by IZO in its declaration of 1919 as 'the culture of artistic invention'. This inventive process was dependent upon establishing 'the objective criteria of artistic value in so far as this is defined as a professional value'. IZO's declaration enumerated these as:

1. material: surface, texture [*faktura*], elasticity, density, weight and other qualities of material
2. colour: saturation, strength, relationship to light, purity, transparency, independence and other qualities of colour
3. space: volume, depth, dimension and other properties of space
4. time (movement): in its spatial expression and in connection with colour, material, composition, etc.
5. form as a result of the interaction of material, colour, space and, in its particular form, composition
6. technique [*tekhnika*]: painting, mosaic, reliefs of different kinds, sculpture, stone structure and other artistic techniques.[37]

This professional dimension was seen as 'the positive achievement of contemporary artistic activity during the last ten years'.[38] INKhUK was conceived as an institution which would move forward from this position toward 'settling questions concerned with the science of art in all its aspects'.[39] The programme of the Institute stressed this: 'The aim of the work of the Institute of Artistic Culture is Science, the investigation of the analytical and the synthetic basic elements of the separate arts and of art as a whole.'[40] From this there arose three types of problems: those related to the theory of different art forms; those related to the theory of the interaction of different art forms; and those related to what Kandinskii called monumental art or art as a whole.[41] Consequently INKhUK originally consisted of three sections each corresponding to the problems stated.

The starting point for these theoretical investigations was to analyse the means by which any form of art acts 'from the point of view of the effect of the artistic means employed on the experiences of the man apprehending it, i.e. on his psyche'.[42] Therefore these artistic means or elements had to be examined and their physiological action on man studied, since this provided 'a bridge to the explanation of their influence on man's psychology'.[43] Such 'facts' as that the colour blue leads to paralysis were considered of value only in so far as they illuminated art's psychological dimension. By studying painting in its colour and surface form, architecture and sculpture in its spatial and volumetric form, music in its sound and time form, dance in its spatial and temporal form, and poetry in its rhythmic sound and time form, the INKhUK theoreticians intended to establish a scientific explanation for the intuitive element in creativity and so establish a scientific basis for art.

The first period of the existence of INKhUK was inspired by this idealistic and eclectic spirit. The problems discussed ranged over such widely disparate fields as an examination of the basic painterly elements by Kandinskii, the elements of sculpture by Korolev, the elements of poetry by Rozanov, the elements of music, and the similarity of plastic and musical experiences. One of the meetings was devoted to the practical occupation of making graphic representations of musical works. For this, preludes by Skryabin and Bach were chosen. Separate musical chords were translated into their colour equivalents (steady notes black, unsteady notes white). The composer Shenshin demonstrated the possibility of translating from one art into another by correlating the musical composition of a Liszt work with the formal composition of a Michelangelo tomb.

Other papers dealt with children's art, African sculpture, the Russian folk woodcut, folk dancing and singing.[44] Shemshurin read a paper entitled 'The Evolution of Form' based on an analysis of ancient writing in which he compared the disintegration of form to the experiments of the Futurists. He concluded that 'in art the ideology of spirit or nature operates. The science of art must control this ideology ... There are no untalented artists, there are only untalented observers.'[45]

Kandinskii, in the hope of 'finding the root of a general law' for painting and in the pursuit of 'the possibility of establishing a link between the law of painting and the laws of music, sculpture, poetry, architecture and dance', circulated a questionnaire to all INKhUK members.[46] In this he asked members which art form affected them most intensely and what it was specifically in this art form that had the power to do so. Kandinskii wanted to know if members had made any investigations into the effect that elements of artistic expression (such as colour in painting) had on the psyche, and if so, how such experiments had been conducted, under what conditions and whether they had been published.

After these general enquiries Kandinskii asked members to answer specific questions and to execute certain tasks relating to painting. This section of the questionnaire was divided into two parts. The first was concerned primarily with form and the second with colour. Kandinskii wanted members to describe the sensations they experienced when they looked at different kinds of lines (and combinations of lines, such as technical drawings) and different forms (geometrical and 'free'). Kandinskii also requested participants to draw their impressions of science and life, in both general and specific aspects. He asked members whether the effect of forms changed if the forms were tilted or turned upside down, or placed close to another form (vertically or horizontally). Members were also asked to make combinations of free and geometric forms, initially mixing only rounded forms with rounded forms and sharp forms with sharp forms, but ultimately mixing them together. Finally Kandinskii asked participants to record their changing perceptions of a form or group of forms placed in the centre, top, bottom, right- or left-hand corner of a page.

In the colour section Kandinskii asked members to describe their physical or psychological reactions to a colour which affected them, then to describe their reactions to the primary and secondary colours, assessing the relative strengths and pleasantness of the effects of each colour within each group. Kandinskii asked if any participants experienced the effects of any colour when they merely visualised it and did not see it, and whether any colour was easier to visualise than any other. Investigating the relationship of colour to sound, Kandinskii asked members to say which colour most resembled a canary song, the lowing of a cow, the whistling of the wind. He also requested members to suggest the most appropriate colours for the triangle, the square and the circle, to draw these shapes and to colour them. Moreover, if a basic colour did not seem to the participant to have an affinity with any particular geometric form, Kandinskii asked them to try to find a free form appropriate to it, to draw and colour it, and if possible to explain the reasons for their choice. Finally Kandinskii asked participants systematically to mix the basic forms and colours by making for example a blue patch of undefined shape on a yellow form, then a yellow patch on a red form, and to describe their reactions. The procedure was then to be repeated using precise geometric forms and then free but precise forms. Answers and responses to all the questions were to be placed in an exercise book, following Kandinskii's format.

As this questionnaire makes clear, during this first period of its existence INKhUK was concerned to conduct a systematic investigation into the formal elements within a given work of art. It was interested in examining the synthetic work of art and the correspondences between different forms of art. All this was undertaken from the standpoint that art represented the greatest possible good. There is no evidence of the Constructivist spirit, yet at the same time there are indications in the minutes or *protokol*, that a different approach was emerging. One such indication of future developments is the report given by Franketti concerning 'theoretical work which is being carried out at the Nizhnyi Novgorod Art Studios by the engineer Nesterov in collaboration with the artists. The subject of study is the statics of a construction and the formulation of the laws of composition.'[47] This group wanted to 'apply the functioning elements of technical construction as a standard for painterly composition'.[48] This concern with applying technology to art and with the art work itself separated this group from the Constructivists. The importance of this paper is not the contribution it made to Constructivist theory, but that it was discussed during a period when the investigation of artistic elements in INKhUK was being conducted solely with reference to the perfection and understanding of the work of art *per se*.

By the autumn of 1920, however, the influence of other aesthetic ideas was making itself felt within the Institute, and the INKhUK programme as set down by Kandinskii was proving irksome. As the report of 1923 states:

> There was found to be a fundamental divergence between Kandinskii and some of the members of the Institute. The psychological approach of Kandinskii sharply diverged from the views of those who considered the material, self-contained 'object' to be the substance of creation. Kandinskii left and Rodchenko, Stepanova, Babichev and Bryusova entered the administration.[49]

The move from the subjective, psychological approach of Kandinskii towards the more objective approach of the General Working Group of Objective Analysis (Obshchaya rabochaya gruppa ob'ektivnogo analiza), which held its first meeting on 23 November 1920, culminated in Kandinskii announcing his departure from the Institute on 27 January 1921, whereupon the Section of Monumental Art ceased to function.[50]

> Toward the spring of 1921 the ideology of the Institute was expressed briefly, in one word 'object'. As a later expression of this period of ideology, in part it is possible to point to the journal *Veshch'* organised by a member of the Institute, Lissitzky, in Berlin in the beginning of 1922.[61]

The platform of *Veshch'/Gegenstand/Objet* (*Object*) was printed in the first issue:

> Art as the creation of new objects ... By no means does it follow to suppose that by objects we mean objects of everyday use. Naturally in factory-made utilitarian objects, in the aeroplane or car, we see genuine art. But we do not wish to limit the production of artists to utilitarian objects. Every organised work – a house, a poem or a painting – is an expedient object, not leading people away from life, but helping to organise it.[52]

The journal proclaimed the 'constructive method' and art as the 'organisation of life'. The products of these ideas were mainly categorised by the works of OBMOKhU, Tatlin's counter-reliefs, and Lissitzky's architecturally inspired paintings or PROUNS, in other words abstract objects or works of art.

Object's platform was a kind of half-way house on the way to Constructivism. While retaining a belief in the validity of the work of art *per se*, it combined this with a widening of aesthetic criteria to include industrially made objects. The distinction between the *Object* approach and that of Constructivism was stressed by Lissitzky in his book *Die Kunstismen 1914-1924*. There he defined Constructivism in the following terms, using his own idiosyncratic English:

> These artists look of the world through the prisma of technic. They don't want to give an illusion by the means of colours on canvas, but work directly in iron, wood, glass, a.o. The shortsighteds see therein only the machine. Constructivism proves that the limits between mathematics and art, between a work of art and a technical invention are not to be fixed.[53]

Lissitzky, therefore, was clearly not a Constructivist at this point. Closely allied to Malevich, he did not remain a Suprematist. His concept of the PROUN – 'A station between architecture and painting'[54] – embodied certain spatial principles which relate his work to the type of abstract spatial explorations conducted in real materials by artists like Rodchenko and Klutsis. However, Lissitzky restricted his experimentation within the two-dimensional limitations of the canvas (colour plate III). Although he still retained many of the stylistic traits of Suprematism, his later design work did indicate an approach close to that of Constructivism. Following the departure of Kandinskii from INKhUK, the main work of INKhUK was conducted in the General Working Group of Objective Analysis. The group's programme had been worked out by Babichev.[55] Its investigations were carried out in two main areas, that of theory and that of practical work or laboratory work as it was called in the programme.

1. Theoretical: the analysis of the work of art, the conscious definition of the basic problems of art (colour, texture, material, construction, etc.). The work was conducted with paintings, frequently in galleries.
2. Laboratory: group work according to independent initiative or according to a task (for example all members were presented with work on the theme 'composition and construction').[56]

The group itself was independent of the structure set up by Kandinskii. 'The task of the group is the theoretical analysis of the basic elements of a work of art.'[64]

Neither the creative process, nor the process of perception, the defined aesthetic emotion, is the object of analysis, but those real forms which, created by the artist, are found in the already finished work. Consequently the form of the work and its elements are the material for analysis and not the psychology of the creation, nor the psychology of aesthetic perception, nor the historical, cultural, sociological or other problems of art.[58]

The objectivity of this approach consisted in the fact that it was opposed to individual taste or criticism that was linked to a particular artistic school or trend. The process of investigation was to take the form of observation, systematisation and explanation. 'The process of observation must follow strictly defined, logical paths and methods ... conclusions obtained in this way constitute the material which is the content of the science of art.'[59]

Babichev had, however, defined this 'process of observation' in more detail than the published report of 1923 indicated. In the proposals for the group's course of study which he presented to the meeting of the Presidium of INKhUK on 25 December 1920 he had included experimental scientific investigations of works of art as a whole, the interrelationships of their parts, and their ideology. He had proposed:

1. The investigation of the organisation and the confirmation of the form of organisation of contemporary art.
2. The definition of works of art as a whole and in parts, their manner, type and evolution.
3. The classification of the elements of a work of art on the attendant bases: their changes and new possibilities (the instance of transmigration into synthesis).
4. The element as meaning. The formula of the element. The element as the unit of measurement. Its function.
5. The establishment of an exact terminology. An examination of *a priori* meaning. New formulation.[60]

In the spring of 1921, on the basis of such a programme, the group conducted its theoretical discussions and its laboratory work in the Museum of Western Painting in Moscow, where they analysed Impressionism, Pointillism and the work of Matisse. They also planned a 'scientific art exhibition'.[61] In contrast to the traditional type of exhibitions which were considered to be 'individualistic cliques of "works of art"',[62] the group intended theirs to consist of scientifically investigated material. The exhibits were to be divided into seven categories, corresponding to the artistic elements and their related problems: the problems of colour, volume, space, construction, texture, material and form.[63] Each of these categories was itself subdivided into three sections relating to the problems of form as line, plane and volume.

Despite these brave efforts it proved very difficult to establish absolutely objective criteria and to abolish all suspicion of tendentiousness. In order to define the 'objective criteria' it was necessary to define what were the basic elements constituting a work of art. Tarabukin called these: paint or another material; *faktura*, the texture or the structure of the colour; the techniques of working the material, etc.; all of which were unified by the composition (the principle), and in the whole comprised the art work (system).[64] But agreement on this question proved difficult to establish and from the debates that ensued over definitions of such primary criteria subsequent divisions arose and the next stage of development within INKhUK began.

The theoretical differences became manifest in the appearance of a new group within INKhUK. On 18 March 1921 the First Working Group of Constructivists was officially organised within INKhUK by Aleksandr Rodchenko, Varvara Stepanova and Aleksei Gan.[65] Before the autumn of that year, 'artists remaining at the level of easel painting and not sharing the Productivist platform on which INKhUK stood, left the Institute'.[66] These included Klyun, Drevin and Udal'tsova.[67] The administration was reorganised. Brik became the president, Babichev and Ladovskii members of the administration, and Tarabukin became the secretary. At the same time several new members such as Arvatov and Kushner, both of whom were fervent Marxists and adherents of the concept of production art, entered the Institute.[68]

THE COMPOSITION–CONSTRUCTION DEBATE

The differences which produced these changes had been exposed during a series of discussions concerning the nature of composition and construction and the moment of their differentiation. These debates took place soon after the creation of the General Working Group of Objective Analysis at its meetings held in the spring of 1921 (1, 21 and 28 January, 11 and 18 February, 4, 18 and 25 March 1921).[69] In the course of these discussions it emerged that the group's members had differing and frequently conflicting conceptions of what comprised the basic artistic categories of composition and construction. The main protagonists in the debate were Popova, Ioganson, Bubnova, Bryusova, Stepanova, Korolev, Tarabukin, Rodchenko, Al'tman, Klyun, Babichev, the Stenberg brothers, Medunetskii, Krinskii, Ladovskii, Udal'tsova and Drevin.[70] As the debates progressed attitudes on the part of the participants crystallised and a basic divergence emerged between those artists who considered that construction could exist as a purely aesthetic principle within a two-dimensional art work and those, prominent among whom were the members of the First Working Group of Constructivists, who felt emphatically that material was an integral part of the concept of construction and that therefore it was related to real objects rather than to any medium of painting. Furthermore, these artists concluded that construction contained a utilitarian imperative which limited its pure manifestation to the construction of useful as opposed to aesthetic objects. On 22 April 1921 a meeting was held in which the participating artists presented the practical demonstrations of their ideas. Some of these drawings have fortunately survived and at present form part of the Costakis Collection.[71] They were intended to represent and to elucidate the theoretical conclusions and final positions of the members in visual form.

A general formulation of Construction was arrived at in early March, but was not totally acceptable to all the participants. It stated:

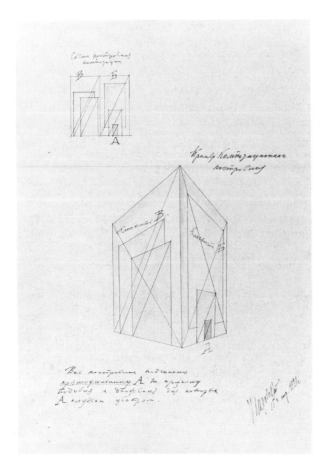

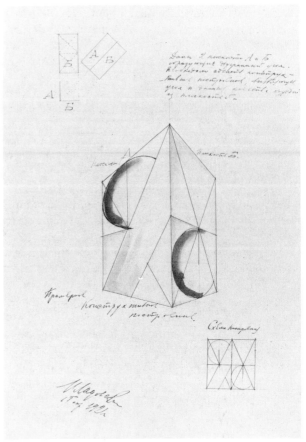

3.1. N. Ladovskii, *Example of a Composed Structure* (*Primer kompozitsionnogo postroeniya*), 15 April 1921, ink, pencil and wash on cardboard, 38 × 27·5 cm. Collection George Costakis, Athens. [Photograph: © George Costakis 1981.]

3.2. N. Ladovskii, *Model of a Constructive Structure* (*Primernoe konstruktivnoe postroenie*), 15 April 1921, ink, pencil and wash on cardboard, 38 × 27·3 cm. Collection George Costakis, Athens. [Photograph: © George Costakis 1981.]

Construction is the effective organisation of material elements.
The indications of construction:
  i. the best use of the materials
  ii. The absence of any superfluous elements
The scheme of a construction is the combination of lines, and the planes and forms which they define; it is a system of forces.
Composition is an arrangement according to a defined and conventional signification.[72]

Individual positions deviated considerably from this *via media*. Ladovskii, for instance as an architect, took three-dimensional constructions as the basis for his formulation. Starting from the position that 'a technical construction is the combination of shaped material elements in accordance with a definite scheme for achieving a forceful effect' he concluded that 'the main indication of construction is that in it there should be no excess materials or elements. The main distinguishing feature of a composition is hierarchy and co-ordination.'[73] In accordance with this definition his composition drawing (plate 3.1) was of a composed structure, governed by the rectangle which generated geometric similarities and displacements. His construction drawing on the other hand (plate 3.2) was of a constructive structure 'which reveals both the angle and the given properties of each of the planes'.[74]

As a sculptor, Babichev gave a rather different definition. For him 'construction is the organic unity of material forms obtained through the exposure of their functions', while 'composition is the continuous interrelation of forms'.[75] The drawings he submitted were based on a purely artistic still life composed of various geometric bodies and were devised to illustrate the absence and presence of the organisational moment. In the composition drawing in plate 3.3 the various bodies exist within planes bearing only a very tangential organisational relationship to

84

each other. In *Construction* (plate 3.4) space and these same elements are organised into an entity which is potentially reconstructable in three dimensions from real materials. The elements are more defined, the space in which they exist is less ambiguous and a sense of volume is conveyed. The structural relationships of the elements are clarified. In *Construction* there is an absence of hazy shadowing around the shapes which in *Composition* seems to emphasise the ambiguities as well as the lack of definition and organisation that Babichev associated with the concept of composition.

Such a position was eschewed by the painters Drevin and Udal'tsova who adopted an extreme stance. Drevin's definition was vague, but at the same time restricted solely to the creation of the two-dimensional art work and in particular to painting. He stated: 'Construction does not have an exact definition. It is possible to find individual indications of construction in painting. Construction in painting is the creation of the object (the work). Composition is the distribution of the parts.'[76]

Those artists who became affiliated with the First Working Group of Constructivists advocated a position at the other extreme from the artistic concept put forward by Drevin and Udal'tsova. Ioganson, for example, denied utterly the two-dimensional nature of construction emphasising that construction was 'the specific utilisation of specific materials' and that 'there is only construction in real space'.[77] His stress on the practical, material and technological dimension led him equally to criticise the constructions of Georgii Stenberg and Medunetskii for being merely the representations of technical constructions.

3.3. A. Babichev, *Composition*, 22 April 1921, pencil on paper, 49·5 × 34·5 cm. Collection George Costakis, Athens. [Photograph: © George Costakis 1981.]

3.4. A. Babichev, *Construction*, 1921, ink, gouache and pencil on paper, 52·1 × 28·2 cm. Collection George Costakis, Athens. [Photograph: © George Costakis 1981.]

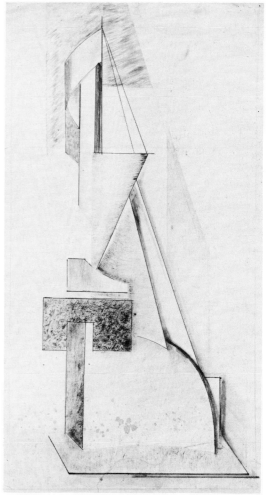

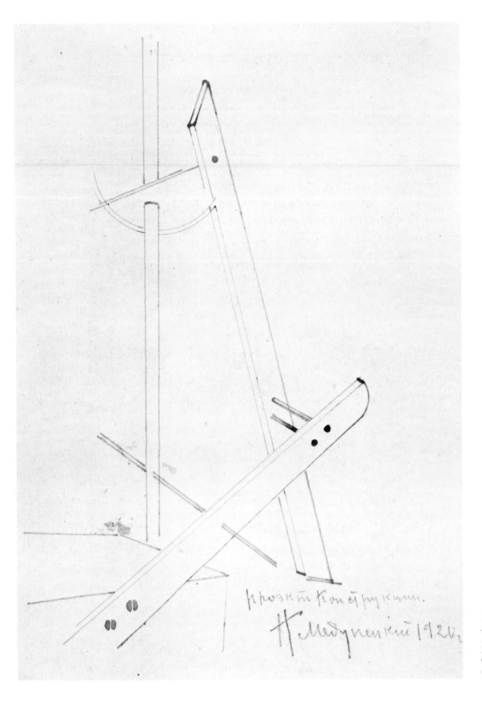

3.5. K. Medunetskii, *Project for a Construction* (*Proekt konstruktsii*), 1920, brown ink on paper, 27 × 19·1 cm. Collection George Costakis, Athens. [Photograph: © George Costakis 1981.]

This criticism serves to highlight the fact that Ioganson's position differs slightly from that of Medunetskii and the Stenberg brothers, who were working closely together at this time. They did not totally dismiss the idea that construction could exist within the two-dimensional art form, but their formulations led them to see it as only effective in the three-dimensional technical construction. Medunetskii declared 'in a painterly construction we realise visual effects, but in a technical one, the force itself. What is construction in technology, is composition in painting. It is balance, both in a painting and in a machine.'[78] Hence Medunetskii's construction drawing (plate 3.5) depicts a three-dimensional structure which, despite certain ambiguities in the relationships of its parts, was made sufficiently clear so as to be reconstructable in three dimensions. Medunetskii's composition drawing on the other hand (plate 3.6) emphasised the lack of materiality and substance of the forms, the absence of any tension between them and their limited existence on one plane.

Like Medunetskii, Georgii Stenberg did not dismiss entirely the idea that construction could exist in painting. For him the elements of construction in painting comprised the material (used efficiently for a given form), form, colour (emphasising and balancing form) and *faktura* (expedient). He saw a resemblance between painterly and technical construction, in so far as a technical construction determines the structural means of the material and its properties such as weight, durability, resilience and resistance, and painterly construction determines the efficient utilisation of the material. The distinction lay with the intentions. In a technical construction 'the system of construction derives from the utilitarian task', whereas in a painterly construction it arises 'from the tasteful distribution of the forms, which are individually constructive'. However, since 'painterly construction developed from the operation of taste ... In so far as the structuring system of a painterly construction is taste, a [painterly] construction is not a construction in its pure form.'[79] The tasteful and technical determinants are illustrated in his brother's drawings (plates 3.7–8).

Popova's stance never attained this degree of commitment to the utilitarian and indicates that she was still firmly attached to aesthetic concerns at this date. Her contributions to the debates clarify the development of her ideas and suggest why she did not become a member of the First Working Group of Constructivists when

3.6. K. Medunetskii, *Composition*, 1920, pencil and orange crayon on paper, 26·6 × 23·4 cm. Collection George Costakis, Athens. [Photograph: © George Costakis 1981.]

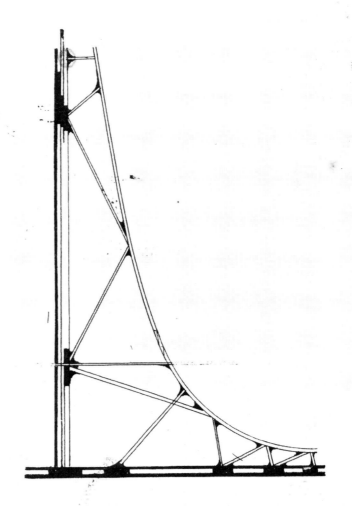

3.7. V. Stenberg, *Construction*, 1920, ink on paper, 25·4 × 19·3 cm. Collection George Costakis, Athens. [Photograph: © George Costakis 1981.]

В.Стенберг.

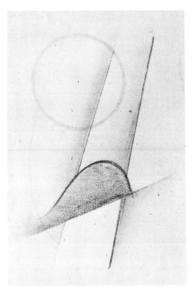

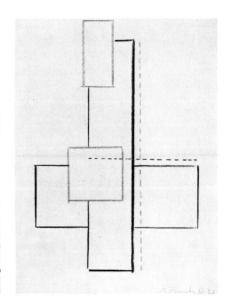

3.8. V. Stenberg, *Composition*, 1920, coloured pencil on paper, 21 × 13·9 cm. Collection George Costakis, Athens. [Photograph: © George Costakis 1981.]

3.9. Popova, *Untitled*, 1921, pencil and ink on paper, 34 × 25 cm. Collection George Costakis, Athens. [Photograph: © George Costakis 1981.]

3.10. L. Popova, *Untitled*, 1921, red and black crayon on paper, 27·6 × 20·7 cm. Collection George Costakis, Athens. [Photograph: © George Costakis 1981.]

it was formed. She acknowledged that there was no organisation in composition although there was a purposeful combining of elements such as volume, material, texture (*faktura*), colour and space. She stated 'construction is purpose and necessity, the expediency of organisation', while 'composition is the regular and tasteful arrangement of material'.[80] However, unlike Stenberg et al., Popova did not reject the function of taste *per se*. This hesitation and still evident distrust of the purely technical is apparent in her final drawings (see plates 3.9–10).

Unlike Popova, Stepanova, who later collaborated with her in the design of clothes and textiles, was a founding member of the First Working Group of Constructivists. However, her contributions to the debate remain ambiguous although more emphatic than those of Popova. As early as the session of 28 January 1921 Stepanova gave a precise formulation of the ideas under discussion:

> Only construction demands the absence of both excess materials and excess elements, in composition it is just the reverse – there everything is based precisely on the excessive... the greater the quantity of excess material and excess elements a composition has, the subtler it is in respect to taste and the more vividly it disassociates itself from construction... we are following the line of reducing the excessive... and are clearly drawn to construction.

For Stepanova, an essential aspect of this distinction lay in the fact that if one element was removed from a composition it did not lose its meaning but resulted merely in the rearrangement of the remaining elements, whereas in a construction the removal of one element would entail the destruction of the whole construction. Stepanova also linked her concept of construction to work in materials. However, the drawings (plates 3.11–12) Stepanova submitted remain very firmly within artistic parameters.

The clearest and earliest formulation of the Constructivist position was provided by Rodchenko. At the very first session he asserted that the concept of composition was an anachronism because it was mere aesthetics and related to concepts of 'taste' and other outmoded artistic ideas. In his view principles of composition had to be replaced by principles of construction and organisation. 'All new approaches to art arise from technology and engineering and move towards organisation and construction.'[81] Construction represented the culmination of centuries of artistic development. To Rodchenko it was part of the same process that had previously produced communist Russia. It was its artistic equivalent. 'As we see in the life of the RSFSR, everything leads to organisation. And so in art everything has led to

88

organisation.'[82] Thus organisation and organisational principles were equated with what Rodchenko called 'pure construction'. Moreover, Rodchenko recognised that a utilitarian element was present in the idea of organisation and construction as early as the INKhUK debate of 21 January 1921, when he stated that 'the real construction is utilitarian necessity'. The *protokoly* of the debates over composition and construction thus establish and confirm Rodchenko's position as a founder of Constructivist theory, as well as of the First Working Group of Constructivists.

By the time the Group of Objective Analysis held its final meeting to discuss composition and construction, the polarisation between the Constructivists and those who remained firmly attached to aesthetic concerns was complete. Therefore almost as soon as the new structure had become effective within INKhUK at the beginning of 1921, a reaction against it was also underway. At the same moment as the First Working Group of Constructivists was organised, the Group of Objective Analysis divided into different groups comprising the Working Group of Architects (Ladovskii and Krinskii) set up on 26 March, the Working Group of Objectivists (Drevin, Udal'tsova, Popova and Vesnin) which held its first session on 15 April, and separate groups of musicians and sociologists.[83] This internal reorganisation took place over the summer and when INKhUK met again in the autumn of 1921 it was a very different body. The members who remained were no longer committed to the concept of fine art. They proposed publishing a collection of essays entitled *From Figurative Art to Construction* which would elaborate and publicise their new ideas.[84]

By 1 January 1922 when the Institute became officially affiliated to the Academy of Artistic Sciences it was an informal organisation of artists and theoreti-

3.11. V. Stepanova, *Composition* (numbered 99), 1921, gouache on paper mounted on grey paper, 22·3 × 18·5 cm. Collection George Costakis, Athens. [Photograph: © George Costakis 1981.]

3.12. V. Stepanova, *Construction*, collage on paper, 35·9 × 22·9 cm. Collection George Costakis, Athens. [Photograph: © George Costakis 1981.]

cians, all of whom were committed to the idea that they should not be creating works of art, but should be concerned with making useful objects.[85] This allegiance to the concept of production art had been made completely explicit on 24 November 1921, when Brik proposed that artists who had rejected easel painting should commence 'real practical work in production'.[86] The essence of his proposals was accepted by INKhUK, and twenty-five artists of the left art, 'under the pressure of the revolutionary conditions of contemporary life', rejected 'pure' art forms and acknowledged that easel painting and their activity as easel painters were futile and *passé*.[87] In the place of pure art they committed themselves to working in industry, espousing 'production art as an absolute value and Constructivism as its only form of expression'.[88] This was a moment of great 'historic significance'.[89] The winter of 1921–2, therefore, saw the systematisation of this new platform and the beginning of the new, third phase of the Institute's existence, a phase which, according to its report, was characterised by 'the scientific and theoretical working out of all questions connected with the idea of production art'.[90]

It is exceedingly difficult to establish the precise identity of the twenty-five artists of INKhUK who signed the famous declaration.[91] Undoubtedly they would be named in the *protokol* of the meeting, to which unfortunately I had no access. However, it can be assumed from the evidence of the report of the Institute's activities published in 1923 that, once INKhUK had become firmly committed to production art and Constructivism, those who continued as active members, in both the theoretical and the practical spheres, did adhere to the credo of Brik, or at least agreed with it substantively, and they can be assumed to have been signatories of the declaration. From the minutes of subsequent meetings those artists who continued to be consistently active in INKhUK included Popova, Stepanova, Rodchenko, Medunetskii, Georgii and Vladimir Stenberg, Aleksandr Vesnin, Babichev, Ioganson and Lavinskii. To these Lobanov adds the name of Rom, possibly the film maker.[92] More speculative is the inclusion of those artists and architects whose consistent participation is more doubtful although they are mentioned in the 1923 report and other sources. These include Krinskii, Ladovskii, Bubnova, Borisov and the other nine artists of OBMOKhU. Aleksei Gan was almost certainly a signatory, although he does not appear after mid-1922, and very seldom before that, in the random selection of *protokoly* that I was able to consult. Naturally visiting speakers at INKhUK such as Malevich in December 1921 should not be considered. Although Al'tman had actively participated in INKhUK debates and gave a talk in May 1922 it is most unlikely (although not impossible) that he was a signatory. This conveniently leaves twenty-five names as potential signatories. Certainly all of those adhered to the ideas of the declaration.

The practical work that members of INKhUK carried out, both individually and acting as a group, between the formation of the Working Group of Objective Analysis in the winter of 1920–1, the total commitment to Constructivism in November 1920 and the publication of its report in 1923, was extensive. According to the 1923 report its activities included the establishment of closer links with the Higher Artistic and Technical Workshops, the VKhUTEMAS, as well as the rather more immediately entertaining tasks undertaken by Popova, Vesnin, Al'tman, Stepanova and others of designing and making sets for theatrical productions. Brik, Arvatov, Kushner and Tarabukin produced theoretical treatises and delivered lectures both inside INKhUK and outside to publicise their ideas. Exhibitions of members' work were held in Moscow over the same period. These included the exhibition The Constructivists (Konstruktivisty) at the Kafe Poetov in Moscow in January 1922, which showed the work of the Stenberg brothers and Medunetskii; the third OBMOKhU exhibition in May 1921; and in September the $5 \times 5 = 25$ exhibition with Aleksandr Vesnin, Lyubov' Popova, Aleksandr Rodchenko, Varvara Stepanova and Aleksandra Ekster.[93] The attempts of INKhUK to 'establish links with a whole range of organisations with the aim of working out the problems of

III. El Lissitzky, *PROUN 99*,
1923, oil on wood, 129·4 × 99 cm.
Yale University Art Gallery, Gift
of the Société Anonyme.

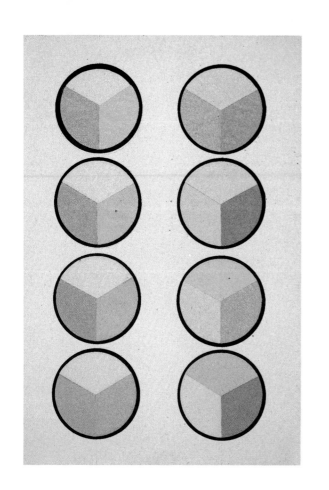

92

production and its scientific presentation' resulted in INKhUK members joining various organisations working on industrial problems.[94] Arvatov joined industrial commissions set up within the cultural departments of the All Union Central Council of Trade Unions (VTsSPS) and its Moscow branch. Brik joined the All Union Central Council of Trade Unions' Central Scientific and Technical Club and also became a member of a committee concerned with the scientific organisation of production which had been set up by the Supreme Council of the National Economy (VSNKh). On a more practical basis Arvatov and Tatlin set up a production laboratory (*proizvodstvennaya laboratoriya*) at the New Lessner (Novyi Lessner) Factory in Petrograd.[95] INKhUK also established links with Proletkul't and played a large part in the reorganisation of Proletkul't on a Productivist basis. Arvatov, Brik and Kushner were particularly active in this respect, and many other members of INKhUK became involved in Proletkul't, including Tarabukin, who gave lectures, and Tatlin who was active in Petrograd.[96]

Within INKhUK itself in its theoretical work the following papers were given:

23 September 1921	Lissitzky	'PROUNS'
17 November 1921	Il'in	'The Politics of the RSFSR in the Field of Art'
8 December 1921	Kemeny	'The Latest Trends in Modern German and Russian Art'
22 December 1921	Stepanova	'Concerning Constructivism'
26 December 1921	Kemeny	'Concerning the Constructive Work of the OBMOKhU'
December 1921	Malevich	'The First Task'
22 February 1922	Toporkov	'On the Dialectical and Analytical Method in Art'
23 March 1922	Borisov	'An Analysis of the Understanding of the Object in Art'
—	Borisov	'The Rhythmics of Space'
—	Krinskii	'The Paths of Architecture'[97]

Papers with a more theoretical and specifically Productivist and sociological character included the following:

20 August 1921	Tarabukin	'The Last Picture has been Painted'
12 October 1921	Brik	'INKhUK's Artistic and Political Tasks'
22 December 1921	Brik	'The Programme and Tactics of INKhUK'
9 March 1922	Kushner	'The Production of Culture'
16 March 1922	Kushner	'The Production of Culture' (part 2)
30 March 1922	Kushner	'The Role of the Engineer in Production'
6 April 1922	Kushner	'The Artist in Production'
13 April 1922	Brik	'What the Artist is to do Now'
October 1922	Arvatov	'Art from the Organisational Point of View'[98]

Papers belonging to the third category were reports of practical work which had been undertaken by the Institute. This practical activity consisted almost entirely of work in the micro-environment of the theatre, although it did also include speculative projects concerning future structures for the everyday environment.

27 April 1922	Popova	*'The Magnanimous Cuckold'*
4 May 1922	Vesnin	*'Phèdre'*
11 May 1922	Al'tman	*'Uriel' Akosta'*
n.d.	Lavinskii	'On Neo-Engineerism'[99]

In addition to this the Institute commissioned the following articles:

Arvatov	'The Aesthetic of Easel Painting'

IV. G. Klutsis, Colour Study relating to his teaching of colour at VKhUTEMAS, *c.* 1926, paper collage and ink on paper, 20·3 × 17 cm. Collection George Costakis, Athens. [Photograph: © George Costakis 1981.]

V. G. Klutsis, Colour Study relating to his teaching of colour at the VKhUTEMAS, *c.* 1926, gouache, pencil and ink on paper, 20·3 × 17 cm. Collection George Costakis, Athens. [Photograph: © George Costakis 1981.]

VI. G. Klutsis, Colour study relating to his teaching of colour at VKhUTEMAS, *c.* 1926, gouache and pencil on paper, 20·4 × 16·7 cm. Collection George Costakis, Athens. [Photograph: © George Costakis 1981.]

Arvatov	'Concretised Utopia'
Rodchenko	'The Line'
Rodchenko	'Artistic Problems'
Popova	'On the New Method in Our Art Schools'

as well as a series of credos from the architects Aleksandr Vesnin and Krinskii, from OBMOKhU artists and from Bubnova, Ioganson, Popova and others.[100]

THE FIRST WORKING GROUP OF CONSTRUCTIVISTS

The First Working Group of Constructivists was formed during the spring of 1921. According to a report published in 1922 the nucleus of the group was set up on 13 December 1920 and consisted solely of Aleksei Gan, Varvara Stepanova and Aleksandr Rodchenko.[101] However, surviving documents suggest the date of 18 March 1921 for the official establishment of the group which by then also included the Stenberg brothers, Konstantin Medunetskii and Karl Ioganson.[102] The disparity in dating is difficult to resolve at present from the scanty documentation available. The earlier date probably refers to the group's more informal beginnings. Once in existence its working nucleus was a 'subsidiary study group' which was determined 'to involve its members in the revolutionary inventive activity of the Constructivists, who in fact had decided to realise in practical terms the communistic expression of material structures'.[103] Their programme stressed many of the ideas, slogans and expressions (such as 'Down with Art', and 'the communistic expression of material structures') which were later developed in greater detail by Gan in his book *Constructivism* published in 1922. The group's initial statements declared that 'art in the past stood in the place of religion. It arose from the mainsprings of individualism' and, as such, was totally irrelevant to the demands of the present 'purifying period'.[104] Instead of creating art, the needs of building a socialist society presented the Constructivist with different tasks:

> It is necessary to establish the discipline of monism and dualism, to master the idealistic world view and the materialistic understanding of the world, the philosophy and theory of scientific communism, to realise the practice of Soviet construction, determine the place which the intellectual productivist of constructivist constructions must occupy in communist life, i.e. in the social production of the future culture; to decide what is expedient in the area of material production and productive relations; to define concretely the meaning of 'intellectual production'; to establish the synthetic act of the coincidence of material production with the intellectual, to arrive at the problem of work; to elucidate the position of work in its historical perspective (slaveholding societies, feudalism, capitalism); to establish the stages of work: before the Revolution – slave work, at present – the liberation of work, and after the final victory of the proletariat – the possibility of exultant work.

To achieve these manifold tasks the group considered that it was essential to 'synthesise the ideological part with the formal part for the real transference of laboratory work onto the rails of practical activity'.[106] According to their programme the Constructivists' only ideological foundation was 'scientific communism, based on the theory of historical materialism'.[107] Their theoretical investigation of Soviet social and material construction was to have impelled the group to move from experimental work outside life into real experiments.

The basis for this 'communistic expression of material structures' was the conversion of 'the specific elements of reality', i.e. tectonics, construction and *faktura*, into volume, plane, colour, space and light. The tectonic (*tektonika*) was defined as emerging from the ideological tenets of communism on the one hand, and, on the other, from the appropriate use of industrial materials. Construction (*konstruk-*

tsiya) represented the process of structuring and organising these mate[ ] *faktura* was the conscious working of the material and using it in an expe[ ] appropriate manner without hampering the tectonic or construction.[ ] three elements were considered to be essential to all categories of industrial production. The Constructivists considered that the material elements comprised the material substance itself (its properties, significance and industrial possibilities) and the intellectual materials which were line, colour, space, plane, volume and light.

Having asserted 'the incompatibility of artistic activity with the functional character of intellectual production', they asserted the 'real participation of intellectual production in the nature of an equal element in the creation of a communist culture'. This term, 'intellectual production', was used as an equivalent for Constructivism. It is evident that it was presented as the explanatory term for a completely new idea. Taking the elements of artistic activity as already established, the Constructivists applied them to 'intellectual production'. This did not make this new area of activity 'artistic activity' but a type of activity which was completely new then, and which corresponds more to our idea of design. The Constructivists were very aware of the delicacy of this balance and the inherent danger that these artistic elements would convert 'intellectual production' back into 'artistic activity'. They were therefore particularly virulent in their attack on 'applied art' and all the ideas related to it, because it endangered the survival of their new concept. It is this fear that explains the extremism of their attack and the lengths to which they went to differentiate Constructivism from 'applied art'.

Nevertheless, it is perhaps important to point out here that their rejection of, and attack on, applied art did in fact leave what they called 'artistic activity' (i.e. easel painting) with rights almost equal to that of 'intellectual production' in the construction of the new communist culture. However, the movement was not merely one way. The Constructivists did not limit their activity to the creation of material values for the new society. They also considered that it was their task to incorporate the need for 'inspiring work', studying the aesthetic aspects of labour and its transformation into 'the exultant work' of communism.[108]

It is here that we have evidence of an interpretation of Marx and the passages in the *German Ideology* where he put forward his most utopian interpretation of what the nature of art would be following the ultimate establishment of communism. He suggested that man would be utterly liberated and that the division of labour which made one man an artist and another a factory worker would be abolished, so that one man would be both a worker and an artist. In this way the distinction between art and work would vanish.

Within this general ideological framework of the First Working Group of Constructivists, individual members elaborated their ideas. Karl Ioganson, for example, in a paper entitled 'From the Construction to Technology and Invention' delivered at INKhUK on 9 March 1922, postulated the existence of two types of construction.[109] One was of an aesthetic or artistic nature and the other was a genuine 'building and technical' construction which could be described as 'important and useful'. Ioganson argued that since Constructivism denied the value of art, for a Constructivist the only construction of any validity was 'an object itself constructively made', 'not for art but for the real translation of it onto the rails of practical necessity'. This led him to condemn as 'false' constructions any which employed the methods and means of past art, including 'such accidental operating with material as is ... practised by Tatlinism'.[110] Ioganson advocated a total abandonment of art and an advance along the path towards technology and invention. However, he drew a distinction between current technology, which was a 'quagmire' full of defects, and technology as 'the application of the laws and rules and discoveries of invention' (i.e. as a body of scientific laws). He concluded with an encapsulation of his own development, which he asserted was the only path open to truly revolutionary artists: 'From painting to sculpture, from sculpture to con-

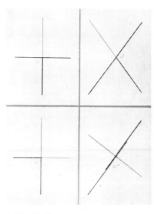

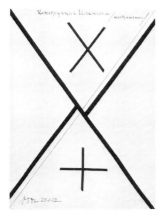

3.13. K. Ioganson, *Construction*, 7 April 1921, graphite and coloured pencil on paper, 31·8 × 24·3 cm. Collection George Costakis, Athens. [Photograph: © George Costakis 1981.]

3.14. K. Ioganson, *Construction (Depiction) – Konstruktsiya (izobrazhenie)*, 23 February 1921, paper collage, graphite and coloured pencil on paper, 45·5 × 33·7 cm. Collection George Costakis, Athens. [Photograph: © George Costakis 1981.]

3.15. K. Ioganson, *Electric Circuit (Depiction) – Elektricheskaya tsep' (izobrazhenie)*, paper collage and coloured pencil on paper, 45·4 × 33·6 cm. Collection George Costakis, Athens. [Photograph: © George Costakis 1981.]

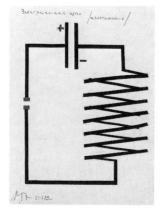

struction, from construction to technology and invention – such is my path and such is and will be the final aim of every revolutionary artist.'[111]

The distinction drawn between the fundamental nature of Tatlin's type of non-utilitarian constructions and those with a 'definite practical aim and purpose'[112] had certain stylistic ramifications. Ioganson stressed the angular qualities that were to characterise the latter: 'The construction of every cold structure in space, or every combination of hard materials, is a right-angled or acute-angled cross.'[113]

This statement reiterates very closely the text inscribed in the verso of Ioganson's drawing *Construction* subtitled 'A Graphic Representation of a Complete Cold Structure in Space' (plate 3.13), executed during the course of the INKhUK debates concerning composition and construction in the spring of 1921.[114] The only difference is that in the 1921 text Ioganson added the following symbols to elucidate his drawing: a', a'', and a'''' indicating the right-angled construction and a''' indicating the obtuse and acute-angled construction. Two later drawings of 23 February 1923 seem to bear a direct relationship to Ioganson's paper and demonstrate clearly his emphasis upon both angular constructions and practical invention.[115] They are close in date to Ioganson's talk at INKhUK and may have been used to illustrate his ideas.

Construction: A Depiction (plate 3.14) synthesises the representations from the earlier drawing, whereas *Electrical Circuit* (plate 3.15) serves as a practical demonstration of his ideas in which all the component elements are rectilinear and their constructional relationships are angular. The theoretical ideas which Ioganson elaborated in 'From the Construction to Technology and Invention' were the underpinning of those three-dimensional works which Ioganson exhibited at the third OBMOKhU exhibition of May 1921 (plate 2.16). Those works exemplified in a practical way his dedication to the angular qualities of the utilitarian structures encountered in contemporary technology.

This latent antagonism between the aesthetic approaches of Tatlin and the OBMOKhU (which formed the backbone of the First Working Group of Constructivists) was made very explicit in the course of a discussion at INKhUK on 26 December 1921, following Kemeny's paper 'Concerning the Constructive Work of the OBMOKhU'.[116] As an ardent supporter of OBMOKhU, Kemeny described their experiments enthusiastically. Although he had earlier acknowledged Tatlin as the 'father of Constructivism', he considered OBMOKhU significant because 'their constructions are material in the truest sense of the word and they emerge from the inner nature of the material used. Their constructions are the first to have moved from the plane into real space.'[117] He drew a distinction between the work of Tatlin as a 'pioneer of Constructivism connected with the practical tasks of the material forms of life', and the OBMOKhU artists whose experimental works he regarded as 'agitation for the life of the future and for communism'.[118]

Vladimir Stenberg opened the discussion by asserting that the work of the OBMOKhU artists was not mere agitation, but that they were 'striving to show practical ways of working and using new materials'.[119] Brik agreed with Kemeny's diagnosis. Holding that production art required the rejection of art and practical participation in industry, he praised the fact that the young artists of the OBMOKhU approached materials and forms without any of the metaphysical inheritance that weighed on Tatlin. Brik considered that their work was primarily agitational, whereas Tatlin 'does not build a material construction but laws of form in general'. The OBMOKhU did not pretend to this and therefore their work was 'a mockery'. Vladimir Stenberg refuted the implication that there was anything utopian in the work of OBMOKhU and reasserted that the basis of their constructions was work with materials,[120] which was an important stage in the creation of future objects. Tatlin, who was present, contested the positions put forward by Brik and Stenberg. He agreed that the creation of utilitarian objects was important and that the solution of this task should not be individual but collective. However, he stressed the need

96

to utilise previous artistic experience in the solution of such tasks and he emphasised the need for serious work. This position is in full accord with that which he expressed in his declaration 'The Work Ahead of Us', that the work with materials in his counter-reliefs was fundamental to the new task.[121] Khrakovskii supported Tatlin's contention that OBMOKhU 'does not feel material but simply copies it'.

When accused of 'knavery', Medunetskii retaliated by accusing Tatlin's Tower of being utopian. 'We talk of real things, and we have never talked of anything else. We took iron, wire, and nothing else.'[122] At another point in the discussion, which had by now been reduced to the level of a slanging match, Georgii Stenberg suggested that they had not dealt with the central issue of whether the old art was necessary for the future work, i.e. whether Tatlin's or their's was the correct path. He asked how the artist was to participate in production and how he was to discover the starting point for the creation of items of mass production. He argued that the artist didn't need slogans but a firm theoretical and practical basis to meet contemporary everyday needs. Ladovskii pointed out that, despite their nihilistic attitude to art, the OBMOKhU were primarily artists, and because their approach was not serious enough and their success was dependent upon their innate talent as artists they would not be the first artists to go into production. More suited to industry were the young artists in VKhUTEMAS. However, as Babichev explained, the fundamental difference between Tatlin and the OBMOKhU was one of form.

> The objects made by OBMOKhU are not appropriate because they are not rooted in any technical work, and it is not clear why they were made (if aestheticism is rejected), because they are in no way utilitarian. These objects are the confirmation of a new mechanical aestheticism. They illustrate of theoretical principles. Tatlin and OBMOKhU do not diverge over the utilitarian task but over the form.[123]

In elucidation of their own principles, the Stenberg brothers and Medunetskii presented a paper at INKhUK on 4 February 1922 entitled 'Constructivism'. Although the complete paper has not been preserved, there is a manuscript entitled 'Theses for the paper Constructivism'.[124] This document's interest lies precisely in the reduced emphasis on the purely ideological and the increased stress on the practical, formal and investigatory approach to the question, suggesting that this new approach may have arisen through the laboratory work of these three Constructivists:

> Constructivism as economy – space
>> utility – the logic of everyday life
>> expediency – the use of the present industrial material with uninterrupted action of its content on the formation of the construction
>> rhythm – the elements of engineering in construction are simultaneously the organising beginnings of its rhythm
>> the basic change of the inner and outer properties of material construction on the basic principles of Constructivism, e.g. the inner properties of a given industrial material and space; the external elements are volume, plane, colour, light and *faktura*[125]

They then enumerated the present tasks of Constructivism and the tasks they envisaged in the future:

> The first laboratory works and their agitational significance
> The abstract solution of the basic problems of Constructivism
> The experimental *oformlenie* of the material and spatial construction and its interrelationship with utility
> The achievements in the field of space, form and rhythm

The communistic expression of material and spatial structures
Russian industry under the banner of Constructivism and its significance on the world market[126]

ALEKSEI GAN

To propagate their ideas the First Working Group of Constructivists proposed publishing a journal, the *Herald of Intellectual Production*,[127] and establishing links with some of the most important economic organisations. This was never effected but the ideas of the group were elaborated and publicised by Gan in his book *Constructivism* published in 1922. As a founder member of the group, Gan based the book on their theoretical positions and practical experience. However, the book was not merely a theoretical treatise intended to publicise the new movement; it was also an agitational publication 'with which the Constructivists began their struggle with the supporters of traditional art'.[128]

This struggle was made necessary by the New Economic Policy of 1921 which re-established a limited market economy and fostered the re-emergence of wealthy bourgeois social elements who could exercise patronage. The issue of patronage became important when government departments were reorganised in 1921 and their budgets reduced so that less money was available for artists.[129] At the same time IZO was reorganised and the avant-garde artists lost their positions and influence there. Simultaneously there was a resurgence of 'realist' artistic groups who were successfully competing with the Constructivists for official patronage.[130]

In this situation Gan was prepared to go to great lengths to prove that Constructivism was the only 'revolutionary' or 'socialist' art form. From the very beginning Gan firmly placed the origins of Constructivism in the immediate post-revolutionary period and attributed its emergence to the active participation of artists in the revolutionary struggle as designers of posters, agit-trains and mass festivals: 'Constructivism is a phenomenon of our days. It arose in 1920 amid the mass action of leftist painters and theoreticians.'

At the basis of Gan's exposition lay a denial of the concept of traditional art as non-socialist, and the identification of Constructivism with Marxism and the new socialist state. Quoting heavily from the *Communist Manifesto*, the writings of Marx, Engels and Lenin, and using a vocabulary heavily dependent on Marxist terminology, Gan argued that art was not an eternal value but was an essentially bourgeois and individualistic product of the non-industrial, primitive and feudal states of society. As part of the bourgeois ideological superstructure, it was destined to disappear with the society that succoured it. Its disappearance was as inevitable as the disappearance of the bourgeoisie with the end of capitalism. In the same way that the proletariat had developed under capitalism, to the point at which it was powerful enough to take power in the socialist revolution, Gan argued that modern technology had produced Constructivism ('the slender child of an industrial culture'), which was ready to occupy the prestigious position recently occupied by art: 'For a long time capitalism has let it rot underground. It has been liberated by the Proletarian Revolution. A new chronology begins with 25 October 1917.'[131]

As 'the first culture of organised labour and intellect', Constructivism was the only possible culture for the new society because art 'was part of the spiritual culture of the past'. Constructivism responded to the new industrial age by rejecting the 'speculative activity of art' and embracing 'intellectual and material production'.

Having preserved the firm material and formal bases of art – i.e. colour, line, plane, volume and movement – artistic work, materially intelligible, will rise to the conditions of purposeful activity, and intellectual and material productions will open up new means of artistic expression. We should not reflect, depict and interpret reality but should build practically and express the planned objectives of the newly active working class, the proletariat. And it is now that the proletarian revolution has conquered ... that the master of colour and line, the combiner of spatial and volumetric solids, and the organiser of mass action – must all become Constructivists in the general business of the building and movement of the many millioned human mass.[132]

Having convinced the reader that the disappearance of art is desirable and inevitable, Gan explained how this was to be achieved. In other words he described the Constructivist approach to the task in question, which he asserted could only be tackled by Constructivism because only Constructivism could unite the ideological with the formal, the artistic with the political.

Gan denied that Constructivism was utopian in the context of the problems that Soviet society was facing in its state of transition from capitalism to communism. He insisted that 'Constructivism does not divorce itself from this basis, from the economic life of our present society.'

Moreover, Gan insisted that Constructivism was 'Marxist', that Constructivists used Marx's theory of dialectical materialism as a guideline for their work, and that all the Constructivists' essential ideas were Marxist: 'Dialectical materialism is, for Constructivism, a compass that indicates the paths and distant objectives of the future ... all its [Constructivism's] essential ideas are to be found in communism.'[133]

Gan then described how Constructivism was based on three principles enunciated in the programme of the First Working Group of Constructivists: tectonics, *faktura* and construction. These had been derived from pre-revolutionary artistic investigations which to Gan were of value precisely because through these investigations Constructivism approached the precision of industrial production in defining the formal qualities of *faktura* and the principles of construction. Gan was even flexible enough at this point to admit that other pre-revolutionary stylistic trends, such as Suprematism, had made contributions to these formal bases. However, to Gan these artists had failed to realise that the nature of art must completely change and that art as such was redundant. The overwhelming superiority of Constructivism was established once again by the fact that it and it alone contributed the principle of 'tectonics'.

These principles, which were fundamental to Gan's conception of Constructivism, were formulated in the following way:

> The *tectonic* ... emerges and is formed on the one hand from the characteristics of communism, and on the other from the expedient use of industrial materials ... The tectonic should lead the Constructivist in practice to a synthesis of the new context and the new form. He must be a Marxist who has outlived art and has a really advanced knowledge of industrial material ...
>
> *Faktura* is the working of the material as a whole and not the working of one aspect of it ... *Faktura* is consciously to select material and use it expediently without halting the movement of the construction or limiting its tectonic.
>
> *Construction* must be understood as the co-ordinating function of Constructivism. If the tectonic unites the ideological and formal, and as a result provides unity of conception, and the *faktura* is the condition of the material, then the construction reveals the actual process of structuring. Thus we have the third discipline, the discipline of the formation of the conception through the use of worked material.[134]

It must be admitted that Gan paid relatively little attention to the formal principles of Constructivism. His main concern and his main importance were to elaborate and demonstrate the ideas of the First Working Group of Constructivists and to justify Constructivism for contemporary Soviet government and society in terms of Marxism, sociology and modern technology.

Gan's extremism was matched by that of Brik. In a paper called 'What are Artists to do Now?' of April 1922, Brik asserted that easel painting was fundamentally opposed 'to the State's point of view, the activities of government bodies in the field of art and to our activity as a circle of the party'.[135] His second contention was that INKhUK should not ally itself to any other artistic group, including any of the 'left' groups. 'For us, union with others, even left groups, is impossible ... The grouping of artists is such now that right and left are being strengthened, the middle is collapsing. And that's good because this middle is more dangerous for us than any groups who agree with us in anything.' In other words Brik was suggesting a constant struggle against both the easel painters and any other artistic groups not sharing completely the attitudes and points of view of INKhUK. Brik, however, at one point seems to throw doubt on the validity of theorising when it comes to the role of the artist in industry.

> The suspicion that the transfer to practical work in production removes the artist from theoretical work has already lost all meaning. Theory doesn't show the way to work, but on the contrary practice dictates the laws which are determined by theory. The artist, working practically in production, draws his strength in this work from his ideology. Consequently all the listed dangers have no serious bases.[136]

He proposed that artists simply go along to factories, in order to be useful to society.

This type of attitude towards working out the practical details of the artist's participation in the productive process was prevalent in INKhUK. Although certain members of INKhUK attended meetings of the relevant committees in various state industrial organisations, INKhUK did not work out a methodology of 'production art'. This was left to the masters themselves, such as Tatlin and Rodchenko, to evolve on the basis of their own practical utilitarian work. Therefore at this particular meeting of INKhUK (13 April 1922) Rodchenko, in disagreement with Brik, proposed that the time had come for INKhUK to organise a series of talks given by invited engineers so that its members could become more closely acquainted with practical production; 'for we have already sufficiently expressed our opinions'. Khrakovskii supported Rodchenko's proposal to consult 'specialists for the explanation of questions relating to production art'. Brik was also attacked over his contention that INKhUK could be characterised as a party organisation. Vesnin and Ladovskii stressed that they considered INKhUK to be a 'theoretical institution', and Babichev accused Brik of adopting a tactic appropriate to the 'provocation of an opposing camp'.[137]

Despite this, however, Brik's paper was not an accidental occurrence. In many ways it represented the culmination of his theoretical work on the ideas of production art which had begun with his first articles in *Art of the Commune*.[138]

Kushner was a rather more serious theoretician of production art. He had become a member of INKhUK in 1921 after the reorganisation, and he lectured extensively in various Proletkul't organisations and at the VKhUTEMAS.[139] Kushner gave four very important papers at INKhUK in March and April 1922. The first talk, entitled 'The Production of Culture',[140] which he presented on 9 March, was concerned with the appearance and development of capitalist forms of production in mechanised industry. Kushner divided objects into two types: the naturally produced and the man-made.[141] The latter were defined by time (production and operation time), space and function. Kushner argued than an object's use-value and cost were interdependent and that cost depended on the amount of time spent on its creation. Concomitantly the longer the object was of use the greater was its value. Therefore to increase the quality of the object one has to decrease the production time or increase the use-time. Kushner then divided the history of objects into three periods. The first was when the object's useful life was limited to one human life (the producer was at the same time the consumer). The second period was when these objects were used by the producer's descendants, i.e. their useful time was increased. In the third period the object left the hands of the producer after production. Production time was decreased and use-time increased. Kushner considered that at this point art emerged as 'an exaggeration of the development of the differentiated function of things'.[142] The art object represents this flowering of the object. 'The object without function' was of course the easel painting.

In his second paper on the same theme, of 16 March 1922, Kushner began with the assertion that the theory of production art must be built upon the basis of mass production.[143] Here Kushner cited the draped dress as an instance of an object dictated not by mass production but by fashion. Production he considered as composed of elements dependent upon the needs of the consumer, and he approached the question of standardisation through a historical appraisal of different periods.

Kushner's third paper, entitled 'The Role of the Engineer in Production', introduced the question of the artist's role in the productive process and within the actual production unit.[144] Kushner began by examining the historical evolution of the engineer's role in the context of a progressively differentiated industrial production, ending with his purely functional role in contemporary industry. Kushner concluded that the engineer's functions were represented by three types of engineer: the engineer-technologist responsible for organising and overseeing the industrial process in the workshops; the engineer-constructor working in the technical office where the calculations were made and designs drawn up; and the engineer-organiser of production working within the entire complex of the modern industrial combine. Kushner recognised the necessity of the engineer's role in modern industrial production yet observed that the engineer was often led by the demands of industry rather than vice versa, and that only when this state of affairs had been reversed would the engineer occupy his rightful place in industrial production. He was especially critical of the engineer-constructors who were responsible for designing new prototypes, and Kushner suggested that the artist's experience of form and material would here be beneficial in producing better designs.

Consequently in his fourth paper, 'The Artist in Production', Kushner examined the definition of the role and significance of that emerging 'discipline taking its beginning on the one hand from engineering, and on the other from art'.[145] In accordance with his previous conclusions Kushner discussed the role which the artist could play in industry with reference not to the craft shops, but to the technical office. Kushner saw the artist in industry not as an executor of objects, but as a new type of engineer, working in co-operation with the others in the technical office.

Apparently during the discussion following this paper a further division among the left artists of INKhUK occurred. It seemed to involve a disagreement between the Productivists (orientated on industry) and the Constructivists with their concern for the material formation of the object. Unfortunately the split is not well documented and I have therefore been unable to establish precise alignments.

ART IN PRODUCTION

At the same time as INKhUK had adopted a '*veshchist*' programme, in 1921, and was moving already towards a more Constructivist platform, a small collection of articles appeared in Moscow under the title *Art in Production*. Published by the Art and Production Subsection of IZO, the collection nevertheless did not seem to represent any coherent viewpoint. Despite the fact that the introductory explanation stated that the publication was inspired by a need to establish the theoretical bases of 'the installation of artistic elements into the life of production ... the transformation of the forms of the production process and the forms of life through art', the articles did not possess any unity in their approach to the 'role of artistic principles in the production process'.[146]

Brik's contribution, entitled 'On the Order of the Day', put forward his definition of the term 'artistic production' (*khudozhestvennoe proizvodstvo*): 'by the term artistic production we simply mean a consciously creative relationship to the production process'.[147] The aim was not 'a beautifully decorated object, but a consciously made object'.[148] Brik pointed to a new form of collective production: 'We want the worker to cease being a mechanical executor of some type of plan unfamiliar to him. He must become a conscious and active participant in the creative process of producing an object.'[149] However, Brik did not clarify how this approach was to be realised practically, i.e. how the consciously made object was to be produced, nor did he elucidate the exact creative relationship between the artistic and the utilitarian. Brik seems to have assumed that, given the right attitude, the formal method of implementing it would arrive of its own accord, and in this way he avoided having to answer one of the most vital questions of the move into production for artists.

Moreover, Brik's attitude had little in common with that put forward by Filippov who considered art to be an element to be applied to the beautification of the environment. Filippov distinguished between two artistic attitudes, the 'reproductive' and 'constructive', corresponding to the 'imitative' and 'productive'.[150] Art in a communist society should 'according to Karl Marx not depict the world but change it'. Only 'constructive' or 'productive' art is capable of achieving this. However, Filippov seems to have seen this productive art as 'the materialisation of painting' and he stated that in fact 'the new easel painting is becoming especially close to production art'. He saw the ultimate aim as gratification 'of the joyful need to decorate life'.[151]

Voronov increased this confusion by treating the concepts of applied and production art as though they were identical phenomena.[152] In a sentence that illogically fused all the different approaches to production art he stated that the new art would be 'really creative fine art, the art of construction, decoration, great production art'.[153] Moreover, Shterenberg's article, which stressed that art in production was now a living reality, really did not make any adequate distinction between applied art and production art, so that it is easy to see how confusions developed.[154] Arkin asserted that 'contemporaneity confirms production art as a basic branch of its artistic culture'; and Filippov, that 'we accept easel painting as a positive artistic achievement, as creative search and design'.[155] The articles, united only in their general commitment to a link between art and industry, did not examine in any detail the problems related to defining the exact nature of the relationship between art and industry, and to what extent, and how, art could combine with the industrial process.

Art in Production indicated that the idea of production art was being discussed by a wide circle of artists and theoreticians outside INKhUK. Although Brik and Torporkov were both members of INKhUK now committed to the Constructivist–Productivist definition of production art outlined above, David Shterenberg (still head of IZO) was an easel painter. His interest in art's connection with industry was not based on a rejection of the value of easel painting. He envisaged fine art coexisting with production art as a separate but not exclusive entity. From his introductory statement and his praise of the decorative work in porcelain, Shterenberg's concept of production art seems closer to decoration. His appearance in *Art in Production* under the aegis of Narkompros indicated a government commitment to production art as a means of raising the aesthetic quality of industrially produced goods, and the role the artist could play in this, but it should not be interpreted as an official move toward the INKhUK stance.

The collection revealed that at this point there was no generally accepted, coherently developed theory of production art. This inevitably led to further confusion when the label 'Productivist' was used to describe a particular artist or theoretician. From this group of essays it emerges that the term 'production art' was not specific, and in its widest sense could be used to denote no more than a very general commitment to the idea of art being involved in industry and with the production of real objects of everyday use. The specific approach the Constructivists and Productivists of INKhUK posited to this problem was the essence of their interpretation of the term. However, in wider circles their approaches were not the only interpretations of the problem.

Art in Production therefore indicated the need to establish a general but solid theoretical basis for the form and concept of production art as opposed to applied art and to propagate this correct understanding of the term – the work in fact that INKhUK had been engaged on during 1921 and continued in 1922. During the 1920s Arvatov, Kushner, Tarabukin and Brik were the chief theorists who undertook this task. Their articles began to appear more frequently in the press in such journals as *Red Virgin Soil*, *Press and Revolution*, *Life of Art* and especially in *Furnace* and *LEF*, both of which adopted Productivist programmes in 1922 and 1923.[156]

The theoretical path followed by these four writers can be seen to consist of two basic approaches. The first consisted of analysing art's development in terms of its formal elements, to prove the inevitability of the emergence of production art. The second consisted of analysing the development of art in terms of sociology, to arrive at the same conclusion. The first theoretical approach argued that the end of painting was a logical product of art's previous development. The second set out to prove the uselessness of fine art in the new social conditions. The assertion that production art was indeed the art of the future was therefore supplied with two theoretical justifications. Tarabukin's arguments, which he explained in *From the Easel to the Machine* were characteristic of the first theoretical trend.[157] Arvatov, whose theories are characteristic of the second line of development, described Tarabukin as understanding nothing about sociology.[158]

NIKOLAI TARABUKIN

Both lines of argument derived from the basic hypothesis that art was *masterstvo*, in other words a skilled activity.[159] In Tarabukin's words:

> Not ideology which can be endlessly varied, nor form by itself, nor materials which are limitlessly different, constitute the concrete sign for the definition of art as a creative category. Only in the very process of work, inspired by the striving towards the most perfect fulfilment of it, lies the sign which discloses the essence of art. Art is the most perfect activity directed towards the mounting [*oformlenie*] of material.[160]

From this starting point Tarabukin viewed the history of painting since Impressionism as a gradual but steady purifying of art, which had removed all extraneous elements. To him the significance of Impressionism was that it asserted the importance of technical skill and freed art from its dependence on an ideological and subjective content. Tarabukin also saw this as a move towards a greater realism. He used the term in a very specialised sense. He wrote:

> I use it in its very widest meaning, and do not identify it with naturalism, which is one of the forms of realism, and the most primitive and naive in its expression. Modern aesthetic understanding of realism has moved from the subject to the

form of the work. The copying of reality is no longer the motive of realistic striving, but, on the contrary, reality has ceased to bear any relationship to the stimulus of creativity.[161]

The artist's task was to create, therefore, real objects which had no prototype in the real world but were 'constructed from start to finish outside lines which could be extended from it to reality'. Tarabukin saw this general tendency manifested in the development of painting from Cubism onwards, in all works where the artist avoided the representational image and chose to work within the material presented by the two-dimensional surface of the canvas. This, Tarabukin argued, led inevitably to the decline of painting itself. 'Work on bare form enclosed art in a narrow sphere, arrested its progress and led to its impoverishment.' Because 'painting was, and remains, a figurative art ... it cannot escape from these limits of the figurative'.[162] So Tarabukin argued that the artist was compelled to reject painting itself and devote himself to making constructions from real materials in real space because in this way the artist 'does not reproduce reality but presents an object as an end in itself'. In other words, 'by its form, construction and material the artist creates a genuinely real object', with a real, not projected, spatial dimension.[163]

At this point Tarabukin examined Constructivism, stressing the internal inconsistencies of the Constructivist standpoint.

Rejecting the aesthetic, the Constructivists had to give themselves another aim which logically developed from the very idea of construction, i.e. a utilitarian aim. Usually we understand construction as a specific form of structure having a utilitarian character of one sort or another, deprived of which it is deprived of all meaning.

But the Russian Constructivists, consciously not seeing themselves as painters, declared their approach to be 'against art' in its typical museum form, and they formed an alliance with technology, engineering and industry without, however, having any specialised knowledge for this and remaining essentially artists *par excellence*.[164]

This contradiction had led, in Tarabukin's opinion, to a dilettante and naive copying of technological and engineering structures, inspired by an intense veneration for industry.[165] For Tarabukin such constructions were meaningless as models for utilitarian structures and could only be justified in purely artistic terms. Thus he condemned the Constructivists as being mere 'aesthetes' and 'champions of "pure" art'.[166]

In juxtaposition to this practice of the Constructivists Tarabukin posited what he called 'production *masterstvo*'. This he defined as fusion between art and industry. 'The problem of production *masterstvo* is not resolved by a superficial connection between art and production but by their *organic interaction*, by linking the very process of work with that of creativity.'[167] This fusion could only be achieved by 'artist-engineers' or 'artist-workers' working at the machine. In this context the Constructivists' constructions were inferior to those created by technology and engineering.

Although valueless as a prototype for any utilitarian object, this type of construction had thrown a bridge over to production and was therefore of immense significance as a 'laboratory experiment in the organisation of material, the working of the *faktura* and the constructive design of its elements, which can be *methodologically* taken into account in production'.[168] Apart from this the only role of any value that the Constructivist could perform in industry was that of a propagandist. Tarabukin argued that the situation of the Constructivist was tragic, because as an artist he was essentially a dilettante and to realise his ideas he required a specialised technical training for which there was no time and which by its narrow nature was alien to his nature as an artist.

Tarabukin concluded that eventually 'production *masterstvo*' would emerge not through the resurrection of fine art, but through the resurrection of industrial production and the values of material culture.[169] However, although he envisaged some regeneration of both art and industry independently, the process by which this was to be achieved was not elucidated by Tarabukin. In fact he made no logical inference concerning the future development of art, leaving this issue vague.

ARVATOV AND *LEF*

Arvatov now came to Tarabukin's aid because his analysis derived from the social and technical aspect of art rather than from its ideological aspect. Arvatov saw the specific qualities of art in terms of sociology, and its function as being 'social and technical' rather than 'social and ideological'.[170] Tracing the development of art from the Middle Ages to the twentieth century, Arvatov asserted that at a given moment artistic production which had always been 'social and technical' became, with the establishment of bourgeois society, determined 'not by social and technical tasks but by social and ideological tasks'.[171] He regarded this development as a betrayal of art's initial essence and therefore considered bourgeois art as an artistic decline. He recognised that art did perform a social function, but explained that in the anarchistic and fragmented nature of social relations under capitalism art was only a substitute for genuine social community. He concluded from this that, in the future society, such a role would be unnecessary and the artist would revert from being an 'organiser of ideas' to being 'an organiser of objects'.[172]

With the disappearance of this ideological function, representational art would also disappear, because it was the means of organising ideas in bourgeois society. Simultaneously easel painting would also disappear because it was 'the commodity form of representational art', 'the social significance of which was compensating for the discord of reality'.[173] In this way Arvatov firmly connected easel painting with the fate of bourgeois society. Easel painting was irrelevant to proletarian society. A painting, 'because it inculcates a passive pleasure in illusion, and leads away from life, is not able to become a fighting instrument in the hands of the proletariat'.[174] Moreover, Arvatov asserted, it could never be proletarian: 'An easel painting, whatever its subject, always will be the product of bourgeois art; even if it is made by a proletarian, because it is [from an] easel and because it is a painting, it is excluded from ever being proletarian.'[175] These conclusions arose from the fact that Arvatov saw bourgeois art as absolute decadence, a view which in turn arose from his very definition of art.[176]

Arvatov proved, in a way parallel to Tarabukin, that the victory of production art would result from the development of art, but he analysed this development in a sociological way. 'The turning point in European art, breaking with Impressionism, was the result of a new stage of social development. The artist's consciousness had evolved under the influence of a very powerful technical progress.'[177] The result of this process, according to Arvatov, was that the artist ceased to paint a picture but started to make it. The significance of this lay in the fact that the creative process began to approach that of the technical industrial process. If formerly the artist's creation 'had resembled the social process of production as much as a watercolour landscape resembled a steam engine',[178] now the work of the new artist went in a completely opposite direction, for now there was a complete coincidence between the artistic method and the general industrial process. 'Artistic work, on a basis of equality, enters the whole collective-cooperative organisation of human activity. The specific instrument of aesthetic painting, the brush, plays an increasingly small role in art; it is supplanted by planes, files, emery paper, drills, etc.'[179] The appearance of a technical intelligentsia in the industrial centres,[180] its attachment to the positivism of the natural sciences, its inventive and technical victories, had, Arvatov maintained, a profound influence on the reorganisation of the process of artistic production. 'The artist calculates, draws, scientifically plans his every step, he considers its social results, he works slowly, he ceases to depend on his moods, his subjective empathies and antipathies – in a word, the process of artistic production is socialised.'[181] The only quality which distinguished these artists from the actual organiser of objects, from the engineer or worker, was the fact that their work was not functional but was still closely connected with the old easel.[182] Arvatov advocated functionalism and stressed that it was essential that 'real working with materials becomes in reality a great organising power, when it is directed to the creation of necessary utilitarian forms, i.e. objects'.[182] This realisation came to artists with the Revolution, when it appeared that 'life no longer justifies artistic objects, which are crushed by form and content'.[183] Production art was the essence of contemporaneity. 'Our epoch is an epoch of industrial collectivism … it creates the possibility of using a mighty and all-enveloping technology consciously to create and build its [society's] life.'[184] In this way all-powerful technology was harnessed to the revolutionary epoch by the Productivists. Subsequently, the laws of industrial production, i.e. the laws of social and technical expediency, were to become the forms of any social activity, including the social activity called art.

Arvatov considered that 'the first task of the working class in art' consisted of the destruction of this 'historically conditioned' division between artistic technique and general social technology.[185] He considered that herein lay the solution to the problem of the merging of art and industry. Wiping out the last distinction between the Constructivist understanding of the object and the industrial object, the Productivists posited the question of the existence of art as a question of industrial production. 'Of high quality, extremely flexible and adaptable in its construction, fulfilling its function as an object most of all in its form, it is the most perfect work of art.'[186] In this way Arvatov regarded the entry of art into production as a task equivalent to improving the artistic process itself.

This left art, in the traditional sense, no place in the new society, because the proletariat, urged to organise reality on the principle of 'conscious utilitarianism', no longer had any need for 'fine' art, and this included, in the Productivist definition, all forms of easel painting. Arvatov argued that the essence of the proletarian world view was 'a social and technological monism', and that the artistic policy of the new class, therefore, should not, and could not, tolerate the existence of any art that was based on the 'individual craft method'.[187] The individualism of the painter was juxtaposed to the 'scientifically organised', 'collective artistic work' of the proletariat. All forms of art, including the applied arts, were discredited by their relationship to individuality. The very word 'art' was discredited, and Tarabukin replaced it with the term 'production *masterstvo*'.[188]

Naturally the products of this skill were distinguished from traditional art products: 'They cease to belong to the realms of the unique or to be preserved in the nature of absolutes. The outlived object will be supplanted by the new; artistic fetishism will die, because the secret of artistic creation, understood now as the highest skill, will be visually exposed.'[189] The direct result of this change in artistic consciousness, which the Productivists themselves called a revolution, was the change in the form 'of the use of artistic values'. An object was accepted and valued not because it answered a definite artistic taste (Arvatov called this 'bourgeois canons'), but because 'in a given situation and for a given task, it is skilfully worked'. Another result of this argument, the 'socialisation of use', was 'the idea that museums, as graveyards of the "eternal" individual values, should be destroyed. In their place will be created general scientific storehouses with an historically necessary and miserly selection of exhibits.'[190]

The greatest problem of all was of course the question of how concretely this merger of art with industry was to be achieved. Obviously the former situation of artists entering the factory with their craft practices was out of the question. Moreover, contemporary engineering, although 'technically completely revolutionary', was 'completely conservative in its aesthetics'. The majority of engineers were 'not able to understand that ... the machine is incomparably more perfect in its form than ... the little designs, eccentricities, and other applied and non-applied wonders from the bag of pure art'.[191] This new task could not be executed by the old type of applied artist nor by the old type of engineer. It could only be done by a new social type – the artist-constructor. However, this new type of worker could not emerge without the reconstruction of the entire system of artistic education, which would transform the art schools into polytechnics, producing 'engineer-constructors, equipped with the whole apparatus of technical knowledge, scientific methods for the organisation of work and with a productivist attitude to form'. These new engineer-constructors, or artist-constructors (Arvatov used the terms interchangeably), were to establish constructive engineering in the industrial enterprises.[192]

Arvatov's thought, best characterised as 'social and technical monism', strove to subordinate all forms of human activity, including art, to the principle of social and technical expediency, which lay at the basis of the industrial process. In art this took the form of defining the creative process as a technical one, and of denying the individual and spiritual impulses of creativity. Equating the spiritual with the material and the aesthetic with the socially useful, it led to a conscious utilitarianism in which the artist was reduced to a social and technical expediency and the result of creativity became the 'useful object'. The philosophy of production art was a 'philosophy of technology'.[193] Monism, collectivism, materialism and internationalism were the defined characteristics of a revolutionary outlook, whereas individualism, idealism, dualism and nationalism were bourgeois. Fine art, as the supreme expression of man's individuality, epitomised the creative activity untrammelled by utilitarian ends. This led to the attack on all forms of 'psychologism'.[194] The assertion that the highest, most perfect form of art was the industrial product led to the advocacy of standardising and rationalising tendencies in art, at the expense of the individuality of the artist and his work – in other words 'technology ... swallowed art'.[195] 'The merging of art with life became the merging of art with technology, became the death of art', from the 'creative essence' of Tarabukin[196] to Arvatov's theories of the sociology of art, which were directed at proving the inevitability of this process. The perfection of man was only the perfection of him as 'an instrument of social action'[197] plugged into the technological process. Collectivised action as the form of artistic life of the new proletarian state was described in many Productivist articles of the early 1920s as a specific form of the ordered Taylorised utopia, which was a widespread ideal at this time.[198]

Arvatov had positively evaluated the contribution of the Constructivists Rodchenko, Tatlin, Stepanova and Popova at the dispute 'Art and Production' at the Central Moscow Proletkul't.[199] The attempt to understand the concrete results of the work of these artists (to which can be added the names of Lavinskii, Medunetskii, the Stenberg brothers and A. Vesnin)[200] led to the conclusion that the institution of 'production art' should be postponed and changed by the present day requirements, i.e. the 'polytechnical transformation ... of the art schools, the organisation of experimental work on model factories and the invention of standard forms of material life, in the fields of furniture, clothes and in other types of production'.[201] In this way the proletariat could work out their own 'aesthetic of social and technical utilitarianism, given not in abstract discussion but in its concrete – either laboratory or private material realisation'.[202]

The future of production art was dependent on the execution of this programme and therefore *LEF* devoted considerable attention to the work carried out by the above mentioned artists. For the theorists of production art in *LEF*, the Constructivists were not Productivists but were merely the precursors of the new, yet to be realised, type of 'engineer-constructor' or 'artist-constructor' who had to combine a complete grasp of artistic skills with a specialised knowledge of technology. In strict terms the only 'Productivists' were theoreticians. Constructivists were the pioneers who held 'in their hands only one banner and that ... ragged', because 'between the construction and the object is a gulf like the one between art and production'.[203] The Constructivists' contribution lay in the fact that they 'represent an end to those who view art as an aim in itself, rebelling against themselves', and because they 'saw a new unprecedented possibility in abstract form. Not the creation of forms of high aesthetics, but expedient constructions of materials'.[204] For Arvatov, abstract non-utilitarian constructions had a methodological significance for the transition to production. He defined the aspects of the industrial as being three: 'the pure material, the method of working, and the purpose of the product'. Therefore it followed that an artist who had no knowledge of how to work with materials in an abstract way was 'utterly meaningless in a factory'.[205] This abstract experimentation in working with materials was exclusively 'laboratory work'. If it was approached as an aim in itself it was already in danger of being aestheticism.

However, in their judgements of projects by the Constructivists there is not always the strict adherence to the principle of 'social and technical expediency'. For example, in assessing the qualities of Lavinskii's project for a town in the air, Arvatov did not condemn it as eccentric or as aestheticism, but praised it as an example of 'maximum expediency', with an 'everyday wholeness like a Japanese house of paper – the difference being in technology'.[206]

The most positive evaluation of the Constructivists' position, and at the same time a highly realistic one, was given by Nikolai Chuzhak, writing in *LEF* in 1923. He stressed the danger of excessive theorising and was critical of the 'fruitless jogging in one place, around the terms produced'.[207] Chuzhak adopted the term 'life-building' (*zhiznestroenie*) to denote the new 'production art' and he considered its most promising expression to be Constructivism. He argued that this fruitless, directionless movement only ceased to be fruitless when 'the idea of production art crystallised into ... Constructivism, where it put out some shoots'.[208] Moreover, in juxtaposing Constructivism and Productivism, he considered Constructivism to be ultimately of more value.

> Constructivists are the only theoreticians [coming] from practical work, at the work bench and the plough (the Productivists are not an example to them ... they tried to go from philosophy) – the Constructivists all the same managed to find some holds in life and they were the first to present the theorists with some hints on material objects, about which – as something still poor, but tangible – it is already possible to speak.[209]

*   *   *

The conclusion of all these theorists was that the Constructivist approach to production art, and therefore Constructivism and production art itself could not be realised without the artist-constructor. The artist-constructor had to bring together in one person, to an almost superhuman degree, the professional equipment of both the gifted artist and the experienced director of technology. This ideal could only be the product of a totally new professional training. It was therefore not accidental that attention became concentrated upon those establishments which could be adapted to provide the necessary artistic and technological expertise within one curriculum. It is in this context that the varied experiments of the Moscow VKhUTEMAS become central to the realisation of Constructivism in practical work and to the whole development of design in the Soviet Union.

4 VKhUTEMAS: THE HIGHER STATE ARTISTIC AND TECHNICAL WORKSHOPS

THE MOSCOW VKhUTEMAS were set up by official decree in 1920 with the intention of training 'highly qualified master artists for industry'.[1] The name VKhUTEMAS was an abbreviation of Vysshie gosudarstvennye khudozhestvenno-tekhnicheskie masterskie - Higher State Artistic and Technical Workshops. They represent an attempt, at least in part, to set up a school of design in post-revolutionary Russia. The theoreticians' conclusions, treated in the preceding chapter, had suggested that the most practical path towards the realisation of the new synthesis between art and life, art and technology, lay through the creation and training of the 'artist-constructor', whose training - partially technical and partially artistic - would enable him to participate fully in the 'constructive' work of forming a socialist environment. The VKhUTEMAS were set up to train such artist-constructors. This chapter will examine the extent to which they succeeded and the extent to which the VKhUTEMAS can be regarded as a school of design dedicated to Constructivist principles.[2]

THE STATE FREE ART STUDIOS

The VKhUTEMAS were set up in 1920 on the basis of the State Free Art Studios (Svobodnye gosudarstvennye khudozhestvennye masterskie).[3] In 1918 the Stroganov School of Applied Art and the Moscow School of Painting, Sculpture and Architecture had been abolished, and together with some private studios they were amalgamated to form the First and Second Free Studios.[4] These were ceremonially opened on 11 and 13 December 1918.[5] Since many of the ideas and experiments undertaken in VKhUTEMAS relate to those of the Free Studios out of which they had developed, it is apposite to examine the latter in some detail at this point. The Free Studios were not inspired by the aim to create a school of design, but by the desire 'to train people in the fine arts to have a complete perception of artistic culture in the fields of painting, architecture, and sculpture' and to provide complete artistic freedom for the development of the individual's artistic abilities. Upholding the principle of absolute artistic freedom in reaction against the repressive nature of the Imperial Academy, the Free Studios declared that, 'recognising within their walls the free existence of all defined artistic trends, the studios give every student the opportunity of developing his individuality in whatever direction he wishes'.[6] With this aim in view artistic education was made free to all students irrespective of previous educational qualifications and it was decided that the studios should embrace all current artistic trends from that academic Realism which had dominated the pre-revolutionary Academy of Arts to Impressionism, Neo-Cézannism, Cubism and Futurism.[7] In other words the teaching staff was to include all shades of artistic opinion from what was described as the extreme right to the extreme left.[8] Archival materials show that, although the students had the ultimate say in the selection of masters by voting, the list of possible candidates was initially drawn up by an artistic commission, and included representatives from all the above mentioned trends.[9] Students were free to add their own candidates to this list.[10] The student voting indicated overwhelming support for the more conservative artistic trends. Arkhipov as the leading representative of the Realist school received 88 votes.[11] According to the classification of the voting reports, the Neo-Impressionist Mashkov received 78, the Impressionists Korovin and Kuznetsov respectively 66 and 35, the Neo-Impressionist Konchalovskii 34, the Post-Impressionist Rozhdestvenskii 21, the Suprematist Malevich 4, and the Futurist (*sic*) Tatlin 8 votes.[12] Irrespective of this distribution, only two representatives from each of the trends were chosen.[13] Had masters been appointed solely on the strength of the student voting, the school would not have undergone any significant alteration. As Kandinskii suggested, the students' mood was essentially Realist and the reform, coming from above, did not respond sufficiently to the students' wishes.[14] However, since the bulk of the students had been members of the unreformed schools the voting may have merely indicated their continued loyalty to former teachers. On the other hand it may only have reflected the fact that the more enterprising students tended to leave the schools before the Revolution if they were dissatisfied.[15] This trend would naturally have left only the less adventurous or less critical elements within the school, to whom the avant-garde were an unknown quantity. Indeed the voting figures should not be taken to show that the reform was itself an avant-garde manoeuvre which did not embrace a wide range of artistic credos. In fact all the non-academic painters were in favour of the reform.[16] The fact that the moderate Mashkov was in charge of administering it is a firm indication of the wide artistic basis of support which it enjoyed. What the voting did indicate, however, was the extent of student antipathy to the so-called Futurists. The quarrels between the avant-garde and the Realists were later to become more acute,[17] and the students' voting pattern here is revealing of factors which later became important in VKhUTEMAS. The presence of a section of the student body that enthusiastically embraced the realistic credo became of especially vital significance in the fine art departments of painting and sculpture. These departments, which had briefly included important avant-garde figures such as Kandinskii, Malevich and Tatlin, were later to become increasingly conservative.

The organisational structure of the Free Studios conformed to traditional artistic categories; they were divided into painting, sculpture and architectural studios. Each group was autonomous, but had equal access to the Institute for the Study of Art which was part of the overall structure of the studios.[18] The painting studios consisted of specialised and individual studios.[19] The specialised studios dealt with specific genres of artistic activity. The masters, derived from all sections of the artistic world, apparently taught in the individual studios.[20] The painting studios also comprised a painting laboratory where students were taught the rudimentary chemical bases of different painterly substances, the analysis of painterly layers, the nature of various grounds (wood, metal, canvas), the culture of materials in art (past and present) and in contemporary industry, instruments and their use, drawing and the use of stencils.[21] The sculpture and architecture studios followed a very similar pattern with an equal emphasis on the students' acquisition of technical skills and knowledge essential to their craft. The Institute for the Study of Art, on the other hand, attempted to introduce the student to the 'emerging science of the study of art'.[22]

The individual studios run by individual masters were intended 'to give the student a clear understanding of the principles of the art of painting through working with it in compositions based on colour, painterly planes (painterly textures) and in relief'.[23] Very little material is available to suggest the precise methods with which this was to be achieved but what is available suggests a great change from the rigidity of traditional methods.[24] Training in the pre-revolutionary art schools had generally consisted of long hours devoted to drawing from plaster casts.[25] Only more advanced students had painted in oils directly from nature.[26]

N. F. Lapshin later described the study of form and volume at Bernshtein's studio, which he had attended with Tatlin, as consisting of 'painting busts in monochrome which were not reminiscent of nature'.[27] In the Free Studios Mashkov taught his students to exploit and identify various stylistic interpretations of reality. Students were given a *nature morte* to paint first in a pointillist style, then naturalistically and then in Mashkov's own Neo-Cézannist style.[28] This type of approach tallies very closely with a description of Aleksandra Ekster's teaching method in Kiev, which consisted of painting the same subject in an Impressionist manner, in a Cézannist manner, and then in a Cubist manner.[29] Malevich taught his students about the theories of Cézanne and Van Gogh, and about the principles of Cubism, Futurism and Suprematism.[30] This type of teaching concerning the relativity of styles did represent an important advance towards a more objective understanding of the role that the various artistic elements as well as the artist's perception played in the creative process – an approach towards Kandinskii's programme for 'positive objective knowledge' and complete freedom for 'the inner life of the artist'[31] and towards the types of investigation which he inaugurated at the INKhUK in 1920. As far as can be judged from the haphazard evidence available, the most important positive contribution that the Free Studios made to the VKhU-TEMAS lay in the artistic experiments that took place there, and the new ideas which were generated by their free discussion of artistic questions.[32]

In comparison with the personal studios there seems to have been considerably less artistic innovation in the specialised workshops. It appears that traditional methods of teaching were retained and that there was no attempt to explore the establishment of a new relationship between the artist and industry. Traditionally great attention had been paid to the students' acquisition of drawing skills and craft techniques with the intention of perfecting their application of ornament to items produced. As far as can be judged from the archival material available, all craft teaching was continued in the Free Studios under the aegis of the same concept of applied art.[33]

'The freedom of the Free Studios consisted in the fact that everyone worked as they wanted to.'[34] Consequently students were given complete freedom to choose the master with whom they wished to work.[35] Restraints had to be imposed on this freedom of choice to prevent the system disintegrating into total chaos. For the first month students could move freely from studio to studio, but at the end of that period they had to choose the studio in which they would work permanently.[36] Thereafter they were only permitted to change studios once a year.[37]

The arrangement of individual studios recalled the Renaissance ideal where students worked under the guidance and direction of a master from whom they learnt their craft. In the Free Studios the student's choice of studio normally implied a general allegiance to the particular artistic practice of the studio master, and the training received and the work produced by the students was strongly determined by him.[39] Vladimir Stenberg's description of Tatlin's and Lentulov's students as producing respectively *Tatlinskie veshchi* (Tatlinesque objects) and *Lentulovskie veshchi* (Lentulovesque objects) may have been an exaggeration,[40] but it highlighted the problem that basic artistic skills and knowledge were not being taught independently from the stylistic credos of the masters. 'It became evident that the Renaissance ideal of the free studios didn't suit us ... The single basis for the objective study of art was lost. The students only mastered the individual methods of the masters.'[41]

Instead of co-ordinating their activities to attain a common goal the studios tended to act as units pulling in diverse directions. Denisov suggested that the failure of the Free Studios lay precisely in this individualistic or anarchistic approach to the problem of artistic education which in future should be organised on a collective basis.[42] However, more relevant was the fact that the purely artistic conception underlying the Free Studios' teaching did not respond to the revolutionary reality of the situation in which they were created, and that they were out of date before the difficulties of their operation had been solved.[43] As Ravdel' pointed out in his report of 1921, 'a year of revolutionary life has forced us to understand that the artist is not an embellisher of life, but a serious moulder of social consciousness and a responsible organiser of the whole of our everyday life'.[44] This realisation had been embodied in a student resolution of June 1920 following a conference of art students which had already argued for a reorganisation of artistic education in Russia according to new principles based on the country's present structure and its current needs.[45]

THE DEVELOPMENT OF THE VKhUTEMAS

In mid-1920 negotiations began to reorganise the Free Studios.[46] On 12 October 1920 Narkompros approved the formation of the VKhUTEMAS,[47] and on 29 November 1920 the school was established by State Decree, signed by Lenin.[48]

The first point of the decree stated the aims of the VKhUTEMAS quite explicitly: 'The Moscow VKhUTEMAS is a specialised educational institution for advanced artistic and technical training, created to prepare highly qualified master artists for industry as well as instructors and directors of professional and technical education.'[49] Training artists for industry was deemed of such vital economic importance that it warranted deferment of active military service.

> On reaching the age limit, students are considered to be in the military reserve but are deferred until completion of their educational obligations. Persons receiving deferment under Point 9, but failing to attend the educational institution are considered deserters and are liable to prosecution under the provisions of martial law.[50]

The strategic importance of such training was emphasised by the priority given to rations for students and teachers.[51] The list of artistic workers receiving rations in April 1922 in Moscow included a high proportion of VKhUTEMAS teachers of all persuasions.[52]

The idea of production art being 'closely related to the transformation of industrial culture on the one hand and to the problem of the transformation of life on the other'[53] had received a certain degree of official interest, sanction and support. The government evidently considered that it could become an important element in rebuilding industry.[54] In August 1918 a sub-department of IZO, the Subsection of Art and Production (Podotdel khudozhestvennoi promyshlennosti) was set up under the direction of Ol'ga Rozanova.[55] This body was responsible for regenerating existing studios and workshops and for organising completely new ones.[56] Relations with industrial enterprises and specialists were initiated and eventually led in the winter of 1919 to the creation of an Art and Production Committee (Khudozhestvenno-proizvodstvennyi sovet).[57] In the spring of 1920 a conference of specialists from both the artistic and industrial sectors was held under the aegis of this new committee. Of the hundred delegates who attended the conference, twenty-three represented the glass and china industries, twenty the printing industry, nine the textile industries, and six came from other unspecified industrial fields. The various official speeches concerned the definition of the role that art could play in industry.[58]

Before this, in August 1919, the Subsection of Art and Production had organised the First All Russian Conference on Art and Production (Pervaya vserossiiskaya konferentsiya po khudozhestvennoi promyshlennosti).[59] Lunacharskii attended the conference and his speech gave qualified support to the ideas of involving art in production and of improving the qualities of industrial manufacture: 'If we are really going towards socialism, we must give production more importance than pure art ... There is no doubt that art in production [*khudozhestvennaya promyshlennost'*] must be closer to human life than pure art is.'[60] He went on to suggest that other Commissariats (especially those concerned with the economy) should participate in the solution of this problem and that all should work together in this field.

As a result of this type of discussion, the Scientific and Technical Department of the Supreme Council of People's Commissars set up an Art and Production Commission (Khudozhestvenno-proizvodstvennaya komissiya). This body held its task to be 'the development and encouragement of artistic creativity among the People'.[61] The motivations guiding the adoption of such a policy were indicated in a brief statement towards the end of their declaration: 'With the restoration of our wrecked industry, artistic and industrial [*khudozhestvenno-proizvodstvennoe*] creativity must play an enormous role in the matter of Russia's importance on the international exchange market.'[62] The Central Institute of Labour (Tsentral'nyi institut truda – TsIT) organised in 1921 represented one concrete step towards achieving this, its aim being to study problems connected with productive processes in their social and aesthetic aspects. Gastev, the poet who lauded the industrial vision in his work, was appointed the director, and Lenin expressed his support by giving it the rare privilege of having at its disposal a fund of convertible foreign currency.[63]

The establishment of the VKhUTEMAS should not therefore be seen solely as a product of artistic developments, but should also be viewed as a part of, and to a certain degree as a culmination of, this coherent government policy of improving the quality of industrial production.

THE GENERAL STRUCTURE OF THE SCHOOL

Before the VKhUTEMAS is examined in detail it should be stressed that at no point was it pedagogically a static entity. The school's structure and course programmes were constantly changing under the impact of practical experience and theoretical developments. Certain changes in emphasis occurred in association with primarily administrative matters such as the changes of *rektor* (the *rektors* were Ravdel', 1920–3; V. Favorskii, 1923–6; and P. Novitskii, 1926–30), and with the 1927–8 change in name from the VKhUTEMAS to the VKhUTEIN (Vysshii gosudarstvennyi khudozhestvenno-tekhnicheskii institut – Higher State Artistic and Technical Institute), which was accompanied by a changed set of statutes.[64]

The history of VKhUTEMAS can be divided roughly into three periods, which correspond to the tenures of the three different *rektors*. The first period, covering 1920–3 under Ravdel', was a time of exploration and experiment. Popova may have exaggerated when she stated that the structure and teaching programmes changed every month,[65] but they were certainly in a constant state of flux. Although often haphazard, it was a necessary part of the transition towards creating a school of design. The structure and staff inherited from the Free Studios had to be moulded to the new industrial tasks. This was achieved with varying degrees of success by the various departments. The faculty reports of 1923 exposed the extent to which the real conditions of the workshops belied the fine theoretical phraseology of the teaching programmes.[66]

The second period, from 1923 to 1926 under Favorskii, was one of consolidation of the experimentation of the initial period and of practical achievements based on this. In accordance with the government's reform of higher education in 1923, the teaching programmes were revised and various changes were made.[67] Production workshops became operational in executing orders for various outside enterprises as a way to establish more concrete links with industry.[68] The high point of VKhUTEMAS activity was the success which greeted the VKhUTEMAS exhibits at the Exposition Internationale des Arts Décoratifs et Industriels Modernes in Paris in 1925 where they were awarded several medals.

Yet 1925, the year of the school's great public triumph abroad, saw also the beginnings of another internal reorganisation. After the academic conference of 1926 these plans became implemented with the aim of 'raising the level of the PRODUCTION FACULTIES which, with the exception of textiles, are in a completely unsatisfactory condition'.[69] Novitskii became *rektor* in mid-1926, and under him the VKhUTEMAS became a more narrowly industrial and technological training institute. This orientation was reflected in the adoption of the new title of 'institute' in 1928. The artistic content of courses became reduced in favour of the technological, and the Basic Course providing the students' artistic foundation was ultimately reduced from two years to one term.[70]

On 30 March 1930 the VKhUTEIN was reorganised and soon after that was dissolved. Various departments became the bases of separate institutes, such as the Moscow Graphics Institute (Moskovskii poligraficheskii institut), the Moscow Architectural Institute (Moskovskii arkhitekturnyi institut) and the art department of the Moscow Textile Institute (Moskovskii tekstil'nyi institut). The Painting and Sculpture faculties were transferred to the Academy of Arts (Akademiya khudozhestv) in Leningrad. The remaining faculties became parts of existing institutes.[71]

Corresponding to these three general periods of development, the overall structure of the course also changed. Initially the course of instruction lasted four years. The first year was spent on the introductory or Basic Course, followed by three years specialisation in one or another of the faculties.[72] In 1923 the preparatory course in the Basic Division was extended to two years, but in 1926 it was reduced to one year and in 1929 to one term.[73] Despite this reduction the total length of the course remained the extended five years.[74] Although the bulk of this time was spent receiving instruction in artistic or technical subjects, every student spent a few hours each week studying the history of art and the rudiments of economics, political science and communism.[75]

Originally the VKhUTEMAS continued the tradition established in the statutes of the Free Studios of accepting all students, especially workers, who wanted to receive artistic training, irrespective of their previous artistic or educational experience.[76] This, however, was an ideal that proved difficult to maintain because the Basic Course demanded a solid knowledge of artistic concepts and a broad educational background. In recognition of the difficulties workers encountered in trying to acquire such preliminary knowledge, the Rabfak (Rabochii fakul'tet - Workers' faculty) was set up in 1921 under the direction of Babichev.[77] Babichev considered that the way to create a school closely corresponding to the needs of the country was not only through organising and equipping production faculties but also through changing the teaching methods of the initial training in the preparatory schools.

> It is necessary to inculcate the student with a professional method of thinking while still in the Rabfak. The student must study artistic form in connection with material. A figurative way of thinking is inadequate for the work of a productivist-utilitarian [*proizvodstvennik-utilitarist*]. Inculcating only a figurative method of thinking ... turns a productivist into a figurative artist. It is essential to replace 'encyclopedic education' with a study of the bases of a chosen specialisation ... Applied art became outmoded when it was understood that an expedient form, conforming to the function of the object and the material, is what makes an object of higher quality than usual.[78]

After completing the course, Rabfak students could enter the VKhUTEMAS. Despite this provision, by 1925 because standards were so various it was felt necessary to introduce the examination of students prior to admission. Thereafter prospective students underwent drawing, painting, modelling and technical drawing tests before being admitted to the VKhUTEMAS.[79] In the same year a pedagogical department was added to the school.

Structural changes also occurred in the seven faculties where the students received their specialist training after the Basic Course (the Painting, Sculpture, Textiles, Ceramics, Architecture, Woodwork and Metalwork faculties). In 1925 there were proposals to reorganise these faculties into larger entities based on rational subject and formal criteria. Thus one plan amalgamated Ceramics, Textiles, Woodwork and Metalwork into the Industrial and Production faculty (Industrial'no-proizvod-stvennyi fakul'tet).[80] This left the other three faculties as the Basic Course, the Architecture faculty, and the Painting and Sculpture faculty. According to the other plan, Graphics, Painting and Textiles became departments within the Plane and Colour faculty (Ploskostno-tsvetovoi fakul'tet); Sculpture and Ceramics formed the Volume faculty (Ob'emnyi fakul'tet) and Architecture, Woodwork and Metalwork faculties became the Spatial faculty (Prostranstvennyi fakul'tet).[81] Although both arrangements seem to have been operational for a while, by 1927 the former classification of faculties had been restored.[82] The only permanent change apparently effected was that in the 1926–7 academic year the Woodwork and Metalwork faculties were combined to form the Dermetfak.[83]

ORIENTATION OF SPECIFIC FACULTIES

Against the background of these structural changes, the body of staff remained on the whole fairly constant. However, among the prime difficulties in trying to establish precise details of staff and their activities (i.e. who taught which courses, in which faculties, at which time) are the haphazard nature of archive materials, the constant changes and the fact that the very multi-disciplinary nature of the courses meant that teachers often taught in more than one faculty. Moreover, it should be stressed that throughout its history the commitment of VKhUTEMAS to design and hence to Constructivism was uneven, varying from faculty to faculty. It was, for instance, entirely absent from the two fine art faculties of Painting and Sculpture which were devoted to figurative art forms and the concept of 'fine art'.

Although the teaching staff of the Painting faculty had initially included such major avant-garde figures as Klyun, Rodchenko, Popova, Aleksandr Vesnin and Baranov-Rossine,[84] by 1923 it completely reflected that department's rejection of abstract experimentation and its commitment to a figurative and realist art that would depict the new heroes of Soviet society. It included such artists as K. Istomin, N. Udal'tsova, S. Gerasimov, I. Mashkov, P. Kuznetsov, R. Fal'k, A. Arkhipov, A. Shevchenko, P. Konchalovskii, A. Drevin, D. Shterenberg and A. Osmerkin. In addition, Favorskii taught theory of composition and Florenskii spatial analysis.[95] The department was divided into three sections: easel painting, monumental painting and decorative painting. These were concerned respectively with the training of instructors and commission painters, monumental painters (frescos and wall paintings), and designers of mass festivals, theatre and cinema sets.[87] Among the graduates of the painting studios of the VKhUTEMAS were such artists as P. Vil'yams, A. Deineka and Yu. Pimenov, all of whom employed experimental techniques within the restrictions of easel painting and within a generalised commitment to a figurative content (plate 4.1).[88]

In 1926 the VKhUTEMAS governing body suggested that the Painting faculty was too tied to the concept and practice of easel painting as such and that 'as well as tasks of pure skill, the Painting faculty should also undertake tasks of a purely utilitarian and production nature and find a way into everyday life, into industry and into the political struggle'.[89]

4.1. A. Deineka, *On the Building Site of the New Workshops* (*Na stroike novykh tsekhov*), 1926, oil on canvas, 209 × 200 cm. Tret'yakov Gallery, Moscow.

4.2. Sculpture in wood by student in the Sculpture faculty at the VKhUTEMAS, 1920s.

4.3. El Lissitzky, Cover for the publication *VKhUTEMAS Architecture* (*Arkitektura VKhUTE-MASa*), 1927.

4.4. S. Telingater, Poster for the theatrical tour of Pavel Lyubov, 1925.

The Sculpture faculty was completely committed to monumental realism and determinedly disregarded all contemporary abstract experimentation with three-dimensional form, including non-utilitarian constructions. Initially the leftist sculpture workshop was run by Boris Korolev and Aleksandr Lavinskii. Working from the model (dressed in a blouse and skirt) the students would produce works with a vaguely Cubistic tendency to reduce form to cubes and prisms, very much in the manner of plate 4.2.[90] By 1923, when Lavinskii joined the staff of the Derfak, his work had become allied to the position of *LEF* and Constructivism generally. The staff of the Sculpture faculty, which included Konenkov, Chaikov and Efimov,[91] concentrated on figurative and monumental sculpture, presenting the students with solutions to sculptural tasks within defined architectural contexts. Motovilov and Plastov were among the students who later became eminent designers of gigantic figurative monuments using simplified forms to depict the heroes and heroines of the Soviet Union.

The Graphics faculty possessed a rather more complicated and varied teaching body displaying a greater emphasis on experimentation than either the Painting or Sculpture faculties. Former members of the avant-garde such as L. Bruni and P. Miturich and more conventional artists such as Favorskii and P. Novitskii (both later *rektors*) and Nivinskii taught in the Graphics faculty. This faculty was divided into three departments: lithography, metallic engraving and bookprinting (including typography and book design).[92] Their aims were to 'develop the students' artistic culture and at the same time acquaint them with all the details of printing skills'.[93] The typography department appears to have been the most artistically progressive section of the Graphics faculty. Amongst other projects it was responsible for designing and producing a small volume of Mayakovskii's verse and a volume on the Architectural faculty in 1927. The covers of both these works adhered to the general typographical principles developed by the Constructivists

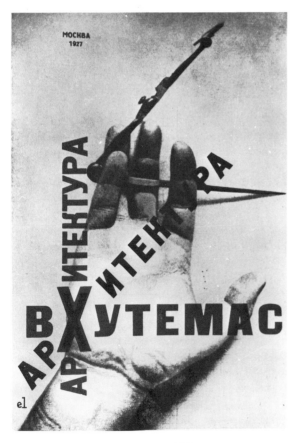

employing a rigid geometrical organisation, asymmetry and sanserif lettering. The architectural cover was based on Lissitzky's self-portrait *Constructor* (plate 4.3),[94] indicating an interest in his experiments in this field (his design for Mayakovskii's *For the Voice* and *A Tale of Two Squares*). These are among the dozen or so works printed by the production workshop of the Graphics faculty.[95] Eminent pupils included Telingater, whose work used experimental compositional devices (plate 4.4), and those working in a more mainstream realist or caricature style such as the Kukryniksy (Kupriyanov, Krylov and Sokolov).

A certain lack of commitment to the concept of design could also be clearly discerned in the Textile and Ceramics faculties which, with the Woodwork and Metalwork faculties, were those faculties within the VKhUTEMAS that were explicitly oriented towards production. The Textile faculty retained a fairly traditional attitude towards cloth, its decoration and the types of motif suitable for this, although employing more modernistic motifs than hitherto. The faculty was divided into two departments: weaving and printing. Graduates from the former were called 'artist-engineers' and from the latter 'artist-colourists'.[96] The examples of the faculty's work displayed at the 1925 exhibition in Paris represented a fairly eclectic mixture of elements derived from modern painting, industry and peasant flower prints (plate 4.5). Later a contemporary Western observer pointed out that in the faculty's designs 'modern machinery and industrial development suggest the motifs. Out of conventionalized aeroplanes, tractors and so on, ingenious and attractive patterns are made.'[97] Remaining essentially figurative, these designs did not represent any move to revolutionise either the concept of designing textiles or attitudes towards the utilisation of artistic motifs in their decoration. Also, as far as can be judged, there was no attempt in the curriculum to relate textiles directly to dress design. Therefore, although Stepanova taught textile composition in the faculty from 1924 until 1925, she does not seem to have been able to break down the department's conservatism or induce it to adopt the innovations which she and Popova had introduced into this area of design in their own work.[98] Tugendkhol'd's judgement of 1923 seems to have endured. He then praised the students' investigation of the artistic and industrial processes and their social and economic ramifications but he found in the examples of textiles they produced 'little that is modern, new or bright'.[99]

The Ceramics faculty does not emerge very clearly from the available documentation, in terms of either its teaching activities or its practical achievements. Its task was to prepare ceramic artists for the porcelain, earthenware and glass industries. Training involved sculptural modelling and painting as well as a knowledge of ceramic and glass technological processes.[100] By 1926 the faculty had established a close relationship with the Dulevskii Factory where many of its students were sent to acquire practical experience of industrial processes and where many of its graduates such as Sotnikov and Kozhin were ultimately employed.[101] From 1927 until 1930 Tatlin taught in the Ceramics faculty and formulated a course on the design of objects for everyday use (*konstruirovanie* or *proektirovanie predmetov byta*) which postulated a much firmer link with the inherent qualities of the material and with the organic quality of living forms in nature.[102]

Standing rather on its own by the nature and scale of its concerns was the Architecture faculty.[103] Organised in November 1920 on the basis of the architectural department of the Moscow School of Painting, Sculpture and Architecture which had become the Architectural faculty in the Second State Free Art Studios in 1918, the faculty's aim was to train architect-artists who would be 'highly qualified master composers in the field of the artistic design of buildings and planning . . . and builders, having knowledge of contemporary technology and the economics of building'.[104] The system of training was initially based on a 'consciously analytical approach to architecture in contrast to the emotional taste of the pre-reformed school'.[105] The faculty's programme defined its aim as the com-

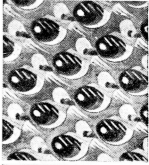

4.5. Fabric designs executed by students in the Textile faculty at the VKhUTEMAS. [Reproduced in *Ekran*, No. 16, 1925.]

bination of 'contemporary scientific truths and artistic truths with the culture of human living space', to achieve 'the fusion of art with life and a full artistic expression of the social and spiritual strivings of contemporary society'. It strove 'towards a methodological study of the laws of the beautiful in architecture and the solution of utilitarian and technical tasks with an inclination towards their artistic and architectural expression'.[106]

During the 1920s the Architectural faculty was not only the leading architectural school in the Soviet Union, but it also acted as 'the central clearing house in the continuing search for new fundamental concepts that will form the theoretical basis of the new architecture'.[107] It was a professional forum of considerable substance in its own right during the whole existence of the VKhUTEMAS–VKhUTEIN and incorporated a wide diversity of architectural approaches. Apart from the traditionalists, the main protagonists were the Rationalists and the Constructivists.

The Rationalist architects of the Association of New Architects (Assotsiatsiya novykh arkhitektorov – ASNOVA), founded by Ladovskii, Krinskii and Dokuchaev in 1923, were primarily concerned with the aesthetic and formal problems of contemporary architecture and the scientific investigation of the fundamental principles of architectural form. They considered that 'a new revolutionary architectural form can only be created on the basis of the latest achievements of science and technology'.[108] Between 1923 and 1930 ASNOVA moved from 'the analytical and rational method ... of creating the entire composition on the basis of a functional and technical foundation to the method of emotionally saturated form, taking into account its psychological and ideological influence'.[109] This change was reflected in Ladovskii's development of the psychological-analytical method and the establishment of a 'psychological-analytical laboratory' within the Architectural faculty in November 1926. The aim of this laboratory was to acquaint the architect with 'the laws of perception and the ways in which they act'.[110] The first two years of the architectural student's training were conducted under the influence of ASNOVA, because Ladovskii was primarily responsible for the Space discipline in the Basic Course. Only in the third, fourth and fifth years did the student become exposed to other approaches.

Amongst the most important of these by the end of the 1920s was that of the Constructivist architects who in 1925 had formed the Association of Contemporary Architects (Ob'edinenie sovremennykh arkhitektorov – OSA), under the leadership of Moisei Ginzburg and the Vesnin brothers. These architects were concerned to 'bring into existence a new architectural form which functionally arises from the purpose of a given building, its material construction and production conditions, answering the specific task and promoting the socialist construction of the country'.[111] This was to be achieved by the creation of a 'materialist working method' which would minimise the individualistic and aesthetic factors in the design process.[112] Developed by Ginzburg, this functional method consisted primarily in decomposing the unified work process of the architect. The factors with which the architect had to deal were first divided into those that were 'characteristic of the epoch as a whole' (i.e. relating to the particular economic and social conditions of the USSR, the collective socialist client, the requirements of the five-year plans) and those that were 'the specifics of a particular building brief'. The objective design process then consisted of four stages: first the spatial organisation of a building was established by using functional flow diagrams and equipment schemes which would also take into account technical, environmental and structural factors. Secondly, the complex of volumes thus produced was analysed in terms of perception and the consideration that the final material form of the building should express its functional essence. Thirdly, these stated intentions were translated into the specific forms of a given building. Finally, the problem was reassembled and an organic unity restored to the design. At this point the architect's individual intuition, which Ginzburg strove to eradicate from the design process, still intruded.[113]

Although Ginzburg was responsible for teaching the theory of architectural composition at VKhUTEMAS–VKhUTEIN from 1926,[114] this functional method was only fully formulated by the closing years of the 1920s and therefore had a limited impact on the VKhUTEMAS students. Perhaps more directly influential as paradigms of the Constructivist approach were practical designs by the Vesnin brothers such as their design for the Palace of Labour of early 1923.

Coexistence between these various modernists and the highly traditionalist staff retained from the Architectural faculty of the Moscow School of Painting, Sculpture and Architecture proved to be impossible. A statement of October 1922 recorded that

1. The Architectural faculty is divided into two groups according to their ideological tendencies: the academic, and the latest architectural researches ...
2. Both groups are completely autonomous in their conception of their tasks ... and in their teaching methods ...
3. The general programme of the faculty is worked out by a Presidium with the agreement of both groups.[115]

These two departments were known respectively as the First or Academic Department (Akademicheskoe otdelenie) and the Second Department or Department of United Workshops (Otdelenie ob'edinennykh masterskikh).[116] The profundity of this split was indicated by the fact that in the autumn of 1922 two leading members of the staff, I. Golosov and K. Mel'nikov, felt it necessary to create yet a third division within the faculty by establishing a New Academy (Novaya akademiya) or Workshop (Studio) of Experimental Architecture (Masterskaya eksperimental'noi arkhitektury) which was intended to occupy a central position, both practically and theoretically between the two and thus to 'reconcile the elements of the traditional system of architectural training with the most modern teaching methods'.[117]

These splits and manoeuvres were one manifestation of the diversity that existed within the Architectural faculty, which could never be described as merely Constructivist. Moreover, given the relatively late development of architectural Constructivism, this was perhaps inevitable. What is surprising is that the Architectural faculty managed to function at all and be as successful and as productive as it was both in terms of the number of students it trained and in the quality of its designs.[118]

The course was basically divided into theoretical and practical disciplines. The former were taught by lectures, seminars and laboratory work. They comprised subjects like physics, chemistry, mechanics, perspective, geometry, history of art, and social and political disciplines. They increased in complexity and specificity as the course progressed so that by the third, fourth and fifth year they included building art, the strength of materials, metal and wooden construction, surveying, technology of building materials, urban construction, reinforced concrete, heating and ventilation, plumbing, the history of architecture and the theory of architectural composition.[119] The practical subjects were taught in the studios and initially the department stressed the artistic aspects since it was here that the errors of past historical eclecticism lay. All factions were united on this point. The first and second year were spent on the Basic Course; however, when this was reduced to one year, second year architectural students still continued those investigations of the formal elements in architecture which had formed the foundations of the Basic Course. This knowledge was synthesised in certain 'production tasks', i.e. 'projects with a defined and specific purpose, for architectural buildings or complexes' which concerned finding the means to demonstrate the expressivity of

1. architectural volume and in particular the expressive qualities of surface
2. the mass and the weight of architectural volume
3. architectural constructions
4. architectural space[120]

This artistic emphasis was continued in the further three years of the course during which particular attention was paid to architectural composition. One VKhUTEMAS student sharply criticised the architectural workshops for their 'aesthetic and painterly relish of angles, volumes and space' in formal exercises 'divorced from life' and 'out of touch with industry', and advocated instead 'a new, serious move in the direction of production architecture'.[121]

The third, fourth and first half of the fifth year were spent studying in the following sections: monumental architecture (under V. Krinskii), decorative-spatial architecture (under N. Ladovskii), planning (under N. Dokuchayev), communal architecture (head not known), a 'laboratory', and a model-making studio (obligatory for all students, and run by A. Efimov).[122] By the beginning of the 1926-7 academic year these sections had been reorganised into housing; public buildings, factories and industrial complexes; planning; and decorative-spatial architecture which comprised the planning of residential zones, parks, gardens and urban areas.[123] These categories of activity were closely related to the contemporary needs and requirements of the Soviet State and design problems were taken from those currently being undertaken by the construction industry and public authorities. Each student had to solve problems related to these sections each year and this ensured that they experienced the whole range of architectural approaches which were embodied in the department. In the summer the students were given practical experience of working on building sites and the final six months of the course was devoted to an independent diploma project which answered contemporary social, political and economic needs.[124]

Despite the diverse views of the teaching staff and the lack of a specifically Constructivist orientation, the Architectural faculty was important as a centre of innovation during the 1920s. The progressive staff were often simultaneously teaching either on other VKhUTEMAS courses or in other architectural schools. Aleksandr Vesnin, for example, taught drawing and colour for seven hours a week in the Woodwork faculty, while El Lissitzky taught principles of architecture in the Dermetfak;[125] Ladovskii and Krinskii both also taught in the Basic Course, and Moisei Ginzburg taught architectural history and theory at the Moscow Higher Technical School (Moskovskoe vysshee tekhnicheskoe uchilishche — MVTU).[126] Whilst there was considerable interfaculty movement among the VKhUTEMAS staff, the archival material does not suggest that it extended to the students. Beyond the time they spent in the Basic Course, the architecture students, for example, did not co-operate practically or theoretically with those in the Wood and Metal Workshops of Dermetfak, who were examining the problems of interior and furniture design. This was merely one case of a central problem underlying the whole school's existence.

This lack of unity among the VKhUTEMAS faculties was also attributable to a fundamental difference of artistic allegiance among the teaching personnel of the school, who were divided essentially into three camps. In 1923 *LEF* categorised these in the following way.

> *The Purists* [easel painters] (Shevchenko, Lentulov, Fedorov, Mashkov, Fal'k, Kardovskii, Arkhipov, Korolev, etc.)
> *The Applied artists* (Filippov, Favorskii, Pavlinov, Nivinskii, Sheverdyaev, Egorov, Norvert, Rukhlyadev, etc.)
> *The Constructivists* and *Productivists* (Rodchenko, Popova, Lavinskii, Vesnin and others)[127]

Each group naturally had a very different concept of what the VKhUTEMAS should be and struggled to secure the realisation of their particular artistic ideology. The VKhUTEMAS was therefore prey to a constant struggle between them, especially in the initial three years. *LEF* described this struggle and the tactics the Constructivists had to employ.

The purists strive for the complete separation of the production faculties from 'sacred' art, which the applied artists resist in conjunction with the Constructivists and the Productivists.

The position of the Constructivists and the Productivists is extraordinarily complicated. On the one hand they have *to fight the purists* to defend the Productivist line, on the other, they have *to press the applied artists*, in an attempt to revolutionise their artistic consciousness.[128]

By 1923 the deterioration of the situation and the inauguration of reform proceedings, prompted the publication of a declaration signed by Brik, Rodchenko. Lavinskii, Tarabukin, Stepanova, A. Vesnin, Babichev, Popova, the Stenberg brothers and Medunetskii. This statement announced that 'the ideological and organisational *breakdown of VKhUTEMAS* is an accomplished fact' because it is 'cut off from the ideological and practical tasks of the present, and from the future of proletarian culture'.[129] The document proceeded to present an outline of actual conditions in the various departments.

The production faculties are empty. The machines are being sold off or are being leased. The staff is being reduced.

To make up for this, the individual painting and sculpture studios for second and third rate artists and easel painters are blossoming luxuriantly.

The Graphics faculty, one of the most important for the Productivists, has been specially marked out, and given the same status as the 'fine' art faculties; moreover, the main emphasis is on craft, hand-work fields – etching, engraving – while the mass, machine and modern work are kept in the background.

The Basic Division, where the preliminary training of the young students takes place, is completely in the hands of the 'purists', easel painters from the Wanderers to the Cézannists. There is no talk about production. There is no whiff of any kind of social task. No posters, caricatures, social satire, or grotesque depictions of everyday life – only timeless, spaceless, partyless, 'pure', 'sacred' painting and sculpture, with its landscapes, still lifes and naked models.

Rabfak is in the same position.[130]

The document ends with eight demands which the Constructivists hoped would deal with the 'artistic reaction' that had manifested itself in the VKhUTEMAS and with the re-emergence of bourgeois artistic concepts, especially that of easel painting, and would set the school back on the true Constructivist and Productivist path.

1. To reduce significantly the 'pure' half of VKhUTEMAS and expand the production side.
2. To amalgamate the industrial faculties, and to include in this the Graphics faculty.
3. To reorganise the Graphics faculty, and to exclude from it all mysticism and handicraft.
4. To establish the teaching of the social forms of fine art in the Painting faculty such as the poster, the caricature, the grotesque depiction of everyday life, cartoon and satire.
5. To introduce the compulsory teaching of the basic production disciplines into the syllabuses of Rabfak and the Basic Division.
6. To link VKhUTEMAS with centres of the State economy and political education.
7. To organise within VKhUTEMAS a systematic method of dealing with orders for the execution of practical artistic tasks.
8. To make the productivists equal to the 'purists' in diploma rights, and give them the name engineer-artist.[131]

This document was evidently the product of a meeting at INKhUK because it is signed by the Constructivists as members of INKhUK, and it relates to the reorganisation of VKhUTEMAS that was currently being considered by the chief administration for professional education. This declaration was almost certainly intended to exert some influence upon the course that reorganisation would take, and by presenting their position in this way the Constructivists were obeying *LEF*'s injunction to assert their ideas. As such, the document may not be free from a certain degree of tactical exaggeration and dramatic hyperbole. However, the complaints of the *Lefovtsy* may not have been exaggerated. In 1927, when yet another reorganisation of the Institute was underway, Novitskii admitted that 'until recently, despite its name .... the VKhUTEMAS gave too much attention to "pure" art, mainly painting'.[132] This fine art emphasis was apparent in the numerical distribution of the students. In 1924 the school contained 1,445 students, of which the largest number, 463, were studying in the Basic Division, 242 were in architecture, 364 in painting, 72 in sculpture, 137 in graphics, 81 in textiles, 47 in ceramics, 22 in Derfak and 17 in Metfak.[133] In this context the two documents in *LEF* together merely emphasise the extent to which the Constructivists had to fight for such areas of dominance as they had in this pluralistic school. That dominance was most successfully asserted in the Basic Course and the Wood and Metalworking faculty, Dermetfak.

THE BASIC COURSE

The Basic Course was perhaps the major achievement of VKhUTEMAS and that aspect of its activity which reflected the influence of INKhUK most clearly. In its underlying conception and specific programmes, the Basic Course reflected both the Institute's early scientific investigation of artistic criteria and its later Constructivist orientation towards the synthesis of this science of art with technological and social functions, which was to comprise the discipline of the 'artist-constructor'. Irrespective of what their future training would be, the Basic Course provided VKhUTEMAS students with 'the bases of a general artistic education':[134] a sound grounding in theoretical and practical work with the elements of artistic form, and the fundamentals of spatial relationships. INKhUK, moreover, explicitly claimed a 'close organic relationship, with VKhUTEMAS and with the Basic Course in particular:

> The vast majority of the Institute's members are also professors at the VKhUTE-MAS. Their practical work in the studios is inevitably and naturally conducted in ideological union and dependence on INKhUK. That hard line of conduct, that friendship and solidarity of the left professors of VKhUTEMAS is undoubtedly based on the situation outlined above.
>
> Moreover, besides the formal working out of the programmes for the workshops, INKhUK itself took part in the work of VKhUTEMAS. The very principle of the disciplines, introduced at the VKhUTEMAS, was worked out at INKhUK, precisely at the time when the Institute was concentrating its attention on the basic problems of easel painting. Finally the organisation and work of the pedagogical section of INKhUK is a result of this connection – its establishment was dictated by natural necessity.[135]

The closeness of the relationship between the two institutions is emphasised by the fact that some students from the production faculties of VKhUTEMAS are also known to have been members of INKhUK and to have attended INKhUK meetings. It is known, for instance, that in March 1922 Rodchenko invited his students to an INKhUK meeting at Brik's flat.[136] A rather disrespectful poem appears to have resulted from this meeting, suggesting that caution should be observed before attributing to INKhUK an undue influence over the student body.

The VKhUTEMAS students went to visit INKhUK
They arrived hungry and angry ... they weren't interested
in Boris Kushner's long talk about wrapper dresses.

They decided: INKhUK members are pseudo-constructivists.
And wrapper dresses are a bourgeois enterprise.
We advise the members of INKhUK to take themselves in hand.

We will not tolerate it, if at INKhUK,
to Anatolii Borisov's paper on palmistry,
INKhUK ladies come in wrapper dresses and gowns,
And Brik, Mayakovskii and Babichev in badly fastened trousers.[137]

The VKhUTEMAS embodied an altogether less frivolous more professional approach. The aim of the Basic Division was therefore to provide a 'general artistic and practical, scientific, theoretical, social and political education, and to provide a system of knowledge essential for the specialist faculties'.[138] It consequently consisted of three educational strands: the study of those 'basic artistic disciplines which organise a work of art, their practical application in specialised industries, and the fundamentals of a specialised and professional education'.[139] Therefore in addition to the purely artistic and practical subjects, all students received tuition in chemistry, physics, mathematics, geometry, the theory of shadows, military training, scientific theory of colour, a foreign language and the history of art.[140] It should, of course, be stressed that a large part of each student's training was occupied by this diverse range of studies. Of greatest interest in the present context, however, are those aspects of the VKhUTEMAS education that reflected emerging conceptions about the proper training for the new 'artist-constructor'. In the Basic Course this was expressed in the attempt to evolve a systematic and objective method for inculcating an understanding of the artistic elements, both separately and in terms of their interrelationships, as an essential artistic basis for the synthetic activity required in later specialisation. This is therefore the focus of my description.

THE EVOLUTION OF THE BASIC COURSE

It is exceedingly difficult to establish the precise content and structure of the artistic and practical aspects of the one year Basic Course which was given for the first three years of the Basic Division's existence. In 1920 there seem to have been five disciplines (*distsipliny*); 'the idea was to study each in turn so that an exclusive circle resulted'.[141]

1. Maximum revelation of colour – Popova
2. Revelation of form through colour – Osmerkin and Fedorov (Cézanne)
3. Simultaneity of form and colour on the plane – Drevin
4. Colour on the plane (Suprematism) – Klyun
5. Construction – Rodchenko[142]

As INKhUK had stressed, the disciplines were based on the type of formal and objective investigation into and analysis of artistic elements and compositional principles carried out by the Institute. 'Each task must present and solve an aspect of those factors which form the synthesis of the work of art ... each task forms a part and not the whole, and is therefore analytical and not formal.'[143]

These disciplines, as is evident from their titles, were based almost entirely on the art of painting, although reflecting the emerging terminology of Constructivism. Even Rodchenko's discipline entitled Construction (*Konstruktsiya*) concentrated on those artistic elements related to the creation of a two-dimensional work of art. His programme of 1921[144] for the discipline consisted of two sections: the construction of forms and colour, and the construction of painterly space. The first part included exercises in structure using diagonals, pyramids, verticals, horizontals and their combinations, as well as exercises in colour (such as harmony, contrast, their interrelations) and exercises based on working with form and colour to produce a construction (as, for example, depth by using colour). According to Galina Chichagova, who was taught discipline no. 5: Construction by Aleksandr Rodchenko on the Basic Course at the VKhUTEMAS in *c*.1920, the still life that Rodchenko first presented to them consisted of a piece of plywood, a lacquered square, to the right a bent figure from aluminium, a piece of rolled white paper and a grey photographic developing tray shot with blue. In the foreground was a frosted glass ball.[145]

The second section of Rodchenko's programme was divided into three parts: form, colour and *faktura*. The exercises with form involved the depiction of structures with two horizontal centres, or two vertical centres, a linear construction in contrast to a plane, or a linear construction as a structural skeleton. The exercises in colour consisted of colour constructions based on colour contrast, interrelationships of colour and textural contrasts, related colour intensities, etc. Those in *faktura* consisted of instruction in the textural working of a surface (relief, washes, polishing, scratching), the effects of weight, intensity, depth, lightness provided by such processing, and the application of the contemporary mechanics of painting (the use of new instruments).

These obviously overlapping and stylistically based disciplines were reorganised some time during 1921 or 1922, reflecting the theoretical changes at INKhUK in their greater commitment to Constructivism. The content was expanded and systematised to reflect an increasing concern with the problem of three-dimensional form, but at the same time the total number of disciplines was reduced to four:

1. Colour construction taught by Aleksandr Vesnin and Lyubov' Popova
2. Spatial construction taught by the architects Dokuchaev, Krinskii and Ladovskii
3. Graphic construction taught by Rodchenko, Kiselev and Efimov
4. Volumetric construction taught by Lavinskii[146]

It was important that, although separated, these disciplines were intended in a more explicit way than before to synthesise into a complete approach. 'Each discipline is not isolated from the others, but is as one element of a unified complex, where all the disciplines mutually amplify and elucidate each other, solving a general compositional task with the specific formal means of each discipline.'[147]

By 1923 these disciplines had been reorganised into three foci of study or *kontsentry*: plane and colour (*ploskostno-tsvetovoi*), volume and space (*ob'emno-prostranstvennyi*), and space and volume (*prostranstvenno-ob'emnyi*). The plane and colour *kontsentr* included all the disciplines relating to painting and graphics, colour and line on a two-dimensional surface, i.e. the former disciplines of colour construction and graphic construction. The volume and space *kontsentr* consisted of all disciplines related to three-dimensional form in a sculptural and plastic way (i.e. volumetric construction), and the *kontsentr* of space and volume dealt with architectural disciplines, formerly spatial construction.[148] Sometime between 1923 and 1925 these *kontsentry*, while remaining three in number, had been reorganised and relabelled colour and plane (*tsveto-ploskostnoi*), graphics (*graficheskii*) and volume and space (*ob'emno-prostranstvennyi*).[149] This structure was also operational in 1927.[150] However, between 1927 and 1929 a further reorganisation of the *kontsentry* took place so that by 1929 there were four *kontsentry*: space (*prostranstvennyi*), volume (*ob'emnyi*), colour (*tsvetovoi*) and graphics (*graficheskii*).[151]

Whatever its internal changes, the aim of the Basic Division was consistently to give 'the new student the knowledge and skills of artistic *masterstvo*, being general to all the fine arts, and the basis for the new synthetic art'.[152] For this reason during the first year the students studied the minimum programme for all the *kontsentry*.[153] Specialisation only began in the second year when students took the maximum programme of the *kontsentr* related to their chosen specialisation.[154] Students in painting, graphics and textiles studied in the plane and colour *kontsentr*; students in metalwork, woodwork, sculpture and ceramics worked in the volume and space *kontsentr*; architectural students worked in the space and volume *kontsentr*.[155] The method of teaching employed was 'collective according to which the tasks and methods of solution are worked out by a subject committee in the presence of a student representative. In order to systematise the tasks, practical links are established between the *kontsentry* and in the second year between the disciplines and industry.'[156] The students' work was also judged collectively by the staff with the whole workshop present.[157] Since the disciplines had been a prototype stage for the *kontsentry*, it is most appropriate to discuss the Basic Course's detailed content in terms of the latter.

THE PLANE AND COLOUR *KONTSENTR*

The plane and colour *kontsentr* was orientated towards the study of the properties of colour, the relationship between colour and form and between volume and mass both in space and on the plane. The teachers of the course included K. Istomin, A. Drevin, N. Udal'tsova, L. Popova, A. Vesnin, A. Osmerkin, E. Mashkevich, G. Fedorov, V. Khrakovskii, A. Ivanov, P. Sokolov, I. Zav'yalov and V. Toot.[158] The chief member of the subject committee was K. Istomin, and later V. Khrakovskii.

In 1923 the *kontsentr* combined all the graphic and painting disciplines; however, by 1925 the graphic disciplines had been organised into a separate, independent *kontsentr* – the graphics *kontsentr*. Prior to their amalgamation in 1923, colour had been taught in the discipline of colour construction under the direction of A. Vesnin and L. Popova. The aim of this discipline had been to teach 'colour as an independent organisational element, and not as figurative, optical decoration; to take it as an element to its utmost concreteness'.[159] It therefore consisted of an analysis of the qualities of colour (tone, weight, tension, relations to other colours, the working of pigment to realise colour), and its interrelationship to other artistic elements (i.e. line, plane, construction and *faktura*). The more elaborate programmes of the *kontsentr* developed from the basis of Popova and Vesnin's programme.

The scientific and theoretical study of colour in its optical manifestations was pursued in the physics course.[160] The plane and colour *kontsentr* concentrated on the purely painterly or artistic aspects of the manifestations of colour.

The plane and colour *kontsentr* must acquaint the student with typical examples of figurative surfaces, and with their formal nature; it must make it apparent that every surface has its inherent colour form, figuration and composition. In this way it is essential to acquaint the student with the surfaces of volumes, moving surfaces and planes.
1. The surface of a mass. Here the main task is that colour gives a particular quality to the surface of an object with the aim of conveying qualities of abstraction or materiality to our perceptions.
2. A moving surface (fluid). Its formal nature, the fluid nature of perception, in principle boundless, the absence of depth and clearly expressed two-dimensionality must all be examined. The form of colour peculiar to particular surfaces must be elucidated. The figuration of such surfaces will be constructed in volumes, and the composition – on the axes of the stretching surfaces or on the axes of the central volumes.
3. The principles of figurative surfaces must be taught, i.e. that it is limited in principle, by limits both vertical and horizontal and with an evident prevalence of vertical limitations. The limitation of the surface gives it a visual completeness in our perception; such a surface is therefore visual. The main theme of such figurative surfaces will be space.

It is essential to show the compositional principles governing all the above mentioned surfaces.[161]

Hence the types of problem given to students to solve included that of co-ordinating colours spatially in relation to figurative planes, and in relation to light sources; colour on static and moving surfaces; the introduction of a static element on to moving coloured surfaces; the transformation of a moving coloured surface into a static one and vice versa. Students also examined the interrelationship between line and colour, and angle and colour (see colour plates IV–VI). Moreover, these tasks were related to the manifestation and use of colour in historical works of art such as medieval painting and Egyptian fabrics and sarcophagi.[162]

It is clear from this evidence that, although much of the formal analysis had continued from Vesnin's and Popova's initial syllabus, the accent of the plane and colour *kontsentr* as taught was on precisely those figurative qualities of colour which Vesnin and Popova had eschewed. At the 1926 Academic Conference the Basic Division made this orientation explicit, by stating that this course concentrated on the interrelationship between colour and natural form and the problem of the transmission of this form onto the canvas, and stressing that the method employed was *realisticheskii* – realist.[163]

THE GRAPHICS *KONTSENTR*

The graphics part of the plane and colour *kontsentr*, which later became the independent graphics *kontsentr*, was taught by Rodchenko, Bruni, Miturich, Pavlinov, Gerasimov and Sherbinovskii.[164] The course, formulated by Pavlinov and Favorskii and accepted by the graphics *kontsentr*, was initially based on the programme of the graphic construction discipline taught by Rodchenko, Kiselev and Efimov, and consisted of the formal analysis of graphic elements. 'The course acquaints the student with the graphic elements and their properties (the line, the point, the spot), and with the compositional approach to the linear design of a surface.'[165]

In accordance with this aspiration the course was divided into four sections:

1. the line and the point
2. the static line
3. the two-dimensional plane (the spot)
4. volume: the representation of volume[166]

Each task was tackled in black and white and then in colour. Special tasks were devised with particular relevance to the material that would be the predominant concern of particular faculties. For instance there were tasks related to the use of line with clay for the Ceramics faculty, and with wood for the Woodworking faculty.[167]

In his speech to the Academic Conference in 1926, Pavlinov stressed the fact that 'the drawing programme is built on the bases of an objective formal method' and that 'the weight of the programme lies in the construction of a constructive volume'.[168] However, he also made it clear that the course by this time had a firmly figurative content. The aim of the course was, he asserted, to develop to a maximum the student's active perception of nature in the structure of a realistic drawing.[169] In this it reflected Pavlinov's view that the complex psychological process of drawing consisted of two aspects: the organisation of the conception and the organisation of the depiction which had to be taught simultaneously.[170] By 1926 the course concentrated on the 'construction of constructive volumes' and, therefore, beginning with the principles for the depiction of an isolated object, it led the student to an understanding of space and its depiction in the following sequence: mass and construction; volume, groups of volumes; space.[171] 'Each task emphasises the elucidation of one or another of the elements of drawing – mass, weight, volume, etc. – and in this sense, sets itself up as a training model.'[172] The first task was to depict the structure of the mass of an extended object, in its simplest organisational form. For this purpose the example of the human figure was taken and the students studied the distribution of mass along the various axes, the way it moved and its concentrations.[173]

Initially to promote the perception of nature and the basic principles governing its depiction, quick five- to ten-minute drawings were made, using a variety of media (watercolour, pen and ink, etc.). These gave way to more prolonged studies of several hours duration. For example, the second exercise consisted of two-hour drawings of the figure concentrating on the compositional organisation of the paper's surface in relation to the depth of the form depicted. The third exercise consisted of four-hour drawings made from nature, which synthesised the previous two exercises.[173] The students then progressed to the structure of volumes. 'In so far as mass was understood chiefly as quantity, i.e. from within, volume, which is produced from mass by the formation of the surface of mass, is understood through the inner movement according to this surface.'[174] In order to study these qualities the students used first plaster casts, then the head of a living model, and finally a partially nude figure. In these studies the volume of the complete object was stressed as opposed to its structure or function. The fourth task in the series was intended to cultivate the perception of spatial relationships in their entirety and therefore consisted of the study of a group of volumes (figurative or abstract), each individual volume being considered not only in its internal complexities but in relation to the group as a whole and as part of the internal volumetric and spatial relationships of this whole. The graphics course ended with an examination of the principles and methods by which space was depicted on a two-dimensional plane. This consisted almost entirely of exercises in perspective, foreshortening and perspectival relationships.[175] The course had thus provided a formal vocabulary which could in theory have been utilised in both realistic and non-realistic representation, since abstract studies were included among the exercises, using figurative elements. Ultimately, however, in actuality the course, at least from c. 1923, was firmly linked with non-abstract, figurative art.[176]

THE VOLUME AND SPACE *KONTSENTR*

The volume and space *kontsentr* taught the artistic disciplines related to volume and space and their interrelationships.[177] The staff, consisting mainly of sculptors who did not teach in the production faculties, included Iodko, Korolev, Chaikov, Niss-Gol'dman and Lavinskii.[178] The syllabus of the *kontsentr* was based on the former discipline no. 4 of 1922, volumetric construction, which had studied form in its three-dimensional manifestation. This had included the transmission of three-dimensional form onto the two-dimensional canvas; the study of volume as the sum of painterly elements (colour, plane, surface, texture, space, line); the interrelationship of volume and space; space as a part of a structure; the spatial plane and its qualities; and the study of shadows.[179]

The aim of this *kontsentr* was 'to acquaint the student with the structure of three-dimensional bodies ... and to convey an awareness of the determined relations of the tensions, as reproduced and observed in material'.[180] The teaching programmes and exercises reflected this aim. According to one programme the investigation of volume began with exercises concerning the three-dimensional structure of volume.[181] Using simple three-dimensional geometric bodies (the cube, cylinder, plane), the students examined the nature of relief and the principles governing volumetric composition. From this they progressed to studying the interrelationship of volumes, the nature of mass as the quantity of material from which volumes are composed, weight as the interrelationship of the parts of a volumetric body, the plastic axes of movement which co-ordinate the movement of the individual parts of the composition, and the nature of this movement and rhythm within a given volume.[182] The exercises were related to simple geometrical bodies, then to more complex forms (still lifes of simple objects such as jugs) and ultimately to the complex geometry of completely organic forms.[183]

THE SPACE AND VOLUME *KONTSENTR*

The teaching programmes of the space and volume *kontsentr*, ultimately known as simply the space *kontsentr*, were the work of the architects N. Ladovskii, N. Dokuchaev and V. Krinskii.[184] The course was taught by these members of staff together with others including Turkus, Lamtsov and Balikhin (who later became head or *dekan* of the whole Basic Division in the last phase of its existence).[185] The course aimed 'to give a formal basis to the spatial arts (to architecture and to those production, decorative and fine arts connected with it), to develop a perception of spatial forms, and to provide the fundamental compositional skills for their organisation'.[186] Professor Krinskii, who chaired the subject committee, defined the *kontsentr*'s task as 'the systematic study of the properties of large forms, the properties of their clarification, and the principles of their organisation in specific conditions'.[187] An early programme of the *kontsentr* indicated that the essence of the course consisted of examining the means by which space was defined (e.g. superimposition), and the means by which it could be transformed (methods of expansion, contraction, widening, lengthening, etc.).[188] By 1926 this programme

4.6. Example of a student solution to the problem of frontal composition (*frontal'naya kompozitsiya*) in the space *kontsentr*, undated photograph. [Reproduced in Krinskii, et al., *Elementy*, 1934.]

4.7. Example of a student solution to the problem of volumetric composition (*ob'emnaya kompozitsiya*) in the space *kontsentr*, undated photograph. [Reproduced in Krinskii, et al., *Elementy*, 1934.]

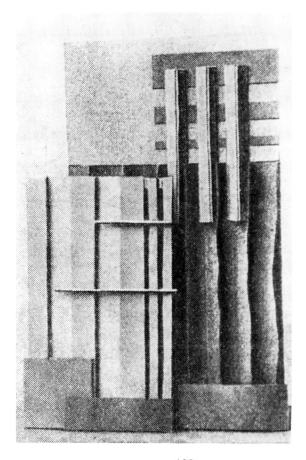

128

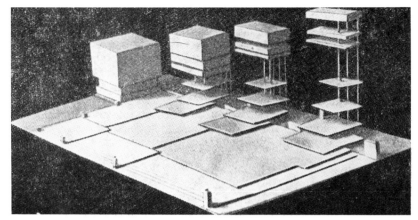

had been elaborated and organised into four main parts.[189] The first part concerned types of forms and their properties (the geometric aspect of forms, size, their position in space, mass, *faktura*, colour, lighting). Each of these properties was examined together with its possible alterations. Subsequently the student studied the basic principles governing the construction of spatial forms. These comprised primarily scale (as an expression of the size of a form and its relationship to man), unity (as the organisation of the form from the point of view of a moving observer) and intensity.[190] Students then progressed to a study of formal relationships and proportions, which included an examination of the factors of rhythm, dynamism and stasis, weight and proportion.[191] Finally the students studied the principles and methods of composition in space which included frontal composition of a flat surface, volumetric composition and composition using spatial depth.[192] The Architectural faculty's book, published in 1927, described some of the teaching exercises. The first exercise was to produce an expressive flat surface as the simplest type of surface. In this the surface was understood as a two-dimensional form that faced the observer frontally and was of minimal thickness. The surroundings were not to be taken into consideration. This was intended to be an exercise which dealt with composition in its most static and hermetic form. The second exercise concerned the creation of an expressive volume and thus developed and elaborated the conditions governing the first exercise. Volume being understood as the three-dimensional form perceived as the observer moves around it, the elements of volume were not independent but inter-dependent entities, which formed the centre of the system created by the movement of the observer. The third exercise was directed at creating an expression of a volume's weight and mass, demonstrating mass as the basic impression of a form and the visual tensions created by weight and support in a form. The fourth exercise demanded that the student create an expressive form defining space and then distribute additional forms within that space. Thus the student revealed the depth of a given space, its relationship to the main form, and the relationship of that form to the surrounding space and forms. All these exercises were executed in three-dimensional models. Fortunately examples have been preserved of students' solutions to exercises in this *kontsentr*. Reproduced here are solutions to the problem of frontal composition (plate 4.6), volumetric composition (plate 4.7), rhythm in space (plate 4.8), and space in depth (plate 4.9).[193]

In this way the disciplines and then the *kontsentry* of the Basic Division, although later often oriented towards more figurative ends, provided the student with an artistic vocabulary and grammar as his preparation for specialisation and the acquisition of specialised artistic and technological knowledge and skills essential for the 'artist-constructor'. Of all the production faculties, that which came the nearest to achieving the fusion of the artistic and the technical was the Dermetfak.

4.8. Example of a student solution to the problem of rhythm in space (*ritm v prostranstve*) in the space *kontsentr*, undated photograph. [Reproduced in Krinskii, et al., *Elementy*, 1934.]

4.9. Example of a student solution to the problem of the composition of deep space (*glubinno-prostranstvennaya kompozitsiya*) in the space *kontsentr*, undated photograph. [Reproduced in Krinskii, et al., *Elementy*, 1934.]

129

DERMETFAK – THE WOOD AND METALWORK FACULTY

In 1926 the Woodwork faculty (Derevoobrabatyvayushchii fakul'tet) was merged with the Metalwork faculty (Metalloobrabatyvayushchii fakul'tet) to form the combined Dermetfak.[194] The staff of the Dermetfak included many of the major Constructivist figures. Rodchenko, who became the deputy head or *prodekan* of the Metfak (Metalwork faculty) in 1922,[195] was responsible for formulating the artistic programmes of that department and in the new Dermetfak continued to teach artistic design (*khudozhestvennoe proektirovanie*).[196] Gustav Klutsis, who had taught colour theory in the Woodwork faculty from 1924, continued to do so in Dermetfak, where he also helped to teach the space discipline.[197] Lamtsov taught spatial theory.[198] Lissitzky, who had taught briefly at the VKhUTEMAS prior to his departure from the Soviet Union in 1921, joined the Dermetfak in 1926 to teach the formal principles of architecture (*formal'nye printsipy arkhitektury*), the design of furniture (*proektirovanie mebeli*) and the design (*oformlenie*) of architectural interiors.[199] In 1927 Vladimir Tatlin also joined the faculty and ran a course on the culture of materials (*kul'tura materialov*) and the design of separate items of everyday use (*proektirovanie otdel'nykh predmetov byta*).[200] Under his guidance, students produced a type of furniture which differed radically from that made under the influence of Lissitzky and Rodchenko.[201]

Derfak was set up on the basis of the carpentry and wood-engraving studios of the former Stroganov School and for a long time it reflected the craft-orientated nature of that training. Between 1920 and 1922 the artistic disciplines – the composition of furniture (I. N. Varentsov), the composition of wooden architecture (S. E. Chernyshev) and carving (N. K. Kruzhupov) – clearly demonstrated that tendency.[202] Composition of furniture, for instance, lasted four years, starting with very simple objects such as shelves and progressing to more complex furnishings and interiors. A great deal of attention was devoted to the decoration of surfaces and furniture styles. The composition of wooden architecture, of two years duration, concentrated on the internal organisation and external structure of wooden buildings, some of which were intended for permanent occupation, while others were of a more transient and decorative character such as exhibition pavilions. Carving, which lasted three years, was concerned with decorative panels, reliefs and architectural detailing. These disciplines were still directed towards producing applied artists. However, under the influence of new teachers such as Kiselev who became the *dekan* of Derfak in 1922 and Lavinskii who joined the staff in 1923, the syllabus changed in accordance with contemporary needs and introduced 'principles of mass machine production' with the aim of training 'highly qualified specialist organisers and constructors of objects for the wood industry – engineer-artists'.[203] Such engineer-artists were more specifically defined as furniture designers who would be able to organise the interiors of clubs, libraries and hostels and to design interiors for forms of transport and transport centres (train compartments, buses and stations), as well as devising light fitments and being able to work on standardisation.[204] The new programme had a strong technological basis, and consisted of four sections: scientific and technical disciplines comprising subjects such as technology of materials, study of materials, machines and production techniques; production disciplines which comprised trends and methods of contemporary industry such as principles of mass production, application of wood to new structures, the scientific principles of combination furniture and the furnishing of interiors, design of furniture and furnishing for housing, factories, state buildings and schools, the preparation of models and furnishings, the organisation and implementation of a project; economic disciplines such as the economics of factory administration and work organisation, accounting, conditions and the future of the wood industry; finally historical disciplines comprising art history, social history, 'the criticism of the fetishism of form', history of styles, and stylistic compo-

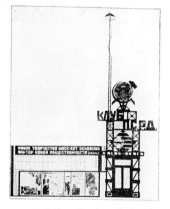

4.10. I. Lobov, Design of a façade for a workers' club, *c.* 1925.

4.11–12. B. Zemlyanitsyn, Design for interior of a workers' club, showing screens folded back to give access to stage and with screens extended to divide interior space for study groups, c. 1925.

sition.[205] By the mid-1920s these basic four sections had been expanded by the addition of a fifth section comprising abstract artistic work with volumes, which was taught by Lavinskii.[206]

In 1923 Lavinskii took over teaching the course on the composition of furniture now renamed the design of furniture - furniture construction (*proektirovanie mebeli - mebelestroenie*). Simultaneously he tried to establish a Constructivist method which would combat both Derfak's engineering bias and its decorative tendencies. The results of his work are most clearly evident in the designs which Derfak exhibited at the Exposition Internationale des Arts Décoratifs et Industriels Modernes held in Paris in 1925. These comprised designs and equipment for a rural reading room (*izba-chital'nya*) and an urban workers' club. The work was undertaken under the direction of Lavinskii and Chernyshev.[207]

The workers' club designs were only executed as drawings. They included the façade, which was intended to proclaim the club's function and thus be an agitational element (plate 4.10). The club's furnishings were intended to function within any given building and therefore were economical, frequently capable of performing several functions and folding up or extending. So, for instance, there were special showcases for literature which extended to divide the room in half (plate 4.11). Special bookcases were developed so that they could be closed up completely when not required or could be used for the display of books in a half-opened or fully opened way (plate 4.12). The concern to save space prompted the design for a coat rack capable of holding forty-eight coats, numbered (plate 4.13). Equally demonstrating this concern for the precise practical functioning of the club was the hexagonal reading table the central circular portion of which moved so that the books could be easily available to each of the six readers (plate 4.14). In the same way the rectangular table had a section which could be lowered or raised for reading, and flaps so that the size of the table could be adjusted for other purposes. These tables and chairs particularly, with their slender structural supports, demon-

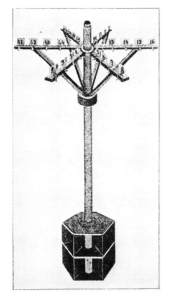

4.13. (above) E. Artamonov, Design for coat hanger for a workers' club, c. 1925.

4.14. (right) B. Zemlyanitsyn, V. Kul'ganov, Hexagonal and rectangular reading tables for a workers' club, c. 1925.

4.15. Derfak students making the model of the Rural Reading Room exhibited in Paris in 1925.

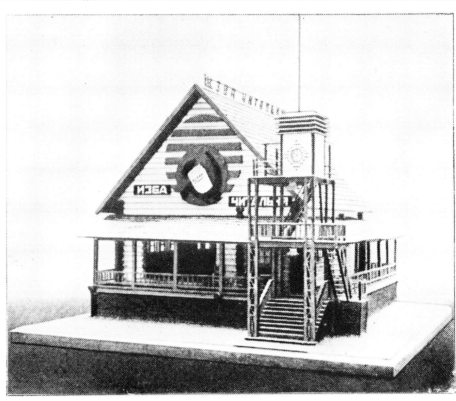

4.16. Model of the Rural Reading Room exhibited at the Exposition Internationale des Arts Décoratifs et Industriels Modernes, Paris, 1925. [Reproduced in *Exposition Internationales des Arts Décoratifs et Industriels Modernes, Catalogue*, Paris 1925.]

strate a great concern for economy, to the point of potential instability, which suggests that metal tubing might have been a more appropriate·material for their execution.

The rural reading room was actually made in model form (plates 4.15–16). It is far more indebted to tradition and in particular to the vernacular forms of Russian wooden architecture. Despite the industrial language of the tribune, clock and radio mast executed in wood, which again acts as an external advertisement of the

132

reading-room's function, the bulk of the building with its steep roof is heavily reliant on traditional building types. The tower and the provision of the veranda suggest a parallel with rural church architecture – a similarity which might have been a consideration in its design, since at this point the government and hence the Constructivists and VKhUTEMAS were concerned to replace the old ideology and way of life with the new. The fact that the building was coloured, painted white with red corners,[208] reinforces the similarity. It was decorated with a hammer and sickle and a book depicting Lenin's name. The reading room was intended to cater for 250 people.[209] The furniture inside was of a much less industrial nature than the exterior. The table which changed into a seat was based on traditional models (plate 4.17) and had a deliberately rustic quality. In contrast to the workers' club furniture the material was more emphatically wooden and it had a greater feel of solidity.

This feeling of solidity and the influence of traditional forms was also evident in the librarian's counter which could be rearranged to create a small stage (plate 4.18). The detailing on this particularly recalls a more decorative less rigidly functional impetus than in the table designs of the workers' club. It is more material and labour intensive than these. This is clear when it is compared to Lavinskii's own rural reading room design of 1925 where despite the structural exigencies of using wood, and therefore the need for a greater mass in furniture than when exploiting the greater tensile strength of metal, there is much greater geometric clarity in the structural elements of the furniture (plate 4.19).[210] There were Constructivist elements in Derfak's rural reading room design, such as the tower with its open skeletal framework and its asymmetrical disposition of functional elements; however, there were also remnants of a more eclectic approach. These suggest that by 1926 and its fusion with Metfak, Derfak was on the way to evolving a Constructivist design method but that such a method had not yet been fully established.

The Metfak was originally organised in December 1921 on the basis of the former jewellery studios of the Stroganov School of Applied Arts, from which it inherited both staff and students.[211] In 1922 Rodchenko took over the task of reorganising the studios, equipping them in a manner suitable to more utilitarian tasks, and formulating an entirely new curriculum.[212] He was concerned with the artistic aspect of design, and the technical aspect of the course was devised and taught by the engineer Malishevskii.[213]

The Metfak had two aims: 'to train highly qualified masters in designing and making items of everyday use which would be distinguished by their suitability to function, strength and beauty ... secondly ... these masters ... in industry must promote improvement in the quality of industrial products.'[214] In other words the Metfak was to produce 'artist-constructors' who would be 'constructors in the making of objects not in the applied sense, but "constructor-inventors" of new efficiently [tselesoobrazno] organised objects'.[215] With this aim in view, the Metfak had by 1926 established firm links with the State steel industry and machine shops where the students could have practical experience of mass production.[216]

The technical aspect of the course consisted of giving 'the student a clear understanding of the means and methods and of the industries working with metal ... secondly the ability to construct and design using the established formulas ... of the theoretical subjects; thirdly the ability to execute an exercise economically using a knowledge of the market with reference to an object and assortment of materials'.[217] The student therefore became acquainted with both the theoretical and practical aspects of working with metal, having received instruction relating to the physical and chemical properties of metal, together with instruction relating to, and practical experience of, specific processes such as galvanising, enamel work, casting, turning, forging, smelting, chasing and mounting. In addition the student was taught the rudiments of economics and accounting, which augmented the general instruction in political economy, social structure and communism.[218]

4.17. A. Kokorev, Design for a table which could be transferred into a seat for the Rural Reading Room, 1925.

4.18. S. Gorbachev, Design for a librarian's counter in the Rural Reading Room, which could be transformed into a stage, 1925.

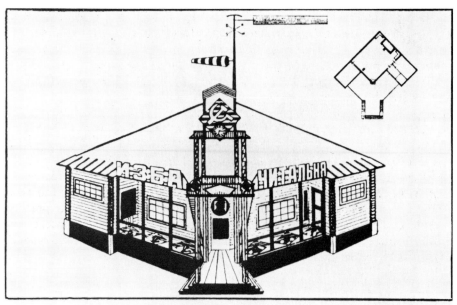

4.19. A. Lavinskii, Design for a rural reading room, 1925, exterior and interior. [Reproduced in *Sovetskoe iskusstvo*, No. 4/5, 1925.]

The artistic aspect of the course was initially formulated and taught by Rodchenko. It consisted of two main parts – the construction of objects: projects and models (*konstruirovanie veshchei: proekty i modely*), which was concerned with the working out and articulation of the object's form, and composition (*kompozitsiya*), which was concerned with the artistic treatment of the object's surface.[219] This delineation coincided with the twofold aim of the faculty to train 'highly qualified specialists for the metal producing industry in the field of the material formation of the object and the artistic treatment of the metal, having in view the application of this new knowledge and skill to a new culture of life and to the mass production of artistically designed goods'.[220]

Instruction in construction was intended to lead to 'the development of the student's resourcefulness and powers of observation and ultimately to the development of inventive initiative, or new means or methods in the matter of the material formation of the object'.[221] This 'inventive initiative' was only one element in the development of the skills and knowledge required for the material formation of the object. Rodchenko argued that 'the principles for the material formation of the object arise from the special purpose of the given object, the material, the production process, the inventive initiative, and the elements of the artistic treatment of

134

the external form'.[222] These methods of dealing with the treatment of the external form of the object were taught in composition. This artistic treatment was regarded as the 'unification of the principles of the external decoration of the object with the technical working of metal. Simplicity and coherence must be the principles governing this superficial working of the object's surface ... Unprincipled aesthetic decoration is strictly excluded.'[223]

In addition to these two approaches to the design of an object Rodchenko taught technical drawing as an essential basic skill for designers. The course of technical drawing was 'to develop an ability to draw quickly any object or detail in any position, its internal arrangement and its dynamic potential'.[224] In other words, it served the purpose of teaching a student how to look at an object, to remember the principles of its mechanism, the way it functioned and its structure, and to make him aware of the possibility of applying these principles to his own design practice.

By 1928 Rodchenko had evolved a system for combining these approaches and methods into a total comprehensive schema.[225] This consisted of seven tasks which the student was to execute:

1. The selection of ready made objects
2. The simplification of goods already in production
3. The elaboration of these
4. The creation of a new variant
5. Proposals for an entirely new product
6. Designs for a complete set of goods
7. Design for furnishing a complete building[226]

The first task was devised to make the student acquainted with existing products and to develop his critical faculties in relation to these objects and in so doing to develop his own ideas concerning the culture of objects. The student therefore had to select a series of existing products to furnish a housing unit or social area (e.g. shop, library, club, etc.), to photograph or draw these and to criticise them. In the second exercise the student was to concentrate on one existing object, 'remove the applied art and the non-working parts, reveal the basic construction and factual appearance and suggest a colour and textural solution'. During their practical work in the workshops the students were expected to execute their own designs. Also working with ready-made products (such as lamps) in the third task, students were expected to make the object's functional structure more complex, in order to make it more convenient to use and more modern in colour and texture, and to exploit new materials (for example making a lamp from metal that would extend). The fourth exercise required students to design a completely new type of an existing object (such as a knife or a teapot), to satisfy contemporary artistic and technical requirements (plate 4.20). The student was then expected to tackle the task of creating completely new objects to serve the needs of the new society. These needs were expressed in such problems as the equipment of Soviet co-operative shops, or traffic lights. This task developed into one of designing a series of objects (employing one principle of construction, material, colour and texture) for a building requiring a unified type of furnishing. The final exercise synthesised the experience acquired in the solution of the preceding design tasks in designing an interior complete in every detail. The type of interiors chosen related specifically to the requirements of the new Soviet State, and included such buildings as communal hostels, state and collective farms, libraries, auditoria and parks of culture and rest.[227] This final task formed the substance of the students' graduation project (*diplomnaya rabota*).

According to archive material these diploma projects were to be 'socially useful, consumer-efficient designed objects, satisfying the formal principles of creative activity, technical simplicity, functional efficacity [*tselesoobraznost'*], and economy of both execution and use'.[228] Specific projects executed included designing the interior for any mode of public transport, and the organisation of cultural bases at

4.20. Z. Bykov, Cooking utensils which collapse into a small package, *c*.1926. [Reproduced in *Sovremennaya arkhitektura*, No. 1, 1926.]

transport centres (exclusive of living or administrative accommodation). The latter was to be organised to satisfy the eating, sanitary and hygienic needs of passengers and to provide them with economic, cultural and purchasing facilities. The students were expected to provide detailed plans of equipment, furnishings, the internal distribution of space and projected plans of movement within the building.[229]

The characteristics which were to be sought in the solution of such tasks – clarity, simplicity of construction, effectiveness of its practical application and rationality in its production – also lay behind Dermetfak's investigation into the use of standardised units. Rodchenko had approached this problem in a purely artistic way in his non-utilitarian constructions when, working entirely with standard-sized pieces of wood, he had explored the variety of constructions that could be produced with them (plates 1.27–8). The use of the standard unit was therefore a part of the formal vocabulary of non-utilitarian Constructivism. Of course its importance in the design process derived pre-eminently from the techniques and economics of production. The rationalistic basis of the Constructivist credo demanded the most

4.21. A. Galaktionov, Designs for exhibition equipment composed entirely of standardised units (*vystavochnoe oborudovanie*), *c*. 1928. [Reproduced in *Daesh'*, No. 3, 1929.]

На путях
к стандарту

(ВЫСТАВОЧНОЕ ОБОРУДОВАНИЕ. ПРОЭКТ А. А. ГАЛАКТИОНОВА)

Высший художественно-технический институт (Вхутеин) выпустил в нынешнем году 12 инженеров-художников (металлистов), окончивших дерево- и металлообрабатывающий факультет.

Выпускникам было предложено несколько производственных тем для дипломных работ. В число этих тем входили: рационализированная кабинка аэроплана, оборудование плоучего дома отдыха, оборудование станции автобусного междугороднего сообщения, особо интересное оборудование зимнего поезда-тяговоза и т. д. Выполненные выпускниками работы представляют собою большой интерес с точки зрения практического применения изготовленных вещей.

Особенно интересной является работа выпускника **А. А. Галактионова**, представляющая собой оборудование торговых и выставочных помещений.

Оборудование это сконструировано так, что все оно состоит из железных труб, досок, кругов и соединительных частей. При чем все эти части являются стандартными.

Сборка оборудования не требует большой затраты рабочей силы.

Оборудование легко приспособляется под все виды товаров и удобно укладывается в транспортные клади. В оборудование входят: полки, витрины, столы, стойки, палатки и т. д., необходимые для выставки и продажи изделий и эксонатов, а также щиты.

Все комбинации оборудования, собирающиеся из стандартных частей, легко приспособляются к любому помещению. Непригодные части легко заменяются другими.

Если бы работа тов. **Галактионова** была реализована в виде специального производства стандартных частей оборудования, она оберегла бы много средств, тратящихся на оборудование недолговечных, и притом не всегда художественно совершенных, различного рода выставок.

На снимках показана в чертежах и макетах работа тов. **А. А. Галактионова**.

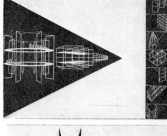

Стандартные элементы, из которых собирается выставочное оборудование.

Отв. редактор: **М. Костелевская** Изд. „РАБОЧАЯ МОСКВА".

Мособлит № 45.782. З. Т. 1.172. Тираж 14.000 О.т.в. в 7-й тип. „Искра Революции" Мосполиграф. Москва, Арбат, Филиповский пер. 13.

136

economic alternative to a given design problem, and the industrial ethic inherent in Constructivism was inevitably reasserted when confronted with problems of industrial manufacture. Under the conditions of the mid-1920s, all aspects of rationalisation and economy were part of the general currency of debate and the national reconstruction effort. A nationwide 'Regime of Economy' was launched by the Party Central Committee in June 1926, and was followed in March of the following year by another decree launching a campaign for the 'Rationalisation of Production' on all fronts.[230] For Constructivism, however, standardisation possessed the added attraction of stressing the impersonal aspect of design and minimising the role of subjective criteria. 'The establishment of standard units is the aspect which, limiting anarchic and individualistic methods of work, serves the task of bringing the artist closer to industry, and bringing the creative work of the artist into an organised and planned channel.'[231] An illustration of the type of work that was carried out in this field is the exhibition equipment designed by A. A. Galaktionov (plate 4.21), which consisted 'entirely of standardised

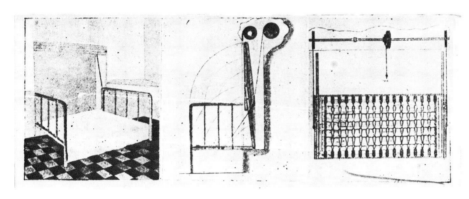

4.22. B. Zemlyanitsyn, Folding chair (*skladnoi stul*), 1927–8, made under the direction of Lissitzky in the latter's studio. [Reproduced in *Stroitel'stvo Moskvy*, No. 10, 1929.]

4.23. N. Sobolev, Design for a folding bed (*otkidnaya krovat'*), 1927–8. [Reproduced in *Stroitel'stvo Moskvy*, No. 10, 1929.]

4.24. B. Zemlyanitsyn, Combined cupboard and table for a hostel (*shkaf-stol dlya obshchezhitiya*), 1927–8. [Reproduced in *Stroitel'stvo Moskvy*, No. 10, 1929.]

steel tubes, panels, circles and connecting parts'.[232] Easily mounted and dismantled, the equipment could be used for displaying goods or exhibits, and was flexible enough to be easily adapted to any building. These standard elements formed window displays, chairs, circular and rectangular kiosks, and bookshelves of enormous variety.

In accordance with its commitment to meeting and answering contemporary needs in Soviet society, the Dermetfak paid particular attention to producing models of furniture that would save space, either by performing two or more functions in the home or by collapsing easily when not in use to maximise the limited living area available.[233] This space-saving preoccupation was determined by, and was a response to, the enormous housing shortage of the 1920s in the Soviet Union when it was quite usual for whole families to live in one small room.[234] One solution proposed to this urgent and basic problem was to design objects which fulfilled only one function but collapsed after use, such as Zemlyanitsyn's folding chair produced in the workshop of El Lissitzky (plate 4.22).[235] This item displays similarities with the Bauhaus approach to the use of industrial materials. However, it obeys the need for economy and the structural elements have been reduced to a minimum both in bulk and in number. Sobolev's folding bed (plate 4.23) also used metal so that with its greater tensile strength the structural components would be lighter and less cumbersome and would occupy less space than if made from wood.[236]

Dermetfak also produced more complicated items which could perform a dual function. These included Zemlyanitsyn's cupboard, the door of which could be lowered to form a table and when not required could be raised out of the way, liberating the space it had occupied for other purposes (plate 4.24).[237] One of the most complex of these multi-purpose items was Morozov's project of 1926 for a

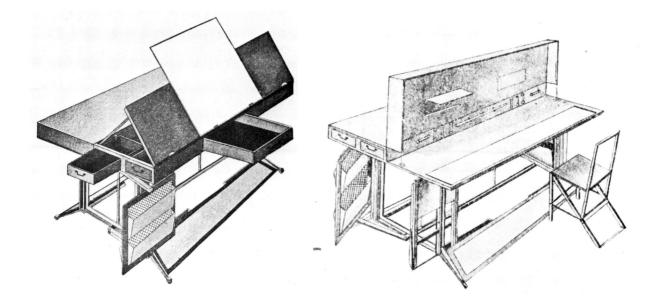

table which could serve as a draughtsman's desk, a writing desk and a dining table (plates 4.25–6). The lower part of the table provided storage for four folding chairs which could be brought out as required. Moving flaps containing pockets for storing papers and magazines were affixed to the lower supports. The top of one half of the table opened vertically to reveal a horizontal eating area. Eating utensils were stored in the vertical section: the horizontal section extended for eating. The table also contained an adjustable drawing board and a series of drawers for storing writing and drawing materials and instruments.[238]

These are sophisticated and well thought out solutions to the space-saving problem and their success and that of Dermetfak's course can be ascertained by comparing these designs with those which the same students executed earlier for the 1923 VKhUTEMAS exhibition. Two items from that exhibition, a folding bed by Galaktionov and a bed which doubled as a chair by Sobolev (plate 4.27), still refer very strongly to traditional concepts of furniture and in the case of Sobolev are materially and labour intensive. Comparison of these objects with later models by the same students, Sobolev's later folding bed (plate 4.23) and Galaktionov's exhibition furniture (plate 4.21) in particular, which were based entirely on standardised structural elements and could be easily and cheaply mass produced since they were economic both in terms of material and production time, emphasises the degree to which the Dermetfak students had, in fact, imbibed the principles of simplicity, clarity and economy and the extent to which they had developed their own 'inventive initiative'. These concerns and the reasons which gave rise to them continued to be operational throughout the 1920s and continued to characterise individual design items of the late 1920s, although Dermetfak's later course tended to concentrate on the design of total schemas for the entire organisation and furnishing of specific buildings.

From this account it would emerge that to a certain extent the VKhUTEMAS (the Basic Division and Dermetfak in particular) played a role in the development of modern design in the Soviet Union not dissimilar to that which the Bauhaus played in Germany. The personal links between the two institutions were not insignificant. Lissitzky taught at the VKhUTEMAS prior to leaving Russia in 1921 and after his return in 1926. During his stay in Germany he had considerable contacts with the German School and retained these, for within the Dermetfak he was the official consultant on foreign connections.[239] Kandinskii, who inaugurated INKhUK in 1920 and taught briefly at the Free Studios and the VKhUTEMAS, continued his pedagogical

4.27a–b. (below) Models of multi-functional furniture. A bed which also serves as an armchair by Sobolev and a folding bed by Galaktionov (*makety kombinirovannoi mebeli: Sobolev, krovat' – kreslo; Galaktionov: skladnaya krovat'*), c. 1923. [Reproduced in *LEF*, No. 3, 1923.]

СОБОЛЕВ. Кровать—кресло.

ГАЛАКТИОНОВ. Складная кровать.

practice at the Bauhaus.[240] By 1928 these personal links were ramified by the proposition of Hannes Meyer (then director of the Bauhaus) that a student exchange should be organised between the two institutions.[241] There is no evidence to suggest that this exchange became operational, but in 1930 Hannes Meyer accompanied by a small group of students went to work in Moscow.[242] The occasion was marked by an exhibition, the catalogue to which stressed the need for rectifying certain errors in the Bauhaus practice, among which was the lack of a firm ideological basis.[243]

* * *

The objects produced in Dermetfak embody the Constructivist approach in that the form of the object is determined by the material from which it is made, the use for which it is intended and the technological considerations of both its functioning and its system of initial manufacture. However, it should be stressed that as far as is known none of these prototypes was adopted for mass production. Although there were provisions in the course, especially in the summer practicals, for students to work in real industry, their primary experience of the implementation of their designs was inevitably in the faculties' workshops. This implementation was performed there under craft conditions and it did not therefore proffer the student any feedback upon his conception from the experience of real production constraints. There had been serious attempts to establish effective links with industry and to finance VKhUTEMAS by setting up a series of production workshops, of which Metfak had one employing six workmen.[244] However, lack of finance and capital prevented this blossoming into a full-scale industrial venture which would have been a substitute for the lack of direct production experience in design work.

4.28-9. Students working in the Derfak workshops during the 1920s.

This is not to say that the students did not eventually move on to work in an industrial context. As far as can be traced, the first designers trained in Dermetfak graduated in 1928. Of this class of twenty, only two went to work directly in factories. Four joined various experimental and organisation institutes. The others joined various industrial trusts and organisations connected with the wood, chemical and rubber industries.[245]

The people who taught these VKhUTEMAS courses that we have identified as the most 'Constructivist' in their orientation, that is the Basic Course and the Dermetfak, had taken various stands in INKhUK about what they considered the nature of the design task to be. The courses they taught were therefore programmatically devised to demonstrate the practical implications of their theoretical views. However, the random nature of the documentation preserved, and the chaotic disorder of post-Civil War life in Russia, make it quite impossible to attempt precise or detailed correlations between any particular person's theories and their courses.

Naturally, the Basic Course, as it was taught, particularly in the later years, by a very eclectic body of staff, became a curriculum that represented many and varying allegiances. Never did it lose, however, the fundamental structure which it had been given by the teaching staff who came to it from INKhUK. Fundamental to the Basic Course's whole conception were the structured disciplines, later preserved as *kontsentry*, which were organised according to formal artistic criteria and represented the training in an objective artistic vocabulary, which the Constructivists saw as the essential prerequisite for the artist-constructor. The purity of this analytical training was the main casualty of the dilution process.

Reinforcing this internal dilution process within the Basic Course itself were external factors operating within the wider school. As a result of the aesthetic pluralism of the school as a whole, the commitment to integrated education and the very concept of design were very unevenly distributed throughout the faculties. The weakness of interfaculty integration in the later years of the course clearly had a direct feedback upon the nature of the Basic Course itself. Nevertheless the Basic Course remained the only point of integration, and when it was finally dissolved in 1929 the dispersal of the faculties into independent entities was inevitable.

The Dermetfak offers a somewhat more close-up view of the relationship between theory and practice. On the basis of the present research, the one qualified exception to the general picture of poor and random documentation of teaching intentions is Rodchenko. In the evolution of his programmes for Dermetfak the operation of an interactive process whereby the factual experience of implementing a course led in turn to modifications of its theoretical bases was clearly visible. The sadness, in a sense, of the whole VKhUTEMAS experience was the extent to which this evolutionary process was crippled and distorted – in the end aborted – by the material circumstances in which it operated. The cyclical interaction of theory with practice, the feedback from one to another, was a positive element of the Constructivist view of the relationship between material design, in its very broadest sense, and the wider environment. Among the many factors which prevented this process ever achieving a 'correct' equilibrium were the disorder and disjointedness (caused by material scarcities) which necessarily accompanied lectures and workshop sessions, and which represented for many students the dominant reality of their training.

VII. L. Popova, Costume design for Actor No. 2 (*prozodezhda aktora No. 2*) in Crommelynck's play *The Magnanimous Cuckold*, 1921, watercolour, gouache and pencil on paper, 33 × 23 cm. Private collection, Sweden.

FOLLOWING PAGES

VIII. V. Stepanova, Designs for sports clothing (*sportodezhda*), 1923. [Reproduced in *LEF*, No. 2, 1923.]

IX. V. Stepanova, Textile design, *c.*1924, pencil, ink and gouache on paper. Private collection, Moscow.

Проэкты спорт-одежды

X. L. Popova, Textile design,
c. 1924, pencil and inks on paper.
23·4 × 19·1 cm. Private collection,
London.

5 THE OBJECT AND THE CONSTRUCTIVIST MICRO-ENVIRONMENT

CONSTRUCTIVIST research and education produced many designs but few finished objects. Even fewer were the items that had resulted from any approximation to the role of 'artist-constructor' as they had conceived it. The principal reason why few projects got beyond the drawing board was the material poverty that dominated all Soviet activity in the 1920s. Material and technological standards of a higher level were required for producing industrial prototypes than for producing drawn designs and traditional artworks. This factor was especially significant at the beginning of the decade, when industrial production was at a third of pre-war levels and only just beginning to recover from the disruption and devastation of the First World War and the Civil War.[1] The lack of material resources and equipment at VKhUTEMAS had affected the extent to which designs could be executed within the studios,[2] and outside of this specific institution there was little possibility for acquiring the necessary feedback or experience. Industry had not recovered sufficiently to have established studios to assist this process, neither had it been reorganised to make provisions for the role of the artist in the production process such as the Constructivists conceived. When Tatlin entered the New Lessner Factory, for example, in the early 1920s, he found it impossible to work because the system was geared either to technical specialists such as engineers or to applied artists who did not assist in the material formation of the product but merely added the decorative elements to an already formulated structure.[3] A contemporary commentator stressed this situation:

> The State in the form of Narkompros created a very large number of points of contact in the form of all those artistic and technical workshops ... yet, despite all these efforts, production has remained for art a complete mystery, and vice versa, with this difference, that art has been active and production passive.[4]

It has been widely asserted that the Constructivists' move into the factory and mass production was not successful, but it should be stressed that as far as is known only Tatlin, Stepanova and Popova did actually attempt to work in specific factories and to put their ideas concerning the role of the artist-constructor into practical operation. Tatlin's Lessner venture was not successful, but that of Stepanova and Popova in the textile industry was more so. This may be attributed to the fact that superficially their task did not differ significantly from that of the traditional concept of the applied artist working in this branch of industry. Although apart from textiles Constructivist designs were not mass produced and the Constructivists' attempt at direct engagement in industry was not successful, this does not diminish the value of the investigations themselves as efforts to realise their objectives, within the limited possibilities of the time.

The objects that will be examined in this chapter fall into several categories: textile and clothing design, furniture, agitational stands, kiosks and theatre. These were the potential components of a totally Constructivist environment, but only on the rarest occasions and under the artificial conditions of exhibition displays and theatrical sets were they ever able to be assembled into real prototypes of what that environment might be. Given the acuteness of the Soviet housing shortage during this period, Constructivists were not even able to transform their own living accommodation into concrete demonstrations of their design ideas. This chapter will not present an exhaustive examination of Constructivist designs. It seeks only to highlight those features of the objects concerned which are salient to the mainstream Constructivist view of the design process. Within an examination of the whole Constructivist movement and its evolution, the detailed enumeration of all known or extant designs would be out of place. Certain works by Tatlin have also been examined in the context of 'Organic' Constructivism in Chapter Seven. The examples discussed here are taken in ascending order of their physical scale.

DESIGNS FOR TEXTILES AND CLOTHING

The two categories of design for textiles and for clothing[5] are treated together because Popova and Stepanova, on the basis of their experience at the First State Textile Print Factory in Moscow (the former Tsindel' Factory),[6] formulated an approach to textile and clothing design that stipulated the close interdependence of the two activities.

As far as can be ascertained, only four Constructivists became involved in textile design and dress design: Rodchenko, Stepanova, Popova and Tatlin. Of these only Stepanova and Popova entered mass production and formulated a Constructivist approach and methodology to work in the area that correlated the two design processes. Neither Tatlin nor Rodchenko presented such a radical reassessment of the design process for cloth and clothing. Rodchenko did not synthesise the two

5.1. A. Rodchenko, Design for a cotton print (*sitets*), *c.* 1924. [Reproduced in *LEF*, No. 2, 1924.]

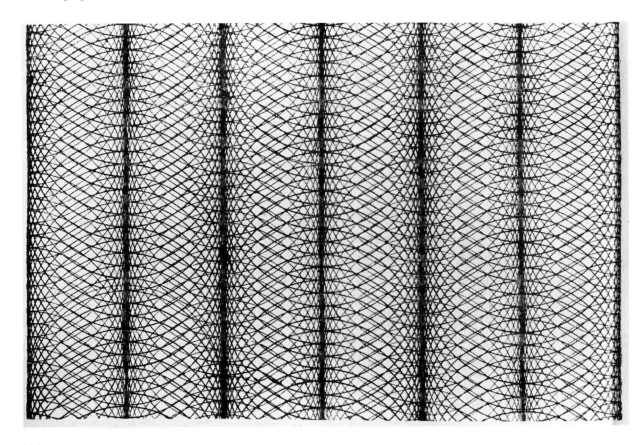

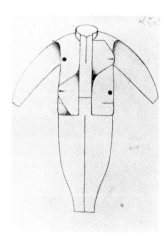

5.2. A. Rodchneko, Costume design for Glebov's play *Inga*, 1929.

processes although at different times he did produce textile designs (plate 5.1),[7] and was involved in creating designs for working clothes (plate 1.33)[8] and theatrical costumes (plate 5.2). The costume designs for *Inga*, in accordance with the contemporary nature of the play, were specifically devised to illustrate the move towards, rather than the achievement of, the rationalisation of clothing, and were in actuality overlaid with contemporary aestheticism.[9] Thus they represent a simplification of established clothing types rather than a postulation of radically new concepts.

Tatlin's work in the Department of Material Culture (Otdel material'noi kul'tury), which he ran at the Petrograd GINKhUK, was concerned with evolving prototypes of mass clothing as well as being involved in other areas of design. The aims of the department were expressed in its three basic areas of investigation: '(1) the investigation of material as the formative starting point of a culture, (2) the investigation of contemporary everyday life as a known form of material culture, and (3) the synthetic formation [*oformlenie*] of material and, resulting from such formations, the construction of models for the new everyday life'.[10] Tatlin's search for new forms for simple objects of everyday life led him to produce several new clothing designs, between 1923 and 1925, the most well known of which comprise a coat and a simple workman's suit (plate 5.3).[11] The coat was cunningly devised so that it could be used for all seasons, a removable flannel lining making it suitable for autumn and a fur lining for winter. The cut was wide over the shoulders and torso, tapering in towards the legs so that heat could not escape downwards, and the material did not cling but allowed air to circulate freely, conserving heat and preserving hygiene. The cut allowed for freedom of movement and natural positions: the pockets were placed according to the length of arms. The suit was designed according to similar principles.[12]

In both items Tatlin concentrated on ordinary working clothes which were based firmly on the volumes of the human body. There is an absence of any tendency to compress the human form into a geometrical format and there is no decoration. Tatlin evidently made serious attempts to promote these designs in the clothing industry, becoming a member of a Committee on Standard Clothing at the Decorative Institute in Leningrad in 1925 and possibly securing at least a nominal approval for the mass production of one of his designs.[13] However, there is no evidence that any of Tatlin's designs were in fact produced industrially. Equally there is no indication that Tatlin embarked upon the design of textiles. Although both he and Rodchenko presented clothing designs that offered solutions to the new social functions of clothing and that simplified existing formats, the more radical task of effectively rethinking the whole cloth and clothing design process within the framework of existing industry was performed mainly by Popova and Stepanova.

Both considered that the way to rationalise textile design was through linking it firmly with the principles governing dress design. Stepanova stressed their concept in an article of 1929.

> The basic task of the textile artist today is to link his work on textiles with dress design ... to outlive all the craft methods of working, to introduce mechanical devices ... to be involved in the life of the consumer ... and most importantly to know what happens to the cloth after it is taken from the factory.[14]

As Arkin pointed out, it was this approach, relating the decoration of cloth not only to the type of material used, but also to the exact purposes for which that material was intended, that made the work of Stepanova and Popova in the area of textile design not merely 'applied art', but design.[15] Therefore the textile designs of these two artists should be examined in relation to principles which they formulated for the design of clothing. Stepanova expounded their concepts in an article entitled 'Present Day Dress – Production Clothing'.[16] She completely rejected the pre-revolutionary concept of fashion which had stressed form and decoration and

organised material to achieve aesthetic effects regardless of the physical movements required in everyday life. In its stead she posited a concept of dress design in which the primary consideration was the function clothing was called upon to perform.

> Fashion which psychologically reflects a way of life, customs and aesthetic taste, gives way to clothing organised for work in different fields as defined by social movements, clothing which can *prove itself only in the process of working in it*, not presenting itself as having an independent value outside real life, as a special type of 'work of art'.[17]

Hence Stepanova argued clothing should not be regarded, as hitherto, in its static state on the model, but as an object which is in perpetual motion in the performance of a specific work task.

148

Today's clothing must be looked at in action, without this there is no clothing, just as a machine is meaningless without the work it produces.

The whole decorative and ornamental aspect of clothing is destroyed with the slogan '*comfort and the appropriateness of dress for a given productive function*'.[18]

As an essential expression of its modernity and functionalism this clothing designed for the masses was to 'turn from the craft system of production towards mass industrial production'.[19] In this way clothing would lose its 'ideological' significance and become a part of material culture.

The form of Constructivist designed clothing should therefore be determined only by the function the clothes must perform. In Stepanova's words:

In the organisation of modern dress it is necessary to go from the function to its material formation. From the special characteristics of the work for which it is designed to the system of the cut ... the form, i.e. the entire external appearance of the clothing, will become a form ... deriving from the requirements of the function and its material realisation [*osushchestvlenie*].[20]

Although aesthetic criteria were energetically dismissed as organising factors in the process of dress design, Stepanova did admit the existence of an aesthetic element within dress, but stressed that this emerged only as a by-product of this perfect adaptability of form to function, and the mode of production. 'The aesthetic elements are replaced by the process of production, the very sewing of the costume ... not the application of decoration to the costume, but the sewing itself, necessary to the cut, will provide the form of the costume.'[21] As the machine aesthetic derived from the aggregate of its logically functioning components and its overall suitability to function, clothing was also to be considered beautiful in as far as it possessed clarity, simplicity, functionality, economy of line and perfect accord between its interdependent and interfunctioning parts. On the basis of these criteria Stepanova classified clothing according to two basic categories: production clothing (*prozodezhda – proizvodstvennaya odezhda*) required for working, and sports clothing (*sportodezhda – sportivnaya odezhda*) for relaxation. *Prozodezhda* was defined as 'working clothes differentiated according to profession and industry'.[22] The danger of uniformity and monotony was overcome by the very variety of forms of work and industrial enterprises, which all demanded particular features within the overall schema.

Among the first practical realisations of such clothing were the work-suit which Stepanova made for Rodchenko (plate 5.2) and the actors' overalls which Popova designed for Meierkhol'd's production of *The Magnanimous Cuckold* in 1922 (colour plate VII).[23] Rodchenko's work-suit, resembling a jump-suit aggressively demonstrating its fastenings and its storage pockets, transformed these essential components into significant formal elements. Otherwise it was extremely simple, and economic in cut, sewing and material. It was a very specialised and individual garment. Popova's actors' overalls were more generalised. In executing the set and costume designs for the play Popova had set herself three tasks, one of which concerned *prozodezhda*.

Putting aside the aesthetic principle of the historical, national, psychological or everyday nature of clothing, in this particular task I wanted to find a general principle of *prozodezhda* for the professional work of the actor in connection with the essentials of his present professional role.[24]

Having rejected the decorative role normally assigned to theatrical costumes, Popova devised overalls which would facilitate the actor's movements on the stage. In doing this Popova approached the costumes as prototypes of production clothing and as functional components of the total Constructivist micro-environment which was created on the stage. As such the actors' working clothes could be regarded as an exercise within the specific context of the theatre which would have implications for the real environment.

In a manuscript entitled 'The Costume as an Element of the Material Design' which Popova wrote about this time and which explicitly relates to the production of *The Magnanimous Cuckold*, Popova elaborated this approach and outlined the method she had adopted in designing the costumes for the play. She stated that she had been governed by three major considerations which she regarded as the three crucial elements of dress design: the ideological, the analytical and the technical. These three obviously parallel the three principles of tectonics, *faktura* and construction.

The ideological aspect, for Popova, consisted of regarding 'the costume as a material element of the theatrical production as a whole, in relation to the other material elements ... in relation to the laws of biomechanics and as the product of the material design of the set according to the utilitarian principle.' The second or analytical aspect comprised 'analysing the costume as a plastic object into its constituent elements - its construction, its linear, volumetric and spatial form, its colour, texture, rhythm and movement'. The technical aspect consisted of 'studying the material and its mode of production'.[25] Of course, these last two aspects in particular provided a preliminary theoretical background for Popova's later work in the textile and clothing industry.

Accordingly the actors' costumes, designed to allow complete freedom of movement and facilitate the acrobatic and mechanistic actions of the actors, consisted of working overalls made of plain, unadorned blue material cut in a simple geometry based on the forms of the human body. This basic uniform - skirts for women and jodhpurs for men - was elaborated to differentiate the various personages, such as a cape for Actor No. 7 or goggles and a type of duffel coat for Actor No. 6, the Burgomaster. Such additions could hardly be described as decorative. They performed an identifying, rather than ornamental function. Stepanova's costume designs for Meierkhol'd's production of *The Death of Tarelkin*,[26] also in 1922 (plate 5.4), followed a similar pattern. 'The costumes, of a sporting cut, made from cloth of two colours, stressed flexibility, and the movement of the human body and were made without any specific theatrical decorativeness.'[27] Unfortunately the

5.4. V. Stepanova, Costume designs for the Meierkhol'd production of Sukhovo-Kobylin's play *The Death of Tarelkin*, 1922. [Photograph: Courtesy Arts Council of Great Britain.]

originally colourful costumes when viewed from the auditorium became a muddy yellow colour.

With regard to the other category of clothing, *sportodezhda*, Stepanova stressed that although its form varied according to the sport, it should be characterised by 'a minimum of clothing, ease of putting on and wearing, and the special significance of colour effects to distinguish individual sportsmen and sports groups'.[28] To assist the task of identification Stepanova suggested the use of badges, emblems, forms and colour. Of these she considered colour to be the most satisfactory because of the necessarily large areas over which sports events take place and the large numbers of spectators to which they must communicate.

Stepanova's practical application of these ideas concerning the functional use of colour combination in sports clothing was illustrated by four designs which accompanied her article in *LEF* (colour plate VIII).[29] Consisting of simple shirts, shorts and skirts, they utilised three colours, white, red and black, which were organised in terms of strictly rectilinear and geometrical motifs. Since these decorative elements performed a purely functional role in these ensembles they did not contradict the functional principle of Constructivism, nor did they detract from the garments' overall simplicity and freedom. However, despite this functionalism and the overt rejection of style, the exuberance of the decorative elements betrayed the fact that the simplification in dress[30] and its organisation on new principles was also related to the emergence of stylistic concepts. This was evident in the angularity of the *prozodezhda* and in the geometrical motifs which were employed in strict combinations in the sports clothing and textile designs.

All the *prozodezhda* designs utilised plain, unpatterned material which did not obscure but gave a clear expression to the structure and form of the clothing. It could be argued that these bore little relationship to textile design which was a decorative task, bound up with traditional concepts of ornament and with embellishing rather than with reorganising material culture. Furthermore, textile design was a relatively superficial element in the restructuring of the entire environment in accord with Constructivist principles. If the Constructivists' acceptance of the invitation to work at the First State Textile Print Factory represented a pragmatic retreat from their ideal, at the same time it was also a positive decision to become involved with a task, which, however peripheral to long-term and large-scale Constructivist objectives, was an immediately realisable opportunity to begin practical work with mass production in industry. Undoubtedly, the success of the venture was in part due to the fact that the role of the artist in the productive process of textiles was an established practice and easily assimilated into the factory's organisation, approximating more to traditional concepts of the applied arts. On the other hand it was also a result of the Constructivists' commitment to the venture. Popova is reported to have said that nothing gave her greater satisfaction than seeing a dress with material bearing her design, and, as Brik asserted, for these artists 'a cotton print is as much a product of artistic culture as a painting'.[31]

Both Stepanova and Popova saw the replacement of traditional Russian plant and flower patterns by geometrically based designs as an essential aspect of the rationalisation of cloth production in accordance with Constructivist principles. They saw their task as consisting of 'the eradication of the firmly embedded ideal regarding the high artistic value of a hand-drawn design [*risunok*] as the imitation and copying of painting; the battle against naturalistic design in favour of the geometricisation of form; and propagandising the industrial tasks of the Constructivist'.[32] Therefore the patterns that Popova and Stepanova designed for the textile industry consisted of rigorous combinations of Euclidean geometric forms (plate 5.5, colour plate IX). Observing a strict economy of artistic means, each design exploited the potential of one or two such forms in combination with an equally restricted colour range of one or two colours with black and white. Through the repetition and mutual development of these simple entities quite complex patterns

5.5. L. Popova, Textile design for a lightweight cloth (*risunka legkoi tkani*), *c.* 1924. [Reproduced in *LEF*, No. 2, 1924.]

5.6. A. Ekster, Designs for mass-produced clothing and production clothing, *c.* 1923. [Reproduced in *Krasnaya niva*, Nos. 21–2, 1923.]

were produced. For instance, in one design (colour plate X) Popova introduced a shift in the pattern, a *sdvig* or dislocation of the rhythm. Such designs were heavily reliant on the investigations of structure, colour and interpenetrating planes which Popova had conducted in her architectonic paintings (colour plate I).

In pursuit of her integrated concept of the whole garment problem, Popova went on to design clothes that would utilise these readily reproducible, geometrical patterns (colour plates XI–XII). These were simple and uncomplicated garments consisting of blouses and skirts, but with a conscious elegance, which hardly fulfilled the strictly functional criteria set up for *prozodezhda*. This deviation from defined objectives was certainly an indication of how Constructivist practice was having to be modified under influence of the transitional period in which it was working out its ideas.[33] Nevertheless, these simple clothes did illustrate the attempt to integrate cloth design and clothing design within the real conditions of industrial practice.

An element of 'beauty' in the traditional sense had unquestionably become overt in Constructivist practice at this point. However, the extent to which Popova and Stepanova succeeded in achieving some genuine interaction and equilibrium between their new aesthetic and the other factors in design, is well indicated by comparing their work with that of Aleksandra Ekster, in which geometrical ornament completely dominates all other concerns. Since the 1920s Ekster has often erroneously been referred to as a Constructivist because she had participated in the $5 \times 5 = 25$ exhibition of 1921. However, despite certain common interests she never adopted a rigorously Constructivist position either in theory or in practice, as her work in the fields of theatrical and fashion design clearly demonstrates.

Ekster's theoretical statements concerning rational clothing design for mass production did utilise many of the principles also put forward by Popova and Stepanova. Ekster stressed the need for clothing to possess the qualities of 'appropriateness, hygiene, psychology and harmony of proportions with the human body' and for it 'to be suitable for the workers and for the kind of work which will be done in it'.[34] Considerations of function were combined with investigations into the material components of clothing. Ekster attempted to correlate form with material and concluded that coarse wool was suitable for a 'form composed of right angles ... without any unnecessary additional vertical rhythm of folds ... soft, wide materials (wool, silk – given the appropriate treatment) make it possible to do more complex and varied silhouettes for clothes ... elastic materials ... make it possible to make clothing for movement (dancing) and the working out of more complicated forms (circles, polygrams)'.[35]

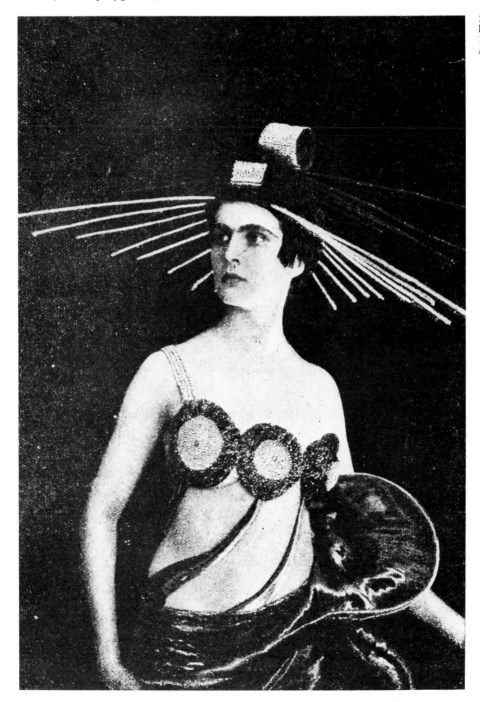

5.7. A. Ekster's costume for Aelita, in a scene from the film *Aelita*, 1924. [Photograph: National Film Archive, London.]

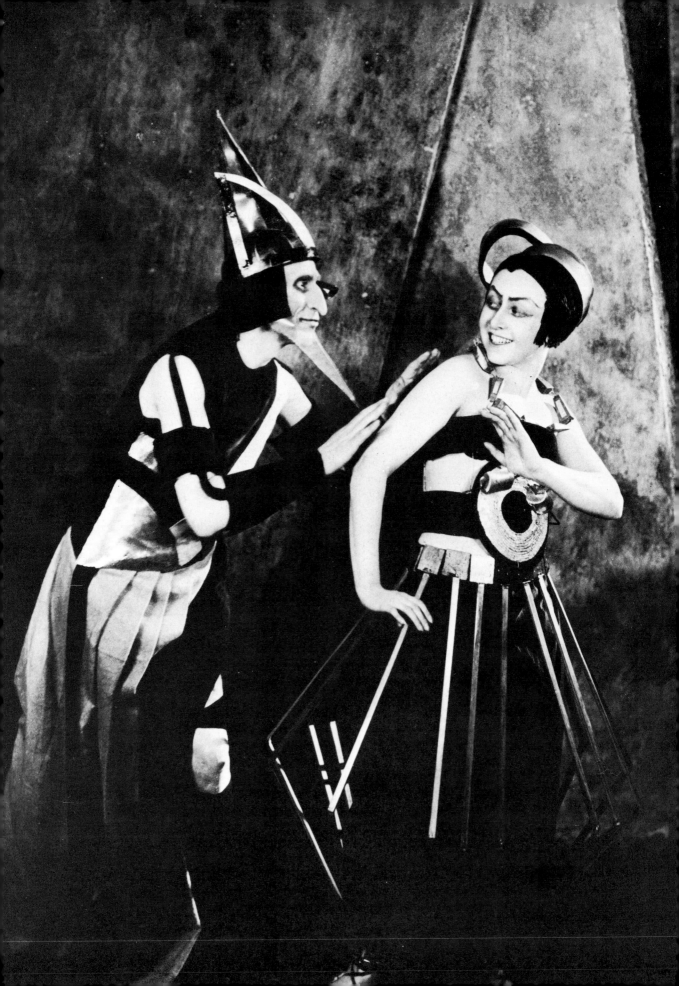

In accordance with these principles Ekster designed garments which would fulfil multiple functions, responding to the varied types of activity upon which people were engaged in everyday life (plate 5.6). As Ekster explained: 'From the first scheme it is possible to make a walking outfit ... taking off the outer part we get a dress for special occasions, and finally, taking off the blouse, we have an under dress – a working dress.'[36] The adaptability of this ensemble obviated the need for a large number of clothes, which in any case the material scarcities of the time made impossible. The principle of practicality evident in conception extended to the process of manufacture. 'All ... are simple in their silhouettes, material and cut, so that the amount of sewing should be minimal.'[37] The man's coat has only four seams but variety was provided by exploiting the texture of the materials by cutting with and against the nap.[38]

However, Ekster certainly never discarded considerations of elegance and beauty *per se*. Even in her work for mass production she used decorative devices and stressed that 'clothing for mass use must consist of the simplest geometrical forms such as the rectangle, square, triangle' and that rhythm and variety in the content of these forms would be provided through colour.[39] It is therefore not surprising that aesthetic factors dominate her creations for the Studio of Fashion (Atel'e mod) and her costume designs for the film *Aelita*.[40] In both these branches of work considerations of strict utility played no role, and Ekster's use of geometrical forms as decorative elements stressed the essentially painterly nature of her approach to clothes. Aelita's costume (plate 5.7) billowed out into extravagant vegetable protrusions more reminiscent of Art Nouveau than Constructivism, and her maid's trousers (plate 5.8), constructed of rectangular metallic strips, seemed designed to impede rather than facilitate movement. It is significant that whereas Stepanova and Popova used the theatre to realise *prozodezhda* Ekster produced these decorative fripperies – a difference which was fundamental in their approach.

Looking back, in 1929, Stepanova herself sadly recognised the limitations to achieving that role in the clothing industry to which the 'artist-constructor' aspired. She observed that under contemporary conditions 'in the industrialised factory ... the artist ... preserves all the features of the handicraftsman ... a handicraft graphic artist'. From this she concluded that 'the only correct path would be if the artists participated in the work of designing the garments themselves'.[41] Modest though the products were that Stepanova and Popova achieved in their ventures into the textile industry, they did display some real attempt to reassess design solutions in this important area of Soviet life and to correlate the constraints and potentials of function, material and production processes with the new formal vocabulary into a coherent design method for this particular area of production.

FURNITURE

There is no evidence to suggest that any Constructivists went to work in furniture factories in the way that they entered the textile industry. They did, however, devote considerable energy to the problem of furniture design. Tatlin, for instance, devised and built several variants of a particular form of oven (plate 5.3), which was intended to combine maximum heat output with minimum fuel consumption.[42] The VKhUTEMAS students of Dermetfak under the guidance of Lissitzky, Rodchenko and Tatlin approached solutions to some of the problems affecting furniture design in relation to contemporary Soviet living conditions. Although none of their designs entered mass production, the Constructivists did formulate an approach to the problems encountered in this field.

One of the earliest attempts to design a whole Constructivist interior environment, and one of the few ever achieved, was Rodchenko's Workers' Club (plates 5.9–10) designed and executed for the Exposition Internationale des Arts Décoratifs

5.8. A. Ekster's costumes for Ikushka and the Martian officers, in a scene from the film *Aelita*, 1924. [Photograph: National Film Archive, London.]

155

5.9. Installation photograph of Aleksandr Rodchenko's Workers' Club at the Exposition Internationale des Arts Décoratifs et Modernes, Paris, 1925. [Photograph: A. H. Barr, Jr., Archives, Library, The Museum of Modern Art, New York.]

5.10. A. Rodchenko, Model of his Workers' Club exhibited in Paris, 1925. [Reproduced in *Sovremennaya arkhitektura*, No. 1, 1926.]

et Industriels Modernes in Paris in 1925. The workers' club emerged in the 1920s as a 'social condenser' which would foster the growth of the new communist society and the new Soviet man by acting as a focus for promoting the total re-education and restructuring of society. Such a club was 'the centre of the new communist way of life', and as such was not to be devoted exclusively to political activities: 'At the same time it must be built for amusement and relaxation. The club must, if it can, show how the new life must be built.'[43] It is this ideological concept which underlines the importance of Rodchenko's practical demonstration of just how such a club should be organised in accordance with Constructivist principles.

The design of the club was therefore based on real and existing as opposed to hypothetical or potential material conditions. Hence its organisation, and the design of the furniture it contained was based on two principles: 'Economy in the use of the floor of the club room and of the space which the object occupied with its maximum useability.'[44] This involved devising wooden furniture for 'simplicity of use, standardisation and the necessity of being able to expand or contract the numbers of its parts'.[45] This was achieved by making many of the items collapsible so that they could be removed and easily stored when not in use, such as for example the tribune, folding screen, display board and bench (plate 5.11). Intended to cater for every type of activity and all aspects of club life, the club contained chairs and tables, cabinets for exhibiting books and journals, storage space for current literature, display windows for posters, maps and newspapers, and a Lenin corner.[46] For talks, meetings and demonstrations of the 'living newspapers' there was an orator's tribune (*tribun dlya oratora*) with moveable screens for films and slides.[47] The furniture was painted in four colours, white, red, grey, black, either alone or in combination, and this scheme seems to have become a kind of colour-canon within Constructivism. Rodchenko's designs for this club consisted of strictly rectilinear combinations of Euclidean geometric forms. These epitomised the concerns displayed in his teaching activity in Dermetfak – the rethinking of structure, strict economy in the use of materials, functionalism both of use and of production and the elaboration of space-saving devices. An open skeletal framework – evident in many of the pieces demonstrated – made them exceedingly light and the jointing permitted folding. In the furniture which he designed for the play *Inga* in 1928 (plate 5.12), discussed below, a certain fluidity and solidity of form replaced the rather austerely angular and schematic constructions of 1925. There was a return to the more traditional type of furniture structures in the *Inga* designs.

Rationalisation and standardisation were to remain, however, the prime concerns in the furniture designs of El Lissitzky. He became involved in this field in 1925 when he returned to Russia and moved increasingly towards a Constructivist standpoint.[48] Reviewing his own activity in 1940, he criticised himself and other artists for having approached the problem of furniture design too theoretically, paying more attention to drawing designs than to the practical activity of actually making furniture:

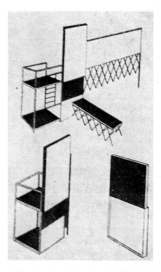

5.11. A. Rodchenko, Design for folding tribune, screen and display stand, for the Workers' Club, forming part of the Soviet display at the 1925 Paris exhibition. [Reproduced in *Sovremennaya arkhitektura*, No. 1, 1926.]

> We approached the work problematically and we ignored the concrete reality of carpentry. If we did spend money, then it was on lectures and designs and not on building prototypes ... True some artists and architects talked about the 'question' of furniture in the first years of the Revolution. But I know of none who actually made a chair or a table ... We should take good models which have been realised in the world of furniture, and we should learn to make them accurately and firmly from the standpoint of the material used, its overall finish and its durability. And then when we have become good humble carpenters, we will be able to attain the ideal, i.e. to outstrip the capitalists.[49]

This strongly expressed commitment to socialism was more than a *post hoc* justification. In his major treatise on furniture, 'The Artistic Pre-Requisites for the Standardisation of Furniture' of 1928, Lissitzky also denounced the bourgeois solution to the design of mass-produced objects because it consisted merely of applying a style in the form of classic, gothic or rococo patterns.[50] He asserted that mass production (the production of objects as if by a collective master) placed the making of objects on a highly scientific and methodical basis, making it possible to produce objects organised on the basis of aesthetic fundamentals. 'We do not need the external artistic qualities of "fashion", but the realizations of the profound bases of style.'[51] Rejecting the application of ornamentation, Lissitzky defined these fundamentals of style by examining a series of objects and concluding that there were five qualities which produced their expressive qualities:

5.12. A. Rodchenko, Design for a chair for Glebov's play *Inga*, 1929.

1. They represent themselves, they do not depict something completely different – THEY ARE HONEST.
2. The eye takes them in as a whole – THEY ARE PRECISE.
3. They are simple, not from any poverty of formative energy or imaginative fantasy, but from richness, striving towards laconism – THEY ARE ELEMENTARY.
4. Their form, as a whole and in detail, could be made from circles and lines – THEY ARE GEOMETRICAL.
5. – They were made by man's hands by means of the working parts of the modern machine – THEY ARE INDUSTRIAL.[52]

Based on the experience of mechanisation and mass production the task of the designer was to create a series of new aesthetic canons independent of bourgeois proclivities for style. Lissitzky concluded that the formal aspects of furniture comprised the expressivity of its tectonic structure, volume, the combination of

5.13. El Lissitzky, Seat designed for the International Fur Trade Exhibition, Leipzig, 1930.

5.14. El Lissitzky, Seat designed for the International Fur Trade Exhibition, Leipzig, 1930, showing its construction.

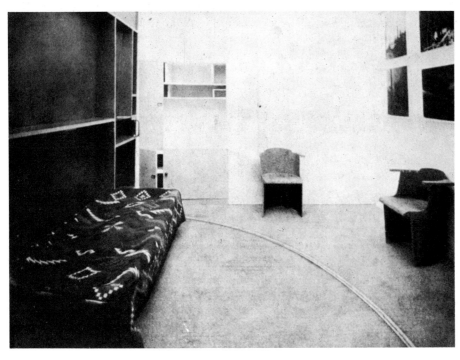

5.15. El Lissitzky, Living room and bedroom in a flat in a House of the Commune, International Hygiene Exhibition, Dresden, 1930.

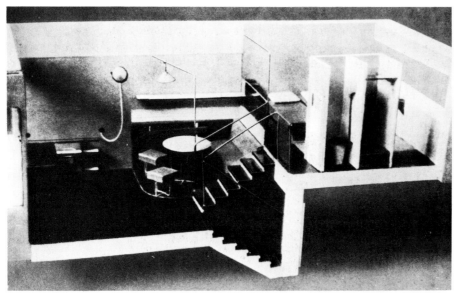

5.16. El Lissitzky, Design for one room apartment in house designed by Milinis and Ginzburg for Ministry of Finance employees, 1934.

volumes and spatial profiles, scale, proportions, modules and rhythms. These factors operate within an examination of the artistic factors, the properties of a material, texture (*faktura*) and colour, always with ultimate reference to the function. Working in this way the designer could produce objects which would be expressive of new Soviet life.[53]

Lissitzky's theoretical propositions found a practical exposition in his designs. The chair designed for the Russian pavilion at the International Fur Trade Exhibition in Leipzig in 1930 (plates 5.13-14) was specifically devised for exhibition use.[54] It was composed of two pieces that could be easily dismantled, transported and reassembled. The main piece forming the back and sides of the chair was cut from one piece of plywood which could be bent around the seat. It was reinforced vertically at the sides. Two small supports joined at right angles to this main piece provided arm rests. The seat of the chair also consisted of one piece of wood. Screwing the seat and back together and adding the arm rests consumed little time. The absence of complex joinery ensured ease and cheapness of production. The possibility of transporting the chair flat in a dismantled form prevented serious damage. The chair was additionally economic in that it exploited a material in which Russia was rich, and utilised this resource not extravagantly. The chair consisted of only four pieces of wood, and, although the area of plywood used was large, the back piece of the chair was fairly thin to retain sufficient elasticity and flexibility for curving around the seat.[55]

Lissitzky used this chair in his design for the layout and furnishings of a room in a communal house he executed for the International Hygiene Exhibition in Dresden in 1930 (plate 5.15). The bed folded into the wooden construction, which then could presumably be swung back against the adjoining wall along the rail in the floor. Thus space used to house the bed at night could be completely liberated as living space during the day. However, Lissitzky did not employ the folding away principle for the one room apartments in the Narkomfin building in Moscow of 1928-9 (plate 5.16).[56] The flats were split into two levels, corresponding to a sleeping (and washing) section and to a living (and eating) section. The furniture designed by Lissitzky in co-operation with his wife was mainly built-in, thereby permitting the maximum exploitation of the space available but creating a rather rigid format which potentially reduced its flexibility to individual needs.

THE CONSTRUCTIVE TENDENCY

5.17a–b. K. Malevich, Architectural models (*arkhitektony/planity*), *c.* 1922–5, plaster. Whereabouts unknown. [Photographs: Courtesy the Galerie Gmurzynska, Cologne; Stedelijk Museum, Amsterdam.]

Lissitzky's work in the field of furniture design, including his theoretical formulations and teaching work at the VKhUTEMAS, had allied him with Constructivism. However, it should be remembered that earlier he had been a pupil of Malevich, a member of UNOVIS, and closely connected with Suprematism. At this juncture it is perhaps apposite to stress the difference between Constructivism and what could be called a Constructive tendency which arose under the impetus of artistic synthesis

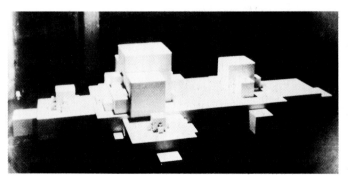

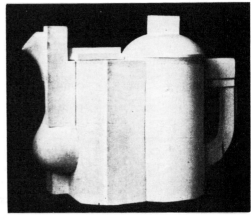

5.18. K. Malevich, I. Chashnik, N. Suetin, Suprematist porcelain designs, *c.* 1922. [Reproduced in *Russkoe iskusstvo*, No. 2/3, 1923.]

XI. L. Popova, Design for a textile and for a dress using a similar print, *c.* 1924, pencil and inks on paper, 72·5 × 34 cm. [Photograph: Courtesy Galerie Gmurzynska, Cologne.]

XII. L. Popova, Design for a flannelette print and a coat and skirt using these, *c.* 1924, pencil and watercolour on paper, 61 × 28 cm. [Photograph: Courtesy Galerie Gmurzynska, Cologne.]

and revolutionary ideas and events, and operated in other artistic persuasions such as Suprematism, encouraging other artists to use their art in the transformation of the environment and the design of everyday objects like furniture.

In 1921, Malevich, who had inaugurated Suprematism, wrote to his pupil Ku-dryashev, pronouncing that Suprematism should adopt a more 'Constructive' approach to the present requirements of reorganising the world.[57] Later the same year he announced to INKhUK: 'I want to recreate the world in a Suprematist mould' and he expressed his desire to 'rebuild the world according to a non-objective system'.[58] In practical pursuit of his new objectives, Malevich devoted himself from 1919 onwards to making drawings and models of three-dimensional bodies which he projected as buildings or complete housing complexes and to which he gave the name *planity* or *arkhitektony* (plate 5.17).[59] However, Malevich's structures, while exploiting the axial massing of volume in space, were complicated, symmetrical and asymmetrical accretions of regular rectangular forms. Unrelated to any real specificity of function, material, manner of construction, size or scale, and expressed solely in formal terms, these experiments had more in common with the earlier utopian visions of Zhivskul'ptarkh than with the Constructivists' later attempts to

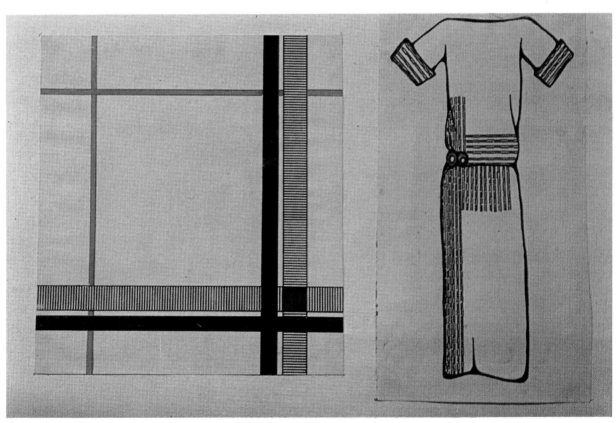

Т. Клуцис 22 г.

formulate and implement a rigorous design method. On a more mundane level Malevich did design some Suprematist cups and saucers (plate 5.18). Taking the sphere and the cube as his basic modules he reinterpreted the forms of these items of crockery into these shapes, without regard to functional requirements, manufacturing processes or materials. The results are cumbersome and comic. In many ways the more traditional practice of decorating conventional cups and saucers with two-dimensional Suprematist forms was much more successful, and Malevich's disciples Suetin and Chashnik produced some attractive items.[60] However, Malevich's followers also approached more prosaic tasks, such as the design of furniture utilising Suprematist principles.

In 1927 Suetin designed several items of furniture for a competition being held by the wood industry (Drevtrest – Wood Trust) of Leningrad.[61] According to Szymon Bojko, Suetin designed this furniture for mass production on the principle of the square becoming a cube and the circle a sphere.[62] In other words the basic forms of the Suprematist painterly vocabulary were given three-dimensionality for the purpose of designing three-dimensional objects. Although Suetin's design drawings are not very clear they do indicate the absence of any coherent or rigorous design method involving considerations of function or the nature of the material used, and they do demonstrate the tendency to view design merely as the process of translating the traditional shape of objects into Suprematist elements. The objects have not been re-thought out or re-structured and the consciously artistic approach to form has in no way been suppressed. This is particularly evident in Suetin's design for a sideboard (plate 5.19) where the traditional symmetrical format has been translated into Suprematist planes decorated with rectangles. The functional aspect of both production and use has been subordinated to the artistic in a way typical of this movement into design among non-Constructivist artists. Despite its good intentions, in reality it amounted to little more than what the Constructivists attacked as applied art.

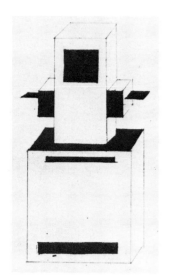

5.19. N. Suetin, Design for a sideboard, 1927, pencil on paper, 22 × 40 cm. [Photograph: Courtesy Galerie Gmurzynska, Cologne.]

KLUTSIS AND THE AGITATIONAL STAND

Returning to the work of Constructivism proper, and to the next larger scale of activity beyond furniture, an example of the rigorous implementation of Constructivist principles is provided by the agitational stands of Gustav Klutsis. In 1922, to celebrate the fifth anniversary of the Revolution and the Fourth Congress of the Comintern, Klutsis designed a series of 'radio-orators', 'radio-tribunes' and 'cinema-photo stands', with three-dimensional and dynamic slogans, for the streets and squares of Moscow.

Fourteen of these designs specifically labelled as agitational stands or 'radio-orators' were exhibited in Riga in 1970.[63] One of these was executed in 1925 for the exhibition accompanying the Fifth Congress of the Comintern.[64] The remaining thirteen designs apparently date from 1922. The stand *The International* (*Internatsional*) was actually erected inside the Moscow Hotel where the delegates to the Congress were staying.[65] The stands were designed to perform specific agitational functions: displaying photographic material and posters or giving a spatial and audio-visual presence to revolutionary slogans. Some stands were very simple in construction and performed only one function, such as the variants in plate 5.21 and the . stand *News of the Whole World* which consisted of two screens.[66] Far more complex were stands like *Design for a Screen and Tribune* (plate 5.20), which combined visual and oral functions, a screen and a speaker's platform. To emphasise the active and passive elements of the structures, loudspeakers were red whereas stands were black. The clarity of this construction and its multiple functions were further developed in the *Design for a Screen-Tribune-Kiosk* also of 1922 (colour

XIII. G. Klutsis, Design for a screen-tribune-kiosk for the Fourth Congress of the Comintern and the fifth anniversary of the October Revolution, 1922 (*Ekran-tribuna-kiosk*), 1922, watercolour and ink on paper, 24·6 × 16·5 cm. Collection George Costakis, Athens. [Photograph: © George Costakis 1981.]

163

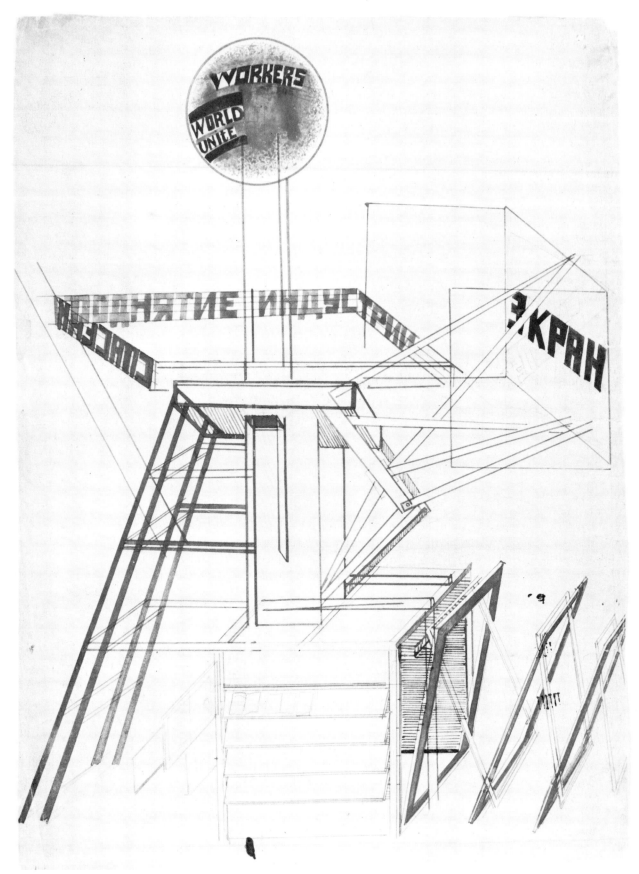

5.20. G. Klutsis, Design for *Propaganda Stand, Screen and Loudspeaker Platform*, 1922, pencil, ink and watercolour on paper, 32·9 × 24 cm. Collection George Costakis, Athens. [Photograph: © George Costakis 1981.]

plate XIII) where a stand for a political speaker, a screen for the display of newsreels, a bookstand for the display of literature and a board for posters were all incorporated into one single construction.

In all of these agitational radio-orators and tribunes the component elements of each structure, whether a book display stand, microphone or screen, were revealed without disguise, and construction was reduced to the essential supports. Many of the components of these tribunes which Klutsis devised became established features of Constructivist design. Rodchenko in his Workers' Club of 1925 (plate 5.11) employs a very similar structure for a book display stand, and his folding screen equally seems to be based on Klutsis' prototype. The compression of several functions into a small overall unit is a concept common to both Constructivists. Klutsis' use of words in the red, white or black of his tribunes as verbal announcements to arrest the attention of the passer-by made the tribunes also effective demonstrations of agitational graphics in three dimensions. Such use of slogans made the agitational content of the tribune effective even when it was not in use as a disseminator of verbal propaganda.

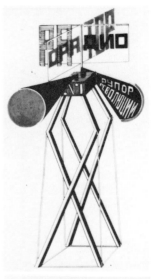

All the stands were light structures painted red, black and white and made from materials easily available (wood, canvas, cables). They recall the stands made by the Stenberg brothers for their works at the third ОВМОКhU exhibition in 1921 (plates 2.15–16). Observing the principles of strict economy and so constructed from strips rather than from blocks of material, Klutsis' stands derived their stability from a multiplicity of vertical, diagonal and horizontal supports. The resultant abundance of long thin lines gave the structures a certain lightness and fragility. Although material scarcity encouraged this method of construction, in many of the stands the geometry of the straight lines and their interactions seem to have provided a design impetus in their own right.

KIOSKS

As small-scale, light, temporary, sometimes transportable structures, the kiosks developed from the formal and practical experimentation with the agitational stands. Intended for propaganda as opposed to agitational tasks they were concerned with the constant dissemination of written, rather than oral information. Their first widespread construction and use was at the All Union Agricultural Exhibition of 1923.[67]

Those architects who were by now leading the extension of Constructivist principles into architecture were not involved in this exhibition, although several future members of their group of Constructivist architects did participate, notably Nikolai Kolli. However, Moisei Ginzburg's inclusion of several pavilions and kiosks by Constructivist artists in his book *Style and the Epoch* of 1924[68] was solid evidence that the leading theoretician of emergent architectural Constructivism considered these small-scale structures as valuable explorations towards a new formal vocabulary for the larger architectural scale.

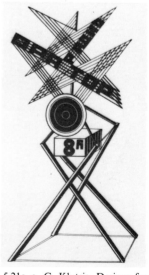

Ginzburg's *Style and the Epoch*, originally conceived as a series of lectures to the Moscow Architectural Society and the Russian Academy of Artistic Sciences, was a sophisticated analysis of architectural history, designed to prove the correctness of a broadly constructive architecture for the social, historical and technological conditions of the new Soviet State. In an appendix to this theoretical statement of Constructivist architecture Ginzburg included forty-one illustrations from 'the so far very small quantity of actually erected structures' which 'have been affected by a feeling for new forms to a greater or lesser extent, and which can therefore have some kind of generic significance in the formation of the new formal language of architecture'.[69]

Ginzburg's illustrations not unnaturally included work by the Vesnin brothers

5.21a–c. G. Klutsis, Designs for Radio Orators, 1922, ink and gouache on paper, a and b: 17·8 × 24·3 cm, c: 17·7 × 13·8 cm. Collection George Costakis, Athens. [Photograph: © George Costakis 1981.]

165

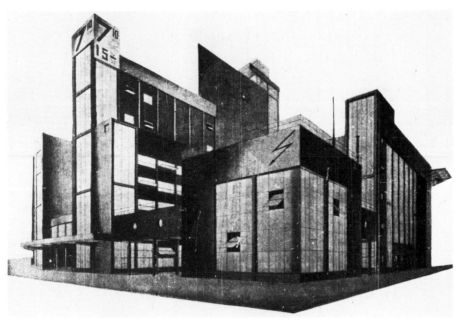

5.22. A. Burov, Design for a theatre, 1923. [Reproduced in Ginzburg, *Stil' i epokha*, 1924.]

who were among the leaders in this search for a new formal language for architecture. He reproduced Aleksandr Vesnin's model for the staging of *The Man who was Thursday* of 1922–3 and the Vesnin brothers' design for the Moscow Palace of Labour, which had already been recognised as the first consistently Constructivist architectural design in its clear spatial and structural response to the new social task. The Vesnins had been awarded third prize whereas Ginzburg's entry for the Palace of Labour competition of 1922–3 had been structurally inarticulate and was unplaced. By 1923–4, when Ginzburg was seriously forming the historical and theoretical basis for Constructivist architecture, the influence of the Vesnins' experiments in extending the formal explorations of the kiosks and theatrical sets was already clearly emerging in the work of the VKhUTEMAS students who later formed the membership of OSA (the Constructivist architectural group which formed around Ginzburg and the Vesnin brothers in 1925).[70] A typical project was that by Burov for a theatre (plate 5.22).[71]

Important to architects as an arena to work out their ideas in the design and construction of small-scale impermanent pavilions, the All Union Agricultural Exhibition was also important to artists because it gave them the opportunity of co-operating with architects in producing pavilions that would synthesise the artist's and the architect's skills. The artists Ekster, Nivinskii and the Stenberg brothers participated in the decoration of pavilions including the simple relief decorations of the Arable Farming Pavilion (plate 5.23).[72] Ekster, who together with Nivinskii was responsible for all the painting at the exhibition, also executed the decorations for the *Izvestiya* Pavilion (plate 5.24).[73] The whole incoherent structure was a badly digested assembly of abstract artistic elements (heavily reliant

5.23. A. Ekster, V. and G. Stenberg, Decorative panel for Field Cultivation Pavilion at the All Union Agricultural Exhibition, Moscow, 1923.

5.24. A. Ekster, V. Mukhina and
B. Gladkov, *Izvestiya* VTsIK
Pavilion at the All Union Agricul-
tural Exhibition, Moscow, 1923.
[Reproduced in Ginzburg, *Stil' i
epokha*, 1924.]

on the Eiffel Tower and Tatlin's monument) and strongly recalling the work of Rodchenko and Zhivskul'ptarkh (plate 2.8).[74] Although the diagonally intersecting composition of writing and imagery on the panels framing the entrance was a device later used in Constructivist graphics, the overall structure was too eclectic and determinedly decorative to be termed Constructivist. At the other extreme was the completely realistic panel Ekster executed for the Forestry Pavilion which remained purely decorative rather than organisational in concept.[75] Here, as elsewhere, Ekster embued the enterprise in which she participated with the spirit of applied art.

Even Lavinskii's kiosk, designed as the stand for the State Publishing House (Gosizdat) at the exhibition (plate 5.25), with its rounded roof supported by a plethora of rectangular pillars, was of almost classical symmetry in comparison with another of his kiosk designs (plate 5.27) for the same organisation. According to Neznamov, the later variant was actually built on Revolution Square (Ploshad' Revolyutsii) in Moscow.[76] Lavinskii's later variant moved away from pre-established models. Still symmetrical and based on the square it too allowed all round visibility for the display of literature. Yet it used a new geometry, rather than one derived from historical styles, with its tapering base and dynamically angled sides. The constructional simplicity of this structure answered the new production requirements and the exigencies of economy in response to material shortages.

Ginzburg also illustrated Gan's kiosk (plate 5.26) as a significant contribution to Constructivist architectural development.[77] Gan who is chiefly remembered as a theorist of the movement because of his treatise *Constructivism*, was also engaged in artistic activity, mainly as a typographer and graphic designer although he also designed kiosks and furniture. When shut, the rectangular structures of his kiosk were minimised by the varied lettering which was used as a utilitarian (identification) and decorative element, and by the coloured rectangular panels in the doors. When unfolded the doors and the walls of the two irregular asymmetrically arranged rectangular structures formed a series of ample shelves and surfaces for the display of books and papers. When not in use the kiosk was very compact and occupied a minimal space.

The Rural Kiosk (plate 5.28) which Gan designed for country areas, although it used metal and glass, was largely made from wood, which was cheap and plentiful and was the traditional building material in the countryside. The kiosk had two

5.25. A. Lavinskii, Kiosk for the State Publishing House at the All Union Agricultural Exhibition, Moscow, 1923. [Reproduced in Ginzburg, *Stil' i epokha*, 1924.]

5.26. A. Gan, Book kiosk for the sale of literature and stationery, *c.* 1923. [Reproduced in Pertsov, *Reviziya levogo fronta iskusstv*, 1925.]

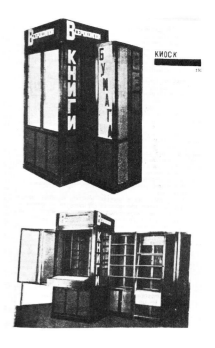

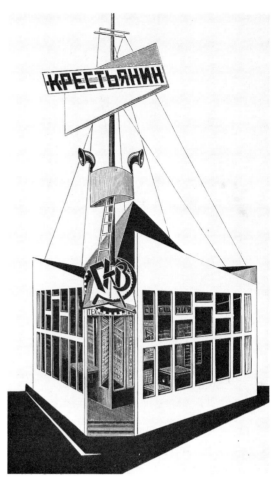

functions, commercial and social. Intended for the sale of literature, it was also to act in conjunction with the clubs (replacing the former function of the church), to contribute to the sovietisation of the countryside and actively to participate in the agitation for a new life in these areas.[78] Socially it was to act as a community centre and a cultural link with the town through the post, radio and cinema (it was provided with a radio and a film screen). The design of the kiosk reflected these aims as well as responding to material and climatic conditions. Gan devised the kiosk so that it acted not only as a centre of information but also as a piece of permanent visual propaganda. It was based on a triangular form so that each facet proclaimed its function and its messages through the windows. This faceting also had a more mundane purpose. The facets were cut with a steep incline so that the snow and rain were channelled to fall in three directions keeping the entrance clear. The overall form provided a new language for wooden architecture and was a visual reminder of the changes taking place, creating an immediately identifiable point in the villages, distinctive from them yet not in a totally alien material or mode – a symbolic, but also a functioning centre for the new ideology.

In 1922 Gan also designed a smaller piece of urban furniture – a street trading stand (plate 5.29) for the Moscow Agricultural Industry (Mossel'prom). This was a small folding structure, apparently made from wood, which could be carried to its destination and then erected, and after use easily folded up again to be carried away. It contained a tray with a moveable glass lid for selling stationary supplies, papers or cigarettes. Gan considered the design and production of such items important evidence that 'Constructivism has not only theoretically solved the problem of rationalising artistic work but is indeed already putting into practice its new forms, and participating in the building of the material culture of the present'.[79]

5.27. A. Lavinskii, Kiosk for the State Publishing House, c. 1924. [Reproduced in *Exposition Internationale des Arts Décoratifs et Industriels Modernes*, 1925.]

5.28. A. Gan, Design for a rural kiosk (*derevenskii kiosk*), c. 1924. [Reproduced in *Sovremennaya arkhitektura*, No. 1, 1926.]

5.29. A. Gan, Folding sales stand (*skladnoi stanok*) designed for Mossel'prom, c. 1922–3. [Reproduced in Pertsov, *Reviziya levogo fronta iskusstv*, 1925.]

THEATRE AS THE ASSEMBLED MICRO-ENVIRONMENT

Even these relatively complete Constructivist exteriors and interiors – the kiosks and the workers' clubs – represented only isolated realisations within environments which, although slowly evolving, remained solidly organised on traditional social principles and clothed in traditional material forms. Even full-scale architecture would have been in the same position at this date. The one arena of creative endeavour in which it was possible to realise experimental syntheses of 'new ways of life' with corresponding total environments was the theatre.

Chuzhak wrote in the very first issue of *LEF*:

> In the theatre, Constructivism . . . united Constructive furnishings (the decor, the props and the costumes) – designed to show, if not the objects themselves, at least their models – with 'Constructive' gestures, movements and pantomime (the biomechanics of Vsevolod Meierkhol'd) – the actors organised according to rhythms.[80]

Meierkhol'd's system of biomechanics (*biomekhanika*) aimed at removing superfluous or unproductive motions, gestures and expressions from the actor's technique, thereby inaugurating a kind of theatrical Taylorism. 'We are always dealing in art with the organisation of material. Constructivism demands that the artist become an engineer as well. Art must be based on scientific principles; all the work done by the artist must be conscious.'[81] As a means of linking the theatre with the proletarian dictatorship, Meierkhol'd discarded psychological realism and the role of individual emotions, reducing acting to an impersonal, scientific and mechanical process. The theatre was to present the ideal proletarian, well-skilled and well-organised. The concept of biomechanics was influenced by circus acrobatics, the conventions of *commedia dell'arte* and the Chinese and Japanese theatres. Like these it cultivated the economy and intensity of the stylised gesture.

5.31. (right) Scene from Crommelynk's play *The Magnanimous Cuckold*, produced by Vsevolod Meierkhol'd, Moscow, 1922. The actors are wearing costumes designed by Popova and utilising the acting apparatus she designed. The actors are, from left: Babanova as Stella, Il'inskii as Bruno, Zaichikov as Estrugo and Dobriner as the Nurse. [Photograph: Society for Cultural Relations with the USSR, London.]

5.30. L. Popova, Acting apparatus for *The Magnanimous Cuckold*, 1922. [Photograph: Society for Cultural Relations with the USSR, London.]

According to Chuzhak's definition the first complete expression of theatrical Constructivism was *The Magnanimous Cuckold* which opened in Moscow on 15 April 1922, produced by Meierkhol'd and acted on a machine designed by Popova.[82] Meierkhol'd explicitly acknowledged the role which Popova's machine had played in his overall handling and direction of the play, and he clearly felt that a full and real Constructivist synthesis had been achieved here between content and form.

> I consider it my duty to point out that in the creation of the performance the work of Professor L. S. Popova was significant . . . that the model of the construction was accepted by me before the beginning of the planning of the play and that much in the tone of the performance was taken from the constructive set.[83]

The play, written by Fernand Crommelynck, was a French farce set in a mill. It was completely devoid of any revolutionary content. As in all Crommelynck's plays passion was reduced to an absurdity. The miller Bruno, tortured by jealous doubts concerning his young faithful wife Stella, compels her to accept the advances of his friend so that he can make sure of her infidelity instead of merely imagining it. He then insists that she accept the overtures of all the villagers so that he will be able to discover her lover. Finding it unbearable Stella eventually runs off to happy monogamy. For the performance the actors wore production clothing (*prozodezhda*) and used Popova's acting apparatus to execute their biomechanics. To facilitate their mechanical movements, Popova had transformed the mill into an intricate apparatus of platforms, revolving doors, ladders and scaffolding (plates 5.30–1).[84] It retained only a slight link with a mill in its wheels, which at tense moments during the play rotated at differing speeds. Composed of several levels, the framework resembled traditional scenery stripped of its illusionistic canvas to reveal its basic structure. As a machine for acting, Popova's construction conveyed the urbanism of city life. The industrial urban environment held the secret to social progress, and Popova's machine therefore possessed an additional ideological implication in that it reflected the attempt in real life to build the industrial bases of socialism with primitive methods.

It does not diminish Popova's achievement in any way to suggest that the idea of a skeletal apparatus was originally that of the Stenberg brothers and Medunetskii, who were initially commissioned by Meierkhol'd to design the set.[85] Their sketches are no longer extant, but according to Vladimir Stenberg they planned a three-dimensional skeletal structure.[86] It is not improbable that their conception provided the basis for Popova's design. In 1921 Popova had been commissioned by Tairov to design the sets and costumes for *Romeo and Juliet*, and her resulting set was a complex construction of perspectival confusions and ambiguous planes defined by colour (plate 5.32).[87] Although the skeletal element was present in the

5.32. L. Popova, Design for the set of Shakespeare's play *Romeo and Juliet*, intended for production at the Kamernyi Theatre, Moscow, 1921, oil on board. Private collection, Moscow.

5.33. L. Popova, Drawing of the set for *The Magnanimous Cuckold*, 1922, collage, ink and gouache on paper, 32·7 × 23·8 cm. Tret'yakov Gallery, Moscow. [Photograph: Courtesy Arts Council of Great Britain.]

design for the mass festival produced in co-operation with Aleksandr Vesnin (plate 2.1) and although Popova had explored it two-dimensionally in her architectonic paintings (colour plate I), there is no evidence that she had been engaged on intensive explorations of it conducted in three-dimensions, with real materials, prior to the set for *The Magnanimous Cuckold*. Her drawn design for the set was conceived two-dimensionally (plate 5.33), and she did not make any structural or three-dimensional relationships explicit. Only after it was constructed did Popova, finding it too detailed, work on it as a three-dimensional structure, adjusting the proportions considerably.[88] In its final form it was therefore more the result of practical laboratory work than of abstract design activity.

At the INKhUK discussion of *The Magnanimous Cuckold*, on 27 April 1922, Popova's statement stressed that her designs had been concerned 'to translate the task from the aesthetic plane onto the Productivist plane', and that she had viewed this as an opportunity for the 'concrete definition and realisation of my personal theoretical and practical professional work ... formulated as equipping a theatrical action with material elements'.[89] Of the three tasks she had set herself in the realisation of this aim, one concerned *prozodezhda*, the remaining two concerned the set itself:

> The organisation of the material elements of the spectacle as an apparatus, a kind of installation or contrivance for the given action. In this respect utilitarian suitability must serve as the criterion, and certainly not the solution of any formal and aesthetic problems ...
>
> The second task was to introduce material elements ... so as to co-ordinate the entire process of this action; to this end the movements of the doors and window, and the rotating of the wheels were introduced into the basic score of the action; by their movement and speeds these were to underline and intensify the kinetic value of each movement of the action.[90]

In 1922 Meierkhol'd also produced *The Death of Tarelkin*, a nineteenth-century comedy by Sukhovo-Kobylin.[91] The decor (plate 5.34) designed by Stepanova differed from that of Popova's machine. Instead of being a multi-levelled structure it consisted of smaller individual constructions, painted a sanitary and neutral white, that did not produce any varying levels for the action but were distributed along the surface of the stage. Stepanova explained that they had been conceived as circus devices, each piece of apparatus performing two or three functions. 'The task had been to provide apparatus-objects as instruments for playing on the stage.'[92] When the actors were imprisoned they went through a kind of mincer which landed them in a square compartment (plate 5.35). These devices were not always successful and the actors complained of the dangers attending their malfunctioning, but they did accentuate the changes in emphasis that Meierkhol'd had administered to the play. Originally Tarelkin was a minor and forgotten functionary mistakenly placed on an obituary list. Meierkhol'd transformed him into a merry prankster, outwitting the police from whom he escaped on a trapeze. Stepanova's constructions were like performing apparatuses – essential to the enactment of this drama. Whereas Popova's full height infrastructure for the entire play presented a new concept of the stage as an all-embracing apparatus for acting rather than an illusionistic and passive background, Stepanova's individual constructions essentially replaced traditional types of stage decor and props. Stepanova did little more than distribute the Constructivist objects over the surface of the conventional stage, whereas Popova's structure maximised the spatial potential of the whole volume in which the hypothetical 'world' of the play was built. Not surprisingly it was Popova's solution which provided the basis for subsequent Constructivist experimentation.

It was here in the theatre, at the very beginning of the 1920s, that Constructivist ideas of the interrelation of the environment with life – albeit hypothetical, but active and real – became first demonstrated and tested. The theatre acted as a micro-environment in which it was possible to explore spatial and material structures which could act as prototype components of a new, completely Constructivist environment. Only at the very end of the decade did it become possible to contemplate the achievement of a similar synthesis at the full scale of the whole urban environment. The first manifestation of the role which the Vesnin brothers were to play in transmitting Constructivist principles and formal language from the theatre into the larger environment was Aleksandr Vesnin's multi-tiered skeletal set for *The Man who was Thursday*, directed by Tairov at the Kamernyi Theatre in 1923 (plate 5.36).[93] This was a direct development of Popova's structure for *The Magnanimous Cuckold*, extending the principles of internal organisation and the methods of construction which Popova had used. Vesnin's structure for this play expanded Popova's relatively simple assemblies into a much more rigorous, multi-levelled and viable construction. These qualities are better seen in the model than when confined within the conventional proscenium arch of the Tairov stage where its whole industrial quality as a free-standing machine was lost. Furthermore, as is clear from the photographs, the model's asymmetry and industrially inspired forms were unfortunately adapted to the theatre for the production and much of the three-dimensional presence and spatial excitement of the design was lost. Initially the design was an almost literal illustration of Ginzburg's arguments in *Style and the Epoch* that

> Under the influence of the changed conditions of life, of the importance of contemporary economics, of technology and all their consequences, our aesthetic emotion has been changed – the very nature of it ... Under the influence of the machine a conception of the beautiful as that organisation of material which perfectly suits the particulars of the case, which most economically satisfies the given purpose, and which is most condensed in form and concise in movement is being hammered into our thinking.[94]

For Ginzburg these changes and the dynamic qualities of the machine would give rise to a new Constructivist architecture which would be functional, economic and asymmetrical in organisation. *The Man who was Thursday* was a vital step towards the realisation of such an architecture.[95] However, in 1923 that was a distant

5.34. Acting apparatus designed by V. Stepanova for *The Death of Tarelkin*, 1922. [Photograph: Society for Cultural Relations with the USSR, London.]

5.35. Third act from Sukhovo-Kobylin's play *The Death of Tarelkin*, produced by Meierkhol'd in 1922, with designs by Stepanova. In this scene the prisoner goes through the meat grinder to end up in the prison cage. [Photograph: Society for Cultural Relations with the USSR, London.]

prospect. Certainly Vesnin's set maximised the potential of the Constructivist theatre to deal with such objectives in an experimental way – although Vesnin's exploration was conducted in terms of the architecture of the set rather than the properties or costumes. The latter particularly were based on accepted types and did not postulate new solutions.

THE REASSERTION OF THE REAL OBJECT

5.36. A. Vesnin, Model of the set for the production of Chesterton's *The Man who was Thursday* at the Kamernyi Theatre, Moscow, 1923. [Reproduced in Ginzburg, *Stil' i epokha*, 1924.]

Popova's second Constructivist theatrical project with Meierkhol'd was *The Earth in Turmoil* of 1923.[96] In contrast to the absence of props in *The Magnanimous Cuckold*, the props for *The Earth in Turmoil* were extensive and were derived from the real world. These were itemised in her plan for the production.

1. Basic Structure
2. Details: a. car
   b. tractor
   c. a three-dimensional screen
   d. continual agitational slogan attached to the structure
   e. a slogan on the tractor
3. A film projector, film camera, films, slides, *Cinema Truth* [*Kino pravda*]
4. Objects: a coffin
   a red pall
   a small machine gun
   bicycles
   weapons

5.37. First act from Tret'yakov's play *The Earth in Turmoil* (*Zemlya dybom*) adapted from Martinet's *La Nuit* and produced by Meierkhol'd. It shows how screens and revolutionary slogans were attached to Popova's acting apparatus during the performance. [Photograph: Society for Cultural Relations with the USSR, London.]

a field kitchen
3 field telephones
one camp bed
one field pack
one large table
maps
2 typewriters
2 aeroplanes (Godunov's system)

5. Lighting by searchlights. Coloured bulb for Burbus's lantern
6. Noises
7. Music. A military orchestra
8. Parade (military section)
9. Pyrotechnics
10. Costumes: peasant group   70
    his highness   1
    Burbus's staff   13
    group of civilians: men   7   women   3[97]

The huge wooden construction (plates 5.37-8) which dominated the stage resembled a gantry crane. In comparison with the machinery of *The Magnanimous Cuckold* its potential was limited and its role in the action less crucial. It was used merely as an apparatus from which to hang the film screen and various agitational and revolutionary slogans such as 'We shall build a new world' and 'Long live the

176

Union of Workers and Peasants'.[98] However, although the apparatus did have a limited role, its resemblance to a crane emphasised the fact that in this instance Popova was directly utilising an image taken from the world of industrial technology. It had undergone only a minor artistic transformation: a reduction in size, a detachment from its rails accompanied by the retention of the wheels for mobility.

5.38. L. Popova, Photomontage of the set for *The Earth in Turmoil* (*Zemlya dybom*), 1923, photomontage and collage on plywood. Only part of this work remains. [Photograph: © George Costakis 1981.]

This direct connection with the real world was reiterated in the props. Whereas in *The Magnanimous Cuckold* these had been minimal, in *The Earth in Turmoil* they were many and consisted almost entirely of the products of modern technology (plate 5.39) especially as expressed in the military field (field telephones, machine guns, aircraft).

Popova made this aspect explicit in an explanatory note published in *LEF*.

The design treatment for the play is on the plane of a living and not an aesthetic influence, with the agitational aspect of the show being the centre of attention ... the props ... do not change for decorative purposes but are taken from surrounding reality and introduced onto the stage in their normal form as far as the structure of the theatre permits ... The objects are chosen in line with relating the play's plot to the present tasks of building the Republic and with creating the opportunity for an agitational commentary on the play.[99]

This suggests a significant change of direction in the development of Constructivism in the theatre. In *The Magnanimous Cuckold* the apparatus could not be identified immediately as a specific machine but was rather an artistic synthesis and intepretation of the mechanical elements of a machine, resembling an abstracted machine. This abstract element was absent from *The Earth in Turmoil* where the artistic interpretation was not substituted for the mechanical, but where it was itself replaced by real mechanical objects taken from the real world. This implied a re-evaluation of the 'aesthetic' and what possessed aesthetic value. Whereas the former

production had been motivated by the idea of art (Constructivism) transforming life, in the second production the fusion of art and life, and the imperative to transform life itself led to the idea of the 'artistic' being a direct product of the real world of objects. In other words life was transforming art and the concept of what was 'beautiful'.[100]

This change of direction referred not only to the theatre, but to most areas of Constructivist activity such as literature where the reporting of facts was held to be superior as an artistic ideal to 'creative writing'.[101] This development had been inherent in the Constructivists' principle of making objects for the real world, their idealisation of the machine and their rejection of 'creativity' *per se*. The production of *The Earth in Turmoil* marked a stage in this process whereby Constructivism setting out to transform the environment was itself being transformed by that environment, returning to existing reality as a source of inspiration, of imagery and as a starting point for artistic work. The process of the decline of Constructivism had in fact begun. As a contemporary critic pointed out, '*The Earth in Turmoil* . . . contains a whole series of compromises with the old theatre.'[102]

This trend away from the abstract construction for theatrical decor and back to the real object was evident in Rodchenko's designs for the play *Inga*.[103] In a declaration issued at the time Rodchenko stated that his aim in his designs for the decor was to explore the possibilities of folding away wooden furniture.[104] He viewed this as a rational attempt to solve a problem of Soviet reality because Russia was rich in wood, and wooden furniture which could be easily folded away and

5.39. Last act from *The Earth in Turmoil*, 1923, where the peasants are converted to support the Revolution and are gathered around the agricultural implement. Popova's gantry crane structure is in the background. [Photograph: Society for Cultural Relations with the USSR, London.]

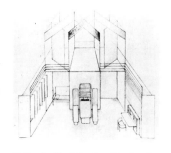

5.40. A. Rodchenko, Design for the set for the play *Inga*, 1929.

stored was a rational solution to the housing problems of everyday life. He betrayed a disenchantment with the design of furniture that performed a dual function. 'It is not possible for a table transformed into a bed to perform its straightforward duties'.[105] The overall scheme for the club (plate 5.40) was certainly less rigorous than that of 1925 (plate 5.9). Although this was partly a response to the exigencies of the theatrical action, it was also reiterated by the individual items of furniture. Although the tables retained a strict angularity, the design for the chair (plate 5.12) betrayed a concern for comfort and solidity expressed in an increased heaviness and more traditional approach to the use of material.[106] Whereas Rodchenko used

5.41. I. Rabinovich, Model of the Martian city as it appears in the film *Aelita*, 1924. [Photograph: National Film Archive, London.]

5.42. Scene from the film *Aelita*, showing Ekster's costumes and the set by V. Simov, 1924. [Photograph: National Film Archive, London.]

the curve in a functional way for the chairs of his Workers' Club of 1925, in the furniture for *Inga* he introduced the curve as a more arbitrary and decorative element to round off the angularity of otherwise completely unadorned forms. No extraneous elements are introduced yet there is a very striking change. The skeletal mode of construction which exposed and celebrated the internal and basic structure of an item of furniture or theatrical apparatus, reducing it to its essential components, was discarded in favour of the smooth flat surface which reclothed and redisguised the underlying structural skeleton of the object. The sets designed for *Inga* confirmed Beskin's prognosis that *The Earth in Turmoil* sounded the death knell for Constructivism in the theatre.[107]

STYLISATION

This chapter has examined a small selection of Constructivist designs, chosen either as successful examples of the formulation and operation of a Constructivist method in their specific field, or to indicate certain trends within Constructivism as a movement. The most extensive Constructivist experimentation with real materials in real space with specific functions was achieved in the theatre. The absence of response from the real world characteristic of that medium was also, in another way, responsible for the small quantity and compromised nature of Constructivist design work produced in concrete industrial fields. Despite this, certain conclusions can be drawn.

In theory the Constructivist-designed object was completely bereft of external, *a priori* factors of style. Based on the scientific study of objective criteria it represented a completely impersonalised and empirically derived, utilitarian product. However, when the actual products of this design process are examined certain visual characteristics they have in common become apparent. These visual similarities suggest that Constructivism evolved its own formal language amounting to a style, and that in the circumstances under which it had to operate the Constructivist 'design method' often entailed, in practice, the utilisation of these formal features as a pre-established vocabulary. The Constructivist system of organising form became expressed in skeletal angular structures, in rectangularity, simplicity, economy of line and material and a geometric solution to surface arrangements.

The danger and consequence of this development was that the characteristics of objects produced by the 'Constructivist method' could be used completely without any reference to the genuine method that had originally generated them.[108] A good example of the essentially decorative application of these elements was Rabinovich's model for the Martian city in *Aelita* (plates 5.41–2). Constructivism had strongly stated its opposition to the concept of 'applied art' and 'decoration' on the one hand, and any fixity or canonisation of form on the other. The trends that emerged were antithetical to the very essence of Constructivism itself, in that they reduced the Constructivist 'method' to a set of rules which could be applied mechanically to decorative tasks and surface solutions rather than as a system for the organisation of material according to the principles of tectonics, *faktura* and construction. Nevertheless, given the uncomprehending and technologically unpropitious climate within which these pioneer designers worked, their achievements were remarkable.

6 CONFINEMENT:PHOTOMONTAGE AND THE LIMITED DESIGN TASK

As the last chapter showed, Constructivism had failed in its primary objective of totally transforming the environment. Constructivist-designed objects had not entered into mass production and the Constructivists' attempts to engage directly in industry had been only partially successful. With the impossibility of working in industry the Constructivist artist lowered his sights to more practical problems such as the small-scale, well-defined design task, and in particular to typographical, poster and exhibition design, which fitted more neatly into traditional artistic categories, and which were less affected by the pressures of material scarcities.

The term 'Constructivist graphic design' seems to be somewhat contradictory. Constructivism was primarily concerned with three-dimensional utilitarian structures. Although two-dimensional experiments did have a place in laboratory work, and during the Civil War Constructivist artists had directly engaged in work on agitational posters, slogans and panels, such activity was essentially incidental to the main tasks of Constructivism as embodied by the three principles of tectonics, *faktura* and construction. However, instead of remaining essentially incidental to the main tasks of Constructivism, this type of activity became one of the dominant areas of practical work for many Constructivists during the second half of the 1920s.

Within these defined and limited areas of work, the photograph and particularly photomontage became an increasingly important feature of solutions to design tasks. This development reinforced the trend which had become apparent in the re-emergence of the object in theatrical Constructivism and the concern with contemporary technology which had led to an artistic dependence upon, and a limited return to, the real object.

In this chapter it will also be argued that the use of the photograph and photomontage reflected wider changes in the artistic environment: the re-emergence of easel painting, and in particular the re-emergence of Realism as an aggressively active artistic style. Fostered by Party preferences for an art comprehensible to the masses Realism became a positive element in the cultural atmosphere of the time and the Constructivists' use of the photograph will be interpreted here as a compromise with that powerful move towards Realism and the attempt to create a popular Soviet art. The mechanical and objective fixation of reality in photography and its use in photomontage tended ultimately to reinforce the influence of the real object which was depicted and which formed its subject matter. The photograph provided a way of being realistic without resorting to painterly Realism, but at the same time it gradually eroded the Constructivist principles with which it was initially manipulated. The photograph and photomontage therefore were at once a symptom and a cause of the decline of Constructivism, and of its increasing compromise with existing, as opposed to projected, reality.

The process of confinement was recognised as early as 1924 when Neznamov

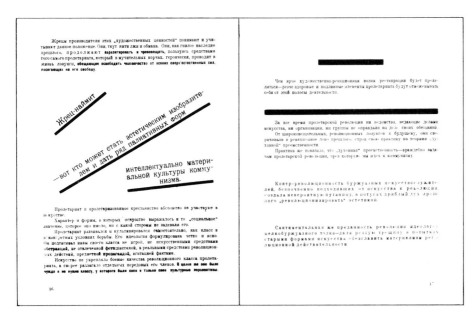

6.1. A page from Aleksei Gan's book *Constructivism* (*Konstruktivizm*), 1922.

writing in *LEF* acknowledged that the two chief areas of practical activity for Constructivists were designing advertising posters and constructing models.[1] Gan was even more explicit in the value which he gave to the general area of graphic design. Looking back in 1928 he asserted that in practical terms the Constructivists had been able to demonstrate the principles of their school most consistently in the areas of 'graphics, cinematography and architecture'.[2] He considered that in the area of graphics, which he defined as agitational literature (books, magazines, and newspapers), the Constructivist had been able to formulate an 'artistic and produc-

6.2. A. Gan, Cover for the Constructivist architectural journal *Contemporary Architecture* (*Sovremennaya arkhitektura*), No. 4, 1926.

6.3. A. Gan, Poster for the First Exhibition of Contemporary Architecture, Moscow, 1927.

6.4. V. and G. Stenberg, Poster for the film *Springtime* (*Vesnoi*), 1930. [Photograph: Courtesy Arts Council of Great Britain.]

6.5. A. Lavinskii, Poster for Eisenstein's film *Battleship Potemkin*, 1925.

tionist' method which was designed to achieve the maximum social and artistic impact because it considered not only production techniques, and artistic criteria, but also social and political requirements and the psychological factors governing the viewer's response.[3]

Gan himself had worked primarily as a typographer. In his theoretical treatise *Constructivism* of 1922 he had used typography for the active reinforcement of his message. He had slung short sharp phrases diagonally across the pages like slogans on banners, he had utilised heavy underlining and different thicknesses of type, and he had varied spacing and used different type faces (serif and sanserif) to emphasise his points. He had even enclosed his statement that 'Art is dead' within black borders. All these efforts had given the pages of his book the visual impact of a poster (plate 6.1).

Gan, who had been a constant associate of the architectural group of Constructivists, OSA, had been responsible for the layouts and covers of the group's journal, *Contemporary Architecture* since it commenced publication in 1926 (plate 6.2). In 1927 Gan designed the poster for OSA's exhibition, the First Exhibition of Contemporary Architecture (plate 6.3). Under his direction the First Working Group of Constructivists had become increasingly involved in typography and graphic design.[4]

Gan himself seems not to have made any intensive use of photomontage; for other Constructivists, however, it became a central area of concern in their two-dimensional design work. Many Constructivists explored this field, including Popova, Stepanova, Lavinskii and Medunetskii. Among the most well known examples of graphic designs by erstwhile Constructivists are the film posters designed by the Stenberg brothers throughout the 1920s (plate 6.4). They rarely utilised photomontage but employed principles of dynamism and structure which had been evinced in a more startling form in their three-dimensional work, and which were obscured, diluted and eventually obliterated by the figurative content demanded by the posters. Lavinskii did use some photomontage in posters such as the one he devised for Eisenstein's film *Battleship Potemkin* in 1925 (plate 6.5). However, the Constructivists who became the chief practitioners of photomontage were Gustav Klutsis, El Lissitzky (a late adherant to Constructivism) and Aleksandr Rodchenko. These will be the central figures of this study for they demonstrate most clearly the developments, attainments and the ultimately fatal defects of the attempts to implement Constructivist principles in this field.

Graphic art and photomontage rose to prominence as Constructivist activities in an artistic situation where Realism was re-emerging as an aggressive artistic credo.[5] The tradition of a realist and didactic art had never been totally extinguished in Russia. During the Civil War the requirements of agitation and propaganda had fostered the creation of images which could be easily identified by a largely illiterate population. Although avant-garde groups and the more traditional artists like the Wanderers had been hit by material shortages their creative and exhibiting activity had continued during the Civil War period despite having been reduced.[6] The preoccupation of Western art historians with those artists who came through from the pre-revolutionary avant-garde has created a quite distorted impression of the cultural and aesthetic norms of the climate in which these artists operated in the 1920s. During the early 1920s other artistic movements were making themselves felt very strongly and asserting conceptions of progressive art which differed from those of the avant-garde. In order to understand therefore the impact Realism had on the climate of the time it is necessary briefly to examine these groups.[7]

In 1922 Realism was revitalised by the formation of that aggressive artistic organisation the Association of the Artists of Revolutionary Russia (Assotsiatsiya khudozhnikov revolyutsionnoi Rossii, hereafter referred to by its abbreviation AKhRR). It was established following a discussion at the forty-seventh 'exhibition of the Wanderers (Peredvizhniki) on 4 March 1922.[8] Radimov, the president of that society, declared that 'artists in our society must depict accurately in painting and sculpture the events of the Revolution, they must portray its leaders and participants, and illustrate the role of the People – the simple toilers – the workers and peasants'.[9]

Narkompros and INKhUK were attacked for their Futurism and Katsman accused those artists (who had appropriated the epithet 'left' for themselves) of being politically reactionary because their art was that of the 'Imperial French bourgeoisie'.[10] From the first, AKhRR considered the task of revolutionary painting to be the depiction of revolutionary events, and combined this with an uncompromisingly Realist stance and a stern rejection of all artistic experimentation. The artistic credo of AKhRR was 'heroic realism', as it declared at its first exhibition in May 1922: 'The revolutionary day, the revolutionary moment, is an heroic day, an heroic moment, and we must now in the monumental forms of heroic realism reveal our artistic experience.'[11] No precise definition of 'heroic realism' as an artistic method was formulated. In practice it entailed depicting with documentary accuracy themes related to the Revolution and social reconstruction, and aggressively opposing any formal artistic investigations. A fine though not typical example of such an approach is the famous painting by Brodskii, *Lenin at Smol'ny* of 1930 (plate 6.6).

6.6. I. Brodskii, *Lenin at Smol'nyi* (*Lenin v Smol'nom*), 1930, oil on canvas, 190 × 287 cm. Tret'yakov Gallery, Moscow.

Its dedication to Realism as an artistic style and the Revolution as subject matter quickly gained AKhRR official support. Having assured the Central Committee of the Party of its allegiance, AKhRR was advised by that body to go into the factories and depict the workers in their everyday life.[12] Krupskaya, who had condemned the Futurists as 'spokesmen for the worst elements in the art of the past',[13] gave her support as head of Glavpolitprosvet to the venture. Skachko, the head of Glavpolitprosvet's art department, was closely associated with the group and gave them their name. Finally in 1928 AKhRR received the ultimate stamp of official approval when the entire Politburo made an official visit to its tenth exhibition – the first time that any exhibition had been accorded such an honour.[14]

AKhRR exhibitions were frequent and they concentrated on specific themes, such as the Red Army (their second, fourth and tenth exhibitions, 1922, 1923 and 1928 respectively) and revolutionary life and work (third, sixth and seventh exhibitions held in 1922, 1924 and 1925 respectively). The revolutionary and contemporary nature of their themes and the realistic style of their works ensured them a ready market. The Red Army Museum and the Museum of the Revolution were their main patrons, utilising AKhRR works to supplement scarce photographic material for their displays.[15] Despite well-founded criticisms levelled at both the artistic quality of AKhRR (their technical prowess was often lamentable) and their aggressiveness, this official patronage ensured their economic viability and continued existence. The association played in the field of the visual arts a role equivalent to that of RAPP in literature.[16] It was the most powerful of the Realist groups dominating the artistic situation at the end of the 1920s and spearheading the attack on those artistic innovations of the avant-garde, collectively termed Formalism.

The rise to cultural prominence of AKhRR was symptomatic of a more general artistic trend away from the art of the avant-garde among the younger generation of artists in the mid-1920s. These young artists advocated a return to conventional forms of easel painting and proposed a return to a figurative subject matter and realistic image. Proof that such a trend existed is provided by the plethora of new artistic groups which were formed during NEP, all of which, despite variations in their artistic credos, argued for the necessity and validity of figurative art. Amongst the earliest of these groups is NOZh (Novoe obshchestvo zhivopistsev – New Society of Painters) organised in 1920–1 by former pupils of Malevich, Tatlin and Ekster.[17] Their manifesto, printed in the catalogue of their first exhibition in November 1922 declared, that as 'former left artists' they considered the 'analytical period in art is finished'.[18] They criticised Constructivism's nihilistic attitude to art, its mechanised conception of man, its fetishism of the machine and its enshrinement of technology as an absolute value, and the fact that lacking any real opportunities for realising their ideas the Constructivists had reached a cul-de-sac. NOZh declared, 'We wish to create real works of art ... We believe in the art of the future ... that its means and properties are still able to systematise the feelings of a revolutionary environment. We believe that the future will bring a new form of painting, corresponding to the tempo of modernity and contemporary psychology.'[19]

A similar artistic disillusionment with Constructivism was experienced by the students of the Second State Free Art Studios who formed the membership of the art group Bytie (Objective Reality).[20] Organised in 1921 as 'a protest against the extremism of left art' and Constructivism's rejection of easel painting, they declared that 'only by rejecting the use of painterly techniques as an end in themselves is it possible for Russian painting once again to become social'.[21] This was to be achieved by concentrating on the 'problem of the content or subject matter of art'.[22] In 1924 in response to the similarity of their ideas NOZh joined Bytie, and in 1926 the remnants of the Knave of Diamonds amalgamated with Bytie.[23]

The formation of OST (Obshchestvo khudozhnikov-stankovistov – Society of Easel Painters) in 1925 was a result of dissatisfaction not only with Constructivism but also with the artistic inadequacies of AKhRR, the pseudo-Cézannism of NOZh and the stylistic weaknesses of the other painting groups of this time.[24] Most of OST's members had studied at the Free Studios and were graduates from the VKhUTEMAS.[25] They had therefore been strongly influenced by the formal experiments of the time and by the interest in technology. Among their members Vil'yams had been director of the Museum of Painterly Culture from July 1922 to July 1923,[26] Lyushin had made a model in 1919 for an Interplanetary Communication Station and Vyalov had experimented with reliefs.[27] They declared that art should participate in the building of socialism but that this art should be easel painting and should combine 'revolutionary contemporaneity and clarity in the choice of subject' with 'a striving towards absolute mastery in the field of easel painting, drawing and sculpture'.[28] The works produced by the group until it dissolved in 1930 were of an eclectic nature, concentrating on industrial themes such as Deineka's *On the Building Site of the New Factory Workshops* (plate 4.1) or urban life and physical culture.

These groups formed the bases of artistic life during the 1920s. The aggressive tactics of AKhRR, strengthened by official support, led to the absorption of the other groups and a considerable weakening of the avant-garde's position by the end of the 1920s. Eventually in 1932 the party's decree 'On the Reformation of Literary and Artistic Organisations' led to the dissolution of all existing artistic and literary groups and made provisions for the setting up of a single Union of Artists which would impose a uniform ideological control over both style and subject matter.[29] That organisation equated artistic work in the building of socialism with Socialist Realism as an artistic theory and practice directed by the Party.[30] However, prior to this endorsement of AKhRR's artistic credo, the government's general artistic policy, expounded in its declaration of political impartiality in the arts of 1925 had sheltered and fostered the aggressive activity of the extreme proletarian artists (AKhRR) who were advocating Realism directly to reflect and thus participate in the political struggle.[31] In many respects the Constructivists' adoption of photomontage can be seen as an attempt to develop an alternative form of agitational art which could win government support yet still be in accordance with Constructivist principles.

THE DEVELOPMENT OF PHOTOMONTAGE

Artistically the use of the photograph was based on, and developed from, the experiments in collage which had also formed the basis for the emergence of non-utilitarian constructions. Both Russian and West European artists had already explored the possibilities of using photographs as collage elements in the pre-war period. Malevich, for example, had incorporated a photograph into his painting entitled *Woman at a Tram-Stop*.[32] However, it has been commonly accepted that this practice had first been extensively developed by the Berlin Dadaists, and that they had invented the term 'photomontage' to describe this new technique.[33] From its inception therefore photomontage was intimately connected with the 'anti-art' stance of Dada and its specific nihilistic agitational aims. Used as a 'ready-made' image the photograph was combined with other extraneous materials such as cuttings from magazines and newspapers, drawings and lettering, to produce images that would destroy the complacency of the post-war world.

The same qualities of the photographic image and photomontage that recommended it to the Dada movement also made it attractive to the Constructivists. The photograph integrated the worlds of the machine (technology and industry) with the world of art.[34] It was an image produced by a mechanical apparatus (the camera) which could be infinitely reproducible by mechanical means. In this way, each photograph was an original and thus destroyed the mystique attached to the concept of the unique work of art, and was truly a 'mass' art form.[35]

Although it developed from the technique of Cubist collage, photomontage performed a different function. The representational qualities of the image and the ideas it engendered in combination with other elements were more important than its material or tactile presence in the work.[36] The concrete quality of the photograph and of photomontage brought the work into direct contact with the real world. In one direction this ultimately led to the ready-mades of Duchamp, in the other to the use of photographic representation of objects as substitutes for the objects themselves. This had the additional advantage of extending thematically the range of subjects that could be treated. *LEF* explained:

By photomontage we mean the use of the photographic print as a figurative means. The combination of photographs changes the composition of graphic images.

The meaning of this change is that *the photograph is not the drawing of a visual fact but the exact fixation of it*. This precision and documentary quality give the photograph a power to influence the viewer that the graphic image is never able to attain.[37]

It was precisely this ability to present a concrete image linking the everyday life of the viewer with the political and social precepts of the Communist Party that made the photograph used in photomontage such a valuable propaganda weapon. Abstract political and social ideas, commands and necessities could be brought within the scope of the comprehension of even the most illiterate peasant. Klutsis later repudiated any debt to the Dadaists in developing photomontage and asserted the independence of the Russian movement, firmly placing its origins in Soviet agitational work of the years 1919–20.

> There are two general tendencies in the development of photomontage. The first originated in American advertising. This so-called publicity-formalistic photomontage is widely used by the Dadaists and Expressionists of the West. The second line developed independently on the soil of the Soviet Union. The second line is agitational–political photomontage, which has developed its own method, principles and laws of construction . . .
>
> In the USSR, photomontage appeared in the 'left' front of art when non-objective art was already finished . . .
>
> Photomontage as a new artistic method appeared in the USSR in 1919–20 . . . the first photomontage in the USSR was the artist G. Klutsis' *Dynamic City*, where the photograph was first used as an element of texture and figurativeness mounted according to the principle of different scales.[38]

KLUTSIS AND THE POLITICAL POSTER

Whereas in the West photomontage was no more than just another branch of art, Klutsis saw it as being, in the Soviet Union, one part of a total system of interrelated forms of socially reconstructive activity.

> The proletarian revolution presented the spatial arts with a series of completely new complex tasks: designing socialist cities, communal housing, parks of culture and rest, green towns, agricultural villages, workers' clubs . . . clothing, mass spectacles, and workers' rooms. The new tasks called into being new types and forms of artistic work. Among these is photomontage.[39]

Therefore for Klutsis the ideological element and more specifically the communist political element was an essential factor in photomontage. His definition of photomontage made this explicit. 'One must not think that photomontage is the expressive composition of photographs. It always includes a political slogan, colour and graphic elements.'[40]

Klutsis claimed that *The Dynamic City* of 1919 (plate 6.7) was the first photomontage.[41] This may seem very early, but since Klutsis executed another photomontage for Lenin's Plan of Electrification in 1920 his dating of 1919 would not seem to be exaggerated.[42] Klutsis' inscription on *The Dynamic City* read, 'Voluminally spatial Suprematism + photomontage. The overthrow of non-objectivity and the birth of photomontage as an independent art form.'[43] He thereby asserted his claim to be the Russian pioneer of photomontage, although his use of the German term indicates that at the time of writing this inscription he was aware of the German term and of the movement which produced it. Either he wrote the inscription at the time of making the montage, in which case he was aware of contemporary Dada experiments and was basing his work on theirs, or the inscription was a later addition and he merely borrowed the name and developed, as he asserted, photomontage independently of the Germans. It has proved almost impossible to establish any precise relationship to the Dada experiments, and it is possible that photomontage developed independently in the Soviet Union.[44]

Klutsis' photomontage *The Dynamic City* was evidently closely related to the painting of the same name he executed in 1919–20 (colour plate XIV) under the influence of Suprematism, Lissitzky's PROUN compositions, Malevich's paintings and the spatial principles of the latter's architectural models and drawings.[45] Although Klutsis' painting and his photomontage differ slightly they have a common structure: a series of rectangular and cuboid bodies are grouped along a diagonal axis against the background of a spherical structure. The apparent three-dimensionality of these bodies is ambiguous since their interrelationships, recessions and protrusions do not produce a coherent three-dimensional structure.

In the photomontage (plate 6.7) Klutsis used photographs of the building surfaces of American skyscrapers (their concrete walls encompassing numerous floors and multitudinous windows) to form the sides of various rectangular structures composing the elements of this dynamic city. He also added photographs of workmen at the extremities of these structures. The placing of these figures suggested that he intended to present this flying city as a world in microcosm with its own centre of gravity enabling men to stand apparently upside down on the lower ends of the buildings.[46]

Klutsis used the photograph in this instance as an element representing existing reality to establish a specific relationship to real life in what is otherwise an abstract composition. As such it had parallels with Picasso's collages, the relative scale of the matter treated suggesting the different approach. The photographs related Klutsis' projected structure to the real world more directly than a painting of the

6.7. G. Klutsis, *The Dynamic City* (*Dinamicheskii gorod*), *c*. 1919, photomontage. Whereabouts unknown. [Reproduced in *Izofront*, 1931.]

6.8. G. Klutsis, *Sport*, 1922, photomontage. Whereabouts unknown. [Reproduced in *Izofront*, 1931.]

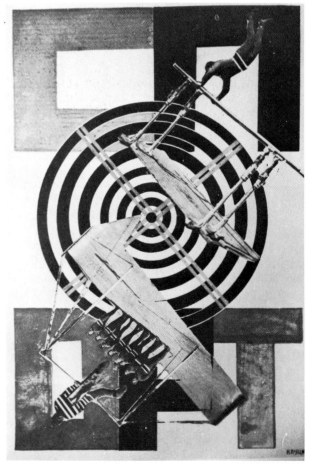

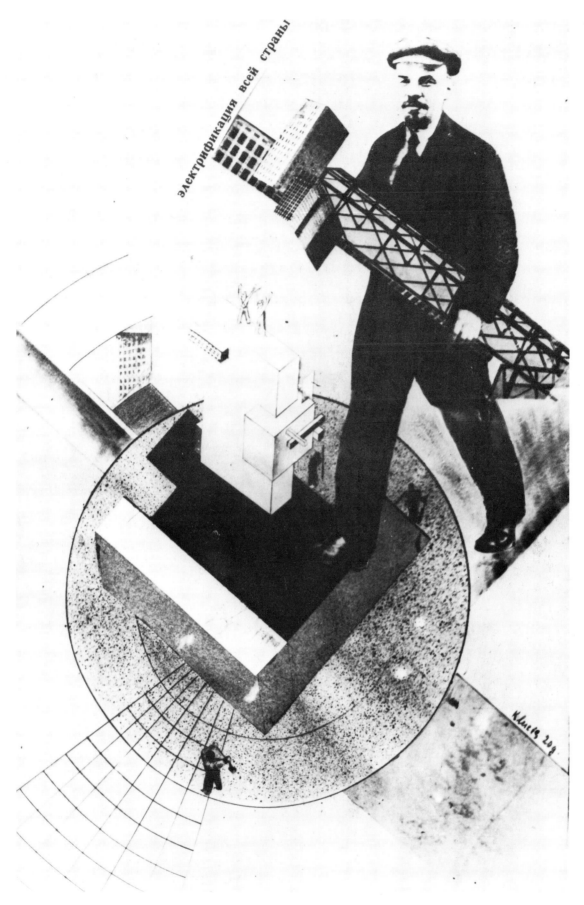

электрификация всей страны

same structure could have done. Ceasing to be an abstract composition it became the representation of an abstract concept of the modern technological city. The introduction of the photographs of real building surfaces communicated to the viewer that the concept lay within the realm of the possible. Klutsis utilised the familiar to make the unfamiliar seem less improbable.

In 1920 to mark Lenin's fiftieth birthday and the introduction of his Plan of Electrification at the Eighth Congress of the Soviets Klutsis used photomontage in the design of two posters with a specifically agitational subject matter: *The Old World and the World being Built Anew* and *The Electrification of the Entire Country* (plate 6.9).[47] In the latter a striding Lenin holds an openwork iron structure (presumably an electricity pylon), and four ray-like structures emanating from the centre emphasise the ideological message of progress. The contrast to *The Dynamic City* is immediately apparent. The earlier photomontage was primarily conceived as an abstract composition to which realistic photographic images had been affixed. The photographs gave a concrete element to a utopian and otherwise purely artistic conception. The importance of *Electrification* lay in the fact that it was conceived as a poster with a specific agitational aim and it carried a specific ideological content.[48] Already the specifically agitational content was the dominant concern, taking precedence over purely artistic considerations.

Klutsis' penchant for diagonally based compositions was a constantly reiterated element in his work. He used it in 1922 in the photomontage *Sport* (plate 6.8) where against the large chunky lettering of the word 'Sport' – a sanserif type which was becoming current at this time and was typical of Constructivist typography[49] – the images of gymnasts were superimposed on a rotating structure composed of concentric circles. Any equilibrium in the design was destroyed by the figures (on the gymnastic equipment) set at strong diagonals to give dynamism to the whole

6.10. G. Klutsis, Poster entitled *Male and Female Workers All to the Election of the Soviets* (*Rabochie i rabotnitsy vse na perevybory sovetov*), 1930.

6.11. G. Klutsis, Poster for the Anti-Imperialist Exhibition, (*Anti-imperialisticheskaya vystavka*), 1931.

composition. Their attachment to two of the four spokes on the wheel introduced a circular, rotating motion.

These experiments formed the basis for Klutsis' work with political posters which he produced intensively during the late 1920s. Despite the trend towards a reduced number of component images, and the greater dominance of photographic and typographic elements over graphic ones, these posters continued to be organised according to the formal predilections of Constructivism, and to employ strict colour combinations of red, black and white in conjunction with the photographs. Klutsis exploited his techniques to produce the series of 'Posters 1930–1933' forming part of the agitational and ideological struggle for the First Five Year Plan.[50] One of the most striking images from this series was *We will repay the Coal Debt to our Country* (colour plate XV) in which the three figures are united by the rhythm of the ascending parallel of their diagonally advancing legs, giving them the coherence and dynamism of a chorus line. In the poster *Male and Female Workers All to the Election of the Soviets* of 1930 (plate 6.10) Klutsis again employed a primarily diagonal arrangement of ascending triangular hands, beginning with small hands and growing larger.[51] The lines of lettering set at a contrasting diagonal emphasised the dynamic effect with the use of large initial letters.[52] This was described as 'the best of all the election posters' because of its 'expressive strength' and 'political actuality'.[53]

Gradually during the 1930s Klutsis' work became increasingly organised on symmetrical principles and in contrast to the simple, solid type-face which had been employed by the Constructivists, Klutsis began to use a serif type with a more flamboyant structure, and varying thicknesses. This development could be seen to have its beginning in the poster Klutsis designed in 1931 for the Anti-Imperialist Exhibition (plate 6.11) where he used serif type mixed with the Constructivists' sanserif heavy type-face. His cover of 1935 for *Peasant Woman* combined three different types, all of a more traditional, ornate nature, which were incorporated into a circular, completely symmetrical and static composition centred on a painted, not photographic image.[54]

LISSITZKY AND THE PHOTOGRAPH IN EXHIBITION DESIGN

In contrast to Klutsis, Lissitzky seems to have been involved with typography before he became interested in photomontage. His early work such as the design for Mayakovskii's *For the Voice* was still influenced by Suprematist stylistic devices although the way in which he formed the book with an index, so that 'the book form is given a functional shape in keeping with its specific purpose', allied him to Constructivism's fusion of the technical and the artistic.[55] His principles of 'optics instead of phonetics' and that 'the idea should be given form through the letters'[56] also were put into practice in *Die Kunstismen* (colour plate XVI).

Lissitzky seems to have become interested in the potential of the photograph in the early 1920s when he began to experiment with photograms, in which additional elements were added in successive exposures. One of the earliest examples is *Self-Portrait: The Constructor* of 1924 (plate 6.12). In this work the photographic image of a hand holding a pair of compasses was fused with the images of Lissitzky's head against a background of graph paper, his personal letter-heading, the letters *XYZ*, and a circle.[57] This compound image indicating Lissitzky's activity as a typographer and constructor juxtaposed elements of reality, according to their significance for the subject without regard for their natural proportions, and traditional perspectival relationships. This approach corresponded to photomontage, and made it possible to incorporate different viewpoints, themes and subjects within the scope of one composite image, almost as a type of motionless moving picture or 'montage' in Eisenstein's sense outside of the film.[58]

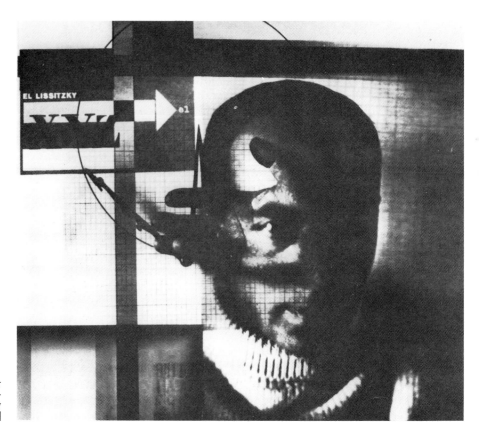

6.12. El Lissitzky, *Self-Portrait: The Constructor*, 1924, photogram. [Photograph: Courtesy Galerie Gmurzynska, Cologne.]

Lissitzky applied the technique of photomontage in the design of exhibition layouts.[59] One of the finest examples of his exploitation of photomontage in this area was the frieze which he composed with Sen'kin for the International Press Exhibition, Pressa, at Cologne in 1928 (plate 6.13), which aimed to show various aspects of Soviet life and the tasks facing the press in educating the masses.[60] This compilation of images was accompanied by a structure representing the rollers of printing machines to which were affixed the various types of images it produced (plate 6.14). This already pointed towards a choice of descriptive photographs utilised without the addition of any elements other than typographical. Such an approach is found in the entrance to the Soviet pavilion at the International Hygiene Exhibition at Dresden in 1930 (plate 6.15), and in his cover for *The USSR in Construction* of 1933 (plate 6.16).

6.13a-b. El Lissitzky, Collages for the Pressa exhibition, Cologne, 1928.

RODCHENKO AND THE OBJECTIVE FUNCTION OF THE PHOTOGRAPH

Rodchenko's development had incorporated many of the aspects of Constructivist graphics which have already been discussed in this chapter. His friend and collaborator Mayakovskii later emphasised the role Rodchenko had played in this field and his contributions to Soviet photomontage and graphic design. 'In the past three years ... [he] has given graphic art a completely new orientation.'[61]

However, there is no evidence to suggest that Rodchenko produced collages incorporating printed matter of a photographic or representative nature (printed realistic images) before 1922. Prior to this he had been working on abstract compilations of materials (plates 1. 26-7), and his first collages were based primarily on the exploitation of isolated letters, words or phrases cut from newspapers and magazines, interspersed with plain coloured or patterned strips and variously shaped pieces of paper. In a collage of 1919 (plate 6.17) the strips of paper forming the basic structure of two intersecting diagonals provide a framework for the composition of the printed matter, which is confined to lettering. Such experiments bore a strong similarity to the typographical compositions of the Futurists and the collages of the Dadaists.[62] These similarities were acknowledged by *Kino-Fot* in 1922, where the difference between montage as employed by the French Dadaists and by the Russian Constructivists was explained in terms of the new ideological content with which the Constructivists endowed the technique.[63]

Certainly it was immediately applied to the area of book design. In 1923 Rod-

FOLLOWING PAGES

6.16. El Lissitzky, Cover of *The USSR in Construction* (*SSSR na stroike – UdSSR im Bau*), No. 9, 1933.

XIV. G. Klutsis, *The Dynamic City* (*Dinamicheskii gorod*), 1919-20, oil with sand and concrete on wood, 87 × 64·5 cm. Collection George Costakis, Athens. [Photograph: © George Costakis 1981.]

6.14. El Lissitzky, Transmissions, part of the layout of the Pressa exhibition, Cologne, 1928. [Photograph: Courtesy Galerie Gmurzynska, Cologne.]

6.15. Entrance to the Soviet Pavilion at the International Hygiene Exhibition, Dresden, 1930. [Photograph: Courtesy Galerie Gmurzynska, Cologne.]

USSR im Bau

DAS SECHZEHNTE JAHR
DER REVOLUTION

9

VEREINIGUNG DER STAATSVERLAGE RSFSR

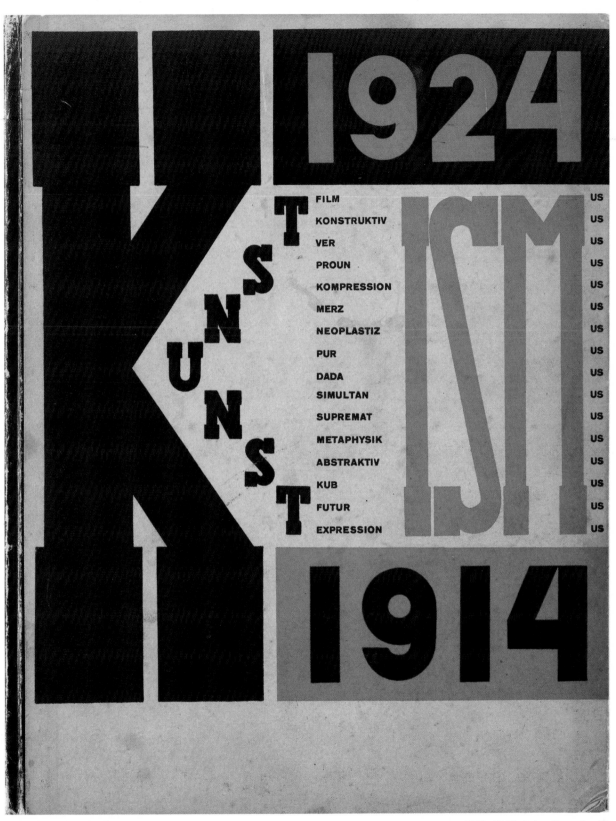

XV. (left) G. Klutsis, Poster entitled *We shall repay the Coal Debt to our Country* (*Vernem ugoľnyi dolg strane*), 1930, *c.* 102·5 × 72 cm. Collection The Museum of Modern Art, New York.

XVI. El Lissitzky, Cover for *Die Kuntismen*, 1925. Private collection, London.

XVII. A, Rodchenko, Cover for the series *Mess Mend*, by Dzhim Dollar (Marietta Shaginyan), Moscow 1924. *c.* 17 × 13 cm.

XVIII. A. Rodchenko, Designs for logos for the Soviet Aeroplane agency, Dobrolet. [Reproduced in *LEF*, No. 2, 1923.]

chenko illustrated Mayakovskii's poem *About This* with a series of ten photomontages made up of material from advertisements, magazines, newspapers and personal photographs of Mayakovskii and Lili Brik.[64] The cover (plate 6.18) was based on Lili Brik's face, and in the illustrations, as for example plate 6.19, Rodchenko used the Briks' telephone number, 67–10, and telephone wires stretching across a skyline of American skyscrapers set at a diagonal to link the top right where Mayakovskii, attentively listening to a receiver as large as himself, sits tortured by jealousy (the primeval quality of which is indicated by the dinosaur) and the lower left-hand corner where the telephone mouthpiece is answered only by a yawning housekeeper. The series of photomontages as a whole was characterised less by a dependence on lettering than by a juxtapositioning of images.

Rodchenko employed the same approach in the *Crisis* photomontage, also of 1923 (plate 6.20), which depicts people falling from two aeroplanes onto a disintegrating urban landscape. Like the Dadaists, Rodchenko exploited the objective descriptive content of the photograph to give reality to impossible but allegorical images, conveying coherent ideas.

The political and social commitment evident in this photomontage was more overt in the advertising work Rodchenko did in collaboration with Mayakovskii. For them advertising was a means of directly engaging in the consolidation and expansion of the economy under NEP which was an essential prerequisite for the political survival of the Soviet State. 'In every military victory, in every economic success 9/10 is the result of the skill and power of our agitation. Advertising is industrial, commercial agitation.'[65] In some later recollections Rodchenko described the manner of their creative enterprise.

6.17. A. Rodchenko, *Untitled Collage*, 1919, various papers on paper.

6.18. A. Rodchenko, Cover for Mayakovskii's poem *About This* (*Pro eto*), 1923, photomontage.

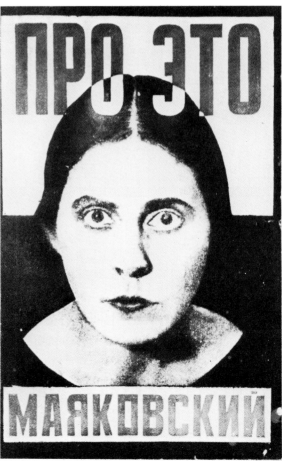

The work on Soviet advertising went at full speed. Volodya wrote the texts on the piano in the evening. In the day he took the orders or delivered them. Two students from VKhUTEMAS and I drew until morning. The whole of Moscow was adorned with our productions. The signboard of the Moscow Association for Processing Agricultural Products. All the kiosks were ours. The signboard of the State Publishing House. Black, red, gold. The State Rubber Trust, the State Universal Stores, *The Small Light* ... We did almost fifty posters, almost a hundred signboards, packets, wrappers, illuminated signs, advertising columns, illustrations in journals and papers.[66]

The products of their co-operation were typified by his posters for the Rubber Trust, such as the one for dummies of 1923 'There have never been and are no better dummies. You'll want to suck them until old age' (plate 6.21).[67] Utilising photomontage Rodchenko also designed posters such as the advertising poster for Vertov's 1924 film *Cinema Eye* (plate 6.22) and bookcovers such as the series for Dzhim Dollar's (Shaginyan's) *Mess Mend* published in 1924 (colour plate XVII).

Apparently one of Rodchenko's first forays into the area of typography was his work on the design of film titles for Vertov's documentary newsreel *Cinema Truth* from 1922 to 1924. Treating the titles as integral parts of the cinematic whole, Rodchenko devised three types of title: those in large type slung boldly across the screen, titles in which the letters receded in size creating an illusion of depth and moving titles which unfolded as the film progressed. As a result, 'from being a dead point in the film the titles became an organic part of it' (plate 6.23).[68] Rodchenko exploited this experience in his two-colour logo designs for the Soviet aeroplane agency Dobrolet (colour plate XVIII).

The posters and his book designs combined his experience both with photomontage and with typography. In the same year, 1922, Rodchenko began work on the magazine *Kino-Fot*, and in 1923 he took over the design work for the layout and

6.19. (facing page left) A. Rodchenko, Photomontaged illustration for Mayakovskii's *About This* (*Pro eto*), 1923.

6.20. (facing page right) A. Rodchenko, *Crisis* (*Krizis*), 1923, photomontage.

6.21. (facing page left) A. Rodchenko, Advertising poster for the Rubber Trust, 1923. The text by Mayakovskii reads: 'There have never been and are no better dummies. You will want to suck them until old age.'

6.22. (facing page right) A. Rodchenko, Poster for Vertov's film *Cinema Eye* (*Kino glaz*), 1924.

6.23. A. Rodchenko, Film titles for Vertov's film *Cinema Eye*, 1922, as illustrated in *Kino-Fot*, No. 5, 1922.

covers of *LEF*, a task he retained throughout the journal's publication and until the last number of *Novyi LEF* appeared in 1928.[69] In the early numbers he sometimes created photomontages (plate 6.24) but in the later issues he often used a complete photograph without intercutting or juxtaposition (plate 6.25). This reflected a change in the direction of Rodchenko's own interests.

From 1924 Rodchenko gradually began to concentrate less on photomontage and more on producing the photographic image itself. In that year he began to take photographs.[70] In manipulating the camera Rodchenko used unusual viewpoints, exploiting to the full the camera's optical eccentricities and potential. He considered that the artist was able to train the eye to receive visual impressions simultaneously from all sides, and that this corresponded to the consciousness of contemporary man.[71] The artist's duty was therefore to disclose new facets and aspects of reality in his work.

> In order to teach man to look in a new way it is necessary to photograph ordinary, familiar objects from totally unexpected viewpoints and in unexpected positions, and to photograph new objects from various vantage points so as to give a complete impression of the object.
>
> We are taught to look in a routine, inculcated manner. We must discover the visible world. We must revolutionise our visual thinking.[72]
>
> We must remove the cataract from our eyes.

The camera was the means to 'change the usual way of looking at things' because, Rodchenko argued, 'the lens of the camera is the pupil of the eye of the cultured man in socialist society'.[73] Rodchenko used the photograph not as a means of straightforward social or political propaganda but as a means of visual re-education; to expand man's consciousness of the environment. The mechanised eye of the camera (a visual machine) was to act as the educative eye of socialist man (i.e. to enable him to perceive reality through the machine and the machine aesthetic). In this approach, Rodchenko and the Constructivists could be seen to have acknowledged still further the restraints of reality and the need for a very prolonged propaganda and educational process to create the prerequisites for their concept of design.

For Rodchenko, this process involved a thorough investigation of the photograph, the camera and photographic techniques. It was typical of Constructivism at this time that this preoccupation with the machine and its products and processes, led, through its own momentum, back to an objective fixation of reality and thereby to the representational image. Many of Rodchenko's experiments in this vein were reproduced in the pages of *Novyi LEF*. In 1928, for example, Rodchenko produced a series of photographs based on exploring the qualities of transparent objects in light (plate 6.26).

> A crystal vase was placed on glass and above it an electric lamp hidden by a dark disk to avoid spoiling the plastic form. The shot was taken from below through the glass at a distance.
>
> In order for this to be comprehensible it is necessary to look at the shot from below raising it above your head parallel to the ceiling.
>
> In photograph No. 2, a glass was set on a glass rosette upturned. The light comes from below left through the edge of the rosette.
>
> In photograph No. 3, a hanging electric lamp was placed behind a jug of water ... The light source came from behind the base of the jug's handle.[74]

The image as recorded on the film was utilised as the finished product. Therefore apart from defining the visual experiment itself the artist did not intrude in the process. The finished image of the environment was an objective reflection (however mechanised and unusual) of the existing environment. Although Rodchenko's experiments with the camera were inspired by a formal analysis of the photograph as an artistic image this development in his work, on the whole, points to a return to the integrated object, existing reality and the present urban and rural environment as a starting point for his work, a return to the representational image and to a limited, but explicitly artistic, experimentation with it.

*   *   *

6.26. A. Rodchenko, Experiments photographing transparent objects, 1928. [Reproduced in *Novyi LEF*, No. 3, 1928.]

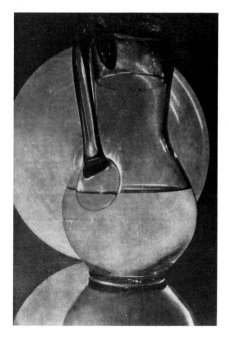

Recognising the impossibility of working within the existing industrial framework of the Soviet Union in the early years of the 1920s, the Constructivists in general eagerly embraced graphic design as an area of work which could respond to their social and political imperatives, and through which they could participate in the construction of a Socialist society, although at one remove from the material constructions they initially envisaged producing. This field had originally been an incidental form of experimentation, as for example in Gan's designs for *Constructivism*, but as the 1920s progressed Constructivists became increasingly reliant upon it for their economic survival. This trend was intensified by the pressure of the cultural climate of the time towards Realism. This gradual confinement of Constructivist activity within generally two-dimensional display tasks led to a consequent limitation of their own aspirations. Where they had previously sought to restructure the whole living environment from the inside, they now were only able to exercise their creativity within the relatively cosmetic and transient medium of photomontage and exhibition display design. The dimension of social construction had been pared away, leaving them with merely artistic tasks. At the same time, the use of photomontage and the photograph led them back to the real image, and thus to traditional concepts of art and its representational role.

Constructivism's demise took place against the emergence of Socialist Realism which reasserted that primarily didactic, socially involved and naturalistic tradition of Russian culture which in the nineteenth century had been expressed in the theories of Chernyshevskii and Dobrolyubov and in the artistic practice of the Wanderers. In the social emphasis which the Constructivists placed on their work they also belonged to this tradition, but their complete rejection of art as a valid activity and their contempt for Realism as an aesthetic principle placed them in conflict with groups who based their aesthetic credo on a complete acceptance of this tradition and of Realism as an artistic style. The objective reflection of reality in the photograph used in photomontage brought Constructivism back into this tradition and as such was a vehicle of Constructivism's decline.

7 ORGANIC CONSTRUCTION: HARNESSING AN ALTERNATIVE TECHNOLOGY

THE PRECEDING chapters have examined Constructivism as a movement which took its inspiration from the world of the machine and from the principles of mechanised production. In this chapter I wish to put forward the hypothesis that in addition to this mainstream, mechanically inspired Constructivism there existed a tendency which could be characterised by the term 'Organic Constructivism'.

This organic tendency developed neither theoretically nor practically to a sufficient degree for it to be considered as an entirely separate movement. However, the organic features which characterised the Constructivist work of both Tatlin and Miturich suggest that these represented more than mere personal foible on their part. Both Tatlin and Miturich derived the inspiration for their design work from organic forms and the world of nature, rather than from mechanical forms and the world of contemporary technology. While rejecting mechanical work with the already established geometric forms of technology, they preserved the basic principles of Constructivism (the principles of tectonics, *faktura* and construction), and extended them to investigate the underlying substances of technological form itself, the very bases of technology. Their observations and explorations of natural phenomena led them to advocate the use of curvilinear forms and principles of movement, and these became the motivating conceptions for their designs for various flying apparatuses. It is these works that formed the main substance of Organic Constructivism, and they also provide the visual and theoretical evidence for postulating the existence of such a trend. The organic characteristics of these works lay both in their formal qualities and in the fundamentally non-mechanical and intuitive approach which determined their organisation.

Before these works are examined in detail, however, this organic element within Constructivism will be briefly related to a general trend of aesthetic thought and practice within the activity of the twentieth-century Russian avant-garde to which the term 'organic' could also be applied. In this context Organic Constructivism would appear to be a specific manifestation of an organic trend within twentieth-century Russian progressive art, rather than an entirely isolated or eccentric phenomenon.

THE ORGANIC TREND

The primary representative of such a trend was the artist and musician Mikhail Matyushin, who took for himself the glory and prestige of having inaugurated this 'organic' trend. Writing in 1923, he asserted, 'I was the first to signal the return to nature.'[1] His claim has been corroborated by a later scholar who asserted that 'his path of creativity is the organic perception of the world'.[2]

As early as 1911, at the Union of Youth exhibition, Matyushin had shown a study of the roots and branches of trees.[3] He considered that these natural forms were the most perfect manifestations of the movement of matter and his observation that such organic matter naturally grew in curves fostered his interest in curved volumes. He called his artistic approach (and the studio he later organised in the Petrograd State Free Art Studios) Spatial Realism (*prostranstvennyi realizm*). Matyushin's Spatial Realism was based on an entirely new perception of nature and on a process of learning from nature 'by observing her freely without clinging to familiar details'.[4] To facilitate this new perception of nature Matyushin developed the concept of *zorved* or See-Know, which he announced at GINKhUK on 13 April 1923.[5] *Zorved* related the conscious process of cognition to an intuitive perception of connections which were not immediately apparent. It was based on the idea that both cognition and physical vision could be developed beyond their present limits. Matyushin defined his new concept thus:

> *Zorved* is in essence the very act of seeing (full observation through 360 degrees) and it will become the primary virgin soil for experiment.
>
> *Zorved* signifies a physiological change from former ways of seeing and entails a completely different way of representing the seen.
>
> *Zorved* for the first time introduces observation and experiment of the hitherto closed 'back plane', all that space which remains outside the human sphere because of insufficient experiment.[6]

As a first step towards implementing this new concept, Matyushin had devised a series of eye exercises which were intended to extend man's field of vision to a full 360 degrees, enabling him eventually to see through the back of his head into that space which at present was utterly closed to him.[7]

Matyushin believed that the current understanding and perception of three-dimensional space was inadequate because it was one-directional, i.e. it moved outward from the front of the observer into space. He argued that three-dimensional space also extended behind the observer, and that this concept of multi-directional space was confirmed by the way a cell grew out from the centre in all directions simultaneously. The aim of the artist therefore was to depict this totality of three-dimensional space, and to do this he needed to develop a perception of the visual from the back of his head.[8] Once he had developed this total vision (i.e. with no limitations above, below, to the sides or the back) he would perceive 'the sense of a new dimension emerging – a dimension which has no top, no bottom, no sides. [and in which] direction plays no role.'[9] In other words Matyushin argued that it was through this intensified awareness of the three-dimensional that a further, fourth dimension would become perceptible.[10]

In 1923 at the Exhibition of Works by Petrograd Artists of All Trends, 1919–1923 (Vystavka kartin Petrogradskikh khudozhnikov vsekh napravlenii, 1919–1923), Matyushin exhibited a volumetric wooden cube consisting of intersecting planes, which was intended to demonstrate the transformation of an object growing into another dimension.[11] This process of growth led Matyushin to observe the complementary form: 'A form possesses three basic units and three supplementary ones. The basic ones are: the straight Line, the Square and the Cube. The complementary ones are the Curve, the Circle and the Sphere.'[12] These theories provided the basis for Matyushin's theoretical and practical work on colour. He had begun observations of the sun rising and setting during the First World War but continued the work more systematically at GINKhUK where he studied colour changes in relation to ordinary and extended vision. The preliminary conclusions of this work were published in 1932 in a book entitled *The Laws Governing the Variability of Colour Combinations: A Reference Book on Colour*.[13] This work was intended to provide essential information on colour for designers and architects working on practical tasks connected with reconstruction in the Soviet Union.

In this work Matyushin demonstrated how colour is stronger when it is perceived together with its residual attendant colours which intensify its brilliance and resonance. The complementary colour always darkens the basic colour with ordinary vision. Extended vision frees the basic colour from its complement and intensifies the colour value of the environment. Matyushin also posited the existence of a third colour which could be used to integrate any two colours.[14] Relating colour to form Matyushin concluded that warm tones (such as orange and red) correspond to curved forms, and cold tones (blue, etc.) correspond to angular forms.[15]

This intuitive approach to natural phenomena as the first step towards their scientific analysis is closely paralleled by the organic element in the work of the extraordinary Futurist poet Velimir Khlebnikov. Khlebnikov's literary work was only one aspect of his enormous visionary output.[16] His 'organic' approach to visual form is most manifest in his speculations concerning the nature of the future environment. These he outlined generally in 'The City of the Future', but he elaborated and described more concretely the type of architecture he envisaged, in an article entitled 'Houses and Us'.[17] In 'Houses and Us' Khlebnikov projected, in varying detail, thirteen different types of building.[18] The illustrations of five of these intended structures were recently discovered in the archive of Pushkinskii Dom (Pushkin House), Leningrad, and are reproduced in plate 7.1.[19] The first

7.1. V. Khlebnikov, Sheet of drawings for architectural structures, c. 1920, ink on paper. Pushkinskii Dom, Leningrad.

building is a chess house (*dom shakhmaty*). The basic structure was to be a metallic honeycomb made to receive standardised living units made from glass. These units, called glass huts (*steklokhaty*), enabled the owner to travel from place to place without straying outside his little glass home. The glass box or hut could be transported easily by train or steamer to the owner's destination where they could easily be installed in another chess house. This chess-board-like structure comprised the empty moorings awaiting the travelling glass living unit. The middle structure, entitled beehive house (*dom ulei*), again consisted of a lattice structure formed into a tall funnel enclosing enormous grounds which contained a fountain.[20] The lattice structure, like that of the chess house, awaits its travelling glass occupants. The three tall thin structures, identified as poplar houses (*doma topoli*) were towers encircled by rings containing cabins. These had access to the tower for lifts. The house in the form of a flower is a cup house (*dom chasha*).[21] Four or five rooms were to be housed in the dome which was to be constructed of glass. Khlebnikov also envisaged spiral formations of cabins around a central tower, which would facilitate movement.[22] The house on the extreme right of the plate is the film house (*dom plenka*). Between metallic needle structures, a flexible room cloth (*komnatnaya tkan'*) was to be slung across to form rooms of any required shape or size. Khlebnikov considered that this type of building would be the most suitable for hospitals or hotels. In this building even the idea of a coherent structural entity is absent.

All of Khlebnikov's projected structures are characterised by their lack of solid, traditional materialism, by their transparency, and by their formal construction based on, but not copied from, growing forms in nature. The absence of rectilinearity in the forms of the buildings and the extensive use of the curved line confirms Khlebnikov's explanation that 'the town itself is made from the first experience of a plant of a higher order' and that it is a kind of forest made from glass.[23]

Khlebnikov's housing forms were related to his concept of the urban organism as a growing entity. He envisaged a new type of city in which traditional heavy, earth-hugging architecture would be replaced by structures soaring into the sky, bringing light and sunshine into the homes of the inhabitants. It was a dynamic conception, intended for inhabitants freed from the restraints of gravity, who would utilise flying extensively as a means of travel.[24] The separate buildings, to be interconnected at various levels, were set in a rural environment so that man could be surrounded by natural phenomena. In this way the harmony between man and the natural world could be re-established and man could live at peace with the animals.[25] Similarly Khlebnikov housed the heroes of his poem 'I and E: A Story of the Stone Age' in a flower house (*dom tsvetok*), suggesting that natural simplicity and high culture united would produce a new harmonious utopia.[26]

Khlebnikov's ideas of flight and weightlessness may have been ultimately influenced by those of the Russian philosopher Nikolai Fedorov, who envisaged an extraordinary complex system of counteracting and regulating magnetic and gravitational forces on a cosmic scale so that ultimately the whole earth would become a space ship travelling through the universe at will.[27] On the other hand they are closely related to the linguistic investigations that Khlebnikov undertook in connection with his literary work. In those studies he detected an inner, universal language inherent in the sounds and syllables of words, which conveyed a meaning independent of the apparent meaning of the word. Hence Khlebnikov discerned qualities of heaviness or earthiness in some words, for instance *'voda'* (water), *'techet'* (flows), and lightness in others, such as *'ptitsa'* (bird), *'letit'* (flies).[28] He considered 'heaviness' to be antipathetical to art. Khlebnikov's perception of a basic harmony between various natural phenomena was also expressed in his theories of the complicated laws governing time and the occurrence of specific events.[29]

TATLIN AND KHLEBNIKOV

Although there is no evidence to suggest a particularly close personal relationship between Tatlin and Khlebnikov, they were acquaintances, if not friends, and did seem to display a considerable respect for each other as artists operating in related fields. It is known that Tatlin admired Khlebnikov greatly, considered him a genius and recited his poetry throughout his life.[30] Khlebnikov for his part had visited the 0.10 and Store exhibitions (Petrograd, 1915, and Moscow, 1916) and had displayed a knowledge of, and admiration for, Tatlin's counter-reliefs in a poem he wrote about him in 1916.[31]

Despite the fact that Tatlin evidently had considerable admiration for Khlebnikov's ideas, there is no direct evidence to suggest that he was specifically influenced by Khlebnikov's models in the two particular design tasks they both tackled. These were the problem of a flying machine, and the problem of buildings for the future town.

The outward skeletal structure of Tatlin's Tower (plate 2.9), holding in place its revolving internal structures of glass, did bear a resemblance to Khlebnikov's architectural ideas of transparency and dynamism as expressed in the glass huts and the receptive metallic structures of the chess houses. Tatlin's concern to fuse

his building with its spatial environment and to open up its interior recalled Khlebnikov's concern to bring light and air and nature into his projected town of the future, ultimately by elevating it completely into space.[32] The Tower was, however, a rather ambiguous structure in this respect. As an alternative to existing urban structures, it was interpreted by contemporaries as celebrating the machine and contemporary technology on the American model, rather than as a reassertion of a closer relationship to nature and the natural environment via that technology. Tatlin's declaration 'The Work Ahead of Us' had not militated against this technological or mechanistic interpretation of the Tower. However, in Tatlin's later statements and work the proximity of his ideas to those of Khlebnikov became more apparent. This was first demonstrated in the theatre.

In 1917 Tatlin and Khlebnikov had briefly co-operated on a production of three plays by Khlebnikov, *Death's Mistake*, *Madame Lenin* and *Thirteen in the Air*, but the spectacle was never realised.[33] After Khlebnikov's death, Tatlin produced *Zangezi* in 1923 basing his decor on Khlebnikov's attitude to words as the expressive elements and the fundamental building units of literary works.[34] In a contemporary article Tatlin explained:

> The production of *Zangezi* is built on the principle: 'the word is a unit of building, material is a unit of organised volume'. According to Khlebnikov's own definition, the over-story is the 'architecture from the stories' and the story is 'architecture from words'. He regards words as he would plastic material. The properties of this material permit one to operate on them for the construction of a language state.
>
> This attitude of Khlebnikov gave me the opportunity to direct work on the production. Parallel to the oral construction it was decided to introduce material construction.[35]

Tatlin's designs for the production, which took place at the Museum of Painterly Culture in Petrograd on 9 May 1923, are known from one photograph of the actual production (plate 7.2), one model of the stage set (plate 7.3), one drawing by Tatlin of the set (plate 7.4) and one woodcut by N. Lapshin' of the performance (plate 7.5). From these photographs, reviews and Tatlin's own statement the production can to a limited extent be reconstructed in its basic elements.[36] Tatlin stated, 'Khlebnikov took sounds as elements . . . to reveal the nature of these sounds I have taken surfaces of different materials which have been treated in different ways.'[37]

7.2. Tatlin's production of Khlebnikov's poem, *Zangezi*, in the Hall of Museum of Painterly Culture, Petrograd, 9 May 1923.

7.3. V. Tatlin, Model for the set of Khlebnikov's poem, *Zangezi*, 1923. Whereabouts unknown. It corresponds to the 20th section of the poem. The figure on the left seems to represent Laughter and on the right, Sorrow. [Reproduced in Fülop-Miller, *Mind and Face of Bolshevism*, 1927.]

7.4. V. Tatlin, Sketch of the set for *Zangezi*, 1923. [Reproduced in Fülop-Miller, *Mind and Face of Bolshevism*, 1927.]

7.5. N. Lapshin, *The Performance of Zangezi*, 1923, woodcut. Russian Museum, Leningrad.

The varieties of these textures and materials, suggested in plate 7.2, provided visually 'a simple and clever parallel to the oral material of the poem'.[38] Differently painted boards were carried to emphasise the different nature of sounds. Tatlin considered *Zangezi* to be 'a song in the language of the stars' which had arrived like a ray of light from the philosopher to the crowds below.[39] He demonstrated this (plate 7.2) by placing the poet (representing Khlebnikov) at the top of a special structure, with a line of figures reaching up to him. To simplify the rather complex structure of the poem Tatlin used a projector (plate 7.5) 'to guide the attention of the spectator, to introduce order and consistency ... also to emphasise the nature of the materials'.[40] The production was not a success, because despite these visual precautions it did not seem to cohere into a theatrical or comprehensible whole.[41] However, it did reveal the extent to which Tatlin himself admired Khlebnikov and saw a compatibility between their respective artistic methods.[42]

THE ORGANIC DIMENSION IN TATLIN'S PRODUCT DESIGNS

These fundamental similarities between Tatlin's approach and that of Khlebnikov seem to go much deeper, as a closer examination of Tatlin's design work will indicate.[43] Running throughout Tatlin's work from the first had been a constancy of curvilinear formal vocabulary which indicated an underlying intuitive sympathy with the natural world and with the organically evolved relationships of material and form that characterise it. What plainly began as an intuitive sympathy emerged in his later creative period as an increasingly positive assertion of the value of the intuitive approach for its own sake, and an increasing preoccupation with organic form *per se*.

The curved surfaces of his pre-construction works such as *The Nude* (plate 1.3), *The Sailor* (plate 1.5) and *The Fisherman* (colour plate XIX) prefigured the interpenetrating curved surfaces of the corner counter-reliefs (plate 1.13) and the two spirals of the Monument to the Third International (plates 2.9–11, 13). They are encountered in a more muted form in Tatlin's sets for Khlebnikov's play *Zangezi* in 1923 (plates 7.2–4).

There was, however, a far greater reliance on the purely organic curved form in several designs produced while Tatlin was teaching at the vKhUTEIN. The *myagkii* 'venskii' stul (soft bentwood, literally: 'Viennese', chair) produced by Rogozhin in 1927 under Tatlin's direction was based on the supportive tensile strength of curved wood (plate 7.6).[44] It was built without any metallic springs: 'in the seat metal springs are replaced by switches of ... wood. These switches joined under the seat produce a form with a weight resistance ... of more than 100 kilos ... When you sit on the chair the wooden switches bend easily and create a spring thanks to which it is as comfortable to sit on the chair as in a soft armchair.'[45] This method of construction also enabled the sitter to shift his weight for greater comfort over long periods of sitting.

In commenting upon the chair himself Tatlin lamented the fact that most Soviet furniture designs were copies of Western models and utilised materials like tubular steel which was unavailable in the USSR. As an alternative, he advocated the study of other materials like wood which was plentiful and cheap in the USSR and not expensive to work.

In addition he argued that the inherent qualities of such materials (as for instance their resistence to cold) often made them more suitable for Russian conditions than metal. As a further example of his approach Tatlin illustrated a sleigh which he and the students had designed (plate 7.7) and which had the advantages of being lighter, more durable and warmer to handle in the cold than its metallic Western counterpart. Tatlin also describes in outline the teaching method he had adopted in Dermetfak: 'A group of my students conduct experiments into the different interrelations of materials, trying to find in the material itself preconditions [leading] towards a [particular] form. And from different materials we obtain the same objects.'[46] He elucidates further: 'We take and analyse an existing object, we make use of technical structures as forms for everyday objects, and finally we use the phenomena of living nature. Such are the basic tasks in the work of organising new objects in the new collective everyday life.'[47] The design method and the nature of the culture of materials which Tatlin advocated is illuminated in his article 'The Problem of Correlating Man and the Object':

> The method of thinking based on the culture of materials gives us the opportunity to take into account both the properties of individual materials and the most advantageous aspects of their interrelationships. Thus in creating an object the artist is equipped with a palette of different materials based on their properties with which he works. Here colour, texture [faktura], strength, elasticity, weight, durability, etc. are studied.
>
> Confronted with the task of creating a specific everyday object with a defined function, the culture of materials artist studies all the properties of appropriate materials and their interrelations, the organic form (man), for which the object

7.6. Rogozhin, Soft bentwood (literally: 'Viennese') chair (myagkii 'venskii' stul), 1927, made in Tatlin's studio in Derfak. [Reproduced in Stroitel'stvo Moskvy, No. 10, 1929.]

7.7. V. Tatlin and the Derfak students, Design for a sleigh. [Reproduced in Rabis, No. 48, 1929.]

in question is being made, and finally the social aspect – this man is a worker and will use the object in question whilst leading a working life.

Here the maximum functionality of the object must be studied, which can be achieved on condition that there is a comprehensive understanding of the properties of materials. This factor gives us the opportunity for an ingenious material selection for a functional object and the introduction of completely new materials which have not been used hitherto. This produces a completely exceptional result – an original object which radically differs from the objects of the West and America. The latter aspect is very important in so far as our way of life is built on completely different principles . . .

Our way of life is built on healthy and natural principles and the Western object cannot satisfy us. We must look for completely different points of departure in the creation of our objects.

Therefore I show such a great interest in organic form, as a point of departure for the creation of new objects.[48]

The other major piece of design which obeys these imperatives and very firmly indicates a more 'organic' approach was a nursing cup for infants (plate 7.8), which Tatlin produced himself in the ceramics studio of the VKhUTEIN.[49] The soft curved forms of the design with the nipple-shaped mouthpiece suggest that it directly derived from the form of the human breast which it was intended to replace. As far as can be judged this is the first example of Tatlin's interest in curved forms leading him to adopt an organic form from the natural world as the basis for a design. The mass variant of this item was produced by Sotnikov, Tatlin's student, and was almost identical to Tatlin's model except for the fact that it had a slit in the top which enabled it to be clipped into a basket so that large numbers could be transported easily without spillage (plates 7.9–10).[50]

The nursing cup and the chair, both belonging to the later 1920s, indicated a far greater reliance on the purely organic curved form as a design factor determining the overall structure of the object than had been apparent in Tatlin's earlier design work immediately following the completion of the Tower. The approach which these two later items embodied was not unrelated to the investigations into materials that Tatlin had conducted at GINKhUK and to his published statements on the culture of materials.[51] However, Tatlin expounded the nature of this new relationship to technology more explicitly in his statement 'Art into Technology' of 1932.[52] In this declaration Tatlin rejected the mechanical application of technology to art, and emphasised instead the organic relationship which existed between the material and its tensile capacity. He stressed that the form was a product of the interaction of these two factors. In formulating this position Tatlin, while acknowledging a link with the other Constructivists, recognised that his approach was different. He condemned them for their stagnating methods and for their mechanical application of artistic techniques evolved in their purely formal work to the larger tasks of design.

The Constructivists, in inverted commas, also operated with materials, but secondarily, for the sake of their formal tasks, mechanically fastening technology to their art. Constructivism, in inverted commas, did not take into account the organic connection between material and its tensile capacity in its work. Essentially it is only as a result of the dynamics resulting from these interrelationships that a vital and inevitable form is born. It is not very surprising that the Constructivists, in inverted commas, turned into decorators or became occupied with graphic work.[53]

In contrast to what he saw as the mainstream Constructivists' pursuit of inspiration *from* technology, Tatlin suggested that the initiative should lie with the artist: 'the artist should provide technology with a series of new interrelationships between

form and material'.[54] He stressed that the artist's work was a counterpart to technology, not dictated by it but contributing to it in a purely artistic way. He saw it as the artist's present task to introduce into everyday life 'a series of forms dictated by complex curvatures'.[55] Thus he rejected the Euclidean geometricity and technological forms of such artists as Rodchenko. He is reported to have said, 'I loved Rodchenko so much, but he went along a path of geometrical thinking not understanding me. In *Object* they called me the father of Constructivism. I was never that . . . I want to make the machine with art and not to mechanise art – there is the difference in understanding.'[56] The practical project in which Tatlin explicitly exemplified his new approach, and expressed his conception of the synthesis of art with life, was his flying apparatus.[57] Tatlin described it as 'the most complex form' in his artistic development (from simple material structures to more complicated ones), as a form which 'answers the needs of the moment in the conquering of space by man'.[58]

7.8. V. Tatlin, Child's nursing vessel, 1928–9, porcelain. Private collection, Moscow.

7.9. A. Sotnikov, Mass variant of the drinking vessel for infants, created under Tatlin's guidance at the VKhUTEMAS, *c.* 1930. [First reproduced in Gray, *Great Experiment*, 1962.]

7.10. A. Sotnikov, Drawing of the tray in which his vessels were to be fixed so that they could be carried without difficulty.

THE *LETATLIN*

Tatlin's machine for human flight was called the *Letatlin*, which was a play on his name and the Russian word, '*letat'*', meaning 'to fly'. It was built between 1929 and 1931 (plate 7.11).[59] From 1931 until 1933 Tatlin headed Narkompros's Scientific Laboratory for Investigating the Plastic Arts. There in a tower at the Novodevichii Monastery on the outskirts of Moscow, put at his disposal by Narkompros, Tatlin developed and built this air bicycle.[60] He called it an air bicycle because it was not motorised but propelled by man like a bicycle. Tatlin moreover intended it to become an item of everyday use,[61] liberating every man from the confines of gravity and enabling every man to fly and to move freely in space.[62] It was deliberately not motorised because his primary objective was to give man the freedom of individual flight, the feeling of moving through space like a bird, without the noise of aeroplanes or the loss of the feeling of being surrounded by space that was incurred by travelling in them. When asked what had prompted him to work on the air bicycle Tatlin had explained: 'The dream is as old as Icarus . . . I too want to give back to man the feeling of flight. This we have been robbed of by the mechanical flight of the aeroplane. We cannot feel the movement of our body in the air.'[63] A by-product of this dream was an intention to decrease the contamination and discomfort of the

FOLLOWING PAGES

7.11. V. Tatlin, The *Letatlin* as exhibited in the Pushkin Museum of Fine Arts, Moscow, 1932.

7.12. V. Tatlin with the wing of the *Letatlin* in the Novedevichii Monastery, Moscow, *c.* 1932. [Photograph: Angelica Rudenstine.]

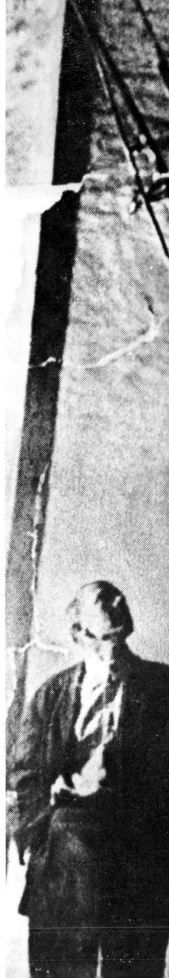

contemporary urban environment: 'The air bicycle will relieve the town of transport, of noise, and overcrowding, and will cleanse the air of petrol fumes.'[64]

Having rejected the traditional concept of air transport, Tatlin also rejected the harsh forms of the structures devised by modern aviation. He is reported to have said: 'The engineers made hard forms. Evil. With angles. They are easily broken. The world is round and soft.'[65] Consequently Tatlin insisted that his air bicycle should be based on the principles of soft rounded form. He stated, 'My apparatus is built on the principle of utilising living organic forms.'[66] In this particular case Tatlin based his forms on those of birds, since their physique is totally adapted to the mechanism of flight. He kept young cranes as pets and the result of his observations of their physical structure and its adaptation to the problem of flight was the gigantic bird-like form of the *Letatlin*. The overall resemblance to a bird is particularly evident in plates 7.11 and 7.13 and the structure of the wing strengthens this similarity (plate 7.12).

Tatlin's observations of the flight of small birds provided the basis for the mechanics of the *Letatlin* as well as for the form. 'I observed young cranes learning to fly. I bought some cranes and went to school with them. Young cranes are as helpless against the wind as human beings.'[67] As the pilot Artseulov commented, the *Letatlin* 'reproduced the principle of a bird's flight ... not only the mechanics of the way the wings work but the very forms are the result of the study of organic (bird) forms'.[68] Tatlin had preserved the ratio between the weight of a bird's wings and its total weight which is one to six (total weight of the *Letatlin* was 32 kg, surface of wings 12 square metres and load per square metre 8 kg).[69] The *Letatlin* worked on the same principles as a glider: it had three wing positions and a tail piece that could also be used to propel and direct the machine. 'The man lies in the middle on his stomach, you put your hands and feet in the stirrups and go up against the wind [plate 7.14].'[70]

In accordance with the organic inspiration determining the form, structure and function of the *Letatlin*, unprocessed, organic materials were used. They were chosen specifically for their flexibility and their suitability to function. The manner of working the materials was determined by the function and form of the whole structure. In this way material, function and form were fused, in accordance with Constructivist principles.

214

The hardest part of the flying machine – the fuselage [plate 7.12] – is made on the principle of a 'basket' formed from elastic components which makes it possible for it to sustain hard jolts and blows without damage.

The wing stays are formed as a complicated octagon of bent wood and have great powers of resistance to the rotations and the twistings of the wings. They are strengthened by a piece of whalebone which can be bent and straightened out again without becoming deformed. The bent wooden details required special moulds in which the wood was placed for pressing with the help of steam or moisture...

In this entire construction, material has been selected on the principle of function and best possible use. The wood was therefore not sawn, but cloven to the desired thickness to preserve the fibres in their full length. According to requirements ash, linden, willow, cork, silk ropes, whalebone and even white tanned leather were used. The moving parts were mounted on ball bearings. The fabric is of silk.[71]

In addition Tatlin had been very concerned to provide a solid scientific basis for his flying apparatus. Apparently, he had even gone to the lengths of consulting the great Russian aeronautics expert Tsiolkovskii about it. The proportions which Tsiolkovskii had used to prove the non-viability of human powered flight seem to have determined those proportions of the Letatlin. Nevertheless, Tsiolkovskii apparently considered that the Letatlin could be a viable proposition and had advised Tatlin to use organic forms for the wings. He had also stressed that Tatlin had the advantage of being an artist in this respect, not merely a calculator.[72] Ultimately, as Tsiolkovskii recognised and Tatlin himself stressed, Tatlin's approach had been pre-eminently artistic. In an interview with Zelinskii in 1932, Tatlin acknowledging this is reported to have said:

I don't want people to take this thing purely as something utilitarian. I have made it as an artist. Look at the bent wings [plate 7.12]. We believe them to be aesthetically perfect... like a hovering seagull... But I count upon my apparatus being able to keep a person in the air, I have taken into account the mathematical side, the resistance of the material and the surface of the wings. We have to learn to fly with it in the air, just as we learn to swim in the water or ride a bicycle.[73]

In his declaration Tatlin had referred to the *Letatlin* as an 'artistic construction', and had stressed that the task of the artist differed from that of the technician in its creative content.[74] In the *Letatlin* Tatlin was fulfilling the role he had defined. The fact that the *Letatlin* never really flew does not detract from the significance of the project as a fusion of the artistic and the utilitarian through the organic or as an example of Tatlin's concept of design for the new life.

The movement which had begun with Tatlin's three-dimensional non-utilitarian constructions found a significant end in this embodiment of a dream.[75] An early credo in the Soviet State Archives throws a new and sharper light on Tatlin's conception of the artist's role in the new society. These theses for an article entitled 'The Initiative Unit in the Creativity of the Collective' were probably written in 1919.[76] The 'initiative unit' (*initsiativnaya edinitsa*) was the term Tatlin used to describe the new type of artist produced by the artistic response to the political and social revolution of 1917. The term was explicitly intended to convey the collective, non-individualistic essence of the new creative activity which Tatlin envisaged and which he called 'invention'.

The initiative [or initiative-taking] unit is the collector of the ENERGY of the collective, which is directed towards cognition and invention. The initiative unit serves as the link between invention and the creativity of the mass.

The viability of the collective is confirmed by the number of initiative units selected by it ... Invention is always the solution of the impulses and wishes of the collective and not of the individual.

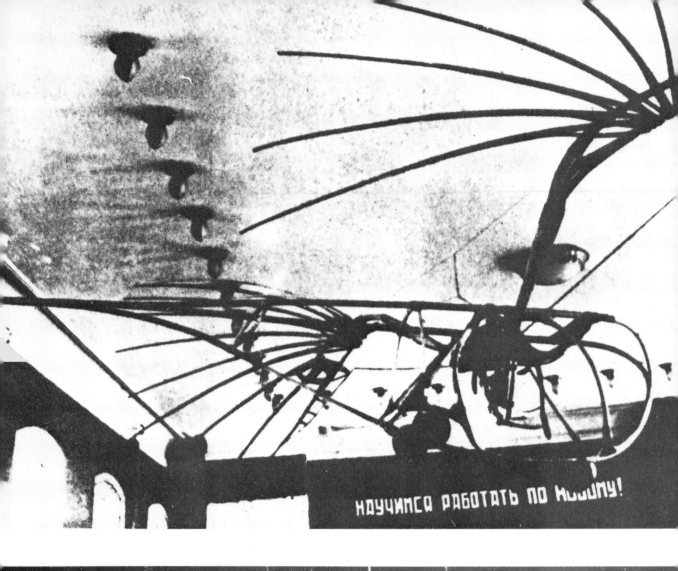

НАУЧИЛСЯ РАБОТАТЬ ПО НОВОМУ!

The world of numbers as that nearest to the architectonics of art gives us (1) confirmation of the existence of the inventor, (2) a full organic union between the [initiative] unit and the collector of numbers. There are no mistakes in Khlebnikov's example.[77]

The reference here to Khlebnikov seems to sharpen the focus on two central elements of Tatlin's approach. In evoking Khlebnikov's analogy between 'word' and 'number' Tatlin emphasises his own idea of design, or 'invention', as a maximal distillation of patterns out of nature. In linking the 'initiative unit' with the 'collector of numbers' Tatlin stresses his conception of the artist as a catalyst and focussing lens for natural and societal processes, not as an autonomous 'personality'. In this way Tatlin underlines both the organic nature of the process of design and the organic quality of the relationship existing between the designer and society. Depicting the creative unit as merely the manifestation of the collective's creative powers on the one hand reduces the individual importance of such a creative unit, yet on the other imbues that unit with the collective power and elevates him as the embodiment of the collective's creativity, as beyond question the only being able to distil from natural forces and to design for the new world.

MITURICH AND THE DYNAMIC OBJECT

The ideas and principles which had inspired Tatlin's design work bear a strong similarity to those which governed the utilitarian activity of Petr Miturich, in particular his designs for his undulators or *volnoviki*.[78] Like Tatlin, Miturich had a profound respect for the work of Khlebnikov. During the Civil War Miturich had created a whole series of three-dimensional constructions in many of which he not only explored Khlebnikov's poetry in visual terms, but also explicitly based his artistic approach upon Khlebnikov's ideas. From Khlebnikov's concept of *bol'shoe chuvstvo mira* (a great feeling for the world), which included the 'five and more senses', Miturich developed his own theory of a sixth sense, that he called simply *chuvstvo mira* (a feeling for the world).[79] This *chuvstvo mira* was conceived as 'an essential cognitive power' that gave man a heightened insight into natural phenomena and enabled him to transcend the limitations of perception through five senses, and to see the world more clearly.[80] As such it was an essential element in man's approach to nature. 'We are not talking of some kind of dark metaphysical imaginings, but of a perfectly concrete sense of the world. Without the prerequisite of this sense one should not approach natural phenomena, they will not open themselves up, they will not submit.'[81] The perceptions gained through *chuvstvo mira* enabled discoveries to be made in both science and art. It was in fact that force which creates new images in art, new understandings in science and new forms in technology. It is one and the same force acting in art, science and technology.

For Miturich this sixth sense of a 'feeling for the world' was fundamental to the creative process both in the arts and in the sciences. However, he argued that it developed particularly during the artistic creative process, enabling the artist to transcend the limitations of normal perception. Although not a mystical or specifically inspirational artistic element, this sixth sense could apparently be consciously developed only through art. The artist was able to perfect his *chuvstvo mira* through the artistic work and the non-artist could develop it by contemplating a work of art in which this *chuvstvo mira* was present. The quality of a work of art *per se* was dependent on the extent to which it contained a *chuvstvo mira*.

Artistic training and aesthetic education therefore were concerned with the development of this sixth sense rather than with the transmission of technique. Miturich considered the latter to be not only useless but positively harmful because it enabled the student to acquire the technical means of producing a work of art

7.13. The *Letatlin* without its covering fabric, as exhibited at the Pushkin Museum of Fine Arts, Moscow, 1932. [Reproduced in *Vystavka rabot*, 1932.]

7.14. V. Tatlin demonstrating how to control the *Letatlin*, 1932. [Photograph: Angelica Rudenstine.]

217

from which this *chuvstvo mira* could be absent. 'The development of motor skills for the hand of the artist is bad; it prevents expression of a *chuvstvo mira*, and coarsens it. The hand of the artist must be as obedient to thought as a seismograph.'[82] For Miturich, the automatic content of their courses and the mechanical conveyance of technique were the weaknesses of both the VKhUTEMAS and the traditional Academy. 'The programmes for the art schools, both under the 'left' and 'right' trends, pursued the mastering of motor skills through the [artificial] study of separate elements. The difference consists only in the body of the elements.'[83]

In Miturich's opinion only the art and the artist embodying a feeling for the world were truly creative and innovative. These could reveal completely new aspects of the world. Such art was able to influence science and technology by revealing new forms and directions.

> Art embodying in itself the content of a new feeling for the world is really creative art because it produces that which did not exist before. Such art leads the observer to new ways of seeing the world, all things, their new evaluations and reciprocal connections. This art is really being effective and mobilising new forces.[84]

Miturich stressed that because of this an artistic education which developed this sixth sense was an essential prerequisite for giving everyone a full education, especially scientists, and that 'one must learn to read paintings. This is as necessary as being able to read and write.'[85] He suggested that the great scientists had already realised this and that is why they had turned to art's progressive forces.

In its relation to the utilitarian imperative Miturich's thought linked up with mainstream Constructivist theory outlined in Chapter Three. Although he never completely abandoned aesthetic activity and continued making figurative drawings throughout this period, Miturich did suggest that artistic activity should be 'projecting activity'[86] (i.e. concerned with the formulation of projects – design), that it was of more than artistic significance and that it could play a major role in forming a new environment. However, in a manner very close to Tatlin's, he considered that artistic forms of perception could function as guidelines for scientific investigation, rather than vice versa, and that the connection between art and technology was via natural phenomena rather than via the machine.

Mainstream Constructivism had extolled the transformatory role of art and the artist only implicitly. In Organic Constructivism this was explicit. Embodying *chuvstvo mira*, art opened up the world of nature, and provided new possibilities for technological development. The artist's task was 'to investigate and learn what is happening around him' in a thorough and disinterested way.[87]

Miturich seems to have started applying this approach to the problems of aerial movement several years before Tatlin began work on his *Letatlin*. It seems that Miturich had become interested in the technical problem of flying as early as 1914, and had begun to construct an ornithopter in 1916, continuing this work in 1917.[88] These investigations were pursued intermittently because Miturich was involved in the fighting during the First World War and Civil War (from 1916 to 1921 he served in various military capacities).[89] In 1921 Miturich discussed his ideas with Khlebnikov, reporting that he felt an affinity in their ideas, and in the same year he constructed his first ornithopter.[90] The chronology of events does not suggest that the primary impulse towards aviatory experiments was provided directly by Khlebnikov. Moreover, a letter of 14 March 1922 in which Khlebnikov expressed sympathy with the subjugation of the skies implied that Miturich's ideas were independently generated.[91] In 1923 Miturich began to teach drawing at the VKhUTEMAS and he continued to do so until it closed in 1930.[92] According to his notes, Miturich continued work on the models over that whole period concurrently with other projects such as figurative drawings and book covers.[93]

In 1922 Miturich asserted that he had solved the problem of flight without a

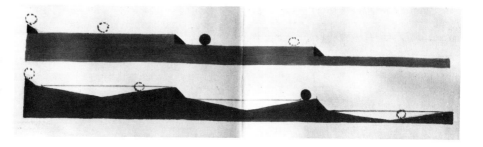

7.15. P. Miturich, Experiment for comparing the speeds of curved and straight paths (*Opyt sravneniya skorostei vol'noobraznym i pryamolineinym putem*), 1920s, ink and gouache on paper, *c.* 26 × 34 cm. Private collection, Moscow.

motor using the principle of wave-like motion or *volnovoe dvizhenie*.[94] This principle, which he also called *kolebatel'noe dvizhenie*,[95] was based on the thesis that the curved line conserves and produces more energy than the straight line. To prove this, Miturich constructed an apparatus (plate 7.15) which consisted of three lengths of wood, each a metre long, and each containing two grooved paths. One path was completely horizontal and the other one went through a curvature of one centimetre in the metre, starting and ending at the same level as the horizontal path. The three pieces were joined together to produce two pathways each of three metres in length. Two metal balls were set off, simultaneously, to travel down the length of the apparatus. Although the ball on the horizontal path had less distance to travel, the ball on the curved path completed all three lengths of the course while the other ball had only completed two lengths.[96] The ball on the curved path was thus travelling at approximately one and a half times the speed of the other ball.

Miturich directly related the principle of *volnovaya tekhnika* (wave technology) to his observations of natural phenomena. He had found that this form of movement was basic to all types of creature. He was particularly interested in the snake, for which it was equally effective on land and in the water.[97] He compared the snake's movements with those of winged creatures, concluding that the basic principle was the same in both cases, but that it was adapted according to the particular function of the two types of animals.[98]

Miturich used this principle of *volnovoe dvizhenie* in his flying apparatus and in a whole series of constructions to each of which he gave the general name of a *volnovik* (undulating mechanism or undulator). He defined this mechanism as one

7.16. P. Miturich, *The Flyer* (*Kryl'ya*), 1921, model of a flying apparatus made from wood, rubber, paper and string, *c.* 18 × 20 cm. Private collection, Moscow.

'which moves with the help of a wave-like vibration of its body or surface',[99] i.e. by means of *volnovoe dvizhenie*. Between 1922 and 1935 he applied for five patents on various forms of *volnoviki*. The first of these was the *Wings* (*Kryl'ya*) of 1921 (plate 7.16) otherwise called *Flyer* (*Letun*).[100] In contrast to Tatlin's apparatus, here the figure was suspended vertically and propelled itself by means of a complex system of levers which operated three sets of wings. After this Miturich's next project appeared to be the boat (*lodka*, plate 7.17).[101] In this project Miturich based the *volnovik* directly on the form and motion of a fish. He evolved further designs based on a fish form: one variant was adapted to move on land as well (plate 7.18); another was constructed in model form.[102] Utilising a similar (but more explicitly) fish form Miturich designed an airship (plate 7.19) which utilised the same principles in the air.[103] A glider followed (plate 7.20) which was based on a horizontal undulating movement as opposed to a vertical oscillation.[104] By 1935 Miturich had applied this principle to movement over the surface of the ground in a design which he entitled *Caterpillar* (*Gusenitsa*, plate 7.22). This was based on the principle of

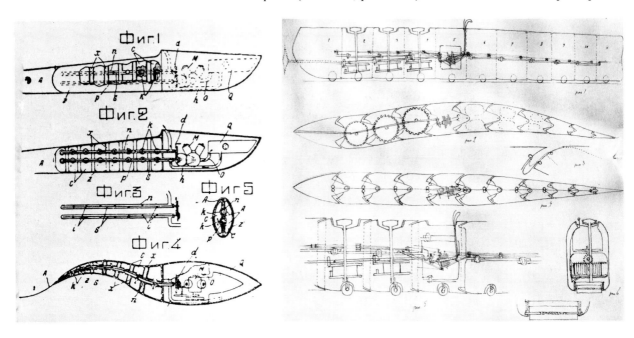

7.17. P. Miturich, Drawing of a boat *volnovik* (*lodka volnovik*), undated, *c*. 1930, pencil and ink on paper, *c*. 32 × 20 cm. Private collection, Moscow.

7.18. P. Miturish, Drawing of a boat *volnovik* (*lodka volnovik*), *c*. 1930, pencil on paper, *c*. 20 × 30 cm. Private collection, Moscow.

movement and form of the caterpillar.[105] In addition to these projects Miturich constructed two further models of a ship using the form of a tadpole (colour plates XX–XXI) and a small model (plate 7.21) showing the principle of the interconnecting segments needed in the articulation of such designs as the boat (plate 7.17) and airship (plate 7.19).

All these *volnoviki* were constantly being modified and adapted by Miturich until his death in 1956. Despite the natural basis of their forms and principles of movement Miturich expressed dissatisfaction with them, feeling that he had not arrived at their final formal solution and that much still had to be done. In 1944 he wrote:

> Even these *volnoviki*, many of which are made into models, please me so little in their exteriors that I do not conceive their form. They still lack the compact form in which energy plays and awaits its material fulfilment. The feeling of the play of strengths in still undefined forms leads to the destruction of regularity, i.e. the elementary position essential for a construction. So a new science of oscillating [or undulating] wave movement is born.[106]

Despite this dissatisfaction with his small items, Miturich extended the principle of *kolebatel'noe dvizhenie* to the design of a town as a complete physical environment.

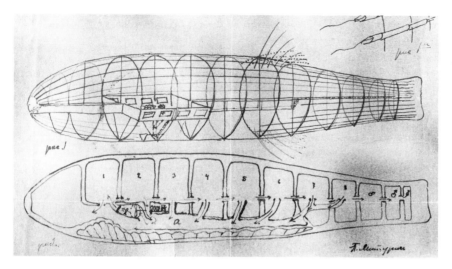

7.19. P. Miturich, Drawing of a boat *volnovik* (*lodka volnovik*), *c.* 1930, ink on paper, *c.* 21 × 32 cm. Private collection, Moscow.

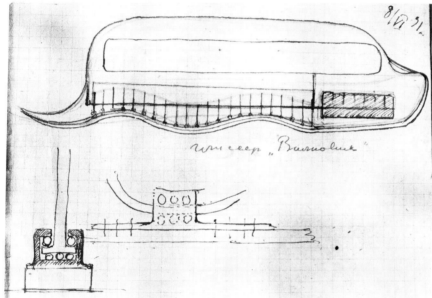

7.20. (below left) P. Miturich, Drawing of a glider *volnovik* (*glizzer volnovik*), 1931, pen and ink and pencil on paper, *c.* 21 × 30 cm. Private collection, Moscow.

7.21. (above) P. Miturich, Model demonstrating a mobile joint as envisaged for the *volnoviki*, *c.* 1930–4, wood, metal, *c.* 15 × 5 cm. Private collection, Moscow.

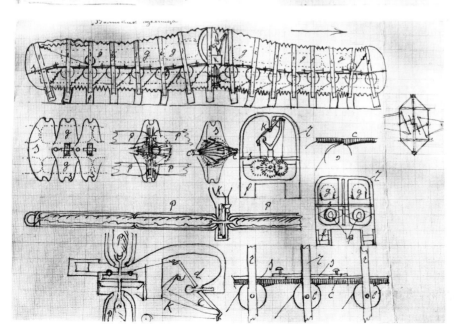

7.22. P. Miturich, Drawing of a caterpiller *volnovik* (*gusenitsa volnovik*) 1935, ink on paper, *c.* 20 × 30 cm. Private collection, Moscow.

221

MITURICH AND THE DYNAMIC RHYTHM ENVIRONMENT

In a treatise entitled 'The Dynamics of Town Roads' Miturich explained his idea that towns should be organised according to the wave principle, outlining precisely how this was to be achieved, and how the existing structure of the town and its network of roads would disappear.[107] He explained that nature grows in the way a tree grows and that towns should also grow in harmony with natural rhythms. Moreover this path of development was pre-eminently economic because his principles saved energy: 'transport through a town costs as much as 1,000 kilometres by water or the railways. Transport deficiencies explain the form of towns and of transport ... It is here that wave dynamics can play a transformatory role.[108] Miturich proposed placing his town on a high bank or raised ground near the water and near the railways, in order to exploit fully the possibilities of these cheap forms of transport. All the food supplies would be delivered to this central high point. Unloading goods would be most economical because it would to a large degree be effected by utilising the incline of the land. The success and effectiveness of the plan depended on the port and the station being close together, forming the centre of the town. The transportation of goods from the port to the railway station was to be achieved by a funicular railway.

Given this urban nucleus with its concentration and centralisation of supply depots, the town's communication network was to spread out from this centre. The network consisted of three types of road, fast, medium and slow. The speed of the roads and their position, on or under the ground, depended on their purpose. Roads for pedestrians and cyclists, for instance, would be above ground because they would not require steep inclines to speed their progress. Miturich explained the advantages of his scheme:

> The whole town is cut out like a net made of adjoining circles, each arc of which gives one the shortest route in any direction on account of the curved paths. This is lacking in a rectilinear system. In the middle of the arc the living quarters are built. Then the city will become as if transparent for human dynamics. At the same time the system of roads will disappear. The façades of houses will fall away, but this doesn't mean that architecture and its artistic aspect will disappear.[109]

On the contrary, Miturich asserted that architectural structures would flourish because they would 'be formed from the point of view of the people moving around at all kinds of speeds and on different levels', and would be the work of the 'artist-architect'.[110]

In this way Miturich had extended the application of Constructivist principles (*faktura*, tectonics, construction) via his intuitive method of *chuvstvo mira* beyond the construction of everyday objects (in his case *volnoviki*) to a total reconstruction of the environment itself. Miturich could not seriously be categorised among the disurbanist town planners who had flourished at the turn of the decade, as his proposals had none of that technical basis they derived from their architectural training.[111] He was not arguing from any specifically Marxist standpoint, but rather from the concept of economy and the principles of construction as found in nature. By applying ideas he had initially worked out on the artistic plane to the scientific and technological plane, Miturich seemed to have evolved what amounted to an alternative approach to the utilisation of natural forces to produce energy and a different concept of energy itself.

Today this has been labelled as 'alternative technology', and Miturich shared with this latterday movement an explicit opposition to contemporary technology on the American model. Judging American technology wasteful and 'American comfort to be monotonous and boring', Miturich compared America to a 'hen house of cultural food production'.[112]

This is probably the ideal classical world for a condensed form of commercial democracy. Although one must overcome the monstrous stupidities of the discomfort of our everyday life, the American world does not tempt me. I would be revealed as a chicken which could no longer become a pheasant. In our situation we can still hope for something beautiful for which it is worth living. The worst is that the chicken itself no longer hopes to become a pheasant.[113]

Miturich's criticism of American society and technology indicated a strong allegiance to communism and to the possibilities of the Soviet system, under which he lived. The disillusionment which he voiced here in 1944 arose from the fact that he had witnessed the socialist state of Soviet Russia adopting the same path of technological development as was followed by capitalist America. His criticisms of American technology and the industrial culture to which it gave rise were, of course, in total conflict with the explicit Americanisation of the mainstream Constructivists, and this too allies Miturich with Tatlin, in the pursuit of other, organic, solutions to the problems of everyday life.[114]

*   *   *

Neither the *Letatlin* nor the *volnoviki* were ever built as operational entities. Miturich's ideas and theories concerning the efficiency and energy-conserving qualities of *kolebatel'noe dvizhenie* never received the full scientific investigation that he constantly solicited. Miturich's town, conceived to utilise the new dynamic rhythm, never got beyond the drawing board. In their pursuit of generative principles for design, however, these ideas and experiments in fact penetrated deeper into the structural principles operating in nature than did conventional Constructivism. Where the latter was merely investigating essentially man-made phenomena produced by the industrial technology of the early twentieth century, Organic Constructivism sought to examine the external natural bases underlying all technologies. Their conclusions seriously questioned many of the assumptions made by mainstream twentieth-century technology. Like many such prescient investigations, the work of Miturich and Tatlin was dismissed at the time as fantasy, and this dimension of it has been ignored ever since. With a consciousness aroused by today's discussions of an 'alternative' technology, however, it is now possible to recognise the value of their achievements in pointing down precisely that path. The central importance of Tatlin is reflected in the way that this one man's oeuvre embodied both the development and the counter-development. His original founding works of Constructivism had been inspired by that contemporary technology which he ultimately came to reject; it was then by means of those very analytical weapons it had put into his hands that he was able to posit an 'alternative'.

8.1. Organisers of the Erste Rus-
sische Kunstausstellung photo-
graphed in one of three avant-
garde rooms on ground floor of
Galerie van Diemen, Unter den
Linden, Berlin, 1922 – from left:
D. Shterenberg, head of IZO,
Mar'yanov, there on behalf of the
Cheka, N. Al'tman, N. Gabo, and
Dr Lütz, director of Galerie van
Dieman. In the background are
paintings by Shterenberg and an
Archipenko sculpture, in the
foreground Gabo's *Torso* of 1917,
now lost, presumed destroyed.
[Photograph: Miriam Gabo, Lon-
don.]

8 POSTSCRIPT TO RUSSIAN CONSTRUCTIVISM: THE WESTERN DIMENSION

CHAPTERS SIX and Seven have indicated how, in its later stages, Constructivism developed along two major paths. One led to a concentration on small-scale, well-defined design tasks such as typographical layouts. The other led to the re-examination of the technological bases of Constructivism pursued by Tatlin and Miturich. The subsequent fates of the Constructivist artists were pre-eminently tied up with work of the former category, that is with small design tasks.

Popova had of course died in 1924. During the 1930s Stepanova, her colleague at the textile factory, together with Rodchenko and Lissitzky, became increasingly involved with the selection of photographs, the composition of photomontages and the design of typographical layouts for official publications such as *The USSR in Construction* (*SSSR na stroike*). This activity involved a more intense relationship with the realistic photograph, its potential and the methods of its production and manipulation, all of which was expressed in the inventive photography of Lissitzky and Rodchenko.

Theatrical design became another outlet for their artistic creativity and means of earning a livelihood. Rodchenko had designed stage sets for *The Bedbug* (*Klop*) and *Inga* during the 1920s, and after the completion of his *Letatlin*, Tatlin primarily secured his living by designing stage sets for the Moscow Arts Theatre. On the card which he completed for the Moscow Union of Artists in 1951, Tatlin stated that 'from 1934 until now I have been working in the theatre as an artistic director. Between 1934 and 1951 [I designed] 80 productions.'[1] The accompanying list of theatres for which he worked included the Red Army Theatre, the Theatre of the Moscow Soviet, the Central Children's Theatre and the Theatre of the Lenin Komsomol. An account of the sets and costumes he designed for Sukhovo-Kobylin's classic play *The Affair* (*Delo*) at the Red Army Theatre in 1940 complimented Tatlin on the fact that 'he is leaving formalism and beginning to realise reality in a realistic manner'.[2]

This return to 'realism' was reflected in the fact that concurrent with his theatrical work and continual modifications to the *Letatlin*, Tatlin also produced numerous realistic drawings and oil paintings.[3] A return to such traditional artistic genres was not confined to Tatlin. Rodchenko also worked in these media, creating works which were primarily figurative.[4]

During the 1930s the Stenberg brothers continued their already prolific work in poster design and became involved in the decorations for Red Square for the anniversary of the Revolution. After Georgii Stenberg's death in 1933, his brother Vladimir continued this work. Medunetskii's subsequent career is difficult to trace. He left Moscow about 1925 to work in provincial theatres. Vladimir Stenberg met him again but has no precise details concerning his ultimate fate, suggesting that he died some time in the later 1930s or early 1940s.[5]

Lissitzky continued his work in typography and simultaneously became very much involved with exhibition design. He died in 1941 having worked until tuberculosis made it impossible. His stands for the *Pressa* exhibition in Cologne and elsewhere are rightly famous for their innovatory spatial and graphic arrangements.

Klutsis also continued to work in the area of posters and photomontage until the end of the 1930s. As an early member of the Bolshevik Party he was arrested in 1938. He is exceptional among the Constructivists in that most of them were not subjected to any physical repression.

Miturich had, of course, never completely abandoned realism or the figurative tradition. Throughout the 1920s and beyond he continued to produce finely observed drawings. He survived financially by illustrating books and executing the occasional graphic design task. He was noted for his rather sensitive figurative drawings which continued to be appreciated and which he had been producing throughout his artistic career. Despite his unflagging efforts his preoccupation and experiments with his *volnoviki* never came to practical fruition.[6]

The students of these men found it easier to establish themselves fruitfully within the framework of public institutions. Shapiro, who had been one of Tatlin's assistants, later worked as an architect in Leningrad and designed several minor public buildings such as the Baths.[7] Sotnikov worked in the Dulevskii Porcelain Factory designing ceramics. The students of the Metfak as indicated in Chapter Four joined various industrial enterprises, and it is to be assumed that their designs became more attuned to the economic and social demands of the First and Second Five Year Plans. The massive constructional tasks of these Plans meant that anyone with an originally architectural background, like Aleksandr Vesnin, could find a ready market for skills in that area.

It was the formal basis of the Constructivists' design work that had become a disputed area and they could continue their activity quite happily if acknowledging and accepting these restraints. They retreated from prominence leaving the Socialist Realists on the one hand and the more narrow technologically trained designers on the other. In artistic fields, the Constructivists' sociological and political commitments lived on, albeit in a completely different form, in Socialist Realism. In the field of product design, however, the design task as they had conceived it virtually ceased to exist under the economic exigencies of the heavy-industry oriented Five Year Plans. What small-scale functional objects were produced naturally employed totally different stylistic languages, so that the similarity of basic political and social positions is not immediately discernible.

In these circumstances it is not fruitful or apposite to judge Constructivism in terms of its impact, or otherwise, upon the immediately subsequent period in the Soviet Union. A primary concern of this study has been to establish chronological and biographical facts which do not lend themselves to recapitulation here. What has emerged from the study is firstly, a movement that created an exceptionally rich body of formal investigation, and secondly, a far more complex, analytical and theoretical base than had been revealed hitherto.

Within the scope of this study it has only been possible to begin the process of opening up this set of subtle theories concerning the nature of the design process and its component elements. Some indication of the boldness and sophistication of the Constructivists' analyses emerges in the INKhUK debates and in the programmes for transmitting and nurturing the discipline of 'artist-constructor', formulated within VKhUTEMAS. Tatlin's and Miturich's pursuits of their 'organic' approach established the, then wholly unexplored, notion of the multi-dimensionality of technology. The whole history of Constructivist involvement in photomontage demonstrated that the pursuit of the 'real' identified with Constructivism, and 'realism' as understood in the arts, were not inherently divorced phenomena, but possessed profound common roots which made possible the apparently contradictory transmutation within the work of individual Constructivists. In all its aspects Constructivism was permeated by that central component which crucially distinguishes it from the Western art movement that appropriated the name, and which fuelled the whole movement in Russia. That central component was its specific revolutionary and social commitment. The Constructivists' attempts to analyse how that commitment should influence the shaping of material demonstrated the inseparability of that process from some set of social principles and priorities, though it is a relationship that can be beneficially or disadvantageously used.

BERLIN 1922

Although Constructivism ceased to be a vital force in the cultural and artistic life of the Soviet Union during the 1930s, its precepts and example did not disappear completely without producing some reverberation and exerting some influence on cultural developments in the rest of Europe. This reverberation and influence still find their echoes today in the works of Western artists and sculptors. The nature of the influence which Russian Constructivism exerted first in the 1920s and then later was to a very large extent determined by the manner in which the West first encountered Constructivism and by how, having confronted Constructivism, it understood its theoretical precepts and assimilated them.

It is, therefore, historically important that the West made its first visual acquaintance with Russian Constructivism on a large scale in 1922, when the Erste Russische Kunstausstellung opened at the Van Diemen Gallery in Berlin.[8] Arranged in conjunction with the Committee to Help the Starving during the 1921–2 famine in Russia, the exhibition naturally had an official tone and represented the whole range of artistic trends then active in post-revolutionary Russia. It included works by artists who still used an Impressionist technique, such as Yuon, works by former academicians like Arkhipov, and Cézannists, like Mashkov, as well as the work of more avant-garde artists like the Suprematist Malevich and the Constructivists Rodchenko and Tatlin. However, despite the presence of more conservative paintings, it was precisely the exhibits of the newest trends and groups, in particular Suprematism and Constructivism, which captured the interest of the German press and exhibition-going public.[9]

Prior to this event some information about artistic life in Russia had been available to limited artistic circles in Germany. When El Lissitzky, for instance, left Russia for Berlin at the end of 1921, he is said to have taken with him a copy of 'The Programme of the First Working Group of Constructivists' and photographs of their work.[10] Having trained at Darmstadt before the First World War, Lissitzky was a fluent German speaker, and he succeeded in publicising Russian ideas in Germany. Together with the Russian writer Il'ya Erenburg, he was responsible for publishing the journal *Object*, the first issue of which appeared in Berlin in 1922.[11] Its trilingual title implied, and its subtitle made explicit, its intention to act as an 'An International Review of Contemporary Art'. Announcing that 'The Blockade of Russia is Coming to an End', *Object*'s declaration was appropriately printed in the three languages (Russian, German and French) of the journal's title. However, despite this international flavour, the dominant language of the journal was Russian. There were a few articles and poems in other languages, but the majority of the articles, especially those concerning art and architecture, were in Russian. Moreover, they concentrated primarily on Western developments such as Purism or De Stijl and included articles by Theo van Doesburg, Le Corbusier and Ozenfant. The artistic questionnaire which *Object* conducted revealed a similar bias, and answers from Léger, Severini, Gleizes and Lipchitz were printed in Russian. The journal also contained an article in Russian describing the exhibitions in Berlin.[12] The Western orientation of the journal's contents and its linguistic emphasis suggest that it was primarily intended to educate a Russian-speaking audience in the art of the West rather than a Western audience in the art of Russia.

The most important exception to this general trend and the most important article informing the West on Russian developments was 'Exhibitions in Russia' by 'Ulen', which appeared in the first issue. Written in German, this article provided a fairly superficial, but relatively objective, avant-garde account of purely artistic developments in Russia after the Revolution. Having briefly outlined the artistic groupings of the pre-revolutionary period, the author concentrated on various IZO exhibitions, naming among other participants, Rozanova, Klyun, Puni, Malevich and Rodchenko 'Ulen' stressed that the most important exhibition of 1919 was Non-Objective Creation and Suprematism because it represented 'the conclusion of painting as colour expression'. Although the Stenbergs' exhibition was mentioned, more attention was given to Gabo and Pevsner's Tverskoi Boulevard exhibition which accompanied the publication of their *Realistic Manifesto*. In the forefront of new trends 'Ulen' placed Tatlin's Monument, OBMOKhU and UNOVIS, although he did not explore the vital differences in approach between these artists. He concluded:

> Everything achieved here continues in the new Russian art schools. They are the fields of battle for the rallying cries 'Art in Life' (not outside it) and 'Art is One with Production'. One of the most glorious revolutions has taken place in the former Russian Academy.[13]

Such statements suggested that *Object* had an affinity with Constructivism. Yet, as has already been pointed out in Chapter Three, it would be completely mistaken to regard *Object* as a Constructivist journal which embodied or purveyed Constructivist ideas. With the exception of Punin's article in Russian concerning that transitional and seminal work, Tatlin's Monument to the Third International, there was no article in *Object* on Constructivism and certainly nothing on the rigorous theoretical ideas adopted in the spring of 1921 by the First Working Group of Constructivists. Although *Object*'s declaration seems to possess at moments a superficial resemblance to Constructivist ideas, this quickly disappears under more careful scrutiny. For instance, the journal's declaration announces that '*Object* will champion constructive art, whose mission is not after all to embellish life, but to organise it' and amplifies this in explaining the magazine's name: 'We have called our periodical *Object* because, to us, art means nothing other than the creation of new objects.'[14]

Such ideas seem remarkably similar to the Constructivists' expressed intention of abandoning the creation of art objects to devote themselves to designing and making prototypes of everyday objects for mass production. However, *Object*'s declaration also makes it clear that, for *Object*, the creation of objects did not entail the abandoning of art, but a broadening of its artistic definition. *Object* did not abolish artistic creation or declare art dead; on the contrary *Object* asserted that art works could be useful objects and equally that useful objects could be defined as art. This expansion of artistic categories was made explicit.

> Naturally it is our opinion that useful objects produced in our factories – aeroplanes, perhaps, or automobiles – are also the products of true art; but we do not wish to see artistic creation restricted to these useful objects alone. Every organised piece of work – whether it be a house, a poem, a painting – is a practical object ... Basic utilitarianism is far from our thoughts. *Object* regards poetry, plastic form and drama, as essential 'objects'.[15]

Such a programme could be readily understood within the widened objectives of artistic creativity being pursued in the West at this time by movements like De Stijl. *Object* did not expound the more violently anti-aesthetic and more rigorously utilitarian theory of Constructivism.

In a very similar way *Object*, unlike the Constructivists, did not adopt a definite political stance. Although it declared that it was 'aloof from all political parties because it is not occupied with the problems of politics but of art', yet it also stressed that it was not apolitical and could not envisage new forms in art without changes in social forms.[16] It is precisely *Object*'s lack of specificity which makes it stand in opposition to the positive and emphatic, social, political and industrial commitment of the Constructivists.

Despite its theoretical vagueness *Object* has been regarded as seminal in bringing the new ideas of post-revolutionary Russian art to the West. Available in German and French, *Object*'s declaration was one of the few sources that Western artists interested in Russian developments could read. Yet that declaration presented, in 1922, a view of art and artistic concepts that the Constructivists had abandoned more than a year before. Whatever information *Object* did give on Russian art, it certainly did not provide any firm theoretical guidelines or a solid ideological context for an understanding of Constructivism. Consequently, Western artists had not been given the type of background knowledge that would have enabled them to understand the works by Constructivist artists which were on display in 1922 at the Erste Russische Kunstausstellung. Without such preliminary information as 'The Programme of the First Working Group of Constructivists', these works were understandably seen primarily within a purely artistic context. The advanced theoretical and practical lessons the Constructivists had drawn from these experiments as well as from the Revolution were not apparent to the German observer.

Moreover, the works by Constructivists which were on display did not contradict this impression, since they were created in the period preceding 1922, before there had been any significant results from the move into production. The exhibition contained spatial constructions by Vladimir and Georgii Stenberg, Konstantin Medunetskii, Karl Ioganson, Vladimir Tatlin and Aleksandr Rodchenko, as well as experimental work produced by the Basic Course at the VKhUTEMAS.[17] These exhibits consisted either of abstract three-dimensional art works such as Tatlin's *Counter-Relief* (No. 569), which had been produced long before 1921 and the creation of the First Working Group of Constructivists, or of works like the spatial constructions of Ioganson, Medunetskii and the Stenberg brothers, which belonged to the category of laboratory work. Laboratory work consisted of abstract experimentation undertaken, not for its own sake, nor in response to any specific utilitarian requirement, but with an ultimately utilitarian application in view. Obviously there was no ambiguity about the former category. Tatlin's work had been created as an art work, pure and simple, and was perceived as such. However, in the latter case of laboratory works there was very little visual indication of any utilitarian content and visually very little to make any adequate distinction between these experiments and works of art. In the absence of statements to the contrary, it is therefore not surprising that these works were regarded pre-eminently as aesthetic objects, and that as a consequence German observers saw Constructivism as being primarily an artistic movement. The presentation of such works within an exhibition format would only confirm such an interpretation. The sociological and ideological dimension of Constructivism was inevitably obscured by the similarity of these works to art objects and by the inaccessibility of the Russian theoretical debates which had resulted from the Constructivists' acceptance of the wider implications of such explorations.[18] Without evidence to the contrary it was natural for the Germans to understand the Constructivists' works they viewed in the exhibition as merely art works.

Unfortunately the catalogue to the exhibition did little to remedy such an impression. Although it did allude to the true position of the Constructivists, the latters' ideas were not expounded at length, so that the profundity of their ideological and industrial commitment was not conveyed. The Constructivists' position was explained in very general terms, and not without ambiguity, by David Shterenberg in his introduction.

Tatlin, the Constructivist, . . . was the first in Russia to present the counter-relief developed from the surface area, which actualizes real material in space. Tatlin is represented in the exhibition by non-objective works which indicate a stage in the transition to production art. His Monument to the Third International can be cited as his first essay in this direction.

There are still further ramifications of these art movements to the left: the representatives of one of them renounce canvas altogether, strive towards production art and currently produce a whole series of non-objective constructions which reveal no utilitarian characteristics. Rodchenko who belongs to this group is represented by strong Suprematist and Constructivist works. He is moving now in the direction of utilitarian architectonic constructions.[19]

This statement conveys the impression that the Constructivists were beginning to move towards a production art, but it gives no real indication that by the time of the exhibition the move into production had been explored theoretically and that there had been attempts to initiate it practically as well. There was no mention of the Constructivists' attempt to evolve a course of training for the artist-constructor at the VKhUTEMAS, or of Tatlin's work at the New Lessner Factory in Petrograd. Such omissions naturally did not help to reduce the emphasis on the non-utilitarian and formal nature of the exhibits themselves.

Moreover, this artistic bias was undoubtedly not contradicted by the type of émigré Russian artist who was then present in Berlin.[20] Among them was Gabo who had come to the West in association with the exhibition, of which he was an active organiser.[21] Gabo's works exhibited at the Van Diemen Gallery included *Spatial Constructions*, *A B* and *C* (Cat. Nos. 546-8) and *Kinetic Construction* (*Time as a New Element of the Plastic Arts*) (Cat. No. 550). The 'constructed' qualities of these works and their titles displayed certain affinities with those constructions exhibited by the First Working Group of Constructivists. Two works which have remained in the West – Medunetskii's *Construction* (colour plate II) and Gabo's *Kinetic Construction* (plate 1.53) – reveal a very similar approach to exploring a linear form extended into and interacting with space. Such visual similarities encouraged the placing of such works within the same category of 'constructive' or 'constructivist' art objects. At the same time, Gabo's uncompromisingly aesthetic stance, and his lack of political commitment to Bolshevism (which his emigration made explicit), gave this new category of art objects an ideology which concealed the basic theoretical and ideological antagonisms that existed between Gabo and the First Working Group of Constructivists. Moreover, Gabo's cogent expositions of 'the Constructive idea' and his use of the term 'constructive' to describe his works acted also to camouflage the differences which existed in Russia between the constructive artist and the Constructivist. Thus these two categories of activity which radically diverged in their ultimate aspirations became subsumed under the one aesthetic theory enunciated by Gabo. This identification reinforced the West's concept of Constructivism as an aesthetic.

Depoliticised by their emigration to the West, Russian Constructivist experiments were viewed by the Germans solely within an aesthetic context. Contemporary German reactions to the 1922 exhibition confirm this. One critic wrote: 'In the place of the delicate colour harmonies of France or the mystical strivings of Germany, the Russians have revealed a stronger movement towards a greater plasticity and spatial force.'[22] Although the German critic Fritz Stahl asserted that 'in the whole of this art there is nothing at all that is really revolutionary', it was generally acknowledged that the Russians' work demonstrated 'an audacity and freedom, a determination to rethink and recreate all values – such as Europe has not seen for decades'.[23] At the same time certain German critics did detect the implications of the Russians' three-dimensional constructions. However, the Germans' statements only emphasise their ignorance of the fact that the Russians had accepted these implications. For instance, even a sensitive and well-informed critic

XIX. V. Tatlin, *The Fisherman* (*Rybak*), *c.* 1912, watercolour and wash on paper, *c.* 28 × 35 cm. Russian Museum, Leningrad.

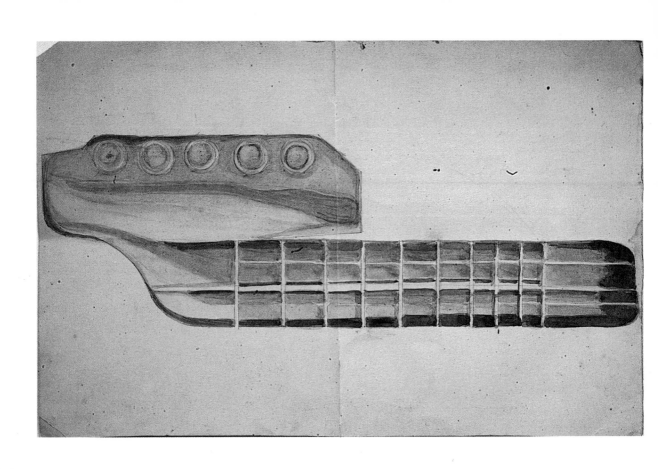

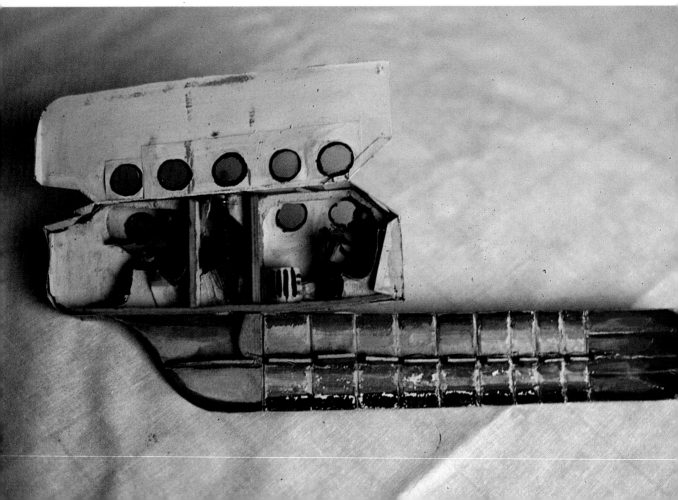

who was able to discern the essential qualities of the Constructivists' works on display did not know that the Constructivists had embraced practical work in industry. Having posed the question as to whether there was a Russian art as such, this critic concluded:

> No ... The Russian exhibition is rather an exhibition of artistic problems, investigations, experiments and laboratory explorations. This is concentrated brain work. Here it is not yet a question of achievements, but of the preliminary stages in the creation of a grammar for a new artistic esperanto ...
>
> A naive striving towards building and constructing objects, which we have, but which are still lacking in Russian technology, has led the Russians to a primitive imitation of machines and architecture in their fine art ...
>
> Essentially the Russian Constructivists should have been sufficiently consistent to draw the ultimate conclusion and in the place of useless aesthetic games to have entered into practical work; and instead of constructing likenesses of machines to have become worker-productivists creating genuine machines.[24]

Such statements suggest that the Germans simply did not know that the Russian Constructivists had explored the theoretical and practical implications of their abstract three-dimensional experimentation in depth, and on that basis had begun to develop a whole methodology of design.

The importance of the 1922 exhibition in establishing the Western 'aesthetic' view of Constructivism is fundamental. Both Russian and European commentators pinpoint 1922 as the year for Constructivism's arrival in the West. Hans Richter in 1924 declared that 'Constructivism appeared first in Russia and was brought to Germany in 1922'.[25] Equally, Matsa stressed that 'Western Constructivism developed in Germany and Holland under the influence of Russian Constructivism'.[26] The work of the Russian Constructivists which was exhibited at the First Russian Art Exhibition in Berlin in 1922 was such that, taken together with the stance of *Object*, and the presence of emigré artists like Lissitzky and Gabo, promoting their own ideas, it gave the West a picture of Russian Constructivism which was eminently more accessible and digestible to them than the actual rigorously anti-aesthetic, politically and socially utilitarian Russian movement. Moreover, in the context of little or no accurate information about what Constructivism was in Russia this 'aesthetic' view encountered no opposition.

THE CONTEXT OF INFORMATION

Prior to 1922 visual and theoretical information concerning Constructivism in particular and Russian art in general had been even more limited and erratic. *Object*'s editorial declaration had talked of a blockade of Russia existing up to 1922. Such terminology suggests a termination of all contact and flow of information. In actuality there had been some contacts. As early as 1919 Kandinskii had published a general account of artistic life in Soviet Russia in the Berlin journal *Die Freiheit*.[27] Even before this there had been attempts to establish permanent and effective contacts with the West. In November 1918 the Petrograd journal *Life of Art* announced that an International Office (the Mezhdunarodnoe byuro otdela izobrazitel'nykh iskusstv) had been set up within the Department of Fine Arts.[28] This body was to be directed by a committee consisting of Lunacharskii, Shterenberg, Punin, Tatlin and Kandinskii and included Dymshits-Tolstaya who was responsible for the everyday running of the office.[29] The purpose of this International Office was to effect 'the unification of the progressive fighters of the new art in the name of constructing a new universal artistic culture', a first step in the creation of which was to be the organisation of an International Congress of Russian and German artists.[30]

XX. P. Miturich, Drawing of a transport *volnovik*, 1920s, pencil, watercolour and gouache on paper, *c.* 20 × 30 cm. Private collection, Moscow.

XXI. P. Miturich, Model of a transport *volnovik*, 1920s, oil, gouache, paper, cardboard, rubber, *c.* 8 × 27 cm. Private collection, Moscow.

One of the first actions of the newly established International Office had been to commission the artist Ludwig Bähr when he left Russia in December 1918 to contact German artistic organisations, convey the Russians' greetings and appeal for international unity in the creation of the new artistic culture.[31] In the summer of 1919 a message from the Arbeitsrat für Kunst (Workers' Art Council), signed by Bruno Taut, Walter Gropius, Cäsar Klein and Max Pechstein, was received. This was followed by news about the Novembergruppe and the West-Ost group and by information about the 'new Weimar Academy' and its approach to an organic synthesis of the arts.[32] However, perhaps encouraged by the initial message from Germany in the summer of 1919, in September the International Office announced its intention of publishing a journal, *Art International*, the first number of which was to contain articles by Lunacharskii, Tatlin, Malevich, Khlebnikov and others.[33] At the same time the Office declared that it was sending 'artistic ambassadors' to the West: 'comrade Kamp to Italy and comrade Krainy [alias Umanskii] to Germany and Austria-Hungary'.[34] Although the journal did not appear, one permanent result of the existence of the International Office seems to have been the departure of Umanskii for Germany and the appearance in the West of one of the fullest and earliest accounts of Russian artistic developments during the revolutionary period.

This informative document was Umanskii's book entitled *New Art in Russia, 1914-1919* (*Neue Kunst in Russland 1914-1919*), completed in Munich in February 1920 and published later the same year. In conjunction with writing the book Umanskii also published several articles on the latest developments in Russian art. These appeared in the Munich journal *Der Ararat*.[35] Both the publication of the articles and the writing of the book predated the most radical artistic developments in Russia, the founding of the Moscow INKhUK in May 1920 and the emergence within that body of the First Working Group of Constructivists in March 1921. It also predated the appearance of Tatlin's Tower, exhibited in November and December 1920. Inevitably, therefore, while Umanskii's book contained much information of a very lucid and thorough kind concerning pre- and immediately post-revolutionary artistic developments in Russia, events had moved so fast that by the time of its publication, and certainly by mid-1921, its exposition of these latest developments was out of date. Umanskii did not mention Constructivism, but he talked at length of Tatlinism as a radical aesthetic movement which had not just created 'a new word in the language of art but a new art language'.[36]

> Tatlinism maintains that the picture as such is dead. The picture surface is too narrow to contain the three-dimensional, and new problems require richer technical means for their solution. Moreover there is a disdain for the necessity to create 'pictures' and 'works of art' to entertain or, even better, repel the initiated. Thus in 1915 Tatlin developed Machine Art which stems from Picasso's and Braque's experiments of 1913. Art is dead - Long live art, the art of the Machine, with its construction and logic, its rhythm, its components, its metaphysical spirit - the art of the Counter-Reliefs. This finds no material unworthy of art: wood, glass, paper, metal sheeting, iron, screws, nails, electrical fittings, slivers of glass scattered across surfaces, the ability of separate parts to move, etc. - all of these have been declared legitimate instruments of the new art language. The grammar and aesthetic of this language require the further mechanical training of the artist and a closer relationship to his omnipotent ally - the sovereign machine. One must define the art of the counter-relief as ... the triumph of the intellect and the material ...[37]

This extract closely resembles the text of Umanskii's article which appeared in *Der Ararat* in January 1920, entitled 'Tatlinism or Machine Art'. It was evidently Umanskii's words and sentiments that inspired George Grosz and John Heartfield to produce their poster at the Dada exhibition five months later, in June 1920, which boldly announced 'Art is Dead. Long live the Machine Art of Tatlin.'[38] This Dada identification with Tatlin inevitably offered a distorted picture of Tatlin's work. As Umanskii pointed out, 'a babbling Dadaism would be impossible in Modern Russia'.[39] However, Umanskii had emphasised, and Grosz and Heartfield had publicised, the nihilistic attitude towards traditionally accepted art forms and materials which was embodied in Tatlin's counter-reliefs. This nihilism was later developed to an extreme in the ideas and theories of the First Working Group of Constructivists. What Grosz and Heartfield could not grasp in June 1920 was the extent of the Constructivists' aesthetic nihilism by the spring of 1921 and the fact that it was accompanied by a very positive identification with, and participation in, the political, industrial and educational construction of a communist society in Russia.

Writing in early 1920, Umanskii could not deal with Constructivism, which had not yet fully developed in Russia, nor could he illustrate Tatlin's Tower. However, he was able to give a fairly detailed account of Punin's article on Tatlin's project, published in 1919, which conveyed the essential ideas inspiring the monument.[70] Umanskii placed Tatlin's Tower within the context of Lenin's Plan for Monumental Propaganda and described it as 'a living machine', which was a 'technical and rational instrument for achieving utilitarian goals'.[41] He perceived that the monument questioned the traditional division between art and technology and between the different branches of the arts, and that, as such, it does 'contradict the most fundamental artistic assumptions and justifies raising the question as to whether Tatlinism is a temporally conditioned abberation of artistic ultra-materialism'.[42] Therefore, despite the fact that there was no visual documentation of Tatlin's monument available, the essential concepts of the project were conveyed by Umanskii in his book, and in a short article which appeared in the March 1920 issue of *Ararat* as part of a survey of the 'The New Monumental Sculpture in Russia'. The further systematic exploration and extension of Tatlin's ideas which followed the exhibition of the monument in Russia and which established the political and industrial imperative of Constructivism could obviously not be described by Umanskii. Yet he had presented a kernel of ideas from the transitional period in Constructivism's development which could have provided a clue to understanding the concepts of the First Working Group of Constructivists had other evidence and information been forthcoming. In actuality, the picture of Russian art which Umanskii had presented to Germany in 1920 was not radically altered by the 1922 exhibition. It was merely visually amplified.

IZO's attempts to inform the West about Russian artistic developments were continued by INKhUK. At some point, probably about 1921, INKhUK had striven to establish some international contacts. Its report, published in 1923, mentioned Holland, Switzerland, Hungary, Berlin, Paris and Tokyo. Lissitzky was named as the contact for Berlin and Paris; Brik and Kemeny for Germany; Bela Uitz for Hungary; Bubnova for Tokyo; and Petrus and Alma for Holland.[43] In many instances these contacts probably amounted to little more than a mailing list, providing an initial point of departure for any information being sent to the West. Moreover their real effectiveness probably postdates Lissitzky's departure after which vital Western centres were dependent to a large extent upon his viewpoint, which as the *Object* declaration makes clear lacked the vigour of the Constructivists' position.

There are, however, important exceptions to be made to this general picture of communications, and these concern the Hungarians. The failure of the Hungarian Revolution had led progressive and socialist artists into emigration along with their political leaders. The main centres of these émigrés were Berlin, Vienna and Moscow. Hungarian knowledge of and interest in Russian art is manifest in their émigré art journals and activities. On 13 November 1920 the Hungarian avant-garde group MA held a special Russian evening in Vienna where slides of work by

Kandinskii, Malevich, Rodchenko, Stepanova, Udal'tsova, Tatlin and others were shown.[44] Umanskii delivered the lecture and undoubtedly conveyed very much the picture of Russian art presented in his book. However, more up to date knowledge of Russian art was soon available to the Hungarians. In the early summer of 1921 the artist Bela Uitz, also editor of the Hungarian magazine *Unity* (*Egység*) published in Vienna, visited Russia to attend the Congress of the Third International in Moscow. There they met Jolan Zsilagyi. Through her they became acquainted with the VKhUTEMAS where she was a student. It is quite likely that they met Rodchenko and his confrères at the VKhUTEMAS.

It was probably as a result of this visit that the second number of *Unity* for 1922 contained a general article on Russian art by Bela Uitz and translations of both 'The Programme of the First Working Group of Constructivists' and *The Realistic Manifesto* by Gabo. These two important statements were accompanied by illustrations of the work of Vladimir Stenberg, Karl Ioganson, Naum Gabo, the OBMOKhU artist Prusakov, and a general view of the third OBMOKhU exhibition which showed clearly the type of two- and three-dimensional experimental works being made and exhibited in Soviet Russia. This was, as far as can be traced, the first publication of the Russian Constructivists' ideas outside Russia. Unfortunately, it was in Hungarian and the Hungarian artists in Vienna had little contact with their Austrian counterparts. So, while this statement had some impact on Hungarian artists, it is doubtful whether this would have spread to the German speaking community around them.

The Hungarian artist Alfred Kemeny also visited Russia in 1921. His visit seems to have been of longer duration than that of Bela Uitz. He was introduced to Naum Gabo by David Shterenberg, head of IZO, and in a quasi-official capacity was introduced by Gabo to all the important artists in the VKhUTEMAS and the Russian avant-garde generally.[45] According to Gabo, he was also given photographs. Kemeny became a great supporter of the OBMOKhU, advocating their merits forcefully at INKhUK on 26 December 1921 in one of two papers he presented to the Institute.[46] Later, when he returned to Germany, he collaborated with Moholy-Nagy on the publication of a manifesto 'Dynamic-constructive Force System' ('Dynamisch-konstruktive kraftsystem') and issued a manifesto with Kallai, Peri and Moholy-Nagy in which the Russian Constructivists' fusion of the ideological and the formal was divided once more into two distinct but equally valid areas of activity. In this way purely formal investigations into 'a dynamic (mobile) constructive system of forces' was elevated to the same importance as the communist tasks confronting the Russian Constructivist.[47] Thus Kemeny and, through him, Moholy-Nagy seem to have assimilated certain formal elements from the Russians' non-utilitarian constructions and combined them with certain ideological aspects of the Russian Constructivists' platform without publicising the real principles of that movement. Their compromise stance was ultimately not so dissimilar to that of Lissitzky's journal *Object*. Kemeny's first-hand knowledge of Russian Constructivism was thus not really effective in promoting a true understanding of that movement in the West, either before or after the 1922 exhibition.

The Western perspective on what was happening in Russia had the opportunity to alter significantly with the Exposition Internationale des Arts Décoratifs et Industriels Modernes in Paris in 1925. Konstantin Mel'nikov's design for the Soviet pavilion was one of the most visually exciting contributions to the exhibition, and its bold geometry was startlingly new amid the neo-classically ornamented displays from other countries. Justifiably, 'it took first place at the exhibition and as a result drew a lot of attention'.[48] Mel'nikov's pavilion expressed the new era in Russia, but more significant, with respect to Constructivism, was Rodchenko's realisation of a totally Constructivist environment in the form of the Workers' Club. In this project Rodchenko's abstract three-dimensional experimentation with standardised units and Euclidean geometric forms which had formed the crux of his non-utilitarian constructions provided the basis for his practical design work. The spatial clarity of the Constructivists' work displayed at Berlin in 1922 was here transformed by Rodchenko into the economically constructed chairs and tables, and the cleverly devised space-saving folding unit consisting of a film screen, political display board and agitational tribune. Also on display were the teaching programmes and products of the Wood and Metalwork faculties of the VKhUTE-MAS.[49] At Paris in 1925 the West had the opportunity to see for the first time the nature of the Constructivists' theoretical extension, and practical application, of those principles which had lain at the basis of their 'laboratory work' on display at Berlin in 1922. In Paris the new Constructivist approach to design in the creation of a new communist environment became manifest.

There is a certain irony in the fact that Constructivism's principles were first displayed clearly in Paris in 1925. Despite the continuing experimentation of Le Corbusier, the centre of radical innovation in design and architecture was undoubtedly Germany. There was no French equivalent of the Bauhaus. In the Paris of 1925, given over to elegance and the decorative use of fine materials, only the clarity of the Russian Constructivists' geometry could attract – its theoretical austerity could find no creative reverberation in Parisian design.[50] The ideological, political and social implications of the Constructivists' ideas were ignored. It was only external geometric style which had any impact because it was most accessible, both culturally and visually, to the West.

Since the 1920s the influence which Constructivism has exerted on Western art has remained within the boundaries set up by the two exhibitions of 1922 and 1925. For American sculptors, like George Rickey, working in the 1960s, it was the Constructivists' approach to space, movement, material and processed geometric form, found in the latter's laboratory work and non-utilitarian constructions, which was associated with Constructivism. It was these principles which the Americans adopted and continued to explore. Contemporary sculptors have continued to experiment with a body of principles which provided only a starting point for the socially and politically committed work of the Russian Constructivists in the 1920s. The geographic, linguistic and cultural inaccessibility of the Russian Constructivists' theoretical statements and debates has removed the full impact of Russian Constructivism from Western understanding.

Russian Constructivists were aware that such a transposition of meaning was taking place and that the term 'Constructivism' was being used with a different meaning by artists and critics in the West. Aleksei Gan, the theoretician of the First Working Group of Constructivists, in his major treatise *Constructivism*, published in 1922, elaborated this very point in his concluding section, entitled 'Constructivism in the West'.[51] Gan recognised that concepts of the 'constructive' and 'construction' were being propounded by various progressive Western journals. In particular he quoted a statement from *L'Esprit Nouveau* – 'the new spirit is the spirit of Construction' – and cited *De Stijl*'s assertion that 'the new collective style derives from a constructive beginning'.[52] Gan even acknowledged that the Western and Russian Constructivisms were part of a general post-war phenomenon in Europe, where the concepts of Work, Clarity and Organisation had become the symbols of a belief in a new art.

However, it is precisely at this point that Gan distinguished the Russian phenomenon from its Western counterpart, and his distinction hinges precisely on the concept of art. Gan argued that, for the West, Constructivism was merely the name given to the new artistic trend. 'They [the West] simply call the new art Constructivism,' he asserted.[53] He particularly singled out Erenburg and Lissitzky for blame. 'The basic mistake,' he stressed, 'of comrade Erenburg and comrade Lissitzky consists in the fact that they cannot tear themselves away from art.'[54] Gan stressed that the Russian Constructivists had dispensed with art and that it was the Revolution which ensured that this would happen. Gan argues:

... Constructivism is not only our phenomenon.

It develops from living conditions which arise from the condition of the productive forces.

And depending on the conditions of the productive forces, i.e. depending on the different social forms, it adopts different inclinations.

The social and political structure of the R.S.F.S.R., and the structure of capitalist Europe and America are completely different.

Naturally, Constructivism is not the same.

Our Constructivism has declared uncompromising war on art, because the means and properties of art are not powerful enough to systematise the feelings of the revolutionary milieu. It is cemented by the real success of the Revolution and its feelings are expressed by intellectual and material production.

In the West Constructivism fraternises with art ...

Our Constructivism has set itself a clear aim: to find the communist expression of material structures.

In the West Constructivism flirts with politics, declaring that the new art is outside of politics, but that it is not apolitical.

Our Constructivism is aggressive and uncompromising: it wages a severe battle with parasites, with left and right painters, in a word with all, who even slightly defend the speculative aesthetic activity of art.

Our Constructivism is fighting for the intellectual and material production of a communist culture.[55]

8.2. Students working in the Metfak of the VKhUTEMAS—on the left Migunov and on the right Bykov—producing utilitarian articles for the new communist Russian society.

BIOGRAPHICAL SKETCHES

AL'TMAN, Natan Isaevich (1889–1970)

Born at Vinnitsa, from 1903 to 1907 Al'tman attended the Odessa School of Art where he studied under Kostanda, Ladyzhenskii and Iorina. In 1911 he went to Paris where he attended the Russian Academy of M. Vasil'eva. One of his most famous works was his Cubist-inspired portrait of the poetess Anna Akhmatova. From 1915 until 1917 he taught at the private school of M. Bernshtein in Petrograd. Between 1918 and 1920 he taught at the Petrograd State Free Art Studios. For the first anniversary of the Revolution in 1918 he designed the decorations for Uritskii Square, Petrograd, transforming the Aleksandr column and the surrounding buildings into colourful Cubo-Futurist constructions. Al'tman was also involved with the Department of Fine Arts (IZO Narkompros) and its journal *Art of the Commune* (*Iskusstvo kommuny*, 1918–19). He was a member of the Moscow INKhUK and on 11 May 1922 he spoke there about his decorations for Gutskov's play *Uriel' Akosta* produced by Granovksii at the Jewish Theatre. These were elegant three-dimensional abstract structures with an aesthetic, not an industrial, Constructivist basis. In 1922 he exhibited with Chagall and Shterenberg. In 1928 he went to Paris where he worked until 1935. In the 1920s and later he worked a great deal in theatrical and graphic design as well as painting.

ARVATOV, Boris Ignat'evich (1896–1940)

Arvatov was a major theoretician of production art. Born in Kiev, the son of a lawyer, Arvatov was educated at the Riga gymnazium and from 1915 attended Petrograd University where he studied in the Faculty of Physics and Mathematics. He was a member of the Socialist Revolutionary Party until 1917. In 1919 or 1920 he joined the Communist Party and until 1921 he was a commissar on the Polish front. In 1921 he became a member of the Moscow INKhUK where he actively participated in discussions concerning the nature of production art. In 1922 he delivered a paper entitled 'Art from the Organisational Point of View' ('Iskusstvo s tochki zreniya organizatsii'). He also belonged to RAKhN. From 1918 he was an academic secretary in Proletkul't. His first published work on art was an elementary introduction to the classic Doric temple (*Gorn*, No. 4, 1919). He wrote extensively on the theatre, Constructivism and production art. For Arvatov, production art, i.e. the work of the new type of 'engineer-constructor', would be the only form of creativity in the new society. Constructivism was a step towards this. Arvatov described his social status as 'intellectual' and his profession as 'art critic and Marxist' (TsGALI, fond 941, op. 10, ed. khr. 23). He was a member of Glavpolitprosvet within the Commissariat of Enlightenment. In 1923 he became ill as a result of having suffered shell shock at the front during the war and the rest of his life was spent in a psychiatric hospital. Despite this he maintained an intense corresponding contact with the journal *LEF* (1923–5) and *Novyi LEF* (1927–8), to which he was a frequent contributor. Arvatov continued to maintain a lively interest in artistic affairs and cultural developments, to the extent of writing to Zelinskii asking for information about the 'new group of literary Constructivists' (TsGALI, fond 1604, op. 1, ed. khr. 12). In 1930 a collection of his writings was published as a book, *About Agitational and Production Art* (*Ob agitatsionnom i proizvodstvennom iskusstve*), for which Rodchenko designed the cover. In 1935 Arvatov's friends Eisenstein, Brik and Shklovskii wrote to the Commissariat of Health on his behalf (TsGALI, fond 1923, op. 1, ed. khr. 1579).

BABICHEV, Aleksei Vasil'evich (1887–1963)

Born in Moscow, Babichev studied mathematics at Moscow University for a year before becoming a sculptor. During 1905–6 he studied at the private studios of I. Dudin and Konstantin Yuon, and from 1907 to 1912 attended the Moscow School of Painting, Sculpture and Architecture where he studied painting and sculpture with K. Korovin and S. Volnukhin. In 1913–14 he travelled through Europe visiting Vienna, Berlin, Paris (where he studied at the Académie de la Grande Chaumière under A. Bourdelle), Italy and Greece. Back in Moscow in 1915–17 he ran his own sculpture studio. He was involved in the decorations of Moscow for May Day 1918 and was also actively engaged in Lenin's Plan for Monumental Propaganda, in connection with which he organised his own sculpture collective called Monolit. In 1918 Babichev joined the staff of the First State Free Art Studios, Moscow, where he taught in the general sculptural studio and decorative sculpture studio. He continued working at the VKhUTEMAS teaching and evolving the syllabus for the volume discipline in the Basic Course. From 1920 to 1924 he was an active member of the Moscow INKhUK, responsible for formulating the programme of the General Working Group of Objective Analysis. In 1926 he joined the Realist group AKhRR and became president of the group's sculptural section. In 1925–30 he ran the art department of the preparatory faculty for workers (Rabfak). During the 1930s he continued teaching in various schools, such as the Moscow Architectural Institute.

BOGDANOV (MALINOVSKII), Aleksandr Aleksandrovich (1873–1928)

A politician, philosopher and doctor, Bogdanov was born in Grodno province. A member of the Social Democrats from 1897, in 1899 he graduated from Khar'kov University in medicine. In 1904 he joined the Bolsheviks but was expelled in 1919 because of his criticism of Lenin's tactics. He was active during the 1905 Revolution. In 1907 he was arrested and exiled. During the First World War he worked as a doctor at the front. With Gor'kii and Lunacharskii, Bogdanov was a member of the 'Forward' group (Vpered) and an organiser of the Party School at Bologna and Capri. Bogdanov was one of the founders of Proletkul't and a member of its central committee until December 1920 when he was dropped because of pressure from Lenin. Like Gor'kii and Lunacharskii, Bogdanov had believed in 'God Building' (bogostroitel'stvo), i.e. in the mystical, religious unity of the proletariat which through the Revolution and socialism would elevate man to the full realisation of his potential, so that he would be like a god. Bogdanov also posited the concept of the three-fold path to socialism: the political, economic and cultural. These ideas he prom-

oted in his books and in articles which were published in Proletkul't's journal *Proletarian Culture* (*Proletarskaya kul'tura*). After 1921 he ceased to work in Proletkul't and devoted himself to scientific work, dying in 1928 from an experimental blood transfusion.

BRIK, Osip Maksimovich (1888–1945)

A literary critic, Brik originally trained as a lawyer in his native city of St Petersburg. He was an active member, together with Shklovskii, of that pre-revolutionary centre of Formalism, the Society for the Study of Poetical Language (OPOYAZ). Both Osip and his wife Lili Brik were close friends of Vladimir Mayakovskii. After the Revolution Brik actively participated in artistic affairs and in discussions concerning the nature of the new art for the new State. From 1918 he worked in the Department of Fine Arts (IZO Narkompros), attending meetings, participating in the reorganisation of art education, acting as commissar of the Petrograd State Free Art Studios during 1919, editing and contributing articles to IZO's journals *Art of the Commune* (1918–19) and *Fine Art* (1919). During the Civil War Brik also worked for the Russian Telegraphic Agency (ROSTA). From 1920 until 1924 he was an active member of the Moscow INKhUK and an important supporter of Constructivism. On 24 November 1921 Brik made his famous proposal to INKhUK that all artists who rejected easel painting should commence 'real practical work in production'. Twenty-five artists supported him and INKhUK adopted an ostensibly Constructivist platform. From 1923 Brik worked on the journal *LEF* (1923–5), and was a co-founder of *Novyi LEF* (1927–8), where he wrote extensively on photography and design. However, his interests became increasingly concentrated on literature. In 1923 he published his story *Not a Fellow-Traveller* (*Ne poputchitsa*, Moscow, 1923) and in 1929 wrote the scenario for Pudovkin's film *The Heir of Genghis Khan*, continuing this type of work in the 1930s. Towards the end of the 1920s he became very active in promoting the ideas of a literature of fact and he contributed to the compilation *The Literature of Fact: The First Collection of Material by Workers on LEF* (*Literatura fakta: pervyi sbornik materialov rabotnikov LEFa*, Moscow, 1929). After Mayakovskii's death in 1930, Brik wrote extensively about his friendship with Mayakovskii and about the latter's work.

BRUNI, Lev Aleksandrovich (1894–1948)

A painter and graphic artist, Bruni was born at Malaya Vishera now in the Novgorod district. He was the son of the architect A. A. Bruni and the nephew of the academician N. A. Bruni. Between 1904 and 1909 he attended Princess Tenisheva's school in St Petersburg, and then, from 1909 until 1912, the Academy of Arts (Akademiya khudozhestv) where he studied under F. Rubo, N. Samokish and Ya. Tsionglinskii. In 1912 he went to Paris where he attended the Académie Julian. Returning to Petrograd he exhibited with the World of Art group (Mir iskusstva, 1915). His flat, No. 5 at the Academy in Petrograd, became a meeting point for various members of the avant-garde at this time, such as Lur'e, Tatlin, Udal'tsova, Punin, Miturich and others. After having mildly flirted with Cubism and Futurism in such works as the *Rainbow* (*Raduga*, 1916), Bruni experimented in working with materials in three dimensions, the results of which he called *Painterly Work in Materials* (*Zhivopisnaya rabota materialov*, see *Izobrazitel'noe iskusstvo*, No. 1, 1919, p. 33). He taught at the Shtiglits' Central School of Technical Drawing in Petrograd in 1920-1. In 1923 he moved to Moscow and joined the staff of the VKhUTEMAS where he taught drawing in the Graphics faculty. In 1925 he became a member of the Four Arts group (Chetyre iskusstva). This corresponded to his rejection of avant-garde experimentation and the return in his own work in the 1920s to figurative description and realism. From 1930 he taught at the Moscow Textile Institute. In 1935 he became the director of the Studio of Monumental Painting at the Moscow Architectural Institute (Moskovskii arkhitekturnyi institut) then at the Academy of Architecture (Akademiya arkhitektury SSSR). During the 1930s he did a lot of illustrative work for journals such as *Thirty Days* (*30 dnei*).

CHICHAGOVA, Galina Dmitrievna
(1891–1967)
and
CHICHAGOVA, Ol'ga Dmitrievna
(1892–1956)

From 1920 both sisters studied at the Moscow VKhUTEMAS graduating from the Graphics faculty. They both became members of Gan's First Working Group of Constructivists and exhibited with the group at the 1924 First Discussional Exhibition of Associations of Active Revolutionary Art (Pervaya diskussionaya vystavka ob'edinenii aktivnogo revolyutsionnogo iskusstva, Moscow, 1924). The sisters specialised in illustrating children's books such as *Where Crockery comes from* (*Otkuda posuda*, Moscow, 1924) and *For Children: About the Newspaper* (*Detyam o gazete*, Moscow). Both Galina and Ol'ga were represented at the Pressa exhibition in Cologne in 1928.

CHUZHAK (NASIMOVICH),
Nikolai Fedorovich (1876–1937)

A writer, literary critic and theoretician of production art, Chuzhak was also a long-standing member of the Bolshevik Party. In *c*.1914 he had been arrested and exiled to Siberia where he did extensive research into Siberian literature and in 1916 published a book on the local poets and their work (*Sibirskie poety i ikh tvorchestvo*). After the Revolution he was active in the Bolshevik underground in Vladivostock where he edited various party journals and newspapers including the *Red Banner* (*Krasnoe znamya*). In 1919 he became a member of the Far Eastern Futurist group Creation (Tvorchestvo) which included Nikolai Aseev, David Burlyuk and and Sergei Tret'yakov. Chuzhak edited the group's journal of the same name (June–December 1920, Vladivostok; April 1921, Chita – in all seven issues). Chuzhak's theory of art was expressed most fully in *Toward the Dialectic of Art* (*K dialektike iskusstva*, Chita, 1921). For Chuzhak, art was conditioned by dialectical materialism and therefore was ceaselessly evolving and creating new ideological or material values. This concept enabled him to support consecutively Symbolism, Futurism and production art. In 1922 Chuzhak moved to Moscow where he joined the editorial board of *LEF* in 1923. However, he split from *LEF* the same year because he considered *LEF*'s artistic practice greatly diverged from its theory. He castigated Brik's novel *Not a Fellow-Traveller* (*Ne popuchitsa*, 1923) for contradicting communist perspectives (unpublished review, TsGALI, fond 340, op. 1, ed. khr. 11), and he was equally critical of Mayakovskii's *About This* (*Pro eto*, 1923). From 1925 onwards he became an enthusiastic proponent of the 'literature of fact' (*reportage*), contributing to *Novyi LEF* (1927-8) and in 1929 editing a collection of articles entitled the *Literature of Fact: The First Collection of Materials by the Workers of LEF* (*Literatura fakta: pervyi sbornik materialov rabotnikov LEF*). From 1926 until 1932 he edited the journal published by the Russian Society of Former Political Prisoners.

DENISOVSKII, Nikolai Fedorovich
(1901–)

Born in Moscow, Nikolai was the son of the graphic artist Fedor Platonovich Denisovskii. From 1911 until 1917 he attended the Stroganov School of Applied Art in Moscow and later the State Free Art Studios where he studied under the artist Georgii Yakulov. In 1918 Denisovskii participated in the decorations of the city of Moscow for the revolutionary festivals and from 1919 until 1920 he worked on the production of posters for the windows of the Russian Telegraphic Agency (Okno ROSTA). Denisovskii was a founding member of OBMOKhU and he participated in all the group's exhibitions (1919, 1920, 1921, 1923). He was also one of the organisers of OST (1925-32). In the mid and late 1920s he worked as an illustrator on such journals as *Crocodile* (*Krokodil*) and executed paintings and watercolours on the theme of industrial construction.

EKSTER (née GRIGOROVICH), Aleksandra Aleksandrovna (1882-1949)

Born at Belostok, near Kiev, Ekster graduated from the Kiev Art School in 1906. In 1908 she went to Paris where she studied at the Académie de la Grande Chaumière under Carlo Delvall. The following year Ekster set up a studio in Paris and became acquainted with Picasso, Braque, Apollinaire and with the Italian Futurist Marinetti. From 1909 until 1914 Ekster travelled extensively between Paris and Russia, playing a very important role in the dissemination of Cubist and Futurist ideas in Russia. She also visited Italy. Her own work at this time displayed the influence of these new ideas. Her assimilation of Cubism was accompanied by a decorative interest in colour and rhythm as is epitomised by *Still Life* (*Natyurmort*, 1913-15) or *Wine* (*Vino*, 1914). During this period she participated in many important avant-garde exhibitions in both Russia and France, including Contemporary Trends (Sovremennye techeniya, St Petersburg, May 1908), Burlyuk's Link exhibition (Zveno, Kiev, autumn 1908), the sculptor Izdebskii's Salons (No. 1, Odessa and Kiev, December 1909-March 1910; and No. 2, St Petersburg and Riga, May-July 1910), Salon des Indépendants (Paris, March-May 1912 and March-April 1914), La Section d'Or (Paris, October 1912), Union of Youth (St Petersburg and Riga, 1910; and at St Petersburg, winter 1913-14), and Espozione Libera Futurista Internazionale (Rome, April-May 1914). From 1914 she remained in Russia where she participated in major avant-garde exhibitions, including Tramway V (Petrograd, March 1915) and The Store (Moscow, spring 1916). Her painting moved towards abstraction as in *Venice* (*Venetsiya*, 1916). In 1916 she began working for Tairov's Kamernyi Theatre in Moscow. Her experiments in theatrical design included treating the costumes as fluid plastic entities, reducing the set to movable three-dimensional geometric forms (Annenskii's *Famira Kifared*, 1916), organising the stage dynamically using complex arrangements of brightly coloured curtains to intensify the action (Wilde's *Salomé*, 1917) and using bridges to create multi-levels (Shakespeare's *Romeo and Juliet*, 1920-1). At Odessa in 1917-18 Ekster worked in a children's school where she taught four to eight year olds the abstract study of form and rhythm. From 1918 until 1921 she taught at her own studio in Kiev where among her students were Isaak Rabinovich and Pavel Tchelitchew. Ekster's studio also apparently participated in the painting of agit-ships with abstract designs and the decoration of Kiev for May Day 1918 and for the first anniversary of the Revolution. In 1921 Ekster exhibited with Vesnin, Popova, Rodchenko and Stepanova at $5 \times 5 = 25$ in Moscow. She showed abstract works entitled *Planar and Colour Structures* (*Ploskostno-tsvetovye postroeniya*, 1921), concerned with 'colour construction based on the laws of colour' (A. Ekster, $5 \times 5 = 25$. *Katalog vystavki*, Moscow, 1921, Nos. 21-5). In 1921-2 Ekster taught at the Moscow VKhUTEMAS. However, she was not committed to Constructivism and her approach remained essentially decorative. This was epitomised by her work in fashion design which consisted of fairly frivolous individual, essentially *haute couture* items as well as more austere prototypes for mass-produced clothing and for production clothing (*prozodezhda*). In 1923 she was responsible (together with Nivinskii) for all the painterly decorations on pavilions at the All Russian Agricultural Exhibition in Moscow (Vserossiiskaya sel'skokhozyainstvennaya vystavka). Her work included decorating the International pavilion and designing (with Gladkov) the *Izvestiya* pavilion. In 1923 she began work on the spatially exciting sets and costumes for the Martian scenes in the film *Aelita*, based on Aleksei Tolstoi's novel, and produced by Protazanov. In 1924 she emigrated, settled in Paris, and from 1925 taught with Léger and in her own studio. She also continued to work in the area of ballet and theatre design.

FAVORSKII, Vladimir Andreevich (1886-1964)

Having received his initial artistic training from K. Yuon and I. Dudin, Favorskii studied in Munich in 1906-7. From 1907 to 1912 he attended Moscow University where he studied art history. He began to exhibit his work in 1911. From 1918 he taught at the Second State Free Art Studios in Moscow. In 1921 he became a professor at the VKhU-TEMAS, teaching in the Graphics faculty, and from 1923 until 1925 he was *rektor* of the VKhUTEMAS. In 1929 Favorskii left the VKhU-TEIN and in 1930 became a professor at the Moscow Graphics Institute (Poligraficheskii institut). Although tolerant of avant-garde experimentation, Favorskii's own work was always firmly representational and his favourite medium was the woodcut. With Bruni and Shterenberg he belonged to the Four Arts group (Chetyre iskusstva).

GABO (PEVZNER, Naum (Neemiya) Borisovich), Naum (1890-1978)

Born in Bryansk, Gabo received a scientific education. He graduated in 1910-11 from Kursk gymnazium and entered the medical faculty of the University of Munich. In

9.1 Naum Gabo in his studio in Berlin in the mid-1920s.

1911–12 he attended Wölfflin's art historical lectures and in 1912 went on a walking tour through Italy visiting art collections at Venice, Milan and Florence. In 1913–14 he visited his brother Antoine Pevsner in Paris and had the opportunity to study Cubist paintings. In 1914 he went with his brother Aleksei to Denmark and then to Norway where he made his first constructions in 1915. *Constructed Head No. 2* of 1916 epitomises his approach at this time. Made from pieces of metal welded together, the internal structure of the form was revealed, incorporating space within itself. In 1917 he returned to Russia and settled in Moscow, where he worked in his brother Antoine's studio at the State Free Art Studios and participated in the frequently violent artistic debates of the period. In August 1920 he summed up his ideas in *The Realistic Manifesto* (*Realisticheskii manifest*) co-signed by his brother Antoine and published to accompany the exhibition of their works held in the open air on Tverskoi Boulevard, Moscow. At this exhibition Gabo showed his three-dimensional constructions which he called *postroeniya*. Gabo was unable to accept the utilitarian imperative of the Russian Constructivists, and in 1922 he left Russia for Berlin.

GAN, Aleksei Mikhailovich
(1889–*c.* 1940)

Little is known of Gan's life and it has proved difficult to establish where he received his artistic training if any.

During the 1910s he seems to have been associated with various Futurist groups and to have worked in the theatre. His connections with the artistic avant-garde seem to have been established by 1917–18 when, with Tatlin and Rodchenko, he helped to prevent pillaging in Moscow (A. Rodtchenko, 'Vladimir Tatlin', *Opus International*, No. 4, 1967, p. 17). Certainly by 1918 Gan was associated with Malevich closely enough to be a signatory, together with Malevich and Morgunov, of a manifesto attacking the conservative elements within the Artists' Union. The manifesto was entitled 'The Problems of Art and the Role of its Suppressors' ('Zadachi iskusstva i rol' dushitelei iskusstva', *Anarkhiya*, No. 25, 23 March 1918; printed in English translation in K. S. Malevich, *Essays on Art, 1915–1933*, ed. T. Andersen, London, 1969, Vol. 1, pp. 49–50). It has been suggested that Gan was experimenting with photomontage as early as 1918. From 1918 until 1920 he was attached to the theatrical department (TEO – Teatral'nyi otdel, Nar-

243

9.2. Aleksei Gan in the early 1920s.

kompros) where he was in charge of revolutionary festivals and mass spectacles. Gan's play *We* (*My*) for which Rodchenko designed costumes (see Karginov, *Rodchenko*, fig. 151, p. 180) was never produced. Gan was a member of the Moscow INKhUK and a founder member, together with Rodchenko and Stepanova, of the First Working Group of Constructivists. As an elaboration of the group's ideas he published his treatise *Constructivism* (*Konstruktivizm*, Tver', 1922), which had a striking typographical layout to reinforce its iconoclastic message. In 1922-3 he published and edited the journal *Kino-Fot* which dealt with the cinema and photography, both fields in which Gan was very interested. By 1924 Gan, always an extremist and true to his slogan 'we declare uncompromising war on art', had split with Rodchenko and Stepanova ('the Constructivists of *LEF*') as well as with other Constructivists including the Stenberg brothers ('the Constructivists of the Kamernyi Theatre'). However, he continued to lead the First Working Group of Constructivists, which then included Ol'ga and Galina Chichagova, L. Sanina, Grigorii Miller, N. Smirnov, A. Mirolyubova and with which Shestakov seems also to have been associated. The group and Gan worked in the fields of furniture, kiosk, clothing, book and poster design, exhibiting some of their projects at the First Discussional Exhibition (Pervaya diskussionnaya vystavka ob'edinenii aktivnogo revolyutionnogo iskusstva, Moscow, 1924). Gan designed kiosks for the distribution of books in both urban and rural areas. He also wrote extensively on artistic, cinematic and theatrical developments. In 1925 he attended the First Meeting of Workers on *LEF* (Pervoe soveshchanie rabotnikov LEFa), held in Moscow, 16 and 17 January 1925. Gan belonged to the group of Constructivist architects, OSA, and from 1926 until 1930 he worked as artistic editor, designing the posters, covers and typographical layouts for the group's journal *Contemporary Architecture* (*Sovremennaya arkhitektura – SA*). In 1927 Gan was the president of the committee that organised OSA's First Exhibition of Contemoprary Architecture, held in Moscow. In 1928 he joined the October Group (Oktyabr').

GINZBURG, Moisei Yakovlevich
(1892-1946)

Born in Minsk, the son of an architect, Ginzburg was the theoretician of architectural Constructivism. He received his grounding in classical architecture in Italy where he graduated from the architectural faculty of the Milan Academy of Art in 1914. Untouched by Futurism he returned to Russia where he attended in 1914-17 the Riga Polytechnical Institute (then evacuated in Mos-cow) with its emphasis on engineering. From 1917 until 1921 he worked in the Crimea. In 1922 he became a professor at the Moscow Institute of Civil Engineering (Moskovskii institut grazhdanskikh inzhenerov) where he taught a course on Renaissance architecture. In 1922 Ginzburg also started to teach a course on architectural composition in the Architectural faculty of the Moscow VKhUTEMAS. His ideas relating to that course were embodied in his book *Rhythm in Architecture* (*Ritm v arkhitekture*, Moscow, 1923). Ginzburg's entry for the Palace of Labour Competition in 1923 was spatially and structurally inarticulate and he recognised the superiority of the Vesnin brothers' design as 'the first realisation of the method of Constructivism'. Ginzburg laid the theoretical foundations of architectural Constructivism in his book *Style and the Epoch* (*Stil'* i *epokha*, Moscow, 1924) in which he argued the correctness of a constructive architecture to answer the social, historical and technological conditions of the new Soviet State. He illustrated over forty structures which pointed towards such a new formal language for architecture. In 1925 around him was formed the group of Constructivist architects, OSA. Ginzburg edited the group's journal *Contemporary Architecture* (*Sovremennaya arkhitektura – SA*, 1926-30). In this magazine many of the theoretical positions and practical procedures for architectural Constructivism were formulated and elaborated: Ginzburg presented his 'functional method' and the group published its experiments with apartment types some of which were later used by Ginzburg and Milinis in their living quarters for the employees of the Commissariat of Finance (Narkomfin Building, Moscow, 1928-30). *SA* kept Russian designers informed of technological and design developments in the West and was responsible for organising the large Exhibition of Contemporary Architecture in 1927 in Moscow, which covered recent architectural developments, both in Russia and in the West.

IOGANSON, Karl Val'demarovich
(*c.* 1890—1924)

Little is known of Karl Ioganson, who is often confused with Boris Ioganson, a Socialist Realist. According to Khan-Magomedov, Karl Ioganson graduated from the Riga Art School (*Pionere der sowjetischen architektur*). He is named by Oginskaya as one of the artists in the Latvian Rifles Regiment working alongside Klutsis in Moscow in 1918-19 (Oginskaya, *Klutsis*, p. 10). This suggests that Ioganson came from Latvia, probably of Swedish parentage. Like Klutsis he may have worked at the State Free Art Studios and then at the VKhUTEMAS in Moscow and thus became associated with the other artists of the OBMOKhU. Ioganson definitely became a member of the Moscow INKhUK in 1920 and he joined the First Working Group of Constructivists when it was set up. At INKhUK on 9 March 1922 he delivered a paper entitled 'From Construction toward Technology and Invention' ('Ot konstruktisii k tekhnike i izobreteniyu') in which he distinguished between constructions of a primarily aesthetic character such as Tatlin's and those constructions which were genuinely useful technological constructions which could be fruitful for the future. Although he was evidently not a member of the OBMOKhU, Ioganson did participate in their third exhibition which opened in Moscow on 22 May 1921. The works he exhibited there seem to have been made from strips of wood and metal and were clearly based on Euclidean geometry. These may have been similar to those which Ioganson contributed to the 1922 Erste Russische Kunstausstellung in Berlin where he exhibited four sculptures (Nos. 551-4), one entitled *Relief*, and the other three *Bautechnische Konstruktion*. In 1924 he was working at a rolling stock mill, the 'Prochatnik'.

KANDINSKII, Vasilii Vasil'evich (1866-1944)

Born in Moscow, Kandinskii grew up in Odessa where his family settled in 1871. From 1886 until 1892 he studied law and political economy at Moscow University where in 1893 he was appointed a lecturer in the law faculty. Despite a successful academic career Kandinskii decided to become an artist and went to Munich in 1897 where he studied with Anton Azbé and Franz von Stuck. In Munich Kandinskii organised the Phalanx group in 1901 and later, in 1909, became the chairman of the New Artists' Association (Neue Künstlervereinigung München). In 1911 Kandinskii completed his treatise *Concerning the Spiritual in Art* (*Über das Geistige in der Kunst*), published in January 1912 in Munich. The Russian text 'O dukhovnom v iskusstve' was read by Dr Nikolai Kul'bin at the All Russian Congress of Artists in St Petersburg on 29 and 31 December 1911, and was later published in the transcripts of the Congress (*Trudy Vserossiiskogo s'ezda khudozhnikov*, Petrograd, 1914, vol. 1, pp. 47-76). At the same time Kandinskii was instrumental in founding the Blue Rider group (Blaue Reiter) which published a magazine in 1912 and organised exhibitions. The group's first exhibition included works by the Russian artists David and Vladimir Burlyuk and their second included works by Larionov, Goncharova and Malevich. Although resident in Germany, Kandinskii did begin to exhibit in Russia from 1904 onwards with various associations including the Moscow Association of Artists (Moskovskoe tovarishchestvo khu-

dozhnikov, February 1904, March 1905, 1907) and the Union of Russian Artists (Soyuz russkikh khudozhnikov, winter 1908-9). Kandinskii participated in the Izdebskii Salons (Salon 'Izdebskii', Odessa and Kiev, winter and spring 1909-10; St Petersburg and Riga, summer 1910). At the 'Salon 2' (Kiev, December 1910) Kandinskii exhibited over fifty works including Improvisations and Compositions which were apparently being shown for the first time in Russia. From 1910 Kandinskii also exhibited with the Knave of Diamonds (Moscow, winter 1910-11, January 1912). In 1914 Kandinskii returned to Russia where he joined IZO in 1918 and became a member of IZO's International Office (Mezhdunarodnoe byuro). Kandinskii was very active in various areas of pedagogical and artistic life: he taught at the State Free Art Studios from 1918; he was active in setting up the Museum of Artistic Culture (Muzei khudozhestvennoi kul'tury), of which he became the director, and he was among the founders of INKhUK in May 1920. After leaving INKhUK in early 1921 Kandinskii was appointed to the founding committee of RAKhN of which he became one of the first vice-presidents. Kandinskii was also head of the Academy's physical and psychological section, for which he devised the programme. In 1921 Kandinskii left for Germany where he joined the staff of the Bauhaus, teaching there until 1933 when he left Germany and settled in France.

KHLEBNIKOV, Velimir (Viktor) Vladimirovich (1885-1922)

Khlebnikov was a Futurist poet whose ideas and theories exerted an immense influence on the avant-garde artists, especially on Miturich and Tatlin. Khlebnikov's father was a guardian of the Kalmyk people, a teacher and ornithologist. From 1903 until 1908 Khlebnikov attended Kazan' University where he studied mathematics and natural sciences. In 1906 he was arrested for belonging to a revolutionary group. In 1908 he entered St Petersburg University where in 1909 he transferred to the Faculty of Eastern Languages. He met Burlyuk and Kamenskii, and became a member of the Futurist group *Hylaea*, which was connected with Matyushin and Guro in St Petersburg. This was followed by a period of intense literary activity during which he contributed poems to various Futurist publications including *A Trap for Judges* (*Sadok sudei*, St Petersburg, 1910). At this time he developed in his poetry the concept of the transrational, *zaum'*, according to which the component elements of words, consonants and sounds, expressed ideas which formed a type of universally comprehensible proto-language which it was the task of the poet to uncover. He also commenced work on his theory of numbers which explained the development of history in terms of mathematics. In 1916 he organised the Government of Time (*Gosudarstvo vremeni*), which consisted of 317 presidents ruling the Earth. In 1916 he served briefly in the Ninety-third Reserve Regiment. During 1917 he was involved in the revolutionary upheavals in Moscow and Petrograd. He was constantly without money, starving and in poor health. In 1921 he visited Persia with the Red Army and in 1921 returned to Moscow. In 1922 he went with Miturich to Santalovo where he died.

KLUTSIS (KLUCIS), Gustav Gustavovich (1895–1944)

Klutsis was a Latvian artist who was born near Ruiena and whose father was a forestry worker. In 1912 he began his artistic training at the Art School in Riga under Purvit, Rozental and Tilberg. From 1915 until 1917 he attended the school run by the Society for the Encouragement of the Arts in Petrograd. While in Petrograd he also painted scenery for the Okhta Workers' Club. According to Rakitin, during 1905 Klutsis, although only ten years old, participated in the Revolution. His eldest brother was arrested and exiled. In 1917 Klutsis joined the notoriously ruthless Ninth Regiment of Latvian Rifles, participating in the defence of Smol'ny and travelling with the government to Moscow. There he sketched Lenin and his fellow soldiers and designed posters and decorations for May Day 1918. He was active in the art studio organised by Vol'demar Andersen and showed his work at the Regiment's first exhibition. He described his portraits of Lenin as composed of 'cubistic volumes, sharp angles and intersecting planes' (Klutsis, 'Avtobiografiya', MS, private archive, Moscow). During 1918 Klutsis studied in Moscow with Il'ya Mashkov. In August 1918 he entered the Second State Free Art Studios in Moscow, where he studied initially with Korovin, then with Malevich and finally, after Malevich left for Vitebsk (summer 1919), with Pevsner who took over Malevich's studio. In 1920 Klutsis exhibited his work with Pevsner and Gabo on Tverskoi Boulevard in Moscow. He visited Malevich in Vitebsk and exhibited with Malevich's Suprematist UNOVIS group both in Vitebsk (1920) and in Moscow (1921). In 1920 Klutsis joined the Communist Party and in 1921 he graduated from the VKhUTEMAS. Prior to his graduation Klutsis seems to have opened an independent studio with Sen'kin within VKhUTEMAS which exemplified the UNOVIS approach (see *Put' Unovisa*, No. 1, January 1921). Klutsis dated his move from abstract into agitational and analytical art to 1920–1. His work had progressed from the Cubist-inspired portraits of Lenin via the Suprematism of *The Dynamic City* (*Dinamicheskii*

gorod, *c*.1919) to a more Constructivist attitude to form and material. According to his wife, the artist Kulagina, while still at the VKhUTEMAS as a student (i.e. 1920–1), Klutsis made models of constructions from wood and paper and studied materials intensively. Photographs of such work indicate that Klutsis combined the pure Euclidian geometry of Suprematism with the materiality, space and volume of working with real materials in three dimensions. In 1922 Klutsis applied these experiments to utilitarian ends when he designed a series of agitational stands and radio-orators to celebrate the fifth anniversary of the Revolution and the Fourth Congress of the Comintern. In 1923 within the VKhUTEMAS Klutsis and Sen'kin proposed the organisation of the Workshop of the Revolution (Masterskaya revolyutsii) to train artists, agitators and Productivists to fulfil contemporary requirements. Klutsis was also involved with the journal *LEF* (1923–5). From 1924 until 1930 he taught colour in the Wood and Metalwork faculty (Dermetfak) of the VKhUTEMAS. In 1925 Klutsis was active in organising the Russian contribution to the Exposition International des Arts Décoratifs et Industriels Modernes in Paris. During the 1920s he became increasingly involved in the theory and practice of photomontage, using it extensively in his agitational posters and decorations for the revolutionary festivals. In 1928 he was a founder member of the group October (Oktyabr').

KLYUN (KLYUNKOV), Ivan Vasil'evich (1873–1943)

Born at Bol'shie Gorki (now in the Vladimir District), Klyun began his artistic studies in Kiev. In the 1890s he attended the art school run by the Society for the Encouragement of the Arts in Warsaw. Then he moved to Moscow where he studied in the private studios of Rerberg, Fisher and Il'ya Mashkov. In 1910 he made contact with the Union of Youth and contributed to their last exhibition in St Petersburg, in winter 1913–14. At this time he began also to work in three dimensions, producing Cubo-Futurist inspired sculptures and reliefs, the most famous example of which is *Rapidly Passing Landscape* (*Probegayushchii peizazh*) exhibited in 1915. Friendly with Malevich and Matyushin, in 1915 he supported Suprematism. Subsequently he joined Malevich's *Supremus* group and collaborated on the magazine. He also illustrated and contributed an essay to Malevich and Kruchenykh's *Secret Vices of the Academicians* (*Tainye poroki akademikov*, Moscow, 1915). He participated in various exhibitions including Tramway V (Petrograd, March 1915), 0.10 (Petrograd, January 1916), The Store (Moscow,

March 1916), and the Knave of Diamonds (Moscow, November 1916 o.s.). In 1918 he participated in the decorations of Moscow for the first anniversary of the October Revolution. Between 1918 and 1921 he directed the Central Exhibitions Bureau of the government's Department of Fine Art (Tsentral'noe vystavochoe byuro, IZO Narkompros). During the same period he taught at the State Free Art Studios and then at the Moscow VKhUTEMAS. Until 1921 he was also a member of INKhUK. In 1924 he became a member of the Four Arts group (Chetyre iskusstva) which was indicative of his move in the mid-1920s away from Suprematism towards a representational and figurative painterly style, the dominant feature of which was a resemblance to the purism of Ozenfant and Le Corbusier.

KRINSKII, Vladimir Fedorovich (1890–1971)

Born in Ryazan', Krinskii trained as an architect at the St Petersburg Academy of Arts (Akademiya khudozhestv), which he attended from 1910 to 1917 originally to become a painter. In 1919 he joined the architectural section of Narkompros. From 1919 until 1920 he was a member of Zhivskul'ptarkh, where he began to investigate the aesthetic bases for a new architecture. Towards the end of 1920 he joined the Moscow INKhUK, participated in the discussions of construction and composition within the Group of Objective Analysis and the Architects' Working Group. Between 1920 and 1923 Krinskii executed a whole series of experiments relating to the problems of colour and form, colour and spatial composition, and colour and graphic composition. He designed various projects, including a skyscraper for the Lubyanka Square (now Dzerzhinskii Square). He also participated in competitions for the Soviet pavilion at the 1925 Paris exhibition and the Lenin Mausoleum. In 1923 Krinskii was a founding member of the rationalist ASNOVA, which sought to establish 'the rational bases of quality in architecture' through the objective study of architectural form. From the end of 1920 he taught in the VKhUTEMAS in Moscow, where with Ladovskii and Dokuchaev he taught the discipline of spatial construction, which became the space and volume *kontsentr* in 1923. The results of his teaching experience were enshrined in the book *Elements of Architectural and Spatial Composition* (*Elementy arkhitekturno-prostranstvennoi kompozitsii*, Moscow, 1934), written together with I. Lamtsov and M. Turkus. During the 1930s his architecture became more classical but he continued his pedagogical activity at the Moscow Architectural Institute (Moskovskii arkhitekturnyi institut - MAI).

KUSHNER, Boris Anisimovich (1888–1937)

Born in Minsk, Kushner made his entrance into literature with a collection of poems entitled *Semaphores* (*Semafory*) published in 1914. In Petrograd he became associated with the Futurists and a frequent contributor to the IZO journal, *Art of the Commune* (*Iskusstvo kommuny*, 1918–19). In 1919 he was the leading organiser of the 'Communist-Futurists' group (kommunisty-futuristy – Komfut) which sought to fuse communism with Futurism because 'all forms of everyday life, morals, philosophy and art must be recreated on communist principles' (*Iskusstvo kommuny*, No. 8, 1919, p. 3). He lectured extensively in various organisations belonging to the Proletkul't. From 1921 he was also an active member of the Moscow INKhUK where he delivered, in 1922, a series of four papers concerning the nature of production culture and the role of the artist in the production process. In 1921 he joined a commission under the jurisdiction of the Supreme Council for the National Economy (VSNKh) to investigate the scientific organisation of industry. Such concerns obviously lay at the base of his wider interest in the total organisation of society according to Taylorist principles, and at one point in 1922 he suggested that in the future communist society all should eat, work, sleep and listen to music at the same time (*Gorn*, No. 2–7, 1922, p. 112). Kushner lectured at the Moscow VKhUTEMAS where he taught a course on the evolution of man-made objects, which was called 'The Dialectics of Material Culture and Art' (Dialektika material'noi kul'tury i iskusstva). He became a member of the editorial board of *LEF* (1923–5) and *Novyi LEF* (1927–8) and contributed frequently to both journals. Kushner also wrote literary sketches of Western Europe, America and the Caucasus. Some time in the 1930s he was arrested and seems to have died in a prison camp.

LADOVSKII, Nikolai Aleksandrovich (1881–1941)

The acknowledged leader and theoretician of Soviet Rationalist architecture, Ladovskii was born in Moscow and from 1914 to 1917 he trained as an architect at the Moscow School of Painting, Sculpture and Architecture. From 1919 until 1920 he belonged to Zhivskul'ptarkh, where his ideas concerning the importance of spatial composition in architecture began to crystallise. During this time he executed a series of architectural projects investigating dynamic composition. In 1920 Ladovskii joined the Moscow INKhUK where he belonged to the Group of Objective Analysis and to the Architects' Working Group, which was established in May 1921 and which later formed the nucleus of AS-

247

NOVA, created in 1923. Ladovskii, a founder of ASNOVA and leader, gave primacy to space and spatial composition in the form-making process, relegating construction to a secondary role. He sought to establish the rational bases of architectural form and in this connection set up a laboratory to study the psychological and physiological perception of three-dimensional form. This was located in the Moscow VKhUTEMAS where from 1920 he taught the spatial discipline (later the space and volume *kontsentr*) on the Basic Course. Ladovskii also organised the Society of Urbanist Architects (Ob'edinenie arkhitektorov urbanistov - ARU) in 1928, and until the mid-1930s was active in formulating new concepts for urban planning, the reconstruction of Moscow and the 'Green Town' (*zelenyi gorod*).

LAVINSKII, Anton Mikhailovich (1893-1968)

9.4. Anton Lavinskii in the 1920s.

Lavinskii was born in Sochi. His father was a customs official and his mother a cook. He trained as an architect at the Baku Technical College from which he graduated in 1913. He practised briefly in the Caucasus before going to St Petersburg to attend the Academy of Arts (Akademiya khudozhestv) where he studied sculpture under Shervud. In 1915 he was mobilised. In 1917 he returned to Sochi where he organised a sculpture studio and worked on a local political committee. In 1918 he returned to Petrograd to study with Shervud and then with the progressive Matveev. There Lavinskii participated in Lenin's Plan for Monumental Propaganda, with a monument of Karl Marx erected in Krasnoe Selo and a statue of Saltykov-Shchedrin. In 1919 he collaborated with Sinaiskii on a monument to the October Revolution. Lavinskii's work at this time was still firmly in the figurative tradition. In spring 1919 he began to teach sculpture at the Saratov State Free Art Studios. In connection with his pedagogical interests he attended the conference of art students in Moscow in summer 1920. In Moscow he became acquainted with members of INKhUK. He joined INKhUK and participated in the debates of the General Working Group of Objective Analysis. At INKhUK on 26 January 1922 Lavinskii delivered a paper entitled 'Engineerism' ('Inzhenerizm') in which he put forward general theoretical principles concerning the engineering quality of form-making in an advanced industrial society and discussed the practical application of these principles in his project for the City of the Future. Lavinskii's City on Springs was circular and organised into sectors with vertical zoning. In 1920 Lavinskii joined the VKhUTEMAS where he ran the general studio in the Sculpture faculty with Korolev and taught volumetric construction (later the

volume and space *kontsentr*) on the Basic Course. From 1923 until 1926 Lavinskii worked in the Woodwork faculty (Derfak) where he taught furniture design (*proektirovanie mebeli*), initially called furniture composition (*kompozitsiya mebeli*). In 1921 for the second production of Mayakovskii's play *Misteriya-buff* Lavinskii designed the set (with Kiselov and Khrakovskii) as a multi-levelled massing of solid structures with industrial connotations. His kiosk for the state publishing house Gosizdat at the 1923 All Russian Agricultural Exhibition in Moscow (Vserossiiskaya sel'skokhozaistvennaya vystavka) presented a novel solution to book display, and it was selected by Ginzburg for illustration in *Style and the Epoch* (*Stil' i epokha*, 1924) as one of those structures which were significant for Constructivist architecture because they displayed a feeling for new forms. Between 1924 and 1925 Lavinskii designed a whole series of kiosks for Gosizdat and other state trading companies such as Mossel'prom. In 1925 the students of Derfak's designs for a workers' club and a rural (hut) reading room (*izba-chital'nya*) were exhibited in Paris. In the mid-1920s Lavinskii designed rural reading rooms, a radio tribune and also worked on designs for lamps and display stands. He also designed posters and book covers. In 1927 he was involved in the decorations for the tenth anniversary of October in Moscow, and also worked on an educational film entitled *The Radio*. In 1928 he collaborated with Lissitsky on the design of the Soviet section at the Pressa exhibition in Cologne. In the 1930s Lavinskii returned to sculpture and continued to work primarily in this medium until his death.

LISSITZKY (LISITSKII, Lazar' Markovich), El (1890-1941)

Lissitzky was born at Pochinok near Smolensk. His family was middle class and Jewish. From 1903 he studied art with Pen who also taught Chagall. In 1909 after an unsuccessful attempt to enter the St Petersburg Academy Lissitzky went to Germany where he studied architecture at the Technische Hochschule in Darmstadt from 1909 until 1914. In 1912 he seems to have returned briefly to Russia and worked in an architectural office in St Petersburg. During 1912 and 1913 he visited Paris, where he met Zadkine, and toured Italy, visiting Venice, Pisa and Ravenna, of which his sketches remain. In 1914 he returned to Russia where he worked briefly in Zadkine's studio in Vitebsk. Declared unfit for military service, Lissitzky from *c.* 1915 to 1917 attended the Riga Polytechnical Institute, which had been evacuated to Moscow. He also worked with the architect Velikovskii. In December 1917 he exhibited in Moscow with the World of

Art group (Mir iskusstva). After the Revolution Lissitzky was actively involved in Jewish cultural activities including the establishment of the Yiddish publishing house Kultur Lige in 1919, the Society for the Encouragement of Jewish Art and the Exhibition of Paintings and Sculpture by Jewish Artists (Vystavka kartin i skul'ptury khudozhnikov evreev, Moscow, summer 1918). He also illustrated books with Jewish themes including *An Unholy Story* by Broderson (*Sichas Chulin*, Moscow, 1917) and the *Great Kid* (*Chad Gadyo*, 1917 and 1919). In 1918 Lissitzky joined IZO Narkompros. In May 1919 he was invited by Chagall to teach architecture and graphics at the Vitebsk Art School. After Malevich's arrival, in the summer of 1919, Lissitzky came under his influence, adopted Suprematism and became a member of Malevich's UNOVIS group. Inspired by Malevich and Suprematism, in 1919–20 Lissitzky developed his concept of the PROUN, which was 'a half-way station between architecture and painting', the name of which may have been derived from 'Project for the affirmation of the New' (*Proekt utverzhdeniya novogo*) or 'For the School of the New Art' (*Pro uchilishche novogo iskusstva*). While in Vitebsk Lissitzky also designed decorations for the revolutionary festivals and agitational posters such as his Suprematist *Beat the Whites with the Red Wedge* (*Klinom*

krasnym bei belykh, 1919). In 1920 Lissitzky became a member of the Moscow INKhUK, and on 23 September 1921 he delivered to the members of INKhUK a paper explaining his new concept of the PROUN. He was appointed to the teaching staff of the Moscow VKhUTEMAS in 1921 and seems to have worked there before travelling abroad. In 1922, in co-operation with the writer Il'ya Erenburg, Lissitzky published the journal *Object* (*Veshch'/Gegendstand/Objet*) in Berlin. This embraced a compromise between traditional concepts of the work of art and the concept of production art advocated by Constructivism, since the position of *Object* extended the concept of art rather than attacking it. During the 1920s Lissitzky travelled extensively between Russia and Europe acting as a valuable link between his colleagues working in Russia and avant-garde architects and artists in the West. In 1922 he designed the catalogue cover and participated in the Erste Russische Kunstausstellung in Berlin. He also was a member of ASNOVA. Abroad he established firm contacts with the avant-garde: with Dada artists at the Congress in Düsseldorf, with De Stijl in Holland, with the Bauhaus in Weimar. He participated both in exhibitions, designing a PROUN room for the Grosse Berliner Kunstausstellung in 1923, and in avant-garde journals, designing covers for *Broom* (1922),

9.5. El Lissitzky (right) in Germany with Fritz Stammberger, who was a worker on Rote Fahne during the 1920s.

249

publishing articles on PROUNS (*De Stijl*, No. 6, 1922) and collaborating with Mies van der Rohe on the magazine *G*. In 1923 he designed the layouts for Mayakovskii's book of poetry *For the Voice* (*Dlya golosa*, Berlin, 1923), and published portfolios of his PROUN lithographs and of his lithographed figures for *Victory over the Sun* (*Sieg über die Sonne*, Hanover, 1923). In Switzerland to recover from tuberculosis in 1924, Lissitzky worked on No. 8/9 of Schwitters' magazine *Merz*, edited *Die Kunstismen* with Hans Arp, did typographical work for the Pelican Ink Company, and co-operated with Mart Stam, et al., on the journal *ABC. Beiträge zum Bauen*. From 1925 onwards Lissitzky lived primarily in Russia although he continued to visit the West intermittently. From 1925 until 1930 he taught the design of architectural interiors (*oformlenie arkhitekturnykh inter'erov*) and furniture design (*proektiro-vanie mebeli*) in the Wood and Metalwork faculty (Dermetfak) of the Moscow VKhU-TEMAS. Lissitzky's theoretical and practical work in the area during the late 1920s allied him clearly to Constructivism. In 1925 he completed his utopian and impractical *Wolkenbügel* (skyscraper) design and in 1926 he edited with Ladovskii the first and only issue of the journal *ASNOVA News* (*Izves-tiya* ASNOVA). Far more practical and Constructivist were his projects for the interiors of communal housing blocks and his design for an interior of one of the flats in Ginzburg and Milinis' House for the Employees of the Commissariat of Finance (Narkomfin), on Novinskii Boulevard, Moscow (1928–30). In 1929 Lissitzky worked on a model for Meier-khol'd's proposed production of Sergei Tret'yakov's *I want a Child* (*Ya khochu re-benka*). In the second half of the 1920s Lissitzky became increasingly involved in exhibition design: projecting the Raum der Abstrakten for the Internationale Kunstaus-stellung (Dresden, 1926); organising the Soviet contribution to the Pressa exhibition (Cologne, 1928); designing the Russian Typographical Exhibition (Vsesoyuznaya poli-graficheskaya vystavka, Moscow, 1927), designing the Soviet sections at Film und Foto (Stuttgart, 1929), Internationale Hygiene-Ausstellung (Dresden, 1930), and Internationale Pelz-Ausstellung (Leipzig, 1930). From the early 1930s Lissitzky had been experimenting with collage, photography, photograms and photomontage. In the later 1930s he worked extensively with photography and photomontage, designing the typographical and photographic layouts for magazines such as *USSR in Construction* (*SSSR na stroike*) for whom he worked from 1932 onwards. In 1928 Lissitzky joined the group October (Oktyabr'), and in 1930 published his survey of Soviet architecture, *Russia: The Reconstruction of Architecture in the Soviet Union* (*Russland. Die Rekonstruktion der Architektur in der Sowjetunion*, Vienna, 1930). During the 1930s Lissitzky continued to work in the fields of graphic and exhibition design, although his deteriorating health imposed certain limitations on his activities. He was appointed artist-architect to the Gor'kii Park of Culture and Rest in Moscow and to the Agricultural Exhibition of 1934. Lissitzky's last works were anti-fascist posters such as *Provide more Tanks* (*Davaite pobol'she tankov*, 1941).

LUNACHARSKII, Anatolii Vasil'evich (1875-1933)

Born in Poltava in the family of a state councillor, Lunacharskii was educated at the gymnazium in Kiev and then at Zurich University. In 1899 he was arrested as a member of the Moscow Social Democratic Circle. He was exiled to Kaluga, Vologda and Totma. In exile he met Bogdanov. In 1904 he met Lenin in Paris. Both Lunacharskii and Bogdanov at this point joined the Bolsheviks. At the request of Lenin in 1905 Lunacharskii worked in St Petersburg on the journal *New Life* (*Novaya zhizn'*). In 1906 he was arrested and in 1907 he was exiled for a second time. He lived on Capri with Gor'kii. Together with Gor'kii and Bogdanov, Lunacharskii was responsible for organising the party schools on Capri and in Bologna. As a member of the Forward group (Vpered) he broke with Lenin. From 1911 to 1915 Lunacharskii lived in Paris, but in 1915 in Switzerland he became reconciled with Lenin. In May 1917 Lunacharskii returned to Russia; in July he was arrested, in August he rejoined the Bolsheviks. After the October Revolution Lunacharskii was appointed head of Narkompros, and he retained this post until 1929. During this period Lunacharskii published several plays and wrote extensively on art and artistic affairs. A highly cultivated man, Lunacharskii was generally tolerant of the avant-garde and their experimentation, so long as they did not claim artististic hegemony or the right to speak on behalf of the Party. From 1929 to 1933 he worked in several capacities in areas related to education and culture. In 1929 he was appointed president of a committee to direct scholarly and teaching institutions under the Central Executive Committee (TsIK); in 1930 he was elected a member of the Academy of Sciences and he became director of the Pushkin House (Pushkinskii dom) in Leningrad. In 1933 Lunacharskii was appointed ambassador to Spain but he died en route.

LUR'E, Artur Sergeevich (1892–1964)

An avant-garde composer, Lur'e was head of the musical department of the Commissariat of Education (MUZO Narkompros) between 1918 and 1921. During this period he wrote revolutionary-inspired marches, one of which, based on Mayakovskii's poem, 'Our March' ('Nash Marsh', 1918) was illustrated by Lur'e's friend Petr Miturich. He was a frequent visitor at Bruni's flat, No. 5 at the Academy of Arts in Petrograd, where artists like Tatlin, Udal'tsova, Puni, Al'tman, Miturich, Klyun and others also tended to congregate. In January 1921 following an investigation of MUZO Lur'e was dismissed and apparently he emigrated soon after this. He lived in America and worked at Princeton University.

MALEVICH, Kazimir Severinovich (1878–1935)

Malevich began his professional artistic studies at the Drawing School in Kiev between 1895-6. He later attended the Moscow School of Painting, Sculpture and Architecture in 1904-5 and studied with Rerberg from 1905 to 1910. In 1910 Malevich participated in the Knave of Diamonds exhibition and in 1912 he contributed to the Donkey's Tail exhibition. From 1911 onwards he was an active member of the Union of Youth group and a close friend of Matyushin. His initial works were influenced by Western developments as well as the native art forms of the icon and the *lubok*. In 1913 Malevich designed the decorations and costumes for the Cubo-Futurist opera *Victory over the Sun* (*Pobeda nad solntsem*) which was performed in St Petersburg in December 1913 and for which Matyushin composed the music and the poet Kruchenykh wrote the libretto. In his concern to develop a new pictorial language, Malevich developed alogism, based on his experiments with Cubism and Futurism, but more particularly on the principle of *zaum'* or the transrational sense of language, developed by Kruchenykh and Khlebnikov. The painting *An Englishman in Moscow* (*Anglichanin v Moskve*), with its irrational juxtaposition of objects such as a fish, a church and a candle completely regardless of scale, epitomises such concerns. In December 1915 at the 0.10 exhibition in Petrograd Malevich launched Suprematism, 'the new realism', which he defined as the 'supremacy of pure emotion', and which consisted of primary Euclidean geometric forms in pure colours against a white background. To explain the ideas which prompted him to develop this abstract art form Malevich published a manifesto at the exhibition and subsequently a small leaflet entitled *From Cubism to Suprematism: The New Painterly Realism* (*Ot kubizma k suprematizmu. Novyi zhivopisnyi realizm*) which with amendments appeared in three editions. In 1916 Malevich gathered together a group of artists to publish a Suprematist journal entitled *Supremus*. This group included Popova, Klyun, Rozanova, Udal'tsova and

Pestel'. After the Revolution Malevich became a member of IZO and of the International Bureau. In the autumn of 1918 he began teaching at the First State Free Art Studios in Moscow. Also in 1919 Malevich designed the costumes and sets for Mayakovskii's play about the Revolution, *Mystery-Bouffe* (*Misteriya-buff*), produced by Meierkhol'd to mark the first anniversary of the Revolution. The Sixteenth State Exhibition: K. S. Malevich, His Path from Impressionism to Suprematism, held in Moscow in 1919-20, comprised 153 of Malevich's works. In the summer of 1919, at the invitation of Chagall, Malevich went to Vitebsk. There he ousted Chagall and became director of the Vitebsk Institute of Art and Practical Work (Vitebskii khudozhestvenno-prakticheskii institut). In 1920 at Vitebsk Malevich founded the UNOVIS group which included Lissitzky, Chashnik, Suetin, Ermolaeva and others. Klutsis was active in the Moscow branch of UNOVIS. In 1922 Malevich returned to Petrograd and became a professor at the newly reinstated Academy of Arts (Akademiya khudozhestv) and a member of GINKhUK of which he became director (1923–6) and where he ran the Formal and Technical Department (Formal'no-tekhnicheskii otdel) in the Section of Painterly Culture. From 1919 Malevich turned away from painting canvases to design cities and individual dwelling units, creating small-scale architectural models in plaster. These he called variously *planity* and *arkhitektony*. These investigations formed the bulk of his work at the GINKhUK. In 1927 Malevich went to Berlin, and visited the Bauhaus. His ideas received wider circulation in his Bauhaus book, *The Non-Objective World*. When he returned to Russia Malevich left a large number of works in Germany and these works later entered the Stedelijk Museum, Amsterdam, and the Museum of Modern Art, New York. Towards the end of the 1920s Malevich returned to painting, producing primarily figurative works and reworkings of his peasant themes of the 1910s.

MATYUSHIN, Mikhail Vasil'evich (1861–1934)

Born in Nizhnii Novgorod (now Gor'kii), Matyushin originally trained as a musician at the Moscow Conservatory, from 1876 to 1881. From 1882 he played the violin in the Court orchestra. In 1889 he began to attend the school run by the Society for the Encouragement of the Arts in St Petersburg, and to study with the Impressionist Tsionglinskii in whose studio he met his future wife, the writer and artist Elena Guro. In 1900 he visited Paris. From 1906 to 1908 he studied with the World of Art painters Dobuzhinskii and Bakst at the Zvantseva Art

School in St Petersburg. In 1909 he joined Kul'bin's Impressionist group and in 1910 together with Guro he founded the Union of Youth group. After meeting Malevich, Kruchenykh and Mayakovskii, Matyushin's and Guro's flat became an important meeting place and intellectual centre for the avant-garde. In 1913 Matyushin edited and published a translation of Gleizes and Metzinger's book *Du cubisme* and published an article on its central ideas in the Union of Youth journal (*Soyuz molodezhi*, No. 3, pp. 25–34) in which he linked Cubism to the concept of the fourth dimension formulated by the Russian philosopher Uspenskii. In the summer of 1913 the first congress of Russian Futurists, which Malevich and Kruchenykh attended, took place at Matyushin's *dacha* in Ususikirkko, Finland. Also in 1913 with Malevich, Khlebnikov and Kruchenykh, Matyushin published *The Three* (*Troe*) in memory of Elena Guro who died that year. In 1913 Matyushin wrote the music for the opera *Victory over the Sun* (*Pobeda nad solntsom*) for which Khlebnikov had written the prologue, Kruchenykh the libretto, and for which Malevich had designed the sets and costumes. In 1914 Matyushin created his first non-objective work entitled *Colour-Form* (*Tsvet-forma*). The same year he wrote the music for Kruchenykh's *Conquered War* (*Pobezhdennaya voina*). From 1918 Matyushin taught in the State Free Art Studios in Petrograd and later in the painting department of the Academy (Akademiya khudozhestv) where he organised his studio of spatial realism. He directed the Department of Organic Culture at the Petrograd GINKhUK where he continued to evolve and develop his system of extended vision called 'see-know' (*zorved*), which combined the development of physical vision with that of spiritual intuition. By means of *zorved* man would be released from the spiritual and physical cage of three dimensions. Matyushin's concern for underlying organic unity led him to investigate the interrelationship between form and colour, and its physical and psychological effect on the viewer. In 1932 his research into colour was published as *The Laws governing the Variability of Colour Combinations: A Reference Book on Colour* (*Zakonomerost' izmenyaemosti tsvetovykh sochetanii. Spravochnik po tsvetu*, Moscow and Leningrad, 1932).

MAYAKOVSKII, Vladimir Vladimirovich (1893–1930)

A Futurist poet born at Bagdadi, Georgia, Mayakovskii moved with his family to Moscow after his father's death in 1906. Whilst still at school in 1908 he joined the Bolshevik party and was briefly imprisoned. From 1908 he had attended art classes, and in 1911 he entered the Moscow School of Painting, Sculpture and Architecture. There in the autumn of 1911 he met David Burlyuk who encouraged his poetry. He joined Burlyuk's Cubo-Futurist Hylaea group and toured Russia with them reciting his verses and scandalising the Russian bourgeoisie. Mayakovskii was also a signatory of the Russian Futurists' manifesto *A Slap in the Face of Public Taste* (*Poshchechina obshchestvennomu vkusu*, 1912). Mayakovskii welcomed the Revolution and was active during 1917 with Punin in the left wing of the Union of Art Workers (Soyuz deyatelei iskusstv), demanding autonomy for art. In 1918 he became a member of IZO Narkompros in Petrograd, where he set up a publishing venture Art of the Young (Iskusstvo molodykh – IMO) and contributed to IZO's journal *Art of the Commune* (*Iskusstvo kommuny*). Mayakovskii's play about the Revolution, *Mystery-Bouffe* (*Misteriya-buff*), was acted on the anniversary of October and Mayakovskii toured workers' organisations lecturing about it. During the Civil War he designed propaganda and information posters for the Russian Telegraphic Agency (ROSTA). In 1923 he founded the magazine *LEF* (1923–5), revived as *Novyi LEF* (1927–8), which acted as a platform for the Futurist, Formalist and Constructivist avant-garde. Mayakovskii collaborated with Rodchenko on the production of advertising posters for government trading organisations. Mayakovskii composed the slogan or rhyme while Rodchenko devised the visual component. Mayakovskii asserted that such work was as important as poetry, which he continued to compose. The aggressively realist Russian Association of Proletarian Writers (RAPP), which had continually attacked Mayakovskii and *LEF*, was finally triumphant. Mayakovskii became a member of RAPP. His plays *The Bedbug* (*Klop*, 1929, for the final act of which Rodchenko designed the set and costumes) and *The Bath House* (*Banya*, 1930) were very badly received. In 1930 Mayakovskii committed suicide.

MEDUNETSKII, Konstantin Konstantinovich (1899–c. 1935)

Born in Moscow, Medunetskii commenced his artistic training in 1914 at the Stroganov School of Applied Arts in Moscow where he specialised in stage design. He continued his training at the State Free Art Studios where, with the Stenberg brothers, Georgii and Vladimir, he studied under Yakulov. On May Day 1918 with Vladimir and Georgii Stenberg he decorated the Post Office on the Myasnitskaya (now Kirov Street – ulitsa Kirova) in central Moscow and was also involved in decorating Moscow for the first anniversary of October. Medunetskii was a founder member of OBMOKhU which held its first exhibition in the spring of 1919. Medunetskii participated in all four of the group's exhibitions (1919, 1920, 1921, 1923). In January 1922 Medunetskii and the Stenberg brothers exhibited their spatial structures and constructions at the Kafe Poetov in Moscow. In the catalogue entitled *The Constructivists* (*Konstruktivisty*) they issued the first published declaration of the principles of Constructivism. At this exhibition Medunetskii showed six works with the title *Construction of a Spatial Structure* (*Konstruktsiya prostranstvennogo sooruzheniya*) which were numbered nine to fourteen. Presumably these were very similar to those he exhibited at the third OBMOKhU exhibition in spring 1921. In 1920 he became a member of INKhUK and he was one of the first members of the First Working Group of Constructivists when it was set up within INKhUK. On 4 February 1922 Medunetskii, together with the Stenberg brothers, presented a paper to INKhUK entitled 'Constructivism' ('Konstruktivizm'). This elaborated the principles governing their approach to and interpretation of Constructivism. In 1922 four of Medunetskii's constructions were exhibited at the Erste Russische Kunstausstellung in Berlin. Exhibit No. 556, entitled *Raumkonstruktion*, was bought by Katherine Dreier for the Société Anonyme and is now in the Yale University Art Gallery. Medunetskii worked constantly with the Stenbergs over this period. Together they designed sets and costumes for Tairov's productions at the Kamernyi Theatre in Moscow. In 1923 with the Stenbergs he visited Paris on tour with the Kamernyi Theatre Company. All three exhibited their work at the Galerie Paul Guillaume and they visited Picasso, but were disillusioned by his classical canvases. (This information was supplied by Vladimir Stenberg in conversation with the author, April 1974.) In 1925, under the direction of D. Shterenberg, Medunetskii worked with Kostin on models for commercial kiosks for the Soviet section of the Paris Exposition Internationale des Arts Décoratifs et Industriels Modernes. These models were exhibited in the Octagonal Hall of the Grand Palais. In the second half of the 1920s Medunetskii continued to work in the field of theatrical design but independently from the Stenbergs. In 1935 Medunetskii was still listed in *Theatrical Moscow* (*Teatral'naya Moskva*) although, according to Vladimir Stenberg, he died shortly after this.

MITURICH, Petr Vasil'evich (1887–1956)

Born in St Petersburg, from 1899 until 1905 Miturich attended the Pskov Military School, from which he was expelled for reading illegal literature. Between *c.* 1906 and 1909 he studied at the Art School in Kiev, graduating with honours. During this period he was considerably influenced by the work of Vrubel'. From 1909 until 1916 he attended the St Petersburg Academy of Art (Akademiya khudozhestv) where he studied in the battle painting class under the direction of Samokish. Whilst a student he decorated the façade of a house in Kiev for the architect Eisler and painted a mural under the direction of the artist Sokol. It seems that as early as 1914 Miturich became interested in aviation. In 1915 his class went to the front. He started exhibiting in the same year and was mentioned by the critic N. Punin in *Apollon* (No. 4/5, 1916). According to family documents, in 1916 Miturich attended a school of military engineering. However, there is no information as to the location of the school or to the nature and duration of Miturich's studies there. In 1916 Miturich began to serve in the Eleventh Siberian Division on the German front. After the Revolution he was elected the head of communications for his Division and he continued to serve as a soldier until 1921. In 1918 he acted as a representative for Narkompros concerning art education in schools. During this period Miturich was closely associated with the avant-garde artists in Petrograd and frequented the flat of his life-long friend Lev Bruni. In 1920 Miturich served in a camouflage unit in Moscow. Despite his military duties, Miturich also, between 1918 and 1922, worked on a series of painted three-dimensional structures. Made from paper, cardboard and wood, these interacted with their surrounding spatial environment to differing degrees of intensity. They were developed from his experiments with Cubism and Futurism, and were primarily abstract. Miturich gave these works titles such as *Spatial Graphics* (*Prostranstvennaya grafika*), *Spatial Poster* (*Prostranstvennyi plakat*) and *Spatial Painting* (*Prostranstvennaya zhivopis'*). They extended his interests in the properties of line which had been displayed when he had devised a set of painted cubes (*kubiki*) which formed his *Graphic Alphabet* (*Graficheskaya azbuka*, 1919). Some of Miturich's spatial posters were based on and illustrated specific transrational (*zaum'*) poems by Velimir Khlebnikov. Miturich's love and admiration for the poet led him to look after Khlebnikov during his last illness (until his death in 1922). Miturich also designed the cover for Khlebnikov's *Zangezi*. From 1923 until 1930 Miturich taught drawing in the Graphics faculty of the Moscow VKhUTEMAS. His artistic production consisted almost entirely of drawings and was firmly figurative. In 1925 he joined the eclectically realist but moderate Four Arts group (Chetyre iskusstva). However, concurrently with his realistic drawings which he continued to create and exhibit until his death, Miturich was also intensively engaged on investigating the economic and energy-saving potential of wave-like motion (*kolebatel'noe dvizhenie*). In 1922

9.6. Petr Miturich in his studio in 1921 with his spatial paintings of 1920–1.

he declared that his flying apparatus called *Wings* (*Kryl'ya*) or *The Flyer* (*Letun*) had solved the problem of flight without a motor, by using this wave-like motion. From 1922 until his death Miturich continued to investigate this principle and to apply it to the design of apparatuses which he called *volnoviki*, and which would be able to travel through the air, through water (his fish-shaped, *Boat* (*Lodka*), 1931) and on land (*The Caterpillar* (*Gusenitsa*), 1935). Miturich even extended this principle to the organisation of a complete city.

NAUMOV, Aleksandr Il'ich (1899–1928)

Born in Moscow, Naumov attended the Stroganov School of Applied Art in Moscow from 1909 until 1917. In 1918 he was involved in decorating the Rogozhsko-Simonovskii district of Moscow and the Safanov Theatre on Taganskaya Square for the first anniversary of the October Revolution. From 1918 he was a student at the State Free Art Studios in Moscow where he studied in the studio without a supervisor, graduating from the VKhUTEMAS in 1921. Naumov was a member of the OBMOKhU and he seems to have contributed to all four of the group's exhibitions (1919, 1920, 1921, 1923). Naumov worked primarily in the fields of poster (advertising, cinema and theatre posters), book, exhibition and theatre design. When designing film posters, Naumov frequently worked with Prusakov, a former member of OBMOKhU, and with Borisov and Zhukov. They sometimes signed themselves as the 'OBMOKhU' although their use of the term no longer related to the specifically agitational quality of the original group.

PERTSOV, Viktor Osipovich (1898–   )

Primarily an art critic, Pertsov during the 1920s also wrote on questions concerning production art. He had worked for Narkompros in the Ukraine before moving to Moscow where he joined Gastev's Central Institute of Labour (Tsentral'nyi institut truda – TsIT) and became active in Proletkul't. He attended the big meeting of LEF in January 1925 and in response to the dissolution which he had witnessed delivered a paper on 8 May 1925 at the Moscow Proletkul't, entitled 'Revising LEF' ('Reviziya LEFa'). In this he exhorted LEF to purify itself and to reassert its position as an urban, industrial and international movement against art and aestheticism.

**PEVSNER (PEVZNER, Natan Borisovich)
Antoine (1886–1969)**

Born in Orel, from 1902 to 1909 Pevsner attended the art school in Kiev where he was influenced by the work of Vrubel' and by the landscapes of Levitan. In 1909 he went to St Petersburg to attend the Academy of Arts (Akademiya khudozhestv) but quickly returned to Orel where he remained until 1911, except for a tour of old Russian monuments in 1910. From 1911 to 1914 he lived in Paris, where he became friendly with Archipenko and Modigliani. During 1913 he began to experiment in his drawings with the faceting of form derived from Cubism. In 1914 he returned to Russia and during 1914–15 worked in Moscow where he was influenced by the paintings in Shchukin's collection, especially those of Matisse, on whose work he based his *Dance* (*Tanets*, 1915). In 1915 Antoine joined his brothers Aleksei Pevzner and Naum Gabo in Norway, remaining there until all three returned to Russia in 1917 and settled in Moscow. In 1918 Antoine became a professor of painting at the State Free Art Studios and then at the VKhUTEMAS. In 1920 Antoine signed his brother Naum's *Realistic Manifesto* (*Realisticheskii manifest*) (appearing in the printed version as Noton Pevzner) and exhibited his two-dimensional painterly explorations of structure together with Gabo's three-dimensional constructions on Tverskoi Boulevard in Moscow. In 1923 he left Moscow and finally settled in Paris. Through the encouragement of his brother Naum he began to work in three dimensions, producing *Head of a Woman* in 1925. In 1926 in collaboration with Naum he designed the decor for Diaghilev's production of *La Chatte*.

POPOVA, Lyubov' Sergeevna (1889–1924)

Born into a wealthy family at Ivanovskoe near Moscow, Popova was educated at the gymnazium in Yalta and then at the Arsen'ev gymnazium in Moscow. She trained as a teacher before commencing her artistic studies with both Stanislav Zhukovskii and the Impressionist Konstantin Yuon whose studio was on the Arbat, Moscow. There she may have met Nadezhda Udal'tsova and Vera Mukhina who also studied there. In 1909 Popova visited Kiev, saw Vrubel''s paintings and may have also seen the Vrubel' exhibition of that year. What she did see impressed her greatly. (L. S. Popova, untitled notes, MS, private archive, Moscow.) In 1910 Popova visited Italy and was strongly influenced by the art of the Renaissance and particularly Giotto. Between 1910 and 1911 she visited various Russian towns of architectural and artistic interest including Rostov, Yaroslavl', Suzdal', Novgorod and Pskov. Popova spent the winter of 1912–

13 in Paris where she worked in the studio of La Palette under the direction of Le Fauconnier and Metzinger. Her paintings of this period reflect this interest in Cubist analysis. In Paris Popova visited the studios of Zadkine and Archipenko and also became acquainted with Futurist ideas. In the summer of 1914 she revisited Italy and France and in 1916 travelled to Turkestan. For some time between 1912 and 1915 she worked in Tatlin's studio together with Aleksandr Vesnin and others. In 1914 Popova exhibited her Cubist paintings at the Knave of Diamonds (Moscow, spring 1914) and at Tramway V (Petrograd, March 1915). In 1915 Popova began to produce reliefs of a limited three-dimensionality such as *Jug on a Table* (*Kuvshin na stole, rel'ef*, 1915, Tret'yakov Gallery, Moscow) which she exhibited at 0.10 (Petrograd, January 1916). Popova exhibited her first non-objective canvases at the Knave of Diamonds exhibition in November 1916 in Moscow where she exhibited six paintings entitled *Painterly Architectonics* (*Zhivopisnaya arkhitektonika*). By this time Popova had become a member of Malevich's Suprematist circle, collaborating with him on the publication of the journal *Supremus*, for which she did many designs. She described her development over these years in the following terms: 'A Cubist period (the problem of form) was followed by a Futurist period (the problem of movement and colour) and the principle of abstracting the parts of an object was followed logically and inevitably by the abstraction of the object itself ... The problem of depiction was replaced by the problem of the construction of form and line (post-Cubism) and colour (Suprematism)' (*Katalog posmertnoi vystavki khudozhnika konstruktora L. S. Popovoi*, Moscow, 1924, p. 6). During the Civil War Popova apparently worked in IZO Narkompros and also became involved in teaching in Proletkul't. In 1918 she had joined the teaching staff of the State Free Art Studios and when the studios became the VKhUTEMAS she and Aleksandr Vesnin taught colour construction on the Basic Course. A member of INKhUK from 1920, Popova actively participated in the debates of the General Working Group of Objective Analysis especially in the crucial discussions concerning the nature of composition and construction. She presented papers to INKhUK concerning her design for *The Magnanimous Cuckold* (*Velikodushnyi rogonosets*) in 1922 and in response to their commission wrote a paper 'Toward the Question of the New Methods in our Art School' ('K voprosu o novykh metodakh v nashei khudozhestvennoi shkole'). In 1920 Popova collaborated with Aleksandr Vesnin on a project for a mass festival in honour of the Third International which was to be directed by Meierkhol'd and to take place on Khodyn' Field in Moscow.

9.7. Lyubov' Popova. [Photograph: © George Costakis 1981.]

Although Popova did not become a member of the First Working Group of Constructivists she did contribute, with Rodchenko and Stepanova (two of the founders), to the $5 \times 5 = 25$ exhibition in Moscow. Popova exhibited five works entitled *Experiments with Painterly Force Structures (Opyty zhivopisno-silovykh postroenii)* which she asserted would lead to 'concrete materialised constructions' (*5 × 5 = 25. Katalog vystavki*, 1921). Popova taught a course concerning the formation of objects (*veshchestvennoe oformlenie*) at the Higher State Theatrical Workshops (Gosudarstvennye vysshie tea-tral'nye masterskie – GVYTM) directed by Meierkhol'd. In 1922 she designed the sets and costumes for Meierkhol'd's production of Crommelynck's farce *The Magnanimous Cuckold*, transforming the water mill into a skeletal machine of various levels and dressing the actors in working clothes (production clothing or *prozodezhda*). In 1923 her set for Meierkhol'd's production of *The Earth in Turmoil (Zemlya dybom)* approached the industrial object from a rather more pragmatic standpoint. The set was based on a gantry crane and the properties were not new artistic prototypes but were selected from already existing objects. Some time in the second half of 1923 or at the very beginning of 1924 Popova together with Stepanova started to design textiles for mass production at the First State Textile Print Factory, previously the Tsindel' Factory, in Moscow. In conjunction with the textile prints Popova also produced dress designs. From its founding in 1923 Popova was also a collaborator on *LEF*. In 1924 she died of scarlet fever.

PRUSAKOV, Nikolai Petrovich (1900–52)

Born in Moscow, Prusakov received his artistic education at the Stroganov School of Applied Art which he attended from 1911 until 1918. He then studied at the State Free Art Studios and eventually graduated from the VKhUTEMAS. In 1919 he became a member of the OBMOKhU and he seems to have contributed to all the group's exhibitions (1919, 1920, 1921, 1923). By 1924 Prusakov had become a member of the First Working Organisation of Artists (Pervaya rabochaya organizatsiya khudozhnikov) which exhibited models of monuments and buildings, montage and paintings at the First Discussional Exhibition of Organisations of Active Revolutionary Art (Pervaya discussionnaya vystavka ob'edinenii aktivnogo revolyutsionnogo iskusstva, Moscow, 1924). During the 1920s Prusakov was actively engaged in the production of film posters some of which he designed in co-operation with Naumov, a former member of OBMOKhU, Borisov and Zhukov. He contributed to the Second Exhibition of Film Posters (Vtoraya vystavka Kinoplakata, Moscow, 1926). He also worked in the areas of exhibition and theatrical design.

PUNI (POUGNY, Jean), Ivan Al'bertovich (1892–1956)

Puni was born in Kouokkala, Finland, which is near Leningrad. His father was a violinist and his mother from the gentry. From 1900 until 1908 he attended the gymnazium and then the Military Academy in St Petersburg, and in 1909 he rented a studio in St Petersburg. Between 1910 and 1912 he visited Italy and France. In Paris he studied at the Académie Julian and stayed with Annenkov. In Russia he exhibited with the Union of Youth (St Petersburg, winter 1911–12 and winter 1913–14), but he broke with them in 1914. In Paris in 1914 he exhibited at the Salon des Indépendants. On his return he organised the exhibitions Tramway V (Petrograd, March 1915) and 0.10 (Petrograd, January 1916). At Tramway V, Puni exhibited his first three-dimensional works such as *The Card Players* (*Igroki v karty*, 1913–14, No. 54), inspired by Cubism and the textural possibilities of collage. He also showed *objet trouvé* works such as a still life composed of a hammer on a board (*Natyur-mort*, No 57). The following year at 0.10 Puni exhibited his first Suprematist-inspired three-dimensional abstract sculptures, *Painterly Sculptures* (*Zhivopisnaya skul'ptura*), and issued an explanatory Suprematist declaration (co-signed by his wife, Kseniya Boguslavskaya) stating that 'a picture is a new conception of abstract, real elements, independent of meaning'. Malevich also published his famous Suprematist manifesto at this exhibition. In 1918 Puni participated in the decoration of Petrograd for May Day and for the first anniversary of the October Revolution. At the invitation of Chagall in 1919 he went to Vitebsk where he taught for a while before returning to Petrograd. From there Puni went to Finland and finally to Berlin. In 1921 he settled in Berlin and exhibited at Der Sturm gallery. In 1923 he moved to Paris where he lived until his death.

PUNIN, Nikolai Nikolaevich (1888–1953)

An art historian and critic, Punin was born in St Petersburg. His father was a military doctor. From 1899 to 1907 he attended the Tsarskoe Selo Classical Gymnazium. In 1907 he entered the University of St Petersburg where he initially studied law, transferring to history and finally to art history. In 1913 he was invited to join the newly formed Department of Russian Art at the Russian Museum in St Petersburg. From 1913 until 1916 he contributed regularly to the art journal *Apollon*, and edited the art section of *Northern Notes* (*Severnye zapiski*) and *Russian Icon* (*Russkaya ikona*). In 1917 he was a member of the Union of Art Workers and of the movement Freedom to Art (*Svoboda iskusstvu*). In 1918 he joined IZO Narkompros and became deputy head and then head of the Petrograd section. During the Civil War he worked as a commissar of the Hermitage Museum, the Russian Museum and the Petrograd State Free Art Studios. He was also on the editorial board of IZO's journals *Art of the Commune* (1918–19) and *Fine Art* (1919). As head of the Petrograd IZO Punin took an active role in the implementation of Lenin's Plan for Monumental Propaganda, the organisation of art studios for workers and the decoration of the city for the revolutionary festivals. From 1919 to 1920 Punin was a deputy in the Petrograd Soviet of Peasant Soldier and Worker Deputies. In 1919 he gave lectures on art to workers which were later published as *The First Series of Lectures* (*Pervyi tsikl lektsii*, Petrograd, 1920), and Punin was also the first commentator on Tatlin's Monument to the Third International. Punin was a founder organiser of the Museum of Artistic Culture (Muzei khudozhestvennoi kul'tury) in Petrograd in 1921 and of the Petrograd GINKhUK, which was established on the basis of the museum in 1924. In GINKhUK Punin directed the section of general artistic ideology. From 1919 to 1925 Punin had taught the history of artistic form at the State Free Art Studios (later the Academy of Arts). From 1926 to 1931 he lectured on contemporary European art at the State Institute of Art History in Leningrad (Gosudarstvennyi institut istorii iskusstv). Until the beginning of the 1930s Punin continued to work in the Russian Museum where he organised a section dealing with the latest trends in Russian art. From 1932 he was head of the Department of Art History at the All Russian Academy of Arts (Vserossiiskaya Akademiya khudozhestv – VAKh), and in 1944 he became head of the art history department of Leningrad University. From c. 1925 to 1938 he was married to the poetess Anna Akhmatova. During the 1930s Punin was apparently arrested several times and exiled.

RODCHENKO, Aleksandr Mikhailovich (1891–1956)

Rodchenko's father was a peasant from the district of Smolensk who worked as a property man for a theatre in St Petersburg, where Rodchenko was born. Brought up and educated in Kazan', from 1910 until 1914 Rodchenko attended the Art School there, where he met Varvara Stepanova whom he subsequently married. In 1913 a local exhibition of his work in Kazan' included two tempera works depicting a carnival against a fantastic architectural background. These were heavily influenced by Beardsley and Art Nouveau, and especially by their Russian equivalent the World of Art group. In February 1914 Rodchenko attended a Futurist meeting in Kazan' and bought a photograph of Mayakovskii. After graduation Rodchenko moved to Moscow where he entered the graphics department of the Stroganov School of Applied Art with which he rapidly became disillusioned. 'We continually redrew Barshchevskii. Had enough. Left. Began to work independently with painting' (A. M. Rodchenko, 'Chernoe i beloe', MS, private archive, Moscow). At this time between 1915 and 1916 Rodchenko became acquainted with the Moscow avant-garde, including Tatlin, Popova and Malevich. He contributed to the fourth Contemporary Painting Exhibition (Sovremennaya zhivopis', Moscow, 1916), and at the invitation of Tatlin he participated in The Store (Moscow, spring 1916) where he exhibited Cubist collages (1914–15) and his first experimental works with compass and ruler which he had commenced in 1915. In 1917 Rodchenko designed some lamps from overlapping and intersecting planes of material for the Kafe Pittoresk in Moscow, which Yakulov, Tatlin and other artists were decorating. In 1918 Rodchenko joined IZO Narkompros and seems to have been particularly active in the

Museums Office (Muzeinoe byuro) and with Rozanova in the Subsection of Art and Production (Podotdel khudozhestvennoi promyshlennosti). Also in 1918 Rodchenko seems to have begun making three-dimensional constructions which he exhibited together with his *Black on Black* (*Chernoe na chernom*, 1918) painting at the Tenth State Exhibition – Non-Objective Creation and Suprematism (Bespredmetnoe tvorchestvo i Suprematizm, Moscow, 1919). In 1920 Rodchenko executed a series of works which explored the line 'as a factor of construction' (Rodchenko, $5 \times 5 = 25$. *Katalog vystavki*, Moscow, 1921). From 1919 Rodchenko was a member of Zhivskul'ptarkh which as its name suggests was concerned with establishing a synthesis of the spatial arts and in this way evolving designs for new building types (e.g. communal housing, etc.). In 1920 Rodchenko was one of the initial members of the Moscow INKhUK and remained an active participant until it closed. Together with Gan and Stepanova he was a co-founder of the First Working Group of Constructivists in March 1921. In 1921 Rodchenko participated in the third OBMOKhU exhibition where he displayed a series of hanging constructions which explored the structure of pure Euclidean geometric forms. In 1921 he also contributed to the $5 \times 5 = 25$ exhibition in Moscow where he displayed three canvases covered simply with the three primary colours and titled *Pure Red Colour* (*Chistyi krasnyi tsvet*), *Pure Yellow Colour* (*Chistyi zheltyi tsvet*) and *Pure Blue Colour* (*Chistyi sinyi tsvet*). From 1920 until it closed in 1930 Rodchenko taught at the VKhUTEMAS where he was initially responsible for discipline no. 5: Construction, on the Basic Course. He also taught in the Metalwork faculty (Metfak) which he directed from 1922 onwards and where he taught courses on the formation of objects: projects and models (*konstruirovanie veshchei: proekty i modely*) and composition (*kompozitsiya*). In 1923 Rodchenko began to design posters for various government trading organisations in collaboration with Mayakovskii whom he had first met in 1920. Mayakovskii composed the slogan and Rodchenko supplied the visual component. Rodchenko was initially assisted by students from the VKhUTEMAS, but ultimately Levin and Lavinskii took over the work. From 1923 to 1925 Rodchenko worked on *LEF* and then on its continuation *Novyi LEF* (1927–8), for which he designed the covers and layouts, and to which he contributed articles, photomontages and photographs. In 1923 Rodchenko designed the photomontages illustrating Mayakovskii's *About This* (*Pro eto*, Moscow, 1923). He used photomontage in the posters for Vertov's *Cinema Truth* (*Kino pravda*) and *Cinema Eye* (*Kino glaz*). In 1924 Rodchenko himself began to work as a photographer. In 1925

Rodchenko designed the interior and furnishings of the Workers' Club which formed part of the Soviet exhibit at the 1925 Paris Exposition Internationale des Arts Décoratifs et Industriels Modernes and in connection with this he visited Paris. Rodchenko had first become involved with the theatre when he did some designs for a production of Gan's play *We* (*My*, *c.* 1919-20). In 1929 he designed the sets and costumes for *Inga* and also for the final act of Mayakovskii's *The Bed Bug* (*Klop*, 1929) produced by Meierkhol'd. Rodchenko also worked in the cinema. He devised captions for Vertov's *Kino pravda* in 1922, and in 1927 he was involved on the film *The Journalist* (*Zhurnalist*). In the late 1920s Rodchenko devoted increasingly more time to typography, graphic design and to photography itself. Together with Stepanova he executed many designs for publications such as *USSR in Construction* (*SSSR na stroike*) during the 1930s.

ROZANOVA, Ol'ga Vladimirovna (1886-1918)

Born at Malenki in Vladimir Province, Rozanova attended the Bol'shakov Art School and the Stroganov School of Applied Art, Moscow, from 1904 until 1910. In 1911 she moved to St Petersburg where she became a member of the Union of Youth group exhibiting with them in December 1911. In St Petersburg she also attended E. Zvantseva's Art School from 1912 to 1913. From 1912 onwards she was also engaged on illustrating her husband Kruchenykh's poetry and other Futurist books such as *Game in Hell* (*Igra v adu*, 2nd edition, 1913), *Te li le* (1914), *Transrational Book* (*Zaumnaya kniga*, 1915) and *Universal War* (*Vselenskaya voina*, 1916). Rozanova also wrote *zaum'*, transrational Futurist verse (see *Iskusstvo*, No. 4, 1919, p. 1; and *Balos*, Tiflis, 1917). In 1913 she published her major statement on art, 'The Bases of the New Creativity and the Reasons for its Misinterpretation' ('Osnovy novogo tvorchestva i prichiny ego neponimaniya', *Soyuz molodezhi*, No. 3, 1913, pp. 14-22). Rozanova participated in most of the major avant-garde exhibitions of the period including Tramway V (Petrograd, March 1915), 0.10 (Petrograd, January 1916) and The Store (Moscow, March 1916). In 1916, after having experimented with Cubism and Futurism, Rozanova adopted Malevich's Suprematism. She acted as Malevich's editorial secretary on the journal *Supremus*, which was prepared for publication but never printed. Prior to the Revolution Rozanova had also worked in the applied arts designing embroideries and textiles, including some for the decorative section of *Supremus*. After the Revolution she joined Proletkul't and at the same time became a member of IZO Narkompros where she directed the subsection

concerned with the applied arts (Podotdel khudozhestvennoi promyshlennosti) and was responsible for the reactivation and establishment of art, applied art and craft workshops. She organised studios and workshops in such towns as Bogororodsk, Ivanovo-Voznesensk and Mster. In 1919 an enormous posthumous exhibition of her work was held in Moscow, and her work was also taken to Berlin for the Erste Russische Kunstausstellung of 1922.

SEN'KIN Sergei Yakovlevich (1894-1963)

Born near Moscow, from 1914 until 1915 Sen'kin attended the Moscow School of Painting, Sculpture and Architecture. He studied in Malevich's studio at the Second State Free Art Studios in Moscow from 1918 to 1919, and maintained contact with Malevich at Vitebsk. Apparently during 1920 he worked as an army artist in the Urals. In 1920 he recommenced his full-time artistic education at the Moscow VKhUTEMAS The UNOVIS journal (*Put' Unovisa*, No. 1, January 1921) reported that by 15 November 1920 Sen'kin and Klutsis together had set up their own independent studio at the VKhUTEMAS, where Klutsis' paintings and Sen'kin's investigations into form-making exemplified the 'new practical realism' of UNOVIS. In 1921 Sen'kin exhibited in the VKhUTEMAS Students' Cézanne Club and in 1922 he showed Suprematist works at the exhibition Association of the New Trends in Art (Ob'edinenie novykh techenii v iskusstve, Petrograd). In the summer of 1923 Sen'kin and Klutsis together attempted to organise the Workshop of the Revolution (Masterskaya revolyutsii) within VKhUTEMAS which would establish 'a body of artists, agitators ... productivists with the general aim of socially and culturally influencing the mass' (*LEF*, No. 1 (5), 1924, p. 155). By this time Sen'kin's affiliation had moved from Suprematism to Constructivism and he was associated with the journal *LEF* (1923-5). In 1928 he became a member of the group October (Oktyabr') and the same year collaborated with Lissitzky on the photomontage display at the Pressa exhibition in Cologne. During the 1920s and later he designed mass festivals, posters, books and magazines. In the 1920s he worked primarily with photomontage.

SHESTAKOV, Viktor Alekseevich (1898-1957)

Born in Orel, Shestakov received his training at the Moscow VKhUTEMAS which he attended from 1920 to 1924. Shestakov seems to have been a member of Gan's latter day First Working Group of Constructivists because in 1924 he wrote an article entitled 'The Equipment of Everyday Life' ('Armatura povsednevnogo byta') for a brochure issued by the group entitled *Constructivism*. As a self-declared Constructivist, Shestakov also participated in the so-called First Meeting of the Workers of the Left Front of the Arts (Pervoe soveshchanie rabotnikov LEFa) which took place in Moscow, 16 and 17 January 1925. From 1922 until 1927 Shestakov worked as a theatrical designer at the Theatre of the Revolution (Teatr revolyutsii) in Moscow. There in 1923 he designed the set for *Lake Lyul* (*Ozero Lyul'*) by A. Faiko, which included pieces of slatted furniture that could be refolded and rearranged to fulfil multiple functions. One chair performed as many as six functions. He was awarded a gold medal in Paris in 1925. From 1927 onwards Shestakov designed sets for Meierkhol'd's theatre including *Krechinskii's Wedding* (*Svad'ba Krechinskogo*) by A. Sukho-Kobylin in 1929.

SHTERENBERG, David Petrovich (1881–1948)

Born in Zhitomir, an avant-garde artist strongly influenced by the French School, Shterenberg lived in Paris from 1906 where he received his artistic training during 1906–12 at the École des Beaux-Arts and at the Académie Vitti studying with Van Dongen and others. In 1917 he returned to Russia where from 1918 until 1921 he was head of IZO Narkompros. In 1921 he became the head of the art department of the Chief Administration for Professional Education within Narkompros (Glavprofobr). From 1920 until 1930 he taught in the Painting faculty of the VKhUTEMAS. In 1922 he organised the Erste Russiche Kunstausstellung. In 1925 he was the director of the Russian section at the Exposition Internationale des Arts Décoratifs et Industriels Modernes in Paris. Never an extremist, Shterenberg in 1925 was one of the founders of OST to which he belonged until 1930.

SOTNIKOV, Aleksei Georgievich (1904–)

Of peasant stock, Sotnikov studied in a technical school after the Revolution. From 1925 to 1928 he attended the Art School in Krasnodar and in 1928 he entered the VKhUTEIN in Moscow where he studied in the Ceramics faculty. He was a student on Tatlin's course concerning 'the design of new everyday objects' (*proektirovanie novykh bytovykh veshchei*). In this connection Sotnikov designed the mass variant of the infant's drinking vessel devised by Tatlin. Sotnikov later helped Tatlin to construct the *Letatlin* in his studio in the Novodevichii Monastery. From 1934 Sotnikov worked at the Dulevskii Porcelain Factory where much of his work was concerned with depicting animals and birds as sculpture in porcelain. In 1976 a major exhibition of his work was held in Moscow.

STENBERG, Vladimir Avgustovich (1899–1982) and STENBERG, Georgii Avgustovich (1900–1933)

The Stenberg brothers were born in Moscow to a Russian mother, but their father was a Swede who in 1921 returned to Sweden. They retained their Swedish nationality until 1933. Encouraged to paint by their father who was himself a painter, from 1912 until 1917 they both attended the Stroganov School of Applied Art in Moscow where they studied under V. Egorov and A. Yanov. They continued their studies at the First State Free Art Studios where they studied in Yakulov's studio. During the Civil War they designed propaganda posters. For May Day 1918, together with Medunetskii and Denisovskii, they decorated the Post Office on the Myasnitskaya (now Kirov Street – ulitsa Kirova), and alone, the Napoleon Cinema and Railway Workers' Club on Krasnosel'skaya. Vladimir decorated various buildings for the first anniversary of the Revolution including the River Transportation Office on Chistoprudnyi Boulevard which he adorned with the figure of a sailor and a worker. The Stenbergs were founder members of the OBMOKhU which held its first exhibition in the spring of 1919. The Stenbergs participated in all four of the group's exhibitions (1919, 1920, 1921, 1923). In January 1922 together with Medunetskii they exhibited their spatial paintings and constructions at the Kafe Poetov in Moscow. In the catalogue boldly titled *The Constructivists* (*Konstruktivisty*), they issued the first published declaration of the principles of Constructivism. In all Georgii and Vladimir exhibited thirty-one works including three-dimensional works made from metal, glass and wood entitled *Construction of a Spatial Structure* (*Konstruktsiya prostranstvennogo sooruzheniya – KPS*) which they considered to be experiments towards new types of buildings, and therefore with an ultimately utilitarian application. These works included some which they exhibited at the third OBMOKhU exhibition in Moscow in April 1921. In 1920 the brothers joined the Moscow INKhUK and became members of the First Working Group of Constructivists when it was set up within INKhUK. On 4 February 1922 the Stenbergs together with Medunetskii delivered a paper to INKhUK entitled 'Constructivism' ('Konstruktivizm') which elaborated the principles governing their approach to and interpretation of Constructivism. The Stenbergs had started working in the theatre in 1915, and from 1922 until 1931 they worked for Tairov at the Kamernyi Theatre in Moscow, designing plays including *The Yellow Blouse* (*Zheltaya koftochka*, 1922) with Medunetskii. In 1923 together with Aleksandra Ekster and Nivin-

skii they worked on the decoration of pavilions at the 1923 Agricultural Exhibition (Vserossiiskaya sel'skokhozyaistvennaya vystavka, Moscow). In 1923 they also toured Europe with the Tairov Company, exhibiting their work in Paris and visiting Picasso, who disillusioned them with his classical canvases. During the 1920s the brothers designed a large quantity of film posters which they signed initially '2 STEN' and then '2 STEN-BERG 2'. From 1928 onwards the Stenbergs were in charge of the November decorations for Red Square and Vladimir continued to be responsible for these until 1948. Georgii was chief artist to the Gor'kii Park of Culture and Rest in Moscow and also designed interiors for the VEO in Moscow and for a Palace of Culture in Leninskaya Sloboda. He also did colour schemes for the settlement at Dneprostroi and submitted a project for the Palace of Soviets (Dvorets sovetov). Both brothers worked in graphic design for magazines such as the *Construction of Moscow* (*Stroitel'stvo Moskvy*). From 1929 until 1932 both brothers taught drawing at the Moscow Architectural Construction Institute (VASI). After Georgii's death in a road accident in 1933 Vladimir worked alone and later collaborated with his son.

STEPANOVA, Varvara Fedorovna (1894–1958)

Born in Kovno (now Kaunas) in Lithuania, Stepanova attended the Art School in Kazan' from *c*. 1910 to 1911. There she met Aleksandr Rodchenko whom she subsequently married. In 1912 Stepanova moved to Moscow where she studied with the Impressionist Konstantin Yuon and Il'ya Mashkov. From 1913 until 1914 she attended the Stroganov School of Applied Art in Moscow. After the Revolution, together with Rodchenko, Stepanova worked in the Museums Office (Muzeinoe byuro) of IZO Narkompros and she also taught in the Fine Art Studio of the Academy of Social Education (Akademiya sotsial'nogo vospitaniya) from *c*. 1921 onwards. Stepanova participated in various exhibitions organised by IZO, including the Fifth State Exhibition and the Tenth State Exhibition – Non-Objective Creation and Suprematism (Bespredmetnoe tvorchestvo i Suprematizm, Moscow, 1919). Like Rodchenko, Stepanova was an initial member of the Moscow INKhUK to which she presented a paper on 22 December 1922, entitled 'On Constructivism' ('O konstruktivizme'). Stepanova was also a co-

9.8. Georgii and Vladimir Stenberg together with Konstantin Medunetskii in the early 1920s. [Photograph: A. B. Nakov.]

261

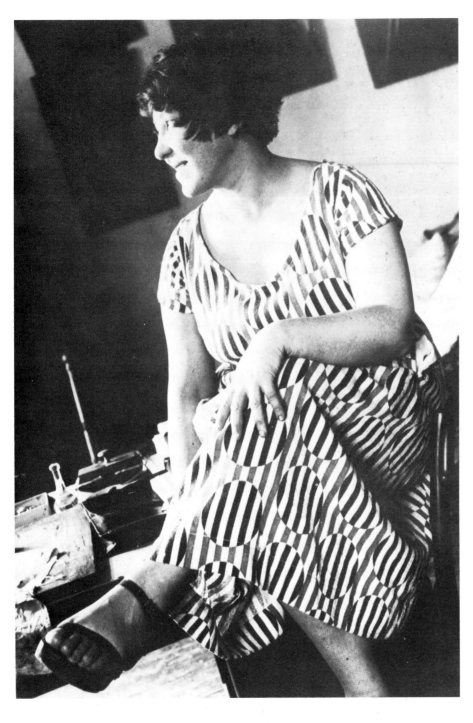

9.9. Varvara Stepanova in the 1920s. [Photograph: Courtesy Galerie Gmurzynska, Cologne.]

founder with Gan and Rodchenko of the First Working Group of Constructivists. In September 1921 she contributed to the Moscow $5 \times 5 = 25$ exhibition where she exhibited compositions based on the mechanical and geometrical analysis of the human figure. In the catalogue she declared that 'Technology and industry have presented art with the problem of Construction as effective action, not contemplative figurativeness' ($5 \times 5 = 25$. *Katalog vystavki*, 1921). In 1922 Stepanova designed the set and costumes for Meierkhol'd's production of Sukhovo-Kobylin's play *The Death of Tarelkin* (*Smert' Tarelkina*). For this she devised a series of collapsible structures made from slatted wood and painted white which reinforced the action of the play and which would also perform multiple functions. The costumes were made in two contrasting colours to reinforce the function and dynamism of the actors' actions. Stepanova also did the designs for Zhemchuznyi's *Book Evening* (*Vecher knigi*, 1924). From 1923 onwards Stepanova was closely involved with the journal *LEF* (1923–5) and *Novyi LEF* (1927–8). From 1924 until

1925 Stepanova taught in the Textile faculty of the VKhUTEMAS. During the same period she designed textiles for the First State Textile Print Factory (Pervaya gosudarstvennaya sittsenabivnaya fabrika), formerly the Tsindel' Factory. In conjunction with this activity Stepanova also worked on problems of production clothing (*prozodezhda*) and sports wear (*sportodezhda*), both theoretically, in her articles, and practically, in her designs. In 1919 Stepanova had become involved with the Futurist poets and herself wrote transrational (*zaum'*) poetry, producing collaged and handwritten books such as *Gaust chaba*, *Toft*, *Zigraf* and *Rtny khomle*. In 1922 Stepanova was involved with Gan's cinematic and photographic journal *Kino-Fot* to which she contributed woodcuts of celebrities like Charlie Chaplin. In 1925 Stepanova began to work on the design of posters with Mayakovskii and towards the end of the 1920s her activity in this area increased. During the 1930s Stepanova worked primarily in graphics and typographical design devising the layouts for publications such as the *USSR in Construction* (*SSSR na stroike*).

SUETIN, Nikolai Mikhailovich (1897-1954)

Born at Myatlevskaya Station in the Kaluga district, Suetin served as a soldier in Vitebsk from 1915 until 1917. From 1918 until 1922 he attended the Art School (Vysshii khudozhestvennyi institut) at Vitebsk, becoming a member of Malevich's UNOVIS group in 1919. After Malevich left Vitebsk in 1922 Suetin, together with other members of the group, Chashnik, Yudin and Ermolaeva, followed him to Petrograd. There Suetin worked in the Formal and Theoretical Department (Formal'no-teoreticheskii otdel) which was run by Malevich within the Petrograd GINKh-UK. Suetin assisted Malevich with his Suprematist architectural constructions (*arkhitektony* and *planity*). Between 1927 and 1930 he worked in the experimental laboratory of the Institute of Art History (Institut istorii iskusstv). From 1923 onwards Suetin also worked in the State Porcelain Factory in Petrograd where he decorated porcelain (some with Suprematist designs). In 1932 he became the factory's artistic director and continued working there until 1952. In 1935 Suetin painted Malevich's coffin with the Black Square.

TARABUKIN, Mikhail Aleksandrovich (1889-1956)

Tarabukin was born in Moscow. In 1918 after he graduated from the University of Moscow (Faculty of Historical and Philosophical Sciences) he began to write and publish articles on art. He was an important member of the Moscow INKhUK throughout its existence from 1920 to 1924. He was the Institute's secretary and took an active part in the debates concerning production art and Constructivism. In this connection he liaised with the VKhUTEMAS. On 20 August 1921 he delivered a paper at the Institute entitled 'The Last Picture has been Painted' ('Poslednyaya kartina napisana') which formed the basis for his major book *From the Easel to the Machine* (*Ot mol'berta k mashine*, Moscow, 1923). In *Towards a Theory of Painting* (*Opyt teorii zhivopisi*), published the same year, Tarabukin presented 'a formal analysis of the elements of painting'. From 1924 until 1928 Tarabukin was a corresponding member of GAKhN where he belonged to the theoretical section and delivered papers concerning conventional art historical themes and issues such as 'The Impressionist Still Life' ('Natyurmort u impressionistov', 7 December 1927). After his study of Bogaevskii was published in 1928 he was attacked as a Formalist. His work did not appear in print until 1973 and his doctoral thesis on the Russian artist Vrubel' was published posthumously in 1974. During the 1930s he taught art history at the Lunacharskii Institute of Theatrical Art (Gosudarstvennyi institut teatral'nogo iskusstva im. A. V. Lunacharskogo).

TATLIN, Vladimir Evgrafovich (1885-1953)

Born in Moscow, Tatlin grew up in Khar'kov in the Ukraine. His father was an engineer and his mother was a poetess who died in 1887. Tatlin commenced his artistic training at the Moscow School of Painting, Sculpture and Architecture which he attended between 1902 and 1904. From 1904 he studied at the Penza Art School (Penzenskoe khudozhestvennoe uchilishche) under Goryushkin-Sorokopudov and Afanas'ev, who was a member of the Wanderers, a critical Realist group established in the nineteenth century. After graduating from the Penza School (Tatlin's graduation certificate is dated 1910), Tatlin briefly returned to the Moscow School of Painting, Sculpture and Architecture, from which he did not graduate. During his two periods of training at the Moscow School Tatlin had studied under Korovin and Serov. The whole period of Tatlin's artistic education had been interrupted by trips abroad as a sailor. In 1903-4 he had visited Egypt and later Turkey, Syria and Libya. Around 1907-8 Tatlin began to associate with Larionov and Goncharova, the leaders of the avant-garde, and he exhibited with them for the first time at the Second Izdebskii Salon in Odessa (December 1910). However, after participating in their Donkey's Tail exhibition (Oslinyi khvost, Moscow, April-March 1912) Tatlin moved away from their group. In the spring of 1911 Tatlin began to exhibit with the Union of Youth group in St Petersburg and continued to contribute to their exhibitions until early 1914. Tatlin also participated in exhibitions of the Knave of Diamonds (Moscow, spring 1913) the World of Art (Moscow, winter 1912–13) and Contemporary Painting (Sovremennaya zhivopis', Moscow, winter 1912–13, spring 1914). Tatlin was also involved in illustrating Futurist books such as A. Kruchenykh and V. Khlebnikov's *The World Backwards* (*Mir s kontsa*, Moscow, 1912) and V. Mayakovskii, V. Khlebnikov and A. Kruchenykh's *The Missal of the Three* (*Trebnik troikh*, Moscow, 1913). Sometime around 1911 Tatlin organised a teaching studio at 37 Ostozhenka, Moscow, and among those who attended were Aleksandr Vesnin (from 1912 until 1913) and Lyubov' Popova. Tatlin's paintings of this period such as *The Nude* (*Naturshchitsa*, 1913, Tret'yakov Gallery, Moscow) combined an awareness of Western avant-garde developments with a strong interest in native Russian traditions. Tatlin was also active in the area of theatrical design executing projects for Glinka's opera *A Life for the Tsar* (*Zhizn' za Tsarya*, now titled *Ivan Susanin*, 1912–13) and Tomashevskii's play *Tsar Maximilian and his unruly Son Adolf* (*Tsar' Maksimilian i ego nepokornyi syn Adol'f*, 1911). In 1913 Tatlin travelled to Berlin and then to Paris where he visited Picasso and Lipchitz and may have met Archipenko. It seems that after his return to Russia, Tatlin began to make three-dimensional painterly reliefs (*zhivopisnye rel'ef*) which he first displayed at the First Exhibition of Painterly Reliefs (Pervaya vystavka zhivopisnykh rel'efov) held at his studio in Moscow, 10–14 May 1914, and at the Tramway V exhibition (Petrograd, March 1915). In 1915 Tatlin began to make more spatially dynamic reliefs slung across corners which he called corner counter-reliefs (*Uglovye kontr'-rel'efy*). These he exhibited at 0.10 (Petrograd, January 1916) organised by Ivan Puni, and at The Store (Moscow, spring 1916). From 1918 until 1919 Tatlin was head of the Moscow branch of IZO Narkompros where he was responsible for the general running of the department, including the implementation of Lenin's Plan for Monumental Propaganda. In response to this experience he commenced his own project for a monument which was later dedicated to the Third International. Over the same period Tatlin also taught painting in the Moscow State Free Art Studios. Sometime in late 1919 Tatlin moved to Petrograd, where, until 1921, he taught in the State Free Art Studios there, setting up his 'Studio of Volume, Material and Construction' (*Masterskaya ob'ema, materiala i konstruktsii*). In November 1920 he exhibited his model of the Monument to the Third International at the studio of the former Academy of Arts where it had been made in Petrograd. In December 1920 he took the model to Moscow where he exhibited it at the Eighth Congress of the Soviets. In 1921 it was reported to the Moscow INKhUK that Tatlin was working with the Petrograd Proletkul't and that he had also attempted to organise a new type of design workshop at the New Lessner Factory (Novyi Lessner) in Petrograd but that he had been thwarted and continually referred to the technical drawing office. Tatlin was also active in the Petrograd Museum of Artistic Culture (Muzei khudozhestvennoi kul'tury) and particularly in setting up the Petrograd GINKhUK within which he organised and directed the Department of Material Culture (Otdel material'noi kul'tury). This was concerned with 'the formation of materials' and applying these experiments to the organisation of life and mass production (V. Tatlin, 'Otchet o rabote za 1923 i 24 gg.'). In pursuit of these interests Tatlin designed workers' clothing and five variants of an economical oven. On 27 May 1923 he presented his ideas concerning the role of the artist-constructor in the factory in a paper entitled 'Material Culture (Against Tatlinism)' ('Material'naya kul'tura (Protiv Tatlinizma)'). Also in May 1923 Tatlin organised and produced Khlebnikov's *Zangezi* at the Petrograd GINKhUK. From 1925 until 1927 he worked in Kiev where he directed the Department of Theatre, Cinema and Photography (Teokino-foto otdel) within the Painting faculty at the Kiev Art School (Kievskii khudozhestvennyi institut) (TsGALI, fond 681, op. 3, ed. khr. 26, list 272). It was here apparently that he began to teach the culture of materials (*kul'tura materialov*). In 1927 Tatlin returned to Moscow to work at the VKhUTEIN where he taught 'the construction or projection of new everyday objects', both in the Wood and Metalwork faculty (Dermetfak) and in the Ceramics faculty. From 1930 to 1933 Tatlin worked in his Scientific and Experimental Laboratory (Nauchno-issledovatel'skaya laboratoriya) under Narkompros which was situated at the Novodevichii Monastery in Moscow. There he worked on his project for a flying machine—the *Letatlin*. In 1932 the three variants of the *Letatlin* were exhibited in Moscow at the Pushkin Museum of Fine Arts, and Tatlin continued to experiment with it until his death. In the 1930s Tatlin returned to figurative painting, executing many portraits and flower pieces. Tatlin also worked in the area of theatrical design, devising decorations and costumes for such productions as Sukhovo-Kobylin's classic play *The Affair* (*Delo*) at the Red Army Theatre, Moscow, in 1940. In 1941 Tatlin may have worked on camouflaging the city of Moscow. He died in 1953 from food poisoning.

9.10. Vladimir Tatlin before the Revolution.

UDAL'TSOVA, Nadezhda Andreevna
(1886-1961)

Born in Orel, Udal'tsova commenced her artistic studies in Moscow at the Moscow School of Painting, Sculpture and Architecture and at Yuon's Art School where she studied under Yuon, Dudin and Ul'yanov. In 1908 she worked with Kim. In 1911 Udal'tsova went to Paris where she attended the Académie de La Palette and received instruction from Metzinger, Le Fauconnier and Segonzac, from whom she assimilated the principles of Cubism. Typical of the type of Cubist work she produced at this time and later is the work *At the Piano* which was exhibited in Berlin in 1922 and is now in the Yale University Art Gallery. In 1913 Udal'tsova returned to Russia and worked in Tatlin's studio in Moscow together with Aleksandr Vesnin and Lyubov' Popova. She continued working in a Cubist idiom and exhibited her canvases at the Knave of Diamonds exhibition of 1914, Tramway V, and 0.10. By the end of November 1916 her affiliation to Malevich and Suprematism was established. She joined the group which gathered around Malevich in 1916-17 with the aim of publishing *Supremus*, conceived as a Suprematist magazine. Under the influence of Suprematism Udal'tsova not only produced Suprematist canvases and gouaches but also applied the brightly coloured geometric shapes (and fragments of these) to designs for handbags, fabrics and dresses. In 1917 Udal'tsova participated in the decoration of the Kafe Pittoresk in Moscow with Yakulov and Tatlin. In 1918, Udal'tsova became a member of the Moscow Section of IZO and was very active in assisting in the decoration of Moscow for May Day 1918. From 1918 she also taught at the State Free Art Studios. In 1920 she became acquainted with the painter Aleksandr Drevin whom she subsequently married. Udal'tsova was an active member of the Moscow INKhUK but she and her husband left the Institute in 1921 in protest against the dominating position of the Constructivist credo within that body. Drevin and Udal'tsova maintained the primacy of painting and early in the 1920s became committed to a return to the object in painting. From 1921 until 1930 Udal'tsova taught in the Painting faculty at VKhUTEMAS.

VESNIN, Aleksandr Aleksandrovich
(1883-1959)

Born in Yur'evets on the Volga, Aleksandr Vesnin worked as a painter and designer but also, and primarily, as an architect, frequently in partnership with his brothers Leonid (1880-1933) and Viktor (1882-1950). Between 1907 and 1911 Aleksandr Vesnin had studied painting with the Impressionists Tsionglinskii and Yuon. In 1912 he graduated from the Institute of Civil Engineers, St Petersburg, and from 1912 worked in Tatlin's studio in Moscow, where he met Popova, Udal'tsova and other avant-garde artists. In 1913-14 he visited Italy. The pre-revolutionary architectural work of the Vesnin brothers was eclectic, including the classical Sirotkin House at Nizhnii Novgorod for which Aleksandr painted the ceiling and a stripped style functionally determined by the frame construction for commercial and industrial buildings. Some time during 1916-17 Aleksandr served in the army. For May Day 1918 he collaborated with Viktor on decorations for Moscow's Red Square and later all three brothers were involved in designing a base for Aleshin's monument to Karl Marx. In 1920, with Lyubov' Popova, Aleksandr designed a mass festival in honour of the Third Congress of the Comintern, which never took place. Aleksandr Vesnin was a member of the Moscow INKhUK and in 1921 was one of those artists who adopted Osip Brik's call for INKhUK members to 'commence real practical work in production'. In 1921 Vesnin had participated in the $5 \times 5 = 25$ exhibition where he displayed 'Structures of Coloured Space by means of Lines of Force'. In April 1922 he delivered a paper to INKhUK outlining his 'Credo' by which he attempted to extend the principles of Constructivism towards the scale of architecture. From 1921 Vesnin taught at the Moscow VKhUTEMAS, where together with Popova, he taught colour construction (later the plane and colour *kontsentr*) on the Basic Course, and drawing and colour in the Woodwork faculty. He also taught in the Architecture faculty. In 1922-3 Vesnin designed the set for *The Man who was Thursday* at the Kamernyi Theatre, Moscow, as an asymmetrical, industrially inspired skeletal construction. This clarity of structural articulation seems to have been influential in determining the final form for the Vesnin brothers' Palace of Labour project of 1923. In 1925 Aleksandr, Leonid and Viktor Vesnin formed together with Moisei Ginzburg the nucleus of the group of architectural Constructivists, OSA, which extended the principles of the First Working Group of Constructivists into architecture. Ginzburg, the theoretician of architectural Constructivism and evolver of its 'functional method' with Aleksandr Vesnin, the practical experimenter, edited OSA's journal *Contemporary Architecture (Sovremennaya arkhitektura – SA)*. During the 1920s the Vesnin brothers were very influential as teachers at the VKhUTEMAS and as designers of projects for various competitions including the Moscow Office of the *Leningrad pravda*, the Arkos auction house and the telegraph offices. In 1928 Aleksandr Vesnin joined the October group and in the 1930s taught at the Moscow Architectural Institute.

NOTES TO THE TEXT

NOTES TO THE INTRODUCTION

1. G. Rickey, *Constructivism: Origins and Evolution* (London, 1967).
2. S. Bann, *The Tradition of Constructivism* (London, 1974), p. 177.
3. I. Matsa, *Sovetskoe iskusstvo za 15 let. Materialy i dokumentatsiya* (Moscow and Leningrad, 1933).
4. *Konstruktivisty. K. K. Medunetskii, V. A. Stenberg, G. A. Stenberg* (Moscow, Kafe Poetov, 1922).
5. 'Programma uchebnoi podgruppy rabochei gruppy konstruktivistov INKhUKa', 1921, MS, private archive, Moscow.
6. *ibid.*
7. A. B. Nakov, *2 Stenberg 2* (London, Annely Juda Fine Art, 1975).
8. See 'Programma uchebnoi podgruppy konstruktivistov INKhUKa', 1921, MS, private archive, Moscow, where the term is first used.

NOTES TO CHAPTER ONE

1. A. Kemeny in 'Protokol zasedaniya INKhUKa', 8 December 1921, MS, private archive, Moscow. See also C. Gray, *The Great Experiment: Russian Art, 1863–1922* (London, 1962), p. 140, and subsequent commentators.
2. A. Abramova, 'Tatlin – (1885–1958). K vos'midesyatiletiyu so dnya rozhdeniya', *Dekorativnoe iskusstvo*, No. 2, 1966, pp. 5–7.
3. Some of these were later placed in the State Archive of Literature and Art (TsGALI), Moscow.
4. See the catalogue *V. E. Tatlin: Zasluzhennyi deyatel' iskusstv RSFSR 1885–1953. Katalog vystavki proizvedenii* (Moscow, 1977), p. 1.
5. This is according to the card Tatlin completed for the Moscow Union of Artists (*Moskovskii soyuz sovetskikh khudozhnikov*) of which he joined the theatrical section in 1932 ('Lichnaya kartochka chlena MOSSKha. Tatlin, Vladimir Evgrafovich', 1951, GTG, 59/2874). Further biographical information is supplied by *Mastera sovetskoi arkhitektury ob arkhitekture* (Moscow, 1975), vol. 2, pp. 68–75; Troels Andersen, *Vladimir Tatlin* (Stockholm, Moderna Museet, 1968); and *V. E. Tatlin*. The latter states that Tatlin left the Moscow School in 1903 (*V. E. Tatlin*, p. 2).
6. This is according to an information form entitled 'Svedenie' filled out by Tatlin, GTG 91/223.
7. See D. E. Gordon, *Modern Art Exhibitions, 1900–1916* (Munich, 1974), vol. 2.
8. The date of 1913 is given for Tatlin's work *The Bottle* by Andersen, *Vladimir Tatlin*, p. 34. The 1977 catalogue gives 1913 as the year Tatlin began working on the reliefs (*V.E. Tatlin*, p. 3). Nikolai Khardzhiev insists that Tatlin's first counter-relief was constructed not in 1913 but in 1914, after Tatlin's visit to Picasso's studio in Paris, where the latter's three-dimensional works provided the direct inspiration for Tatlin's reliefs ('Appunti', *Paragone (Arte)*, Vol. 16, No. 183, May 1966, p. 77). On the other hand, E. F. Kovtun suggests that Tatlin began working on the reliefs as early as 1912 ('Iz istorii russkogo avangarda (P. N. Filonov)', in *Ezhegodnik rukopisnogo otdela pushkinskogo doma na 1977 god* (Leningrad, 1979), p. 217). This is almost certainly too early since Tatlin exhibited them for the first time at the First Exhibition of Painterly Reliefs (Pervaya vystavka rel'efov 1913–14) held at his studio on the Ostozhenka (No. 37) between 10 and 14 May 1914 (*V. E. Tatlin*, p. 4). Subsequently he exhibited them at the Tramway V exhibition of 1915 where he showed six reliefs dated 1914 and one relief of 1915 (Gordon, *Modern Art Exhibitions*, Vol. 2, p. 869). The earliest date given to the reliefs in the contemporary literature was 1913–14 which was given in the brochure *Vladimir Evgrafovich Tatlin* (Petrograd, 1915). Since this date applies to the type of reliefs which were already more abstract than *The Bottle*, this suggests that the second half of 1913 is a not unlikely date for that work and for Tatlin commencing work on the reliefs.
9. This explanation was presented by Camilla Gray and has generally been adopted by subsequent commentators (Gray, *Great Experiment*, p. 146, and Andersen, 'Notes on Tatlin', in *Vladimir Tatlin*, pp. 6–7, 12).

There are tremendous difficulties concerning the precise dating of Tatlin's trip to Paris. The date given by Tatlin himself is very vague – 1913–14 ('Lichnaya kartochka chlena MOSSKha. Tatlin, Vladimir Evgrafovich', 1951, GTG, 59/2874). Gray gives late 1913 for Tatlin's visit to Paris (*Great Experiment*, p. 144). Andersen gives 1913 for the trip generally and suggests that Tatlin may have travelled to Berlin in April 1913, citing as evidence a card to Shkol'nik, the secretary of the Union of Youth group, which reports that Tatlin will not be in Moscow from 26 April 1913 (*Vladimir Tatlin*, p. 12). A date as early as 1912 has been suggested for Tatlin's visit to the West (*Mastera sovetskoi arkhitektury*, Vol. 2, p. 69). However, it is more likely that Tatlin went to Paris in the spring or summer of 1913 (*V. E. Tatin*, p. 3). Dating Tatlin's visit to the spring and summer of 1913 would be appropriate since Picasso would then still have been occupying the studio at 242 Boulevard Raspail of which photographs exist showing some of his constructions *in situ*, such as

The Guitar surrounded by drawings ('Oeuvres et images inédites de la jeunesse de Picasso', *Cahiers d'Art*, No. 11, 1950, pp. 281-2). There is no evidence to suggest that after Picasso moved his studio to 5 bis rue Schoelcher he reinstated the constructions in the same way.

Some fascinating stories concerning this visit to the West are preserved in the memoirs of contemporaries. Valentina Khodasevich relates how in Berlin Tatlin apparently posed as a blind bandore player at the exhibition of Russian folk art, and that, despite the fact that he was a great success and carefully saved his money for France, he was too poor to stay in Paris long ('Bylo . . .', *Dekorativnoe iskusstvo*, No. 3, 1980, p. 40). Gray says that while Tatlin was in his guise as blind musician in Berlin Kaiser Wilhelm gave him a gold watch (*Great Experiment*, p. 144). According to the sculptor Lipchitz, when Tatlin visited him in Paris in 1913 Tatlin asked Lipchitz to take him to see Picasso. Evidently impressed by what he had seen, or dismayed by Picasso's refusal to employ him as a servant, Tatlin suddenly sat down on the pavement as they walked home and mumbled, 'There's something behind it . . . I'll break his neck for him' (A. M. Hammacher, *Jacques Lipchitz* (New York, 1970), p. 69). Picasso in conversation with Larionov confirmed that Tatlin had visited him and that Tatlin had also asked to work as Picasso's servant so that he could stay in France longer (D. Vallier, 'L'Art abstrait en Russie. Ses origines – ses premières manifestations 1910-1917', *Cahiers d'art*, No. 33/5, 1960, p. 285). D. Danin's memories of Tatlin's own recollections suggest that Tatlin presented himself as a musician to Picasso playing for him on his bandore and that Picasso gave him some tubes of paint ('Uletavl', *Druzhba narodov*, No. 2, 1979, p. 223).

10. Tatlin, 'Svedenie', p. 1, and Tatlin 'Anketnyi list', 14 January 1919, TsGALI, fond 680, op. 1, ed. khr. 1018, list 432.

11. Picasso, untitled works, Nos. 104-7, at the Knave of Diamonds (Bubnovyi valet) exhibition, January 1912; Picasso, *Composition* (gouache), No. 101, Knave of Diamonds, March-April 1913; and Picasso, *Nature morte* (drawing), No. 112, Knave of Diamonds, January-February 1914 (Gordon, *Modern Art Exhibitions*, Vol. 2, pp. 539, 686, 786). Shchukin bought *Friendship* (1908) in 1913 and by the end of 1913 his collection contained forty canvases by Picasso including *Woman with a Fan* (1908), *The Factory at Horta del Ebro* (1909) and *Three Women* (1909), all now in the Hermitage Museum, Leningrad. The date for the purchase of Picasso's *Friendship* is given in W. Rubin, ed., *Pablo Picasso: A Retrospective* (New York, Museum of Modern Art, 1980), p. 88. For the contents of Shchukin's collection, see Ya. Tugendkhol'd, 'Frantsuzskoe sobranie S. I. Shchukina', *Apollon*, No. 1/2, 1914. The list of works which Tugendkhol'd gives is reprinted in V. Marcadé, *Le Renouveau de l'art pictural russe* (Lausanne, 1971), pp. 271-7. Picasso's works in the collection appear on p. 276.

12. This painting is usually dated 1911-12. John Golding on stylistic grounds attributed it to 1912 (*Cubism: A History and an Analysis, 1907-1914* (London, 1971), p. 103, nn. 1-2). It is dated to May 1912 in Rubin, *Picasso*, p. 156.

13. For the story behind this development, see Golding, *Cubism*, p. 103.

14. G. Apollinaire, *Les Peintres cubistes* (Geneva, 1950), p. 7. Although collage existed long before it was adopted by the Cubists, Cubism elevated it to the point of being accepted as high art and made it an artistically respectable technique. During the nineteenth century, scrapbooks employed collage techniques often incorporating photographs.

15. *ibid.*, p. 39.

16. Golding, *Cubism*, p. 104; quoted from Sabartès, *Picasso* (London, 1949), p. 241.

17. Golding, *Cubism*, p. 105.

18. *ibid.* As Golding points out, the use of extraneous material, the exploration of unorthodox technical procedures, and the ability to see the aesthetic possibilities in objects and materials hitherto not thought to have any artistic value led to the 'ready-mades' of Dada and to the Surrealists' *objets trouvés* and the juxtaposition of incongruous materials to evoke new sensations and images.

19. As for example *The Guitar* of 1912 and the less descriptive *Bottle and Guitar* of 1913. A few examples of Picasso's constructions were photographed by Kahnweiler and reproduced by Apollinaire in *Les Soirées de Paris*, No. 18, 15 November 1913.

20. Troels Andersen, *Malevich* (Amsterdam, Stedelijk Museum, 1970), pp. 70, 92.

21. *Vselenskaya voina* (Petrograd, 1916). See *From Surface to Space: Russia, 1916-1924* (Cologne, Galerie Gmurzynska, 1974), pp. 126-9, and *Twentieth Century Russian Paintings, Drawings and Watercolours, 1900-1930* (London, Sotheby and Co., 12 April 1972), pp. 78-9.

22. (Moscow, 1919). See E. Kovtun, 'Varvara Stepanova's Anti-Book', in *From Surface to Space*, pp. 57-63. One copy of the book is reproduced in that catalogue on pp. 143-50.

23. TsGALI, fond 2089, op. 1, ed. khr. 2.

24. Alina Vasil'evna Abramova, who initiated contemporary Soviet research into the 1920s and Soviet design, has completed an extensive study of Tatlin where she discusses this type of difficulty ('Tatlin', 1960s, MS, private archive, Moscow).

25. Andersen, *Vladimir Tatlin*, p. 50, and *V. E. Tatlin*, p. 29. The latter gives the title as *Painterly Relief: Panel No. 1 (Zhivopisnyi rel'ef. Doska No. 1)*.

26. According to Khardzhiev there exists a Cubist drawing by Tatlin which was inscribed by Malevich: 'A Drawing by Tatlin. He took lessons in Cubism from me. K.M.' (*K istorii russkogo avangarda* (Stockholm, 1976), p. 88). Khardzhiev, moreover, suggests that Tatlin's experimentation with Cubism took place under Malevich's supervision prior to Tatlin's experimentation with the reliefs.

27. The date of 1913 for *The Nude* is taken from N. Punin, *Tatlin (Protiv kubizma)* (Petrograd, 1921). However, the dating of the other painting presents some problems. The title *Moryak. Avtoportret* is given by Andersen, although he does not date the painting (*Vladimir Tatlin*, p. 31). Punin called it simply *The Sailor (Matros)* and dated it 1912. It may therefore be the painting exhibited as *The Sailor* at the Union of Youth exhibition from 27 December 1911 until 23 January 1912 (*Soyuz molodezhi*, St Petersburg, No. 84; Gordon, *Modern Art Exhibitions*, Vol. 2, p. 526). On the other hand, Tatlin exhibited a *Self-Portrait* at the Donkey's Tail exhibition in Moscow between 24 March and 21 April 1912 (*Oslinyi khvost*, No. 256; Gordon, *Modern Art Exhibitions*, Vol. 2, p. 566). These titles most probably refer to the same painting. If they do, this would suggest that *The Sailor: A Self-Portrait* was produced in 1911 (probably in late 1911); if not, that it was produced at the beginning of 1912. Although the curvilinear quality of forms and space is less pronounced in *The Sailor: A Self-Portrait*, than in *The Fish Seller* of *c.*1911, the striking similarities in the handling of the paint in these two works and the richness of textures created, makes it tempting to suggest that

the two works were produced within a relatively short space of time during the winter of 1911–12.
28. N. Punin, 'Obzor techenii v iskusstve Peterburga', *Russkoe iskusstvo*, No. 1, 1923, p. 18. The art historian Nikolai Khardzhiev also shares the view that for Tatlin's painting *The Nude* (1913) the influence of Russian artistic traditions was more important than Western innovations ('Appunti', *Paragone (Arte)*, Vol. 16, No. 183, May 1965, p. 77).
29. D. Danin recalled this in his memoirs of Tatlin ('Tatlin', MS, private archive, Moscow, p. 4, and Danin, 'Uletavl', p. 222). This would tend to discredit Camilla Gray's suggestion that Tatlin discovered icon painting through Goncharova (*Great Experiment*, p. 142). However, it is likely that Goncharova with her extensive social contacts, would have been able to facilitate Tatlin's entry to view private icon collections which may otherwise have been closed to him.
30. *Vystavka drevne russkogo iskusstva, ustroennaya v 1913 godu v oznamenovanie chestvovaniya 300-letiya tsarstvovaniya doma Romanovykh* (Moscow, 1913). The icon impressed Matisse also when he visited Moscow in 1911. Matisse praised the icons as 'authentic popular art'. He is reported to have said, 'Here is the primary source of artistic endeavour. The modern artist should derive inspiration from these primitives.' Such words reported in the Russian press undoubtedly underlined the Russian avant-garde's interest in its native heritage ('Matiss o Moskve', *Utro Rossii*, 27 October 1911; translation taken from Yu. Rusakov, 'Matisse in Russia in the Autumn of 1911', *Burlington Magazine* May 1975, p. 288). Although Matisse made this statement during his visit to Russia in November 1911, this would not necessarily have been the first time he had seen Russian icons. N. Khardzhiev argues that he may have encountered Russian icons in Paris in 1906 at the exhibition of Russian art organised by Diaghilev ('Matiss o russkikh khudozhnikakh', *Iskusstvo*, No. 12, 1969, p. 58). The inclusion of icons in that exhibition serves to indicate the consistent interest taken in these native artefacts by progressive Russian artists since the turn of the century.
31. The Futurists collected and exhibited children's art. They were also responsible for the discovery of the now celebrated Georgian primitive artist Pirosmanashvili, whose work, from the collections of Le Dantyu and Il'ya Zdanevich, they displayed at the Target exhibition (*Mishen'*) in Moscow, April 1913 (Gordon, *Modern Art Exhibitions*, Vol. 2, p. 709). It is interesting to note a parallel interest among Futurist poets. Roman Jakobson recalled that he collected children's folklore and incantations which contained sounds liberated from meaning which were completely *zaumnye* ('Art and Poetry: The Cubo-Futurists', in S. Barron and M. Tuchman, eds., *The Avant-Garde in Russia 1910–1930: New Perspectives* (London and Cambridge, Mass., 1980), p. 18).
32. B. Lubetkin, 'The Origins of Constructivism', lecture given to Cambridge University School of Architecture, 1 May 1969, tape recording. There are no extant reliefs which correspond to this description by Lubetkin; however, this is not proof that such reliefs did not exist. The use of the wallpaper in *The Bottle* relief could well have had this kind of antecedent. It is clear that Tatlin himself sought to place his work in the context of Russian as opposed to Western art. In this early period before Lubetkin's departure from Russia there are no grounds to suppose that Tatlin would give his work this Russian emphasis for political reasons. In his lecture Lubetkin dated the icon exhibition 1912.

33. V. Markov, *Printsipy tvorchestva v plasticheskikh iskusstvakh. Faktura* (St Petersburg, 1914), pp. 54, 56, 60. This quotation was first suggested by Jean-Paul Marcadé to Margit Rowell (M. Rowell, 'Vladimir Tatlin: Form/Faktura', *October*, No. 7, 1978, p. 94 text and n. 21). I have retranslated the text.
34. Punin, *Tatlin*, p.
35. V. Khodasevich, 'Bylo . . .', *Dekorativnoe iskusstvo*, No. 3, 1980, p. 41. Khodasevich's account of Tatlin working does suggest a very intuitive and spontaneous creative relationship with the material. However, the existence of sketches by Tatlin which are related to the reliefs, and which in some cases seem to be preliminary studies for the corner counter-reliefs, implies that Tatlin did not always work in the way Khodasevich describes (see A. Rudenstine, ed., *Russian Avant-Garde Art: The George Costakis Collection* (London, 1981), Nos. 1109, 1111; and *Constructivism and the Geometric Tradition: Selections from The McCrory Corporation Collection* (New York, 1979), No. 186 illustrated p. 19).
36. Khodasevich, 'Bylo . . .', p. 41.
37. Gray, *Great Experiment*, pp. 178–9, and I. Puni, *Sovremennaya zhivopis'* (Berlin, 1923), p. 30.
38. The Russian Futurists had used wallpaper to print their early literary manifestos such as *Sadok Sudei*. It was also used in Cubist collages by Picasso and Braque. Thus the material itself here represents a very concrete link with the indigenous and foreign avant-garde movements which dominated Tatlin's artistic environment.
39. These are the captions given in the brochure *Vladimir Evgrafovich Tatlin*, p. 2. They are subtitled here 'Pervaya vystavka rel'efov' 1913–14'. It should be noted that these are both dated 1914 by Andersen in *Vladimir Tatlin*, p. 35. The whereabouts of both are unknown.
40. Andersen, *Vladimir Tatlin*, p. 41. Originally illustrated in Punin, *Tatlin*.
41. Andersen, *Vladimir Tatlin*, p. 49.
42. The brochure *Vladimir Evgrafovich Tatlin* subtitled two works (plates 1.8–9) 'painterly reliefs' (*zhivopisnye rel'efy*) followed in parentheses by 'The First Exhibition of Reliefs, 1913–1914' (Pervaya vystavka rel'efov, 1913–1914). The three other works illustrated in the brochure were of a more intensively three-dimensional nature and each bore the title *Corner Counter-Relief* (*Uglovoi kontr-rel'ef*) and the date 1914–15.
43. S. I. Isakov, 'K "kontr-rel'efam" Tatlina', *Novyi zhurnal dlya vsekh*, No. 12, 1915, and A. A. Strigalev, 'O nekotorykh novykh terminakh v russkom iskusstve XX veka', *Problemy istorii sovetskoi arkhitektury*, No. 2, 1976, p. 67.
44. *Vladimir Evgrafovich Tatlin*, pp. 1–3, gives this title to the works.
45. See Punin, *Tatlin*, and Andersen, *Vladimir Tatlin*, p. 42. In the latter it is titled *Hanging Corner-Relief. Selection of Materials: Iron, Aluminium, Primer* (*Visyashchii uglovoi rel'ef. Material'nyi podbor: zhelezo, alyuminii, levkas*). However, a comparison of this plate with that reproduced in the brochure *Vladimir Evgrafovich Tatlin*, p. 3, would indicate that they are the same relief. Therefore I have adopted the dating and title as given in the brochure. It is interesting to note that Nikolai Tarabukin, writing in 1922, mentioned that after the 'corner counter-relief' Tatlin created a 'central counter-relief'. Tarabukin considers this to have created a far more active relationship with the spatial environment than the corner counter-relief because it broke not only with the plane but also with the wall and this could be viewed from more than one position. He therefore compares it with the work of the ОВМОКhU

artists Medunetskii and Vladimir and Georgii Stenberg (*Ot mol'berta k mashine* (Moscow, 1923), p. 9). This would imply a completely free-standing or free-hanging relief. There are no photographs of any reliefs by Tatlin which exactly answer this description. However, Punin's list of Tatlin's work includes a central relief. It is possible that this refers to plate 1.9, which is not affixed to a wall but may have been affixed to a convex corner of a wall, thus allowing different angles of vision within about 250 degrees as opposed to the more limited range of viewpoint for the corner counter-relief (Plate 1.13).

46. U. Boccioni, 'The Technical Manifesto of Futurist Sculpture', 1912; translation taken from U. Apollonio, ed., *Futurist Manifestos* (London, 1973), p. 52.

47. *ibid.*, p. 63.

48. *ibid.*

49. V. E. Tatlin, T. Shapiro, I. Meerzon and P. Vinogradov, 'Nasha predstoyashchaya rabota', *VIII s'ezd sovetov. Ezhednevnyi byulleten' s'ezda VTsIK*, No. 13, 1 January 1921, p. 11.

50. According to Khardzhiev, Marinetti's First Futurist Manifesto which appeared in *Le Figaro* on 20 February 1909 was published in Russia soon after ('Appunti', pp. 78–80). A report on Italian Futurism which included a Russian translation of 'Futurist Painting. The Technical Manifesto' ('La pittura futurista, Manifesto tecnico'), which had been signed by Boccioni, Carrà, Russolo, Balla and Severini, appeared in *Apollon* in 1910 (P. Buzzi, 'Pis'ma iz Italii', *Apollon*, No. 9, 1910, pp. 17–18). Russian translations of 'The Exhibitors to the Public' ('Gli espositori al pubblico') and the Manifesto of Futurist Painting were printed in *Soyuz molodezhi*, No. 2, 1912, pp. 23–8, 29–35. More extensive collections of Futurist manifestos were published in Russia in 1914 (V. Shershenevich, *Manifesty italianskogo futurizma. Sobranie manifestov* (Moscow, 1914), and G. Tasteven, *Futurizm* (Moscow, 1914)). Tasteven's collection included five manifestos, three of which were also contained in Shershenevich's. Tasteven's publication of his commentary on Futurism and his collection of manuscripts were perhaps motivated by his friendship with Marinetti, and, according to Khardzhiev it was Tasteven in Paris in 1913 who invited Marinetti to visit Russia. Marinetti arrived in Moscow on 26 January 1914. He spoke at the Polytechnic Museum and at the Small Hall of the Conservatoire on 27 and 28 January 1914. In St Petersburg he spoke at the Kalashnikov Stock Exchange on 1 and 4 February (Khardzhiev, 'Appunti', pp. 78–80). Press coverage was extensive (*Rannee utro*, 25 January 1914; *Vechernie izvestiya*, 25 January 1914; *Nov'*, 27 January 1914; *Nov'*, 29 January 1914). A lively account of the visit is provided by B. Livshits in Chapter 7 ('My i zapad') of his memoirs (*Polutoraglazyi strelets* (Leningrad, 1933), pp. 211–56). A well annotated English translation is provided by J. Bowlt in B. Livshits, *The One and A Half Eyed Archer* (Newtonville, 1977), pp. 181–213.

51. Gordon, *Modern Art Exhibitions*, Vol. 2, p. 724, and Sillart', 'Vystavka futuristskoi skul'ptury Bochchioni', *Apollon*, No. 7, 1913, pp. 61–3.

52. Punin, *Tatlin*, p. 5.

53. D'yakonitsyn has suggested a relationship between the Rayism of Larionov and Goncharova, their works *Rayist glass* and *Mirror* and Tatlin's scientific and technological investigations in his painterly reliefs. D'yakonitsyn does, however, stress the ambiguous aspect of these experiments from the ideological point of view (*Ideinye protivorechiya russkoi zhivopisi kontsa 19 – nachala 20 vekov* (Perm', 1966), p. 161, n. 417).

54. M. Larionov and N. Goncharova, 'Luchisty i budushchniki. Manifest'; printed in V. Parkin, *Oslinyi khvost i mishen'* (Moscow, 1913), p. 13. Rayism is the literal translation of *luchizm, luch* meaning a ray. Rayonism, often used instead of Rayism, comes from the French for *luch – un rayon*.

55. Tatlin illustrated A. Kruchenykh and V. Khlebnikov, *The World Backwards* (*Mir s kontsa*, Moscow, 1912), and V. Mayakovskii, V. Khlebnikov and A. Kruchenykh, *The Missal of the Three* (*Trebnik troikh*, Moscow, 1913).

56. *Vladimir Evgrafovich Tatlin*, pp. 2–3. This brochure was written with Tatin's full co-operation and approval. It has sometimes been assumed that he was the author of the text. Zhadova, however, suggests that it was written by Udal'tsova and Tatlin ('Tatlin – proektirovshchik material'noi kul'tury', in *Sovetskoe dekorativnoe iskusstvo* (Moscow, 1980), p. 205, n. 6).

57. *Poslednyaya futuristicheskaya vystavka kartin, 0.10. Katalog vystvaki* (Petrograd, 1915), Nos. 132–44. See also Gordon, *Modern Art Exhibitions*, Vol. 2, p. 885.

58. E. Adamov, 'Pis'mo iz Moskvy', *Kievskaya mysl'*, 6 May 1915, p. 2; translation taken from Andersen, *Vladimir Tatlin*, pp. 6–7.

59. Punin, *Tatlin*, p. 14.

60. *Tramvai V. Pervaya futuristicheskaya vystavka kartin. Katalog vystavki* (Petrograd, 1915), No. 54, and Gordon, *Modern Art Exhibitions*, Vol. 2, p. 868. For a discussion of this work, see H. Berninger and J. A. Cartier, *Jean Pougny (Iwan Puni) 1892–1956 Catalogue de l'oeuvre, Tome 1: Les Années d'avant-garde, Russie-Berlin, 1910–1923* (Tübingen, 1972), pp. 44–5. The construction which contained a hammer was No. 57 in the Catalogue of the 0.10 exhibition.

61. *0.10 Katalog vystavki*, Nos. 98–120. Puni also showed paintings (Nos. 116–20). Puni had been responsible for the organisation of this exhibition and with his wife Kseniya Boguslavskaya he issued a declaration. An original copy of this printed statement is housed in the Fondation Pougny at the Bibliothèque Nationale, Paris. It is also reprinted in Berninger and Cartier, *Pougny*, p. 52. At the exhibition Puni aligned himself with Malevich; Tatlin exhibited alone.

62. K. Boguslavskaya and I. Puni, 'Deklaratsiya', 1915, in Berninger and Cartier, *Pougny*, p. 52.

63. I. Klyun, untitled declaration issued at 0.10 exhibition; reproduced in Berninger and Cartier, *Pougny*, p. 53.

64. *0.10. Katalog*, No. 24, and Gordon, *Modern Art Exhibitions*, vol. 2, p. 883. This work is now lost and presumably was destroyed. It is known only from press cuttings (see Berninger and Cartier, *Pougny*, p. 65). Sketches survive in Klyun's oeuvre catalogue in the Costakis Collection (see Rudenstine, *Russian Avant-Garde*, Nos. 257, 261).

65. *0.10. Katalog*, No. 23, and Gordon, *Modern Art Exhibitions*, Vol. 2, p. 883. This construction was in the Costakis Collection until 1977 when it was donated to the Tret'yakov Gallery, Moscow (see Rudenstine, *Russian Avant-Garde*, Nos. 132–5).

66. Rudenstine, *Russian Avant-Garde*, in particular No. 294, but see also Nos. 287–98. In all these works pure integral, geometric forms are given three dimensionality. Some of the mobiles (see No. 296) suggest other interests and points of departure which were never exploited. The complete abstraction of these works seems dependent on the formal vocabulary of Suprematism, and colour would perhaps have played a major role. Rozanova's abstract sculptures also exhibited at 0.10 and now also lost are known only through sketches in the Costakis Collection (Rudenstine,

Russian Avant-Garde, Nos. 1036–40). However, their abstract qualities are very advanced.

67. A. Rodtchenko, 'Vladimir Tatlin', *Opus International*, No. 4, 1967, p. 16.

68. This work was illustrated in *Izobrazitel'noe iskusstvo*, No. 1, 1919, p. 33. There is no evidence that it is still extant. A clearer documentary photograph of this construction is held by George Costakis.

69. Reproduced in Gray, *Great Experiment*, pl. 177. Since this work is known to me only through this illustration, I do not know its Russian title.

70. Bruni's work in paintings which was concurrent with such constructions is attested to by canvases like *The Rainbow* (*Raduga*) of 1916, also illustrated in *Izobrazitel'noe iskusstvo*, No. 1, 1919, p. 26.

71. This work was destroyed. It was apparently photographed in Tatlin's studio in Petrograd.

72. N. Punin, 'Kvartira No. 5', MS, private archive, Leningrad. Punin's account has been amplified by information kindly given to me by Bruni's widow, Nina Konstantinovna Bruni, Moscow, April 1978.

73. Shapiro later became an architect and was responsible for building various public buildings such as the Public Baths in Leningrad. It was he who reconstructed the model of Tatlin's Tower for the Tatlin exhibition in Moscow of 1977.

74. Rodchenko acknowledged Tatlin as his master (Rodtchenko 'Vladimir Tatlin', p. 19).

75. Quoted by S. Bojko, 'Rodchenko's Early Spatial Constructions', in *From Surface to Space*, p. 16.

76. *ibid.*

77. This exhibition was subtitled 'Non Objective Creation and Suprematism'. The other participants were Malevich, Klyun, Popova, Rozanova and A. Vesnin. See *Katalog desyatoi gosudarstvennoi vystavki. Bespredmetnoe tvorchestvo i Suprematizm* (Moscow, 1919). Rodchenko's folding works were apparently nos. 214–16. These were made of plywood and painted white. Rodchenko also exhibited *Coloured Non-Objective Sculpture* (*Tsvetnaya bespredmetnaya skul'ptura*), apparently Nos. 217–19. The complete list of Rodchenko exhibits at this exhibition is reprinted in I. Matsa, *Sovetskoe iskusstvo za 15 let. Materialy i dokumentatsiya* (Moscow and Leningrad, 1933), pp. 113–14.

78. A. M. Rodchenko, 'Liniya', MS, private archive, Moscow. Originally written as a paper for INKhUK in 1921 (on INKhUK, see Chapter Three), it was later revised for publication, though it never appeared. A translation of one of these versions of the article is to be found in *From Surface to Space*, pp. 65–7, another was published with a commentary by A. B. Nakov in *Arts Magazine* Vol. 47, No. 7, 1973, pp. 50–2.

79. The *Black on Black* series was part of a whole series of works by Rodchenko based on an abstract investigation of colour. At the Tenth State Exhibition of 1918, he had exhibited numerous works executed in 1918. They had titles such as *Movement of Colour from Form* (*Dvizhenie tsveta ot formy*, no. 187) and *The Abstraction of Colour* (*Abstraktsiya tsveta*, nos. 205–13) (Matsa, *Sovetskoe iskusstvo*, pp. 113–14).

80. Rodchenko, 'Liniya'; translation taken from *From Surface to Space*, p. 66. In this text Rodchenko states explicitly that he is referring to works he created in 1917–18.

81. On OBMOKhU (Society of Young Artists) and its exhibitions, see Chapter Two.

82. Reproduced in *Kino-Fot* and dated 1921.

83. Reproduced in *Kino-Fot*, No. 2, 1922, with the date 1920.

84. Bojko mentions six, but appears to be referring to one construction under two titles, i.e. as 'oval' and 'ellipse'. I have only found pictorial evidence that one construction to which this description could be applied was made (see Bojko, 'Rodchenko's Early Spatial Constructions', p. 17). *Ellipse* is the only one of Rodchenko's constructions to be preserved. It now forms part of the Costakis Collection (see Rudenstine, *Russian Avant-Garde*, No. 1019).

85. This was confirmed by Rodchenko's daughter, V. A. Rodchenko, in the spring of 1974.

86. Conversation with Vladimir Stenberg, November 1974.

87. Rodchenko, 'Liniya'. On the formation of the First Working Group of Constructivists in March 1921, see Chapter Three.

88. Rodchenko's statement in *5 × 5 = 25. Katalog vystavki* (Moscow, 1921).

89. See N. Rozanova, *Petr Miturich* (Moscow, 1972).

90. The art critic Nikolai Punin mentions Miturich's portrait of Lur'e in his autobiographical notes entitled 'Flat No. 5' ('Kvartira No. 5'). Punin's notes are based on the meetings which took place between all the artists of Petrograd in 1915–16 in the Academy of Arts flat of Lev Bruni where Miturich also lived and worked. Among those who regularly gathered in the evenings in Bruni's studio were the immediate circle around Bruni, which included L'vov who was in the army, Punin, Lur'e, Mandel'shtam, Klyuev, Tyrs and Mitrokhin. Punin recalls that on certain evenings they were joined by Puni, Tatlin, Klyun, Popova, Udal'tsova, and Rozanova who brought news of artistic developments in Moscow.

91. Punin, 'Kvartira No. 5', p. 7.

92. There are no other collages by Miturich and there is no indication to suggest that he worked extensively in this medium. On the contrary, there is every reason to believe that this was a unique and eccentric work. It seems not irrelevant to note that in the 1920s when many Constructivist artists were working in photomontage Miturich, as far as I know, never did any photomontage work at all.

93. Rozanova, *Miturich*, p. 7.

94. This work was an illustration to the music by the composer Lur'e. According to his memoirs posthumously published in 1969, Lur'e produced his music *Our March* (*Nash Marsh*) under the 'spontaneous influence' of Mayakovskii's poem of the same name, written in January 1918 ('Nash Marsh', *Novyi Zhurnal* (New York), No. 94, 1969, p. 127). The music was dedicated to his Futurist colleagues (*ibid.*).

95. *Izobrazitel'noe iskusstvo*, No. 1, 1919. They are illustrated on pp. 31 and 35 respectively.

96. Identified by Mai Miturich, Petr Vasil'evich's son.

97. In the exhibition of 1968 two of Miturich's spatial paintings were exhibited, both from the Tret'yakov Gallery. One of these was possibly *Prostranstvennaya zhivopis'*, *No. 14* which was bought by the Museum Office of IZO (*Izobrazitel'noe iskusstvo*, No. 1, 1919, p. 31). I have had difficulty in identifying the other; it is, however, possibly *No. 20*, since I was informed that this was obtained by IZO.

98. Rozanova, *Miturich*, p. 7. It should be noted moreover that for this whole period Miturich continuously was a member of the armed forces, although in various capacities. In 1916 he joined the 11th Siberian Division at the front: he was in the Red Army in 1919 and working in the Moscow camouflage unit in 1920; in 1921 he was working in the painting studio of the Red Army on a design project for a barracks. In 1919 Miturich created a

whole series of cardboard cubes (*kubiki*) which he painted with a vast range of graphic designs: hatching strokes, faces, spots, squares and amorphous elements. The range of this exploration of line in its three-dimensional spatial form is indicated by plate 1.45.

99. For Khlebnikov's poetry, see V. Markov, 'Predislovie', in V. V. Chlebnikov, *Gesammelte Werke* (Munich, 1968), Vol. 1, pp. v–xii, and V. Markov, *Russian Futurism* (London, 1969). The relationship between Khlebnikov and Miturich is fully described in the latter's memoirs (Moe pervoe znakomstvo s Velimirom Khlebnikovym', MS, private archive, Moscow). Miturich's relationship with Khlebnikov was vital and fanatical. Isakov and Miturich drew Khlebnikov's *Vestnik predsedatelya zemylanogo shara* on stone to be reproduced in one hundred copies, when all means of publishing were out of Khlebnikov's reach. Miturich fed Khlebnikov and later nursed him. After Khlebnikov's death Miturich married Khlebnikov's sister, Vera, who was an artist.

100. Miturich, 'Moe pervoe', p. 1.

101. *ibid.*, p. 3. At this time Miturich was living with the Isakovs. In the photograph of his studio (plate 1.39), Sergei Isakov's works can be seen on the left-hand side. Miturich referred to Sergei Isakov as his pupil.

102. *ibid.*

103. *ibid.*, p. 12.

104. *ibid.* When Miturich photographed the works prior to destroying them he mounted them with title, date, etc. The numbering appears to be chronological and in sequence of production; however, there is no absolute proof of this. The plates reproduced here have been taken from these original photographs preserved in a private archive in Moscow.

105. This work was not destroyed. Each panel measures approximately one metre square; the background is now light grey, and the graphic elements are painted in white and a darker grey, possibly very dark blue. It was re-erected for the exhibition in the Tret'yakov Gallery in Moscow in 1968 (see catalogue, *P. V. Miturich: vystavka proizvedenii* (Moscow, 1968)).

106. N. Gabo letter to Dr Werner Hofmann, 12 August 1960, p. 1 (Gabo Papers, Beinecke Rare Book and Manuscript Library, Yale University). Gabo states that he attended Wölfflin's course during the academic year 1912–13. Wölfflin listed the museums and churches which Gabo was to visit and Gabo wrote a report which terminated his study of art history. In response to Dr Werner's inquiry about Worringer, Gabo wrote that he did not know him, but that Professor Lipps' ideas were popular at that time in Munich.

107. N. Gabo, 'The 1922 Soviet Exhibition', *Studio International*, Vol. 182/3, No. 938, p. 171. Also see S. E. Starr and K. Frampton, 'Russian Art in Revolution and Emigration: An Interview with Naum Gabo', unpublished text, Gabo Papers, Beinecke, Yale, pp. 14–15. In this interview Gabo states that he organised the three abstract rooms at the 1922 exhibition.

108. In Moscow, Pevsner did produce works with abstract forms and textural interests such as *Painting with Cork inlaid on Board*, 1923. However, he did not move away from the two-dimensional plane of the painting until he left Russia. His only work exhibited at Berlin was a still life, No. 149 (*Erste Russische Kunstausstellung* (Berlin, Galerie van Diemen, 1922), p. 20). No three-dimensional works by Pevsner were exhibited until June 1924 when in Paris he exhibited six, one of which was dated 1924 (*Constructivistes Russes Gabo et Pevsner: Peintures, Constructions* (Paris, Galerie Per-

cier, 1924), Nos. 10–15). In the introduction to the catalogue Waldemar George pointed out that Pevsner created high reliefs from a painted base. The two reproductions of Pevsner's work in the catalogue confirm this statement and present a logical extension from the textural paintings of 1923. As a contrast they serve to emphasise the fully three-dimensional qualities of Gabo's constructions.

109. N. Gabo, 'Sculpture: Carving and Constructing in Space', in *Gabo, Constructions, Sculpture, Paintings, Drawings, Engravings* (London, 1957), p. 168.

110. Title from *Gabo*, p. 82. In *Egyseg*, No. 2, 1922, p. 8, it was titled *Realist Composition, 1919*. A. Pevsner called it *Construction in a Niche* (*A Biographical Sketch of My Brothers, Naum Gabo and Antoine Pevsner* (Amsterdam, 1964), p. 26).

111. This construction was exhibited at Berlin in 1922 at the First Russian Art Exhibition (*Erste Russische Kunstausstellung*, No. 548, p. 30), and illustrated in the catalogue with the caption *Raumkonstruktion C*. (*Modell zu einer Glasplastik*) (*Spatial Construction C* (*Model for a Plastic Glass*). The title given in my text was the title later given by Gabo to this work in *Gabo*, fig. 17. This work was bought by Katherine Dreier and subsequently lost.

112. 'Russia and Constructivism' – an interview with Naum Gabo by Abram Lassaw and Ilya Bolotowsky, 1956, in *Gabo*, p. 159.

113. N. Gabo and N. Pevsner, *Realisticheskii manifest* (Moscow, 5 August 1920), was translated by Gabo as *The Realistic Manifesto*. The original printed Russian text is reproduced at approximately a quarter its real size in *Gabo*, p. 149, together with Gabo's English translation (*Gabo*, pp. 151–2). I have used Gabo's translation throughout. Although *The Realistic Manifesto* was signed by Gabo and Pevsner (then Natan Pevsner, misprinted Noton Pevsner), Gabo claimed sole authorship for the statement (*Gabo*, p. 158). Aleksei Pevsner confirms Gabo's assertion, describing Gabo's writing of the manifesto and Antoine's request for permission to sign it (*A Biographical Sketch of My Brothers*, p. 24). A fragment consisting of a few pages of the original manuscript text of the manifesto in Gabo's hand is now located among the Gabo papers at the Beinecke Rare Book and Manuscript Library, Yale University. One copy of the printed text is also held by the Beinecke. According to Gabo the manifesto was authorised for publication by the wife of Kamenev, who accepted it without reading it, on the basis of its 'realist title' (*Gabo*, p. 158). It was published to accompany the exhibition of Gabo's and Pevsner's works on Tverskoi Boulevard in central Moscow, which opened on 6 August 1920. According to one authority, often identified as Lissitzky, the exhibition was held in an open bandstand on the boulevard (Ulen, 'Die Ausstellungen in Russland', *Veshch'*, No. 1/2, 1922, p. 19). Apparently this exhibition had an enlivening effect on the traffic and in the evenings the artists found themselves speaking at impromptu meetings (*ibid.*). In a note written many years later (probably in the 1970s), Gabo stated that the manifesto poster was stuck up all over Moscow by students from the VKhUTEMAS (at this point still the Free Studios) on the second day of the exhibition, 7 August 1920. He also identified the exhibitors as himself, Antoine Pevsner, Gustav Klutsis and some other students of his whose names he had forgotten. The exhibition seems to have been fairly small. Gabo stated that he exhibited four or five constructions including the *Head* of 1916, whilst Antoine showed three paintings, Klutsis two and his students an unspecified num-

ber of paintings (N. Gabo, short note, Gabo Papers, private archive, London). Further information concerning the works exhibited on Tverskoi Boulevard is contained in the list of plates in *Gabo*, p. 182. According to this the exhibits comprised *Constructed Head No. 1* of 1915 (pls. 1–2), *Head of a Woman* of 1916–17 (also called *Head in a Niche*, now in the Museum of Modern Art, New York, pl. 7), and *Construction en creux* (earlier version, painted cardboard, later version in wood and plastic, 1921, illustrated in pl. 18).

114. N. Gabo, 'On Constructive Realism', in *Gabo*, p. 174.

115. Pevsner, *A Biographical Sketch of my Brothers*, p. 42.

116. 'Russia and Constructivism', in *Gabo*, p. 158.

117. Gabo and Pevzner, *Realisticheskii manifest*; cited from *Gabo*, p. 152.

118. *ibid*.

119. 'Russia and Constructivism', in *Gabo*, p. 158.

120. This construction, also known as *Standing Wave*, is now in the Tate Gallery. It was made in Russia. Gabo apparently used a bell mechanism for the motor and acquired the metal parts from a scientific laboratory. Given the shortage of such materials in Russia at that time Gabo would have encountered considerable difficulty in acquiring these materials. See N. Gabo, 'The "Kinetic Construction of 1920"', *Studio International*, Vol. 178, September 1969, p. 89.

121. 'Russia and Constructivism', in *Gabo*, p. 160.

122. N. Gabo, letter to Jean Clay, 11 March 1973, p. 1 (Gabo Papers, Beinecke, Yale).

123. Gabo's involvement with decorations for the revolutionary festivals was mentioned by him in his memoirs of the period. He recounted, for instance, how he insisted on receiving food rations to sustain such work. However, it is most difficult to establish the precise nature and extent of his involvement in such activity. Gabo mentioned a similarity between his *Project for a Radio Station* and Tatlin's model for a Monument to the Third Internation (*Gabo*, p. 26). Both share aspirations towards synthesising the arts of sculpture, painting and architecture. However, because of its explicitly articulated agitational function and from the very fact that Tatlin constructed a model of his project, it was more advanced in terms of being a coherently organised structure and of expounding a potentially new role for art in the new society.

124. Gabo and Pevzner, *Realisticheskii manifest*; cited from *Gabo*, p. 152.

125. N. Gabo, 'Constructive Art', *Listener*, Vol. 16, No. 408, 1936, p. 848.

126. G. Klutsis, in *Sovetskie khudozhniki: Avtobiografii* (Moscow, 1937), vol. 1, p. 116.

127. *Ot Unovisa* (Vitebsk, no date); reprinted in L. Zhadova, *Malevich: Suprematism and Revolution in Russian Art, 1910–1930* (London, 1982), p. 298.

128. L. Oginskaya, *Gustav Klutsis* (Moscow, 1981), p. 17.

129. See Popova, *Seated figure*, 1915, and *Italian Still Life*, 1914, reproduced in Gray, *Great Experiment*.

130. L. S. Popova, Untitled MS, private archive, Moscow.

131. The title of this painting is determined by the title which Popova herself inscribed on a postcard reproducing the relief and dated 23 June 1916. The postcard is part of the Costakis Collection (verso and recto are reproduced in Rudenstine, *Russian Avant-Garde*, Nos. 815–16). The relief itself also formerly belonged to Costakis who donated it in 1977 to the Tret'yakov Gallery, Moscow. It is, however, illustrated in Rudenstine, *Russian Avant-Garde*, No. 817. This work was exhibited at

the Last Futurist Exhibition, 0.10, as number 96 (Gordon, *Modern Art Exhibitions*, Vol. 2, p. 883). It was also exhibited at Popova's posthumous exhibition (*Posmertnaya vystavka L. S. Popovoi 1889–1924. Katalog vystavki proizvedenii* (Moscow, 1924), p. 10, No. 16) where it is dated 1915 and illustrated but given the title *The Jug on The Table: A Painterly Relief* (*Kuvshin na stole. Zhivopisnyi rel'ef*).

132. L. S. Popova, 'Zhivopisnyi rel'ef', MS, private archive, Moscow.

133. This work was first exhibited at the Erste Russische Kunstausstellung in Berlin in 1922 where it was bought by Katherine Dreier for the collection of the Société Anonyme. It is now in the collection of Yale University Art Gallery with the rest of that collection. Although this work is not signed or dated it is one of the four works on paper which Popova exhibited in 1922, i.e., Nos. 440–3 in the catalogue, three of which were entitled *Komposition* and the other *Landschaft*. *Komposition* is evidently the title under which this work was exhibited. However, there is a companion piece at Yale which is signed on the verso in Popova's hand, dated 1918, and entitled *Zhivopisnaya arkhitektonika* or *Painterly Architectonics*. The stylistic similarities and interest in intersecting planes would suggest that the same title and date should be applied to this work.

134. L. S. Popova, 'Zhivopisnaya arkhitektonika', MS, private archive, Moscow.

135. The catalogues for the $5 \times 5 = 25$ exhibition were all hand-made, and each copy contained an original work by each of the artists concerned. Popova and Stepanova contributed lino or woodcuts; Rodchenko a series of drawings of coloured lines on squared paper, and Ekster and A. Vesnin, small gouaches.

136. Eight of these works were exhibited at Vystavka iz sobranii G. D. Kostakisa i D. V. Sarab'yanova v institute atomnoi energii im. Kurchatova (Moscow, June 1972) as numbers 19–26.

137. L. S. Popova, 'Raboty 20–21g', signed Moscow, December 1922, MS, private archive, Moscow.

138. *ibid*.

139. For Stepanova's paintings see *Two Figures* of 1920 in Rudenstine, *Russian Avant-Garde*, No. 1083. Stepanova exhibited her first non-objective paintings in 1919. See her declarations (signed Agrarykh) in the catalogue of the Tenth State Exhibition (*Desyataya gosudarstvennaya vystavka. Bespredmetnoe tvorchestvo i suprematizm* (Moscow, 1919); reprinted in Matsa, *Sovetskoe iskusstvo*, pp. 110–11).

NOTES TO CHAPTER TWO

1. A good introduction to the economic and political realities of the period is provided by J. P. Nettl, *The Soviet Achievement* (London, 1967).

2. V. Tatlin, 'Kratkii obzor', MS, private archive, Moscow, p. 1.

3. A. M. Rodchenko, 'Chernoe i beloe', early 1920s, MS of memoirs, private archive, Moscow.

4. A. Lur'e, 'Nash Marsh', *Novyi Zhurnal*, No. 94, 1969, p. 128.

5. V. Mayakovskii, 'Prikaz po armii iskusstva', *Iskusstvo kommuny*, No. 1, 1918, p. 1.

6. I. Puni, 'Sovremennye gruppirovki v russkom levom iskusstve', *Iskusstvo kommuny*, No. 19, 1919, p. 3.

7. N. Punin, 'Obzor techenii v iskusstve Peterburga', *Russkoe iskusstvo*, No. 1, 1923, p. 18.

8. Ya. Tugendkhol'd, *Iskusstvo oktyabr'skoi epokhi* (Moscow, 1928).

9. D. Shterenberg, 'Otchet o deyatel'nosti Otdela izobrazitel'nykh iskusstv Narkomprosa. Istoriya vozniknoveniya kollegii Otdela izobrazitel'nykh iskusstv', *Izobrazitel'noe iskusstvo*, No. 1, 1919, p. 50; reprinted in *Obzor deyatel'nosti Otdela izobrazitel'nykh iskusstv* (Petrograd, 1920), pp. 3–9. For an account of their activities see 'Otchet IZO', pp. 50–1. The union was not a homogeneous body and the strains were evident even at this stage between the right, left and centre.

10. 'Otchet IZO', p. 51. This was the famous meeting Lunacharskii called in the Winter Palace. Fear of government control was a preoccupation of the left wing of the union as well as of the right. Apparently Mayakovskii was one of the few who did not distrust Soviet power (see V. Mayakovskii, *Polnoe sobranie sochinenii* (Moscow, 1961), Vol. 12, p. 596).

11. 'Otchet IZO', p. 51. The report, written by Shterenberg, stated that the conservative artistic elements were to work in this relatively safe zone because of their 'having nothing in common with the working and peasant masses'.

12. *ibid.* According to a Narkompros Resolution and Directive concerning IZO of 28 May 1918, Shterenberg was appointed head of IZO on 29 January 1918; reprinted in *Spravochnik otdela IZO NKP* (Moscow, 1920), p. 3.

13. 'Otchet IZO', p. 51.

14. The five architects were named as Il'in, Dubenetskii, Rudnev, Shtal'berg and Shchuko ('Otchet IZO', p. 51).

15. O. Brik, 'IMO – iskusstvo molodykh', in *Mayakovskomu* (Leningrad, 1940), p. 97. According to Brik, he and Mayakovskii were invited to become members of IZO in the summer of that year by Punin and Shterenberg (*ibid.*, p. 93). However, the first record of his attendance at the meetings is in November 1918 (Mayakovskii, *Polnoe sobranie sochinenii* Vol. 12, p. 216).

16. 'Otchet IZO', p. 52. According to the section of the Department's report reprinted in E. A. Speranskaya, ed., *Agitatsionno-massovoe iskusstvo pervykh let Oktyabrya. Materialy i issledovaniya* (Moscow, 1971), p. 126, n. 190, Tatlin was elected, not appointed, president of the board. He remained the head of the Moscow IZO until May 1919 (V. Tatlin, 'Udostoverenie', TsGALI, fond 681, op. 3, ed. khr. 26, list 273). Tatlin was also elected a deputy by the Union of Artists and Painters to the Art section of the Moscow Soviet ('Professional'nyi soyuz khudozhnikov zhivopistsev', dok. No. 81, 21 November 1917).

17. Report of the Moscow IZO dated July 1917, TsGALI, fond 2306, op. 2, ed. khr. 210, list 1. A section of the report is reprinted in *Agitatsionnomassovoe iskusstvo*, p. 126, n. 190.

18. TsGALI, fond 2306, op. 2, ed. khr. 210, list 1; reprinted in *Agitatsionno-massovoe iskusstvo*, p. 126, n. 190.

19. *ibid. Khudozhestvennaya promyshlennost'* – literally means artistic production. In 1918–19 the term was used to indicate art being applied to tasks other than merely producing works of art. It possessed connotations of craft and applied art.

20. *Gazeta IZO*, No. 1, 10 March 1921; reprinted in I. Matsa, ed., *Sovetskoe iskusstvo za 15 let. Materialy i dokumentatsiya* (Moscow and Leningrad, 1933), p. 102.

21. *Katalog pervoi gosudarstvennoi svobodnoi vystavki proizvedenii iskusstv* (Petrograd, Dvorets iskusstv [Winter Palace], 1919). Other sources give the statistics as 359 artists exhibiting 2,826 works ('Otchet IZO', p. 76).

22. *Gazeta IZO*, No. 1, 1921; reprinted in Matsa, *Sovetskoe iskusstvo*, pp. 67–8.

23. 'Podotdel khudozhestvennogo truda', *Gazeta*

IZO, No. 1, 10 March 1921; reprinted in Matsa, *Sovetskoe iskusstvo*, pp. 67–8.

24. 'Khudozhestvenno - proizvodstvennyi P[od]otdel Izo Narkomprosa', in *Iskusstvo v proizvodstve* (Moscow, 1921), pp. 36–7. This work is also described by Rodchenko in his memoirs 'Chernoe i beloe'.

25. N. Tarabukin, 'Pervaya vserossiiskaya khudozhestvenno-promyshlennaya vystavka', *LEF*, No. 1, 1923, pp. 250–1.

26. 'Polozhenie Otdela izobrazitel'nykh iskusstv i khudozhestvennoi promyshlennosti po voprosu o "khudozhestvennoi kul'tury"', *Iskusstvo kommuny*, No. 11, 1919, p. 4; reprinted in Matsa, *Sovetskoe iskusstvo*, pp. 63–4.

27. 'Obshchii plan programmy nauchno-teoreticheskogo otdela tsentro-sektsii AKIZO Narkomprosa', MS, private archive, Moscow.

28. *ibid.*

29. *ibid.*

30. *Pravda*, 24 November 1918. On 29 December 1918 *Izvestia* printed a warning that Futurism was tainted by bourgeois decadence and therefore harmful to proletarians.

31. A. Lunacharskii, 'O printsipakh gosudarstvennogo priobreteniya khudozhestvennykh proizvedenii', *Iskusstvo kommuny*, No. 1, 1918. It should be noted that Lunacharskii's reply did not mean that he wholeheartedly supported the line of the paper *Iskusstvo kommuny* or of the Futurists in general. He was aware of the danger of their antipathy to the past and of their tendency to talk from the point of view of a specific artistic trend and yet at the same time from the point of view of the government.

32. Lenin to Lunacharskii. Note dated 6 May 1921; reprinted in *Lenin i Lunacharskii. Perepiska, doklady. dokumenty* (Moscow, 1971), p. 281.

33. V. I. Lenin, *O literature i iskusstve* (Moscow, 1957), pp. 555–6.

34. L. Zhadova, 'Lyubov' Popova', *Tekhnicheskaya estetika*, No. 11, 1967, p. 26. There is no reference to any further activity by Popova in *Agitatsionno-massovoe iskusstvo*.

35. The scenario of the spectacle was intended to be by Aksenov, and the direction by Meierkhol'd. It is this projected, but never performed, mass festival which Rene Fülop-Miller illustrates and describes in his book *The Mind and Face of Bolshevism: An Examination of Cultural Life in the Soviet Russia* (London, 1927), pp. 145, 148–9. According to Fülop-Miller's description this theatrical performance was to include 'a cast of of thousands': 'two hundred riders from the cavalry school, two thousand three hundred foot soldiers, sixteen guns, five aeroplanes with searchlights, ten automobile searchlights, several armoured trains, tanks, motor cycles, ambulance sections, detachments of the general recruiting school, of the associations for physical culture, the central direction of military training establishments were to take part, as well as various military bands and choirs.

'In the first five scenes the various sections of the revolutionaries were to have combined to encircle the capitalist fortress and with the help of artillery corps to surround it with a curtain of smoke. Concealed by this dense screen, the tanks were to have advanced to the attack and stormed the bastions, while the flame-throwers were giving out an enormous fireball of changing outline. The silhouette of the illuminated smoke would finally have represented a factory with the watchword of the fight inscribed on the walls: "What work has created shall belong to the workers." After a great parade of troops, the gymnastic associations on motor-vans were to have shown the people of the future engaged in throwing the discus and gathering the hay in sheaves. Then a general dance, with the motto "Hammer and sickle," was to introduce motions representing industrial and agricultural work, the hammer bearers from time to time crossing in a friendly way their instruments with the sickles of the other group. Rhythmic movements performed by the pupils of the public training schools were to have symbolised the phrase, "Joy and strength – the victory of the creators"; now nearing, now retreating from the tribunal, they were finally, in conjunction with the troops, to have been effectively grouped in the "city of the future." The final items of the performance were to have been provided by a display of flying by aeroplanes with searchlights, fireworks, and a great choral singing, accompanied by the orchestras.'

The finished design drawing by Popova and Vesnin originally in the Costakis Collection was donated by Costakis to the Trety'akov Gallery, Moscow, in 1977. The Costakis Collection possesses contemporary photographs of the actual models made for the festival (A. Rudenstine, ed., *Russian Avant-Garde Art: The George Costakis Collection* (London, 1981), Nos. 857, 859–60).

36. *Lenin i Lunacharskii*, p. 660.

37. Zhadova, 'Lyubov' Popova', p. 26.

38. *Agitatsionno-massovoe iskusstvo*, p. 69.

39. *ibid.*, p. 114, no. 32.

40. *ibid.*, p. 106.

41. N. Rozanova, *Petr Vasil'evich Miturich* (Moscow, 1972), p. 6.

42. V. Dmitriev, 'Pervyi itog', *Iskusstvo kommuny*, No. 15, 1919, pp. 2–3. Strangely, as V. Pertsov points out, the greatest impact in decorating the streets of Moscow, Vitebsk and Petrograd in 1918 and 1919 was created by the Suprematists. He attributes the subsequent force of the attack against the left artists precisely to their merging with revolutionary life in this way (*Reviziya levogo fronta v sovremennom russkom iskusstve* (Moscow, 1925), p. 17). The excitement of those days is conveyed in a passage from *Veshch*: 'The older academic artists squandered time by waiting for "normal" times. The younger ones hurried to replace them ... The Russian Futurists, painters and poets alike, cried out during the first days of the Revolution "Bring everything into the streets, get buckets of paint and paint the surroundings"' (Ulen, 'Die Ausstellungen in Russland', *Veshch'*, No. 1/2, 1922, p. 18).

43. *Agitatsionno-massovoe iskusstvo*, p. 96 and p. 126, n. 189.

44. *ibid.*, p. 126, n. 190.

45. Posters by Popova were exhibited at the posthumous exhibition but were all dated 1924. See *Katalog posmertnoi vystavki khudozhnika konstruktora L. S. Popovoi* (Moscow, 1924), p. 12, No. 79.

46. Rozanova, *Miturich*, p. 6.

47. These were exhibited in 1975. See *Varvara Fedorovna Stepanova 1894–1958. Katalog vystavki* (Kostromo, Kostromskoi oblastnoi muzei izobrazitel'nykh iskusstv, 1975), p. 18.

48. N. M. Chegodaeva, 'Plakat' in *Istoriya russkogo iskusstvo* (Moscow, 1957), Vol. 11, p. 72.

49. The list of artists who worked for this department is printed in full in *Agitatsionno-massovoe iskusstvo*, pp. 189–92.

50. *ibid.*, p. 186. The young artists concerned were A. Tyshler, I. Rabinovich, N. Shiffrin, S. Voshmevetskaya, L. Erenburg and M. Genkina.

51. *Agitatsionno-massovoe iskusstvo*, p. 151, n. 5.

52. For a full history of the appearance of this plan, see A. Strigalev, 'K istorii vozniknoveniya Leninskogo plana monumental'noi propagandy', in *Voprosy sovetskogo izobrazitel'nogo iskusstva i arkhitektury* (Moscow, 1976), pp. 213–51. For accounts in English, see J. Bowlt, 'Russian Sculpture and Lenin's Plan of Monumental Propaganda', in H. A. Millon and L. Nochlin, eds., *Art and Architecture in the Service of Politics* (London and Cambridge, Mass., 1978), pp. 182–93, and C. Lodder, 'Lenin's Plan of Monumental Propaganda', *Sbornik: Study Group on the Russian Revolution*, No. 3, 1980, pp. 67–84. Lenin is traditionally acknowledged to have been the author of the Plan for Monumental Propaganda and it is usually referred to as Lenin's Plan. In 1933 Igor' Grabar' recalled how Lunacharskii had announced to a meeting of artists and sculptors some time during the winter of 1917–18: 'I've just come from Vladimir Il'ich. Once again he has had one of those fortunate and profoundly exciting ideas with which he has so often shocked and delighted us. He intends to decorate Moscow's squares with statues and monuments to revolutionaries and the great fighters for socialism. This provides both agitation for socialism and a wide field for the display of our sculptural talents' (I. Grabar', 'Aktual'nye zadachi sovetskoi skul'ptury', *Iskusstvo*, No. 1/2, 1933, p. 155).

53. *Izvestiya VTsIK*, No. 155, 1918.

54. 'O snyatii pamyatnikov, vozdvignutykh v chest' tsarei i ikh slug, i vyrabotke proektov pamyatnikov Rossiiskoi sotsialisticheskoi revolyutsii, in *Sobranie uzakonenii i rasporyazhenii Rabochego i Krest'yanskogo Pravitel'stva*, No. 31, 1918, p. 391. This is also reproduced in V. N. Perel'man, *Bor'ba za realism v izobrazitel'nom iskusstve 20kh godov. Materialy, dokumenty, vospominaniya* (Moscow, 1962), p. 55.

55. 'Spisok lits koim predlozheno postavit' monumenty v g[orode]. Moskve i drugikh gorodakh RSFSR', *Iskusstvo*, No. 2, 1918, p. 4. One million roubles was assigned to erect a monument on the grave of Karl Marx (*Sobranie uzakonenii*, No. 39, st. 508).

56. A. Lunacharskii, 'Monumental'naya agitatsiya', *Plamya*, No. 11, 1918.

57. *ibid.*

58. All these details are from Lunacharskii, 'Monumental'naya agitatsiya'. A series of brochures providing biographical information was also published under the general title *Komu proletariat stavit pamyatniki*.

59. Lunacharskii, 'Ob arkhitekturno-khudozhestvennom oformlenii Moskvy'; cited from Strigalev, 'K istorii', p. 229.

60. It is interesting to note that this work was in fact published by the Petrograd Soviet in 1918 as part of a series of utopian novels which included Thomas More's *Utopia* (first published in Russian in 1903). The first Russian translation of Campanella seems to have appeared in 1906.

61. A. Lunacharskii, 'Lenin o monumental'noi propagande', *Literaturnaya gazeta*, No. 4/5, 29 January 1933; cited from A. Lunacharskii, *Vospominaniya i vpechatleniya* (Moscow, 1968).

62. Concerning the erection of these plaques, see Lunacharskii, 'Monumental'naya agitatsiya', *Plamya*, No. 11, 1918. The plan may also bear some relationship to French revolutionary festivals. Russian interest in the French experience was amply attested by articles in the popular magazines such as *Gorn* and by such publications as Zh. T'erso, *Prazdnestva i pesni frantsuzskoi revolyutsii* (Moscow, 1918).

63. Lunacharskii, 'Lenin o monumental'noi propagande'.

64. For details and examples, see *Agitatsionno-massovoe iskusstvo*, and M. Guerman, *Art of the October Revolution* (London, 1979).

65. Strigalev, 'K istorii', p. 232.

66. See *Iskusstvo kommuny*, No. 13, 1919; No. 15, 1919; No. 17, 1919.

67. 'Otkrytie pamyatnika T. G. Shevchenko', *Iskusstvo kommuny*, No. 1, 1918, p. 4

68. 'Otkrytie pamyatnika Garibal'di', *Iskusstvo kommuny*, No. 14, 1919.

69. Matsa, *Sovetskoe iskusstvo*, p. 36.

70. *ibid.* Works in Saratov are well documented in *Agitatsionno-massovoe iskusstvo*. Over sixty sculptors are listed as participating in a competition for monuments as part of Lenin's plan (not earlier than 1918) in *Iz istorii stroitel'stva sovetskoi kul'tury 1918-1919 Moskva. Dokumenty i vospominaniya* (Moscow, 1964), pp. 38-44.

72. *Izvestiya VTsIK*, 24 July 1918, No. 155, and *Iskusstvo*, No. 2, 1918, p. 15.

73. *ibid.*

74. *Lenin i Lunacharskii*, p. 80. It was one of several letters that Lunacharskii forwarded to Lenin to refute the accusation that Narkompros was inactive in effectively implementing the Plan for Monumental Propaganda (*ibid.*, pp. 84-9). Tatlin expressed distress at Vinogradov's complaints concerning the plan because they discredited IZO (and hence the artists who ran it). The letter is reprinted in full in *Lenin i Lunacharskii*, p. 80. It is undated, but according to A. Strigalev it was written between 18 September and 12 October 1918 ('O proekte Pamyatnika III Internatsionala khudozhnika V. Tatlina', *Voprosy sovetskogo izobrazitel'nogo iskusstva i arkhitektury* (Moscow, 1973), p. 415).

75. *Lenin i Lunacharskii*, p. 80.

76. Strigalev, 'O proekte', p. 426.

77. N. Punin, *Pamyatnik III Internatsionala* (Petrograd, 1920), p. 1. It is difficult to establish with any certainty Tatlin's precise movements at this period, because the sources are somewhat conflicting. Tatlin's letter to the *Rektor* of VKhUTEMAS in 1927 gave 1921 as the year of his move to Petrograd. On the other hand Tatlin's 'Udostoverenie' stated that in 1920 he became a member of the IZO Kollegiya in Petrograd, having ceased to be head of the Moscow IZO in May 1919. It would seem likely that Tatlin moved to Petrograd soon after May 1919. Certainly Tatlin constructed his model in Petrograd which suggests that he was there at least by the beginning of 1920. The fact that he states that he taught for one and a half years at the VKhUTEMAS should not affect the argument since the term 'VKhUTEMAS' was used widely before the official decree was signed, and has been used, *post facto*, to apply to the Free Studios (TsGALI, fond 681, op. 3, ed. khr. 26, list 272-3).

78. N. Punin, 'O pamyatnikakh', *Iskusstvo kommuny*, No. 14, 9 March 1919.

79. For details concerning this dedication, see Strigalev, 'O proekte', pp. 416-18.

80. Punin, 'O pamyatnikakh'.

81. *ibid.*

82. *ibid.* Strange as it seems this idea was utilised to celebrate Stalin's birthday in 1949, when his face was projected into the sky over the Kremlin.

83. Punin, 'O pamyatnikakh'.

84. Strigalev, 'O proekte', p. 416.

85. *ibid.* For a very brief discussion of Tatlin's debt to Russian artistic traditions see Chapter One. The Tsarevich plate was executed by Chekhonin in 1922 to a design by Tatlin of 1922 which was based on Tatlin's earlier design of 1911 for *Tsar Maksimilian and his Unruly Son Adolf*.

86. Punin, 'O pamyatnikakh'.

87. The Kafe Pittoresk which belonged to the Moscow baker Nikolai Filippov was opened on 30 January 1918 at 5 Kuznetskii Most. According to the artist Georgii Yakulov, Filippov had approached him in July 1917 with the proposal of decorating the café. The work on the decorations therefore took place in the second half of 1917. According to Yakulov's account (in a letter dated 19 August 1918 to Lunacharskii), the artists who were called in to help him in this venture were Bruni, Goloshchapov, Bogoslovskaya (sculptor), Golova, Dymshits-Tolstaya, Tatlin, Shaposhnikov, Rybinkov and Udal'tsova (TsGA, RSFSR, fond, 2306, op. 24, d. 54, list 1-2; reprinted in full in *Agitatsionno-massovoe iskusstvo*, p. 128, n. 209). It should be stressed that Yakulov's account omits Rodchenko's name although Rodchenko's memoirs, cited by Karginov, do state that Yakulov invited him as well as Tatlin to work on the café's designs (G. Karginov, *Rodchenko* (London, 1979), p. 91). It is well established that the overall responsibility for the design of the Kafe Pittoresk lay with Yakulov. A gouache, now in the collection of the Musée National d'Art Moderne in Paris, appears to be a study for the café, executed by Yakulov in 1917 (see J. C. Marcadé, 'Oeuvres de Georges Yakoulov et d'Ivan Koudriachov', *Revue du Louvre*, Vol. 23, No. 6, 1973, p. 381).

This description of the café, written by Umanskii in 1920, is particularly evocative of the eclectic nature of the enterprise and its fundamentally figurative nature: 'The Kafe Pittoresk, Yakulov's masterpiece, presents an unusual picture. Counter-reliefs whose effects are heightened by schematic colouring are cleverly hung from the walls. They seem to expand the space with their angular interpenetrating planes, without violating the café's architectonic unity. Avoiding undue aestheticisation, the podium (the place of countless debates on the various questions concerning the new artistic life), the tables, and the benches are also elevated to the status of art objects. Splendid sculptural creations are suspended from the large domed ceiling, the vitreous facets of which are decoratively (but not ornamentally) painted in an appropriate style. Are they aeroplanes? Or dynamos? or dreadnoughts? The observer's ability to recognise objects becomes numbed. However, he feels a presentiment of restless dynamism in these semi-machine, semi-decorative shapes, the construction of which emphasises the enigma of modern machines and is the source of a peculiar disquiet' (K. Umanskij, *Neue Kunst in Russland 1914–1919* (Potsdam/Munich, 1920), pp. 35-6; translation based on that provided by K. P. Zygas, 'The Sources of Constructivist Architecture: Designs and Images, 1917–1925' (Cornell University Ph.D., 1978), p. 13).

88. *Agitatsionno-massovoe iskusstvo*, p. 128, n. 209.

89. *ibid.*

90. I. Erenburg, *A vse-taki ona vertitsya* (Berlin, 1922), p. 26.

91. *Severnaya kommuna*, 17 October 1918, No. 132; reprinted in *Agitatsionno-massovoe iskusstvo*, p. 16.

92. Lur'e, 'Nash Marsh', p. 128.

93. V. Khlebnikov, 'Gorod budushchego' in V. V. Khlebnikov, *Sobranie proizvedenii Velimira Khlebnikova* (Leningrad, 1928-33), Vol. 3, pp. 63-5; and A. Bogdanov, *Krasnaya zvezda* (Petrograd, 1918); first edition 1907.

94. B. A[rvatov], 'Oveshchestvlennaya utopiya', *LEF*, No. 1, 1923, pp. 61-4. Four of Lavinskii's drawings for the proposed city including its overall plan were reproduced on pp. 62-3.

95. A. Lavinskii, 'Inzhenerizm (Tezisy k gorodu budushchego)', MS, private archive, Moscow.

96. A[rvatov], 'Oveshchestvlennaya utopiya', p. 64.

97. S. O. Khan-Magomedov, 'Pervaya novatorskaya tvorcheskaya organizatsiya sovetskoi arkhitektury', *Problemy istorii sovetskoi arkhitektury*, No. 2, 1976, p. 5. According to this article the committee consisted of one sculptor, B. Korolev, and seven architects – including Krinskii and Ladovskii.

98. *ibid.*, p. 6.

99. *Zhizn' iskusstva*, No. 276/7, 24–5 October 1919.

100. *Zhizn' iskusstva*, No. 315, 1919.

101. Punin dated his text July 1920 (Punin, *Pamyatnik*, p. 6). These are the only sketches preserved but it is to be presumed that Tatlin did make other sketches and plans which have been lost. Photographs of the model were published in N. Punin, *Tatlin (Protiv kubizma)* (Petrograd, 1921). In 1967 an additional photograph was published in *Výtvarne uměni*, No. 8–9, 1967.

102. *Zhizn' iskusstva*, 3 March, No. 387; and 30–1 October 1920, No. 596/7.

103. This was in the mosaics studio of the former Academy of Art. The exhibition was accompanied by political meetings and discussions concerning the monument (*Zhizn' iskusstva*, 12 November 1920, No. 607).

104. Tatlin's declaration 'Nasha predstoyashchaya rabota' was published in the journal of the Eighth Congress, *VIII s'ezd sovetov. Ezhednevnyi byulleten' s'ezda VTsIK*, No. 13, 1 January 1921, p. 11.

105. N. Khardzhiev, 'Mayakovskii i Tatlin. K 90-letiyu so dnya rozhdeniya khudozhnika'; reprinted in *Neue russische Literatur. Almanach* (Salzburg, 1978), p. 90.

106. This is the figure that Strigalev gives in 'O proekte'. N. Khardzhiev is in agreement with Strigalev, giving the height of model as 7 metres ('Mayakovskii i Tatlin', p. 90). In *Object*, it was given as 5 metres (Ulen, 'Die Ausstellungen in Russland' *Veshch'* No. 1/2, 1922, p. 19. Erenburg for some reason gave the height as 25 metres (*A vse-taki ona vertitsya*, p. 19).

107. N. Punin, 'Tour de Tatline', *Veshch'*, No. 1/2, 1922; reprinted in Andersen, *Vladimir Tatlin*, p. 57.

108. This theme has been recurrent ever since Lunacharskii expressed horror at Tatlin's project and declared that he would much rather have the Eiffel Tower (*Izvestiya VTsIK*, No. 22, 29 November 1922). Erenburg in *Vse-taki ona vertitsya* compared Eiffel's 300 metres height to Tatlin's 400. Andersen and Zygas also recall the resemblance.

109. Troels Andersen, 'Notes on Tatlin', in *Vladimir Tatlin*, pp. 7–8.

110. John Elderfield, 'Line of Free Men: Tatlin's "Towers" and the Age of Invention', *Studio International*, No. 916, 1969, pp. 162–7.

111. K. P. Zygas, 'Tatlin's Tower Reconsidered', *Architectural Association Quarterly*, Vol. 8, No. 2, 1976, pp. 22, 18.

112. M. Rowell, 'Vladimir Tatlin: Form/Faktura', *October*, No. 7, winter 1978, pp. 102–3. The surviving sketches of Tatlin's designs for *The Flying Dutchman* are now preserved in the Central Bakhrushin Theatrical Museum in Moscow. Illustrations of them appear in *V. E. Tatlin*, 1977, p. 46, and *Sovetskoe iskusstvo*, 17 September 1934.

113. V. E. Tatlin, T. Shapiro, I. Meerzon and P. Vinogradov, 'Nasha predstoyashchaya rabota', *VIII s'ezd sovetov. Ezhednevnyi byulleten' s'ezda VTsIK*, No. 13, 1 January 1921, p. 11.

114. Ulf Linde and Per Olof Ultveldt, 'Report on the Reconstructing', in Andersen, *Vladimir Tatlin*, pp. 26–7.

115. V. E. Tatlin, 'Iskusstvo v tekhniku', *Brigada khudozhnikov*, No. 6, 1932, pp. 15–16; translation taken from Andersen, *Vladimir Tatlin*, pp. 75–6.

116. El Lissitzky, *Russia: An Architecture for World Revolution*, trans. E. Dluhosch (London, 1970).

117. L. Trotsky, *Literature and Revolution* (Ann Arbor, 1960), pp. 246–9.

118. R. Khiger, *Puti arkhitekturnoi mysli* (Moscow, 1933), p. 20.

119. Broby-Johansen, 'Quod felix', *Akademisk Tidskrift*, No. 10, 1926, pp. 134–5; quoted in Andersen, *Vladimir Tatlin*, p. 63.

120. A. Begicheva, 'Vospominaniya o Tatline. Do kontsa ne razgadai', MS, private archive, Moscow, p. 10. The meeting and conversation referred to are said to have occurred on 25 August 1925 (*ibid.*, p. 16). Part of these memoirs were published in 1968 (see A. Begicheva, 'Komisar narkomosa', *Vitchyzna*, No. 2, 1968, pp. 159–70).

121. Begicheva, 'O Tatline', p. 10.

122. L. Lozowick, 'Tatlin's Monument to the Third International', *Broom*, Vol. 3, No. 3, 1922, p. 234. Lozowick suggested that this cosmic symbolism was romanticism 'slipping in by the back door'.

123. Tatlin, 'Iskusstvo v tekhniku', p. 16.

124. B. Lubetkin, 'Architectural Thought since the Revolution', *Architectural Review*, Vol. 71, No. 426, May 1932, p. 202. I have found no Soviet source which spells out fully the text of this slogan.

125. V. M. Lobanov, *Khudozhestvennye gruppirovki za poslednie 25 let* (Moscow, 1930), p. 103. The OBMOKhU held four exhibitions of its work between 1919 and 1923. In 1923 it ceased to function and it last exhibited as a group at Berlin, in 1922 (*ibid.*, p. 105, and V. Komardenkov, *Dni minuvshie (Iz vospominanii khudozhnika)* (Moscow, 1972), p. 72).

126. Lobanov supplies this list of its members (*Khudozhestvennye gruppirovki*, p. 104). A. B. Nakov asserts that the majority of these students came from the studio without a master. (*2 Stenberg 2* (London, Annely Juda Fine Art, 1975), p. 9). However, according to Vladimir Stenberg, he, his brother and Medunetskii at least, were students in Yakulov's workshop (conversation with Vladimir Avgustovich Stenberg, April 1974). Lobanov supports the reminiscences of the artist in his statement that the artists were the pupils of Lentulov and Yakulov (*Khudozhestvennye gruppirovki*, p. 104). Komardenkov states that for a certain time he and some of his comrades studied in Yakulov's studio at the First State Free Studios (*Dni minuvshie*, p. 76).

127. Lobanov, *Khudozhestvennye gruppirovki*, p. 104.

128. *Agitatsionno-massovoe iskusstvo*, p. 70. The Myasnitska is now ulitsa Kirova. The post office is still there – almost opposite the entrance to the studios and residence blocks of the VKhUTEMAS at No. 21.

129. *ibid.*, pp. 92 and 125, n. 167. The group was registered as a collective after May 1919 within the subsection of artistic work of IZO (see *Gazeta IZO*, No. 1, 21 March 1921).

130. *Agitatsionno-massovoe iskusstvo*, p. 125, n. 167, and Lobanov, *Khudozhestvennye gruppirovki*, p. 104. Lobanov states that the group worked in Voronezh as well as elsewhere.

131. F. Bogorodskii, *Vospominaniya khudozhnika* (Moscow, 1959), p. 138. Bogorodskii describes Denisovskii as 'a former president of OBMOKhU'. As I have been unable to trace any archive material relating to the structure and activities of the group, it has been impossible to test the truth of this assertion. According to Bogorodskii, Denisovskii describes this activity as 'terribly revolutionary but probably not intelligible'.

Bogorodskii became a Socialist Realist. His account of the OBMOKhU is therefore highly coloured by his own artistic credo as is his description of the works exhibited at the first OBMOKhU exhibition: 'There were paintings and posters, sculptures and graphics and even abstract works by the young innovators. The majority of these works were of course formalist, but none of the works was signed with the name of the author. On the works was only the mark "OBMOKhU". In this way the collectivity of all their creative impulses was stressed.' He went on to talk of their 'search for new forms of art' being compounded with a mischievousness which meant that their works were regarded as mere curiosities.

132. Lobanov, *Khudozhestvennye gruppirovki*, pp. 104–5.

133. It is the third exhibition of the OBMOKhU which was made the subject of the exhibition Russian Constructivism Revisited, Hatton Gallery, University of Newcastle-upon-Tyne, 1974. The names of these artists are included on the invitation card (Private archive, Moscow; also reproduced in *From Surface to Space*, p. 18). Concerning the two photographs of the exhibition, one was reproduced by Lissitzky in *Veshch'*, No. 1/2, 1922, p. 19, and the other by Matsa in *Sovetskoe iskusstvo*, p. 138.

134. Judging from the photographs these seem to be the only variants of this type of construction exhibited by Rodchenko at the exhibition – a further example of this type of construction is illustrated in *Kino-Fot*.

135. In the catalogue of the exhibition this work was illustrated under the title *Raumkonstruktion* and was listed as No. 556. It was purchased at the exhibition by Katherine Dreier (in company with Marcel Duchamp) for the Société Anonyme. It is now in the collection of Yale University Art Gallery. The exhibition number 556 is still affixed to the base of the work. At some point, subsequently, the number was wrongly listed as 557 and that number has stuck.

136. See *Russian Constructivism Revisited*, No. 85, p. 16; it was reconstructed by Philip Wright.

137. Identified in conversation with V. A. Stenberg, April 1974.

138. See also Nakov, *2 Stenberg 2*, pp. 42–3, 45.

139. Conversation with V. A. Stenberg, April 1974.

140. L. Moholy-Nagy, *The New Vision: From Material to Architecture* (New York, 1930), p. 109. A photograph of this construction, together with a photograph of the third OBMOKhU exhibition and other works by OBMOKhU artists was reproduced in 1922 in the Hungarian journal *Egység* published in Vienna (*Egység*, No. 2, 1922, pp. 7–9). For details concerning the general role Hungarians played in the transmission of Russian material to the West, see Chapter Eight.

141. K. Ioganson, 'Ot konstruktsii k tekhnike i izobreteniyu', 9 March 1922, MS, private archive, Moscow, p. 1. For a fuller examination of Ioganson's ideas, see Chapter Three.

142. 'Otchet gruppy konstruktivistov INKhUKa' 6 September 1921, MS, private archive, Moscow. The other members were Gan and Stepanova.

Notes to Chapter Three

1. This change was evident in all the avant-garde activity of the pre-revolutionary period.

2. N. Tarabukin, *Ot mol'berta k mashine* (Moscow, 1923), p. 8.

3. B. Arvatov, *Iskusstvo i klassy* (Moscow, 1923), p. 83.

4. Certain aspects of the arts and crafts movement in Russia are treated by Camilla Gray in Chapter I of her *The Great Experiment*. It is also dealt with by Tamara Talbot Rice in the latter part of *A Concise History of Russian Art* (London, 1963). A more detailed treatment of the activity of Mamontov and Tenisheva has been given by John Bowlt in his *Russian Art, 1875–1975: A Collection of Essays* (New York, 1976).

The Abramtsevo workshops were organised in the early 1880s. They continued to function through the First World War and by 1920 they had been absorbed by IZO (*Spravochnik Otdela izobraziteľnykh iskusstv Narkomprosa*, Moscow, 1920, p. 98). The craft workshops at Talashkino were set up after Prince Tenishev bought the estate in 1893, but they were closed in 1905 when Princess Tenisheva left for Paris. Craft work from both Talashkino and Abramtsevo was exhibited in Paris at the International Exhibition of 1900.

5. P. S. Strakhov, *Esteticheskie zadachi tekhniki* (Moscow, 1906), pp. 102–3.

6. 'The mode of production of material life conditions the social, political and spiritual life processes in general. It is not the consciousness of men that determines their social being, but on the contrary, their social being that determines their consciousness' ('Preface to a Contribution to the Critique of Political Economy', in K. Marx, *Selected Works* (Moscow, 1950), Vol. 1, p. 329).

7. S. Fitzpatrick, *The Commissariat of Enlightenment: Soviet Organisation of Education and the Arts under Lunacharsky, October 1917–1921* (Cambridge, 1970), pp. 89–91.

8. See *ibid.*, pp. 89–109.

9. Lenin and the Soviet government moved against the Proletkul't in 1920 and brought it under the control of Narkompros because its leaders were demanding complete autonomy and represented almost a rival workers' party. Lenin feared the influence of Bogdanov's 'God Building' ideas, and regretted the influence of Futurism and other bourgeois influences on proletarian cultural organisations ('O proletkul'takh', *Pravda*, No. 270, 1 December 1920).

Gor'kii, Bogdanov and Lunacharskii had all believed in 'God Building' (*bogostroitel'stvo*), i.e. in the mystical, religious unity of the proletariat, and that the Revolution and socialism would elevate man to the full realisation of his potential, so that he would be like a god. Lenin had condemned this deviation and had established a rival Party school at Longjumeau. Gor'kii held that literature was a means of educating and elevating the masses. He considered that the new revolutionary literature should be built upon the foundations of the old, and preferred realism as an artistic method.

10. Prominent among these extremists was A. K. Gastev. For details, see Chapter Four.

11. V. Pertsov, 'Proizvodstvo i iskusstvo', *Organizatsiya truda*, No. 1, 1921, p. 128.

12. 'Kogo predosteregaet Lef', *LEF*, No. 1, 1923, p. 10. This declaration is unsigned; however, the names that appeared as signatories of the first declaration were Aseev, B. Arvatov, O. Brik, B. Kushner, V. Mayakovskii, S. Tret'yakov and N. Chuzhak ('Za chto boretsya Lef', *LEF*, No. 1, 1923, p. 3).

13. *Iskusstvo kommuny* was published by IZO Narkompros in Petrograd. In all, nineteen issues appeared between 7 December 1918 and 13 April 1919. Its list of contributors included those who were to be most prominent in formulating the new theoretical position for art and artists in a socialist society – Brik, Punin and Kushner – as well as others whose role was important in this phase of

the debate but who never became prominent theoreticians, such as Mayakovskii and Al'tman.

14. N. Chuzhak, 'Pod znakom zhiznestroeniya', *LEF*, No. 1, 1923, p. 24. *Komfut* (*Kommunisty-futuristy* – Communist Futurists) was organised in Petrograd in 1919. Their declaration published in *Iskusstvo kommuny*, No. 8, 1919, proclaimed that 'a communist structure demands a communist consciousness. All forms of everyday life, morals, philosophy, and art must be recreated on communist principles. Without this the further development of the communist revolution is not possible.' In a following number of the paper Boris Kushner explained that the concrete programme of the organisation included lectures on 'Marxism, the ideology of the aristocracy, the ideology of the democrats, Futurism, etc.', and that the collective intended to publish brochures on such subjects as 'The Culture of Communism' and 'Futurism and Communism'. Publications in the second priority category included ones on 'Creativity', 'Beauty' and 'Inspiration' (B. K., 'Kommunisty-futuristy', *Iskusstvo kommuny*, No. 9, 1919, p. 3).
15. *Iskusstvo kommuny*, No. 1, 1918, p. 1.
16. Chuzhak, 'Pod znakom zhiznestroeniya', pp. 24–7.
17. O. Brik, 'Drenazh iskusstvu', *Iskusstvo kommuny*, No. 1, 1918, p. 1.
18. B. Kushner, 'Bozhestvennoe proizvedenie', *Iskusstvo kommuny*, No. 9, p. 1.
19. V. Dmitriev, 'Pervyi itog', *Iskusstvo kommuny*, No. 15, 1919, p. 2.
20. 'Primechanie red[aktsii]', *Iskusstvo kommuny*, No. 8, 1919, p. 2.
21. Brik, 'Drenazh iskusstva'.
22. Chuzhak, 'Pod znakom zhiznestroeniya', p. 27.
23. *ibid.*
24. 'Primechanie redaktsii', *Iskusstvo kommuny*, No. 7, 1919, p. 2.
25. N. Punin, cited by Chuzhak in 'Pod zhakom zhiznestroeniya', p. 27.
26. I. Puni, 'Tvorchestvo zhizni', *Iskusstvo kommuny*, No. 5, 1919, p. 1.
27. See Fedorov-Davydov's reviews of Arvatov's *Iskusstvo i klassy* in *Pechat' i revolyutsiya*, No. 3, 1924, and of Tarabukin's *Ot mol'berta k mashine* in *Pechat' i revolyutsiya*, No. 5, 1924.
28. O. Brik, 'Opasnyi estetizm', *Iskusstvo kommuny*, No. 5, 1919, p. 4.
29. Chuzhak, 'Pod znakom zhiznestroeniya', p. 28.
30. See N. Punin, 'Proletariat i iskusstvo', *Izobrazitel'noe iskusstvo*, No. 1, 1919, p. 24, and 'Ot redaktsii', *Izobrazitel'noe iskusstvo*, No. 1, 1919, p. 6.
31. Chuzhak, 'Pod znakom zhiznestroeniya', p. 28.
32. Punin, 'Proletariat i iskusstvo', p. 24.
33. 'Ot redaktsii', *Izobrazitel'noe iskusstvo*, No. 1, 1919, p. 6.
34. *Art* (*Iskusstvo*). *Furnace* (*Gorn*) was first published in 1918 but only five issues appeared before it recommenced publication in 1922. Published by Proletkul't, *Gorn* was concerned with all areas of Proletkul't's activity and interests and was not primarily an artistic publication. *Artistic Life* (*Khudozhestvennaya zhizn'*, 1919–20) provides some information concerning the artistic debates of the period but it concentrated on official IZO matters to a greater extent than *Iskusstvo kommuny*. These publications were supplemented by other smaller journals and publications produced in the capital and provinces – for example the IZO Newspaper (*Gazeta IZO*) published in 1921, and the *Art Workers' Herald* (*Vestnik rabotnikov iskusstv*, Nos. 1–3, 1920–1).

35. *LEF – Zhurnal levogo fronta iskusstv*, 1923–5, and *Russkoe iskusstvo*, Nos. 1–3, 1923.
36. 'Institut khudozhestvennoi kul'tury', *Russkoe iskusstvo*, No. 2/3, 1923, p. 85. In 1918, in the pages of *Iskusstvo kommuny*, Brik had advocated the setting up of a similar institute, although his conception was more utilitarian than that of Kandinskii: 'An institute of material culture should be organised immediately where artists could be trained for work on the creation of new objects for proletarian use, and where they would work on creating the prototypes of these objects, these future works of art' ('Drenazh iskusstvu', p. 1). Full details concerning the background to the formation of INKhUK are given in S. O. Khan-Magomedov, 'Vozniknovenie i formirovanie INKhUKA (Institut khudozhestvennoi kul'tury)', *Problemy istorii sovetskoi arkhitektury*, No. 2, 1976, pp. 24–7. Briefly his story commences with Stepanova's evidence that as early as December 1919 former members of the Union of New Art, Kandinskii, Franketti, Rodchenko, Stepanova, Shestakov and others, had the idea of forming a Committee of Masters (*Sovet masterov*) to protect their professional interests. This body met on 17 and 29 January, 28 February and 6 March 1920. On 6 March the new organisation became the Institute of Artistic Culture. Its organisational period (meetings on 13 March, 3 and 26 April, 5, 14 and 22 May) was completed by May 1920 when it became fully operational. On 5 May the shortened form INKhUK was adopted. The Institute's programme is dated May 1920. See *Institut khudozhestvennoi kul'tury v Moskve (INKhUK) pri otdele IZO NKP. Skhematicheskaya programma rabot Instituta khudozhestvennoi kul'tury po plano V. V. Kandinskogo* (Moscow, 1920); reprinted in I. Matsa, *Sovetskoe iskusstvo za 15 let. Materialy i dokumentatsiya* (Moscow/Leningrad, 1933), p. 126.
37. 'Polozhenie Otdela izobrazitel'nykh iskusstv i khudozhestvennoi promyshlennosti NKP po voprosu "o khudozhestvennoi kul'ture"', *Iskusstvo kommuny*, No. 11, 1919, p. 4; reprinted in Matsa, *Sovetskoe iskusstvo*, pp. 63–4.
38. *ibid.*
39. 'Obshchii plan programmy nauchno-teoreticheskogo otdela Tsentrosektsii AKIZO Narkomprosa', MS, private archive, Moscow, p. 1.
40. *Institut*, in Matsa, *Sovetskoe iskusstvo*, p. 126.
41. *ibid.* Similar researches were conducted in Leningrad under the auspices of the Museum of Artistic Culture (Muzei khudozhestvennoi kul'tury) set up in 1919 and opened in 1921. From this body, the Leningrad INKhUK, more correctly known as GINKhUK – the State institute of Artistic Culture (Gosudarstvennyi institut khudozhestvennoi kul'tury) – was organised in October 1924 and officially ratified in February 1925. Malevich was its first director. Although it was subject to certain changes, basically GINKhUK contained four sections: Matyushin ran the section of Organic Culture (Otdel organicheskoi kul'tury); Tatlin headed that of Material Culture (Otdel material'noi kul'tury); Punin, General Ideology (Otdel obshchei ideologii); and Malevich, the Section of Painterly Culture—Formal and Theoretical (Otdel zhivopisnoi kul'tury – formal'no-teoreticheskii). Filonov and Mansurov also worked in the Institute. Although GINKhUK was eventually absorbed into the structure of the Academy it continued its own theoretical work independently within this body until the early 1930s. For details concerning the history and structure of the Institute, consult L. Zhadova, *Malevich: Suprematism and Revolution in Russian Art, 1910–1930* (London, 1982), pp. 318–20. For

details of Malevich's work there, see *Kazimir Malevitsch zum 100. Geburtstag* (Cologne, Galerie Gmurzynska, 1978), pp. 274–80.

42. *Institut*, in Matsa, *Sovetskoe iskusstvo*, p. 127.

43. *ibid.*

44. These papers were all presented at meetings of the theoretical subsection of INKhUK's Monumental Art section. This information is taken from minutes of INKhUK meetings ('Protokoly zasedanii INKhUKa', MS, private archive, Moscow). A list of papers is also provided in S. O. Khan-Magomedov, 'Sektsiya monumental'nogo iskusstva INKhUKa', *Problemy istorii sovetskoi arkhitektury*, No. 3, 1977, p. 21.

45. 'Protokol zasedaniya INKhUKa', 9 June 1920, MS, private archive, Moscow.

46. The systematic nature of Kandinskii's questionnaire on colour and form which he circulated at INKhUK prefigured his later investigations carried out at the Bauhaus and his conclusions published in *Point and Line to Plane* (*Punkt und Linie zu Fläche*) in 1926. He had also dealt with this question earlier in his treatise 'Concerning the Spiritual in Art' published in Russian as 'O dukhovnom v iskusstve' in *Trudy Vserossiiskogo s'ezda khudozhnikov v Petrograde, dek. 1911- yanv. 1912* (Petrograd, 1914), Vol. I, pp. 47–76. Several drawn and painted responses to Kandinskii's questionnaire still survive. Amongst these is that of Popova in which she painted the circle red, the square blue and the triangle yellow. Other colours formed incomplete parts of geometrical entities. White formed part of a curved elliptical form; black had an acute angle; green formed an obtuse angle; purple an acute angle, and orange part of a circular form.

47. 'Protokol zasedaniya INKhUKa', 1 September 1920, MS, private archive, Moscow.

48. *ibid.*

49. 'Institut khudozhestvennoi kul'tury', p. 85. This report was initially written by A. Babichev for presentation at the Russian Academy of Artistic Sciences (Rossiiskaya akademiya khudozhestvennykh nauk – RAKhN) in October 1922 (MS, private archive, Moscow). In the text cited the only difference between the manuscript and the printed text is that in the manuscript 'the views of the masters' replaces 'the views of those'. According to Khan-Magomedov the divergences between the subjective, psychological method of Kandinskii and the more objective approach of Rodchenko and others emerged in the Autumn of 1920 ('Sektsiya monumental'nogo iskusstva', p. 22). The report states that this occurred soon after the establishment of INKhUK. ('Institut khudozhestvennoi kul'tury', p. 85).

50. 'Protokol zasedaniya INKhUKa', 27 January 1921, MS, private archive, Moscow. For details concerning the formation and activities of the General Working Group of Objective Analysis, see S. Khan-Magomedov, 'Rabochaya gruppa ob'ektivnogo analiza INKhUKa', *Problemy istorii sovetskoi arkhitektury*, No. 4, 1978, pp. 53–6. Kandinskii attended the All-Russian Conference of Heads of Art sections within Narkompros from 19 to 25 December 1920 as the official representative of INKhUK and reported that 'the Institute is on the right path' (see *Vestnik rabotnikov iskusstv*, No. 4/5, 1921, pp. 74–5). After Kandinskii left INKhUK he continued the work which he had started there in the Russian Academy of Artistic Sciences, of which he became the first vice-president after it opened on 16 June 1921. Kandinskii had been a member of the Committee formed in May 1921 as a nucleus for an Academy and with the responsibility for devising plans for the study of artistic questions. (A. I. Kondrat'ev, 'Rossii-

skaya akademiya khudozhestvennykh nauk', *Iskusstvo*, No. 1, 1923, pp. 408–9). At an early meeting of the Academy, probably in the summer or early autumn of 1921, Kandinskii presented 'A Plan for the work of the Academy in the Area of the Fine Arts' ('Plan raboty akademii v oblasti izobrazitel'nykh iskusstv'; see Kondrat'ev, 'Rossiiskaya akademiya khudozhestvennykh nauk', p. 412). The Academy was divided into three major sections – Physical and Psychological, Sociological, and Philosophical. Kandinskii was in charge of the Physical and Psychological section for which he drew up a plan of operation which was accepted by the Academy's governing body as early as 21 July 1921. According to this, the section was to 'discover the inner laws forming a work of art in the sphere of each art form, and on the basis of the results to establish the general principles for a synthetic artistic expression' ('Otchet o deyatel'nosti fiziko-psikhologicheskogo otdeleniya', MS, TsGALI, fond 941, op. 212, ed. khr. 1, list 26; also for further details, see Kondrat'ev, 'Rossiiskaya akademiya khudozhestvennykh nauk', pp. 414–15).

An English translation of Kandinskii's plan as reported by Kondrat'ev is provided in J. Bowlt, *Russian Art of the Avant-Garde: Theory and Criticism, 1902-1934* (New York, 1976), pp. 197–8.

51. 'Institut khudozhestvennoi kul'tury', pp. 85–6. *Veshch'* was published by Lissitzky and Ilya Erenburg (the latter was not a member of INKhUK). Only two issues of the journal appeared.

52. *Veshch'*, No. 1, 1922, p. 2.

53. El Lissitzky and H. Arp, *Die Kunstismen, 1914-1924* (Zurich/Munich/Leipzig, 1925), p. xi. Camilla Gray has described Lissitzky's position as stated here and in *Veshch'* as 'Objectism' (*Great Experiment*, p. 244).

54. Lissitzky and Arp, *Kunstismen*, p. xi.

55. 'Institut khudozhestvennoi kul'tury', p. 85. Babichev's manuscript notes for a programme for the Working Group of Objective Analysis at INKhUK are reprinted as 'Zapiska k programme. Rabochaya gruppa ob'ektivnogo analiza INKhUKa', in D. Sarab'yanov, *Aleksei Vasil'evich Babichev. Khudozhnik, teoretik, pedagog* (Moscow, 1974), pp. 104–5.

56. 'Institut khudozhestvennoi kul'tury', p. 85.

57. N. Tarabukin, 'Polozhenie o gruppe ob'ektivnogo analiza', MS, private archive, Moscow.

58. *ibid.*

59. *ibid.*

60. A. Babichev, 'Doklad', MS, private archive, Moscow.

61. Circular from the Academic Council of INKhUK (Uchenyi sovet INKhUK), dated 1921, private archive, Moscow. Although it was not explicitly stated that the Group of Objective Analysis was the organiser of the exhibition, the approach epitomises that of the group. There is no evidence to suggest that the exhibition was ever held, presumably because the split came before it could be realised. The first and second Museums of Western Painting initially comprised the former collections of the Russian connoisseurs Shchukin and Morozov.

62. Circular, 1921, private archive, Moscow.

63. *ibid.*

64. Tarabukin, *Ot mol'berta*, pp. 13–14. The Russian term *'faktura'* literally means texture but this is inadequate to convey the ideological and artistic overtones which it carries in Russian. *Faktura* suggests the working of the surface of materials. I therefore have retained the transcription of the Russian term. Tarabukin elaborated this analysis

of artistic elements in *Opyt teorii zhivopisi* (Moscow, 1923).

65. 'Pervaya rabochaya gruppa konstruktivtov', MS, private archive, Moscow, p. 2.

66. 'Institut khudozhestvennoi kul'tury', p. 86.

67. *ibid.* These, plus Korolev, are the only members mentioned by name in the report.

68. 'Institut khudozhestvennoi kul'tury', p. 86.

69. There are full typed reports or *protokoly* for eight of these meetings. The debate is elaborated in full in the articles of S. Khan-Magomedov, 'Diskussiya v INKhUKe o sootnoshenii konstruktsii i kompozitsii (yanvar'-aprel' 1921 goda). Problemy, lyudi, dokumenty', *Tekhnicheskaya estetika*, No. 20, 1979, pp. 40–77. It is also discussed in M. Rowell and A. Rudenstine, *Art of the Avant-Garde: Selections from the George Costakis Collection* (New York, Solomon R. Guggenheim Museum, 1981), pp. 25–7, 226–7.

70. The last eight in this list seem to have joined INKhUK on 12 January 1921.

71. On 21 January the group based their discussion on the Cubist and Suprematist work of Malevich who was present ('Protokol zasedaniya INKhUKa', 21 January 1921, MS, private archive, Moscow, reported by V. Rakhitin, 'Malevich and Inkhuk', in *Kazimir Malevitsch*, pp. 290–2). Malevich recognised the existence of composition but not of construction.

72. 'Protokol zasedaniya INKhUKa', 4 March 1921, MS, private archive, Moscow.

73. *ibid.*, 21 January 1921.

74. Inscription on the drawing (see plate).

75. 'Protokol zasedaniya INKhUKa', 11 February 1921, MS, private archive, Moscow.

76. *ibid.*, 4 March 1921.

77. *ibid.*, 11 February 1921.

78. *ibid.*, 18 March 1921.

79. *ibid.*, 4 March 1921.

80. *ibid.*, 21 January 1921.

81. *ibid.*, 1 January 1921.

82. *ibid.*, 21 January 1921.

83. 'Institut khudozhestvennoi kul'tury', p. 86.

84. 'Ot izobrazitel'nosti k konstruktsii.' Although certain articles were written for this it was never issued because of lack of financial resources.

85. Although the report gives 1922 as the date when INKhUK became part of the State Academy of Artistic Sciences – GAKhN ('Institut khudozhestvennoi kul'tury', p. 86), it seems that INKhUK continued to function as a more or less independent body until 1924. The last attendance list is for 1 February 1924 and there may have been a few informal meetings held after that, possibly until the end of March 1924. Those who attended the last recorded meeting included Rodchenko and Stepanova. In January 1924 Babichev, representing INKhUK, met representatives of the Academy to discuss the possibility of affiliating the Institute to the Academy so that INKhUK could be financially subsidised yet maintain its independence. However, the Academy insisted that financial aid meant control.

86. 'Institut khudozhestvennoi kul'tury', p. 86.

87. *ibid.*, p. 88.

88. *ibid.*

89. *ibid.*

90. *ibid.*

91. The information bureau called them '25 masters of left art' ('Institut khudozhestvennoi kul'tury', p. 88).

92. Although Rom is not mentioned by the report in *Russkoe iskusstvo*, he is cited by Lobanov as an example of one of the twenty-five artists who went into industry (*Khudozhestvennye gruppirovki*, p. 101).

93. *ibid.* The $5 \times 5 = 25$ exhibition took place in Moscow in September 1921. The five artists who participated in the exhibition – Aleksandra Ekster, Aleksandr Vesnin, Lyubov' Popova, Aleksandr Rodchenko and Varvara Stepanova – each exhibited five works. Stepanova's declaration stressed her rejection of the contemplative function of art and her acceptance of 'CONSTRUCTION as positive activity' ($5 \times 5 = 25$. *Katalog*, p. 3). Lyubov' Popova made the most explicit statement of the group: 'All the present experiments are figurative and must be regarded only as a series of preparatory experiments towards concrete material constructions' (*ibid.*, p. 7).

94. 'Institut khudozhestvennoi kul'tury', p. 88.

95. *ibid.*

96. *ibid.* INKhUK was also responsible for setting up relations with artists in Vitebsk and Petrograd and outside Russia.

97. 'Institut khudozhestvennoi kul'tury', p. 88.

98. *ibid.*

99. *ibid.* The date for Lavinskii's paper is not given by *Russkoe iskusstvo*, however Khan-Magomedov gives 26 January 1922 as the date when Lavinskii delivered his paper ('A. M. Lavinskii. Put' v proizvodstvennoe iskusstvo', *Tekhnicheskaya estetika*, No. 1, 1980, p. 20). Although *Russkoe iskusstvo* reports the title of Lavinskii's paper as 'On Neo-Engineerism', Lavinskii's manuscript (undated) is entitled 'Engineerism (Theses)' ('Inzhenerizm (Tezisy)') and ends with 'Theses toward the City of the Future' ('Tezisy k gorodu budushchego') (see A. Lavinskii, 'Inzhenerizm', MS, private archive, Moscow). It is possible but very unlikely that Lavinskii presented two papers to INKhUK with such very similar titles. I therefore assume that the MS gives the correct title.

100. 'Institut khudozhestvennoi kul'tury', p. 88. It should be noted that the majority of these commissions were executed, if not always published. Arvatov's article 'Oveshchestvlennaya utopia' was published in *LEF*, No. 1, 1923, pp. 61–4. Rodchenko's paper 'The Line' ('Linya') was apparently delivered to an INKhUK meeting on 26 November 1921 and exists in manuscript form, dated 1921 (private archive, Moscow). Two English translations are available – A. Rodchenko, 'The Line', with introduction and notes by Andrei Boris Nakov, *Arts Magazine*, Vol. 47, No. 7, 1973, pp. 50–2, and A. Rodchenko, 'Line', trans. John Bowlt, in *From Surface to Space*, pp. 65–7. Popova's article 'K voprosu o novykh metodakh v nashei khudozhestvennoi shkole' exists in manuscript form and is dated 1921 (private archive, Moscow). Popova seems to have worked on this problem with some interest, since several drafts of the paper exist.

101. 'Front khudozhestvennogo truda. Materialy k vserossiiskoi konferentsii levykh v iskusstve. Konstruktivisty', *Ermitazh*, No. 13, 1922, p. 3.

102. 'Programma uchebnoi podgruppy rabochei gruppy konstruktivistov INKhUKa', 1921, typescript, private archive, Moscow. This 'Programme of the Subsidiary Study Group of the First Working Group of Constructivists' states that the First Working Group of Constructivists was set up in March 1921. This programme does differ slightly from 'The Programme of the Working Group of Constructivists of INKhUK' ('Programma rabochei gruppy konstruktivistov INKhUKa', 1921, MS, private archive, Moscow), and from the text of the 'The First Programme of the Working Group of Constructivists', also of 1921, which was printed in the Moscow magazine *Ermitazh* in August 1922 ('Pervaya programma rabochei gruppy konstruktivistov', *Ermitazh*, No. 13, 1922, pp. 3–4). The *Ermitazh* version in turn differs from the variant of the programme published by the Hun-

garian magazine *Egység* in Vienna in 1922 ('A konstruktivistak osoportjanak programma', *Egység*, No. 2, 1922, p. 5). The Hungarian version included a list of slogans which the *Ermitazh* had not included. An English translation of the *Egység* version of the programme was made by Gabo and printed in *Gabo*, p. 153, under the title 'The programme of the Productivist Group'. Gabo's statement on p. 153 that he has translated the text from *Egység*, the strong textual similarities, the inclusion of the slogans and the identical layout and numbering confirm that the text he had translated was the 'The Programme of the Working Group of Constructivists' printed in *Egység* in 1922. In the West the term 'Constructivist' was used to refer to works of a purely aesthetic nature, and by 1957 Gabo was himself using the term to describe his work. Gabo frequently referred to the Constructivists as Productivists in order to differentiate their creative position from his own. In this particular instance the transposition is not surprising, but confusing. Subsequent commentators have relied on Gabo's translation and have referred to the text as 'The programme of the Productivist Group'. Another confusion which has arisen about this document concerns its authorship. Rodchenko and Stepanova were cited by Gabo as the authors and subsequent publications have reiterated this. In fact, the manuscript documentation and printed sources state clearly that Aleksei Gan, along with Stepanova and Rodchenko, was a founding member of the group and an author of its manifesto (see 'Programma uchebnoi podgruppy rabochei gruppy konstruktivistov', 'Programma rabochei gruppy konstruktivistov INKhUKa', and 'Konstruktivisty', *Ermitazh* No. 13, 1922, p. 3).

103. 'Programma uchebnoi podgruppy'.
104. Gan, *Konstruktivizm*.
105. 'Programma uchebnoi podgruppy'.
106. 'Programma rabochei gruppy konstruktivistov INKhUKa', MS, private archive, Moscow.
107. *ibid.*
108. *ibid.* All the above account is based on this manuscript.
109. K. Ioganson, 'Ot konstruktsii k teknike i izobreteniyu', 9 March 1922, MS, private archive, Moscow, p. 1.
110. *ibid.*
111. *ibid.*, p. 2.
112. *ibid.*, p. 1.
113. *ibid.*, p. 2.
114. Rudenstine, *Russian Avant-Garde Art*, Nos. 67–8.
115. *ibid.*, Nos. 96–7.
116. 'Protokol zasedaniya INKhUKa', 26 December 1921, MS, private archive, Moscow. Alfred Kemeny (1896–1945) was a Hungarian art critic and theoretician who was a member of the Hungarian avant-garde group MA. In Moscow in 1921, David Shterenberg, then head of IZO, introduced him to Gabo, through whom he became acquainted with the personalities and works of other members of the Russian avant-garde. Gabo also supplied him with photographic material and texts, including that of *The Realistic Manifesto*. Kemeny attended some INKhUK meetings and delivered two talks there in December 1921: 8 December 'The Latest Trends in Contemporary German and Russian Art' ('Noveishie napravleniya v sovremennom nemetskom i russkom iskusstve'), and on 26 December 'Concerning the Constructive Work of the OBMOKhU' ('O konstruktivnykh rabotakh OBMOKhU'). Returning to Berlin in 1922 he issued a manifesto with Moholy-Nagy, entitled 'Dynamische-konstruktivisches Kraftsystem', printed in the March edition of *Der Sturm*, which relied very heavily on Russian ideas. Gabo accused them of plagiarism (Draft of a letter, undated, private archive, London). Kemeny was involved with Kallai, Moholy-Nagy and Peri in writing another manifesto which was published in *Egység* in 1923. An English translation of this text is printed in *The Hungarian Avant-Garde: The Eight and the Activists* (London, Hayward Gallery, 1980). Later Alfred Kemeny also published articles about contemporary Russian art in Germany. Among these was 'Die abstrakte Gestaltung vom Suprematismus bis heute', *Das Kunstblatt*, No. 8, 1924, pp. 245–8.

117. 'Protokol zasedaniya INKhUKa', 8 December 1921.
118. *ibid.* Kemeny disregarded Tatlin's corner counter-reliefs. It is interesting to note that Kemeny also put Rodchenko in the same category with Tatlin.
119. 'Protokol zasedaniya INKhUKa', 8 December 1921.
120. *ibid.* Stenberg said, 'Most important for us is the work with material.'
121. This should be related to Tatlin's conception of the artist as an essentially collective creative entity (see Chapter Seven).
122. 'Protokol zasedaniya INKhUKa', 8 December 1921.
123. A. Babichev, untitled notes, private archive, Moscow, p. 1.
124. 'Tezisy po dokladu "konstruktivizm"'. This is conserved in a private archive in Moscow.
125. *ibid.*, p. 1.
126. *ibid.*, pp. 1–2. *Oformlenie* means design or mounting to do with the external appearance of an object. *Khudozhestvennoe oformlenie* means decorative design. It does not denote the completely different approach to design which was embodied in Constructivism and in the emergence of the concept of design. I therefore have once again chosen to retain the Russian word to suggest the sense of the evolution of these concepts over the period in question.
127. *Vestnik intellektual'nogo proizvodstva.*
128. Gan, *Konstruktivizm*, p. 1. Sections of this book appear in translation in Bann, *Constructivism*, pp. 33–42.
129. See A. Nove, *An Economic History of the USSR* (London, 1972), pp. 83–118, for details of the New Economic Policy. For the reorganisation of Narkompros and the effects of NEP in the cultural sphere, see Fitzpatrick, *Commissariat of Enlightenment*, especially Ch. 10.
130. See Chapter Six for details of these groups. Gan was very disconsolate about official artistic ideas: 'The communists of Narkompros who direct artistic affairs differ more from the non-communists outside Narkompros. They also belong to the camp of "the beautiful" as "the last prisoners of the eternal"' (*Konstruktivizm*, p. 1).
131. *ibid.*, p. 19. This somewhat conflicts with his previous statement that Constructivism arose from immediate participation in revolutionary activities.
132. *ibid.*, p. 53.
133. *ibid.*, p. 55.
134. *ibid.*, pp. 61–2.
135. 'Chto delat' khudozhniku poka?' Brik delivered this paper to a meeting of the Academic Council of INKhUK on 13 April 1922 (see 'Protokol zasedaniya uchenogo soveta INKhUKa', No. 10, 13 April 1922, MS, private archive, Moscow).
136. *ibid.*
137. *ibid.*
138. A very typical exposition of his ideas is to be

found in 'Khudozhnik i kommuna', *Izobrazitel'noe iskusstvo*, No. 1, 1919. This platform remained Brik's position even while he was head of INKhUK in 1922. Although Brik continued to attend INKhUK meetings until 1924 (his signature appears on the last attendance list of 1924), in 1923 his attentions moved increasingly in the direction of literary work (with the appearance of the journal *LEF*) and criticism (e.g. his novel *Ne poputchitsa*). Following this a split within the left front occurred in 1923. Chuzhak wrote a review of the novel asserting that it was not needed as art of the present day and that it contradicted communist perspectives (see 'Osoboe mnenie', written to *LEF* as a review which remained unpublished (TsGALI, fond 340, op., 1, ed. khr. 11, 14.2.1923)). The rift between Chuzhak and *LEF* was completed at the point when he criticised Mayakovskii's *Pro eto* as well. Although perhaps not so important as a theoretician of production art Brik did have considerable importance as an organiser, galvanising his confrères into activity. Stenberg referred to this during the debate at INKhUK on 26 December 1922 ('Protokol zasedaniya INKhUKa', MS, private archive, Moscow).

139. 'Institut khudozhestvennoi kul'tury', p. 88.

140. 'Proizvodstvo kul'tury'.

141. To make this distinction clear in Russian, Kushner used the term *'predmet'* to apply to objects generally and he used the word *'veshch''* to denote objects that are man-made. To preserve this distinction I have merely added the 'man-made' to object when it is appropriate. B. Kushner, 'Proizvodstvo kul'tury', 1922, MS, private archive, Moscow.

142. *ibid.*

143. B. Kushner, 'Rol' inzhenera v proizvodstve', MS, private archive, Moscow. The date for this paper is given in 'Institut khudozhestvennoi kul'tury', p. 88, as 30 March 1923. This paper was also printed in *LEF* under the title 'The Organisers of Production'. See B. Kushner, 'Organizatory proizvodstva (Doklad, chitannyi v Institute khudozhestvennoi kul'tury 30 marta 1922g.)', *LEF*, No. 3, 1923, pp. 97–103.

144. Kushner, 'Rol' inzhenera v proizvodstve', part 2, MS, private archive, Moscow.

145. B. Kushner, 'Khudozhnik v proizvodstve', MS, private archive, Moscow, paper delivered at INKhUK, 6 April 1922.

146. *Iskusstvo v proizvodstve* (Moscow, 1921), p. 4.

147. O. Brik, 'V poryadke dnya', in *Iskusstvo v proizvodstve*, pp. 7–8.

148. *ibid.*, p. 8.

149. *ibid.*

150. A. Filippov, 'Proizvodstvennoe iskusstvo', *Iskusstvo v proizvodstve*, pp. 9–12.

151. *ibid.*

152. V. Voronov, 'Chistoe i prikladnoe iskusstvo', in *Iskusstvo v proizvodstve*, pp. 19–27.

153. *ibid.*, p. 27.

154. D. Shterenberg, 'Pora ponyat'', in *Iskusstvo v proizvodstve*, pp. 5–6.

155. D. Arkin, 'Izobrazitel'noe iskusstvo i material'naya kul'tura', in *Iskusstvo v proizvodstve*, pp. 13–18. Filippov, 'Proizvodstvennoe iskusstvo', p. 11.

156. *Krasnaya nov'*, *Pechat' i revolyutsiya*, *Zhizn' iskusstva*. The Proletkul't journal *Gorn* adopted a Constructivist stance in accordance with the generally Productivist ideas expressed by Proletkul't theorists as for example 'the art of the new world will be production art or it will not be at all' (V. Pletnev, 'Na ideologicheskom fronte', *Pravda*, 27 September 1922).

157. *Ot mol'berta k mashine.*

158. See reviews of Tarabukin's books as for example in *Pechat' i revolyutsiya*, No. 5, 1924, pp. 292–9.

159. *Masterstvo* denotes a theoretical and manual mastery of formal, artistic and technical elements. I have retained the Russian term since mastery in English does not express so clearly this combination of technical skill, craftsmanship and workmanship that the Russian term conveys.

160. N. Tarabukin, *Ot mol'berta k mashine* (Moscow, 1923), p. 7. A full translation of this book into French was made by A. B. Nakov (see N. Tarabukin, *Le Dernier Tableau* (Paris, 1972)).

161. Tarabukin, *Ot mol'berta*, p. 7.

162. *ibid.*, p. 13.

163. *ibid.*, p. 9.

164. *ibid.*, p. 10. This definition of construction is rather at odds with Tarabukin's own attempt to apply 'construction' as a purely artistic term (*Ot mol'berta*, pp. 13–15). It should be noted that there is considerable confusion and ambiguity in Tarabukin's use of the term 'Constructivism'. At one point he referred to Constructivism as an art movement concerned with the creation of works of art (*Ot mol'berta*, pp. 7, 18), and yet he also defined it as a movement with a strictly utilitarian content (*ibid.*, p. 10). This inconsistency continued in his juxtaposition of the practice of 'Constructivism' and the ideal concept of 'production *masterstvo*' (production skills) (*ibid.*, pp. 18–19).

165. Tarabukin, *Ot molberta*, pp. 10–11. It should be noted that Lunacharskii also criticised the Constructivists (and the Productivists) for their aping of technology. 'The factory and the mill, the most powerful organising forces, and the foundation stone not only of the future rule of man over nature but also of socialism ... nevertheless must be perceived as an hostile principle, while, as Engels said, the productive powers of man govern man himself. Our Russian theoreticians, like Brik ... are most decidedly not in a position to understand this. It seems to them that this comprises the proletarisation of life, and that all functions of human society will be reduced to mechanical production, to the production of mechanically, at best physiologically, helpful objects or even (it seems he doesn't say this but in actual fact this idea dominates the Constructivists in everything) in the mimicry of the machine. For Tatlin mimics the machine ... this is a machine on which it is impossible to work. This is a peculiarly ape-like technicism' (Lunacharskii, 'Vstupitel'naya stat'ya', in G. Kaizer, *Dramy* (Moscow/Leningrad, 1923); quoted from A. V. Lunacharskii, *Ob izobrazitel'nom iskusstve* (Moscow, 1966), Vol. 1, p. 475). Lunacharskii likened the Constructivists to monkeys given spectacles and putting them on their tails because they are unable to guess that they are to go on the nose. 'They all play at being engineers, but they don't know as much of the essence of machinery as a savage' ('Teatr RSFSR', *Pechat' i revolyutsiya*, No. 7, 1922).

166. Tarabukin, *Ot mol'berta*, p. 11. Tarabukin regarded the two-dimensional work of the Constructivists as even more absurd and representing a return to representational art that was more ridiculous than Suprematism because it represented structures that were to be built. It is evident in this context that the two-dimensional works referred to were laboratory works by the Constructivists.

167. Tarabukin, *Ot mol'berta*, p. 21.

168. *ibid.*, p. 19.

169. *ibid.*, p. 35.

170. In Russian these terms are *sotial'no-technicheskii* and *sotsial'no-ideologicheskii* (see B. Arvatov, *Iskusstvo i klassy* (Moscow, 1923), p. 12).

171. Arvatov, *Iskusstvo i klassy*, p. 12.
172. B. Arvatov, *Iskusstvo i proizvodstvo* (Moscow, 1926), p. 23.
173. *ibid.*, p. 72.
174. B. Arvatov, 'Utopiya ili nauka', *LEF*, No. 4, 1924, p. 18.
175. Arvatov, *Iskusstvo i klassy*, p. 34.
176. This was recognised by contemporary art critics. See A. Fedorov-Davydov's review of *Iskusstvo i klassy*, in *Pechat' i revolyutsiya*, No. 3, 1924, and I. Matsa, 'Sovetskaya mysl' v 20e gody', in *Iz istorii sovetskoi esteticheskoi mysli* (Moscow, 1967), pp. 46–7.
177. B. Arvatov, *Natan Al'tman* (Berlin, 1924), p. 34.
178. *ibid.*, p. 35.
179. *ibid.*, p. 51.
180. Arvatov considered these new technicians to be the 'most radical and transitional members of the new intelligentsia' (Arvatov, *Iskusstvo i proizvodstvo*, p. 70).
181. Arvatov, *Natan Al'tman*, p. 51.
182. Arvatov, *Iskusstvo i proizvodstvo*, pp. 72–3.
183. Tarabukin, *Ot mol'berta*, p. 84.
184. Arvatov, *Iskusstvo i proizvodstvo*, p. 88.
185. *ibid.*, p. 96. It should be noted that in Russian the term *'tekhnika'* stands for technics, techniques, and for engineering. It therefore has much of the meaning which is English is given to the word 'technology', although in Russian there is another word *'tekhnologiya'* which also stands for technology.
186. Arvatov, *Iskusstvo i proizvodstvo*, p. 91.
187. *ibid.*, p. 103.
188. Tarabukin, *Ot mol'berta*, p. 35.
189. Arvatov, *Iskusstvo i proizvodstvo*, p. 127.
190. *ibid.*, p. 129.
191. *ibid.*, pp. 90–1.
192. *ibid.*, p. 93.
193. *Filosofiya tekhniki* (see Tarabukin, *Ot mol'berta*, p. 41); compare this with the definition by O. Spengler that 'technology is tactics and an activity with a defined aim' (*Decline of the West*, London, 1923)).
194. I. Grossman-Roshchin describes the tendency as 'it must in all fields fight under the banner of anti-psychologism' ('Sotsial'nyi zamysel futurizma', *LEF*, No. 4, 1924).
195. I. Matsa, *Iskusstvo epokhi zrelogo kapitalizma na zapade* (Moscow, 1929), p. 242.
196. Tarabukin, *Ot mol'berta*, p. 17.
197. S. Tret'yakov, 'LEF i NEP', *LEF*, No. 2, 1923, p. 75.
198. In the beginning of the 1920s B. Kushner put forward a rather horrifying description of the logical development of this theory. He stated that in the city of the future everyone should dance at the same time, everyone should listen to music at the same time, 'communist socialised poetry must uphold the intense voice to the degree of a roar listened to simultaneously by a large crowd' ('Reforma formy', *Gorn*, No. 2/7, 1922, p. 112).
199. 'Protokol doklada t. Arvatova v tsentral'nom moskovskom Proletkul'te, 27 marta 1923', *Gorn*, No. 8, 1923.
200. By this time the First Working Group of Constructivists, consisting of Gan and Miller, etc., had broken with 'the pseudo-Constructivists' and writers of *LEF*. See their statement 'Pervaya rabochaya gruppa konstruktivistov' in the '*Pervaya diskussionnaya vystavka ob'edinenii aktivnogo revolyutsionnogo iskusstva*' (Moscow 1924); reprinted in Matsa, *Sovetskoe iskusstvo*, p. 317.
201. Arvatov, 'Utopiya ili nauka', p. 17.
202. *ibid.*
203. B. Arvatov, 'Oveshchestvlennaya utopiya', *LEF*, No. 1, 1923, p. 61.
204. *ibid.*
205. B. Arvatov, 'Proletariat i levoe iskusstvo', *Vestnik iskusstv*, No. 1, 1922, p. 10. Tarabukin has exactly the same opinion concerning the significance of non-utilitarian constructions.
206. Arvatov, 'Oveshcestvlennaya utopiya', pp. 62–3. Arvatov's description of the project is accompanied by four detailed illustrations of the project.
207. Chuzhak, 'Pod znakom', p. 31. The journal *LEF* (*Zhurnal levogo fronta iskusstv - Journal of the Left Front of the Arts*) was published in Moscow from 1923 to 1925. The editorial board included B. Arvatov, N. Aseev, O. Brik, B. Kushner, V. Mayakovskii (editor), S. Tret'yakov and N. Chuzhak. Later it became *Novyi LEF* (*New LEF*), published 1927–8.
208. Chuzhak, 'Pod znakom', p. 31.
209. *ibid.*, p. 32.

NOTES TO CHAPTER FOUR

1. *Izvestiya VTsIK*, 25 December 1920.
2. This theme formed the basis of an article by V. Barooshian, 'VKhUTEMAS and Constructivism', *Soviet Union*, Vol. 3, part 2, 1976, pp. 197–207. Although the fullest account of the VKhUTEMAS to appear outside the Soviet Union so far, this still remains very general.
3. *Izvestiya VTsIK*, 25 December 1920. The Russian word *'masterskie'* can mean both 'studios' and 'workshops'. I have rendered it as 'studios' here to stress the continuing fine-artistic profile of the Free Studios, and used 'workshops' to stress the consciously industrial orientation of the later VKhUTEMAS.
4. 'Reorganizatsiya khudozhestvennykh zavedenii v Moskve', *Izvestiya VTsIK*, 7 September 1918. According to the archive, this decree was dated 8 September 1918 (TsGALI, fond 681, op. 1, ed. khr. 28, list 42). In Petrograd the existing Academy was also dissolved and the Pegoskhumas (Petrogradskye gosudarstvennye svobodnye uchebnye masterskie - Petrograd State Free Teaching Studios), renamed in 1919 the Svobodnye masterskie, were opened on 10 October 1918 (M. Spasovskii, 'Khudozhestvennaya shkola', *Argonavty*, No. 1, 1923). According to Spasovskii the professors appointed to teach in these studios included Andreev, Ioffe, Al'tman, Karev, Tatlin and Matyushin. The students were themselves responsible for choosing the artists they wished to supervise the studios ('Instruktsiya vyborov rukovoditelei svobodnykh khudozhest-vennykh masterskikh', in *Spravochnik Otdela izobrazitel'nykh iskusstv Narkomprosa* (Moscow, 1920), pp. 33–5). As Matsa points out, Spasovskii's account is not completely accurate. Spasovskii names the commissars of the Free Studios as Karev (1918), Brik (1919) and Shkol'nik (1920); however, Matsa states that Al'tman, Punin and Shterenberg also filled this post (I. Matsa, *Sovetskoe iskusstvo za 15 let. Materialy i dokumentatsiya* (Moscow/Leningrad, 1933), p. 151). State Free Art Studios were also set up in Ryazan', Kazan', Saratov, Penza, Voronezh, and Tver' (see 'Svedeniya o khudozhestvennom obrazovanii na 1918/19 akad. god', in Matsa, *Sovetskoe iskusstvo*, p. 155). A full list is printed in *Spravochnik IZO*, pp. 46–9.
5. 13 December 1918 was the date of the opening of the Second State Free Art Studios in Moscow, when Lunacharskii delivered his famous speech (TsGALI, fond 681, op. 1, ed. khr. 118, list 538–51).
6. 'Afisha pervykh gosudarstvennykh svobod-

nykh khudozhestvennykh masterskikh', MS, private archive, Moscow.

7. It is interesting to note that at this juncture, 1918, Tatlin was categorised as a Futurist (TsGALI, fond 680, op. 1, ed. khr. 1018, list 105).

8. Matsa, *Sovetskoe iskusstvo*, p. 150.

9. TsGALI, fond 680, op. 1, ed. khr. 1018, list 105–6.

10. *ibid.*, list 110. See also 'Instruktsiya vyborov rukovoditelei svobodnykh gosudarstvennykh khudozhestvennykh masterskikh', *Izvestiya VTsIK*, 7 September 1918.

11. TsGALI, fond 681, op. 1, ed. khr. 1018, list 196.

12. *ibid.*

13. These were classified as Realism–Naturalism (Arkhipov and Malyutin), Impressionism (Kuznetsov and Korovin), Neo-Impressionism (Mashkov and Konchalovskii), Post-Impressionism (Rozhdestvenskii and Fal'k), Suprematism (Malevich and Morgunov), Futurism (Tatlin and Kandinskii) (TsGALI, fond 680, op. 1, ed. khr. 1018, list 106). Ultimately many more were appointed. An undated list (*ibid.*, list 428) names 50 artists and architects teaching in the Free Studios.

14. V. Kandinskii, 'K reforme khudozhestvennoi shkoly', *Iskusstvo*, No. 1, 1923, p. 405.

15. Many important figures such as Malevich, Tatlin and Rodchenko had failed to complete their courses for this reason.

16. TsGALI, fond 680, op. 1, ed. khr. 1018, list 1. In connection with this it should be noted that a conference of young artists and students in May 1918 resolved that art schools should be free, in the sense that each student should be free to select his own instructor and have absolute freedom in every manifestation of his creative work ('Rezolyutsiya konferentsii uchashchikhsya iskusstva', *Anarkhiya*, 12 May 1918).

17. L. Khlebnikov, 'Bor'ba realistov i futuristov vo VKhUTEMASe', in *Lenin i Lunacharskii. Perepiska, doklady, dokumenty* (Moscow, 1971), p. 706.

18. 'Skhema uchebnogo plana gosudarstvennykh svobodnykh khudozhestvennykh masterskikh', in *Spravochnik IZO*, pp. 27–8.

19. There has been little information available on the nature of these two types of studios. I have based my distinction on archive material in TsGALI, fond 681, op. 1, ed. khr. 1018, but the precise delineation remains unclear.

20. There were also studios without supervisors but it is difficult to ascertain how these worked. According to Kandinskii the experiment was 'not very successful and almost pitiable' (Kandinskii, 'K reforme khudozhestvennoi shkoly', p. 401) and the studios were empty.

21. *Spravochnik IZO*, p. 27.

22. *ibid.*, p. 29. The 'Instruktsiya izucheniya iskusstva' is printed in full on pp. 29–32.

23. TsGALI, fond 681, op. 2, ed. khr. 65, list 58.

24. It should be stressed that the Civil War and the tremendous fuel and food shortages hampered the practical implementation of these programmes, as contemporary accounts show. 'The students of the First and Second State Free Schools, in Moscow, during the present heating crisis go barefoot into the forest to collect firewood and bring it themselves on sledges in order to heat their studios' (D. Shterenberg, 'Nasha zadacha', *Khudozhestvennaya zhizn'*, No. 2, 1920, p. 5). Archival evidence supports this description (TsGALI, fond 681, op. 2, ed. khr. 25, list 17).

25. For historical details concerning the Moscow School of Painting, Sculpture and Architecture, see N. A. Dmitrievna, *Moskovskoe uchilishche zhivopisi, vayaniya i zodchestva* (Moscow, 1959). For the Stroganov, see E. N. Shul'gina, 'Stroganovskoe uchilishche', in Z. N. Bykov, ed., *Moskovskoe vysshee khudozhestvenno-promyshlennoe uchilishche (byvshee Stroganovskoe) 1825–1965* (Moscow, 1965), pp. 11–36.

26. N. F. Lapshin, 'Avtobiograficheskie zapiski', 1941, GRM, fond 144, ed. khr. 452, list 1.

27. *ibid.*, list 4. Lapshin later taught at the VKhUTEMAS but there are no records of the teaching methods he employed there.

28. A. Goncharov, 'VKhUTEMAS', *Tvorchestvo*, No. 4, 1967, pp. 15–16.

29. Taken from the evidence of a former pupil of Aleksandra Ekster in Kiev, in conversation with the author, November 1974. According to A. B. Nakov, the sequence of styles was Fauvism, Cubism and Abstraction (*Alexandra Exter* (Paris, Galerie Jean Chauvelin, 1972), p. 38).

30. K. Malevich, 'Programma zanyatii v masterskikh uchebnogo 1919 i 1920 goda', TsGALI, fond 681, op. 1, ed. khr. 845, list 353.

31. V. Kandinskii, 'Masterskaya Kandinskogo. Tezisy prepodavaniya', TsGALI, fond 680, op. 1, ed. khr. 845, list 351–2.

32. Gabo's reminiscences of the VKhUTEMAS seem to apply more accurately to the Free Studios. These were indeed 'both a school and a free academy' where 'many ideological questions between opposing artists ... were thrashed out', which 'had a much greater influence on the development of constructive art than all the teaching' (N. Gabo, 'Russia and Constructivism', in *Gabo: Constructions, Sculpture, Paintings, Drawings, Engravings* (London, 1957), p. 157).

33. Malishevskii, 'Otchet metfaka', TsGALI, fond 681, op. 2, ed. khr. 177, list 201.

34. Matsa, *Sovetskoe iskusstvo*, p. 151.

35. 'Instruktsiya vyborov rukovoditelei svobodnykh gosudarstvennykh khudozhestvennykh masterskikh', *Izvestiya VTsIK*, 7 September 1918.

36. 'Protokol soveta glavnykh masterov SVOMASa', 21 October 1918, TsGALI, fond 680, op. 1, ed. khr. 1018, list 200. The arrangement of one month of free movement among the studios was initiated by the Moscow Free Studios and may not have been in practice in the other Free Studios.

37. 'Instruktsiya vyborov rukovoditelei'.

38. The parallel with craft workshops extended to the nomenclature. A student was called a *podmaster'e* or apprentice.

39. This was not always so. The Stenberg brothers for instance worked in the studio of Yakulov, an eclectic modernist who produced rather Expressionistic work (see Kafe Pittoresk, Chapter Two). The reason given by Vladimir Stenberg was that Yakulov allowed them to do exactly as they wished (conversation with V. A. Stenberg, April 1974).

40. Conversation with V. A. Stenberg, April 1974.

41. Ravdel' 'Otchet', TsGALI, fond 681, op. 2, ed. khr. 47, list 37.

42. V. Denisov, 'O khudozhestvennoi shkole', *Zhizn' iskusstva*, No. 8, 1921.

43. Writing in 1923 Kandinskii criticised both the extreme, rather anarchic freedom of the Svobodnye masterskie and the extreme regulation and strict syllabuses of the VKhUTEMAS as forms of artistic education ('K reforme khudozhestvennoi shkoly', *Iskusstvo*, No. 1, 1923, p. 000).

44. Ravdel', 'Otchet', TsGALI, fond 681, op. 2, ed. khr. 47, list 37.

45. TsGALI, fond 681, op. 2, ed. khr. 25, list 23.

46. The evidence suggests that the original impetus for reorganising the First and Second State Free Art Studios came from within the Directory of the Studios. By September 1920 they had appealed to the Scientific and Technical Department

of VSNKh (Vysshii sovet narodnogo khozyaistva – Supreme Soviet of the National Economy) with the idea of establishing a specialist school of 'artistic and technical education on the basis of strict conformity to the contemporary needs of the RSFSR' (TsGALI, fond 681, op. 2, ed. khr. 2, list 21).

47. A. V. Abramova, 'VKhUTEMAS-VKhUTEIN: 1918-1930', in Bykov, *Moskovskoe vysshee khudozhestvenno-promyshlennoe uchilishche*, p. 40.

48. TsGALI, fond 681, op. 2, ed. khr. 25, list 21.

49. *Izvestiya VTsIK*, 25 December 1920.

50. *ibid.*

51. S. Bojko, 'VKhUTEMAS', in *The 1920s in Eastern Europe* (Cologne, Galerie Gmurzynska, 1975), p. 20.

52. The list is reprinted in Matsa, *Sovetskoe iskusstvo*, pp. 251-2. It includes Popova, Rodchenko and Pevsner. The VKhUTEMAS won the right to rations with its new status. In July 1920 the Free Studios had requested special rations (TsGALI, fond 681, op. 2, ed. khr. 20). One of the difficulties encountered in assessing the size of the VKhUTEMAS at this time was that students remained on the ration list for survival even when no longer attending the school.

53. 'Ot redaktsii', in *Iskusstvo v proizvodstve*, p. 3.

54. The government approved of the idea that art should participate in raising the quality of industrial goods. The Constructivist approach, however, with its violent opposition to the validity of fine art and easel painting and its advocacy of abstract formal experimentation and extreme technicisation, was less officially popular.

55. 'Khudozhestvenno-proizvodstvennyi podotdel IZO NKP', in *Iskusstvo v proizvodstve*, p. 34; reprinted in Matsa, *Sovetskoe iskusstvo*, p. 64. According to his own memoirs, Rodchenko also worked in this department (A. Rodtchenko, 'Vladimir Tatlin', *Opus International*, No. 4, 1967, p. 18).

56. A full list of workshops existing under the Department is given in *Spravochnik IZO*, pp. 96-104, and *Iskusstvo v proizvodstve*, pp. 37-9.

57. *Iskusstvo v proizvodstve*, p. 36. This body contained representatives, workers from the textile, building, china painting and other trades (*ibid.*, p. 34). The declaration of this committee embodied many of the ideas that were discussed in Chapter Three: 'The construction of a new socialist life cannot be managed without a fundamental transformation of the existing external forms of everyday life, in order to realise the necessary conditions for the liberation of work, and to embellish and develop the everyday life of the worker, to replace the monotonous and dull forms in this life for beautiful and joyful ones, it is necessary to develop the production of artistic objects of everyday life in all ways and to diffuse them widely throughout the life of the workers.

'Combining in itself the elements of art and industry, art production [*khudozhestvennaya promyshlennost'*] apart from this basic aim ... must pursue the task of raising the artistic and general cultural level of the masses, promoting art's rapprochement with industrial work, and developing the master worker in the worker' ('Deklaratsiya khudozhestvenno-proizvodstvennogo soveta Narkomprosa (1920 g.)', in Matsa, *Sovetskoe iskusstvo*, p. 65).

58. For details, see *Iskusstvo v proizvodstve*, pp. 34-5.

59. For full details, see the publication of its proceedings *Pervaya vserossiiskaya konferentsiya po khudozhestvennoi promyshlennosti avgust 1919* (Moscow, 1920).

60. 'Rech' narodnogo komissara po prosve-

hcheniyu A. V. Lunacharskogo', in *Pervaya vserossiiskaya*, pp. 63-4.

61. For details of this body, see N. Kol'tsova, 'Programma-deklaratsiya khudozhestvenno-proizvodstvennoi komissii', *Tekhnicheskaya estetika*, No. 10, 1967, pp. 14-15. Kol'tsova has printed in full the declaration of its aims.

62. Kol'tsova, 'Programma', p. 15.

63. On the formation of TsIT, see E. H. Carr, *Socialism in One Country, 1924-1926* (London, 1970), Vol. 1, pp. 409-11. TsIT subsequently organised short-term labour training courses in basic knowledge of industrial processes for semi-skilled factory work. TsIT closed in 1938 when Gastev was arrested. Its courses had been especially popular in the late 1920s because they were quicker and cheaper than those organised by Narkompros.

64. The question of renaming the VKhUTEMAS was raised by Narkompros on 9 September 1925 (TsGALI, fond 681, op. 2, ed. khr. 22, list 97). The VKhUTEMAS soviet had put the issue of the change of name forward to Glavprofobr (the organ directing higher education) at the beginning of 1927, but the actual statutory change did not seem to take effect until 1928.

65. L. Popova, untitled MS, private archive, Moscow.

66. See TsGALI, fond 681, op. 3, ed. khr. 42.

67. The commission set up under the chairmanship of the Impressionist Yuon had decided to return to the former Academic system of training. However, this was combatted by the Constructivists as well as Favorskii and other members of the staff.

68. There is little information available on the precise working of the production workshops. They seem to have been run independently of the faculties to enable the students to have practical experience of working with machines (see TsGALI, fond 681, op. 2, ed. khr. 29).

69. See TsGALI, fond 681, op. 2, ed. khr. 177, and D.A., 'VKhUTEMAS', *Izvestiya VTsIK*, 5 February 1927.

70. 'O reorganizatsii masterskikh 1926', TsGALI, fond 681, op. 2, ed. khr. 185.

71. Abramova, 'VKhUTEMAS-VKhUTEIN', p. 68. The real successor to the VKhUTEIN was the Moscow Higher Artistic and Production School (formerly the Stroganov), Moskovskoe vysshee khudozhestvenno-promyshlennoe uchilishche (byvshee Stroganovskoe), set up in 1945.

72. *Izvestiya VTsIK*, 25 December 1920.

73. N. Adaskina, 'VKhUTEMAS. Ego rol' v formirovanii osnovnykh printsipov sovetskoi khudozhestvennoi pedagogiki 1920kh godov', in *Voprosy russkogo i sovetskogo iskusstva. Materialy itogovoi nauchnoi konferentsii, yanv. 1972* (Moscow, 1973), p. 188.

74. The last six months was devoted to a diploma project.

75. Early provisions for this, made in response to Lenin's stipulations (V. I. Lenin, *Polnoe sobranie sochinenii*, Vol. 52, p. 17, and Vol. 35, p. 174), were expanded when the 1922 government decree established an educational minimum for political subjects in all institutes of higher education (historical materialism; capitalism and the proletarian revolution; the political structure and social tasks of the RSFSR ('Postanovlenie soveta narodnykh komissarov', 1 November 1922, copy sent to VKhUTEMAS, 23 November 1922 – TsGALI, fond 681, op. 2, ed. khr. 9, list 20). It is interesting to note that Boris Kushner taught a course entitled 'Dialektika material'noi kul'tury i iskusstva' (Dialetics of Material Culture and Art). It consisted of seventeen lectures of two hours each in which he traced the evolution of objects up to the advent

of mass production, and into the post-industrial society of communism. He examined the essence of industrial culture, the theory of standardisation and aesthetics in relation to future communist culture, in which there would be a 'unity of arts of the synthetic utopia' (B. Kushner, 'Programma kursa dialektiki material'noi kul'tury i iskusstva', TsGALI, fond 681, op. 2, ed. khr. 49, list 3–4). This seems to belong to the early period of VKhU-TEMAS.

76. There are few indications of the sociological structure of the VKhUTEMAS. However, the Textile faculty produced such an analysis in 1925–6 in which it stated that of a total of 168 students, 57 were the children of workers, 33 of peasants, 64 of Soviet civil servants while only one was a child of a 'non-working element' (TSGALI, fond 681, op. 3, ed. khr. 42, list 23).

77. D. Sarab'yanov, *Aleksei Vasil'evich Babichev. Khudozhnik, teoretik, pedagog* (Moscow, 1974), p. 73, and N. Babicheva, 'Rabfak iskusstv', *Dekorativnoe iskusstvo*, No. 7, 1965, pp. 27–8. In 1923 the Rabfak was reorganised as the Edinyi khudozhestvennyi rabfak iskusstv (United Artistic Rabfak of Arts) and theatrical and musical departments were opened.

78. From Babichev archive; quoted in Abramova, 'VKhUTEMAS-VKhUTEIN', p. 44.

79. K. G. Dorokhov, *Zapiski khudozhnika* (Moscow, 1974), pp. 22–3.

80. This plan seems to have been based on the form of 'Osnovy postroeniya VKhUTEMASa kak VUZa' (TsGALI, fond 681, op. 2, ed. khr. 93, list 368–9). It is undated but according to N. Adaskina it is from 1923 ('VKhUTEMAS', p. 172). In this document the production faculty is of the same composition as in the 1925 plan but Painting, Graphics, Architecture and Sculpture are separate faculties making five in all, without the Basic Division. However, in practice the faculties remained independent operational entities.

81. The plans seem to have been the work of Toot (see V. Toot, 'Doklad Libermana', 11 August 1925, TsGALI, fond 681, op. 2, ed. khr. 22, list 67). In this report Toot presented two variants for reorganisation. In both instances the total number of faculties was reduced to four. In one case they would consist of:
1. Basic Course
2. Architecture faculty
3. Production faculty
4. Painting and Sculpture faculty
In the other of:
1. Basic faculty
2. Plane faculty (Painting and Textiles)
3. Volume faculty (Sculpture and Ceramics)
4. Spatial faculty (Architecture, Wood and Metalwork)

82. See *Spravochnik VKhUTEMASa*.

83. 'Otchet za 1926–1927 chebnyi god po fakul'tetu obrabotki dereva i metalla vysshego khudozhestvenno-tekhnicheskogo instituta', TsGALI, fond 681, op. 3, ed. khr. 42, list 65.

84. TsGALI, fond 681, op. 2, ed. khr. 65, list 90.

85. 'Spisok professorov i rektorov zhivopisnogo otdela', TsGALI, fond 681, op. 2, ed. khr. 65, list 149. A list of July 1924 gave the staff as Kardovskii, Shevchenko, Fal'k, Shterenberg (all in the easel department), Chernyshev (monumental) and A. A. Vesnin and Kuprin (theatrical) (TsGALI, fond 681, op. 2, ed. khr. 103, list 18). See also TsGALI, fond 681, op. 2, ed. khr. 160, list 50–1. Arkhipov was an academic painter. Both Udal'tsova and Drevin had been members of IN-KhUK but had left when it adopted a Constructivist platform (see Chapter Three). Mashkov, Konchalovskii and Fal'k had all been members of

the Knave of Diamonds group and had experimented with a Neo-Cézannist painterly style. Both Shevchenko and Fal'k had experimented with Cubism. None of these artists had adopted abstraction. Drevin's and Udal'tsova's brief flirtation with this had ended in 1921 when they declared their rejection of all abstraction.

86. TsGALI, fond 681, op. 2, ed. khr. 65, list 153.

87. TsGALI, fond 681, op. 2, ed. khr. 93, list 368–9. For the teaching programmes of the Painting faculty, see TsGALI, fond 681, op. 2, ed. khr. 46, list 11–24.

88. For details of their work, see V. Kostin, *OST (Obshchestvo stankovistov)* (Leningrad, 1978).

89. 'Zhivopisnyi fakul'tet', TsGALI, fond 681, op. 2, ed. khr. 174, list 378.

90. S. O. Khan-Magomedov, 'A. M. Lavinskii. Put' v "proizvodstvennoe iskusstvo"', *Tekhnicheskaya estetika*, No. 1, 1980, p. 20.

91. TsGALI, fond 681, op. 2, ed. khr. 65, list 95.

92. TsGALI, fond 681, op. 2, ed. khr. 93, list 368–9.

93. TsGALI, fond 681, op. 2, ed. khr. 65, list 74.

94. Lissitzky returned to Russia in 1925 and was teaching in the Architectural faculty of the VKhU-TEMAS in 1927. In that year Lissitzky taught furniture design for four hours a week to the third year students, he taught the design of architectural interiors for three hours a week to the fourth year and the formal principles of architecture for four hours a week to the fifth year (TsGALI, fond 681, op. 3, ed. khr. 26. list 313–14).

95. *Dlya golosa* and *Rasskaz dva kvadrata*. TsGALI, fond 681, op. 2, ed. khr. 29.

96. TsGALI, fond 681, op. 3, ed. khr. 26.

97. M. Villard, 'A Soviet Art School', *The Arts*, Vol. 16, No. 6, 1930, p. 409.

98. Concerning Stepanova's work at VKhUTE-MAS, see TsGALI, fond 681, op. 2, ed. khr. 103, list 18. For a discussion of Popova's and Stepanova's work in textile production and clothing design, see Chapter Five.

99. Ya. Tugendkhol'd, 'Vystavka proizvodstvennykh fakul'tetov VKhUTEMASa', *Izvestiya VTsIK*, 30 December 1923. This article is reprinted in V. P. Tolstoi, ed., *Sovetskoe dekorativnoe iskusstvo. Materialy i dokumenty 1919–1932. Farfor, fayans, steklo* (Moscow, 1980), pp. 157–9.

100. TsGALI, fond 681, op. 2, ed. khr. 65.

101. See 'Protokol zasedaniya', 7 July 1926, TsGALI, fond 681, op. 2, ed. khr. 174, list 2.

102. See TsGALI, fond 681, op. 2, ed. khr. 160, list 43.

103. During this period architecture was also taught at the Moscow Higher Technical School, MVTU, and in Petrograd-Leningrad at the Academy of Arts, the Polytechnic Institute, the Institute of Civil Engineers and the Institute of Architecture (see V. E. Khazanova, *Sovetsksaya arkhitektura pervykh let Oktyabrya* (Moscow, 1970), p. 201). Of these the VKhUTEMAS was the most committed to modern architecture.

104. *Raboty arkhitekturnogo fakul'teta VKhU-TEMASa 1920–1927* (Moscow, 1927), p. vii.

105. 'Programma arkhitekturnogo fakul'teta', TsGALI, fond 681, op. 2, ed. khr. 14, list 16.

106. *ibid.*, list 16–17.

107. TsGALI, fond 681, op. 2, ed. khr. 93, list 94.

108. V. Petrov, 'ASNOVA za 8 let', *Sovetskaya arkhitektura*, No. 1/2, 1931, pp. 48–51.

109. *ibid.*

110. *Izvestiya ASNOVA*, No. 1, 1926, p. 7. For further details concerning this laboratory, see S. O. Khan-Magomedov, 'Psikhotekhnicheskaya laboratoriya VKhUTEINa', *Tekhnicheskaya estetika* No. 1, 1978, pp. 16–22.

111. 'Zayavlenie ob'edineniya sovremennykh ar-

khitektorov "OSA" v khudozhestvennyi otdel glavnauki Narkomprosa', April 1926; reprinted in V. Khazanova, ed., *Iz istorii sovetskoi arkhitektury 1926-1932. Dokumenty i materialy* (Moscow, 1970), p. 69.

112. M. Ginzburg, 'Konstruktivizm v arkhitekture', *Sovremennaya arkhitektura*, No. 5, 1928, pp. 143-5.

113. M. Ginzburg, 'Konstruktivizm kak metod laboratornoi i pedagogicheskoi raboty', *Sovremennaya arkhitektura*', No. 6, 1928, pp. 170-6. For a lucid examination of the functional method, see C. Cooke, 'Nikolai Krasil'nikov's Quantitative Approach to Architectural Design: An Early Example', *Environment and Planning B*, No. 2, 1975, pp. 3-20.

114. See M. Ya. Ginzburg, 'Programma po kursu teorii arkhitekturnoi kompozitsii', TsGALI, fond 681, op. 2, ed. khr. 14, list 29.

115. See 'Polozhenie ob arkhitekturnom fakul'tete', 3 October 1922, TsGALI, fond 681, op. 2, ed. khr. 14, list 12. Khazanova, *Sovetskaya arkhitektura*, p. 200, dates this document as 1923.

116. 'Otchet o deyatel'nosti arkhiteturnogo fakul'teta VKhUTEMASa za pervye tri trimestra', TsGALI, fond 681, op. 2, ed. khr. 174, list 399.

117. Khazanova, *Sovetskaya arkhitektura*, p. 200, and TsGALI, fond 681, op. 2, ed. khr. 14, list 5. According to the latter (a statement by Golosov and Mel'nikov) their studio had been in existence for two years prior to October 1922.

118. According to Khan-Magomedov, based on TsGALI, the architectural students in February 1924 numbered 242, and in November 1925, 241 ('U istokov sovetskogo dizaina: derevoobdelochnyi fakul'tet VKhUTEMASa (VKhUTEINa)', *Tekhnicheskaya estetika*, No. 2, 1980, p. 13, n. 12).

119. *Raboty arkhitekturnogo fakul'teta*, pp. vii, xi.

120. *ibid.*, p. 10.

121. Vkhutemaska, 'Levaya metafizika', *LEF*, No. 4, 1923, pp. 219-20. The author of the article is identified as E. Semenova by Z. Minto in her introduction to the reminiscences of E. Semenova, 'Vkhutemas, Lef, Mayakovskii', published in *Trudy po russkoi i slavyanskoi filologii* (Tartu), No. 9, 1966, p. 288.

122. 'Osnovnye polozheniya ob otdelenii arkhitekturnogo fakul'teta', TsGALI, fond 681, op. 2, ed. khr. 65, list 95.

123. *Raboty arkhitekturnogo fakul'teta*, p. xi.

124. *ibid.*, xi-xii. Ten architectural students worked on the All Russian Agricultural Exhibition of 1923 in Moscow (TsGALI, fond 681, op. 2, ed. khr. 174, list 391).

125. TsGALI, fond 681, op. 2, ed. khr. 65, and op. 3, ed. khr. 26, list 317.

126. *Iz istorii sovetskoi arkhitektury 1926-1932*, p. 87.

127. 'VKhUTEMAS', *LEF*, No. 2, 1923, p. 174 (emphasis as in original).

128. *ibid.*, p. 174.

129. 'Razval VKhUTEMASa. Dokladnaya zapiska o polozhenii vysshikh khudozhestvenno-tekhnicheskikh masterskikh', *LEF*, No. 4, 1923, pp. 27-8 (quotes from p. 27).

130. *ibid.*

131. 'Razval VKhUTEMASa', p. 28. The production faculties were defined in an earlier *LEF* article as the discipline of colour, volume and construction ('VKhUTEMAS', *LEF*, No. 2, 1923, p. 174). *LEF* considered its weapons in the fight to secure dominance for its interests to be 'example, agitation and propaganda' (*LEF*, No. 2, 1923, p. 9).

132. Reported in D.A., 'VKhUTEMAS', *Izvestiya VTsIK*, 5 February 1927.

133. TsGALI, fond 681, op. 1, ed. khr. 95, list 72;

op. 2, ed. khr. 28, list 47; ed. khr. 65, list 186; and ed. khr. 51, list 96.

134. K. Istomin, 'Programma masterskoi zhivopisi osnovnogo otdeleniya'; reprinted in M. N. Yablonskaya, *Konstantin Nikolaevich Istomin* (Moscow, 1972), pp. 140-1. See also TsGALI, fond 681, op. 2, ed. khr. 53, list 61.

135. 'Institut khudozhestvennoi kul'tury. Otchet o deyatel'nosti INKhUKa', *Russkoe iskusstvo*, No. 2/3, 1923, pp. 86-7. A. Vesnin, Popova, Krinskii, Lavinskii, Ladovskii, Rodchenko, Stepanova, Babichev, Kushner (as well as Drevin, Udal'tsova and others who left before INKhUK adopted its Constructivist platform) all taught at the VKhUTEMAS. The question of a junction between INKhUK and the State Free Art Studios had been discussed at the INKhUK meeting of 14 June 1920. Although it had been proposed by Ravdel', director of the Studios, it was rejected because 'INKhUK as a scientific establishment could not take on the problems of practical teaching (Protokol No. 6, 14 June 1920, of the theoretical section of monumental art, MS, private archive, Moscow).

136. For instance Z. Bykov and Akhtyrko (INKhUK list, private archive, Moscow). Moscow INKhUK meetings frequently took place in such casual surroundings because it didn't have official accommodation.

137. Untitled poem, private archive, Moscow.

138. TsGALI, fond 681, op. 2, ed. khr. 72, list 60.

139. 'Osnovy postroeniya VKhUTEMASa kak VUZa', TsGALI, fond 681, op. 2, ed. khr. 93, list 368-9.

140. 'Osnovnoe otdelenie. Obshchaya teoriya podgotovki', TsGALI, fond 681, op. 4, ed. khr. 24, list 11. Some of the programmes are given in detail in TsGALI, fond 681, op. 2, ed. khr. 49, list 1-23.

141. 'Zapis' besedy s G. D. Chichagovoi i, MS, private archive, Moscow, p. 1.

142. 'Zapis'', p. 1. A small illustrated brochure published in 1920 by the VKhUTEMAS students (illustrated by Arkhtyrko, poems by Chichagova, Babichev and others), entitled *Distsipliny VKhUTEMASa*, confirms this structure. It suggests, moreover, that Discipline No. 4 was taught by Klyun. It has been suggested that Ekster also taught Discipline No. 1 briefly prior to her departure from Russia ('Zapis'', p. 1), but I have found no further archival corroboration of this.

143. TsGALI, fond 681, op. 2, ed. khr. 177, list 3.

144. A. Rodchenko, 'Distsiplina No. 5', 1921, MS, private archive, Moscow. This course would seem to be a more specific variant of Rodchenko's programme 'Konstruktsiya zhivopisnogo prostranstva', dated 1920-1 and reprinted in R. O. Antonov, 'Evolyutsiya khudozhestvenno-konstruktorskikh programm fakul'teta obrabotki dereva i metalla VKhUTEMASa', *Khudozhestvenno-konstruktorskoe obrazovanie*, No. 4, 1973, p. 205. An English translation of this programme is reprinted in G. Karginov, *Rodchenko* (London, 1979), pp. 170-1. The title is translated as 'The Structure of Pictorial Space' and it is dated 1920. It defines the different elements (lines, planes and volumes) which are co-ordinated by factors such as rhythm, colour and *faktura*.

145. G. Chichagova, 'VKhUTEMAS', in D. Eliot, ed., *Alexander Rodchenko* (Oxford, Museum of Modern Art, 1979), p. 106.

146. See L. Popova and A. Vesnin, 'Distsiplina No. 1', MS, TsGALI, fond 681, op. 2, ed. khr. 46, list 26, and 'Raspisanie osnovnogo otdeleniya', 4 July 1922, TsGALI, fond 681, op. 2, ed. khr. 48, list 34.

147. TsGALI, fond 681, op. 3, ed. khr. 222, list 14.

148. This account is based on 'Osnovy postroeniya VKhUTEMASa kak VUZa', TsGALI, fond 681, op. 2, ed. khr. 93, list 368.

149. 'Protokol VKhUTEMASa', 2 February 1925, TsGALI, fond 681, op. 2, ed. khr. 72, list 60.

150. See *Spravochnik VKhUTEMASa*, p. 9.

151. 'Moskovskii vysshii gosudarstvennyi khudozhestvenno-tekhnicheskii institut. Diplom 1929-1930 g.', printed sheet, private archive, Moscow.

152. 'Osnovnoe otdelenie', TsGALI, fond 681, op. 2, ed. khr. 160, list 8.

153. 'Osnovy postroeniya VKhUTEMASa kak VUZa', TsGALI, fond 681, op. 2, ed. khr. 93, list 368.

154. When the Basic Division was reduced to a year this format was preserved; specialisation occurred under the aegis of the faculties rather than in the Basic Division (L. Marts, 'Propedevticheskii kurs VKhUTEMASa-VKhUTEINa', *Khudozhstvenno-konstruktorskoe obrazovanie*, No. 2, 1970, p. 45).

155. TsGALI. fond 681, op. 2, ed. khr. 93, list 368.

156. 'Doklad osnovogo otdeleniya', undated, probably 1925, TsGALI, fond 681, op. 2, ed. khr. 152, list 39.

157. *ibid.*

158. L. Marts, 'Propedevticheskii kurs', p. 56. Adaskina adds the name of Bruni to this list of teaching staff ('VKhUTEMAS', p. 180).

159. L. Popova and A. Vesnin, 'Distsiplina No. 1', TsGALI, fond 681, op. 2, ed. khr. 46, list 26.

160. The theoretical curriculum for the physical study of colour was devised by Fedorov and the practical aspect of the course was conducted by S. Kravtsov and the artist Gustav Klutsis. Historical theories of colour were studied, as well as the most recent colour theories. The student was taught about its physical properties and principles, the action of colour on surfaces, the reflection of colour from coloured surfaces, the development of colour, the mixing of colours, etc. The students studied the anatomy and the physiology of the eye, the harmony and contrast of colours and the basic psychological elements governing the perception of colour ('Programma prakticheskikh zanyatii po kursu "uchenie o tsvetakh" ', TsGALI, fond 681, op. 2, ed. khr. 65, list 123).

161. TsGALI, fond 681, op. 2, ed. khr. 65, list 124-5.

162. 'Programma po tsvetnoi distsipline', TsGALI, fond 681, op. 2, ed. khr. 154, list 90, and K. Istomin, 'Programma po distsipline tsveta. Pervyi kurs osnovnogo otdeleniya'; reprinted in Yablonskaya, *Istomin*, p. 141.

163. V. Khrakovskii, 'Doklad', 1926, TsGALI, fond 681, op. 2, ed. khr. 177, list 8-9.

164. Marts, 'Propedevticheskii', p. 49. Adaskina in listing the teaching staff of this *kontsentr* adds the names of Drevin, Efimov, Kiselev, Rodionov and Shevchenko ('VKhUTEMAS', p. 186).

165. TsGALI, fond 681, op. 3, ed. khr. 26, list 59. Unfortunately I have not been able to establish the programme of the earlier discipline of graphic construction.

166. TsGALI, fond 681, op. 3, ed. khr. 126, list 59.

167. *ibid.*

168. 'Doklad predsedatelya graficheskogo kontsentra professora Pavlinova', TsGALI, fond 681, op. 2, ed. khr. 177, list 8.

169. *ibid.*, list 9.

170. P. Pavlinov, *Dlya tekh kto risuet. Sovety khudozhnika* (Moscow, 1965), p. 68.

171. Marts, 'Propedevticheskii', p. 51, and

TsGALI, fond 681, op. 3, ed. khr. 222, list 15.

172. TsGALI, fond 681, op. 2, ed. khr. 177, list 9.

173. Marts, 'Propedevticheskii', pp. 51-2.

174. TsGALI, fond 681, op. 3, ed. khr. 222, list 16.

175. Marts, 'Propedevticheskii', pp. 52-4.

176. V. Favorskii, 'Zabyt′ "igru v inzhenera" ', *Brigada khudozhnikov*, No. 4/5, 1932.

177. TsGALI, fond 681, op. 2, ed. khr. 93, list 374.

178. Marts, 'Propedevticheskii', p. 60, and Adaskina, 'VKhUTEMAS', p. 183. Marts points out that Korolev, although accepting the formal approach of INKhUK, had left that istitution when it had adopted a Productivist programme.

179. 'Distsiplina No. 4. Ob'em i prostranstvo', TsGALI, fond 681, op. 2, ed. khr. 46, list 25.

180. Niss-Gol'dman, 'Doklad', 1926, TsGALI, fond 681, op. 2, ed. khr. 177, list 270-2.

181. 'Ob'emno-prostranstvennyi kontsentr', TsGALI, fond 681, op. 2, ed. khr. 65, list 133-4. This confirms the rather more detailed account of Marts ('Propedevticheskii', pp. 62-4). Marts based her account on a programme of 1929 (TsGALI, fond 681, op. 3, ed. khr. 222, list 16) which is more detailed.

182. TsGALI, fond 681, op. 2, ed. khr. 65, list 133-4.

183. Marts, 'Propedevticheskii', pp. 62-4.

184. These teaching methods were finally incorporated into a detailed and well illustrated volume – V. F. Krinskii, I. V. Lamtsov and M. A. Turkus, *Elementy arkhitekturno-prostranstvennoi kompozitsii* (Moscow, 1934). This was republished in a smaller format in 1968 by Stroiizdat, Moscow. Both volumes contain appendices in which the teaching programmes which the three architects employed at VKhUTEMAS, VKhUTEIN and the Moscow Architectural School, 1923-33, are reprinted.

185. Marts, 'Propedevticheskii', p. 65, and Adaskina, 'VKhUTEMAS', p. 185.

186. 'Doklad predsedatelya prostranstvennogo kontsentra professora Krinskogo', 1926, TsGALI, fond 681, op. 2, ed. khr. 177, list 9.

187. *ibid.*

188. TsGALI, fond 681, op. 2, ed. khr. 65, list 134.

189. This programme is described in TsGALI, fond 681, op. 2, ed. khr. 177, list 10. For a detailed exposition of these exercises and the entire programme of the *kontsentr*, especially the maximum taken by the architectural students, see Krinskii, et al., *Elementy*.

190. Marts, 'Propedevticheskii', pp. 66-8.

191. TsGALI, fond 681, op. 2, ed. khr. 177, list 10.

192. *ibid.*, list 10-11.

193. Further examples of the work of architectural students in this *kontsentr* are to be found in *Raboty arkhitekturnogo fakul'teta VKhUTEMASa 1920-1927* (Moscow, 1927). Many of these are reproduced in V. Quilici, *L'architettura del construttivismo* (Bari, 1969), pl. 33-41, and other isolated examples appear in various other Western histories.

194. 'Otchet za 1926-1927 uchebnyi god po fakul'tetu obrabotki dereva i metalla Vysshego khudozhestvenno-tekhnicheskogo instituta', TsGALI, fond. 681, op. 3, ed. khr. 42, list 65. This rationalisation occurred because of adverse reports of the conditions in both faculties which were in a 'most sorry state' with 'completely inadequate equipment, no room for study, no laboratory and no workshops' ('Protokol zasedaniya pravleniya VKhUTEMASa' TsGALI, fond 681, op. 2, ed. khr. 174, list 17).

195. TsGALI, fond 681, op. 2, ed. khr. 48, list 93.

196. 'Fakul'tet obrabotki dereva i metalla', TsGALI, fond 681, op. 2, ed. khr. 160, list 42–3.
197. *ibid.*, and TsGALI, fond 681, op. 3, ed. khr. 26, list 312.
198. TsGALI, fond 681, op. 2, ed. khr. 160, list 42–3.
199. TsGALI, fond 681, op. 3, ed. khr. 26, list 313–14, 317. In his autobiography ('Avtobiografiya', TsGALI, fond 2361, op. 1, ed. khr. 30, list 17–18) Lissitzky stated that he had started working in Dermetfak in 1925. In his 'Anketa RABPROS', he gave 1926 (*ibid.*, list 14). My work in the VKhUTEMAS archive did not produce an earlier reference than the 1926/7 academic year. An English translation of Lissitzky's autobiography is given in *El Lissitzky* (Cologne, Galerie Gmurzynska, 1976), p. 89. Lissitzky taught furniture design (*proektirovanie mebeli*) four hours a week to third year students and three hours a week to fourth year students (TsGALI, fond 681, op. 3, ed. khr. 26, list 313–14). He taught the formal principles of architecture to fifth year students (*ibid.*, list 317). A late programme of 1930 cites that in the Woodwork section of Dermetfak Lissitzky was teaching the design of interior furnishing and the architectonics of furniture (*proektirovanie vnutrennego oborudovaniya i arkhitektonika mebeli*) ('see TsGALI, fond 681, op. 1, ed. khr. 1118, list 25–6).
200. See 'Protokol Dermetfaka', TsGALI, fond 681, op. 3, ed. khr. 26, list 263; TsGALI, fond 681, op. 2, ed. khr. 160, list 43; and op. 1, ed. khr. 1118, list 25–6.
201. This is discussed in Chapter Seven.
202. TsGALI, fond 681, op. 2, ed. khr. 65, list 38–41.
203. Kiselev, 'Derevoobdelochnyi fakul'tet v nastoyashchem ego vide i programmnyi proekt ego reorganizatsii', 3 October 1922, TsGALI, fond 681, op. 2, ed. khr. 28, list 20.
204. *ibid.*
205. *ibid.*, list 27–9.
206. *ibid.*, list 41.
207. That year Chernyshev's course had been reorganised and retitled 'light wooden architecture' (*legkaya derevyannaya arkhitektura*). The designs for the workers' club involved the students E. P. Artamonov, B. P. Zemlyanitsyn, V. N. Kul'ganov, K. I. Kudryashov, and I. P. Lobov, while the *izba-chital'nya* was the work of S. I. Gorbachev, O. E. Kiselev, A. P. Kokorev, and P. D. Korgashinskii (see TsGALI, fond 681, op. 2, ed. khr. 72, list 63).
208. Khan-Magomedov points out that the building was coloured ('U istokov', p. 15).
209. *ibid.*
210. For details of this project, see M. Lavinskii, 'Izba-chital'nya', *Sovetskoe iskusstvo*, No. 4/5, 1925, p. 96.
211. 'Otchet o deyatel'nosti metalloobrabatyvayushchego fakul'teta za 1921', TsGALI, fond 681, op. 2, ed. khr. 48, list 85, and Malishevskii, 'Doklad', 1926, TsGALI, fond 681, op. 2, ed. khr. 177, list 201.
212. TsGALI, fond 681, op. 2, ed. khr. 177, list 201.
213. TsGALI, fond 681, op. 2, ed. khr. 103, list 18.
214. Malishevskii, 'Doklad', 1926, TsGALI, fond 681, op. 2, ed. khr. 177, list 201.
215. V. Stepanova's account of the organisation of the Metfak cited in A. Abramova, 'Nasledie VKhUTEMASa', *Dekorativnoe iskusstvo*, No. 4, 1964, p. 8. Stepanova (Rodchenko's wife) described the reorganisation of the faculty under Rodchenko as taking place in 1920. However, the archival evidence (TsGALI, fond 681, op. 2, ed.

khr. 48, list 85, and fond 681, op. 2, ed. khr. 34, list 509) suggests that Rodchenko only became involved with the faculty early in 1922.
216. A. Rodchenko, 'Doklad na zasedanii pravleniya VKhUTEMASa', 7 July 1926, TsGALI, fond 681, op. 2, ed. khr. 174, list 1.
217. S. Malishevskii, 'Predlozhenie o programme prepodavaniya', 20 October 1923, TsGALI, fond 681, op. 2, ed. khr. 65, list 137.
218. 'Programmy metalloobrabatyvayushchego fakul'teta VKhUTEMASa', TsGALI, fond 681, op. 2, ed. khr. 48, list 1–13.
219. TsGALI, fond 681, op. 2, ed. khr. 53, list 72. In A. Rodchenko, 'Uchebnyi plan metalloobrabatyvayushchego fakul'teta VKhUTEMASa' (TsGALI, fond 681, op. 2, ed. khr. 65, list 2), these two divisions are called *Konstruktivnoe otdelenie* (Constructive section) and *Otdelenie khudozhestvennoi obrabotki metalla* (Section concerning the artistic working of metal). Neither document is dated so that at this point it is difficult to establish precise sequences.
220. A. Rodchenko, 'Uchebnyi plan metalloobrabatyvayushchego fakul'teta VKhUTEMASa', TsGALI, fond 681, op. 2, ed. khr. 65, list 2.
221. A. Rodchenko, 'Ob'yasnitel'naya zapiska k uchebnomu planu', MS, private archive, Moscow.
222. A. Rodchenko, 'Ob'yasnitel'naya zapiska k programme kursa kompozitsii dlya metfaka VKhUTEMASa professora Rodchenko', MS, private archive, Moscow. A slightly different variant is reprinted in R. Antonov, 'Evolyutsiya khudozhestvenno-konstruktorskikh programm', pp. 212–13. Antonov has dated it 1928–9.
223. *ibid.*
224. A. Rodchenko, 'Tsel' proektirovaniya', MS, private archive, Moscow. Although a detailed programme for Rodchenko's course on technical drawing was not among the material I studied at TsGALI, a fairly detailed exposition of his ideas concerning technical drawing and its importance in the design process is given in A. Rodchenko, 'Tekhnicheskoe risovanie', *Novyi LEF*, No. 11, 1927, pp. 27–36, and No. 11, 1928, pp. 27–8.
225. Antonov, 'Evolyutsiya khudozhestvenno-konstruktorskikh programm', p. 201.
226. This and the following description of these tasks is taken from Abramova, 'Nasledie VKhUTEMASa', pp. 8–10.
227. *ibid.*
228. TsGALI, fond 681, op. 3, ed. khr. 26, list 320.
229. *ibid.*, and TsGALI, fond 681, op. 3, ed. khr. 26, list 264. Abramova gives certain details of one such project by Pavlov ('Nasledie VKhUTEMASa', p. 12).
230. On these campaigns, see for example E. H. Carr and R. W. Davies, *Foundations of a Planned Economy, 1926–1929* (London, 1969), Chapters 13 and 18.
231. A. Rodchenko, cited in Abramova, 'VKhUTEMAS-VKhUTEIN', p. 52.
232. 'Na putyakh k standartu', *Daesh'*, No. 3, 1929. A. A. Galaktionov graduated in 1928 and went to work at the State Scientific Experimental Institute (Gosudarstvennyi nauchnyi eksperimentalnyi institut) on the internal furnishing of buildings (TsGALI, fond 681, op. 3, ed. khr. 231).
233. A. Rodchenko, 'Programma po kursu proektirovaniya metalloveshchei Dermeta', MS, private archive, Moscow, p. 1. Abramova related these characteristics to the 1923 exhibition of Metfak's work (Abramova, 'VKhUTEMAS-VKhUTEIN', p. 52). The Metfak's exhibits are reviewed in *LEF* which illustrated two items produced by Metfak students (Varst, 'O rabotakh konstruktivistskoi molodezhi', *LEF*, No. 3, 1923, pp. 53–6).

234. The clearest and most detailed picture of Soviet housing during this period is given in T. Sosnovy, *The Housing Problem in the Soviet Union* (New York, 1954).

235. Lobov, 'Mebel' fakul'teta po obrabotke dereva i metalla VKhUTEINa', *Stroitel'stvo Moskvy*, No. 10, 1929, p. 10. This chair was part of Zemlyanitsyn's diploma project which was the furnishing of a captain's cabin (TsGALI, fond 681, op. 3, ed. khr. 114, list 14).

236. Lobov, 'Mebel', p. 9.

237. Abramova, 'Nasledie VKhUTEMASa', p. 11.

238. A. Gan, 'Fakty za nas', *Sovremennaya arkhitektura*, No. 2, 1926.

239. TsGALI, fond 681, op. 3, ed. khr. 26, list 276, 313–14, 317. Lissitzky returned to USSR in 1925 making occasional visits to the West. For his life in the West, see S. Lizzitsky-Küppers, *El Lissitzky: Life, Letters, Texts* (London, 1968).

240. V. Kandinsky, *Cours au Bauhaus* (Paris, 1975), and W. Grohmann, *Wassily Kandinsky* (Cologne, 1958).

241. TsGALI, fond 681, op. 3, ed. khr. 243. The letter suggests that this proposal had often been discussed. There was no other correspondence relating to the Bauhaus that I saw except a proposal to exchange photographs. However, at the 1926 Academic Conference, Malishevskii referred to the Bauhaus in his speech (TsGALI, op. 2, ed. khr. 177, list 204–5). Literature on the Bauhaus which appeared in Russia at this time included D. Arkin's article 'VKhUTEMAS i germanskii BAUKHAUZ', *Izvestiya* VTsIK, 5 February 1927; D. Arkin, 'Iskusstvo veshchi na zapade', *Zapad i vostok* (Moscow, 1926), pp. 126–35; and Yu. Semenov, 'V kuznitse novogo stilya', *Krasnaya nov'*, No. 39, 1928. For further details concerning the contacts between European and Soviet designers (particularly architects), see T. N. Samokhina, 'Mezhdunarodnye svyazi sovetskoi arkhitektury v period stanovyleniya Soyuza arkhitektorov SSSR', *Problemy istorii sovetskoi arkhitektury*, No. 2, 1978, pp. 77–80, and, more importantly, I. Kokkinaki, 'K voprosu o vzaimosvyazyakh sovetskikh i zarubezhnykh arkhitektorov v 1920–1930-e gody. Kratkii obzor', *Voprosy sovetskogo izobrazitel'nogo iskusstva i arkhitektury* (Moscow, 1976), pp. 350–82.

As early as 1920, even before the organisation of the VKhUTEMAS, Gropius had written to the Russians pointing out the similarities between the aims of the Bauhaus and those of Russian culture generally in their striving toward a synthesis of the arts (*Khudozhestvennaya zhizn'*, No. 4/5, 1920, pp. 23–4). For a comparison of the programmes of the Bauhaus and the VKhUTEMAS, see Kh. Shedlikh, 'Baukhauz i VKhUTEMAS. Obshchie cherty pedagogicheskoi programmy', *Vzaimo-svyazi russkogo i sovetskogo iskusstva i nemetskoi khudozhestvennoi kul'tury* (Moscow, 1980), pp. 133–56.

242. They formed a group called Red Front. Meyer was principally engaged as a town planner but also taught at the Higher Architectural and Building Institute (Vysshii arkhitekturno-stroitel'nyi institut) (*Baukhauz Dessau 1928–1930. Katalog vystavki* (Moscow, 1931), p. 23).

243. A. Mordvinov, 'Vystavka Baukhauza v Moskve', in *Baukhauz Dessau*, p. 24. The negative aspects of Meyer's work were described as absence of social and ideological content, absence of artistic aspects, the mechanical nature of his method, and the limitation of architecture to a purely functional role. The positive contributions of his work were listed as his working method with its detailed analysis of function, physical and psychological

factors, his rationalisation of design and the production process and the system of architectural education which he had formulated at the Bauhaus.

244. TsGALI, fond 681, op. 2, ed. khr. 103, list 9.

245. According to Stepanova, the 1928 graduates were the first students to graduate from Dermetfak (cited in Abramova, 'Nasledie VKhUTEMASa', p. 8). The archive material does not stipulate whether these were the first graduates ('Spisok studentov okonchivshikh fakul'tet po obrabotke dereva i metalla', TsGALI, fond 681, op. 3, ed. khr. 231). In the final year of the faculty's existence there were twenty-two graduates, but the archive does not give any indication of the posts they finally occupied.

NOTES TO CHAPTER FIVE

1. According to A. Nove, if the gross output of Russian industry in 1913 was indexed at 100, by 1921 it was 31 (*An Economic History of the U.S.S.R.* (London, 1972), p. 68).

2. Narkompros lacked the funds to finance VKhUTEMAS adequately, especially as in certain cases this involved importing expensive machinery from abroad. There are frequent references in the faculty reports to lack of essential equipment in all faculties, hampering the execution of designs, as for example Metfak's report of 1926 (TsGALI, fond 681, op. 2, ed. khr. 177, list 201–5).

3. Arvatov reported to INKhUK on 23 March 1922 that Tatlin had repudiated the counter-reliefs as 'unnecessary objects which he would no longer make' and that Tatlin was already organising work in the Petrograd factories ('Protokol zasedaniya uchenogo soveta INKhUKa', 23 March 1922, MS, private archive, Moscow). *Russkoe iskusstvo* reported that Tatlin and Arvatov had organised a production laboratory (*proizvodstvennaya laboratoriya*) at the New Lessner Factory in Petrograd ('Institut khudozhestvennoi kul'tury', *Russkoe iskusstvo*, No. 2/3, 1923, p. 87).

4. V. Pertsov, 'V styke iskusstva s proizvodstvom', *Vestnik iskusstv*, No. 5, 1922.

5. For a general account of this area, see T. Strizhenova, *Iz istorii sovetskogo kostyuma* (Moscow, 1972), and J. Bowlt, 'From Pictures to Textile Prints', *Print Collector's Newsletter*, No. 1, 1976, pp. 16–20. An English translation of Strizhenova's book has been published under the title *From the History of Soviet Costume* (London, 1977).

6. According to Brik, Popova and Stepanova had been invited to work at the factory by the director ('Ot kartiny k sittsu', *LEF*, No. 2, 1924, p. 34). On 5 January 1924 Stepanova presented a report to INKhUK concerning the position in the factory (V. Stepanova, 'O polozhenii i zadachakh khudozhnika-konstruktivista v sittsenabivnoi promyshlennosti v svyazi s rabotami na sittsenabivnoi fabrike', in 'Protokol zasedaniya INKhUKA', 5 January 1924, MS, private archive, Moscow). This *protokol* does not suggest that a large amount of time had lapsed since Popova and Stepanova entered the factory because INKhUK passed a resolution congratulating the factory on its attitude toward the 'artist-constructor'. This would suggest that Stepanova and Popova worked there no earlier than the autumn and winter of 1923–4. In 1924 at the posthumous exhibition of Popova's work, projects for textile designs (*proekty tekstil'nykh risunkov*) and specimens of printed fabric (*obraztsy nabivnykh tkanei*) were on display. In the catalogue they were all dated 1924 (*Katalog posmertnoi vystavki khudozhnika-konstruktora L. S. Popovoi* (Moscow, 1924), p. 12,

nos. 81–2). Zhadova also dates Popova's work at the factory to the last year of her life, confirming this interpretation, since Popova died on 25 May 1924 ('Lyubov' Popova', *Tekhnicheskaya estetika*, No. 11, 1967, p. 26). Strizhenova placed the entry into the factory in 1921 which is almost certainly too early (*Iz istorii sovetskogo kostyuma*, p. 95).

7. This plate illustrated Brik's article 'Ot kartiny k sittsu', *LEF*, No. 2, 1924, p. 33.

8. Strizhenova implies that Rodchenko himself designed the *prozodezhda* that he is wearing (*Iz istorii sovetskogo kostyuma*, p. 84). However, a photograph of Rodchenko wearing his *prozodezhda* was reproduced in *Sovetskoe iskusstvo* in 1925 where it appeared with the caption 'V. Stepanova – production clothing' (O. Beskin, 'Otvet napravo – zapros nalevo', *Sovetskoe iskusstvo*, No. 6, 1925, p. 8).

9. A. Rodchenko, 'Diskussii o novoi odezhde i mebeli – zadacha oformleniya', in A. Glebov, *Inga* (Moscow, 1929), p. 14.

10. V. Tatlin, 'Otchet issledovatel'skoi raboty za 1923–4g. otdela material'noi kul'tury', 10 November 1924, MS, private archive, Leningrad.

11. These are known through examples published with a commentary under the title 'New Life' ('Novyi byt'), *Krasnaya panorama*, No. 23, 1924, p. 17.

12. *ibid.* The design was theoretically the work of the whole collective of this department of GINKh-UK (*ibid.*), but in reality this consisted of six students only four of whom were active (V. Tatlin, 'Otchet o rabote za 1923 i 24 gg. otdela material'noi kul'tury'. 1 September 1924, MS, private archive, Leningrad).

13. For more detail concerning this, see L. Zhadova, 'Tatlin – proektirovshchik material'noi kul'tury', *Sovetskoe dekorativnoe iskusstvo 77/78* (Moscow, 1980), p. 218, nn. 40–3.

14. V. Stepanova, 'Ot kostyuma – k risunku i tkani', *Vechernyaya Moskva*, 28 February 1929.

15. D. Arkin, *Iskusstvo bytovoi veshchi* (Moscow, 1932), pp. 152–3.

16. Varst, 'Kostyum segodnyashnego dnya – prozodezhda', *LEF*, No. 2, 1923, pp. 65–8. The article is signed 'Varst', a pseudonym that Varvara Stepanova used composed from the first three letters of her Christian name and the first two of her surname. Stepanova also outlined her ideas in a paper that she gave at INKhUK in 1923. An extract from this paper is reprinted in Strizhenova, *Iz istorii sovetskogo kostyuma*, p. 84.

17. Varst, 'Kostyum', p. 65.

18. *ibid.*

19. *ibid.*

20. *ibid.*

21. *ibid.*

22. Specialised clothing including protective clothing (*spetsodezhda – spetsializirovannaya odezhda*) comprised a special category of production clothing (*prozodezhda*) (Varst, 'Kostyum', p. 68).

23. *Velikodushnyi rogonosets.* For a full discussion of the production in its entirety, see A. Law, 'Le Cocu magnifique de Crommelynck', *Les Voies de la création théâtrale* (Paris, 1979), pp. 13–43. It is evident that Popova started working on the costume designs prior to the end of 1921. In Strizhenova, *Iz istorii sovetskogo kostyuma*, p. 81, the design for actor No. 7 is signed and dated by Popova, 1921.

24. L. Popova, 'Vstuplenie k diskussii INKhUKa o "Velikodushnom rogonostse"', 27 April 1922, MS, private archive, Moscow.

25. L. Popova, 'Kostyum kak element material'nogo oformleniya', *c.* 1922, MS, private archive, Moscow.

26. *Smert' Tarelkina.*

27. V. Stepanova, 'Smert' Tarelkina', 1924, MS, private archive, Moscow.

28. Stepanova, 'Kostyum', p. 68.

29. *ibid.*, p. 66.

30. It should be noted that the practical exigencies of material scarcity as well as the changes in the status of women and social understanding of their role in society, exerted a strong pressure towards the simplification of dress. This is very evident in a small collection of do-it-yourself designs for clothing, toys, clubrooms, etc., published under the title *Iskusstvo v bytu* (Moscow, 1925). Some of these designs are reproduced in Strizhenova, *Iz istorii sovetskogo kostyuma*, and consisted of utilising old tea cloths, blankets and scarves to make clothes.

31. D. Arkin, 'L'Artiste et l' industrie', in *L'Art décoratif et industriel de l'URSS* (Moscow, 1925), p. 46, and O. Brik, 'Ot kartiny k sittsu', *LEF*, No. 2 (6), 1924, p. 34.

32. Stepanova, 'O polozhenii i zadachakh khudozhnika-konstruktivista'; also quoted in Strizhenova, *Iz istorii sovetskogo kostyuma*, p. 97.

33. V. Stepanova, 'Tezisy k dokladu "Iskusstvo i proizvodstvo"', paper delivered at INKhUK, 17 February 1921, in 'Protokol zasedaniya INKhUKa', 17 February 1921, MS, private archive, Moscow. Stepanova had theoretically accepted this delay and the impossibility of achieving a synthesis of art and industry immediately.

34. A. Ekster, 'V konstruktivnoi odezhde', *Atel'e*, No. 1, 1923, pp. 4–5.

35. *ibid.*

36. A. Ekster, 'Prostota i praktichnost' v odezhde', *Krasnaya niva*, No. 21, 1923, p. 31.

37. *ibid.*

38. A. Ekster, *Krasnaya niva*, No. 22, 1923, p. 32.

39. Ekster, 'Prostota i praktichnost' v odezhde', p. 31.

40. In the Studio of Fashion Ekster worked with Mukhina and Lamanova whose ideas and designs are discussed by Strizhenova (*Iz istorii sovetskogo kostyuma*, pp. 28ff.). Lamanova and Mukhina designed 'do-it-yourself' clothes for the album *Art in Everyday Life* (*Iskusstvo v bytu*) (Moscow, 1925). In these clothing designs, which were intended to be pragmatic solutions to the current material shortages, they utilised items such as patterned scarves, blankets and old embroidered towels which people might have. Their designs for everyday clothes, while simple in basic structure, easy to sew and economic in materials, compromised with existing solutions and strove towards more traditional concepts of style, elegance and beauty – aesthetic effects which were anathema to the Constructivists.

Aelita, directed by Protazanov, was released in 1924. It was based on Aleksei Tolstoi's novel of the same name. Set in Moscow during the winter of 1920–1, it commenced with a mysterious radio message and culminated in a flight to Mars and a Martian revolution. Its moral was that the practical tasks of social reconstruction should take precedence over fantastic projects. Ekster designed the Martian costumes, Victor Simov the sets on Mars, and Rabinovich the model of the Martian city (*Aelita* (Moscow, no date)).

41. Stepanova, 'Ot kostyuma – k risunku i tkani'.

42. 'Novyi byt', *Krasnaya panorama*, No. 23, 1924, p. 14. Tatlin maintained that such a stove could keep food hot for about thirty hours. Khodasevich recalls Tatlin building the stoves and that they smoked once completed ('Bylo', p. 12).

43. N. Lukhmanov, *Arkhitektura kluba* (Moscow, 1930), pp. 11, 18.

44. Stepanova described this club in some detail (see Varst, 'Rabochii klub. Konstruktivist A. M. Rodchenko', *Sovremennaya arkhitektura*, No. 1, 1926, p. 36). This was donated to the French Communist Party after the exhibition. Rodchenko visited Paris for the exhibition and related his adventures in *Novyi LEF*, No. 2, 1927, pp. 19–21. It should be noted that before the Workers' Club Rodchenko had made designs for the Kafe Pittoresk in 1917 (plate 2.6) and for the interior of the hostel for the delegates to the Third Congress of the Comintern in 1921. Several projects for lamps, etc., have been preserved (see I. Matsa, 'Aleksandr Rodchenko', *Iskusstvo*, No. 7, 1972, p. 36, and G. Karginov, *Rodchenko* (London, 1979), plates 69–71).

However, Yakulov omits Rodchenko's name from the list of artists with whom he worked on decorations for the Kafe. Pittoresk, and Khardzhiev also insists that Rodchenko was not among the participants (see Yakulov's letter in *Agitatsionno-massovoe iskusstvo*, p. 128, n. 209, and N. Khardzhiev, 'Appunti', *Paragone (Arte)*, Vol. 16, No. 183, 1965, p. 75). This would suggest that Rodchenko produced his lamp designs for the Kafe Pittoresk independently, in response to having seen the decorations of the other artists. In any event, Rodchenko's lamp designs represent his early and still essentially decorative and painterly response to the task of applying his artistic experience to the organisation of a utilitarian object. Since the evidence suggests that Rodchenko was not involved on the Kafe Pittoresk, it is improbable that these designs were realised.

45. Varst, 'Rabochii klub', p. 36.

46. A Lenin corner (*ugol Lenina*) became a significant feature of all peasant and workers' clubs after Lenin's death, in 1924. These variants on the traditional Red Corner where the icons stood, were devoted specifically to photographs, statues and the political writings of Lenin.

47. Varst, 'Rabochii klub', p. 36. 'Living Newspapers' such as the Blue Blouse groups enacted current events from an agitational standpoint.

48. Lissitzky, 'Mebel'', 3 April 1940, TsGALI, fond 2361, op. 1, ed. khr. 58, list 12. English and German translations of the text are printed in *El Lissitzky* (Cologne, Galerie Gmurzynska, 1976), pp. 79–80, under the title 'From a Questionnaire on Furniture'. It should be stressed that Lissitzky stated that he entered the Dermetfak in the same year, i.e. 1925 ('Avtobiografiya', TsGALI, fond 2361, op. 1, ed. khr. 58, list 17).

49. Lissitzky, 'Mebel'', TsGALI, fond 2361, op. 1, ed. khr. 58, list 12.

50. Lissitzky, 'Khudozhestvennye predposylki standartizatsii mebeli', 1928, TsGALI, fond 2361, op. 1, ed. khr. 30, list 5.

51. *ibid.*, list 4.

52. *ibid.*, list 7.

53. *ibid.*, list 18–41.

54. From Lissitzky-Küppers, *El Lissitzky*, plates 224–5. This chair was awarded a German patent (Lissitzky, 'Mebel'', list 12), but it is not known whether it was mass produced for the German market.

55. The use of the curve has an interesting significance in Lissitzky's work. In a letter to Oud in 1924, Lissitzky explained his disagreement with the Dutch standpoint: 'The "Universal" =Straight Line + Vertical, does not correspond with the universe, where there are only curvatures and no straight lines. Hence the sphere (not the cube) is the crystal of the universe, but we cannot do anything with it (the sphere) since it is the final state (death); that is why we concentrate on the elements of the cube which can always be re-assembled and destroyed at will (life). A modern machine must have something spherical, since the circular motion is its *advantage*, compared with the straight line to-and-fro motion of the human hand/foot. And if our flat, our house, is an apparatus for accommodating our body (like clothing) why should it not incorporate the spherical?' (Lissitzky, letter to J. Oud; reprinted in *El Lissitzky*, p. 73).

56. The Constructivist architects M. Ginzburg and I. Milinis designed this building in 1928–9 for the People's Commissariat of Finance (Narkomfin).

57. K. Malevich, letter to Kudryashev, 17 August 1921, Costakis Collection.

58. K. Malevich, paper delivered to INKhUK in December 1921, MS, private archive, Moscow.

59. For more details concerning these, see T. Andersen, *Malevich* (Amsterdam, Stedelijk Museum, 1970), Appendix 2. Malevich also used the term 'arkhitekton' to describe his architectural models. The earliest projects are dated 1913 (Khazanova, *Sovetskaya arkhitektura*, p. 23).

60. See *Chasnik* (New York, Leonard Hutton Gallery, 1980).

61. Drevtrest was the organisation in charge of the wood-processing industry. For the competition Suetin designed chairs, a divan bed, shelves, cupboards and sideboards. These designs were exhibited at the Galerie Gmurzynska in Cologne in 1977 (*Die Kunstismen in Russland*, Nos. 160–83). For the competition Suetin adopted a black circle in a square outline as an adaptation of the UNOVIS sign (*ibid.*, p. 168).

62. *ibid.*, p. 168.

63. Some of these were exhibited in that year at an exhibition to commemorate the Fourth Congress of the Comintern (*Katalog vystavki proizvedenii Gustava Klutsisa* (Riga, Gosudarstvennyi khudozhestvennyi muzei, 1970), pp. 31–2, 43–4, Nos. 13–26).

64. *ibid.*, p. 44, No. 26. Klutsis helped to organise and design this exhibition (A. Eght, 'Khudozhnik G. Klutsis', *Dekorativnoe iskusstvo*, No. 11, 1966, p. 8).

65. L. Oginskaya, 'Khudozhnik-agitator', *Dekorativnoe iskusstvo*, No. 5, 1971, p. 37.

66. L. Marts, 'Gustav Klutsis', *Tekhnicheskaya estetika*, No. 1, 1968, p. 29.

67. For further information concerning this exhibition, consult Khazanova, *Sovetskaya arkhitektura*, pp. 167–71.

68. M. Ginzburg, *Stil' i epokha* (Moscow, 1924).

69. *ibid.*, pp. 153–4.

70. Ob'edinenie sovremenykh arkhitektorov, (Society of Contemporary Architects). See Khazanova, *Sovetskaya arkhitektura*, p. 205.

71. Burov was one of a student group that took third prize in the competition for the original layout of the Agricultural Exhibition.

72. *Iz istorii sovetskoi arkhitektury 1917–1925 gg.*, ed. K. N. Afanas'ev (Moscow, 1963), pp. 177, 187. The architect of the pavilion was Zholtovskii.

73. *Ibid.*, pp. 181, 177. The architect was Gladkov.

74. It is difficult to determine who exactly was responsible for particular elements of the superstructure. Gladkov's design resembles that of Rodchenko. The latter was to have designed the Machine building but eventually did not (*Iz istorii sovetskoi arkhitektury*, p. 179). Popova was also originally to have executed the facade of the *polevodstvo* pavilion but there is no evidence to suggest that in the event she was involved in its decoration (*ibid.*, p. 181).

75. Pavil'on 'Lesovodstvo'. Khazanova, *Sovetskaya arkhitektura*, p. 174.

76. P. Neznamov, 'Prom-raboty A. Lavinskogo', *LEF*, No. 3(7), 1924, p. 76d.

77. Ginzburg illustrated it in *Stil' i epokha*, plates XL and XLI. Ginzburg did not date the kiosk but, since his book was published in 1924 and most of the illustrations date from 1922–3, it can be assumed that the kiosk was probably designed over the same period. Gan's kiosk was not designated as a project that was commissioned for the Agricultural Exhibition and it therefore appears to have been an independent project.

78. A. Novinkov, 'Derevenskii kiosk. Proekt – maket. Konstruktivist Aleksei Gan', *Sovremennaya arkhitekura*, No. 1, 1926, p. 35. Although a model was produced, there is no further evidence as to whether this prototype was adopted in actual construction programmes and whether any such kiosk was built.

79. A. Gan, 'Fakty za nas', *Sovremennaya arkhitektura*, No. 2, 1926.

80. N. Chuzhak, 'Pod znakom zhiznestroeniya', *LEF*, No. 1, 1923, p. 32.

81. V. Meierkhol'd, 'Akter budushchego', *Ermitazh*, No. 6, 1922, pp. 10–11.

82. Rudnitskii confirms this view asserting that it was 'the first if not the only production in which the principles of scenic Constructivism were consistently realised' (K. Rudnitskii, *Rezhisser Meierkhol'd* (Moscow, 1969), p. 261). For a detailed examination of the production, see Rudnitskii, *Rezhisser Meierkhol'd*, pp. 260–74.

83. V. Meierkhol'd, 'Pis'mo k redaktsii', *Izvestiya VTsIK*, 9 May 1922.

84. *The Magnanimous Cuckold* was not Popova's first excursion into the theatre. She had designed the costumes for *The Tale of the Priest and his Workman Balda* at the Moscow Children's Theatre and for Lunarcharskii's play *The Locksmith and the Chancellor* (1921) at the Korsh Theatre.

86. After they were deprived of their commission the studio of theatrical art run by Popova was entrusted with its execution (E. Rakitina, 'Lyubov' Popova. Iskusstvo i manifesty', in *Khudozhnik, stsena, ekran* (Moscow, 1975), p. 161). Popova taught object-making (*veshchestvennoe oformlenie*) at the State Higher Theatrical Workshops (Gosudarstvennye vysshie teatral'nye masterskie – GVYTM) which were directed by Meierkhol'd. The programme is preserved among her papers, private archive, Moscow. The Stenberg brothers did later execute theatrical designs for Tairov (see A. Efros, *Kamernyi teatr i ego khudozhniki 1914–1934* (Moscow, 1934)).

86. Conversation with V. A. Stenberg, November 1974.

87. Popova's set had proved so difficult to transpose into reality that Aleksandr Vesnin was called on to adapt her ideas into something more buildable. His designs were ultimately used for the production (Efros, *Kamernyi teatr*).

88. Rakitina, 'Lyubov' Popova', p. 161. Only a day before the posters were to be distributed did she allow her name to be added to the poster.

89. L. Popova, 'Vstuplenie k diskussii INKhUKa o "Velikodushnom rogonostse"', MS, private archive, Moscow. Certain sections of this document have been reproduced by Rakitina ('Lyubov' Popova', pp. 153–4). Portions of Rakitina's citation have been translated by J. Bowlt, 'From Surface to Space: The Art of Liubov Popova', *Structurist*, No. 15/16, 1975–6, p. 87. It should be noted that in the passage quoted Rakitina cites concrete realisation as concentration (*kontsentratsiya*) ('Lyubov' Popova', p. 153). In the typescript I examined the form used is 'concrete realisation' or 'definition' (*konkretizatsiya*).

90. Popova, 'Vstuplenie', p. 1. Translation taken from Bowlt, 'From Surface to Space', p. 87.

91. Aleksandr Sukhovo-Kobylin (1817–1903). For details of the play, see Rudnitskii, *Rezhisser Meierkhol'd*, pp. 273–7.

92. V. Stepanova, 'Smert' Tarelkina', 1924, MS, private archive, Moscow.

93. See Efros, *Kamernyi teatr*, pp. 96–107.

94. Ginzburg, *Stil' i epokha*, p. 000.

95. For a fuller examination of the role the theatre played in extending the ideas and principles underlying the work of the First Working Group of Constructivists into the area of architecture, see C. Lodder, 'Constructivist Theatre as a Laboratory for an Architectural Aesthetic', *Architectural Association Quarterly*, Vol. 11, No. 2, 1979, pp. 24–35. A slightly different emphasis is produced in the later article by K. P. Zygas, 'Cubo-Futurism and the Vesnins' *Palace of Labour*', in S. Barron and M. Tuchman, eds., *The Avant-Garde in Russia, 1910–1930: New Perspectives* (London and Cambridge, Mass., 1980), pp. 110–17.

96. The play was an adaptation of *La Nuit* by Martinet, written by Sergei Tret'yakov, who was a contributor to *LEF*. For details, see Rudnitskii, *Rezhisser Meierkhol'd*, pp. 278–81.

97. L. Popova, 'Montirovka spektaklya "Zemlya dybom"'; cited in Rakitina, 'Lyubov' Popova', p. 163. *Kino pravda* (*Cinema Truth*) was the title of Dziga Vertov's newsreel, to which presumably Popova is referring.

98. A whole series of the slogans devised by Popova for the play *The Earth in Turmoil* form part of the Costakis Collection. Many along with scene titles used are reproduced in Rudenstine, *Russian Avant-Garde Art*, Nos. 888, 890–905.

99. L. Popova, 'Poyasnitel'naya zapiska k postanovke *Zemlya dybom*, v teatre Meierkhol'da', *LEF*, No. 4, 1923, p. 44. Popova recognised that this new revolutionary situation required a different approach and stressed this by using the old slogans to stress the past stage.

100. Rakitina, 'Lyubov' Popova', p. 163.

101. For an exposition of this in literature, see N. Chuzhak, ed., *Literatura fakta. Pervyi sbornik materialov rabotnikov LEFa* (Moscow, 1929).

102. S. Mokul'skii, 'Gastroli teatra Meierkhol'da', *Zhizn' iskusstva*, No. 23, 1924, pp. 12–13.

103. For details concerning the production of *Inga*, see A. Glebov, *Inga* (Moscow, 1929). The play concerned the new role of women in Soviet society.

104. Rodchenko, 'Diskussii o novoi odezhde i mebeli – zadacha oformleniya', p. 12.

105. *ibid.*

106. Rodchenko stressed that the clothes for *Inga* were not presenting a rational solution to the form of dress but indicated the remnants of aestheticism. This element could equally be seen to be present in the furniture designs ('Diskussii', p. 14).

107. E. Beskin, 'Teatral'nyi LEF', *Sovetskoe iskusstvo*, No. 6, 1925, p. 53.

108. The very first issue of *LEF*, in 1923, complained of the emergence of an 'aesthetic constructivism' in the theatre and poetry ('Konstruktivisty', *LEF*, No. 1, 1923, p. 251).

NOTES TO CHAPTER SIX

1. P. Neznamov, 'Proz-raboty A. Lavinskogo', *LEF*, No. 3 (7), 1924, p. 77.

2. A. Gan, 'Chto takoe konstruktivizm', *Sovremennaya arkhitektura*, No. 3, 1928, p. 79.

3. *ibid.*

4. The First Working Group of Constructivists seems to have become less cohesive some time during the second half of 1922 or first half of 1923. Certainly Gan's name disappears from the INKhUK *protokoly* at that point. I have not been able to discover precisely what happened. The group remained with Gan at its head but all the members changed. By the 1924 First Discussional Exhibition it consisted of Gan, Miller, Mirolyubova, Sanina, Smirnov, Galina and Ol'ga Chichagova, Shestakov, etc. The main areas of activity on which they were engaged were equipment, children's literature, typography and *prozodezhda* – specialised working clothing. In 1924 at the exhibition Gan declared all other Constructivists to be pseudo-Constructivists (see Matsa, *Sovetskoe iskusstvo*, pp. 316–7, and V. Pertsov, *Reviziya levogo fronta v sovremennom russkom iskusstve* (Moscow, 1925), p. 56).

5. This was influenced by the inauguration of NEP (New Economic Policy), the subsequent need for tighter ideological control, the dissolution of IZO and the Constructivists' diminished role in directing the artistic life of the country, and Party preferences for Realism. As Gan complained: 'As soon as we had ended the military front of the Civil War and had turned to the peaceful tasks of reconstruction, art experts raised their heads ... and started spouting on about the eternal values of the beautiful' (*Konstruktivizm* (Tver', 1922), p. 11). Gan criticised Marxist aesthetic theory for being reactionary, 'marching under the flag of the Academy' (*ibid.*) and Narkompros for its misguided policy (*ibid.*, p. 14).

6. Over eighty exhibitions were held in Petrograd and Moscow during the period 1917–21. These ranged over the whole gamut of artistic affiliations. For a full list of exhibitions through this period, see *Vystavki sovetskogo izobrazitel'nogo iskusstva. Spravochnik* (Moscow, 1965), Vol. I, pp. 8–88.

7. The re-emergence of Realism and a return to Realism among formerly avant-garde artists was not restricted to Russia during the 1920s. Picasso turned from Synthetic Cubism to a style of monumental Realism such as epitomised by his canvas *Cavalier* of 1921. Vladimir Stenberg recounted how this was felt to be a betrayal by the Russian avant-garde (conversation with the artist, November 1974), but Picasso's path was echoed by that of other French artists, such as Braque, Léger and Picabia, who returned to the representational image in their work, even when, as in Surrealism, this was used to attack the illusion of reality itself.

8. Fifty-four artists participated in this exhibition (*Vystavki*, Vol. 1, p. 94).

9. Reported in *Assotsiatsiya khudozhnikov revolyutsionnoi Rossii. Sbornik vospominanii, statei, dokumentov* (Moscow, 1973), p. 8 (hereafter referred to as *AKhRR*).

10. *ibid.*, p. 9. The Constructivists had equated their artistic credo with the Revolution. For them Realism was the reactionary art; see Chapter Three and in particular the sections on Gan's *Konstruktivizm*.

11. 'Deklaratsiya Assotsiatsii khudozhnikov revolyutsionnoi Rossii', May 1922; reprinted in V. N. Perel'man, ed., *Bor'ba za realizm v izobrazitel'nom iskusstve 20kh godov* (Moscow, 1962), p. 120.

12. *ibid.*, p. 10.

13. N. Krupskaya, 'Glavpolitprosvet i iskusstvo', *Pravda*, February 1921.

14. Perel'man, *Bor'ba*, pp. 10–18.

15. Ya. Tugendkhol'd, *Iskusstvo oktyabr'skoi epokhi* (Leningrad, 1930), p. 30.

16. RAPP (Rossiiskaya assotsiatsiya proletarskikh pisatelei – Russian Association of Proletarian Writers). See E. J. Brown, *The Proletarian Episode in Russian Literature, 1928–1932* (New York, 1953).

17. Lobanov, *Khudozhestvennye gruppirovki*, p. 107. According to Lobanov, the founding artists were Adlivankin, Gluskin, Nyurenberg, Perutskii and N. Popov (*ibid.*, p. 106).

18. 'Nash put'', *NOZh. Pervaya vystavka kartin* (Moscow, 1922); reprinted in Matsa, *Sovetskoe iskusstvo*, p. 308. *Nozh* is also Russian for knife.

19. *ibid.*, p. 311.

20. Lobanov, *Khudozhestvennye gruppirovki*, p. 109. They were mainly students from the studios of the Knave of Diamonds group of artists, in particular of P. Konchalovskii. The members of Bytie were Bunat'yan, S. Sakharov, Sretenskii, Taldykin and A. Lebedev (*ibid.*, p. 110). The Knave of Diamonds was a pre-revolutionary group of Russian artists strongly influenced by contemporary French painting. Their first and only exhibition after the Revolution was held in Moscow, 16 November to 4 December 1917. Exhibitors at this included Klyun, Malevich, Rozanova and Ekster (*Vystavki*, Vol. 1, p. 8).

21. *Katalog vystavki kartin obshchestva khudozhnikov 'Bytie'* (Moscow, 1927); reprinted in Matsa *Sovetskoe iskusstvo*, p. 313.

22. *ibid.*

23. Lobanov, *Khudozhestvennye gruppirovki*, p. 113.

24. 'Platforma OST', in Matsa, *Sovetskoe iskusstvo*, p. 575.

25. A. B. Vil'yams studied in the studio of Korovin, and Konchalovskii; Deineka with Favorskii and Nivinskii, Pimenov with Malyutin, Favorskii and Kardovskii, Vyalov with Kandinskii and Lentulov; S. A. Lyushin with Arkhipov; S. Merkulov with Mashkov; Kudryashev with Malevich (V. Kostin, *OST. Obshchestvo stankovistov* (Leningrad, 1967), p. 16).

26. 'Otchet o deyatel'nosti muzeya zhivopisnoi kul'tury', TsGALI, fond 664, op. 1, ed. khr. 8, list 24.

27. Kostin, *OST*, p. 25.

28. 'Platforma OST', in Matsa, *Sovetskoe iskusstvo*, p. 575.

29. See the decree 'O perestroike literaturno-khudozhestvennykh organizatsii (Postanovlenie TsK VKP(b) ot 23 aprelya 1932)'.

30. 'O politike v oblasti khudozhestvennoi literatury (Rezolyutsiya TsK VKP(b) ot 18 iyunya 1925)'.

31. This trend has been particularly well documented in the field of literature (see H. Ermolaev, *Soviet Literary Theories, 1917–34* (Berkeley, 1963), and Brown, *Proletarian Epsiode*. S. Fitzpatrick has argued that in 1928–9 while the State retained its impartiality in the artistic conflicts, the Party actively supported the Proletarian artistic groups, and that this resulted in a reduction of the government sphere but growth of the party sphere in cultural matters ('The Emergence of Glaviskusstvo: Class War on the Cultural Front, Moscow, 1928–1929', *Soviet Studies*, No. 2, 1971, p. 236).

32. 1913–14, in the Stedelijk Museum, Amsterdam. The Futurists had also used photographs as sources of inspiration as well as experiment (see A. Scharf, *Art and Photography* (London, 1974), pp. 256–68). Larionov had used photographic and cinematic subject matter in his Rayist works exhibited at the Donkey's Tail exhibition in Moscow, 1912 (see S. Compton, 'Art and Photography', *Print Collector's Newletter*, Vol. 7, No. 1, 1976, pp. 12, 14).

33. Raoul Hausmann explained: 'I also needed a name for this technique, and, in agreement with

George Grosz, John Heartfield, Johannes Baader and Hannah Hoch, we decided to call these works *photomontages*. This term translates our aversion to playing the artist, and thinking of ourselves as engineers (hence our preference for workmen's overalls) we meant to construct, to assemble [*montieren*] our works' (*Courier Dada* (Paris, 1958), p. 42; cited from Dawn Ades, *Photomontage* (London, 1976), p. 7).

34. As Klutsis stressed, 'the very word photomontage grew out of industrial culture – the montage of machines, the montage of turbines' ('Fotomontazh kak sredstvo agitatsii i propagandy', *Za bol'shevistskii plakat* (Moscow, 1932), p. 87).

35. For a detailed explanation of the Constructivists' opposition to the unique work of art and the individuality of the artist and subjectivity of the artistic process, see Chapter Three. The documentary quality of photomontage and its mass character meant that it could be regarded as an ideal form of proletarian art and received the same official favour that Lenin bestowed on the cinema. Lenin had said that 'the cinema is, for us, the most important of all the arts' (G. Boltyanskii, *Lenin i kino* (Moscow, 1925), p. 19).

36. The potential metaphorical function of the ready-made image was recognised by Picasso's suggestion that Severini's use of a real moustache to replace its painted form would be more novel if it replaced an eye (recorded in a letter from Papini to Boccioni printed in *Lacerba* on 15 March 1914; cited in Scharf, *Art and Photography*, p. 277).

37. 'Foto-montazh', *LEF*, No. 4, 1924, p. 41.

38. G. Klutsis, 'Fotomontazh kak novyi vid agitatsionnogo iskusstva', *Izofront. Klassovaya bor'ba na fronte prostranstvennykh iskusstv. Sbornik statei ob'edineniya 'Oktyabr''* (Mosow and Leningrad, 1931), pp. 119–26. It should be noted that a rather inaccurate version of this statement is given by Ades in *Photomontage*, p. 15. Most importantly the latter implies that photomontage appeared under the aegis of the journal *LEF* which only commenced publication in 1923. Although Rodchenko did design the layouts and covers for *LEF* (later *Novyi LEF*) and the magazine did constantly act as a propagandiser of photomontage, Rodchenko himself only began to incorporate genuine photographic images into his abstract collage work in 1922. His advent into photomontage proper only occurred in 1923 with his photocollages illustrating Mayakovskii's poem *Pro eto* (*About This*). Rodchenko's and *LEF*'s advent into this field thus postdated the emergence of photomontage in the Soviet Union.

39. Klutsis, 'Fotomontazh', p. 121.

40. *ibid.*, p. 120. Klutsis adopted the term 'photo-slogan-montage' to describe the cover for his book on Lenin in 1924.

41. Klutsis, 'Fotomontazh', p. 125.

42. The dating of 1919 was accepted by the compilers of *Katalog Klutsisa*, p. 35. Oginskaya cites Klutsis' own list of work (*spisok rabot*) as giving 1919 and states that the lithograph of the same title was executed by his wife Kulagina in 1923 (L. Oginskaya, 'Khudozhnik - agitator', *Dekorativnoe iskusstvo*, No. 7, 1971, pp. 36–7). Marts asserts that it was preceded by an earlier photomontage entitled *Blow* (*Udar*) of 1918 but confirms 1919 for the *Dynamic City* ('Gustav Klutsis', *Tekhnicheskaya estetika*, No. 1, 1968, p. 28). In terms of Klutsis' artistic development the dating of 1919 is acceptable in providing a convenient point to mark his changeover from Suprematism to Constructivism and the Constructivist kiosks he was designing in 1922. *Dinamicheskii gorod*, moreover, does not appear to be the very first instance of Klutsis' use of photographic elements. According to Oginskaya and the Riga catalogue an earlier

work entitled *Storm: The Latvian Rifles, 1918* (*Shturm. Latyshskie strelki 1918 g.*), which seems to have been executed for the Fifth Congress of the Soviets, also utilised photographic material (*Katalog Klutsisa*, p. 30, and L. Oginskaya, 'Gustav Klutsis - khudozhnik leninskoi temy', *Dekorativnoe iskusstvo*, No. 4, 1970, p. 37). Another work exhibited in 1970 under the title *In Answer to the Movement of the Left Social Revolutionaries* (*V otvet na levo-eserovskoe dvizhenie*) as a design for a panel for the Fifth Congress of the Soviets in 1918 was described as a photomontage (*Katalog Klutsisa*, p. 35).

43. S. Bojko, *New Graphic Design in Revolutionary Russia* (London, 1972), p. 30.

44. According to *Veshch'*, No. 1, 1922, the blockade of Russia existed until 1920–1. Umanskii published a series of articles in *Der Ararat* in 1920 and his book on Russian art appeared in 1920, but there is no evidence of much information concerning wartime and post-war experiments in the West reaching Russia until 1920–1. Lissitzky apparently only saw photographic experiments in photomontage when he was in the West in 1921. In accounting for Klutsis' development it should be noted that Klutsis had been a pupil of Malevich in Moscow and had visited Vitebsk. He would therefore have had an opportunity to see *Woman at a Poster Column.*

45. Klutsis' sketchbooks in TsGALI, contain sketches of Lissitzky's works including typographical layouts for the *ABC* magazine (TsGALI, fond 1334, op. 2, ed. khr. 239, list 313). Klutsis' painting *The Dynamic City* is in the George Costakis Collection (see Rudenstine, *Russian Avant-Garde Art*, No. 339). The composition has strong affinities with Malevich's architectural models in the use of a strong diagonal axis. The affixing of elements, however, is asymmetrical and there are more spatial ambiguities than in Malevich's works.

46. This also suggests that the dynamic city floats against the background of the world and that the spherical body is probably meant to represent the world. The ultra-modern character of its composition (skyscrapers) could be interpreted as that of modern technology with the worker representing the harnessing of mechanical power to benefit the masses under the Socialist Revolution. As an allegory of the new Socialist city this project has affinities with the cosmic utopianism present in the early post-revolutionary projects of the Constructivists (Lavinskii and Tatlin) discussed in Chapter Two.

47. *Mir staryi i mir vnov' stroyashchiisya* (*The Old World and the World being Built Anew*). See Oginskaya, 'Gustav Klutsis - khudozhnik leninskoi temy', p. 37. Excluding the possibility that *Storm* was a poster, this is the first time that photomontage was used in posterwork in the USSR as a specifically agitational medium.

48. It is interesting to note that Klutsis was among the first artists to exploit the image of Lenin striding forward, to emphasise his role and inspiration. This has remained a powerful and popular image in the Soviet Union, frequently utilised in later propaganda displays and works of art.

49. An approach to this simple chunky type-face was made in the ROSTA posters of the Civil War, such as, for example, Mayakovskii's poster *The Rallying Cry of the Ukrainians and Russians is One: The Polish Sir will not Lord it over the Workers*. However, Klutsis' use of this particular type-face which became popular with the Constructivists was one of the first instances of its use, and dated from the same period as *Kino-Fot* (Nos. 1–6, 1922–3) and Gan's *Konstruktivizm* (1922).

50. From a series entitled *The Fight for the Five Year Plan* (*Bor'ba za pyatiletku*), (*Katalog Klu-*

tsisa, pp. 37–8). The first Five Year Plan had been inaugurated in 1928.

51. An interesting intermediate variant is preserved in the Moscow archive (TsGALI, fond 1334, op. 2, ed. khr. 239, list 9). This gives a valuable insight into Klutsis' working method. The image is far more complex. The hands do not taper to a point from the basis of the detailed photograph and there are too many conflicting diagonals to attain the unity achieved in the final version.

52. Klutsis had used this arrangement previously in a design for a poster exhorting people to fulfil the provisions of the First Five Year Plan entitled *We will fulfil the Plan of Great Works* (*Vypolnim plan velikikh rabot*, 1930) (Klutsis, 'Fotomontazh', p. 129). The dating is taken from *Katalog Klutsisa*, p. 36.

53. *Brigada khudozhnikov*, No. 1, 1931, p. 34.

54. *Krest'yanka*, No. 21, 1935. Although the cover was not signed, Klutsis' widow has identified it as his work, authenticating it in writing as his design (TsGALI, fond 1334, op. 2, ed. khr. 239, list 87). Another variant was published in *Rabis*, No. 10, 1933.

55. *Dyla golosa*. See El Lissitzky, 'Our Book', 1926, in Lissitzky-Küppers, *El Lissitzky*, p. 359. Originally published in *Gutenberg-Jahrbuch* (1926–7).

56. El Lissitzky, 'Typography of Typography', in Lissitzky-Küppers, *El Lissitzky*, p. 355. Originally published in *Merz*, No. 4, 1923.

57. An earlier stage of this photogram – the hand of the Constructor formed the cover for the yearbook of the Architectural Department of VKhUTEMAS published in 1927 (plate 4.2). 'XYZ' is possibly a private witticism referring to the journal *ABC* with which Lissitzky was involved, and possibly suggesting that he had outstripped his confederates. The Unovis sign incorporated a circle and a square. Lissitzky used the photogram technique in his portrait of Kurt Schwitters in which two views of Schwitters' head were fused against the background of *Merz*.

58. It should be noted that articles by Eisenstein, 'Montazh attraktsionov', and by Vertov, 'Kinoki. Perevorot', were printed in *LEF*, No. 3, 1923.

59. Lissitzky had designed an exhibition room for the International Art Exhibition at Dresden in 1926 and for the Niedersächsische Landesgalerie Hanover, 1927–8, as completely artistic environments. These are illustrated in Lissitzky-Küppers, *El Lissitzky*, pl. 186–94.

60. Lissitzky-Küppers, *El Lissitzky*, pls. 206–7. An extension of this involvement with the agitational nature of the photograph used on a monumental scale was undertaken by Sen'kin. In 1930 he became interested in the problem of projecting enormously enlarged photographic images onto the surfaces of walls and fixing such images so that they could act as agitational photographic frescoes.

61. Text from *Novoe o Mayakovskom, Literaturenoe nasledstvo*, Vol. 65 (Moscow, 1958); translated by Bojko, *New Graphic Design* p. 18.

62. See S. Bojko, 'Collages et photomontages oubliés de A. Rodtchenko', *Opus International*, No.10/11, 1969, p. 32.

63. The strong ideological stress in this article which accompanied a reproduction of Rodchenko's photomontage suggests that the article was written by Gan, editor of the magazine of which only six issues appeared.

64. The photographs were by Vasserman, Kapustyanskii and Shterenberg, as acknowledged in V. Mayakovskii, *Pro eto* (Moscow, 1923), p. 2.

65. V. Mayakovskii, untitled notes on agitation and advertising, 1923, MS, private archive, Moscow. For more details concerning this commercial agitation, see L. Oginskaya, 'Mayakovskii v reklame', *Dekorativnoe iskusstvo*, No. 1, 1970, pp. 52–3.

66. A. M. Rodchenko, 'Rabota s Mayakovskim', 1940, MS, Mayakovskii Museum, Moscow.

Mosselprom (Moskovskoe ob'edinenie predpriyatii po pererabotke produktov sel'skokhozyaistvennoi promyshlennosti – Moscow Association for Processing Products of the Agricultural Industry); Gosizdat (Gosudarstvennoe izdatel'stvo – State Publishing House); Rezinotrest (Rezinovyi trest – State Rubber Company); GUM (Gosudarstvennyi universal'nyi magazin – Universal State Stores); *Ogonek* (*The Small Light*, a popular magazine).

The students who helped Rodchenko were in turn, Bykov and Pylinskii, Zhigunov and Sobolev.

67. 'A. M. Rodchenko. Reklam-plakaty s tekstom V. V. Mayakovskogo', *LEF*, No. 5, 1924.

68. 'Konstruktivisty', *LEF*, No. 1, 1923, p. 251.

69. During this period he designed the covers for a multitude of books by Mayakovskii. These included *To Sergei Esenin* (*Sergeyu Eseninu*, 1926); *My Discovery of America* (*Moe otkrytie Ameriki*, 1926) and covers for other writers such as Aseev's *Selected Poems* (*Izbrannye stikhi*, 1930), and books by Erenburg, Pertsov and Tret'yakov.

70. Bojko, *New Graphic Design*, p. 29.

71. A different approach to the concept of expanding vision was embodied in the experiments of Matyushin (see Chapter Seven).

72. A. Rodchenko, 'Puti sovremennoi fotografii', *Novyi LEF*, No. 9, 1928, pp. 38–9.

73. A. Rodchenko, 'K foto v etom nomere', *Novyi LEF*, No. 3, 1928, p. 29.

74. Rodchenko, 'K foto', pp. 28–9.

NOTES TO CHAPTER SEVEN

1. M. Matyushin, 'Tvorcheskii put' khudozhnika', MS, private archive, Leningrad.

2. A. Povelikhina, 'Matyushin's Spatial System', *Structurist*, No. 15/16, 1975–6, p. 64. In this whole discussion of Matyushin I am heavily indebted to the pioneering investigations and generous help of Alina Vasil'evna Povelikhina.

3. *A Sculpture of a Branch* (*Composition*) (*Skul'ptura suchka* (*kompozitsiya*) shown at the Union of Youth exhibition in St Petersburg, December 1911–January 1912 (*Katalog vystavki kartin Soyuza molodezhi v S. Peterburge 5 dekabrya 1911–10 yanvarya 1912* (St Petersburg, 1911), No. 48); also listed in D. E. Gordon, *Modern Art Exhibitions, 1910–1916* (Munich, 1974), Vol. 2, p. 525).

4. Povelikhina, 'Matyushin', pp. 64–5.

5. *ibid*., p. 65. The term '*zorved*' was based on the combination of the roots of two Russian words. Firstly *zor* from *zret'* meaning to see in the sense of physical sight and *zorkii*, meaning sharp-sighted. Secondly *ved* from *vedat'* meaning to see in the sense of know, cognition. This could therefore be rendered in English by 'see-know'. I have preferred to retain the Russian phrase. As Povelikhina has pointed out, this concept combined Eastern and Western philosophies. It is known that Matyushin had read Uspenskii's writings concerning the philosophical and religious conceptions of the East (see Povelikhina, 'Matyushin', p. 70, nn. 5, 8).

6. M. Matyushin, 'Ne iskusstvo a zhizn'', *Zhizn' iskusstva*, No. 20, 1923, p.15.

7. Matyushin set out a whole series of experiments in his manuscript 'Opyt khudozhnika novoi mery' (galley proof with autograph annotations, 26 May 1926, TsGALI, fond 134, op. 2, ed. khr. 21).

Although corrected by the artist the article was never published. In the Department of Organic Culture at the Leningrad GINKhUK, Matyushin and his students conducted a series of experiments into the potentials of sight, sound and touch, thought and concentration. They even devised physical exercises to promote extended vision. As part of this programme of research Matyushin investigated the relationship between sound, form and colour.

8. Matyushin, 'Opyt khudozhnika novoi mery'.

9. Matyushin, 'Opyt khudozhnika novoi mery'. In his own work Matyushin relied heavily on landscape to depict his concept of extended vision along the horizontal. Objects were reduced to flat planes displaced upwards to depict the curve of the earth's surface, as in *Landscape from all sides* (*Peizazh so vsekh storon, c.*1920), illustrated in Povelikhina, 'Matyushin'.

10. Matyushin's interest in the fourth dimension, fostered by the ideas of Lobachevskii, Riman and Minkovskii, was evinced as early as 1913 in *Soyuz molodezhi*, No. 3, 1913, pp. 25–34, where in reviewing Gleizes and Metzinger's book *Du cubisme*, he expounded Hinton and Uspenskii's ideas of the fourth dimension. In *Troe* (1913) he referred to three-dimensional space as a cage. It is not improbable that Matyushin may have been one of the dominant influences in the development of his friend Malevich's concern with the fourth dimension. The theme of the fourth dimension was present in Russian art of the period. Gabo and Pevsner in their *Realistic Manifesto* (1920) saw the fourth dimension as the incorporation of time or movement into the work of art (see Chapter One). Tatlin's perception of the inner tension of materials may very well ultimately be linked to these ideas of Matyushin's. Certainly Tatlin was a member of GINKhUK and was constantly involved in discussions with Matyushin.

11. Povelikhina, 'Matyushin', p. 68.

12. M. Matyushin, 'Nauka v iskusstve', MS; quoted in Povelikhina, 'Matyushin', p. 68.

13. M. Matyusin, *Zakonomernost' izmenyaemosti tsvetovykh sochetanii. Spravochnik po tsvetu* (Moscow and Leningrad, 1932). The book was accompanied by a series of tables, made from strips of coloured papers, which demonstrated the arguments expounded in the text. It was intended to be followed by another volume which did not appear.

14. These experiments were tabulated and exhibited in 1924, 1925 and 1926 in GINKhUK. Malevich took several tables with him when he visited the Bauhaus in 1927. These are now in the Stedelijk, Museum, Amsterdam, having formerly been erroneously attributed to Malevich (Andersen, *Malevich*, p. 136).

15. This principle was illustrated by a piece of wood of a sinuous curved rounded form painted in warm reddish tones and an angular shaped piece painted in cool bluish tones. This piece was exhibited in 1930 and is reproduced in Povelikhina, 'Matyushin', p. 71.

16. The fullest account of Khlebnikov's literary work is given in Vladimir Markov, *Russian Futurism: A History* (Berkeley, 1968).

17. This article was first published in 1930. V. Khlebnikov, 'My i doma', in *Sobranie proizvedenii Velimira Khlebnikova* (Leningrad, 1928–33), Vol. 4, pp. 275–86. The manuscript dates from 1914–15 and was signed with the pseudonym 'Lunev' (*ibid.*, p. 339).

18. These were the bridge house (*dom-most*); poplar house (*dom-topol'*); underwater palaces (*podvodnye-dvortsy*); steamer houses (*doma-parokhody*); film house (*dom-plenka*); chess house (*dom-shakhmaty*); swing house (*dom-kacheli*); hair house (*dom-volos*); cup house (*dom-chasha*); tube house (*dom-trubka*); book house (*dom-kniga*); field house (*dom-pole*); house on wheels (*dom na kolesakh*) (Khlebnikov, 'My i doma', pp. 283–5).

19. This houses the archive of IRLI, the Institute of Russian Literature and Art. For complete details of these drawings, see E. F. Kovtun and A. V. Povelikhina, 'Utes iz budushchego (Arkhitekturnye idei Velimira Khlebnikova)', *Tekhnicheskaya estetika*, No. 5/6, 1976, pp. 40–2. My present account is heavily dependent upon this article, research material and personal discussions, which Evgenii Fedorovich Kovtun and Alina Vasil'evna Povelikhina have kindly made available to me. Unless otherwise stated information concerning the nature of Khlebnikov's dwelling units is taken from his article 'My i doma'.

20. The beehive house (*dom-ulei*) is not mentioned in Khlebnikov's list of thirteen types, but from the description in the article, it appears that this was a variant of the tube house (*dom-trubka*) (Khlebnikov, 'My i doma', p. 284).

21. Khlebnikov seemed to refer to this as a flower house (*dom-tsvetok*) and also mentioned a 'reddish frosted glass dome' (Khlebnikov, 'My i doma', p. 286).

22. Kovtun and Povelikhina, 'Utes iz budushchego', p. 40.

23. Khlebnikov, 'My i doma', pp. 278–9.

24. *ibid.*, p. 277. In his article 'Utes iz budushchego' Khlebnikov developed further the concept of flying and weightlessness so that his new city, existing entirely in space, was inhabited by flying inhabitants with flying, kite-like buildings. 'They walk in the air ... or run through air, snow, through frozen snow crusts of cloud on the skies of time' (*Sobranie proizvedenii Velimira Khlebnikova*, Vol. 4, pp. 296–300).

25. V. Khlebnikov, 'Lebediya budushchego', *Sobranie proizvedenii Velimira Khlebnikova*, Vol. 4, p. 289.

26. 'I i E. Povest' kamennogo veka'. See Kovtun and Povelikhina, 'Utes iz budushchego', p. 41. Also see Khlebnikov 'My i doma', p. 286.

27. Nikolai Fedorovich Fedorov (1828–1903), philosopher. See his major work *Filosofiya obshchego dela*, Vol. 1 (Vernyi, 1906); Vol. 2 (Moscow, 1913). See Vol. 1, p. 293, and Vol. 2, p. 350. There is no direct evidence to corroborate the view that there was a direct relationship between the ideas of Fedorov and those of Khlebnikov and later Miturich and Tatlin, who both undertook the construction of flying apparatuses (Kovtun and Povelikhina, 'Utes iz budushchego', p. 42).

28. V. Khlebnikov, 'Izberem dva slova', *Neizdannye proizvedeniya* (Moscow, 1940).

29. Khlebnikov's writings on the laws of numbers and time were published posthumously as *Otryvok iz dosok sudby* (A Fragment from the Boards of Destiny). He considered that these could ultimately be reduced to the numbers 2 and 3 (V. Khlebnikov, letter to Miturich dated 14 March 1922, in V. Khlebnikov, *Sobranie proizvedenii Velimira Khlebnikova*, Vol. 5, p. 324). Using his laws Khlebnikov had accurately predicted the Russian Revolution of 1917.

30. All reminiscences of Tatlin recall this (see D. Danin, 'Tatlin', MS, private archive, Moscow, p. 8, and A. A. Levashkova, 'O Tatline', MS, private archive, Moscow, p. 3). It is interesting to note that while at Kiev Tatlin's bookshelves contained (according to one eye-witness) 'everything that Khlebnikov had published; one volume of Gogol' and Pushkin, two volumes of Blok, collections of poems by Mayakovskii and Whitman, Dostoevskii's *The Idiot*, stories by Leskov, and Lenin's *Philosophical Notebooks*. On the wall there was a death mask of Leonardo and the head of his 'Angel in Plaster' (Begicheva, 'O Tatline', p. 6).

31. See Khlebnikov, *Neizdannye proizvedeniya*, p. 413, and V. Khlebnikov, 'Tatlin tainovidets lopastei'; reprinted in Khlebnikov *Neizdannye proizvedeniya*, p. 170. Apparently written at the end of May 1916 at Tsaritsyn when Petrovskii and Tatlin visited Khlebnikov there (*ibid.*, p. 413). In English the poem could be rendered thus:

> Tatlin seer of the paddles,
> And stern bard of the screw,
> From the detachment of sun-fishers,
> With his dead hand he knotted
> A spiderweb doll of rigging
> In the shape of an iron horseshoe,
> In a vision pincers
> Look at what he showed
> Blindmen who had gone dumb.
> Such unheard of things
> made of tin, unheard of
> by the brush.

32. A. Abramova refers to Tatlin's plans for a '*gorod vozdukha*' (a city of the air) and to designs he apparently also made for a city built in the midst of nature, including drawings for a modern variant of the *izba* (very small wooden house) (Abramova, 'Tatlin', p. 7). Unfortunately it has proved impossible to establish the precise details of these projects. Nevertheless their existence suggests a strong link with the ideas of Khlebnikov and Fedorov, and adds another dimension to Tatlin's design for the Monument to the Third International.

33. Khlebnikov, *Neizdannye proizvedeniya*, p. 413.

34. *Zangezi* was based on Khlebnikov's ideas of *zaum'* developed between 1915 and 1916. Khlebnikov believed that consonants expressed ideas forming a type of proto-protolanguage and that language thus contained inherent wisdom that man should uncover. Originally language had been a clear and precise means of expression but this had gradually been lost. The task was therefore to recover the original meanings and to build on this foundation a universal language which would lead to the cessation of wars because perfect understanding would have been established. *Zangezi* was one of the few attempts to put this into practice (Markov, *Russian Futurism*, pp. 302–3). For the text of the dramatic poem, see *Sobranie proizvedenii*, Vol. 3, pp. 317–68. Khlebnikov wrote *Zangezi* between 1920 and 1922. It was published in 1922 with a cover designed by Miturich (*ibid.*, p. 386).

35. 'Vvedenie Zangezi', in *Sobranie proizvedenii*, Vol. 5, p. 317. A manuscript lists the different types of poetic language Khlebnikov used in *Zangezi*:
1. *Ptichii yazyk* – bird language
2. *Yazyk bogov* – the language of the gods
3. *Zvezdnyi yazyk* – star language
4. *Zaumnyi yazyk – ploskost' mysli* – transrational language – the plane (or surface) of thought
5. *Razlozhenie slova* – word decomposition
6. *Zvukopis'* – sound writing
7. *Bezumnyi yazyk* – irrational language (*ibid.*, p. 387).

35. V. Tatlin, 'O Zangezi', *Zhizn' iskusstva*, No. 18, 1923, p. 15. State here is used in the sense of ruling government, and perhaps refers to the universal language which would bring peace (see n. 50). 'Over-story' is the literal meaning of *sverkhpovest'*, denoting the story overriding the words and stories within it.

36. Tatlin, 'O Zangezi', p. 15. It should be noted that GINKhUK was also situated in the building of the Museum of Painterly Culture, 9 St Isaac's Square, Petrograd. According to Punin, the poem was read twice (N. Punin, 'Zangezi', *Zhizn' iskusstva*, No. 20, 1923, p. 10). The participants in the production were students from the Academy of Art, the University and the Mining Institute. Tatlin considered that professional actors would carry with them theatrical traditions which would be detrimental to the 'revolutionary' nature of the poem (Tatlin, 'O Zangezi', p. 15). The production was accompanied by lectures: Punin on Khlebnikov's laws of time and Yakubinskii on Khlebnikov's literary work, and an exhibition of material structures by Tatlin all dedicated to the memory of Khlebnikov (Tatlin, 'O Zangezi', p. 15). Reviews of the production include Punin, 'Zangezi', pp. 10–12, and Yutkevich, 'Sukharnaya stolitsa', *LEF*, No. 3, 1923, pp. 181–2.

37. Tatlin, 'O Zangezi', p. 15.

38. Punin, 'Zangezi', p. 10.

39. Tatlin, 'O Zangezi', p. 15.

40. *ibid.*

41. Punin, 'Zangezi', p. 10. Yutkevich insisted that the production was a failure because it was lifeless. Both agreed that it was a rather amateur production lacking the polish and acumen of a professional performance.

42. Tatlin's production of *Zangezi* in 1923 was the only production of three projected by Tatlin which actually materialised. Apparently Tatlin also wanted to produce *Zangezi* in Kiev in 1925 and again in Moscow in 1927 (Begicheva, 'O Tatline', p. 16).

43. According to the memoirs of one of Tatlin's students, Derunov, when the students despaired of solving the design task Tatlin had set them, Tatlin would quote Khlebnikov's words from *Zangesi*: 'I am able! Be able. I will be able' (L. Zhadova, 'Tatlin – proektirovshchik material'noi kul'tury', *Sovetskoe dekorativnoe iskusstvo 77/78* (Moscow, 1980), p. 224, n. 57). Equally, A. Gladkov remembers Tatlin talking about Khlebnikov's utopian fantasies in a very matter-of-fact way ('O V. Tatline', in 'Kniga vospominanii', MS, private archive, Moscow; cited in Zhadova, 'Tatlin – proektirovshchik', p. 228).

44. Camilla Gray attributed this chair to Tatlin (*Great Experiment*, pl. 197). However, in 1929 it was illustrated under this title in *Stroitel'stvo Moskvy*. (Lobov, Mebel' fakul'teta po obrabotke dereva i metalla VKhUTEINa', *Stroitel'stvo Moskvy*, No. 10, 1929, p. 10) where it was described as the diploma work of Rogozhin (a student of Dermetfak) who produced it 'under the direction of V. Tatlin'. The attribution of *Stroitel'stvo Moskvy* has to be accepted as the correct one although Tatlin's influence had evidently been very great and his participation in the design considerable. Rogozhin eventually became an engineer. Tatlin taught in the Dermetfak from 1927 to 1930. The word 'Viennese' (*venskii*) of the chair's title refers to the fact that it was the Viennese firm of Michael Thonet which originally brought this material into mass-produced furniture design. Where Thonet designs never used the material's flexibility, except accidentally, it is typical of Tatlin's approach that this dynamic property was seized upon here and exploited positively.

45. Lobov, 'Mebel' fakul'teta', p. 10. Lobov cites the material as beech switches. In fact as Tatlin's statement makes clear the chair was constructed from glued wooden strips cut on the cross ('Khudozhnik – organizator byta', *Rabis*, No. 48, 1929, p. 48).

46. Tatlin, 'Khudozhnik-organizator byta'.

47. V. Tatlin, 'Problema sootnosheniya cheloveka i veshchi', *Rabis*, No. 15, 1930, p. 9.

48. *ibid.*

49. This is now preserved in a private collection in Moscow. Tatlin taught in the Ceramics faculty from 1927 to 1930, and undoubtedly produced other items, none of which has apparently survived. In 1977, in Moscow, Tatlin's drawn designs

for two milk jugs, a teapot, a tea cup, a sugar basin and a plate were exhibited under the title of *proekty posudy dlya novogo byta* (*V. E. Tatlin. Zasluzhennyi deyatel' iskusstva RSFSR. Katalog vystavki proizvedenii* (Moscow, 1977), Nos. 102–7). These items are in the collection of the Bakhrushin Central Theatrical Museum Tsentral'nyi teatral'nyi muzei imeni A. A. Bakhrushina) in Moscow. Larissa Zhadova illustrated some of these in her article 'Tatlin: proektirovshchik', p. 223. It should be stressed that Tatlin had begun to experiment with ceramics as early as 1923 when he was working in the Department of Material Culture at GINKhUK and these items date from this earlier period. After the Ceramics faculty of the VKhUTEIN was transferred to the Silicate Institute in 1930 Tatlin continued working there until *c.* 1933.

50. It is this mass model which is reproduced in Gray, *Great Experiment*, pl. 199. The split in the top led to the supposition that it was a teapot. The distinction between the two variants has been established by A. V. Abramova.

51. For Tatlin's definition of the aims of the Department of Material Culture (Otdel material'noi kul'tury) and details concerning its activity, see V. Tatlin, 'Otchet issledovatel'skoi raboty za 1923–1924g. Otdela material'noi kul'tury', typescript, private archive, Leningrad, p. 1; cited in Chapter Five. He worked there with Khapaev, N. Nekrasov, E. Kholodov, Sakovich, Zheltikov and Korotkov (*ibid.*).

52. V. Tatlin, 'Iskusstvo v tekhniku', *Brigada khudozhnikov*, No. 6, 1932, pp. 15–16. This declaration was also published in *Vystavka rabot zasluzhennogo deyatelya iskusstv V. E. Tatlina* (Moscow and Leningrad, 1932). An English translation is printed in Andersen, *Vladimir Tatlin*, pp. 75–6.

53. Tatlin, 'Iskusstvo v tekhniku', p. 15.

54. *ibid.*, p. 16.

55. *ibid.*

56. Begicheva, 'O Tatline', p. 9. She also reports that he was opposed to rectilinear geometrical forms even in painting because they were sterile, dead and unnatural.

57. A. Sotnikov, 'Stenogramma vystuplenie na vechere V. E. Tatlina', typescript, private archive, Moscow, p. 1.

58. Tatlin, 'Iskusstvo v tekhniku', p. 16.

59. Abramova, 'Tatlin', p. 7. It is difficult to establish when Tatlin conceived the idea for the *Letatlin*. According to one source Tatlin had been working on it for ten years before 1933 ('Letatel'nyi apparat V. E. Tatlina', *Vechernyaya Moskva*, No. 152, 5 July 1933), and he is reported to have talked about it in Kiev in 1925 (Begicheva, 'O Tatline', p. 17). This would suggest that the idea emerged some time during the early 1920s. This is confirmed by V. Khodasevich who maintains that Tatlin began to talk about constructing a flying apparatus in the mid-1920s ('Bylo', MS, private archive, Moscow, p. 14). However, Zhadova has pointed out that as far back as 1912 Khlebnikov wrote 'Tat[lin] flew off in his flyer' (V. Khlebnikov, 'Obrazchik slovonovshestv v yazyke', *Poshchechina obshchestvennomu vkusu* (Moscow, 1912); cited by Zhadova in 'Tatlin - proektirovshchik', p. 231, n. 74). Tatlin made several models of the *Letatlin* and continued to work on it until his death. Two variants of the *Letatlin* together with two skeletal constructions of the apparatus, uncovered to display the form, were exhibited at the State Museum of Fine Arts in Moscow in 1932. See plate 7.11 and I. Matsa, 'O konstruktivizme', *Iskusstvo*, No. 8, 1971, p. 46.

60. 'Lichnaya kartochka chlena MOSSKha Tatlin', and K. Zelinskii, 'Letatlin', *Vechernyaya Moskva*, 6 April 1933. Tatlin was assisted by Sotnikov, Pavil'onov, Zelenskii and Shchipitsyn (his former students) (Abramova, 'Tatlin', p. 7). Tatlin only mentions Sotnikov and Pavil'onov ('Iskusstvo v tekhniku', p. 16). Tatlin stayed in this studio until 1937 (Danin, 'Tatlin', p. 31).

61. Tatlin, 'Iskusstvo v tekhniku', p. 16. Tatlin had described the glider as the most complicated dynamic form which could be used widely. He hoped that it would become a mass item of use, as cheap as a bicycle (T. Grits and V. Trenin, 'Letatlin', *Yunyi naturalist*, 9 September 1933).

62. Begicheva, 'O Tatline', p. 18.

63. Zelinskii, 'Letatlin'. Tatlin believed that man was descended from flying creatures (Danin, 'Tatlin', p. 28) a suspicion or dream that Khlebnikov shared (Khlebnikov, 'My i doma', p. 286). Mikhail Maksimovich Litvinov, the son of Maksim Litvinov, the Foreign Minister, flew the model for a few yards. According to Matsa, this experimental run with the *Letatlin* took place on a hill at Sal'kovo, Zvenigorod, near Moscow, in the autumn of 1933 (I. Matsa, 'O konstruktivizme', *Iskusstvo*, No. 8, 1971, p. 46). The actual construction was eventually housed in the N. E. Zhukovskii Central State Museum of Aviation and Aeronautics.

64. Begicheva, 'O Tatline', p. 18.

65. *ibid.*

66. Tatlin, 'Iskusstvo v tekhniku', p. 16.

67. K. Zelinskii, 'Letatlin', *Vechernyaya Moskva*, 6 April 1933; translation from Andersen, *Vladimir Tatlin*, p. 78.

68. M. Artseulov, 'O "Letatline"', *Brigada khudoznikov*, No. 6, 1932, p. 17.

69. *ibid.*

70. Zelinskii, 'Letatlin'.

71. Artseulov, 'O "Letatline"', p. 18; translation based on that in Andersen, *Vladimir Tatlin*, p. 76.

72. Begicheva, 'O Tatline', p. 18. Tatlin also gave a paper at the Soviet Ministry of Aviation where his ideas were received with scepticism (*ibid.*, p. 19).

73. Zelinskii, 'Letatlin'. Tatlin also stressed that he had designed the Tower as an 'artistic object'. In answer to the question what is important in art he had answered: 'Above all a feeling for the new artistic measure, and of course taste. Taste - this is the categorical imperative of art. I concentrated my position in the Tower to the Third International. Not everyone understood this' (Danin, 'Tatlin', p. 63).

74. Tatlin, 'Iskusstvo v tekhniku', p. 15.

75. The engineer Matveev was captivated by the *Letatlin* and envisaged it emerging as a practical venture (N. I. Matveev, 'Letayushchii velosiped', *Vechernyaya Moskva*, 5 July 1933).

76. 'Initsiativnaya edinitsa v tvorchestve kollektiva.' The *tezisy* (theses) of this article are preserved in TsGALI, fond 665, op. 1, ed. khr. 32, list 11. Tatlin's article was apparently intended for publication in the journal the *Art International* (*Internatsional iskusstva*, announced in *Iskusstvo*, No. 8, 1919, p. 7) to be published by the International Office (Mezhdunarodnoe byuro) of IZO. The advertisement announced articles by Lunacharskii, Tatlin, Dymshits-Tolstaya, Polyakov, V. Khlebnikov, Malevich and others. The journal was not published, but cover designs by Morgunov, Malevich and Dymshits-Tolstaya are preserved (see TsGALI, fond 665, op. 1, ed. khr. 31, 35). More importantly the texts of several articles are preserved in the archives. These include: A. Toporkov, 'Callisthenics' ('Kallistika'); K. Malevich, 'To the Innovators of the Whole World' ('Novatoram vsego mira'); V. Tatlin, 'The Initia-

tive Unit in the Creativity of the Collective: Theses' ('Initsiativnaya edinitsa v tvorchestve kollektiva. Tezisy'); S. Dymshits-Tolstaya, 'The Intuition of Living Creation' ('Intuitsiya zhivogo tvorchestva'); V. Khlebnikov, 'Artists of the World' (Khudozhniki mira') ('Internatsional iskusstva', TsGALI, fond 665, op. 1, ed. khr. 32).

77. *ibid.*

78. A *volnovik* was an apparatus which moved and was designed according to the principles of *volnovoe dvizhenie*, a wave-like motion.

79. M. Miturich introduction to P. Miturich, 'Chuvstvo mira', *Tvorchestvo* No. 4, 1976, p. 14.

80. M. Miturich, 'Chuvstvo mira', p. 14, and P. Miturich, 'Chuvstvo mira', p. 17. In Russian *chuvstvo* denotes sense in the meaning of sensation (including the five senses), emotion or feeling. Since it combines perception through physical (physiological) sensation with an emotional (psychological) perception, the phrase '*chuvstvo mira*' could be rendered in English by 'a feeling for the world'.

81. P. Miturich, 'Chuvstvo mira', p. 15.

82. *ibid.*, p. 15.

83. *ibid.*

84. *ibid.*, p. 17.

85. *ibid.*

86. *ibid.*, p. 16.

87. *ibid.*

88. Rozanova, *Miturich*, pp. 5-6. Although Rozanova states that Miturich was constructing an ornithopter at this time, Miturich's statement that his first model was constructed in 1921 suggests that this early activity did not result in a model (P. Miturich, 'Vol'novye dvizhiteli', MS, private archive, Moscow, p. 2).

89. Rozanova, *Miturich*, p. 6.

90. P. Miturich, 'Moe pervoe znakomstvo s Velimirom Khlebnikovym', p. 5. Miturich reported Khlebnikov's reaction as an unwillingness to discuss Miturich's inventions because 'technical things were a closed book to him and he understood nothing about them'. The date of the first model is given in Miturich, 'Volnovye dvizhitelva', p. 2.

91. Khlebnikov, *Sobranie proizvedenii*, Vol. 5, p. 324.

92. *P. V. Miturich. Katalog vystavki* (Moscow, 1968), p. 19.

93. P. Miturich, untitled MS, private archive, Moscow. It should be stressed that Miturich's drawings were primarily realistic. In 1921 Miturich was still working on his spatial posters and the *kubiki* (see Chapter One). At this point it should be noted that Miturich had received some technical training when he had attended a military engineering school in 1916, prior to going to the front (Rozanova, *Miturich*, p. 6). His period of attendance was almost certainly less than a year, so the training received was not extensive.

94. P. Miturich, 'Opyt printsipial'noi zashchity svoikh izobretenii', MS, private archive, Moscow, p. 1.

95. The term '*kolebatel'noe dvizhenie*' literally means a rippling, undulating or oscillating movement.

96. P. Miturich, 'Opyt sravneniya skorostei vol'noobraznym i pryamolineinym putem', MS, private archive, Moscow, p. 1. The actual apparatus is still preserved and I saw the experiment performed with exactly the results described in the MS. Miturich was indefatigable in canvassing support for intensive scientific investigations of the principle he had discovered, but although his experiment aroused 'lively interest', none of the scientists he approached pursued it, and not one could explain precisely why it worked.

97. P. Miturich, notebook MS, private archive, Moscow.

98. *ibid.*

99. P. Miturich, 'Volnovaya dinamika', MS, private archive, Moscow, p. 1.

100. Miturich, 'Opyt printsipial'noi zashchity', p. 1. Miturich applied for the patent of *Wings* on 26 April 1922. It had been constructed prior to this in 1921 (Miturich, 'Volnovye dvizhiteli', p. 2). The word '*letun*' comes from the Russian verb *letat'*, to fly. Miturich had visited the exhibition of Tatlin's flying apparatus, but criticised it for its purely formal solution to the problem of self-propelled flight (see P. Miturich, 'Dvenik', MS, private archive, Moscow, entry for 31 March 1934).

101. Miturich took out a patent for this *volnovik* in 1931 (Miturich, 'Opyt printsipal'noi zashchity', p. 1) but it can be presumed that he had been working on it for several years prior to this.

102. Miturich consulted Krzhizhanovskii at the Hydrotechnical Institute on this project. Interest was expressed there but not pursued (V. Pekelis, 'Dobavlenie k odnoi biografii', *Nauka i zhizn'*, No. 10, 1968, p. 118).

103. Miturich applied for this patent in July 1931 (Miturich, 'Opyt printsipial'noi zashchity', p. 1).

104. The patent for this was applied for in 1932 (Miturich, 'Opyt printsipial'noi zashchity', p. 1).

105. *ibid.*

106. P. Miturich, letter dated 10/11 October 1944, private archive, Moscow.

107. P. Miturich, 'Dinamika putei goroda', undated (but written in 1930s), MS, private archive, Moscow.

108. *ibid.*

109. *ibid.*

110. *ibid.*

111. Certain leading Constructivist architects had postulated a 'disurbanist' town-planning schema for the Soviet Union during the early years of the First Five Year Plan, inaugurated autumn 1928. Taking the maxim of Marx that in a communist society there should be no division between work and recreation environments, or between town and country, they had argued a close linear intertwining of the two spread across the whole USSR (see C. Cooke, 'The Town of Socialism', Ph.D. thesis, Cambridge University, 1974).

112. P. Miturich, diary MS, private archive, Moscow, entry for 26 March 1944.

113. *ibid.*

114. Miturich and Tatlin had been friends. They had apparently quarrelled over the latter's friendship with Mayakovskii. (Miturich regarded it as a type of betrayal because of a quarrel between Khlebnikov and Mayakovskii.) Certainly by the early 1930s Miturich and Tatlin were no longer on speaking terms, but these personal differences should not be allowed to obscure the similarity of approach.

NOTES TO CHAPTER EIGHT

1. 'Lichnaya kartochka chlena MOSSKha. Tatlin, Vladimir Evgrafovich', GTG, 59/2874, p. 2.

2. For details of the sets and costumes he designed for this project, see B. Alekseev, 'Novoe v tvorchestve V. E. Tatlina', *Tvorchestvo*, No. 8, 1933, pp. 14–15.

3. Of these many have survived and found their way into TsGALI, fond 2089, op. 2, and into private archives in Moscow.

4. See G. Karginov, *Rodchenko* (London, 1979), pls. 204–5 (1943), pp. 238–9.

5. Conversation with V. A. Stenberg, November 1974.

6. In 1936 and 1938 he participated in the designing of exhibitions (N. Rozanova, *Petr Vasil'evich Miturich* (Moscow, 1972), p. 17). For examples of his later work see *ibid.*, pls. on pp. 81–123.

7. Shapiro is still alive and helped with the exhibition of Tatlin's works in Moscow in 1977.

8. It should be stressed that the Erste Russische Kunstausstellung was the first *Soviet* exhibition in Europe. Prior to that date there had been several exhibitions by Russian émigré artists. In Paris five Russian exhibitions had been held between 1919 and 1921. This number excluded one-man exhibitions by artists like Archipenko, Chagall and Boguslavksii (G. Lukomskii, 'Russkaya vystavka v Berline (Pis'mo iz Berlina)', *Argonavty*, No. 1, 1923, p. 68). In other European cities there had also been exhibitions of work by émigré artists, for instance in Berlin Ivan Puni's work had been exhibited at the Der Sturm gallery in February 1921. However, the significance of the Erste Russische Kunstausstellung lay in the fact that it arrived in Berlin in September 1921 direct from the new Soviet State and that it consisted of works which had been collected by David Shterenberg from artists who had remained in Russia during the revolutionary period. This did not denote a wholehearted acceptance of the Soviet regime but it did indicate at least a passive allegiance. The political positions of the artists included in the exhibition therefore ranged over a very wide spectrum. The exhibition included those whose allegiance was nominal and based on a nationalist sentiment rather than any political agreement with the Bolsheviks, and those artists belonging to the loosely termed 'Futurist' trends which had responded most favourably to the Revolution (Suprematist artists and those who later embraced Constructivism). It also included works by a few of the most recent émigrés such as Puni who had left Russia in September 1920, Kandinskii who left in December 1921, and Gabo who left in the summer of 1922.

9. Ya. Tugendkhol'd, 'Russkoe iskusstvo zagranitsei. Russkaya khudozhestvennaya vystavka v Berline', *Russkoe iskusstvo*, No. 1, 1923, p. 100. The German public's interest should not perhaps be over-estimated. As Lukomskii disparagingly pointed out, on the fifteenth day of the exhibition he received ticket number 1697. He contrasted this with the 15,000 who within the space of two weeks had visited a World of Art exhibition in Paris ('Russkaya vystavka v Berline', p. 68).

10. V. Khazanova, *Sovetskaya arkhitektura pervykh let Oktyabrya 1917–1925 gg.* (Moscow, 1970), p. 196, n. 8. Khazanova does not state her source of information. However, Lissitzky would undoubtedly have had access to, and first-hand knowledge of the First Working Group of Constructivists because he had presented papers at the Moscow INKhUK in September 1921. In addition it should be noted that Aleksei Gan in his book *Constructivism* states that the writer Il'ya Erenburg when 'he left us two months ago … took a wealth of material: photographs of our work, a notebook and a load of impressions' (*Konstruktivizm*, p. 69). Thus it seems established, that *Veshch''s editors had the opportunity and the material in 1922 to present to the West the latest theoretical developments made by the First Working Group of Constructivists. That Veshch' failed to do this was more owing to the aesthetic position of its editors than to any deficiency of material.*

11. *Veshch'*/Gegenstand/*Objet*, No. 1/2, March–April 1922.

12. An idea of the literary, musical and theatrical contributions in *Veshch'* can be gained from a list of the entire contents of the journal printed in English in K. P. Zygas, 'The Magazine Veshch/

Gegenstand/Objet', *Oppositions*, No. 5, fall 1976, pp. 118–21. Unfortunately, Zygas's list is somewhat erratic. I therefore list below those articles specifically relating to painting, sculpture and architecture which appeared in *Veshch'*:

No. 1/2, March–April 1922

a. 'The Blockade of Russia is Coming to an End', in German, French and Russian ('Blokada Rossii konchaetsya')

b. Notices in Russian concerning:
    the March 1922 International Congress of Artists
    the Hungarian magazine *MA*
    the Museum of Artistic Culture in Moscow
    Dada
    reproductions of Gleizes and Léger's work in the magazine *Clarté*
    the Russian magazine *Blow* (*Udar*) published in Paris

c. V. Shklovskii, 'A Letter to Roman Jakobson' ('Pis'mo k Romanu Yakobsonu')

d. A. Gleizes, 'Concerning the Present State of Painting and Its Tendencies' ('O sovremennom sostoyanii zhivopisi i ee tendentsiyakh')

e. Questionnaire: Untitled answers in Russian from Fernand Léger, Gino Severini, Lipshits

f. T. van Doesburg, 'The State of Contemporary Art' ('Sostoyanie sovremennogo iskusstva')

g. 'Ulen', 'Exhibitions in Russia' ('Die Ausstellungen in Russland')

h. Corbusier-Saugnier, 'Contemporary Architecture' ('Sovremennaya arkhitektura')

i. Notices concerning the first international exhibition in Düsseldorf (May–July 1922), in Russian

j. N. Punin, 'Tatlin's Tower' ('Tatlinova bashnya')

No. 3, May 1922

a. 'The Triumphant Train' ('Torzhestvuyushchii oboz'), containing various notices and remarks

b. Notices in Russian about the Venice exhibition, the Paris Congress, the International Congress of Left Artists at Düsseldorf

c. A. Ozenfant and C. Jeanneret, 'Apropos of Purism' ('Po povodu "purizma"')

d. Questionnaire – Untitled answers in Russian from A. Archipenko and Juan Gris

e. 'Concerning Pablo Picasso' ('O Pablo Pikasso'), short notice

f. Raoul Haussman, 'Optophonetics' ('Optofonetika')

g. El [Lissitzky], 'Exhibitions in Berlin' ('Vystavki v Berline')

h. 'Cézanne and Cézannism' ('Sezann i Sezannizm'), article from the French magazine *L'Esprit Nouveau*

13. 'Ulen', 'Die Ausstellungen in Russland', *Veshch'*, No. 1/2, March–April 1922, p. 9. This translation is based on that of K. P. Zygas which appeared as 'The Exhibitions in Russia', in *Oppositions*, No. 5, fall 1976, pp. 125–7; this quote, p. 127.

14. Erenburg and Lissitzky, 'Blokada Rossii konchaetsya', *Veshch'*, No. 1/2 March/April 1922, p. 2. The present translation is indebted to the text printed in S. Lissitzky-Küppers, *El Lissitzky: Life, Letters, Texts* (London, 1968), pp. 340–1.

15. 'Blokada Rossii konchaetsya', pp. 2–3.

16. *ibid.*, p. 3.

17. The three-dimensional work by the Russian Constructivists which was exhibited at the Erste Russische Kunstausstellung in Berlin in 1922 consisted of the following works (titles are taken from the exhibition catalogue, *Erste Russische Kunstausstellung* (Berlin, Galerie van Diemen, 1922)):

Ioganson	551	*Relief*
	552	*Bautechnische Konstruktion III*
	553	*Bautechnische Konstruktion IV*
	554	*Bautechnische Konstruktion*
Medunetskii	555	*Relief*
	556	*Raumkonstruktion*
	557	*Konstruktion*
	558	*Konstruktion*
Rodchenko	559	*Konstruktion*
Stenberg, G.	563	*Konstruktion*
	564	*Raumkonstruktion*
	565	*Raumkonstruktion*
Stenberg, V.	566	*Konstruktion*
	567	*Bautechnischche Konstruktion*
Tatlin	569	*Contre-Relief*

In addition, certain Constructivists also contributed painted works to the exhibition

Klutsis	84	*Konstruktion*
Medunetskii	135	*Komposition*
	136	*Konstruktion*
	137	*Farbige Konstruktion*
Popova	151	*Komposition*
	152	*Farbige Konstruktion*
	153	*Violinen*
	154	*Portrait*
Rodchenko	163	*Gegenstandlos*
	164	*Konstruktion*
	165	*Schwarze Komposition*
	166	*Rote Farbe*
	167	*Komposition*
	168	*Suprematismus*
Stepanova	209	*Komposition*
	210	*Komposition*
	211	*Figuren*

18. D. Shterenberg, 'Zur Einführung', in *Erste Russische Kunstausstellung*, p. 13. My translation is adapted from that by Naum Gabo which appears in *Gabo: Constructions, Sculpture, Paintings, Drawings, Engravings* (London, 1957), p. 155. Among other minor changes I have replaced 'productive art' with 'production art'.

19. Shterenberg, 'Zur Einführung', pp. 13-14. It should be noted that Shterenberg's introduction did nothing to diminish the identification of Gabo with the Constructivists. Shterenberg had stated that 'parallel to the Constructivists stands the sculptor Gabo' and he had then expounded the formal qualities of Gabo's explorations, without elucidating any of the fundamental divergences between Gabo and the Constructivists.

20. Gabo was not the only other artist to arrive in Berlin in 1922. There were many other Russian artists living in Berlin at this time. Ivan Puni had arrived in 1920 and his studio became a meeting place for artists and writers such as Il'ya Erenburg, Raoul Hausmann and Hans Richter. E. Steneberg has compiled a list of Russian writers, poets, philosophers, artists and critics who frequented what has been called the Russian Club or House of Art (Haus der Künste) at the Café Leon in Berlin over the period 1922-3 (*Russische Kunst. Berlin 1919-1932* (Berlin, 1969), pp. 18-19). Although this list appears to be reliable it should be noted for instance that Medunetskii was only in Berlin briefly, for a while in 1923. He and the Stenberg brothers travelled to Berlin and then on to Paris as artists with the Tairov Theatre Company on their European tour of 1923. The Stenbergs are not mentioned by Steneberg as having been in Berlin at this time. It was at the Café Leon that Puni delivered a series of lectures on Russian art which were later published as a book entitled *Contemporary Painting* (*Sovremennaya zhivopis'* (Berlin, 1923)). Puni, who arrived in Berlin on 21 October 1921, exhibited a large number of works at the Der Sturm gallery in February 1921. These included designs and drawings for abstract sculptures – *Zeichnungen und Skizzen zu ungegenständlichen Skulpturen*, from 1915-16 (Nos. 14-26) and 1916 (Nos. 27-52). See *Jwan Puni Petersburg. Gemälde, Aquarelle. Zeichnungen* (Berlin, Galerie Der Sturm, 1921), p. 4. For contemporary photographs of the installation and contents of that exhibition, see H. Berninger and J. A. Cartier, *Jean Pougny*, (Iwan Puni) 1892-1956. *Catalogue de l'oeuvre, Tome I: Les Années d'avant-garde, Russie-Berlin, 1910-1923* (Tübingen, 1972), pp. 124-5, 128-9.

21. N. Gabo, 'The 1922 Soviet Exhibition', *Studio International*, Vol. 182/3, No. 938, p. 171. In this letter Gabo attacked the misconception that Lissitzky was an organiser of the 1922 exhibition. He stated quite categorically that the organisers were Sterenberg (Sternberg in Gabo's transliteration), Mar'yanov (representing the Cheka) Al'tman, himself, and Dr Lutz, the director of the Galerie van Diemen. Gabo included a photograph with his statement which is reproduced in the plate here. Gabo organised the three abstract rooms at the 1922 exhibition.

22. This quote is taken from a German critic cited by Ya. Tugendkhol'd in his article 'Russkoe iskusstvo zagranitsei', p. 101.

23. F. Stahl, 'Russische Kunstausstellung Galerie van Diemen', *Berliner Tageblatt*, Abendausgabe, 18 October 1922 and Tugendkhol'd, 'Russkoe iskusstvo zagranitsei', p.101. A contemporary reaction cited by E. Neuman expressed a similar evaluation of the exhibition: 'it brushed aside with a single stroke the previous work of the Expressionists and brought to light the Abstractionists' ('Russia's "Leftist Art" in Berlin, 1922', *Art Journal*, Vol. 27, No. 1, 1967, p. 22).

24. Cited by Tugendkhol'd, 'Russkoe iskusstvo zagranitsei', p. 102.

25. H. Richter, statement printed in *Sovremennaya arkhitektura*, No. 2, 1926.

26. I. Matsa, *Iskusstvo sovremennoi Evropy* (Moscow and Leningrad, 1926).

27. V. Kandinsky, 'Kunstfrühling in Russland', *Die Freiheit*, Abendausgabe, 9 April 1919. An English translation is printed in K. Lindsay and P. Vergo, eds., *Kandinsky: Complete Writings on Art* (London, 1982), Vol. 1, pp. 428-9.

28. 'Mezhdunarodnoe khudozhestvennoe byuro', *Zhizn' iskusstva*, No. 21, 23 November 1918, p. 6.

29. 'Mezhdunarodnoe byuro pri otdele izobrazitel'nykh iskusstv', *Iskusstvo*, No. 1, 1919, p. 2.

30. 'Mezhdunarodnoe byuro', *Iskusstvo*, No. 1, 1919, p. 2. This short announcement also explained the dual importance of such an artistic international: 'The Social role of art, as a factor harmoniously uniting nations and societies, makes it a powerful weapon in the struggle for the realisation of world socialism. At the same time the spiritual role of art promises socialised humanity the as yet unexperienced joys of a national artistic activity, in creating and understanding art.' Kandinskii elaborated upon the aims of the conference in an article entitled 'Concerning "The Great Utopia"' which was published in 1920 ('O "velikoi utopii"', *Khudozhestvennaya zhizn'*, No. 3, 1920, pp. 2-4). A translation of this text is printed in Lindsay and Vergo, *Kandinsky*, Vol. 1, pp. 444-8). Umanskii also publicised this projected congress and encouraged German artists to attend (K. Umanskij, *Neue Kunst in Russland 1914-1919*

(Potsdam and Munich, 1920), pp. 55–6). Other contacts preceding the 1922 exhibition were made by Malevich who in February 1922 sent a letter to Dutch artists in response to Dutch attempts to establish contacts with Soviet artists (see K. S. Malevich, *Essays on Art, 1915–1933* (London, 1969), Vol. 1, pp. 187–8, 254, and *de Stijl*, No. 79/84, 1927, col. 53).

31. V. Kandinskii, 'Shagi Otdela izobrazitel'nykh iskusstv v mezhdunarodnoi khudozhestvennoi politike', *Khudozhestvennaya zhizn'*, No. 3, 1920, p. 16. This text is translated in Lindsay and Vergo, *Kandinsky*, Vol. 1, pp. 448–54.

32. *ibid*.

33. 'Internatsional iskusstv' *Iskusstvo*, No. 8, 1919, p. 7.

34. 'Mezhdunarodnoe byuro', *Iskusstvo*, No. 8, 1919, p. 7.

35. Articles published by Umanskii included: 'Der Tatlinismus oder die Maschinenkunst', *Der Ararat*, No. 4, January 1920, pp. 12–13; 'Die neue Monumentalskulptur in Russland', *Der Ararat*, No. 5/6, February–March 1920, pp. 29–33.

36. Umanskij, *Neue Kunst in Russland*, p. 19.

37. Umanskij, *Neue Kunst in Russland*, pp. 19–20.

38. Grosz and Heartfield were photographed holding their poster with its message derived from Umanskii's article at the Dada exhibition in Berlin in June 1920. This photograph was reproduced in the almanac *DADA* and is also reproduced in T. Andersen, *Vladimir Tatlin* (Stockholm, Moderna Museet, 1968), p. 18. Grosz visited Russia in 1921 but does not seem to have been impressed with what he saw (*Ein kleines Ja und ein grosses Nein* (Hamburg, 1955)).

39. Umanskij, *Neue Kunst in Russland*, p. 51.

40. Umanskii evidently based his description on Punin's article 'About Monuments' ('O pamyatnikakh', *Iskusstvo kommuny*, No. 14, 9 March 1919). Although Umanskii cites an article by Tatlin from the journal *Iskusstvo*, No. 2, 1919, as his source, I have been unable to trace such an article. It should be stressed that later other commentaries on Tatlin's Tower were published in Germany and elsewhere. Among the earliest was E. Ehrenburg, 'Ein Entwurf Tatlins', *Fruehlicht*, Vol. 1, No. 3, 1921–2, pp. 92–3. The Hungarian journal *MA* printed a translation of Punin's description in Vol. 7, No. 5/6, 1922, p. 31.

41. Umanskij, *Neue Kunst in Russland*, p. 32.

42. Umanskij, *Neue Kunst in Russland*, p. 33.

43. 'Institut khudozhestvennoi kul'tury. Otchet o deyatel'nosti INKhUKa', *Russkoe iskusstvo*, No. 2/3, 1923, pp. 85–8.

44. B. Uitz, *MA*, January 1921. For this and other general information concerning the Hungarian avant-garde, I am indebted to *The Hungarian Avant-Garde: The Eight and the Activists* (London, Arts Council, 1980).

45. This information is taken from N. Gabo, draft in Russian of a letter, undated, probably 1960s, Gabo papers C. 5, vi., private archive, London.

46. For further details concerning Kemeny and INKhUK and the debate surrounding this paper, see Chapter Three.

47. This manifesto is reprinted in an English translation in *Hungarian Avant-Garde*, p. 120. It should be noted that the Hungarians reviewed the 1922 exhibition. See L. Kassák, 'A berlini orosz kiállítás', *MA*, December 1922; A. Kemény, 'Jegyzetek az orosz müvészet berlini kiállításhoz', *Egység*, 4 February 1923; E. Kallai, 'A berlini orosz kiállítás', *Akasztott Ember*, Vol. 1, 1923 No. 1. In addition *MA* printed a translation of Punin's description of the monument ('Tatlin Uvegtornya', *MA*, Vol. 7, No. 5/6, 1922, p. 31).

48. Cited by V.K. in 'Arkhitektura na parizhskoi khudozhestvenno-promyshlennoi vystavke 1925 goda', *Stroitel'naya promyshlennost'*, No. 9, 1925, p. 642.

49. The catalogue accompanying the exhibition included a short article by D. Shterenberg which introduced the work of VKhUTEMAS to the French public. Writing of the Dermetfaks' work (the Wood and Metal-work faculties exhibited their work separately), Shterenberg stressed that 'Ces deux facultés s'efforcent de donner aux objets qu'elles fabriquent des formes inspirées d'une constructivisme utilitaire et adaptées aux besoins réels de notre marché' ('Le Vkhoutemass', *Exposition Internationale des Arts Décoratifs et Industriels Modernes. Union des Republiques Sovietistes Socialistes. Catalogue* (Paris, 1925), p. 76). The 'Salle du Vkhoutemass' was situated in the Grand Palais. The projects of the Wood and Metalwork faculties were not listed in the catalogue but included the Rural Reading Room ((Izba-chital'nya, listed in the catalogue *Exposition Internationale URSS*, p. 73, illustrated on p. 179) drawings, photographs and designs for useful implements. The other exhibits included theatre models and costume designs by Popova for *The Magnanimous Cuckold* and *The Earth in Turmoil*, by Stepanova for *The Death of Tarelkin* (illustrated on p. 189) and by Vesnin for *The Man who was Thursday*; Rodchenko's advertising posters to slogans by Mayakovskii; architectural designs and models by the Vesnin brothers for the Palace of Labour; works by Ginzburg and the architectural faculty of the VKhUTEMAS (a construction by the students was illustrated on p. 180); Tatlin's model for his Monument to the Third International (illustrated on p. 171) and many other items. It should be stressed that a vast quantity of the exhibits were not Constructivist. There was an extensive collection of traditional craft items and also of purely decorative artistic work such as the porcelain designs of Suetin, Chashnik and Malevich. These works responding to the traditional concepts of crafts and the applied arts did not assist the clarification of Constructivist principles. Moreover, Shterenberg, in his article, presented the general aim of the VKhUTEMAS as one of social and utilitarian involvement, stressing that even painting had an important part to play in this respect ('Le Vkhoutemass', p. 76).

50. The inaccessibility of Russian Constructivism to French aesthetic ideas at this time is epitomised by the fact that when the critic André Salmon published his book on modern Russian art in Paris three years later (*Art russe moderne*, 1928) he was able to omit the names and works of the four major innovating masters of the Russian avant-garde in the 1910s and 1920s, Malevich, Tatlin, Matyushin and Filonov. With the exception of Popova no Constructivists were represented in Salmon's volume. Three works by Popova were illustrated and given the title 'compositions'. Two of these were in fact textile designs.

51. 'Konstruktivizm na zapade'.

52. Gan, *Konstruktivizm*, p. 69.

53. *ibid*.

54. *ibid*.

55. *ibid*, p. 70.

SELECT BIBLIOGRAPHY

PRIMARY SOURCES

STATE ARCHIVES IN LENINGRAD

Gosudarstvennyi Russkii muzei:
 fond 100, ed. khr. 249. S. Dymshits-Tol'staya, 'Vospominaniya', undated.
 fond 144, ed. khr. 452. N. Lapshin, 'Avtobiograficheskie zapiski', 1941.

STATE ARCHIVES IN MOSCOW

Tsentral'nyi gosudarstvennyi arkhiv literatury i iskusstva – TsGALI:
 fond 134, op. 2, ed. khr. 23. M. Matyushin, 'Avtobiografiya', undated.
 fond 134, op. 2, ed. khr. 24. M. Matyushin, 'Dnevnik', 1915-16.
 fond 134, op. 2, ed. khr. 21. M. Matyushin, 'Opyt khudozhnika novoi mery'.
 fond 664, op. 1, ed. khr. 8. Muzei zhivopis'noi kul'tury.
 fond 665, op. 1, ed. khr. 32. V. Tatlin, 'Initsiativnaya edinitsa v tvorchestve kollektiva. Tezisy', undated.
 fond 680. Gosudarstvennye svobodnye khudozhestvennye masterskie.
 fond 681. VKhUTEMAS.
 fond 1334, op. 2, ed. khr. 238-9. Klutsis, sketchbooks and designs.
 fond 1334, op. 2, ed. khr. 324. M. Matyushin, 'Chto dobavit' v spravochnik po tsvetu', 1930s.
 fond 2089, op. 1, ed. khr. 2. V. Tatlin, Dva al'boma s figurami, 1913-16.
 fond 2361, op. 1, ed. khr. 30. El Lissitzky, 'Khudozhestvennye predposylki standartizatsii mebeli', 1928.
 fond 2361, op. 1, ed. khr. 58. El Lissitzky, 'Mebel'', 3 April 1940; 'Avtobiografiya', 1940.
Gosudarstvennaya tret'yakovskaya galereya:
 fond 59, ed. khr. 2874. V. Tatlin, Lichnaya kartochka chlena MOSSKha. Tatlin, Vladimir Evgrafovich, 1933.

PRIVATE ARCHIVES IN LENINGRAD

Matyushin, M. 'Tvorcheskii put' khudozhnika', 1930s.

Matyushin, M. 'Novyi prostranstvennyi realizm. Khudozhnik v opyte chetvertoi mery', undated.

Tatlin, V. 'Otchet issledovatel'skoi raboty za 1923-4, Otdela material'noi kul'tury', typescript, 10 November 1924.

Tatlin, V. 'Otchet o rabote za 1923 i 24 gg. Otdela material'noi kul'turv', 1 September 1924.

PRIVATE ARCHIVES IN MOSCOW

Abramova, A. V. 'Tatlin', typescript, 1960s.

Abramova, A. V. 'Zapis' besedy s G. D. Chichagovoi', 1960s.

Babichev, A. Untitled notes and doklady.

Babichev, A. and G. Chichagova, Distsipliny VKhUTEMASa, booklet of lithographs with verses, 1920.

Begicheva, A. 'Vospominaniya o Tatline. Do kontsa ne razgadai', undated.

Danin, D. 'Tatlin', 1940s.

Ioganson, K. 'Ot konstruktsii k tekhnike i izobreteniyu', paper given at INKhUK, 19 March 1922.

Kemeny, A. 'O konstruktivnykh rabotakh OBMOKhU', paper delivered at INKhUK, 26 December 1922.

Kemeny, A. 'Noveishie napravleniya v sovremennom nemetskom i russkom iskusstve', paper delivered at INKhUK, 8 December 1922.

Kushner, B. 'Proizvodstvo kul'tury', 1922, paper delivered at INKhUK.

Kushner, B. 'Rol' inzhenera v proizvodstve', paper delivered at INKhUK, 30 March 1922.

Kushner, B. 'Khudozhnik v proizvodstve', paper delivered at INKhUK, 6 April 1922.

Lavinskii, A. 'Inzhenerizm (Tezisy k gorody budushchego)', paper delivered at INKhUK, 26 January 1922.

Levashkova, A. 'O Tatline', undated.

Miturich, P. 'Dinamika putei goroda', 1930s.

Miturich, P. Dnevnik, 1944.

Miturich, P. 'Moe pervoe znakomstvo s Velimirom Khlebnikovym', undated.

Miturich, P. 'Opyt printsipial'noi zashchity svoikh izobretenii', undated.

Miturich, P. 'Opyt sravneniya skorostei vol'noobraznym i pryamolineinym putem', undated.

Miturich, P. Pis'ma, various dates.

Miturich, P. 'Vol'novye dvizhiteli', undated.

Miturich, P. 'Volnovaya dinamika', 1943.

Miturich, P. Zapisnaya knizhka, undated.

Popova, L. 'K voprosu o novykh metodakh v nashei khudozhestvennoi shkole', dated December 1921.

Popova, L. 'Kostyum kak element material'nogo oformleniya', undated.

Popova, L. 'Raboty 20–21 g.', undated.

Popova, L. 'Sushchnost' distsiplin', undated.

Popova, L. 'Tsely organizatsii Muzeya zhivopisnoi kul'tury', 1921.

Popova, L. 'Vstuplenie k diskussii INKhUKa o "Velikodushnom rogonostse",' paper delivered at INKhUK, 27 April 1922.

Popova, L. 'Zhivopisnaya arkhitektonika', undated.

Punin, N. 'Kvartira No. 5'.

Rodchenko, A. 'Chernoe i beloe', 1920s.

Rodchenko, A. 'Distsiplina No. 5', undated but probably 1921.

Rodchenko, A. 'Liniya', 1921.

Rodchenko, A. 'Programma organizatsii laboratorii pri Gosud. khudozh. masterskikh', 1920.

Rodchenko, A. 'Programma po kursu proektirovaniya metalloveshchei Dermetfaka', typescript, 1922–4.

Rodchenko, A. 'Ob'yasnitel'naya zapiska k uchebnomu planu', undated.

Rodchenko, A. 'Ob'yasnitel'naya zapiska k programme kursa kompozitsii dlya Metfaka VKhUTE-MASa professora Rodchenko', undated.

Rodchenko, A. 'Tsel' proektirovaniya', undated.

Stenberg, G., V. Stenberg and K. Medunetskii, 'Tezisy po dokladu "konstruktivizm"', 1922.

Stepanova, V. 'O polozhenii i zadachakh khudozhnika-konstruktivista v sittsenabivnoi promyshlennosti v svyazi s rabotami na sittsenabivnoi fabrike', paper delivered at INKhUK, 5 January 1924.

Stepanova, V. 'Smert' Tarelkina', 1924.

Stepanova, V. 'Tezisy k dokladu "Iskusstvo i proizvodstvo"', paper delivered at INKhUK, 17 February 1921.

Tarabukin, N. 'Polozhenie o gruppe ob'ektivnogo analiza', undated.

Tatlin, V. 'Kratkii obzor', undated.

Tatlin, V. 'Svedenie', undated.

Protokoly zasedanii INKhUKa, 9 June 1920–5 January 1924, together with INKhUK attendance lists.

'Obshchii plan programmy nauchno-teoreticheskogo otdela tsentrosektsii AKIZO Narkomprosa', undated.

'Otchet gruppy konstruktivistov INKhUKa', Moscow, 6 September 1921.

'Pervaya rabochaya gruppa konstruktivistov. Programma', 1921.

'Programma uchebnoi podgruppy rabochei gruppy konstruktivistov INKhUKa', 1921.

SECONDARY SOURCES

CONTEMPORARY PERIODICALS

Afisha TIM, Moscow, 1926.

Al'manakh, Leningrad, 1930, Nos. 1–10.

Antrakt, Moscow, 1923, Nos. 1–7.

Argonavty, Petrograd, 1923, No. 1.

Arkhitektura i VKhUTEIN, Moscow, 1929, No. 1.

Atel'e, Moscow, 1923, No. 1.

Avangard, Moscow, 1922, Nos. 1–3.

Brigada khudozhnikov, Moscow, 1931–2.

Byulleten' GAKhN, Moscow, 1925–8, Nos. 1–11.

Daesh', Moscow, 1929, Nos. 1–14.

Ermitazh, Moscow, 1922, Nos. 1–15.

Gazeta futuristov (*Da zdravstvuet revolyutsiya dukha'*), Moscow, Mayakovskii, Kamenskii and Burlyuk, No. 1, 1918.

Gorn, Moscow, Proletkul't, 1918–23.

Gryadushchee, Petrograd, Proletkul't, 1918–21.

Iskusstvo, Vitebsk, 1921.

Iskusstvo, Moscow, 1918, Nos. 1–11.

Iskusstvo, Moscow, 1919, Nos. 1–8.

Iskusstvo, Moscow, 1923–8.

Iskusstvo i promyshlennost', Moscow, 1924, Nos. 1–2.

Iskusstvo kommuny, Petrograd, 1918–19, Nos, 1–19.

Iskusstvo i massy, Moscow, 1929–30.

IZO, Vestnik otdela izobrazitel'nykh iskusstv NKP, Moscow, 1921, No. 1.

Izobrazitel'noe iskusstvo, Petrograd, 1919, No. 1.

Izvestiya OBKhON, Moscow, 1929.

Khudozhestvennaya zhizn', Moscow, 1919–20.

Khudozhnik i zritel', Moscow, 1924, Nos. 1–7.

Kino-Fot, Moscow, 1922–3, Nos. 1–6.

Kniga i revolyutsiya, Petrograd, 1920–3.

Krasnaya niva, Moscow, 1923–31.

Krasnaya nov', Moscow, 1921–31.

Krasnaya panorama, Leningrad, 1923–30.

Krasnoe studenchestvo, Moscow, 1925–31.

LEF. Zhurnal levogo fronta iskusstv, ed. B. Arvatov, N. Aseev, O. Brik, B. Kushner, V. Mayakovskii, S. Tret'yakov and N. Chuzhak, Moscow, 1923–5 (1923, Nos. 1–4; 1924, Nos. 1–2(6); 1925, No. 3(7)). It later became *Novyi LEF*, ed. V. Mayakovskii and S. Tret'yakov, Moscow, 1927–8 (1927, Nos. 1–12; 1928, Nos. 1–12).

Makovets, Moscow, 1922, Nos. 1–2.

Na literaturnom postu, Moscow, 1926–32.

Pechat' i revolyutsiya, Moscow, 1921–30.

Plamya, Petrograd, 1918–20.

Proletarskaya kul'tura, Moscow, 1918–20.

Russkoe iskusstvo, Petrograd, 1923, Nos. 1–3.

Sovetskoe iskusstvo, Moscow and Leningrad, 1926–8.

Sovremennaya arkhitektura, Moscow, 1926–30.

Tvorchestvo, Moscow, 1918–22.

Tvorchestvo, ed. I. Naimovich-Chuzhak, Vladivostok and Chita, 1920–1 (1920, Nos. 1–4, 1921, Nos. 5–7).

Veshch'/Gegenstand/Objet, ed. El Lissitzky and I. Erenburg, Berlin, 1922, Nos. 1–3.

Vestnik iskusstv, Moscow, 1922, Nos. 1–5.

Vesnik professional'nogo soyuza khudozhnikov-zhivopistsev v Moskve, Moscow, 1918, No. 1.

Vestnik rabotnikov iskusstv (Rabis), Moscow, 1920–34.

Vestnik teatra, Moscow, 1919–21.

Zhizn' iskusstva, Petrograd, 1918–22.

Zhizn' iskusstva, Petrograd, 1923–9.

Zhizn' i tvorchestvo, Tver', 1921–2.

GENERAL

Aelita (Moscow, undated).

Aksel'rod, L. 'Voprosy iskusstva', *Krasnaya nov'*, No. 6, 1926, pp. 148–61.

Alekseev, B. 'Suetin - vospitatel' khudozhnikov', *Dekorativnoe iskusstvo*, No. 11, 1964, pp. 19–23.

Andersen, T. *Malevich* (Amsterdam, Stedelijk Museum, 1970).

Andersen, T. *Moderne russisk kunst 1910–1925* (Copenhagen, 1967).

Annenkov, Yu. *Dnevnik moikh vstrech* (New York, 1966), 2 vols.

Annenkov, Yu. *Portrety* (Petrograd, 1922).

Assotsiatsiya khudozhnikov revolyutsionnoi Rossii. Sbornik vospominanii, statei, dokumentov (Moscow, 1973).

Arkin, D. 'Chto my vystavlyali v Parizhe. Iskusstvo byta', *Ekran*, No. 16, 1925.

Arkin, D. 'Estetika funktsionalizma. Arkhitekturnaya i khudozhestvenno-promyshlennaya deyatel'nost' Baukhauza', *Brigada khudozhnikov*, No. 2, 1932.

Arkin, D. *Iskusstvo bytovoi veshchi* (Moscow, 1932).

Arkin, D. 'Iskusstvo veshchi', *Kul'turnaya revolyutsiya*, 1929, No. 2, pp. 25–8.

Arkin, D. 'Iskusstvo veshchi', *Ezhegodnik literatury i iskusstva na 1929 god* (Moscow, 1929).

Arkin, D. 'Iskusstvo veshchei na zapade', *Zapad i vostok* (Moscow, 1926).

Arkin, D. 'Khudozhnik i proizvodstvo', *Pravda*, 14 July 1928.

Vetrov, A. [D. Arkin], 'Khoroshee - vrag plokhogo', *30 Dnei*, No. 4, 1926, p. 32.

Arkin, D. 'Mechty o novom stile (Iskusstvo veshchi na zapade)', *Pechat' i revolyutsiya*, No. 12, 1929, pp. 61–9.

Arkin, D. 'O mebeli. Mebel'naya promyshlennost' i rekonstruktsiya byta', *Brigada khudozhnikov*, No. 2, 1932, pp. 19–24.

Arkin, D. 'Promyshlennost' i khudozhnik', *Izvestiya*, 18 July 1926.

Arkin, D. 'Stroitel'stvo i "mebel'naya problema"', *Stroitel'stvo Moskvy*, No. 10, 1929, pp. 7–8.

Arkin, D. 'VKhUTEMAS i germanskii BAUKHAUZ', *Izvestiya*, 5 February 1927.

Arkin, D. 'Voprosy khudozhestvennoi promyshlennosti', *Arkhitektura SSSR*, No. 3, 1941.

Arvatov, B. 'AKhRR na zavode', *Zhizn' iskusstva*, No. 30, 1925.

Arvatov, B. 'Byt i kul'tura veshchi', in *Al'manakh Proletkul'ta* (Moscow, 1925), pp. 75–82.

Arvatov, B. 'Esteticheskii fetishizm', *Pechat' i revolyutsiya*, No. 3, 1923, pp. 86–95.

Arvatov, B. 'Iskusstvo i kachestvo promyshlennoi produktsii', *Sovetskoe iskusstvo*, No. 7, 1925, pp. 39–43.

Arvatov, B. *Iskusstvo i klassy* (Moscow, 1923).

Arvatov, B. 'Iskusstvo i organizatsiya byta', *Pechat' i revolyutsiya*, No. 4, 1926, pp. 83–9.

Arvatov, B. 'Iskusstvo i proizvodstvo', *Gorn*, No. 8, 1923, pp. 257–8.

Arvatov, B. *Iskusstvo i proizvodstvo* (Moscow, 1926).

Arvatov, B. 'Izobrazitel'nye iskusstva', *Pechat' i revolyutsiya*, No. 7, 1922, pp. 140–6.

Arvatov, B. 'K. Malevich. Bog ne skinut', *Pechat' i revolyutsiya*, No. 7, 1922, pp. 343–4.

Arvatov, B. 'Kakoi teatr nuzhen rabochemu klassu', *Gorn*, No. 8, 1923, pp. 250–2.

Arvatov, B. 'Na putyakh k proletarskomu iskusstvu', *Pechat' i revolyutsiya*, No. 1, 1922, pp. 65–75.

Arvatov, B. 'Nastuplenie pravykh', *Zhizn' iskusstva*, No. 26, 1925, pp. 2–3.

Arvatov, B. *Natan Al'tman* (Berlin, 1924).

Arvatov, B. 'O formal'no-sotsiologicheskom metode', *Pechat' i revolyutsiya*, No. 3, 1927, pp. 54–65.

Arvatov, B. 'O khudozhestvennoi kul'turnosti sredi rabochykh', *Sovetskoe iskusstvo*, No. 9, 1925.

Arvatov, B. 'O novom etape v proletarskom khudozhestvennom dvizhenii', *Sovetskoe iskusstvo*, No. 6, 1925, pp. 16–19.

Arvatov, B. *Ob agitatsionnom i proizvodstvennom iskusstve* (Moscow, 1930).

Arvatov, B. 'Oveshchestvlennaya utopia', *LEF*, No. 1, 1923, pp. 61–4.

Arvatov, B. 'Proletariat i levoe iskusstvo', *Zhizn' iskusstva*, No. 26, 1925, pp. 2–3; and *Vestnik iskusstv*, No. 1, 1922, pp. 10–11.

Arvatov, B. 'Protokol doklada t. Arvatova v tsentral'nom moskovskom Proletkul'te, 27 marta 1923', *Gorn*, No. 8, 1923.

Arvatov, B. 'Reaktsiya v zhivopisi', *Sovetskoe iskusstvo*, Nos. 4–5, 1925, pp. 70–4.

Arvatov, B. *Sotsiologicheskaya poetika* (Moscow, 1928).

Arvatov, B. 'Stradayushchie bessiliem', *LEF*, No, 3, 1923, p. 180.

Arvatov, B. 'Teatr kak proizvodstvo', in I. Aksenov, ed., *O Teatre* (Tver', 1922), pp. 113–22.

Arvatov, B. 'Utopiya i nauka', *LEF*, No. 1, 1923, pp. 16–21.

Arvatov, B. 'Veshch'', *Pechat' i revolyutsiya*, No. 7, 1922, pp. 341–2.

Babichev, A. 'O konstruktsii i kompozitsii', *Dekorativnoe iskusstvo*, No. 3, 1967, pp. 17–18.

Bann, S. *The Tradition of Constructivism* (London, 1974).

Barron, S. and M. Tuchman, eds., *The Avant-Garde in Russia, 1910–1930: New Perspectives* (London and Cambridge, Mass., 1980).

Baukhauz Dessau 1928–1930. Katalog vystavki (Moscow, 1931).

Berdyaev, N. *Krizis iskusstva* (Moscow, 1918).

Berninger, H. and J. A. Cartier, *Jean Pougny (Iwan Puni) 1892–1956. Catalogue de l'oeuvre, Tome I: Les Années d'avant-garde, Russie-Berlin, 1910–1923* (Tübingen, 1972).

Beskin, E. 'Teatral'nyi LEF', *Sovetskoe iskusstvo*, No. 6, 1925, pp. 47–60.

Beskin, O. 'Otvet napravo – zapros nalevo (po povodu stat'i t. Pel'she)', *Sovetskoe iskusstvo*, No. 6, 1925, pp. 6–15.

Beskin, E. 'Iskusstvo i klass', *Vestnik rabotnikov iskusstv*, No. 1, 1920, pp. 9–13.

Blyumenfel'd', V. 'Na levom fronte', *Zhizn' iskusstva*, No. 24, 1925, pp. 4–5.

Bogdanov, A. *Elementy proletarskoi kul'tury v razvitii rabochego klassa* (Moscow, 1920).

Bogdanov, A. *Inzhener Menin* (Moscow, 1918, second edition).

Bogdanov, A. *Iskusstvo i rabochii klass*, (Moscow, 1918).

Bogdanov, A. *Krasnaya zvezda. Roman-utopiya* (Petrograd, 1918).

Bogdanov, A. *Kul'turnye zadachi nashego vremeni* (Moscow, 1911).

Bogdanov, A. *O proletarskoi kul'ture* (Moscow and Leningrad, 1924).

Bogorodskii, F. *Vospominaniya khudozhnika* (Moscow, 1959).

Boltyanskii, G. *Lenin i kino* (Moscow, 1925).

Bouch, M. and A. Zamochkine, 'L'Art Pictural Sovietique', *VOKS: Les Arts Plastiques en URSS*, No. 9/10, 1935, pp. 9–33.

Bowlt, J. E. 'From Pictures to Textile Prints', *Print Collector's Newsletter*, Vol. 7, No. 1, 1976, pp. 16–20.

Bowlt, J. E., ed., *Russian Art of the Avant-Garde: Theory and Criticism, 1902–1934* (New York, 1976).

Brik, O. 'Drenazh iskusstvu', *Iskusstvo kommuny*, No. 1, 1918, p. 1.

Brik, O. 'Futurizm', *Gorn*, No. 8, 1923, pp. 253–5.

Brik, O. 'IMO – iskusstvo molodykh', in *Mayakovskomu* (Leningrad, 1940).

Brik, O. 'Khudozhnik i kommuna', *Izobrazitel'noe iskusstvo*, No. 1, 1919.

Brik, O. 'Nash dolg', *Khudozhestvennaya zhizn'*, No. 1, 1919, pp. 3–4.

Brik, O. 'Ne teoriya a lozung', *Pechat' i revolyutsiya*, No. 1, 1929.

Brik, O. 'Ot kartiny k sittsu', *LEF*, No. 2, 1924.

Brik, O. 'Ot kartiny k foto', *Novyi LEF*, No. 3, 1928, pp. 29–33.

Brik, O. 'Predislovie', in B. Arvatov, *Sotsiologicheskaya poetika* (Moscow, 1928).

Brik, O. 'V poryadke dnya', in *Iskusstvo v proizvodstve* (Moscow, 1921).

Brik, O. 'Za novatorstvo', *Novyi LEF*, No. 1, 1927.

Bush, M. and A. Zamoshkin, *Put' sovetskoi zhivopisi* (Moscow, 1933).

Carr, E. H. *Socialism in One Country, 1924–1926* (London, 1970).

Carr, E. H. and R. W. Davies, *Foundations of a Planned Economy, 1926–1929* (London, 1969).

Chegedaeva, N. 'Plakat', in *Istoriya russkogo iskusstva* (Moscow, 1957), Vol. 11.

Chuzhak, N. 'Foto-lito-izo montazh', *Zhizn' iskusstva*, No. 23, 1925, pp. 3–4.

Chuzhak, N. 'Iskusstvo byta', *Sovetskoe iskusstvo*, No. 4–5, 1925, pp. 3–12.

Chuzhak, N. 'Iskusstvo byta', *Sovremennaya arkhitektura*, No. 1, 1927, pp. 21–3.

Chuzhak, N. *K dialektike iskusstv* (Chita, 1921).

Chuzhak, N. *K estetike marksizma* (Irkutsk, 1916).

Chuzhak, N., ed., *Literatura fakta. Pervyi sbornik materialov rabotnikov LEFa* (Moscow, 1929).

Chuzhak, N. 'Literatura zhiznestroeniya', *Novyi LEF*, No. 11, 1928.

Chuzhak, N. 'Most ot illyuzii k materii', *Zhizn' iskusstva*, No. 25, 1925, pp. 5–6.

Chuzhak, N. 'O tom, chto na LEFe', *Zhizn' iskusstva*, No. 24, 1925, pp. 5–6.

Chuzhak, N. 'Pervaya vystavka SSSR i zadachi pechati', *Zhurnalist*, No. 6, 1923.

Chuzhak, N. 'Pod znakom zhiznestroeniya', *LEF*, No. 1, 1923, pp. 12–39.

Compton, S. 'Art and Photography', *Print Collector's Newsletter*, Vol. 7, No. 1, 1976, pp. 12–15.

Deibler, T. and A. Glez, *V bor'be za novoe iskusstvo* (Petrograd, 1923).

Die Kunstismen in Russland 1907–1930 (Cologne, Galerie Gmurzynska, 1977).

Dobrowski, M. 'Constructivism in Soviet Painting', *Soviet Union*, Vol. 3, part 2, 1976, pp. 152–86.

Dorokhov, K. G. *Zapiski khudozhnika* (Moscow, 1974).

D'yakontsyn, L. *Ideinye protivorechiya v estetike russkoi zhivopisi kontsa 19 – nachala 20vv.* (Perm', 1966).

Dzhonson, 'NOT i iskusstvo', *Vremya*, No. 6, 1924, pp. 33–4.

Efros, A. *Profili* (Moscow, 1930).

Efros, A. *Kamernyi teatr i ego khudozhniki 1914–1934* (Moscow, 1934).

Ekster, A. 'Prostota i praktichnost' v odezhde', *Krasnaya niva*, No. 21, 1923, p. 31.

Ekster, A. 'V konstruktivnoi odezhde', *Atel'e*, No. 1, 1923, pp. 4–5.

Ekster, A. 'V poiskakh novoi odezhdy', *Vserossiiskaya vystavka*, No. 2, 1923, pp. 16–18.

Erenburg, I. *A vse-taki ona vertitsya* (Berlin, 1922).

Ermakov, A. 'Lunacharskii i proletkul't', *Druzhba narodov*, No. 1, 1968, pp. 242–7.

Erste Russische Kunstausstellung (Berlin, Galerie van Diemen, 1922).

Exposition Internationale des Arts Décoratifs et Industriels Modernes. Section de l'U.R.S.S. Catalogue des Oeuvres d'Art Décoratif et d'Industrie Artistique exposées dans le Pavilion de l'U.R.S.S. au Grand Palais et dans les Galeries de l'Esplanade des Invalides (Paris, 1925).

Favorskii, V. 'Soderzhanie formy', *Dekorativnoe iskusstvo*, No. 1, 1965, p. 3.

Fedorov-Davydov, A. *Russkoe iskusstvo promyshlennogo kapitalizma* (Moscow, 1929).

Fedorov-Davydov, A. 'Gosplan po delam iskusstva', *Pechat' i revolyutsiya*, No. 2, 1925, pp. 139–44.

Fevral'skii, A. *Desyat' let teatra Meierkhol'da* (Moscow, 1931).

Filippov, A. V., ed., *Khudozhestvennoe oformlenie massovoi posudy* (Moscow, 1932).

Fitzpatrick, S. *The Commissariat of Enlightenment: Soviet Organisation of Education and the Arts under Lunacharsky, October 1917–1921* (Cambridge, 1971).

Fitzpatrick, S. 'The Emergence of Glaviskusstvo: Class War on the Cultural Front, Moscow, 1928–1929', *Soviet Studies*, Vol. 23, No. 2, 1971, pp. 236–53.

'Fotomontazh', *LEF*, No. 4, 1923, p. 41.

From Surface to Space: Russia, 1916–1924 (Cologne, Galerie Gmurzynska, 1974).

From Painting to Design: Russian Constructivist Art of the Twenties (Cologne, Galerie Gmurzynska, 1981).

Fülop-Miller, R. *The Mind and Face of Bolshevism. An Examination of Cultural Life in Soviet Russia* (London, 1927).

Gabo: Constructions, Sculpture, Paintings, Drawings, Engravings (London, 1957).

Gabo, N. *Of Divers Arts* (London, 1962).

Naum Gabo: The Constructive Process (London, Tate Gallery, 1976).

Five European Sculptors: Naum Gabo, Antoine Pevsner, Wilhelm Lehmbruck, Aristide Maillol, Henry Moore (New York, Museum of Modern Art, 1948).

Gan, A. 'Chto takoe konstruktivizm?', *Sovremennaya arkhitektura*, No. 3, 1928, pp. 79–81.

Gan, A. 'Fakty za nas', *Sovremennaya arkhitektura*, No. 2, 1926.

Gan, A. *Konstruktivizm* (Tver', 1922).

Gan, A. 'Spravka o K. Maleviche', *Sovremennaya arkhitektura*, No. 3, 1927, pp. 104–7.

Gastev, A. 'Nasha prakticheskaya metodologiya', *Organizatsiya truda*, No. 1, 1921, pp. 18–19.

Gastev, A. 'Nasha zadacha', *Organizatsiya truda*, No. 1, 1921, pp. 7–17.

Ginzburg, M. *Stil' i epokha* (Moscow, 1924).

Gize, M. 'Iz istorii sovetskoi khudozhestvennoi promyshlennosti', *Iskusstvo*, No. 1, 1961, pp. 26–9.

Golding, J. *Cubism: A History and an Analysis, 1907–1914* (London, 1959).

Gorelov, A. 'Filosofiya konstruktivizma', *Zvezda*, No. 8, 1929, pp. 199–202.

Gorin, A. 'Iskusstvo i proizvodstvo', *Vestnik rabotnikov iskusstv*, No. 1, 1920, pp. 24–6.

Gray, C. 'El Lissitzky's typographical principles', in *El Lissitzky* (Eindhoven, 1965–6), pp. 20–2.

Gray, C. 'The Genesis of Socialist Realist Painting, Futurism, Suprematism, Constructivism', *Soviet Survey*, No. 1, 1959, pp. 32–9.

Gray, C. *The Great Experiment in Russian Art, 1862–1922* (London, 1962).

Grigor'ev, M. 'Krizis formalizma', *Pechat' i revolyutsiya*, No. 8, 1927, pp. 84–92.

Grossman-Roshchin, I. 'Sotsial'nyi zamysel futurizma', *LEF*, No. 4, 1923, pp. 109–24.

'Institut khudozhestvennoi kul'tury, Otchet o deyatel'nosti INKhUKa', *Russkoe iskusstvo*, No. 2/3, 1923, pp. 85–8.

Institut khudozhestvennoi kul'tury v Moskve (INKhUK) pri otdele IZO NKP. Skhematicheskava programma rabot Instituta khudozhestvennoi kul'tury po planu V.V. Kandinskogo (Moscow, 1920); reprinted in Matsa, *Sovetskoe iskusstvo*, pp. 126–39.

Isakov, S. 'Izobrazitel'noe iskusstvo – proletarskoe iskusstvo', *Zhizn' iskusstva*, No. 34, 1923, pp. 15–16.

Iskusstvo SSSR i zadachi khudozhnikov (Moscow, 1928).

Iskusstvo v bytu (Moscow, 1925).

Iskusstvo v proizvodstve (Moscow, 1921).

Iz istorii sovetskoi arkhitekury (Moscow, 1965 and 1970), 2 Vols., 1917–25 and 1926–32.

Iz istorii stroitel'stva sovetskoi kul'tury 1918–1919, Moskva. Dokumenty i vospominaniya (Moscow, 1964).

Izofront. Klassovaya bor'ba na fronte prostranstvennykh iskusstv. Sbornik statei ob'edineniya 'Oktyabr'' (Moscow and Leningrad, 1931).

Kamenskii, V. *Put' entuziasta* (Moscow, 1931).

Kandinskii, V. 'K reforme khudozhestvennoi shkoly', *Iskusstvo*, No. 1, 1923.

Kandinskii, V. 'Muzei zhivopisnoi kul'tury', *Khudozhestvennaya zhizn'*, No. 2, 1920, pp. 18–20.

Kandinskii, V. 'O dukhovnom v iskusstve', in *Trudy vserossiiskogo s'ezda khudozhnikov v Petrograde, dek. 1911–yanv. 1912* (Petrograd, 1914), Vol. 1, pp. 47–76.

Kerzhentsev, P. 'Kommunizm i kul'tura', *Tvorchestvo*, No. 2, 1920, pp. 46–50.

Khan-Magomedov, S. 'A. M. Lavinskii. Put' v "proizvodstvennoe iskusstvo"', *Tekhnicheskaya estetika*, No. 1, 1980.

Khan-Magomedov, S. *O nekotorykh problemakh konstruktivizma* (Moscow, 1964).

Khan-Magomedov, S. 'Pervaya novatorskaya tvorcheskaya organizatsiya sovetskoi arkhitektury', *Problemy istorii sovetskoi arkhitektury*, No. 2, 1976.

Khan-Magomedov, S. *Pionere der sowjetischen Architektur. Der weg zur neuen sowjetischen Architektur in den zwanziger und zu Beginn der dreissiger Jahre* (Dresden, 1983).

Khan-Magomedov, S. 'Pervaya tvorcheskaya organizatsiya pionerov sovetskogo dizaina – gruppa konstruktivistov INKhUKa (1921)', in *Khudozhestvennye problemy predmetno-prostranstvennoi sredy* (Moscow 1978).

Khan-Magomedov, S. 'Traditsii i uroki konstruktivizma', *Dekorativnoe iskusstvo*, No. 9, 1964, pp. 25–9.

Khan-Magomedov, S. 'Vspomnite ob etom proekte!', *Teatr*, No. 3, 1969, pp. 68–70.

Khazanova, V. *Sovetskaya arkhitektura pervykh let Oktyabrya* (Moscow, 1970).

Khiger, R. *Puti arkhitekurnoi mysli* (Moscow, 1933).

Khlebnikov, V. *Neizdannye proizvedeniya* (Moscow, 1940).

Khlebnikov, V. *Sobranie proizvedenii Velimira Khlebnikova* (Leningrad, 1928–33).

Khlebnikov, V. *Zangezi* (Moscow, 1922). Miturich designed the cover.

Kokkinaki, I. 'K voprosu o vzaimosvyazyakh sovetskikh i zarubezhnykh arkhitektorov v 1920–1930-e gody. Kratkii obzor', in *Voprosy sovetskogo izobrazitel'nogo iskusstva i arkhitektury* (Moscow, 1976), pp. 350–82.

Kol'tsova, N. 'Programma-deklaratsiya khudozhestvenno-proizvodstvennoi komissii', *Tekhnicheskaya estetika*, No. 10, 1967, pp. 14–15.

'Konstruktivisty', *LEF*, No. 1, 1923, p. 251.

Kostin, V. *OST (Obshchestvo stankovistov)* (Leningrad, 1978).

Kovtun, E. and A. Povelikhina, 'Utes iz budushchego', *Tekhnicheskaya estetika*, No. 5/6, 1976, pp. 40–2.

Kruchenykh, A. *Lef agitki Mayakovskogo, Aseeva, Tret'yakova* (Moscow, 1925).

Krupskaya, N. 'Glavpolitprosvet i iskusstvo', *Pravda*, February 1921.

Kushner, B. 'Bozhestvennoe proizvedenie', *Iskusstvo kommuny*, No. 9, 1919, p. 1.

Kushner, B. *Demokratizatsiya iskusstva* (Petrograd, 1917).

Kushner, B. *Revolyutsiya i elektrifikatsiya* (Petrograd, 1920).

K[ushner], B. 'Kommunisty-futuristy', *Iskusstvo kommuny*, No. 9, 1919, p. 3.

Kushner, B. 'Komu futurizm?', *Iskusstvo kommuny*, No. 12, 1919, p. 2.

Kushner, B. 'Nam muzyka', *Iskusstvo kommuny*, No. 11, 1919, p. 2.

Lavinskii, A. 'Izba-chital'nya', *Sovetskoe iskusstvo*, No. 4/5, 1925, p. 96.

Lenin i Lunacharskii. Perepiska, doklady, dokumenty, Literaturnoe nasledstvo No. 80 (Moscow, 1971).

Lenin, V. *O literature i iskusstve*, (Moscow, 1957).

Lenin, V. *Polnoe sobranie sochinenii* (Moscow, 1958–65), Vols. 35, 52.

Livshits, B. *Polutoraglazyi strelets* (Leningrad, 1933). An English translation by John Bowlt is published under the title *The One and a Half-Eyed Archer* (Newtonville, Mass., 1977).

Lobanov, V. *Khudozhestvennye gruppirovki za poslednie 25 let* (Moscow, 1930).

Lubetkin, B. 'Architectural Thought since the Revolution', *Architectural Review*, Vol. 71, No. 426, 1933.

Lubetkin, B. 'The Origins of Constructivism', lecture given to Cambridge University School of Architecture, 1 May 1960.

Lukomskii, G. 'Russkaya vystavka v Berline', *Argonavty*, No. 1, 1923, pp. 68–9.

Lunacharskii, A. 'Lenin o monumental'noi propagande', *Literaturnaya gazeta*, No. 4/5, 29 January 1933, in A. Lunacharskii, *Vospominaniya i vpechateleniya* (Moscow, 1968).

Lunacharskii, A. 'Monumental'naya agitatsiya', *Plamya*, No. 11, 1918.

Lunacharskii, A. 'O printsipakh gosudarstvennogo priobreteniya khudozhestvennykh proizvedenii', *Iskusstvo kommuny*, No. 1, 1918.

Lunacharskii, A. 'O Russkom narodnom tvorchestve', *Dekorativnoe iskusstvo*, No. 6, 1958, pp. 5–6.

Lunacharskii, A. *Ob izobrazitel'nom iskusstve* (Moscow, 1966), 2 Vols.

Lunacharskii, A. 'Teatr RSFSR', *Pechat' i revolyutsiya'*, No. 7, 1922.

Lur'e, A. 'Nash Marsh', *Novy Zhurnal* (New York), No. 94, 1969, pp. 127–42.

Malakhov, S. 'Teoriya konstruktivizma', *Pechat' i revolyutsiya*, No. 4, 1929, pp. 54–62.

Kazimir Malevitsch. Zum 100. Geburtstag (Cologne, Galerie Gmurzynska, 1978).

Mandel'shtam, R. *Marksistskoe iskusstvovedenie* (Moscow, 1929).

Markov, V. 'Predislovie', in *V. V. Chlebnikov, Gesammelte Werke* (Munich, 1968), Vol. 1.

Markov, V. *Russian Futurism* (London, 1969).

Mastera sovetskoi arkhitektury ob arkhitekture (Moscow, 1975), 2 Vols.

Matsa, I. *Iskusstvo epokhi zrelogo kapitalizma na zapade* (Moscow, 1929).

Matsa, I. *Sovetskoe iskusstvo za 15 let. Materialy i dokumentatsiya* (Moscow and Leningrad, 1933).

Matsa, I. 'Sovetskaya mysl' v 20e gody', *Iz istorii sovetskoi esteticheskoi mysli* (Moscow, 1967).

Matsa, I. 'Tezisy doklada "Polozhenie iskusstva v SSSR i aktual'nye zadachi khudozhnikov", in *Ezhegodnik literatury i iskusstva na 1929 god* (Moscow, 1929). The paper was delivered at a meeting of the artistic and literary section of the Communist Academy in March 1928.

Matyushin, M. 'An Artist's Experience of the New Space', *The Structurist*, No. 15/16, 1975/6, pp. 74–7.

Matyushin, M. 'Ne iskusstvo a zhizn'', *Zhizn' iskusstva*, No. 20, 1923, p. 15.

Matyushin, M. 'O knige Gleza i Metsanzhe "O kubizme"', *Soyuz molodezhi*, No. 3, 1913, pp. 25–34.

Matyushin, M. 'Sproba novogo v'dchuttya prostoronii', *Nova generatsiya*, No. 11, 1928, pp. 311–22.

Matyushin, M. *Zakonomernost' izmenyaemosti tsvetovykh sochetanii. Spravochnik po tsvetu* (Moscow and Leningrad, 1932).

Matyushina, O. 'Prizvanie', *Zvezda*, No. 3, 1973, pp. 137–53.

Mayakovskii, V. *Polnoe sobranie sochinenii* (Moscow, 1955–61).

Mayakovskii, V. 'Prikaz po armii iskusstv', *Iskusstvo kommuny*, No. 1, 1918, p. 1.

Mayakovskii, V. *Pro eto* (Moscow, 1923).

V. Mayakovskii. materialy i issledovaniya (Moscow, 1940).

Meierkhol'd, V. 'Akter buduschchego', *Ermitazh*, No. 6, 1922, pp. 10–11.

Meierkhol'd, V. 'Lozung oktyabrya iskusstv', *Vestnik teatra*, No. 82, 1921.

Meierkhol'd, V. 'Pis'mo k redaktsii', *Izvestiya*, 9 May 1922.

Meierkhol'd, V. *Stat'i, pis'ma, rechi, besedy* (Moscow, 1968), 2 Vols.

Metody raboty proletkul'ta (Moscow, 1920).

Mokul'skii, S. 'Gastroli Teatra Meierkhol'da', *Zhizn' iskusstva*, No. 23, 1924, pp. 12–13.

Moskva–Parizh 1900–1930 (Moscow, Pushkin Museum of Fine Arts, 1981).

Nakov, A. *Alexandra Exter* (Paris, Galerie Jean Chauvelin, 1972).

Neradov, G. 'Glaviskusstvo', *Sovetskoe iskusstvo*, No. 4/5, 1925, pp. 23–6.

Neznamov, P. 'Prom-raboty A. Lavinskogo', *LEF*, No. 3 (7), 1924.

Nisen, E. *O kubizme* (St Petersburg, 1913); translation of Gleizes and Metzinger's *Du Cubisme*.

Novinkov, A. 'Derevenskii kiosk. Proekt-maket. Konstruktivist Aleksei Gan', *Sovremennaya arkhitektura*, No. 1, 1926, p. 35.

Novitskii, P. 'Osnovy khudozhestvennoi politiki raboche-krest'yanskogo gosudarstva', *Nauka i iskusstvo*, No. 1, 1926, pp. 15–28.

Novitskii, P. 'Restavratory i arkhitekurnyi fakul'tet Vkhuteina', *Sovremennaya arkhitektura*, No. 4, 1928, pp. 109–10.

'O proletkul'takh', *Pravda*, No. 270, 1920.

Obzor deyatel'nosti Otdela izobrazitel'nykh iskusstv (Petrograd, 1920).

'Otchet o deyatel'nosti Otdela izobrazitel'nykh iskusstv Narkomprosa. Istoriya vozniknoveniya kollegii Otdela izobrazitel'nykh iskusstv', *Izobrazitel'noe iskusstvo*, No. 1, 1919.

Paris–Moscou 1900–1930 (Paris, Centre Georges Pompidou, 1979).

Pel'she, R. 'O Nekotorykh oshibkakh "lefovtsev"', *Sovetskoe iskusstvo*, No. 4/5, pp. 13–22.

Perel'man, V., ed., *Bor'ba za realizm v izobrazitel'nom iskusstve 20kh godov* (Moscow, 1962).

Pertsov, V. 'Proizvodstvo i iskusstvo. Obzor literatury', *Organizatsiya truda*, No. 1, 1921, pp. 128–31.

Pertsov, V. 'V stykhe iskusstva s proizvodstvom', *Vestnik iskusstv*, No. 5, 1922.

Pervaya diskussionnaya vystavka ob'edinenii aktivnogo revolyutsionnogo iskusstva (Moscow, 1924); reprinted in Matsa, *Sovetskoe iskusstvo*, pp. 316–7.

Pervaya moskovskaya obshchegorodskaya konferentsiya proletarskikh kul'turno-prosvetitel'nykh organizatsii (Moscow, 1918).

Pervaya vserossiiskaya konferentsiya po khudozhestvennoi promyshlennosti avgust 1919 (Moscow, 1920).

Pevsner, A. *A Biographical Sketch of My Brothers Naum Gabo and Antoine Pevsner* (Amsterdam, 1964).

Pletnev, V. 'Na ideologicheskom fronte', *Pravda*, 27 September 1922.

'Polozhenie otdela izobrazitel'nykh iskusstv v khudozhestvennoi promyshlennosti NKP po voprosu "o khudozhestvennoi kul'ture"', *Iskusstvo kommuny*, No. 11, 1919.

Poslednyaya futuristicheskaya vystavka kartin, 0.10. Katalog vystavki (Petrograd, 1915–16).

Povelikhina, A. 'Matiushin's Spatial System', *The Structurist*, No. 15/16, 1975/6, pp. 64–71.

Puni, I. *Sovremennoe iskusstvo* (Berlin, 1923).

Puni, I. 'Sovremennye gruppirovki v russkom levom iskusstve', *Iskusstvo kommuny*, No. 19, 1919, p. 3.

Punin, N. 'Iskusstvo i proletariat', *Izobrazitel'noe iskusstvo*, No. 1, 1919, pp. 8–24.

Punin, N., ed., *Iskusstvo rabochikh. Kruzhki IZO rabochikh klubov Leningrada i masterskie IZO oblpolitprosveta pri DPR im. Gertsena* (Leningrad, 1928).

Punin, N. 'Mera iskusstva', *Iskusstvo kommuny*, No. 9, 1919, p. 2.

Punin, N. *Noveishie techeniya v russkom iskusstve* (Leningrad, 1927–8), 2 Vols.

Punin, N. 'O pamyatnikakh', *Iskusstvo kommuny*, No. 14, 1919.

Punin, N. 'Obzor novykh techenii v iskusstve Petrograda', *Russkoe iskusstvo*, No. 1, 1923, pp. 21–9.

Punin, N. 'Proletariat i iskusstvo', *Izobrazitel'noe iskusstvo*, No. 1, 1919.

Punin, N. 'Risunki neskol'kikh molodykh', *Apollon*, No. 4, 1916.

Punin, N. *Russkii plakat 1917–1922. V. V. Lebedev* (Petrograd, 1922).

Punin, N. *Russkoe i sovetskoe iskusstvo* (Moscow, 1976).

Punin, N. 'Tour de Tatline', *Veshch'*, No. 1–2, 1922.

Punin, N. *Tsikl lektsii* (Petrograd, 1920).

Punin, N. 'V zashchitu zhivopisi', *Apollon*, No. 1, 1917, pp. 61–4.

5 × 5 = 25. Katalog vystavki (Moscow, 1921).

Quilici, V. *L'Architettura del Construttivismo* (Bari, 1969).

Radlov, N. *O futurizme* (Petrograd, 1923).

Rakitin, V. *L. A. Bruni* (Moscow, 1970).

Redko, A. *Teatr i evolyutsiya teatral'nykh form* (Moscow, 1926).

Rickey, G. *Constructivism: Origins and Evolution* (London, 1967).

Roginskaya, F. 'Novyi realizm v zhivopisi', *Krasnaya nov'*, No. 3, 1926, pp. 236–49.

Roginskaya, F. 'Ocherednye zadachi na fronte proizvodstvennykh iskusstv', *Iskusstvo i massy*, No. 2, 1930, pp. 6–10.

Rozanova, O. 'Osnovy novogo tvorchestva i prichiny ego neponimaniya, *Soyuz molodezhi*, No. 3, 1913, pp. 14–22.

Rudenstein, A., ed., *Russian Avant-Garde Art: The George Costakis Collection* (London, 1981).

Rudnitskii, K. *Rezhisser Meierkhol'd* (Moscow, 1969).

Russian Constructivism Revisited (Newcastle upon Tyne, Hatton Gallery, 1974).

Salmon, A. *Art russe moderne* (Paris, 1928).

Samokhina, T. 'Mezhdunarodnye svyazi sovetskoi arkhitektury v period stanovleniya Soyuza arkhitektorov SSSR', *Problemy istorii sovetskoi arkhitektury*, No. 2, 1978, pp. 77–80.

Sarab'yanov, D. *Aleksei Vasil'evich Babichev. Khudozhnik, teoretik, pedagog* (Moscow, 1974).

Semenov, Yu. 'V kuznitse novogo stilya', *Krasnaya nov'*, No. 39, 1928.

Shershenevich, V., trans., *Manifesty italianskogo futurizma. Sobranie manifestov.* (Moscow, 1914).

Sosnovy, T. *The Housing Problem in the Soviet Union* (New York, 1954).

Sterenburg, D. 'Die kunstlerische Situation in Russland (Zur Ausstellung in der Galerie van Diemen)', *Das Kunstblatt*, Vol. 6, No. 11, 1922, pp. 485–92.

Shterenberg, D. 'Nasha zadacha', *Khudozhestvennaya zhizn'*, No. 2, 1920, p. 5.

Aleksei Sotnikov. Skul'ptura. Katalog vystavki (Moscow, 1976).

Sovetskii reklamnyi plakat 1917–1932 (Moscow, 1972).

Speranskaya, A., ed., *Agitatsionno-massovoe iskusstvo pervykh let Oktyabrya. Materialy i issledovaniya* (Moscow, 1971).

Spravochnik Otdela izobrazitel'nykh iskusstv Narkomprosa (Moscow, 1920).

Steneberg, E. *Russische Kunst Berlin 1919–1932* (Berlin, 1969).

Sternin, G. *Khudozhestvennaya zhizn' Rossii na rubezhe XIX–XX vekov* (Moscow, 1970).

Stiv, 'Pervaya diskussionnaya vystavka', *Vechernie izvestiya*, 17 June 1924.

Strakhov, P. *Esteticheskie zadachi tekhniki* (Moscow, 1906).

Strigalev, A. 'K istorii vozniknoveniya leninskogo plana monumental'noi propagandy', *Voprosy sovetskogo izobrazitel'nogo iskusstva i arkhitektury* (Moscow, 1976), pp. 213–51.

Strigalev, A. 'O nekotorykh novykh terminakh v russkom iskusstve XX veka', *Problemy istorii sovetskoi arkhitektury*, No. 2, 1976, p. 67.

Strizhenova, T. *Iz istorii sovetskogo kostyuma* (Moscow, 1972).

Tarabukin, N. 'Foto reklama i foto-plakat', *Vremya*, No. 10/11, 1924, pp. 43–6.

Tarabukin, N. 'G. Volflin. Istolkovanie iskusstv', *Pechat' i revolyutsiya*, No. 7, 1922, pp. 340–1.

Tarabukin, N. 'INKhUK', *Gorn*, No. 8, 1923, p. 273.

Tarabukin, N. *Iskusstvo dnya* (Moscow, 1925).

Tarabukin, N. 'Iskusstvo dnya', *Pechat' i revolyutsiya*, No. 1, 1920, pp. 244–8.

Tarabukin, N. 'Natsionalizatsiya umstvennogo truda', *Vremya*, No. 8, 1924, pp. 16–20.

Tarabukin, N. 'Natyurmort kak problema stilya', *Sovetskoe iskusstvo*, No. 1, 1928, pp. 42–52.

Tarabukin, N. *Opyt teorii zhivopisi* (Moscow, 1923); both this and the following entry translated and introduced by A. Nakov, in N. Tarabukin, *Le Dernier Tableau* (Paris, 1972).

Tarabukin, N. *Ot mol'berta k mashine* (Moscow, 1923).

Tarabukin, N. 'Pervaya vserossiiskaya khudozhestvenno-promyshlennaya vystavka', *LEF*, No. 1, 1923, pp. 250-1.

Tarabukin, N. 'Problema peizazha', *Pechat' i revolyutsiya*, No. 5, 1927, pp. 37-65.

Tarabukin, N. 'Proletarskii khudozhnik', *Rabochii zhurnal*, No. 3/4, 1924, pp. 135-8.

Tarabukin, N. *Vrubel'* (Moscow, 1974).

Tarabukin, N. 'Zhanr kak problema stilya', *Sovetskoe iskusstvo*, No. 4, 1928, pp. 13-27.

Tasalov, V. *Estetika tekhnitsizma. Kriticheskii ocherk* (Moscow, 1960).

Tasteven', G. *Futurizm. Na puti k novomu simvolizmu* (Moscow, 1914).

Tetlingater. S. Katalog vystavki (Moscow, 1975).

Toporkov, A. *Tekhnicheskii byt i sovremennoe iskusstvo* (Moscow, 1928).

Tramvai V. Katalog vystavki (Petrograd, 1915).

Tret'yakov, S. 'Iskusstvo v revolyutsii i revolyutsiya v iskusstve', *Gorn*, No. 8, 1923, pp. 111-18.

Tret'yakov, S. 'LEF i NEP', *LEF*, No. 2, 1923, pp. 70-8.

Trotsky, L. *Literature and Revolution* (London, 1927).

Tufanov, A. *K zaumi* (Petrograd, 1924).

Tugendkhol'd, Ya. *Aleksandra Ekster* (Berlin, 1922).

Tugendkhol'd, Ya. *Iskusstvo oktyabr'skoi epokhi* (Leningrad, 1930).

Tugendkhol'd, Ya. 'Pamyati L. Popovoi', *Khudozhnik i zritel'*, No. 6/7, 1924, pp. 76-7.

Twentieth Century Russian and Eastern European Paintings, Drawings and Sculptures, 1900-1930 (London, Sotheby & Co., 4 July 1974).

Twentieth Century Russian Paintings, Drawings and Watercolours, 1900-1930 (London, Sotheby and Co., 12 April 1972).

Utopies et réalities en URSS, 1917-1934. Agit-prop, design, architecture (Paris, Centre Georges Pompidou, 1980).

Vardin, I. 'Platforma konstruktivizma', *Na literaturnom postu*, No. 9, 1929, pp. 20-8.

Vardin, I. 'Ideologicheskaya platforma konstruktivizma', *Na literaturnom postu*, No. 10, 1929, pp. 19-34.

Veresaev, V. 'K khudozhestvennomu oformleniyu byta', *Krasnaya nov'*, No. 1, 1926, pp. 160-77.

Vystavki sovetskogo izobrazitel'nogo iskusstva. Spravochnik, ed. E. Butorina (Moscow, 1965), Vol. 1, 1917-1930.

Werke aus der Sammlung Costakis: Russische Avantgarde 1910-1930 (Düsseldorf, Kunstmuseum, 1977).

Women Artists of the Russian Avant-Garde (Cologne, Galerie Gmurzynska, 1979).

Westheim, P. 'Die Ausstellung der Russen', *Das Kunstblatt*, Vol. 6, No. 11, 1922, pp. 493-8.

Zelinskii, K. 'Na velikom rubezhe (1917-1920 gody)', *Znamya*, No. 12, 1957, pp. 147-89.

Zhadova, L. *Malevich: Suprematism and Revolution in Russian Art, 1910-1930* (London, 1982).

Zhadova, L. 'O teorii sovetskogo dizaina 20kh godov', *Voprosy tekhnicheskoi estetiki*, No. 1, 1968, pp. 78-107.

Zhadova, L. 'Sovetskii otdel na mezhdunarodnom vystavke dekorativnogo iskusstva i promyshlennosti v Parizhe, 1925', *Tekhnicheskaya estetika*, No. 10, 1966, pp. 5-8.

Zhadova, L. 'Tsvetovaya sistema M. Matyushina', *Iskusstvo*, No. 8, 1974, pp. 38-42.

Zhadova, L. 'Vkhutemas-Vkhutein', *Dekorativnoe iskusstvo*, No. 11, 1970, pp. 36-42.

Zhukov, 'Levyi front iskusstv', *Kniga i revolyutsiya*, No. 3, 1923, pp. 39-44.

Zygas, K. P. 'The Sources of Constructivist Architecture: Designs and Images, 1911-1925' (Cornell University, Ph.D. thesis, 1978).

GUSTAV KLUTSIS

Klutsis, G. 'Fotomontazh kak sredstvo agitatsii i propagandy', in *Za bol'shevistskii plakat* (Moscow and Leningrad, 1932).

Klutsis, G. 'Fotomontazh kak novyi vid agitatsionnogo iskusstva', in *Izofront. Klassovaya bor'ba na fronte prostranstvennykh iskusstv. Sbornik statei ob'edineniya 'Oktyabr''* (Moscow and Leningrad, 1931), pp. 119-26.

Katalog vystavki proizvedenii Gustava Klutsisa (Riga, Gosudarstvennyi khudozhestvennyi mezei, 1970).

Marts, L. 'Gustav Klutsis', *Tekhnicheskaya estetika*, No. 1, 1968, pp. 28-30.

Oginskaya, L. *Gustav Klutsis* (Moscow, 1981).

Oginskaya, L. 'Gustav Klutsis - khudozhnik leninskoi temy', *Dekorativnoe iskusstvo*, No. 4, 1970, pp. 36-42.

Oginskaya, L. 'Khudozhnik-agitator', *Dekorativnoe iskusstvo*, No. 5, 1971, pp. 34-7.

Shantyko, N. 'Klutsis - illyustrator Mayakovskogo', *Khudozhnik*, No. 2, 1970, pp. 19-20.

EL LISSITZKY

El Lissitzky, *Russia: An Architecture for World Revolution* (London, 1970). First edition in German, *Russland: Die Rekonstruktion der Arkhitektur in der Sowjetunion* (Vienna, 1930).

El Lissitzky and H. Arp., *Die Kunstismen 1914-1924* Zurich, Munich and Leipzig, 1925).

'Ulen' [probably psendonym for Lissitzky], 'Die Ausstellungen in Russland', *Veshch'*, No. 1/2, 1922, p. 19.

El Lissitzky (Eindhoven, Stedelijk von Abbe Museum, 1965-6).

El Lissitzky (Cologne, Galerie Gmurzynska, 1976).

Khardzhiev, N. 'Pamyati khudozhnika Lisitskogo', *Dekorativnoe iskusstvo*, No. 2, 1961, p. 29.

Khardzhiev, N. 'El Lisitskii - konstruktor knigi', *Iskusstvo knigi*, No. 3, 1962.

Lissitzky-Küppers, S. *El Lissitzky: Life, Letters, Texts* (London, 1968).

Lozowick, L. 'El Lissitzky', *Transition*, No. 18, 1929, pp. 284-6.

Richter, H. *El Lissitzky, Sieg über die Sonne. Zur Kunst des Konstruktivismus* (Cologne, 1958).

KONSTANTIN MEDUNETSKII, VLADIMIR AND GEORGII STENBERG

Katalog vystavki. Konstruktivisty K. K. Medunetskii, V. A. Stenberg, G. A. Stenberg (Moscow, Kafe Poetov, 1922).

Abramova, A. '2 Stenberg 2', *Dekorativnoe iskusstvo*, No. 9, 1965, pp. 18–25..

Gerchuk, Yu. 'Golos nemogo kino', *Dekorativnoe iskusstvo*, No. 2, 1968, pp. 40–1.

Gertsenberg, V. and A. Zamoshkin, 'Georgii Stenberg', *Iskusstvo*, No. 5, 1933, pp. 15–36.

Korotkov, S. '2 Stenberg 2', *Moskovskii khudozhnik*, No. 5, 1967, p. 3.

Law, A. 'A Conversation with Vladimir Stenberg', *Art Journal*, Fall 1981, pp. 222–33.

Nakov, A. *2 Stenberg 2* (London, Annely Juda Fine Art, 1975).

'Pamyati G. A. Stenberga', *Stroitel'stvo Moskvy*, No. 9, 1933, p. 38.

PETR MITURICH

Miturich, P. 'Chuvstvo mira', *Tvorchestvo*, 1976, No. 4, pp. 14–17; introduced and edited by Mai Miturich, the son of the artist.

Petr Vasilévich Miturich (1887–1956). K 90-letiyu so dnya rozhdeniya. Katalog vystavki (Moscow, 1978).

Petr Vasil'evich Miturich (1887–1956). Vystavka proizvedenii. Zhivopis', grafika. Katalog (Moscow, 1968).

Pekelis, V. 'Dobavlenie k odnoi biografii', *Nauka i zhizn'*, No. 10, 1968, pp. 114–19.

Rozanova, N. *Petr Vasil'evich Miturich* (Moscow, 1972).

LYUBOV' POPOVA

Popova, L. 'Poyasnitel'naya zapiska k postanovke "Zemlya dybom" v teatre Meierkhol'da', *LEF*, No. 4, 1923, p. 44.

Lyubov' Popova. Ivan Klyun. Vystavka iz sobranii G. D. Kostakisa i D. V. Sarab'yanova v institute atomnoi energii im. Kurchatova (Moscow, June 1972).

Posmertnaya vystavka khudozhnika-konstruktora, L. S. Popovoi 1889–1924. Katalog vystavki proizvedenii (Moscow, 1924).

N. Adaskina, 'Lyubov' Popova. Put' stanovleniya khudozhnika-konstruktora', *Tekhnicheskaya estetika*, No. 11, 1978, pp. 17–23.

Bowlt, J. 'From Surface to Space: The Art of Liubov Popova', *Structurist*, No. 15/16, 1975-6, pp. 80-8.

Brik, O. 'Khudozhnik-konstruktor Lyubov' Sergeevna Popova', *Ogonek*, No. 25, 1924, p. 12.

Murina, E. 'Tkani Lyubovi Popovoi', *Dekorativnoe iskusstvo*, No. 8, 1967, pp. 24–7.

Rakitina, E. 'Lyubov' Popova. Iskusstvo i manifesty', *Khudozhnik, stsena, ekran* (Moscow, 1975), pp. 152–63.

Sarabianov, D. 'Space in Painting and Design', in *From Painting to Design: Russian Constructivist Art of the Twenties* (Cologne, Galerie Gmurzynska, 1981), pp. 48–71.

Tugendkhol'd, Ya. 'Pamyati L. Popovoi', *Khudozhnik i zritel'*, No. 6/7, 1924, pp. 76–7.

Zhadova, L. 'Lyubov' Popova', *Tekhnicheskaya estetika*, No. 11, 1967, pp. 26–8.

ALEKSANDR RODCHENKO

Rodchenko, A. 'Diskussii o novoi odezhde i mebeli - zadacha oformleniya', in A. Glebov, *Inga* (Moscow, 1929), pp. 12–14.

Rodchenko, A. 'K analizu foto iskusstva', *Sovetskoe foto*, No. 9, 1935, p. 31.

Rodchenko, A. 'K foto v etom nomere', *Novyi LEF*, No. 3, 1928.

Rodchenko, A. 'Master i kritika', *Sovetskoe foto*, No. 9, 1935, pp. 4–5.

Rodchenko, A. 'Protiv summirovannogo portreta za monumental'nyi snimok', *Novyi LEF*, No. 4, 1928.

Rodchenko, A. 'Tekhnicheskoe risovanie', *Novyi LEF*, No. 11, 1927, pp. 27–36.

Rodchenko, A. 'Tekhnicheskoe risovanie', *Novyi LEF*, No. 11, 1928, pp. 27–8.

Rodchenko, A. 'Rodchenko v Parizhe. Iz pisem domoi', *Novyi LEF*, No. 2, 1927, pp. 9–21.

Rodchenko, A. 'Perestroika khudozhnika', *Sovetskoe foto*, No. 5/6, 1936, pp. 19–21.

Rodchenko, A. 'Puti sovremennoi fotografii', *Novyi LEF*, No. 9, 1928, pp. 38–9.

Rodtchenko, A. 'Vladimir Tatlin', *Opus International*, No. 4, 1967, pp. 16–18.

Rodchenko, A. 'Reklam-plakaty s tekstom V. V. Mayakovskogo', *LEF*, No. 5, 1924.

Rodchenko, A. 'On Art and on Artists', in *From Painting to Design: Russian Constructivist Art of the Twenties* (Cologne, Galerie Gmurzynska, 1981), pp. 114–21.

314

Rodčenko, A. '"The Line". With Introduction and Notes by Andrei Boris Nakov', *Arts Magazine*, Vol. 47, No. 7, May-June 1973, pp. 50-2.

Rodchenko, A. 'Line', translated by J. Bowlt in *From Surface to Space: Russia, 1916-1924* (Cologne, Galerie Gmurzynska, 1974), pp. 65-7.

Abramova, A. 'A. M. Rodchenko', *Iskusstvo*, No. 11, 1966, pp. 51-9.

Antonov, R. 'A. M. Rodchenko', *Tekhnicheskaya estetika*, No. 2, 1967, pp. 36-9.

Berezin, A. 'Nemerknushchee iskusstvo. Vystavka rabot A. M. Rodchenko v tsentral'nom dome zhurnalista', *Moskovskaya pravda*, 5 October 1968.

Bojko, S. 'Collages et photomontages oubliés de A. Rodtchenko', *Opus International*, No. 10/11, 1969, pp. 30-5.

Bojko, S. 'Rodchenko's Early Spatial Constructions', in *From Surface to Space*.

Elliot, D., ed., *Alexander Rodchenko* (Oxford, Museum of Modern Art, 1979).

Karginov, G. *Rodchenko* (London, 1979).

Katalog vystavki rabot Aleksandra Mikhailovicha Rodchenko (Moscow, 1961).

Khardzhiev, N. 'A. M. Rodchenko. Khudozhnik oformitel' knigi. 1891-1956', *Iskusstvo knigi*, No. 2, 1961, pp. 189-92.

Kirsanov, S. 'Iskusstvo smotret' vpered', *Sovetskoe foto*, No. 2, 1962, p. 25.

Lapshin, V. 'Zhizn' polnaya poiskov', *Tvorchestvo*, No. 9, 1962, pp. 20-1.

Matsa, I. 'Aleksandr Rodchenko', *Iskusstvo*, No. 7, 1972, pp. 31-6.

'Pamyati A. M. Rodchenko', *Sovetskoe foto*, No. 1, 1957, p. 62.

Rakitin, V. 'Ob Aleksandre Rodchenko, novatorstve i traditsiyakh', *Iskusstvo knigi*, No. 2, 1973, pp. 16-19.

Shklovskii, V. 'Aleksandr Rodchenko - khudozhnik-fotograf', *Prometei*, No. 1, 1966, pp. 387-417.

Strakhova, V. 'Sovremennoe i ponyne',*Tvorchestvo*, No. 2, 1969, pp. 24-5.

Urusevskii, S. 'Neskol'ko slov o Rodchenko', *Iskusstvo kino*, No. 12, 1967, pp. 101-5.

Uvarova, I. 'Veshchi tyanut k sebe v poru', *Dekorativnoe iskusstvo*, No. 9, 1968, pp. 29-32.

Verdone, M. 'Rodchenko nell avanguardia', *Bianco e nero*, Vol. 25, No 4/5, 1967, pp. 72-89.

Vol'kov-Lannit, L. *Aleksandr Rodchenko risuet, fotografiruet, sporit* (Moscow, 1967).

Vol'kov-Lannit, L. 'Fata na foto (K rukografii ili k fotografii?)', *Novyi LEF*, No. 11, 1928, pp. 28-36.

Vol'kov-Lannit, L. 'Vmeste s poetami revolyutsii', *Iskusstvo kino*, No. 12, 1967, pp. 85-101.

VAVARA STEPANOVA

Agrarykh, [V. Stepanova], 'Bespredmetnoe tvorchestvo', *in Katalog desyatoi gosudarstvennoi vystavki. Bespredmetnoe tvorchestvo i suprematizm*, (Moscow, 1919); reprinted in I. Matsa, *Sovetskoe iskusstvo za 15 let*, pp. 110-11.

Varst [V. Stepanova], 'Kostyum segodnyashnego dnya - prozodezhda', *LEF*, No. 2, 1923, pp. 65-8.

Varst [V. Stepanova], 'O rabotakh konstruktivistskoi molodezhi', *LEF*, No. 3, 1923, pp. 53-6.

Stepanova, V. 'Ot kostyuma k risunku i tkani', *Vechernyaya Moskva*, 28 February 1929.

Varst [V. Stepanova], 'Rabochii klub. Konstruktivist A. M. Rodchenko', *Sovremennaya arkhitektura*, No. 1, 1926, p. 36.

Stepanova, V. 'Occasional Notes', in *From Painting to Design: Russian Constructivist Art of the Twenties* (Cologne, Galerie Gmurzynska, 1981), pp. 122-44.

Stepanova, Varvara Fedorovna 1894-1958. Katalog (Kostroma, Kostromskoi oblastnoi Muzei izobrazitel'nykh iskusstv, 1975).

Kovtun, E. 'Varvara Stepanova's Anti-Book', in *From Surface to Space: Russia, 1916-1924* (Cologne, Galerie Gmurzynska, 1974), pp. 57-63.

VLADIMIR TATLIN

Tatlin, V. 'Iskusstvo v tekhniku', *Brigada khudozhnikov*, No. 6, 1932, pp. 15-16.

Tatlin, V. 'Khudozhnik - organizator', *Rabis*, No. 48, 1929, p. 4.

Tatlin, V. 'O Zangezi', *Zhizn' iskusstva*, No. 18, 1923, p. 15.

Tatlin, V. 'Problema sootnosheniya cheloveka i veshchi', *Rabis*, No. 15, 7 April 1930, p. 9.

Tatlin, V., T. Shapiro, I. Meerzon and P. Vinogradov, 'Nasha predstoyashchaya rabota', *VIII s'ezd sovetov. Ezhednevnyi byulleten' s'ezda VTsIK*, No. 13, 31 December 1920, p. 11.

Vladimir Evgrafovich Tatlin (Petrograd, 1915).

'Novyi byt', *Krasnaya panorama*, No. 23, 1924, p. 14.

Abramova, A. 'Tatlin (1885-1958). K vos'midesyatiletiyu so dnya rozhdeniya', *Dekorativnoe iskusstvo*, No. 2, 1966, pp. 5-7.

Alekseev, B. 'Novoe v tvorchestve V. E. Tatlina', *Tvorchestvo*, No. 8, 1940, pp. 14-15.

Andersen, T. *Vladimir Tatlin* (Stockholm, Moderna Museet, 1968).

Arkin, D. 'Tatlin i "Letatlin"', *Sovetskoe iskusstvo*, 9 April 1932.

Artselulov, K. 'O Letatline', *Brigada khudozhnikov*, No. 6, 1932, pp. 17-18.

'Letatel'nyi apparat V. E. Tatlina', *Vechernyaya Moskva*, No. 152, 5 July 1933.

'Bez propellera letatel'nyi apparat B. E. [*sic*] Tatlina', *Vechernyaya Moskva*, 11 July 1933.

Danin, D. 'Uletavl'', *Druzhba narodov*, No. 2, 1979, pp. 220-36.

Elderfield, J. 'The Line of Free Men: Tatlin's "Towers" and the Age of Invention', *Studio International*, No. 11, 1969, pp. 162-7.

Grits, T. and V. Trenin, 'Letatlin', *Yunyi naturalist*, 9 September 1933.

Isakov, S. 'K "kontr-rel'efam" Tatlina', *Novyi zhurnal dlya vsekh*, No. 12, 1915, pp. 44–50.

Kronman, E. 'Ukhod v tekhniku. Tatlin i "Letatlin"', *Brigada khudozhnikov*, No. 6, 1932, pp. 19–23.

Lozowick, L. 'Tatlin's Monument to the Third International', *Broom*, Vol. 3, No. 3, 1922, pp. 232–4.

Matveev, N. 'Letayushchii velosiped', *Vechernyaya Moskva*, 3 July 1933.

Punin, N. 'Tour de Tatline', *Veshch'*, No. 12, 1922.

Punin, N. 'Zangezi', *Zhizn' iskusstva*, No. 20, 1923, pp. 10–11.

Punin, N. *Pamyatnik tret'ego internatsionala* (Petrograd, 1920).

Punin, N. *Tatlin (Protiv kubizma)* (Petrograd, 1921).

Rowell, M. 'Vladimir Tatlin: Form/Faktura', *October*, No. 7, winter 1978, pp. 83–108.

Strigalev, A. 'O proekte pamyatnika III Internatsionala khudozhnika V. Tatlina', in *Voprosy sovetskogo izobrazitel'nogo iskusstva i arkhitektury* (Moscow, 1973).

Umanskij, K. 'Der Tatlinismus oder die Maschinenkunst', *Der Ararat*, No. 4, 1920, pp. 12–13.

Umanskij, K. 'Die neue Monumentalskulptur in Russland', *Der Ararat*, No. 5/6, 1920, pp. 29–33.

Volavková-Skořepová, Z. 'Vladimír Jergrafovič Tatlin', *Výtvarné Umění*, No. 8/9, 1967, pp. 407–17.

V. E. Tatlin. Zasluzhennyi deyatel' iskusstva RSFSR 1885–1953. Katalog vystavki proizvedenii (Moscow, 1977).

Vystavka rabot zasluzhennogo deyatelya iskusstv V. E. Tatlina. Katalog (Moscow and Leningrad, 1932).

Yutkevich, S. 'Sukharnaya stolitsa', *LEF*, No. 3, 1923, pp. 181–2.

Zelinskii, K. 'Letatlin', *Vechernyaya Moskva*, 6 April 1932.

Zhadova, L. 'Tatlin – proektirovshchik material'noi kul'tury', in *Sovetskoe dekorativnoe iskusstvo 77/78* (Moscow, 1980), pp. 204–34.

Zygas, K. P. 'Tatlin's Tower Reconsidered', *Architectural Association Quarterly*, Vol. 8, no. 2, 1976, pp. 15–27.

THE VKhUTEMAS

Abramova, A. 'Nasledie VKhUTEMASa', *Dekorativnoe iskusstvo*, No. 4, 1964, pp. 8–12.

Abramova, A. 'VKhUTEMAS-VKhUTEIN: 1918–1930', in Z. N. Bykov, ed., *Moskovskoe vysshee khudozhestvenno-promyshlennoe uchilishche (byvshee Stroganovskoe) 1825–1965* (Moscow, 1965), pp. 39–68.

Adaskina, N. 'VKhUTEMAS. Ego rol' v formirovanii osnovnykh printsipov sovetskoi khudozhestvennoi pedagogiki 1920kh godov', in *Voprosy russkogo i sovetskogo iskusstva. Materialy itogovoi nauchnoi konferentsii yanv. 1972* (Moscow, 1973).

Antonov, A. 'Evolyutisya khudozhestvenno-konstruktorskikh programm fakul'teta obrabotki dereva i metalla VKhUTEMASa', *Khudozhestvenno-konstruktorskoe obrazovanie*, No. 4, 1973, pp. 193–216.

A[rkin], D. 'VKhUTEMAS', *Izvestiya VTsIK*, 5 February 1927.

Arkin, D. 'VKhUTEMAS i germanskii BAUKHAUS', *Izvestiya VTsIK*, 5 February 1927.

Arkin, D. 'L'artiste et l'industrie', *L'Art décoratif et industriel de l'URSS* (Moscow, 1925), pp. 39–47.

A.B., 'Metodicheskoe soveshchanie po vysshemu khudozhestvennomu obrazovaniyu', *Iskusstvo v shkole*, No. 1, 1927, pp. 55–6.

Babichev, N. 'Rabfak iskusstv', *Dekorativnoe iskusstvo*, No. 7/9, 1965, pp. 27–8.

Barooshian, V. 'Vkhutemas and Constructivism', *Soviet Union*, Vol. 3, part 2, 1976, pp. 197–207.

Bojko, S. 'Kak gotovyat dizainerov', *Dekorativnoe iskusstvo*, No. 10, 1964, pp. 20–1.

Bojko, S. 'Vkhutemas', *The 1920s in Eastern Europe* (Cologne, Galerie Gmurzynska, 1975).

Brik, O. 'Shkola konstruktivizma', *Ogonek*, No. 20, 1923, p. 6.

Brona, I. 'Pervye diplomanty Kievskogo khudozhestvennogo instituta', *Sovetskoe iskusstvo*, No. 4, 1927, pp. 51–4.

Brynkhanenko, N. 'Ot rizy k avtomobilyu', *Krasnoe studenchestvo*, No. 4, 1929, pp. 30–1.

Chichagova, G. 'VKhUTEMAS', in D. Eliot, ed., *Alexander Rodchenko* (Oxford, Museum of Modern Art, 1979), p. 106.

'Dekret Soveta narodnykh komissarov o Vysshikh gosudarstvennykh khudozhestvenno-tekhnicheskikh masterskikh', *Izvestiya VTsIK*, 25 December 1920.

Denisov, V. 'O khudozhestvennoi shkole', *Zhizn' iskusstva*, No. 8, 1921.

Dmitrieva, N. *Moskovskoe uchilishche zhivopisi, vayaniya i zodchestva* (Moscow, 1959).

Dokuchaev, N. 'Arkhitektura i nasha shkola', *Stroitel'naya promyshlennost'*, No. 2, 1927, pp. 122–7.

Enk, 'Vystavka diplomnykh rabot poligrafaka Vkhutein', *Iskusstvo v massy*, No. 5/6, 1930, pp. 41–3.

Favorskii, V. 'Zabyt' "igru v inzhenera"', *Brigada khudozhnikov*, No. 4/5, 1932, pp. 10–11.

Goncharov, A. 'VKhUTEMAS', *Tvorchestvo*, No. 4, 1967, pp. 15–16.

Gosudarstvennyi institut istorii iskusstv 1912–1917 (Leningrad, 1927).

Guchev N. and N. Popov, 'Arkhitektura i mebel'', *Arkhitektura SSSR*, No. 9, 1934, pp. 39–49.

'Instruktsiya vyborov rukovoditelei Svobodnykh gosudarstvennykh khudozhestvennyk masterskikh', *Izvestiya VTsIK*, No. 193, 7 September 1918.

Izvestiya OBKhON (Moscow, 1927).

Kandinskii, V. 'K reforme khudozhestvennoi shkoly', *Iskusstvo*, No. 1, 1923, pp. 399–406.

Khan-Magomedov, S. 'U istokov sovetskogo dizaina: derevoobdelochnyi fakul'tet VKhUTEMASa (VKhUTEINa) Tekhnicheskaya estetika, No. 2, 1980.

Khlebnikov, L. M. 'Bor'ba realistov i futuristov vo VKhUTEMASe', in *Lenin i Lunacharskii. Perepiska, doklady, dokumenty*, Literaturnoe nasledstvo, No. 80 (Moscow, 1971).

Khudozhestvennoe obrazovanie. Uchebnye plany muzykal'nykh i khudozhestvennykh vuzov (Moscow, 1927).

'Klubnaya mebel'', *Rabochii klub*, No. 2, 1928.

Konnov, F. 'Ne povtoryat' oshibok Vkhuteina', *Brigada khudozhnikov*, No. 4/5, 1932, pp. 11–12.

Kostin, V. I. *Tat'yana Alekseevna Mavrina* (Moscow, 1966), pp. 65–75, 166–5.

Krinskii, V., I. V. Lamtsov and M. A. Turkus, *Elementy arkhitekturno-prostranstvennoi kompozitsii* (Moscow, 1934).

Kupreyanov, N. 'Poligrafiya v khudozhestvennykh vuzakh', *LEF*, No. 4, 1923, pp. 187–95.

Lakhtin, N. 'Stroitel'stvo i vysshaya shkola', *Stroitel'naya promyshlennost'*, No. 1, 1927, pp. 70–2.

Lavrov, V. 'Arkhitektura Vkhutemasa (rabota arkhitekturnogo fakul'teta Vkhutemasa 1920–1927 gg.)', *Stroitel'stvo Moskvy*, No. 11, 1927, pp. 15–17.

Lobov, 'Mebel' fakul'teta po obrabotke dereva i metalla VKhUTEINa', *Stroitel'stvo Moskvy*, No. 10, 1929, pp. 9–11.

Marts, L. 'Propedevticheskii kurs VKhUTEMASa - VKhUTEINa', *Khudozhestvenno-konstruktorskoe obrazovanie*, No. 2, 1970, pp. 39–114.

Maslov, 'Edinyi respublikanskii institut proletarskogo izobrazitel'nogo iskusstva', *Proftekhnicheskoe obrazovanie*, No. 5, 1930, pp. 43–4.

'Na putyakh k standartu', *Daesh'*, No. 3, 1929.

Novitskii, P. 'O Vysshei khudozhestvennoi shkole', *Zhizn' iskusstva*, No. 34, 1926, pp. 2–3, and No. 35, 1926, pp. 13–14.

Pavlinov, P. 'Bor'ba s graficheskoi negramotnost'yu', *Front nauki i tekhniki*, No. 12, 1933, pp. 62–5.

Pavlinov, P. *Dlya tekh kto risuet. Sovety khudozhnika* (Moscow, 1965).

Programma po proizvodstvennoi praktike dlya studentov arkhitekturnogo fakul'teta VKhUTEMASa na 1926–1927 uchebnyi god (Moscow, 1927).

Raboty arkhitekturnogo fakul'teta VKhUTEMASa 1920–1927 (Moscow, 1927).

'Razval VKhUTEMASa. Dokladnaya zapiska o polozhenii vysshikh khudozhestvenno-tekhnicheskikh masterskikh', *LEF*, No. 4, 1923, pp. 27–8.

'Reorganizatsiya khudozhestvennykh zavedenii v Moskve', *Izvestiya VTsIK*, 7 September 1918.

'Rezolyutsiya konferentsii uchashchikhsya iskusstva', *Anarkhiya*, 12 May 1918.

Rozen, M. 'Nepareryvnaya proizvodstvennaya praktika v khudozhestvennykh uchebnykh zavedeniyakh', *Proftekhnicheskoe obrazovanie*, No. 7, 1930, pp. 37–8.

Sbornik materialov po khudozhestvennomu obrazovaniyu (Moscow, 1927).

2-i Sbornik materialov po khudozhestvennomu obrazovaniyu (Moscow, 1928).

Semenova, S. 'VKhUTEMAS, LEF, Mayakovskii', *Trudy po russkoi i slavyanskoi filologii* (Tartu), No. 9, 1966, pp. 288–306; publication and introduction by Z. Mints, commentary by I. Gazer.

Sen'kin, S. 'Lenin v kommune VKhUTEMASa', in V. Perel'man, ed., *Bor'ba za realizm v iskusstve 20kh godov* (Moscow, 1962), pp. 90–5.

Sidorov, A. 'Vystavka kartin v pomeshchenii VKhUTEMASa', *Pravda*, 15 May 1923.

Spasovskii, M. 'Khudozhestvennaya shkola', *Argonavty*, No. 1, 1923.

Spravochnik VKhUTEMASa i pravila priema na 1927/1928 god (Moscow, 1927).

'Teatral'no-dekorativnoe otdelenie zhivopisnogo fakul'teta Vkhutemasa', *Sovetskoe iskusstvo*, No. 4/5, 1925, pp. 75–6.

VKhUTEIN. Vysshyi gosudarstvennyi khudozhestvenno-tekhnicheskii Institut v Mosvke (Moscow, 1929).

'VKhUTEMAS', *LEF*, No. 2, 1923, p. 174.

Vkhutemaska [E. Semenova], 'Levaya metafizika', *LEF*, No. 4, 1924, pp. 219–20.

Yablonskaya, M. *Konstantin Nikolaevich Istomin* (Moscow, 1972).

Zhadova, L. 'Vkhutemas-Vkhutein', *Dekorativnoe iskusstvo*, No. 11, 1970, pp. 36–42.

RUSSIAN AND SOVIET ARTISTIC GROUPS AND EXHIBITIONS

Donkey's Tail – Oslinyi khvost

First Working Group of Constructivists – Pervaya rabochaya gruppa konstruktivistov

First State Free Art Studios, Moscow – Pervye gosudarstvennye svobodnye khudozhestvennye masterskie

Moscow School of Painting, Sculpture and Architecture – Moskovskoe uchilishche zhivopisi, vayaniya i zodchestva

Petrograd State Free Art Studios – Petrogradskie gosudarstvennye svobodnye khudozhestvennye masterskie

Second State Free Art Studios, Moscow – Vtorye gosudarstvennye svobodnye khudozhestvennye masterskie

The Store – Futuristicheskaya vystavka 'Magazin', Moscow, March 1916

Stroganov School of Applied Art, Moscow – Stroganovskoe khudozhestvenno-promyshlennoe uchilishche

Tramway V. The First Futurist Exhibition – Tramvai V. Pervaya futuristicheskaya vystavka kartin, Petrograd, March 1915

Union of Youth – Soyuz molodezhi

Working Group of Objective Analysis – Rabochaya gruppa ob'ektivnogo analiza

0.10. The Last Futurist Exhibition – 0.10. Poslednyaya futuristicheskaya vystavka kartin, Petrograd, December 1915–January 1916

ABBREVIATIONS

AKhRR	Assotsiatsiya khudozhnikov revolyutsionnoi Rossii – Association of Artists of Revolutionary Russia
ASNOVA	Assotsiatsiya novykh arkhitektorov – Association of New Architects
Derfak	Derevoobrabatyvayushchii fakul'tet – Woodwork faculty at the VKhUTEMAS, Moscow
Dermetfak	Derevo i metalloobrabatyvayushchii fakul'tet – Wood and Metalwork faculty at the VKhUTEMAS, Moscow
GAKhN	Gosudarstvennaya akademiya khudozhestvennykh nauk – Russian Academy of Artistic Sciences
GINKhUK	Gosudarstvennyi institut khudozhestvennoi kul'tury – State Institute of Artistic Culture, Petrograd
Glavpolitprosvet	Glavnyi politiko-prosvetitel'nyi komitet Narkomprosa – Main Political Education Committee of Narkompros
GTG	Gosudarstvennaya tret'yakovskaya galereya – State Tret'yakov Gallery, Moscow
INKhUK	Institut khudozhestvennoi kul'tury – Institute of Artistic Culture, Moscow
IZO	Otdel izobrazitel'nykh iskusstv – Department of Fine Arts in the Commissariat of Enlightenment
LEF	*Zhurnal levogo fronta iskusstv – Journal of the Left Front of the Arts*
Metfak	Metalloobrabatyvayushchii fakul'tet – Metalwork faculty at the VKhUTEMAS, Moscow
Narkompros	Narodnyi komissariat prosveshcheniya – People's Commissariat of Enlightenment
OBMOKhU	Obshchestvo molodykh khudozhnikov – Society of Young Artists
OPOYAZ	Obshchestvo po izucheniyu poeticheskogo yazyka – Society for the Study of Poetical Language
OSA	Ob'edinenie sovremennykh arkhitektorov – Society of Contemporary Architects
OST	Obshchestvo khudozhnikov-stankovistov – Society of Easel Painters
Proletkul't	Proletarskaya kul'tura – Proletarian Culture Movement
Rabfak	Rabochii fakul'tet – Workers' Preparatory faculty
RAKhN	Rossiiskaya akademiya khudozhestvennykh nauk – Russian Academy of Artistic Sciences
TsGA	Tsentral'nyi gosudarstvennyi arkhiv – Central State Archives, Moscow
TsGALI	Tsentral'nyi gosudarstvennyi arkhiv literatury i iskusstva – Central State Archive of Literature and Art, Moscow
UNOVIS	Utverditeli novogo iskusstvo – Affirmers of the New Art
VKhUTEMAS	Vysshie gosudarstvennye khudozhestvenno-tekhnicheskie masterskie – Higher State Artistic and Technical Workshops, Moscow
VKhUTEIN	Vysshii gosudarstvennyi khudozhestvenno-tekhnicheskii institut – Higher State Artistic and Technical Institute, Moscow
Zhivskul'ptarkh	Kollektiv zhivopisno-skul'pturno-arkhitekturnogo sinteza – Collective of Painterly, Sculptural and Architectural Synthesis

INDEX